MW01049881

THE ROYAL INSCRIPTIONS OF AMĒL-MARDUK (561–560 BC), NERIGLISSAR (559–556 BC), AND NABONIDUS (555–539 BC), KINGS OF BABYLON

THE ROYAL INSCRIPTIONS OF THE NEO-BABYLONIAN EMPIRE

THE ROYAL INSCRIPTIONS OF THE NEO-BABYLONIAN EMPIRE
VOLUME 2

The Royal Inscriptions of Amēl-Marduk (561–560 BC), Neriglissar (559–556 BC), and Nabonidus (555–539 BC), Kings of Babylon

FRAUKE WEIERSHÄUSER and JAMIE NOVOTNY

with the assistance of Giulia Lentini

EISENBRAUNS
University Park, Pennsylvania

Printed in the United States of America on acid-free paper.

ISBN 978-1-575069-975

The research and publication of this volume
have been supported by the Gerda Henkel Foundation,
the Alexander von Humboldt Foundation, and
Ludwig-Maximilians-Universität München.

Cover illustration: A bull from the Ištar Gate at Babylon
Drawing by Sabrina Nortey

The text editions in this work were produced using Oracc.
See http://oracc.org for further information.

Library of Congress Cataloging-in-Publication Data

Names: Amel-Marduk, King of Babylonia, -560 B.C., author. | Neriglissar, King of Babylonia, -556 B.C., author. | Nabonidus, King of Babylonia, active 6th century B.C., author. | Weiershäuser, Frauke, editor. | Novotny, Jamie R., editor. | Lentini, Giulia, editor.

Title: The royal inscriptions of Amēl-Marduk (561–560 BC), Neriglissar (559–556 BC), and Nabonidus (555–539 BC), kings of Babylon / [edited by] Frauke Weiershäuser and Jamie Novotny with the assistance of Giulia Lentini.

Other titles: Royal inscriptions of the neo-Babylonian Empire ; v. 2.

Description: University Park, Pennsylvania : Eisenbrauns, [2020] | Series: The royal inscriptions of the neo-Babylonian Empire ; volume 2 | Includes bibliographical references and index.

Summary: "A complete corpus of the extant royal inscriptions of the Neo-Babylonian kings Amēl-Marduk (561–560 BC), Neriglissar (559–556 BC), and Nabonidus (555–539 BC), who were three of the last native kings of Babylonia before the conquest of Cyrus the Great"— Provided by publisher.

Identifiers: LCCN 2020028358 | ISBN 9781646021079 (cloth)

Subjects: LCSH: Amel-Marduk, King of Babylonia, -560 B.C. | Neriglissar, King of Babylonia, ¬-556 B.C. | Nabonidus, King of Babylonia, active 6th century B.C. | Cuneiform inscriptions, Akkadian. | Akkadian language—Texts. | Babylonia—History—Sources. | Babylonia—Kings and rulers.

Classification: LCC PJ3833.A44 A44 2020 | DDC 892/.1—dc23

LC record available at https://lccn.loc.gov/2020028358

Eisenbrauns is an imprint of The Pennsylvania State University Press.
The Pennsylvania State University Press is a member of the Association of University Presses.

The paper used in this publication meets the minimum requirements of the American National Standard for Information Sciences—Permanence of Paper for Printed Library Materials, ANSI Z39.48-1984.

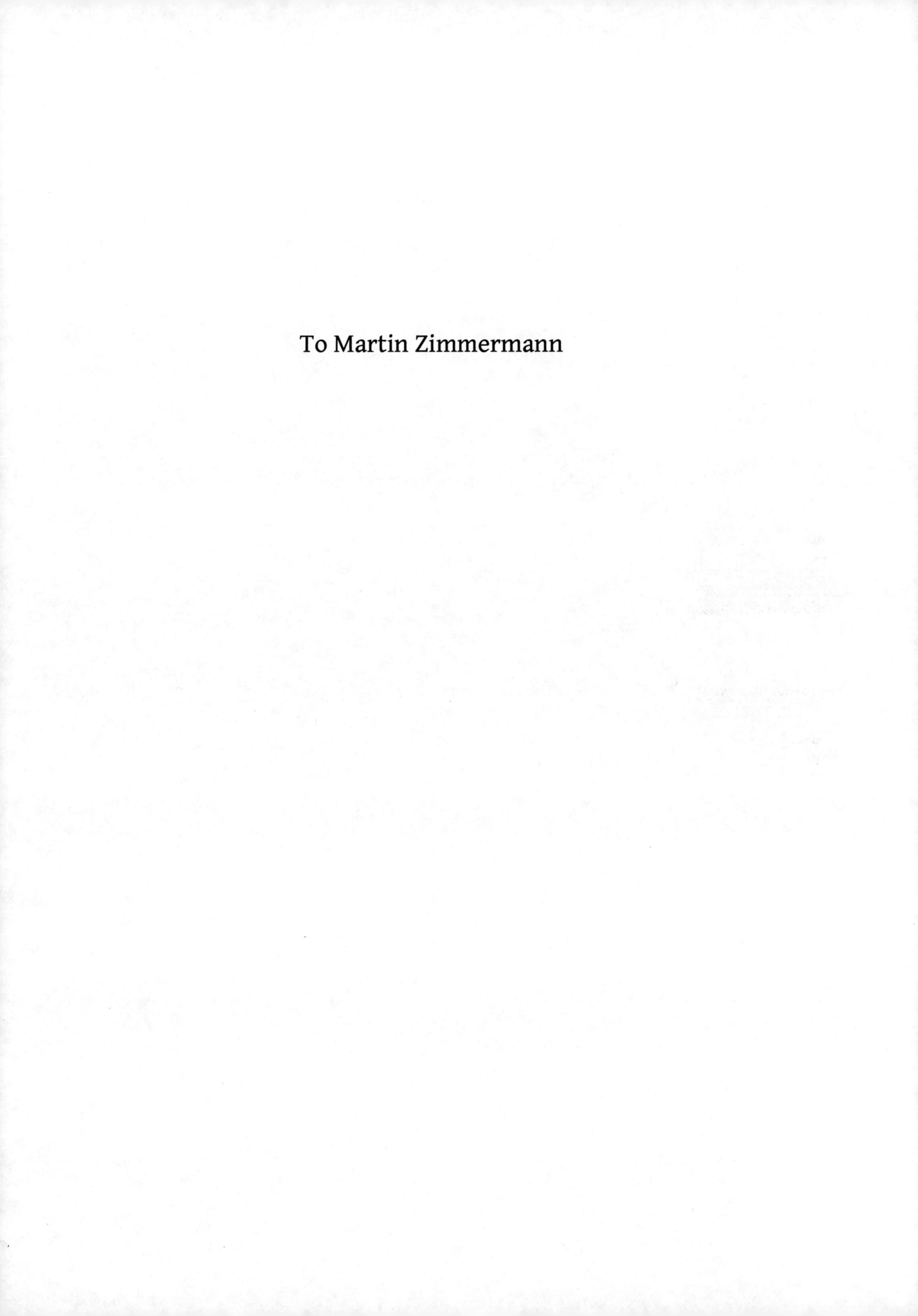

To Martin Zimmermann

Contents

III. Nabonidus — Babylonia

List of Figures

Contents of Scores

(a pdf is available at http://oracc.org/ribo/bab7scores/)

Directors' Foreword

The present series of publications, Royal Inscriptions of the Neo-Babylonian Empire (RINBE), is intended to present a comprehensive, modern scholarly edition of the complete corpus of official inscriptions of the last native kings of Babylon (626–539 BC), which comprises about 230 compositions written on approximately 1,500 clay and stone objects. It is modeled on the publications of the now-defunct Royal Inscriptions of Mesopotamia (RIM) series and the soon-to-be-completed Royal Inscriptions of the Neo-Assyrian Period (RINAP) series. RINBE is the successor of both of the aforementioned publication series. Although some of RINBE's contents have been publicly available online since August 2015 via the "Babylon 7" sub-project of the open-access Royal Inscriptions of Babylonia online (RIBo) Project, the project officially began in June 2017, when we, RINBE's co-founders and directors, established the series' editorial board, its team of consultants, and the books' authors.

During the next couple of years, RINBE will create a complete and authoritative modern presentation of the entire corpus of the royal inscriptions of the six kings of the Neo-Babylonian Empire in three books and in a fully annotated, linguistically tagged, Open Access and Open Data digital format. In addition to this core data, the online version offers substantial metadata and contextualization resources, as well as linkage to further external resources. The online facilities include:

- a catalogue searchable by museum and excavation numbers, publication data, dates, find spot, etc.;
- browsable text editions, with English and German translations;
- exportable JavaScript Object Notation (JSON) versions of the corpus;
- Akkadian glossaries and proper noun indices;
- a search facility to explore texts by transliteration, words, names, as well as by English and German translations;
- a glossary that provides guided search facilities and concordances of all instances of every word; and
- informational pages giving historical background and other kinds of information.

As part of the Munich Open-access Cuneiform Corpus Initiative (MOCCI) based at Ludwig-Maximilians-Universität München's Historisches Seminar (LMU Munich, History Department), RINBE's contents are fully integrated into the Open Richly Annotated Cuneiform Corpus (Oracc) Project, the Cuneiform Digital Library Initiative (CDLI), and the Ancient Records of Middle Eastern Polities (ARMEP) map interface. The print publications, like the RINAP volumes, are published by Eisenbrauns, now an imprint of Penn State University Press. They use the same formatting as the RINAP publications, but with one important addition: Golden Standard Open Access publishing, that is, PDFs is available for free download without an embargo period directly upon publication.

This book, despite being the first volume to appear, is the second volume in the RINBE series. A two-part volume of the inscriptions of Nabopolassar and Nebuchadnezzar II is to follow. All three books are principally prepared by Frauke Weiershäuser and Jamie Novotny, with the input of valuable expertise from members of the series' editorial board and its team of consultants, as well as the cheerful and productive assistance of Giulia Lentini. It is our pleasure to dedicate this first volume to Martin Zimmermann, Professor of Ancient History at LMU Munich, whose tireless efforts to widen the remit of his academic discipline, as taught in Munich, to also include the Ancient Near East resulted in the establishment of the Alexander von Humboldt Chair in the Ancient History of the Near and Middle East in 2015, and this created the research and funding context that enabled us to embark on this ambitious publication project.

We are very happy to express our deep appreciation to the Alexander von Humboldt Foundation and LMU Munich, which through the establishment of the Karen Radner's Alexander von Humboldt Professorship for

Ancient History of the Near and Middle East in 2015 allowed this publication project to find a home at LMU's History Department. Both institutions provided crucial financial support for our work. LMU in particular strategically invested funds in Frauke Weiershäuser's research position, which enabled prioritizing the publication project within MOCCI. In addition, research grants awarded by the Gerda Henkel Foundation (Düsseldorf) to Jamie Novotny in 2018 and to Jamie Novotny and Karen Radner in 2019 helped to quickly implement the work program, especially collating original objects kept in the British Museum (London), the Iraq Museum (Baghdad), and the Vorderasiatisches Museum (Berlin). We would like to express our profound thanks and are enormously grateful for the warm support that RINBE has received from these institutions, especially the Vorderasiatisches Museum, whose new director, Barbara Helwing, has graciously made all relevant finds from the Babylon excavations accessible to us. We are very pleased to cooperate with the VAM's Babylon Project.

Munich
Philadelphia
April 2020

Karen Radner
Grant Frame
The Directors

Foreword from the Director of the Vorderasiatisches Museum

With this volume of The Royal Inscriptions of the Neo-Babylonian Empire publication series (RINBE 2), Frauke Weiershäuser and Jamie Novotny present the complete corpus of known inscriptions of the kings Amēl-Marduk, Neriglissar, and Nabonidus. Through the series' clear structure and inclusion of metadata, RINBE sets the publishing standard for the modern presentation of such ancient inscriptions and, therefore, is an invaluable scholarly resource.

A considerable number of examples of Akkadian inscriptions of these three Babylonian kings are preserved on clay tablets and other inscribed objects (especially mud bricks and barrel-shaped clay cylinders) found during the excavations by Robert Koldewey from 1899 to 1917 in Babylon. The numerous artifacts from the Babylon excavations were divided between Germany and the Ottoman Empire. The share of the finds from Babylon allocated to Germany, including close to 5,000 inscribed objects, is now kept in the collections of the Vorderasiatisches Museum SMB SPK in Berlin. Many text archives from Babylon have previously been collated and published, but a full and comprehensive study of the Babylon collections in Berlin is still on-going. In this regard, the Vorderasiatisches Museum acknowledges and highly welcomes the work that has made the present volume (RINBE 2) possible. This study helps place the Babylon collections in Berlin into a wider historical and cultural context, as well as offers new perspectives of and interconnections between this rich source material. The book also highlights some of the special objects in Berlin that were discovered during Koldewey's excavations. For example, clay cylinder VA Bab 2971 (Nabonidus 2 ex. 1) is an exquisitely-inscribed object that records Nabonidus' rebuilding of the temple of the goddess Ištar; that cylinder is the only complete copy of that text. Therefore, the Vorderasiatisches Museum would like to express its sincere gratitude to the authors of this book for their diligent and careful work.

The Vorderasiatisches Museum Berlin, as one of the many research institutions united under the umbrella of the Staatliche Museen Berlin – Stiftung Preussischer Kulturbesitz, represents a unique archive of world knowledge and, thus, making these archives available to scholars is one of the museum's most important tasks. This has successfully happened here, with the publication of the present book, and the start of the RINBE series marks a promising step towards further research collaboration between the Munich Open-access Cuneiform Corpus Initiative (MOCCI) and the Vorderasiatisches Museum.

Berlin
April 2020

Barbara Helwing

Preface

The preparation of this book, the inaugural volume of the RINBE series, began several years before this series was formally established by Karen Radner and Grant Frame in June 2017. In fact, it began shortly before the official establishment of the Alexander von Humboldt Professorship for Ancient History of the Near and Middle East at Ludwig-Maximilians-Universität München (Historisches Seminar – Abteilung Alte Geschichte) in August 2015. Late in 2014, Radner and Jamie Novotny started discussing plans for long-term, Open Access, digital Assyriology projects. They quickly decided to not only retro-digitize the four published volumes of the sub-series Royal Inscriptions of Mesopotamia: Assyrian Periods (RIMA) and Royal Inscriptions of Mesopotamia: Babylonian Periods (RIMB) of the long-defunct, University-of-Toronto-based Royal Inscriptions of Mesopotamia (RIM) Project led by A. Kirk Grayson, but also to start preparing editions of the remaining first-millennium-BC royal inscriptions, in particular, those of Nabopolassar, Nebuchadnezzar II, and their successors. This led to Novotny preparing Oracc-compatible transliterations of the Neo-Babylonian inscriptions edited in Rocío Da Riva's book The Inscriptions of Nabopolassar, Amel-Marduk and Neriglissar and Hanspeter Schaudig's volume Die Inschriften Nabonids von Babylon und Kyros' des Großen samt den in ihrem Umfeld entstandenen Tendenzschriften. Textausgabe und Grammatik. The first dataset includes the texts of Amel-Marduk and Neriglissar and became the foundation upon which Royal Inscriptions of Babylonia online (RIBo; http://oracc.org/ribo/) was built. In December 2016, Frauke Weiershäuser permanently joined Radner's team and started lemmatizing the inscriptions of Nabonidus, as well as translating them into readable, modern English; she also began preparing new German translations.

It was not until June 2017, however, when Radner and Frame formally established the RINBE series, that the present book really began to take shape. In April 2018, Novotny secured funding from the Gerda Henkel Foundation, and the resultant program of museum research enabled the team to begin transforming the transliterations for the project from non-critical, retro-digitized and lemmatized versions of texts published by other scholars to critical and authoritative editions prepared through first-hand examinations of the originals, thereby ensuring that RINBE 2 contains carefully-prepared, discipline-standard, and peer-reviewed editions.

The present volume is the result of the close and long-term collaboration between Weiershäuser and Novotny. As for the division of labor, the bulk of the work was done by Weiershäuser, RINBE 2's primary author. She collated most of the pieces in the British Museum (London) and all of the available objects in the Iraq Museum (Baghdad) and the Vorderasiatisches Museum (Berlin); wrote most of the book's introduction, and most of the text introductions and on-page notes; and prepared the bibliographies. Novotny, the book's secondary author, prepared the initial transliterations of the Nabonidus inscriptions, the editions of the inscriptions of Amēl-Marduk and Neriglissar, the catalogue of texts and exemplars, and most of the front and back material; collated many exemplars of Nabonidus' "Eḫulḫul Cylinder" (Nabonidus 28); wrote some sections of the book's introduction, most of the commentaries, and some of the on-page notes; created most of the score transliterations; edited the English of the entire manuscript; and produced the final camera-ready copy of book. Weiershäuser and Novotny were assisted by Giulia Lentini, MA, who provided research and editorial support, including the collation of some pieces of Nabonidus' "Eḫulḫul Cylinder" (Nabonidus 28).

Work on the present corpus of inscriptions necessitated travel for collation of previously published inscriptions and for examination of unpublished material. The authors wish to thank the various museums and museum authorities that have aided them in the preparation of this book. In particular, they would like to thank the directors, keepers, curators, and assistants of the British Museum (London), the Vorderasiatisches Museum (Berlin), the Israel Museum (Jerusalem), the Iraq Museum (Baghdad), the Louvre Museum (Paris), and the Yale Babylonian Collection (New Haven). Specifically, the authors would like to express their gratitude to Shaymaa

Abdulzahra, Luma al-Duri, Juliane Eule, Frank Gaedecke, Anna von Graevenitz, Helen Gries, Barbara Helwing, Markus Hilgert, Agnete Lassen, Laura Peri, Nura Qusy, Sonja Radujkovic, Qais Hussein Rasheed, Ilham Shakir, Tawfeeq Abidmohammed Sulatan, Jonathan Taylor, and Ariane Thomas. They and their colleagues have been extremely helpful and have extended to us every courtesy and assistance, sometimes at very short notice.

As is usual with a volume of this scale, numerous individuals aided in the production of the book and online material in some way. While the authors have collated most of the texts themselves, other scholars have kindly collated some texts, provided information on pieces, or aided in some way. These include, in alphabetical order, Selim Adalı, Yigal Bloch, Rocío, Da Riva, Anmar Abdulillah Fadhil, Hussein Flayyeh, Grant Frame, Laith Hussein, Ahmed Ibrahimi, Joshua Jeffers, Enrique Jiménez, Frans van Koppen, Nathan Morello, Olof Pedersén, Karen Radner, Hanspeter Schaudig, Ali Ubaid Shalgham, Jonathan Taylor, Poppy Tushingham, Klaus Wagensonner, and Christopher Walker. In particular, we would like to thank Da Riva and Pedersén for their generous and manifold support. Their deep knowledge of the sources and, in Pedersén's case, of the minutia of excavation work undertaken at Babylon, have greatly improved the quality of the information provided in this volume. The penultimate manuscript was read by Paul-Alain Beaulieu, Johannes Hackl, Christian Hess, and Martin Worthington, all of whom made numerous astute comments, welcome criticisms, and improvements, particularly on the transliterations and translations. In addition, the members of the RINBE editorial board (especially Grant Frame and Karen Radner) and our project consultants generously made time to offer helpful suggestions, especially at the beginning and near the completion of the volume. Their time, care, and generosity are greatly appreciated. Special thanks must be given to Steve Tinney for providing technical support. The authors have tried their best to name everyone who aided in the production of RINBE 2 and, thus, any omissions are unintentional.

The authors' appreciation goes out to the Gerda Henkel Foundation, the Alexander von Humboldt Foundation, and the Ludwig-Maximilians-Universität München for providing financial and material support of the work on the RINBE Project and its online counterpart, RIBo, as outlined in the Preface. Without these institutions' generous assistance, it would not have been possible to complete this volume.

Munich
April 2020

Frauke Weiershäuser and Jamie Novotny

Editorial Notes

The volumes in the RINBE series are modeled upon the publications of the soon-to-be-completed Royal Inscriptions of the Neo-Assyrian Period (RINAP) series, with a few minor modifications. Like the RINAP volumes, the books in this series are not intended to provide analytical or synthetic studies, but rather to provide basic text editions that can serve as the foundations for such studies. Thus, extensive discussions of the contents of the texts are not presented and the core of each volume is the edition of the relevant texts.

In this volume, the order of the texts is based for the most part upon the following two criteria:

(1) The city at which the structure dealt with in the building or dedicatory portion of the text was located. If that information is not preserved on the text, the provenance of the inscribed object is the determining factor.

(2) The type of object upon which the inscription is written (cylinder, brick, tablet, etc.).

Following the practice of the RINAP series, which was in turn modeled on the now-defunct Royal Inscriptions of Mesopotamia (RIM) series, inscriptions that cannot be assigned definitely to any particular ruler are assigned text numbers beginning at 1001. Certain other inscriptions, in particular, any text composed in the name of a ruler's family members (e.g., the king's mother) are given numbers that begin at 2001.

In the volumes of the RINBE series, the term "exemplar" is employed to designate a single inscription found on one object. The term "text" is employed to refer to an inscription that existed in antiquity and that may be represented by a number of more or less similar exemplars. In our editions, exemplars of one text are edited together as a "master text," with a single transliteration and translation. Variants to the "master text" are provided either on page (major variants) or at the back of the volume (minor variants).

Each text edition is typically supplied with a brief introduction containing general information. This is followed by a catalogue containing basic information about all exemplars. This includes museum and excavation numbers (the symbol + is added between fragments that belong to the same object), provenance, lines preserved, and an indication of whether or not the inscription has been collated: c = collated from the original, (c) = partially collated from the original, p = collated from a photograph, (p) = partially collated from a photograph; and n = not collated. The next section is typically a commentary containing further technical information and notes. The bibliography then follows. Items are arranged chronologically, earliest to latest, with notes in parentheses after each bibliographic entry. These notes indicate the exemplars with which the item is concerned and the nature of the publication, using the following keywords: photo, copy, edition, translation, study, and provenance. Certain standard reference works (e.g., the various volumes of "Keilschriftbibliographie" and "Register Assyriologie" published in the journals Orientalia and Archiv für Orientforschung respectively; Borger, HKL 1–3; AHw; CAD; and Seux, ERAS) are not normally cited, although they were essential in the collecting and editing of these texts. While the bibliographies aim at featuring all major relevant items, they cannot be considered exhaustive, as a vast amount of scattered literature exists on many of the inscriptions edited in this volume, with much of this literature of only limited interest for this volume's aim of providing authoritative text editions.

As noted earlier, a distinction is made between major and minor variants to a "master text"; the major variants are placed at the bottom of the page and the minor variants at the back of the book. In brief, major variants are essentially non-orthographic in nature, while minor variants are orthographic variations. Orthographic variants of proper names may at times be significant and thus on occasion these will also appear on the page as major variants. Complete transliterations of all exemplars in the style of musical scores are found in a PDF available on the Open Richly Annotated Cuneiform Corpus (Oracc) platform at http://oracc.org/ribo/scores/. Thus, readers who find the notes on variants insufficient for their needs are encouraged to consult the full reading of any exemplar; such scores, however, are not normally given for brick inscriptions. Objects whose attribution to a particular text is not entirely certain are given exemplar numbers that are followed by an asterisk (*). Moreover, these exemplars are listed in separate catalogues (Likely Additional Exemplars), beneath the main catalogue.

Several photographs are included in this volume. These are intended to show a few of the object types bearing inscriptions of the three kings whose texts are edited in this volume and to aid the reader in appreciating the current state of preservation of some of the inscriptions.

As is normal practice for transliterating cuneiform inscriptions, lower case Roman script is used for Sumerian and lower case italics for Akkadian; logograms in Akkadian texts appear in capitals. The system of sign values in Borger, Mesopotamisches Zeichenlexikon, is generally followed. Italics in the English translation indicate either an uncertain translation or a word in the original, Akkadian language. In general, the rendering of names follows standard modern English translations; for example, Amēl-Marduk (rather than Amīl-Marduk or Evil-Merodach), Belshazzar (and not Bēl-šarru-uṣur), Lâbâši-Marduk (instead of Lā-abâš-Marduk), Nabonidus (rather than Nabû-na'id), and Neriglissar (instead of Nergal-šarru-uṣur). As for the translations of ceremonial names of temples and other buildings given in the present volume — for example, Eurmeiminanki ("House which Gathers the Seven *Me*s of Heaven and Netherworld"), the ziggurat of the god Nabû at Borsippa — these generally follow George, House Most High (for bibliographical abbreviations, see pp. xxiv–xxxii).

There are several differences between the RIM and RINBE styles; the latter follows that of RINAP. Among these, the most notable is that all partially preserved or damaged signs, regardless of how they are broken, appear between half brackets (⸢ and ⸣), following the model of the Oracc platform. Thus, no partially preserved sign has square brackets ([and]) inserted in its transliteration; for example, [DINGI]R and LUGA[L KU]R appear in the transliteration as ⸢DINGIR⸣ and ⸢LUGAL KUR⸣ respectively. This change was made to ensure compatibility of the online RINBE editions with the standards of Oracc, the parent site and project where the LMU-Munich-based Royal Inscriptions of Babylonia online (RIBo) Project, to which RINBE belongs, is housed. This change was implemented in the print version in order to present identical editions in RINBE 2 and on RIBo, in particular, in its "Babylon 7" sub-project. Note, however, that the translations may appear more damaged than their corresponding transliterations indicate, as the translations were prepared according to standard Assyriological practices; for example, ⸢DINGIR⸣ (= [DINGI]R) and ⸢LUGAL KUR⸣ (= LUGA[L KU]R) are translated as "[the go]d" and "king [of the lan]d," and not "the god" and "king of the land."

The bibliographical abbreviations, other abbreviations, and object signatures, whenever possible, follow RIM and RINAP in the print series; e.g., BE is used for prefix of excavation numbers from the German excavations at Babylon rather than Bab, the preferred siglum of some current Assyriological projects and scholars. In general, the museum, collection, and excavation numbers differ slightly in format from the Cuneiform Digital Library Initiative (CDLI) in the printed volumes; e.g., the "Babylon Stele" of Nabonidus (Nbn. 3) appears as EŞ 1327 in this volume, but as Ist EŞEM 01327 on CDLI. However, on RIBo, in both its informational pages and its downloadable catalogue, the format of RINBE's museum, collection, and excavation numbers follows that of CDLI, thereby facilitating better metadata exchange between RINBE and CDLI and easier cross-platform searching of the two projects' catalogues.

In addition to the indices of museum and excavation numbers and selected publications found in RIM volumes, the RINBE volumes also contain indices of proper names (personal names, topographical names, and divine names). Searchable online versions of the manuscripts are maintained on Oracc by the Munich Open-access Cuneiform Corpus Initiative (MOCCI). Web versions of the editions are also hosted on CDLI.

Munich
April 2020

Jamie Novotny
Editor-in-Chief

Bibliographical Abbreviations

AAE	Arabian Archaeology and Epigraphy. Hoboken, New Jersey, 1990–
Abel and Winckler, KGV	L. Abel and H. Winckler, Keilschrifttexte zum Gebrauch bei Vorlesungen. Berlin, 1890
Achämenidenhof	B. Jacobs and R. Rollinger (eds.), Der Achämenidenhof. The Achaemenid Court: Akten des 2. Internationalen Kolloquiums zum Thema »Vorderasien im Spannungsfeld klassischer und altorientalischer Überlieferungen« Landgut Castelen bei Basel, 23.–25. Mai 2007 (=Classica et Orientalia 2). Wiesbaden, 2010
ADAJ	Annual of the Department of Antiquities of Jordan. Amman, 1951–
AfO	Archiv für Orientforschung, vol. 3– (vols. 1–2 = AfK). Berlin, Graz, and Horn, 1926–
AHw	W. von Soden, Akkadisches Handwörterbuch, 3 vols. Wiesbaden, 1965–1981
AJSL	The American Journal of Semitic Languages and Literatures. Chicago, 1895–1941
Akkadica	Akkadica. Brussels, 1977–
Alle soglie della classicità	E. Acquaro (ed.), Alle soglie della classicità. Il Mediterraneo tra tradizione e innovazione. (=Studi di onore di Sabatino Moscati 1). Pisa, 1996
Ancient Mesopotamia Speaks	A.W. Lassen, E. Frahm, and K. Wagensonner (eds.), Ancient Mesopotamia Speaks: Highlights of the Yale Babylonian Collection. New Haven, 2019
ANET^2	J.B. Pritchard (ed.), Ancient Near Eastern Texts Relating to the Old Testament, 2nd edition. Princeton, 1955
ANET^3	J.B. Pritchard (ed.), Ancient Near Eastern Texts Relating to the Old Testament, 3rd edition. Princeton, 1969
AnOr	Analecta Orientalia. Rome, 1931–
AnSt	Anatolian Studies: Journal of the British Institute of Archaeology in Ankara. London 1951–
AoF	Altorientalische Forschungen. Berlin, 1974–
Arabian Studies 2	Proceedings of the Seminar for Arabian Studies 2, Proceedings of the fifth Seminar for Arabian Studies held at the Oriental Institute, Oxford 22nd and 23rd September 1971. Oxford, 1972
Arch.	Archaeologia, or, Miscellaneous Tracts Relating to Antiquity. London, 1770–1992
ArOr	Analecta Orientalia. Rome, 1931–
ARRIM	Annual Review of the Royal Inscriptions of Mesopotamia Project. Toronto, 1983–91
AS	Assyriological Studies. Chicago, 1931–
AuOr	Aula Orientalis: revista de estudios del Próximo Oriente Antiguo. Barcelona, 1983–
AUWE	Ausgrabungen in Uruk-Warka Endberichte. Deutsches Archäologisches Institut, Abteilung Baghdad. Mainz am Rhein, 1987–
Babylone	B. André-Salvini (ed.), Babylone. Paris, 2008
Babylon: Myth and Reality	I.L. Finkel and M.J. Seymour (eds.), Babylon: Myth and Reality. London, 2008
Babylon: Mythos	J. Marzahn and G. Schauerte (eds.), Babylon: Mythos. Munich, 2008
Babylon: Wahrheit	J. Marzahn and G. Schauerte (eds.), Babylon: Wahrheit. Munich, 2008
Bagh. Mitt.	Baghdader Mitteilungen. Berlin, 1960–
Ball, Light	C.J. Ball, Light from the East or the Witness of the Monuments: An Introduction to the Study of Biblical Archaeology. London, 1899
BAR	Biblical Archaeology Review. Washington, D.C., 1975–
BASOR	Bulletin of the American Schools of Oriental Research. New Haven and Boston, 1919–
Bauer, Asb.	T. Bauer, Das Inschriftenwerk Assurbanipals (=Assyriologische Bibliothek, Neue Folge 1–2). Leipzig, 1933
BBVO 26	E. Cancik-Kirschbaum and B. Schnitzlein (eds.), Keilschriftartefakte: Untersuchungen zur Materialität von Keilschriftdokumenten (=Berliner Beiträge zum Vorderen Orient 26). Gladbeck, 2018
BCSMS	Bulletin of the Canadian Society for Mesopotamian Studies, 40 vols. Toronto, 1981–2005

Beaulieu, Nabonidus	P.-A. Beaulieu, The Reign of Nabonidus, King of Babylon 556–539 BC (=Yale Near Eastern Researches 10). New Haven and London, 1989
Becker, AUWE 6	A. Becker., Uruk: Kleinfunde I: Stein (=Ausgrabungen in Uruk-Warka Endberichte 6). Mainz am Rhein, 1993
Beek, An Babels Strömen	M.A. Beek, An Babels Strömen. Hauptereignisse aus der Kulturgeschichte Mesopotamiens in der alttestamentlichen Zeit. München, 1959
Berger, Nbk	P.-R. Berger, Die neubabylonischen Königsinschriften: Königsinschriften des ausgehenden babylonischen Reiches (626–539 a. Chr.) (=Alter Orient und Altes Testament 4/1), Kevelaer and Neukirchen-Vluyn, 1973
Bezold, Cat.	C. Bezold, Catalogue of the Cuneiform Tablets in the Kouyunjik Collection of the British Museum, 5 vols. London, 1889–1899
Bezold, Literatur	C. Bezold, Kurzgefasster Überblick über die babylonisch-assyrische Literatur, nebst einem chronologischen Excurs, zwei Registern und einem Index zu 1700 Thontafeln des British-Museum's. Leipzig, 1886
Biblica	Biblica. Rome, 1920–
BibMes	Bibliotheca Mesopotamica. Malibu, 1975–
BIN	Babylonian Inscriptions in the Collection of J.B. Nies. New Haven, 1917–
BiOr	Bibliotheca Orientalis. Leiden, 1943–
BM Guide[2]	British Museum. A Guide to the Babylonian and Assyrian Antiquities, 2nd edition. London, 1908
BM Guide[3]	British Museum. A Guide to the Babylonian and Assyrian Antiquities, 3rd edition. London, 1922
Böhl, Chrestomathy 1	F.M.T. Böhl, Akkadian Chrestomathy, Volume 1: Selected Cuneiform Texts. Leiden, 1947
Böhl, OpMin	F.M.T. Böhl, Opera Minora. Groningen and Jakarta, 1953
Börker-Klähn, Bildstelen	J. Börker-Klähn, Altvorderasiatische Bildstelen und vergleichbare Felsreliefs, 2 vols (=Baghdader Forschungen 4). Mainz am Rhein, 1982
Boissier, Choix	A. Boissier, Choix de textes relatifs à la divination assyro-babylonienne, 2 vols. Geneva, 1905
Boissier, Seconde note	A. Boissier, Seconde note sur la publication des textes divinatoires du British Museum. Geneva, 1914
Bonatz, Grabdenkmal	D. Bonatz, Das syro-hethitische Grabdenkmal: Untersuchungen zur Entstehung einer neuen Bildgattung in der Eisenzeit im nordsyrisch-südostanatolischen Raum. Mainz, 2000
Borger, Asarh.	R. Borger, Die Inschriften Asarhaddons, Königs von Assyrien (=AfO Beiheft 9). Graz, 1956
Borger, BIWA	R. Borger, Beiträge zum Inschriftenwerk Assurbanipals: Die Prismenklassen A, B, C = K, D, E, F, G, H, J und T sowie andere Inschriften. Wiesbaden, 1996
Borger, HKL	R. Borger, Handbuch der Keilschriftliteratur, 3 vols. Berlin, 1967–75
Boulanger, Naissance de l'écriture	J.-P. Boulanger, Naissance de l'écriture: cunéiformes et hiéroglyphes; Galerie Nationales du Grand Palais, 7 mai – 9 août 1982. Paris, 1982
Boutflower, Book of Daniel	C. Boutflower, In and around the book of Daniel. London, 1923
Briant, From Cyrus to Alexander	P. Briant, From Cyrus to Alexander: A History of the Persian Empire. Winona Lake, IN, 2002
Brinkman, PKB	J.A. Brinkman, A Political History of Post-Kassite Babylonia, 1158–722 B.C. (=AnOr 43). Rome, 1963
Budge, Rise and Progress	E.A.W. Budge, The Rise and Progress of Assyriology. London, 1925
Butler, Dreams	S.A.L. Butler, Mesopotamian Conceptions of Dreams and Dream Rituals (=Alter Orient und Altes Testament 258). Münster, 1998
CAD	The Assyrian Dictionary of the Oriental Institute of the University of Chicago, 21 vols. Chicago, 1956–2010
CDA	J. Black, A. George, and N. Postgate (eds.), A Concise Dictionary of Akkadian. Wiesbaden, 1999
CDLI	Cuneiform Digital Library Initiative (https://cdli.ucla.edu). Los Angeles, CA, 1998–
CDOG 2	J. Renger (ed.), Babylon: Focus mesopotamischer Geschichte, Wiege früher Gelehrsamkeit, Mythos in der Moderne; 2. Internationales Colloquium der Deutschen Orient-Gesellschaft 24.– 26. März 1998 in Berlin (=Colloquien der Deutschen-Orient-Gesellschaft 2). Saarbrücken, 1999
Clay, YOS 1	A.T. Clay, Miscellaneous Inscriptions in the Yale Babylonian Collection (=YOS 1). New Haven, 1915

CLeO 3 — R. Rollinger (ed.), Herodot und das persische Weltreich: Akten des 3. Internationalen Kolloquiums zum Thema "Vorderasien im Spannungsfeld Klassischer und Altorientalischer Überlieferungen" Innsbruck, 24. - 28. November 2008 (=Classica et orientalia CLeO 3). Wiesbaden, 2011

Concepts of Kingship in Antiquity — G. B. Lanfranchi and R. Rollinger (eds.), Concepts of Kingship in Antiquity: Proceedings of the European Science Foundation Exploratory Workshop, Held in Padova, November 28th–December 1st, 2007 (=History of the Ancient Near East Monographs 9). Padova, 2010

Contenau, Manuel 1 — G. Contenau, Manuel d'archéologie orientale: Depuis les origines jusqu'a l'époque d'Alexandre 1. Notions générales (Races, chronologie, langage, écriture, religion, etc. ...). Histoire de l'art (Art archaïque d'Elam et de Sumer). Paris, 1927

COS 1 — W.W. Hallo and K. Lawson Younger, Jr., The Context of Scripture 1: Canonical Compositions from the Biblical World. Leiden, 2002

COS 2 — W.W. Hallo (ed.), The Context of Scripture, Volume 2: Monumental Inscriptions from the Biblical World. Leiden, 2000

CRAIB — Académie des Inscriptions et Belles Lettres, Comptes rendus. Paris, 1857–

CRRA — Compte Rendu de la Rencontre Assyriologique Internationale. [various locations], 1950–

CRRA 14 — La divination en Mésopotamie ancienne et dans les régions voisines, Strasbourg, 1965. Paris, 1966

CRRA 45/1 — T. Abusch, P.-A. Beaulieu, J. Huehnergard, P. Machinist, and P. Steinkeller (eds.), Proceedings of the XLVe Rencontre Assyriologique Internationale, Part I, Harvard University: Historiography in the Cuneiform World. Bethesda, MD, 2001

CT — Cuneiform Texts from Babylonian Tablets in the British Museum. London, 1896–

CUSAS 17 — A.R. George (ed.), Cuneiform Royal Inscriptions and Related Texts in the Schøyen Collection (=Cornell University Studies in Assyriology and Sumerology 17). Bethesda, MD, 2011

D'Agostino, Nabonedo — F. D'Agostino, Nabonedo, Adda Guppi, il deserto e il Dio Luna. Storia, ideologia e propaganda nella Babilonia desl VI sec. A.C. Pisa, 1994

Dandamaev, Political History — M.A. Dandamaev, A Political History of the Achaemenid Empire. Leiden, 1989

Da Riva, GMTR 4 — R. Da Riva, The Neo-Babylonian Royal Inscriptions (=Guides to the Mesopotamian Textual Records 4). Münster, 2008

Da Riva, SANER 3 — R. Da Riva, The Inscriptions of Nabopolassar, Amel-Marduk and Neriglissar (=Studies in Ancient Near Eastern Records 3). Boston and Berlin, 2013

Da Riva, Twin Inscriptions — R. Da Riva, The Twin Inscriptions of Nebuchadnezzar at Brisa (Wadi Esh-Sharbin, Lebanon): A Historical and Philological Study (=Archiv für Orientforschung Beiheft 32). Wien, 2012

Das Altertum — Das Altertum. Berlin, 1955–

Dictionnaire de la Bible 4 — A. Robert (ed.), Dictionnaire de la bible: Supplément 4: Hetzenauer - Justice et Justification. Paris, 1949

Dictionnaire de la Bible 6 — H. Cazelles (ed.), Dictionnaire de la bible: Supplément 6: Mystères - Passion. Paris, 1960

van Dijk, TLB 2 — J. van Dijk, Textes divers (=Tabulae Cuneiformes a F.M.Th. de Liagre Böhl collectae 2). Leiden, 1957

DLZ — Deutsche Literaturzeitung. Berlin, 1880–

Ehring, Rückkehr JHWHs — C. Ehring, Die Rückkehr JHWHs. Traditions- und religionsgeschichtliche Untersuchung zu Jesaja 40, 1–11, Jesaja 52, 7–10 und verwandten Texten (=Wissenschaftliche Monographien zum Alten und Neuen Testament 116). Neukirchen-Vluyn, 2007

Eichmann und Hausleiter, Tayma 2 — A. Hausleiter, R. Eichmann, M. Al-Najem (eds.), M.C.A. Macdonald, H. Schaudig, P. Stein, Tayma II, Inscriptions from the Saudi-German Excavations, Part 1. Riyadh, forthcoming

Ellis, Foundation Deposits — R.S. Ellis, Foundation Deposits in Ancient Mesopotamia (=Yale Near Eastern Researches 2). New Haven and London, 1968

Exile and Return — J. Stökl and C. Waerzeggers (eds.), Exile and Return: The Babylonian Context (= Beihefte zur Zeitschrift für alttestamentliche Wissenschaft 478). Berlin, 2015

Foster, Before the Muses — B.R. Foster, Before the Muses: An Anthology of Akkadian Literature, 2 vols. Bethesda, 1993

Frame, RIMB 2 — G. Frame, Rulers of Babylonia from the Second Dynasty of Isin to the End of Assyrian Domination (1157–612 BC) (=RIMB 2). Toronto, 1995

Frame, RINAP 2 — G. Frame, The Royal Inscriptions of Sargon II, King of Assyria (721–705 BC) (=RINAP 2). University Park, PA, 2020

Frayne, RIME 4	D.R. Frayne, Old Babylonian Period (2003–1595 BC) (=RIME 4). Toronto, 1990
FuB	Forschungen und Berichte, Staatliche Museen zu Berlin. Berlin, 1957–1991
Gadd, History and Monuments	C.J. Gadd, History and Monuments of Ur. London, 1929
Gadd, UET 1	C.J. Gadd, L. Legrain, and S. Smith, Royal Inscriptions (=Ur Excavations Texts 1). London, 1928
Galling, Studien	K. Galling, Studien zur Geschichte Israels im persischen Zeitalter. Tübingen, 1964
Galling, Textbuch^{3}	K. Galling, Textbuch zur Geschichte Israels, 3rd edition. Tübingen, 1979
de Genouillac, Kich	H. de Genouillac, Premières recherches archéologiques à Kich (Fouilles françaises d'El-'Akhymer, Mission d'Henri de Genouillac, 1911–1912), 2 vols. Paris, 1924–25
George, BTT	A.R. George, Babylonian Topographical Texts (=Orientalia Lovaniensia Analecta 40). Leuven, 1992
George, House Most High	A.R. George, House Most High: The Temples of Ancient Mesopotamia (=Mesopotamian Civilizations 5). Winona Lake, IN, 1993
Giorn. della Società As. Ital.	Giornale della Società Asiatica Italiana, 29 vols. Florence, 1887–1920.
Glassner, Chronicles	J.-J. Glassner, Mesopotamian Chronicles (=Writings from the Ancient World 19). Atlanta, 2004
Grayson, Chronicles	A.K. Grayson, Assyrian and Babylonian Chronicles (=Texts from Cuneiform Sources 5). Locust Valley, NY, 1975
Grayson and Novotny, RINAP 3/1	A.K. Grayson and J. Novotny, The Royal Inscriptions of Sennacherib, King of Assyria (704–681 BC), Part 1 (=RINAP 3/1). Winona Lake, IN, 2012
Grayson and Novotny, RINAP 3/2	A.K. Grayson and J. Novotny, The Royal Inscriptions of Sennacherib, King of Assyria (704–681 BC), Part 2 (=RINAP 3/2). Winona Lake, IN, 2014
Gressman, ATAT^{2}	H. Gressman, Altorientalische Texte zum Alten Testament, 2nd edition. Berlin, 1926
Grotefend, Erläuterungen	G.F. Grotefend, Erläuterung der Keilinschriften babylonischer Backsteine mit einigen anderen Zugaben und einer Steindrucktafel. Hannover, 1852
Harper, Literature	R.F. Harper, Assyrian and Babylonian Literature: Selected Translations, with a Critical Introduction. New York, 1904
Heller, Spätzeit	A. Heller, Das Babylonien der Spätzeit (7.–4. Jh.) in den klassischen und keilschriftlichen Quellen. Berlin, 2010
Hilprecht, Explorations	H.V. Hilprecht, Explorations in Bible Lands During the 19th Century. Philadelphia, 1903
HUCA	Hebrew Union College Annual. Cincinnati, 1924–
Hunger, Kolophone	H. Hunger, Babylonische und assyrische Kolophone (=Alter Orient und Altes Testament 2). Kevelaer and Neukirchen-Vluyn, 1968
IEJ	Israel Exploration Journal. Jerusalem, 1950–
ILN	The Illustrated London News. London, 1842–
Imperien und Reiche	M. Gehler and R. Rollinger (eds.), Imperien und Reiche in der Weltgeschichte. Epochenübergreifende und globalhistorische Vergleiche. Wiesbaden, 2014
Iraq	Iraq. London, 1934–
ISIMU	ISIMU: Revista sobre Oriente Próximo y Egipto en la antigüedad. Madrid, 1998–
JA	Journal asiatique. Paris, 1822–
JAC	Journal of Ancient Civilizations. Changchun, 1986–
Jastrow, Religion	M. Jastrow, Die Religion Babyloniens und Assyriens, 2 vols. Gießen, 1905–12
JCS	Journal of Cuneiform Studies. New Haven and Cambridge, MA, 1947–
Jensen, Kosmologie	P. Jensen, Die Kosmologie der Babylonier, Studien und Materialien, mit einem mythologischen Anhang und 3 Karten. Strassburg, 1890
JEOL	Jaarbericht van het Vooraziatisch-Egyptisch Genootschap "Ex Oriente Lux." Leiden, 1933–
JNES	Journal of Near Eastern Studies. Chicago, 1942–
Jordan, Uruk-Warka	J. Jordan, Uruk-Warka nach den Ausgrabungen durch die Deutsche Orient-Gesellschaft (=WVDOG 51). Leipzig, 1928
JRAS	Journal of the Royal Asiatic Society. London, 1834–
Judah and the Judeans	O. Lipschits and J. Blenkinsopp (eds.), Judah and the Judeans in the Neo-Babylonian Period. Winona Lake, IN, 2003
Jursa, Die Babylonier	M. Jursa, M., Die Babylonier. Geschichte, Gesellschaft, Kultur. Munich, 2004.
Kaskal	Kaskal. Rivista di storia, ambiente e culture del Vicino Oriente Antico. Padua, 2004–
Keiser, BIN 2	C. Keiser and J.B. Nies, Historical Religious and Economic Texts and Antiquities (=Babylonian Inscriptions in the Collection of J.B. Nies). New Haven, 1920
King, BBSt	L.W. King, Babylonian Boundary-Stones and Memorial-Tablets in the British Museum, 2 vols. London, 1912
Klauber, PRT	E. Klauber, Politisch-religiöse Texte aus der Sargonidenzeit. Leipzig, 1913

Klengel-Brandt, Turm	E. Klengel-Brandt, Der Turm von Babylon. Legende und Geschichte eines Bauwerkes. Leipzig, 1982
Klio	Klio. Beiträge zur Alten Geschichte. Berlin, 1901–
Koldewey, Ischtar-Tor	R. Koldewey, Das Ischtar-Tor in Babylon (=Wissenschaftliche Veröffentlichungen der Deutschen Orient-Gesellschaft 32). Leipzig, 1918
Koldewey, Königsburgen 1	R. Koldewey, Die Königsburgen von Babylon 1: Die Südburg (=Wissenschaftliche Veröffentlichungen der Deutschen Orient-Gesellschaft 54), Leipzig, 1931
Koldewey, Königsburgen 2	R. Koldewey, Die Königsburgen von Babylon 2: Die Hauptburg und der Sommerpalast Nebukadnezars im Hügel Babil (=Wissenschaftliche Veröffentlichungen der Deutschen Orient-Gesellschaft 55), Leipzig, 1932
Koldewey, Tempel	R. Koldewey, Die Tempel von Babylon und Borsippa (=Wissenschaftliche Veröffentlichungen der Deutschen Orient-Gesellschaft 15), Leipzig, 1911
Koldewey, WEB^4	R. Koldewey, Das wieder erstehende Babylon: Die bisherigen Ergebnisse der deutschen Ausgrabungen, 4th edition. Leipzig, 1925
Koldewey, WEB^5	R. Koldewey, Das wieder erstehende Babylon: Die bisherigen Ergebnisse der deutschen Ausgrabungen, 5th edition. Leipzig, 1990
Koschaker, Rechtsvergleichende Studien	P. Koschaker, Rechtsvergleichende Studien zur Gesetzgebung Hammurapis, Königs von Babylon. Leipzig, 1917
Kuhrt, Persian Empire	A. Kuhrt, The Persian Empire: A Corpus of Sources from the Achaemenid Period. London and New York, 2007
Lambert, BWL	W.G. Lambert, Babylonian Wisdom Literature. Oxford, 1960
Landsberger, Brief	B. Landsberger, Brief des Bischofs von Esagila an König Asarhaddon (=Mededelingen der Koninklijke Nederlandse Akademie van Wetenschappen, Afd. Letterkunde, NR 28/6). Amsterdam, 1965.
Landsberger, MSL 6	B. Landsberger, The Series ḪAR-ra = ḫubullu: Tablets V–VII (=Materials for the Sumerian Lexicon 6), Rome, 1958
Langdon, Building inscriptions	S. Langdon, Building inscriptions of the Neo-Babylonian Empire: Part 1, Nabopolassar and Nebuchadnezzar. Paris, 1907
Langdon, NBK	S. Langdon, Die neubabylonischen Königsinschriften (=Vorderasiatische Bibliothek 4), Leipzig, 1912
Langdon, OECT 1	S. Langdon, The H. Weld-Blundell Collection in the Ashmolean Museum, vol. 1: Sumerian and Semitic Religious and Historical Texts (=Oxford Editions of Cuneiform Texts 1), Oxford, 1923
Legrain, PBS 15	L. Legrain, Royal Inscriptions and Fragments from Nippur and Babylon (=Publications of the Babylonian Section, University Museum, University of Pennsylvania 15). Philadelphia, 1926
Leichty, RINAP 4	E. Leichty, The Royal Inscriptions of Esarhaddon, King of Assyria (680–669 BC) (=RINAP 4). Winona Lake, IN, 2011
Leichty, Sippar	E. Leichty, Tablets from Sippar, 3 vols. (=Catalogue of the Babylonian Tablets in the British Museum 6–8). London, 1986–88
Linssen, Cults of Uruk and Babylon	M.J.H. Linssen, The Cults of Uruk and Babylon: The Temple Ritual Texts as Evidence for Hellenistic Cult Practices (= Cuneiform Monographs 25). Leiden and Boston, 2004
Litke, Assyro-Babylonian God-lists	R. Litke, A Reconstruction of the Assyro-Babylonian God-lists, AN: ^{d}*A-nu-um* and AN: *Anu šá amēli* (= Texts from the Babylonian Collection 3). New Haven, 1998
Longman, Autobiography	T. Longman, Fictional Akkadian Autobiography: A Generic and Comparative Study. Winona Lake, IN, 1991
MDOG	Mitteilungen der Deutschen Orient-Gesellschaft zu Berlin. Berlin, 1898–
MDP	Mémoires de la Délégation en Perse. Paris, 1900–
Meissner, BAW	B. Meissner, Beiträge zum assyrischen Wörterbuch, 2 vols. (=Assyriological Studies 1–2). Chicago, 1931–32
Meissner, Chrestomathie	B. Meissner, Assyrisch-babylonische Chrestomathie für Anfänger. Leiden, 1895
Meissner, Warenpreise	B. Meissner, Warenpreise in Babylonien (=Abhandlungen der Preußischen Akademie der Wissenschaften 1936/1). Berlin, 1936
Ménant, Babylone	J. Ménant, Babylone et la Chaldée. Paris, 1875
Ménant, Manuel	J. Ménant, Manuel de la langue assyrienne. Paris, 1880
Mesopotamia	Mesopotamia. Turin, 1966–
Messerschmidt and Ungnad, VAS 1	L. Messerschmidt and A. Ungnad, Vorderasiatische Schriftdenkmäler der Königlichen Museen zu Berlin vol. 1. Leipzig, 1907
de Meyer (ed.), Tell ed-Dēr 3	L. de Meyer (ed.), Tell ed-Dēr 3: Soundings at Abū Habbah (Sippar). Louvain, 1980
MJ	Museum Journal of the University Museum, University of Pennsylvania, vols. 1–24. Philadelphia, 1910–35
MOCCI	The Munich Open-Access Cuneiform Corpus Initiative. Munich, 2015–

Mofidi-Nasrabadi, Bestattungssitten — B. Mofidi-Nasrabadi, Untersuchungen zu den Bestattungssitten in Mesopotamien in der ersten Hälfte des ersten Jahrtausends v. Chr. (Baghdader Forschungen 23). Mainz, 1999

MSL — B. Landsberger (ed.), Materials for the Sumerian Lexicon. Rome, 1937–

MVAG — Mitteilungen der Vorderasiatisch-Aegyptischen Gesellschaft. Leipzig and Berlin, 1896–1944

NABU — Nouvelles assyriologiques brèves et utilitaires. Paris, 1987–

Naster, Chrestomathie — P. Naster, Chrestomathie accadienne (=Bibliothèque du Muséon 12). Louvain, 1941

Neue Beiträge zur Semitistik — N. Nebes, (ed.), Neue Beiträge zur Semitistik: erstes Arbeitstreffen der Arbeitsgemeinschaft Semitistik in der Deutschen Morgenländischen Gemeinschaft vom 11. bis 13. September 2000 an der Friedrich-Schiller-Universität Jena. Wiesbaden, 2002

Nineveh 612 — R. Mattila (ed.), Nineveh B.C.: The Glory and Fall of the Assyrian Empire. Helsinki, 1995

Novotny, Eḫulḫul — J.R. Novotny, Eḫulḫul, Egipar, Emelamana, and Sîn's *Akītu*-House: A Study of Assyrian Building Activities at Ḫarrān. PhD dissertation, University of Toronto, 2003

Novotny and Jeffers, RINAP 5/1 — J. Novotny and J. Jeffers, The Royal Inscriptions of Ashurbanipal (668–631 BC), Aššur-etel-ilāni (630–627 BC), and Sîn-šarra-iškun (626–612 BC), Kings of Assyria, Part 1 (=RINAP 5/1). University Park, PA, 2018

Nürnberger Blätter — Nürnberger Blätter zur Archäologie, vols. 1–22. Nurnberg, 1984–2004

OBO — Orbis Biblicus et Orientalis. Freiburg, Göttingen, and Leuven, 1973–

OBO 175 — C. Uehlinger (ed.), Images as media: Sources for the cultural history of the Near East and the Eastern Mediterranean (1st millennium BCE) (=Orbis Biblicus et Orientalis 175). Freiburg and Göttingen, 2000

OECT — Oxford Editions of Cuneiform Texts. Oxford, London, and Paris, 1923–

OLZ — Orientalistische Literaturzeitung. Berlin and Leipzig, 1898–

Oppenheim, Ancient Mesopotamia — A.L. Oppenheim, Ancient Mesopotamia: Portrait of a Dead Civilization. Revised edition completed by E. Reiner. Chicago and London, 1964

Oppenheim, Dream-book — A.L. Oppenheim, The Interpretation of Dreams in the Ancient Near East, with a Translation of an Assyrian Dream-book. (=Transactions of the American Philosophical Society NS 46/3) Philadelphia, 1956

Oppenheim, JAOS Suppl. 10 — A.L. Oppenheim and L.F. Hartman, On Beer and Brewing Techniques in Ancient Mesopotamia According to the XXIIIrd Tablet of the Series ḪAR.ra = *ḫubullu* (=Journal of the American Oriental Society Supplementum 10). Baltimore, 1950

Oppert, EM — J. Oppert, Expédition scientifique en Mésopotamie exécutée par ordre du gouvernement de 1851 à 1854 par MM. Fulgence Fresnel, Félix Thomas et Jules Oppert, 2 vols. Paris, 1859–1863

Oracc — Open Richly Annotated Cuneiform Corpus Initiative (oracc.org). 2007–

Orthmann, Der alte Orient — W. Orthmann, Der alte Orient (=Propyläen Kunstgeschichte 14). Berlin, 1975

Orientalia NS — Orientalia. Nova Series. Rome, 1932–

Pagan Priests — M. Beard and J. North (eds.), Pagan Priests: Religion and Power in the Ancient World, Ithaca, NY, 1990

Parker and Dubberstein, Babylonian Chronology — R. Parker and W. Dubberstein, Babylonian Chronology 626 B.C.–A.D. 75 (=Brown University Studies 19). Providence, 1956

PBA — Proceedings of the British Academy. Oxford, 1905–

PBS — Publications of the Babylonian Section, University Museum, University of Pennsylvania, 15 vols. Philadelphia, 1911–26

PIHANS — Publications de l'Institut historique-archéologique néerlandais de Stamboul. Leiden, 1956–

PNA — H.D. Baker and K. Radner (eds.), The Prosopography of the Neo-Assyrian Empire. Helsinki, 1998–

Poebel, AS 15 — A. Poebel, The Second Dynasty of Isin According to a New King-list Tablet (=Assyriological Studies 15). Chicago, 1955

Pognon, Inscriptions sémitiques — H. Pognon, Inscriptions sémitiques de la Syrie, de la Mésopotamie et de la région de Mossoul. Paris, 1907

Pognon, Wadi Brissa — H. Pognon, Les inscriptions babyloniennes du Wadi Brissa (=Bibliothèque de l'École des Hautes Études, IVe section (sciences historiques et philologiques) 71). Paris, 1887

Political Memory — J.M. Silverman and C. Waerzeggers (eds.), Political Memory in and after the Persian Empire (= Society of Biblical Literature Ancient Near Eastern Monographs 13). Atlanta, 2015

Prince, SSS 5 — R.J. Lau and J.D. Prince, Abu Habba cylinder of Nabuna'id (V Rawlinson Pl. 64) (=Semitic Study Series 5). Leiden, 1905

PSAS 40	M.C.A. Macdonald (ed.), The Development of Arabic as a Written Language (=Supplement to the Proceedings of the Seminar for Arabian Studies 40). Oxford, 2010
PSBA	Proceedings of the Society of Biblical Archaeology, 40 vols. London, 1878–1918
1 R	H.C. Rawlinson and E. Norris, The Cuneiform Inscriptions of Western Asia, vol. 1: A Selection from the Historical Inscriptions of Chaldaea, Assyria, and Babylonia. London, 1861
5 R	H.C. Rawlinson and T.G. Pinches, The Cuneiform Inscriptions of Western Asia, vol. 5: A Selection from the Miscellaneous Inscriptions of Assyria and Babylonia. London, 1880–84
RA	Revue d'assyriologie et d'archéologie orientale. Paris, 1886–
Radner, Short History of Babylon	K. Radner, A Short History of Babylon. London, 2020
RB	Revue biblique. Paris, 1892–
Records of the Past	S. Birch (ed.), Records of the Past Being English Translations of the Assyrian and Egyptian Monuments [Series 1], 12 vols. London, 1873–81
Reiner, Astral Magic	E. Reiner, Astral Magic in Babylonia (=Transactions of the American Philosophical Society 85/4). Philadelphia, 1995
Reiner, Your Thwarts in Pieces	E. Reiner, Your Thwarts in Pieces, Your Mooring Rope Cut: Poetry from Babylonia and Assyria (=Michigan studies in the humanities 5). Ann Arbor, 1985
Rép. Géogr.	W. Röllig (ed.), Beihefte zum Tübinger Atlas des vorderen Orients, Reihe B, Nr. 7: Répertoire géographique des textes cunéiformes. Wiesbaden, 1974–
Representations of Political Power	M. Heinz and M. H. Feldman (eds.), Representations of Political Power: Case Histories from Times of Change and Dissolving Order in the Ancient Near East. Winona Lake, IN, 2007
Reuther, Merkes	O. Reuther, Die Innenstadt von Babylon (Merkes) (=Wissenschaftliche Veröffentlichungen der Deutschen Orient-Gesellschaft 47). Leipzig, 1926
RIBo	Royal Inscriptions of Babylonia online (oracc.org/ribo/). Munich, 2015–
Rich, Narrative Babylon	C.J. Rich, Narrative of a journey to the site of Babylon in 1811, now first published: memoir on the ruins; with engravings from the original sketches by the author: remarks on the topography of ancient Babylon, by Major Rennell; in reference to the memoir: second memoir on the ruins; in reference to Major Rennell's remarks: with narrative of a journey to Persepolis: now first printed, with hitherto unpublished cuneiform inscriptions copied at Persepolis. London, 1839
Rich, Second Memoir on Babylon	C.J. Rich, Second Memoir on Babylon; containing an Inquiry into the Correspondence between the Ancient Descriptions of Babylon and the Remains still visible on the Site, suggested by the "Remarks" of Major Rennell, published in the Archæologia. London, 1818
RIM	The Royal Inscriptions of Mesopotamia. Toronto, 1984–2008
RIMA	The Royal Inscriptions of Mesopotamia, Assyrian Periods, 3 vols. Toronto, 1987–1996
RIMB	The Royal Inscriptions of Mesopotamia, Babylonian Periods, 1 vol. Toronto, 1995
RIME	The Royal Inscriptions of Mesopotamia, Early Periods, 5 vols. Toronto, 1990–2008
RINAP	The Royal Inscriptions of the Neo-Assyrian Period. Winona Lake, IN, and University Park, PA, 2011–
RINBE	Royal Inscriptions of the Neo-Babylonian Empire. University Park, PA, 2020–
RINBE 1/1	F. Weiershäuser and J. Novotny, The Royal Inscriptions of Nabopolassar (625–605 BC) and Nebuchadnezzar II (604–562 BC), Kings of Babylon, Part 1 (=Royal Inscriptions of the Neo-Babylonian Empire 1/1) [in preparation]
RINBE 1/2	F. Weiershäuser and J. Novotny, The Royal Inscriptions of Nabopolassar (625–605 BC) and Nebuchadnezzar II (604–562 BC), Kings of Babylon, Part 2 (=Royal Inscriptions of the Neo-Babylonian Empire 1/2) [in preparation]
RINBE 2	The present volume.
RLA	Reallexikon der Assyriologie und Vorderasiatischen Archäologie, 15 vols. Berlin, 1932–2018
Rogers, History	R.W. Rogers, A History of Babylonia and Assyria, 6th edition, 2 vols. New York, 1915
Rolle der Astronomie	H. D. Galter (ed.), Die Rolle der Astronomie in den Kulturen Mesopotamiens. Beiträge zum 3. Grazer Morgenländischen Symposion (23.–27. September 1991) (=Grazer Morgenländische Studien 3). Graz, 1993
Rollinger, Herodots Babylonischer Logos	R. Rollinger, Herodots Babylonischer Logos. Eine kritische Untersuchung der Glaubwürdigkeitsdiskussion an Hand ausgewählter Beispiele: Historische Parallelüberlieferung – Argumentationen – Archäologischer Befund – Konsequenzen für eine Geschichte Babyloniens in persischer Zeit (=Innsbrucker Beiträge zur Kulturwissenschaft Sonderheft 84) Innsbruck, 1993

Routes d'Arabie	A. al-Ghabban, B. André-Salvini, F. Demange, C. Juvin, and M. Cotty (eds.), Routes d'Arabie. Archéologie et Histoire du Royaume Arabie Saoudite. Paris, 2010
RSO	Rivista degli studi orientali. Rome, 1907–
RT	Recueil de travaux relatifs à la philologie de à l'archéologie égyptiennes et assyriennes. Paris, 1870–1923
Rutten, Encyclopédie photographique de l'art	R. Rutten (ed.), Encyclopédie photographique de l'art, 2 vols. Paris, 1935–36
Sack, Amēl-Marduk	R. Sack, Amēl-Marduk 652–560 B.C.: A Study Based on Cuneiform, Old Testament, Greek, Latin, and Rabbinical Sources (=Alter Orient und Altes Testament Sonderreihe 4). Neukirchen-Vluyn, 1972
Sack, Neriglissar	R.H. Sack, Neriglissar: King of Babylon (=Alter Orient und Altes Testament 236). Kevelaer and Neukirchen-Vluyn, 1994
Sass and Marzahn, WVDOG 127	B. Sass and J. Marzahn, Aramaic and Figural Stamp Impressions on Bricks of the Sixth Century B.C. from Babylon (=Wissenschaftliche Veröffentlichungen der Deutschen Orient-Gesellschaft 127). Wiesbaden, 2010
Schaudig, Inschriften Nabonids	H. Schaudig, Die Inschriften Nabonids von Babylon und Kyros' des Großen samt den in ihrem Umfeld entstandenen Tendenzschriften. Textausgabe und Grammatik. (=Alter Orient und Altes Testament 256), Münster, 2001
Scheil, MDP 5	V. Scheil, Textes élamites-anzanites, 2me série (=Mémoires de la Délégation en Perse 5). Paris, 1904
Scheil, MDP 10	V. Scheil, Textes élamites-sémitiques, 4me série (=Mémoires de la Délégation en Perse 10). Paris, 1908
Scheil, MDP 14	V. Scheil, Textes élamites-sémitiques, 5me série (=Mémoires de la Délégation en Perse 10). Paris, 1913
Schrader, KB	E. Schrader (ed.), Keilinschriftliche Bibliothek, Sammlung von assyrischen und babylonischen Texten in Umschrift und Übersetzung, 6 vols. Berlin, 1889–1915
Schuster-Brandis, AOAT 46	A. Schuster-Brandis, Steine als Schutz- und Heilmittel: Untersuchung zu ihrer Verwendung in der Beschwörungskunst Mesopotamiens im 1. Jt. v. Chr. (=Alter Orient und Altes Testament 46). Münster, 2008
Seipel and Wieczorek, Von Babylon bis Jerusalem	W. Seipel and A. Wieczorek (eds.), Von Babylon bis Jerusalem. Die Welt der altorientalischen Königsstädte, 2 vols. Milan, 1999
Semitic Languages	S. Weninger (ed.), The Semitic Languages: An International Handbook (Handbücher zur Sprach- und Kommunikationswissenschaft 36). Berlin and Boston, 2011
Seux, ERAS	M.-J. Seux, Épithètes royales akkadiennes et sumériennes. Paris, 1967
SMEA	Studi Micenei ed Egeo-Anatolici. Rome, 1966–
S. Smith, BHT	S.A. Smith., Babylonian Historical Texts Relating to the Capture and Downfall of Babylon. London, 1924
von Soden, SAHG	A. Falkenstein and W. von Soden, Sumerische und akkadische Hymnen und Gebete. Zurich and Stuttgart, 1953
Sollberger, TCS 1	E. Sollberger, The Business and Administrative Correspondence Under the Kings of Ur (=Texts from Cuneiform Sources 1). Locust Valley, NY, 1966
Sollberger, UET 8	E. Sollberger, Royal Inscriptions Part 2 (=Ur Excavation Texts 8). London, 1965
Spar, CTMMA 4	I. Spar and M. Jursa, Cuneiform Texts in the Metropolitan Museum of Art 4: Temple Archive and Other Texts From the First and Second Millennium B.C. (=Cuneiform texts in the Metropolitan Museum of Art 4). New York, 2014
SPAW	Sitzungsberichte der königlich Preussischen Akademie der Wissenschaften zu Berlin. Berlin, 1882–1918
Stamm, Namengebung	J.J. Stamm, Die akkadische Namengebung (=Mitteilungen der Vorderasiatisch-Aegyptischen Gesellschaft 44). Leipzig, 1939
Strassmeier, Liverpool	J.N. Strassmaier, Die babylonischen Inschriften im Museum zu Liverpool nebst anderen aus der Zeit von Nebukadnezzar bis Darius (=Actes du 6e Congrès International des Orientalistes tenu en 1883 à Leide, 2, Section Sémitique). Leiden, 1885
Strassmeier, Nbn.	J.N. Strassmaier, Inschriften von Nabonidus, König von Babylon (=Babylonische Texte 1–4). Leipzig, 1889
Studies Astour	G.D. Young, M.W. Chavalas, and R.E. Averbeck (eds.), Crossing Boundaries and Linking Horizons: Studies in Honor of Michael C. Astour on His 80th Birthday. Bethesda, 1997
Studies Edhem	Halil Edhem Hâtira Kitabi: Cilt 1 (In Memoriam Halil Edhem Vol. 1) (=Türk Tarih Kurumu yayınları 7/5). Ankara, 1947
Studies Ellis	M.J. Boda and J. Novotny (eds.), From the Foundations to the Crenellations: Essays on Temple Building in the Ancient Near East and Hebrew Bible (=Alter Orient und Altes Testament 366). Münster, 2010

Studies Finkelstein	M. de Jong Ellis (ed.) Essays on the Ancient Near East in Memory of Jacob Joel Finkelstein (=Memoirs of the Connecticut Academy of Arts and Sciences 19). Hamden, CT, 1977
Studies Grayson	G. Frame (ed.), From the Upper Sea to the Lower Sea: Studies on the History of Assyria and Babylonia in Honour of A.K. Grayson (=PIHANS 101). Leiden, 2004
Studies Hallo	M. Cohen (ed.): The Tablet and the Scroll: Near Eastern Studies in Honor of William W. Hallo, Bethesda, MD, 1993
Studies Kienast	G.J. Selz (ed.), Festschrift für Burkhart Kienast zu seinem 70. Geburtstage dargebracht von Freunden, Schülern und Kollegen (=Alter Orient und Altes Testament 274). Münster, 2003
Studies Koschaker	J. Friedrich (ed.), Symbolae ad iura orientis antiqui pertinentes Paulo Koschaker dedicatae. Leiden, 1939
Studies Kramer	B. Eichler (ed.), Kramer Anniversary Volume: Cuneiform Studies in Honor of Samuel Noah Kramer (=Alter Orient und Altes Testament 25). Neukirchen-Vluyn, 1976
Studies Landsberger	H.G. Güterbock and T. Jacobsen (eds.), Studies in Honor of B. Landsberger on his Seventy-fifth Birthday, April 21, 1965 (=Assyriological Studies 16). Chicago, London, and Toronto, 1965
Studies Lehmann-Haupt	K. Regling and H. Reich (eds.), Festschrift zu C.F. Lehmann-Haupts sechzigstem Geburtstage. Vienna, 1921
Studies Mellink	J.V. Canby, E. Porada, B.S. Ridgway, and T. Stech (eds.), Ancient Anatolia. Aspects of Change and Cultural Development. Essays in Honor of Machteld J. Mellink. Madison, 1986
Studies Parpola	M. Luukko, S. Svärd, and R. Mattila (eds.), Of God(s), Trees, Kings, and Scholars: Neo-Assyrian and Related Studies in Honour of Simo Parpola (=StOr 106). Helsinki, 2009
Studies Rochberg	C.J. Crisostomo, E.A. Escobar, T. Tanaka, and N. Veldhuis (eds.), The Scaffolding of Our Thoughts: Essays on Assyriology and the History of Science in Honor of Francesca Rochberg. Leiden and Boston, 2018
Studies Römer	M. Dietrich and O. Loretz (eds.): *dubsar anta-me*, Studien zur Altorientalistik, Festschrift für Wilhelm H. Ph. Römer zur Vollendung seines 70. Lebensjahres mit Beiträgen von Freunden, Schülern und Kollegen (= Alter Orient und Altes Testament 253). Münster, 1998
Studies Stolper	M. Kozuh, W.F.M. Henkelman, C.E. Jones, and C. Woods (eds.), Extraction and Control: Studies in Honor of Matthew W. Stolper (=Studies in Ancient Oriental Civilization 68), Chicago, 2014
Šulmu 4	J. Zabłoka and S. Zawadzki (eds.): Šulmu IV: Everyday Life in Ancient Near East. Papers Presented at the International Conference Poznań, 19–22 September, 1989 (=Uniwersytet im. Adama Mickiewicza w Poznaniu. Seria Historia 182), Poznan, 1993
Sumer	Sumer: A Journal of Archaeology in Iraq. Baghdad, 1945–
Syria	Syria. Paris, 1920–
Tadmor, Tigl. III	H. Tadmor, The Inscriptions of Tiglath-pileser III, King of Assyria: Critical Edition, with Introductions, Translations, and Commentary. Jerusalem, 1994
Tadmor and Yamada, RINAP 1	H. Tadmor and S. Yamada, The Royal Inscriptions of Tiglath-pileser III (744–727 BC) and Shalmaneser V (726–722 BC), Kings of Assyria (=RINAP 1). Winona Lake, IN, 2011
TCS	Texts from Cuneiform Sources. Locust Valley, NY, 1966–
Teloni, Crestomazia	B. Teloni, Crestomazia Assira con Paradigmi Grammaticali. Florence, 1887
Tempel im Alten Orient	K. Kaniuth, A. Löhnert, J.L. Miller, A. Otto, M. Roaf, and W. Sallaberger (eds.), Tempel im Alten Orient. 7. Internationales Colloquium der Deutschen Orient-Gesellschaft 11.–13. Oktober 2009, München. Wiesbaden, 2013
ThLZ	Theologische Literaturzeitung. Leipzig, 1876–
Thompson, Bodleian	R. Campbell Thompson, A catalogue of the Late Babylonian tablets in the Bodleian Library, Oxford. London, 1927
TSBA	Transactions of the Society of Biblical Archaeology. London, 1872–1893
TUAT	O. Kaiser (ed.), Texte aus der Umwelt des Alten Testaments. Gütersloh, 1982–2001
TUAT Erg.	B. Janowski (ed.), Texte aus der Umwelt des Alten Testaments: Ergänzungslieferung, Gütersloh, 2001
UE	Ur Excavations. Oxford, London, and Philadelphia, 1926–
UET	Ur Excavations, Texts. London, 1928–
UF	Ugarit-Forschungen. Internationales Jahrbuch für die Altertumskunde Syrien-Palästinas. Münster, 1969–
Unger, ABK	E. Unger, Assyrische und babylonische Kunst. Breslau, 1927
Unger, Babylon	E. Unger, Babylon: die heilige Stadt nach der Beschreibung der Babylonier. Berlin and Leipzig, 1931

Unger, Babylonisches Schrifttum	E. Unger, Babylonisches Schrifttum. Leipzig, 1921
UVB	Vorläufiger Bericht über die von (dem Deutschen Archäologischen Institut und der Deutschen Orient-Gesellschaft aus Mitteln) der Deutschen Forschungsgemeinschaft unternommenen Ausgrabungen in Uruk-Warka. Berlin, 1930–
UVB 1	J. Jordan and A. Schott, Erster vorläufiger Bericht über die von der Notgemeinschaft der Deutschen Wissenschaft in Uruk-Warka unternommenen Ausgrabungen (=UVB 1). Berlin, 1930
UVB 10	A. Nöldeke, Zehnter vorläufiger Bericht über die von der Deutschen Forschungsgemeinschaft in Uruk-Warka unternommenen Ausgrabungen (=UVB 10). Berlin, 1939
UVB 12/13	H. Lenzen, [XII./XIII.] Vorläufiger Bericht über die von dem Deutschen Archäologischen Institut und der Deutschen Orient-Gesellschaft aus Mitteln der Deutschen Forschungsgemeinschaft unternommenen Ausgrabungen in Uruk-Warka: Winter 1953/54 – Winter 1954/55 (=UVB 12/13). Berlin, 1956
UVB 14	H. Lenzen, [XIV.] Vorläufiger Bericht über die von dem Deutschen Archäologischen Institut und der Deutschen Orient-Gesellschaft aus Mitteln der Deutschen Forschungsgemeinschaft unternommenen Ausgrabungen in Uruk-Warka: Winter 1955/56 (=UVB 14). Berlin, 1958
UVB 18	H. Lenzen, [XVIII.] Vorläufiger Bericht über die von dem Deutschen Archäologischen Institut und der Deutschen Orient-Gesellschaft aus Mitteln der Deutschen Forschungsgemeinschaft unternommenen Ausgrabungen in Uruk-Warka. XVIII : Winter 1959/60. Berlin, 1962
Vanderhooft, Neo-Babylonian Empire	D.S. Vanderhooft, The Neo-Babylonian Empire and Babylon in the Latter Prophets (=Harvard Semitic Monographs 59). Atlanta, GA, 1999
Varia Anatolica	Varia Anatolica. Paris, 1988–
VAS	Vorderasiatische Schriftdenkmäler der Königlichen Museen zu Berlin. Leipzig and Berlin, 1907–
Verbrugghe and Wickersham, Berossos and Manetho	G.P. Verbrugghe and J.M. Wickersham, Berossos and Manetho, Introduced and Translated; Native Traditions in Ancient Mesopotamia and Egypt. Ann Arbor, MI, 1996
de Vogüé, CIS 2	M. de Vogüé, Corpus Inscriptionum Semiticarum 2. Paris, 1889
Wachsmuth, Alten Geschichte	C. Wachsmuth, Einleitung in das Studium der Alten Geschichte. Leipzig, 1895
Walker, CBI	C.B.F. Walker, Cuneiform Brick Inscriptions in the British Museum, the Ashmolean Museum, Oxford, the City of Birmingham Museums and Art Gallery, the City of Bristol Museum and Art Gallery. London, 1981
Waterman, Tel Umar 2	L. Waterman, Second preliminary report upon the excavations at Tel Umar, Iraq, conducted by the University of Michigan, the Toledo Museum of Art and the Cleveland Museum of Art. Ann Arbor, 1933
Weissbach and Wetzel, Hauptheiligtum	F. Wetzel and F.H. Weissbach, Das Hauptheiligtum des Marduk in Babylon, Esagila und Etemenanki (=WVDOG 59). Leipzig, 1938
Wetzel, Stadtmauern	F. Wetzel, Die Stadtmauern von Babylon (=WVDOG 48). Leipzig, 1930
Who Was King	P. Charvát and P.M. Vlčková (eds.), Who Was King? Who Was Not King? The Rulers and the Ruled in the Ancient Near East. Prague, 2010
Winter, On Art in the Ancient Near East 2	I.J. Winter, On Art in the Ancient Near East, Vol. 2: From the Third Millennium BCE (=Culture and History of the Ancient Near East 34/2). Leiden and Boston, 2009
Wiseman, Nebuchadrezzar and Babylon	D.J. Wiseman, Nebuchadrezzar and Babylon. Oxford, 1987
WO	Die Welt des Orients. Wuppertal, Stuttgart, and Göttingen, 1947–
Woolley, UE 5	C.L. Woolley, The Ziggurat and its Surroundings (=Ur Excavations 5). London and Philadelphia, 1939
Woolley, UE 9	C.L. Woolley, The Neo-Babylonian and Persian Periods (=Ur Excavations 9). London, 1962
Worthington, Textual Criticism	M. Worthington, Principles of Akkadian Textual Criticism. Berlin and Boston, 2012
WVDOG	Wissenschaftliche Veröffentlichungen der Deutschen Orient-Gesellschaft. Leipzig, Berlin, and Wiesbaden, 1900–
WZKM	Wiener Zeitschrift für die Kunde des Morgenlandes. Vienna, 1887–
YOS	Yale Oriental Series, Babylonian Texts. New Haven, 1915–
ZA	Zeitschrift für Assyriologie und Vorderasiatische Archäologie. Berlin, 1886–
Zadok, Rép. Géogr. 8	R. Zadok, Geographical Names According to New- and Late-Babylonian texts (=Répertoire géographique des textes cunéiformes 8). Wiesbaden, 1985
ZÄS	Zeitschrift für Ägyptische Sprache und Altertumskunde. Leipzig and Berlin, 1863–

Zawadzki, Fall of Assyria	S. Zawadzki, The Fall of Assyria and Median-Babylonian Relations in Light of the Nabopolassar Chronicle (=Uniwersytet im. Adama Mickiewicza w Poznaniu, Seria Historia 149). Poznan, 1988
ZK	Zeitschrift für Keilschriftforschung und verwandte Gebiet, vols. 1–2. Leipzig, 1884–85
ZOrA	Zeitschrift für Orient-Archäologie. Berlin, 2008–

Other Abbreviations

Akk.	Akkadian
AM	Amēl-Marduk
bibl.	biblical
c	collated
ca.	circa
cf.	*confer* (lit. “compare”)
cm	centimeter(s)
col(s).	column(s)
dia.	diameter
DN	divine name
ed(s).	editor(s)
esp.	especially
et al.	*et alii* (lit. “and others”)
ex(s).	exemplar(s)
fig(s).	figure(s)
fol(s).	folio(s)
frgm(s).	fragment(s)
gen.	gentilic
GN	geographical name
K	Konstantinopel
m	meter(s)
MS	manuscript
n	not collated
n(n).	note(s)
NB	Neo-Babylonian
Nbn.	Nabonidus
Ner.	Neriglissar
no(s).	number(s)
NS	Nova Series/New Series
obv.	obverse
p	collated from photo
p(p).	page(s)
ph(s)	photo(s)
pl(s).	plate(s)
PN	personal name
rev.	reverse
Sum.	Sumerian
var(s).	variant(s)
vol(s).	volume(s)

+	Between object numbers indicates physical join
(+)	Indicates fragments from same object but no physical join

Object Signatures

A Babylon	Collection of the Nebuchadnezzar Museum, Babylon
AH	Signature of objects in the Abu Habba collection of the British Museum, London
ANE	Trinity College, University of Cambridge, Cambridge
AO	Collection of Antiquités Orientales of the Musée du Louvre, Paris
Ash	Signature of objects in the collection of the Ashmolean Museum, Oxford
B	Signature of tablets in the Babylon collection of the Arkeoloji Müzeleri, Istanbul
BE	Prefix of excavation numbers from the German excavations at Babylon
BM	British Museum, London
Bod AB	Signature of objects in the Bodleian Library collection of the Ashmolean Museum, Oxford
Bu	E.A.W. Budge collection of the British Museum, London
CBS	Collections of the Babylonian Section of the University Museum, Philadelphia
CDLI P	Signature of Cuneiform Digital Library Initiative object number
D	Signature of tablets in the Arkeoloji Müzeleri, Istanbul
EŞ	Eşki Şark Eserleri Müzesi of the Arkeoloji Müzeleri, Istanbul
Grolier	Signature of objects in the Grolier collection of the Saint Louis Public Library, St. Louis
Hr	Prefix of excavation numbers from the Turkish excavations at Ḫarrān
IM	Iraq Museum, Baghdad
IMJ	The Israel Museum, Jerusalem
K	Kuyunjik collection of the British Museum, London
Ki	Signature of tablets in the Kish collection of the Arkeoloji Müzeleri, Istanbul
L	Prefix of excavation numbers from the French excavation at Larsa
LB	F.M.Th. de Liagre Böhl Collection, Leiden
Loan Ant	Signature of objects loaned to the Fitzwilliam Museum, Cambridge
MM	Montserrat Museum, Barcelona
MMA	Metropolitan Museum of Art, New York
MS	Schøyen Collection, Oslo
NBC	Signature of tablets in the James B. Nies Babylonian collection of the Yale Library, New Haven
R	H.J. Ross collection of the British Museum, London
S	Prefix of excavation numbers from the American excavation at Seleucia
Sb	Signature of objects in the Susa collection of the Musée du Louvre, Paris
SM	Harvard Semitic Museum, Cambridge, MA
Sp	Signature of objects in the Spartoli collections of the British Museum, London
SPL W	Signature of objects in the Saint Louis Public Library, St. Louis
TA	Prefix of excavation numbers from the German excavations at Tēmā
U	Prefix of excavation numbers from the British-American excavation at Ur
UM	University Museum, Philadelphia
VA	Vorderasiatisches Museum, Berlin
VA Bab	Babylon collection of the Vorderasiatisches Museum, Berlin
VAT	Tablets in the collection of the Vorderasiatisches Museum, Berlin
W	Excavation numbers of the German excavations at Uruk (Warka)
W-B	Signature of objects in the Weld-Blundell collection of the Ashmolean Museum, Oxford
X	Michael C. Carlos Museum, Emory University, Atlanta
YBC	Babylonian Collection of Yale University Library, New Haven

Introduction

During the six years that immediately followed the successful, forty-three-year-long reign of Nebuchadnezzar II (605–562), four kings ascended the Babylonian throne in quick succession. Nebuchadnezzar's son Amēl-Marduk (561–560) reigned for just two years before he was murdered and replaced by his brother-in-law Neriglissar (559–556), who died after ruling over Babylonia for three years and eight months. After only two or three months on the throne, Neriglissar's young and inexperienced son Lâbâši-Marduk (556) was removed during a coup d'état and replaced by Nabonidus (555–539), the man who would be Babylon's last native king. Seventeen years later, in 539, when Cyrus II took control of Babylon and its territorial holdings, the once-great Babylonian Empire founded by Nabopolassar (625–605) came to an abrupt end.

Amēl-Marduk

Amēl-Marduk (biblical Evil-Merodach), whose name means "man of Marduk," became king after his father Nebuchadnezzar II died.[1] His duties, however, probably started earlier, during the final weeks or months of his father's extremely long reign, when Nebuchadnezzar was sick and dying. Despite being the legitimate, designated successor to the Babylonian throne, Amēl-Marduk appears to have faced opposition from the very start of his reign. This is not only suggested by the fact that his reign lasted a mere two years and ended with his murder, but also from later sources that portray him negatively. For example, the Babylonian author Berossos is reported to have stated that he "ruled capriciously and had no regard for the laws" and a fragmentarily preserved, Akkadian propagandistic text records that he concerned himself only with the veneration of the god Marduk, that he neglected his family, and that his officials did not carry out his orders.[2]

Almost nothing is known about his accomplishments. One inscription of his alludes to him having renovated Esagil ("House whose Top Is High") at Babylon and Ezida ("True House") at Borsippa, however, there is no concrete textual or archaeological proof that he actually undertook construction on either of those temples.[3] The fact that inscriptions of his are known from baked bricks and a paving stone does suggest that he did sponsor construction work at Babylon during his short reign. According to the Bible (2 Kings 25: 27–30 and Jeremiah 52: 31–34), Amēl-Marduk liberated the imprisoned, exiled Judean king Jehoiachin after he had spent thirty-seven years in captivity.[4] This is the only political act of Amēl-Marduk that we know about.

---

[1] For studies on his reign, see, for example, Da Riva, GMTR 4 pp. 14–15; Finkel, CDOG 2 pp. 333–338; and Sack, Amēl-Marduk. Nebuchadnezzar had at least ten children: seven sons and three daughters; see Beaulieu, Orientalia NS 67 (1998) pp. 173–201; and M.P. Streck, RLA 9/3–4 (1999) p. 197. As I. Finkel (CDOG 2 pp. 323–342) has convincingly argued on the basis of BM 40474, a late Neo-Babylonian clay tablet inscribed with a plea of a jailed son of Nebuchadnezzar, Nabû-šum-ukīn and Amēl-Marduk might have been one and the same person and, thus, it is very plausible that that Nabû-šum-ukīn changed his name to Amēl-Marduk since Marduk, Babylon's tutelary deity, came to his aid when his father had him imprisoned (with the exiled Judean king Jehoiachin). According to the 5th–7th-century-AD, rabbinical Midrashic text Vayikra Rabbah (XVIII 2), Amēl-Marduk was imprisoned because some officials had declared him king while his father was away.

[2] Respectively, Verbrugghe and Wickersham, Berossos and Manetho p. 60; and Schaudig, Inschriften Nabonids pp. 589–590 P3 (Amīl-Marduk Fragment). Berossos' statement about Amēl-Marduk having "no regard for the laws" might have been based on the fact that Nebuchadnezzar had his son arrested and thrown in jail. The Bible (2 Kings 25: 27–30 and Jeremiah 52: 31–34) and the "Uruk Prophecy" (Beaulieu, Studies Hallo p. 47), however, depict Amēl-Marduk in a positive manner.

[3] In Amēl-Marduk 1, Amēl-Marduk refers to himself as *muddiš esagil u ezida* "the one who renovates Esagil and Ezida," which could be true or simply an honorific title.

[4] The reason(s) for Jehoiachin's release is/are uncertain and subject to scholarly debate. S. Zawadzki (Šulmu 4 [1993] pp. 307–317, esp. p. 315) has suggested that Amēl-Marduk may have released the exiled Judean king in order to gain support among the Judean deportees living in Babylonia since the king's own magnates were constantly opposing him. Another possible explanation is that Amēl-Marduk and Jehoiachin became friends while they were imprisoned together and that former released the latter on account of that (close) friendship; Amēl-Marduk's

Amēl-Marduk's tenure as king came to an abrupt and violent end in the summer of 560, when his brother-in-law Neriglissar had him killed and seized the Babylonian throne for himself.[5]

Neriglissar

Neriglissar, whose name means "O Nergal, protect the king" (Akk. *Nergal-šarru-uṣur*), was not in the direct line of succession, as he was not the son of Nebuchadnezzar or of his immediate predecessor Amēl-Marduk.[6] Instead, he was the son of the Aramaean tribal leader Bēl-šum-iškun[7] and an influential and wealthy landowner[8] who became the important *simmagir*-official[9] of Nebuchadnezzar and later married one of the king's daughters (possibly Kaššaya).[10] By the time he deposed Amēl-Marduk and seized control of the Babylonian throne, Neriglissar appears to have had ample political and military experience and, therefore, was regarded by the court, nobles, and prominent Babylonian families as a better choice of king than Nebuchadnezzar's own flesh and blood; perhaps, his marriage to Kaššaya helped seal the deal. As far as we can tell, Neriglissar's claim to the throne was not contested during the three years and eight months that he was king of Babylon.

During his short reign, Neriglissar sponsored several building activities in important Babylonian cult centers and undertook at least one military campaign. During his third regnal year (557), he marched west with his army to Cilicia, defeated king Appuašu of the land Pirindu, and captured, looted, and destroyed several royal cities of his, including the island fortress Pitusu; Appuašu, however, managed to avoid capture.[11]

Inscriptions record that Neriglissar oversaw projects at or near Babylon and at Sippar.[12] At Babylon, he sponsored renovation of parts of Marduk's temple Esagil ("House whose Top Is High"), especially one of its enclosure walls;[13] restored the Lībil-ḫegalla canal ("May It Bring Abundance"; Babylon's eastern canal) and reinforced its banks; and he repaired a wing of the royal palace that had collapsed into the Euphrates River. At Sippar, his workmen made repairs to the ziggurat of the sun-god Šamaš, Ekunankuga ("House, Pure Stairway of Heaven").

Lâbâši-Marduk

After ruling over Babylonia for three years and eight months, Neriglissar died. His son Lâbâši-Marduk, whose name means "O Marduk, may I not come to shame" (Akk. *Lā-abâš-Marduk*), ascended the throne.[14] The royal court did not approve of him becoming king since he was still a young child and inexperienced and, therefore, had him removed and killed shortly after he assumed power.[15] Nabonidus, who was placed on the throne in his stead,

---

incarceration is recorded in the rabbinical Midrashic text Vayikra Rabbah (XVIII 2), as well as in the Medieval Chronicles of Jerahmeel.

[5] Da Riva, GMTR 4 p. 15; and Wiseman, Nebuchadnezzar and Babylon p. 10.

[6] For studies on his reign, see, for example, Da Riva, GMTR 4 pp. 15–16; Sack, Neriglissar; and van Driel, RLA 9/3–4 (1999) pp. 228–229.

[7] Bēl-šum-iškun is probably identical with the Aramaean tribal leader of the Puqūdu tribe who is mentioned in the Hofkalender inscription of Nebuchadnezzar II (Da Riva, ZA 103 [2013] p. 271 EŞ 7834 v′ 23′). The evidence will be presented in a forthcoming book chapter by R. Da Riva; see also D'Agostino, Alle soglie della classicità p. 121; and van Driel, RLA 9/3–4 (1999) p. 228.

[8] Neriglissar had close connections with the wealthy and influential Egibi merchant family. See van Driel, JEOL 29 (1987) pp. 50–67; and Sack, Neriglissar pp. 23–25.

[9] The precise function/sphere of influence of the *simmagir*-official remains largely unknown today, but it is clear that he was an important official at the king's court, as well as the governor of a large province in the trans-Tigridian area (the *bīt-simmagir* province). For studies about this Babylonian official, see Jursa, Achämenidenhof pp. 96–97; Jursa, Paszkowiak, and Waerzeggers, AfO 50 (2003–04) pp. 255–268; and von Soden, ZA 62 (1971) pp. 84–90. The *simmagir*-official mentioned in the Hofkalender inscription of Nebuchadnezzar II (Da Riva, ZA 103 [2013] p. 271 EŞ 7834 v′ 21′) and in the Bible (Jeremiah 39:3) in connection with the capture of Jerusalem is presumably none other than the future king Neriglissar; for details, see, for example, Jursa, Achämenidenhof pp. 85–88; and Vanderhooft, Neo-Babylonian Empire p. 151.

[10] According to Berossos, Neriglissar married one of Nebuchadnezzar's daughters. P.-A. Beaulieu (Orientalia NS 67 [1998] pp. 199–200) proposes that this princess was most likely Kaššaya.

[11] The events are recorded in the Chronicle of the Third Year of Neriglissar; see Grayson, Chronicles pp. 103–104 for a translation of that text. Neriglissar 7 probably also refers to this campaign.

[12] Neriglissar 1–3 and 6 respectively. In brick inscriptions (Neriglissar 4–5), Neriglissar refers to himself as *muddiš esagil u ezida* "the one who renovates Esagil and Ezida." This is probably true in the case of the former, as inferred from Neriglissar 1 (Esagil Inscription). However, there is no concrete textual or archaeological proof that he actually undertook construction on Ezida at Borsippa. The epithet might simply be an honorific title, rather than one that is based on historical reality.

[13] He also manufactured eight copper *mušḫuššu*-dragons and had them placed in the Ka-Utu-e, Ka-Lamma-arabi, Ka-ḫegal, and Ka-ude-babbar gates of Esagil.

[14] For studies on his reign, see, for example, Da Riva, GMTR 4 p. 16; and Röllig, RLA 6/5–6 (1983) p. 409.

[15] Da Riva, GMTR 4 p. 16. The classical authors Josephus and Berossos erroneously state that Lâbâši-Marduk was king for nine months. Economic and administrative records from Uruk and Sippar support the Uruk King List's statement that he ruled over Babylonia for about three months. His short reign is omitted in the Ptolemaic Canon. Nabonidus' personal involvement in Lâbâši-Marduk's assassination is

states that Lâbâši-Marduk "was untutored in proper behavior (and) ascended the royal throne against the will of the gods"; this biased statement about the impiety of his immediate predecessor, undoubtedly, sought to legitimize Nabonidus' own claim to the throne.[16] Lâbâši-Marduk was not in power long enough for him to accomplish anything and, therefore, it does not come as any surprise that no royal inscription recording his deeds has yet come to light.

Nabonidus

Unlike the four men who sat on the throne of Babylon before him, Nabonidus, whose name means "The god Nabû is praised" (Akk. *Nabû-na'id*), did not have any direct or even indirect family connection whatsoever with his predecessors (see below for further details); he did, however, according to his own inscriptions, serve at the royal court, starting in the reign of Nebuchadnezzar II.[17] When Lâbâši-Marduk, Neriglissar's young and unqualified son, succeeded his father as king, the nobles, courtiers, and Babylonian elite were unhappy and plotted almost immediately to have him removed from the throne. During Lâbâši-Marduk's second or third month as king, these men staged a coup against him and placed an older and more experienced man on the throne: Nabonidus.[18] Despite being over fifty (or sixty) years old,[19] Nabonidus proved to be a suitable choice since he, together with his son Belshazzar (Akk. *Bēl-šarru-uṣur*), ruled over Babylonia for seventeen years.

Contrary to popular belief, which has generally been heavily influenced by a handful of later pro-Cyrus sources (for example, the Cyrus Cylinder and the propagandistic Verse Account), Nabonidus, Babylon's last native king,[20] was a rather successful ruler. Not only did he lead his army on far-flung campaigns, he undertook numerous building activities in Babylonia's most important cult centers and ensured that his land prospered and was financially stable. Nabonidus managed to accomplish a great deal during his tenure as king. Only the highlights of his life and career are provided here.[21]

Nabonidus' Family

Information about Nabonidus' family background is scarce in extant written sources.[22] Unlike Neriglissar, it is certain that Nabonidus did not have any direct family ties to Nabopolassar and Nebuchadnezzar II, although he was part of the royal court (according to some of his own inscriptions). In official texts written in his name, he regularly states that a certain Nabû-balāssu-iqbi ("Nabû has decreed his life") was his father. The king's father's name is usually followed by the epithet "wise prince" (Akk. *rubû emqu*), as it is in two inscriptions of Neriglissar following that the name of king's father, Bēl-šum-iškun.[23] Nabû-balāssu-iqbi, like the father of Neriglissar, might

---

assumed, although there is no direct evidence to prove it with certainty.

[16] Nabonidus 3 (Babylon Stele) iv 34′–42′.

[17] Because Nabonidus was undoubtedly one of the most vibrant personalities of ancient Mesopotamia, it is little surprise that his life and times have received a great deal of scholarly attention. For some recent biographies of him, see, for example, Beaulieu, Nabonidus; D'Agostino, Nabonedo; Dandamaev, RLA 9/1–2 (1998) pp. 6–11; Da Riva, GMTR 4 pp. 16–18; Sack, Studies Astour pp. 455–473; Schaudig, Studies Kienast pp. 447–497; and Weisberg, Studies Astour pp. 547–556.

[18] According to Nabonidus 3 (Babylon Stele) v 1′–7′, "they (the courtiers) brought me (Nabonidus) inside the palace, and all of them fell limp at my feet and (then) kissed my feet. They constantly blessed me being king." Further details about the coup against Lâbâši-Marduk and Nabonidus' ascent to the throne would have been described in the now-missing portion of col. v of that basalt stele. That same inscription records that Nabonidus not only served Nebuchadnezzar II, but also Neriglissar, stating: "I am the strong envoy of Nebuchadnezzar (II) and Neriglissar, the kings who came before me. Their troops are entrusted to my hand" (Nabonidus 3 [Babylon Stele] v 14′–20′). The Adad-guppi stele (Nabonidus 2001 ii 44–48) also records that Nabonidus served both of those kings. These statements, although they come from biased, self-aggrandizing sources, indicate that Nabonidus, like Neriglissar, had years of experience before sitting on the throne. The first known archival text dated to Nabonidus as king of Babylonia is dated to the 26th of June 556 (18-III, Strassmeier, Nbn. 1), for a discussion of the last texts dated to Lâbâši-Marduk and the first tablets dated to Nabonidus, see Frame, Studies Rochberg pp. 287–295.

[19] H. Schaudig (Studies Kienast p. 10) suggests that Nabonidus was born ca. 620 and was about sixty-five years of age when he became king. M. Dandamaev (RLA 9/1–2 [1998] p. 7) proposes that he was born ca. 610 and, thus, was about fifty-five when he ascended the throne. In any case, Nabonidus was (by the standards of the time) quite old when he became king.

[20] Although Achaemenid Persian rule over Babylonia (539–331) was relatively stable, there were a few, short-lived attempts to place a Babylonian on the throne. In 522, Nidinti-Bēl, a man claiming to be the son of Nabonidus and assuming the name of Nebuchadnezzar III, briefly declared himself king when Cyrus II's son Cambyses II died; he was defeated and killed by Darius I. One year later, in 521, a certain Nebuchadnezzar IV revolted and declared himself king; he too was quickly defeated. During the second regnal year of Xerxes I (484), Šamaš-erība and Bēl-šimânni led revolts in Babylonian; both attempts were unsuccessful.

[21] See n. 17 for recent biographies of Nabonidus.

[22] See, for example, Dandamayev, RLA 9/1–2 (1998) pp. 7–8; and Schaudig, Inschriften Nabonids pp. 12–14.

[23] Neriglissar 1 (Esagil Inscription) i 11 and Neriglissar 7 i 11′. In the inscriptions of both kings, it is uncertain if the epithet "wise prince" refers to the king's father or to the king himself. H. Schaudig (Inschriften Nabonids p. 13 [with earlier references]) argued for a reference to

have been an Aramaean tribal chief, but this is far from certain given the present information in cuneiform sources, especially archival texts.[24]

His mother Adad-guppi, whose name means "Adad has saved" (Aramaic *Hadad-ḥappī*),[25] is known from a long, pseudo-autobiographical inscription engraved on two steles from Ḫarrān (Nabonidus 2001 [Adad-guppi Stele]). Although her ancestry is currently unknown,[26] she almost certainly originated from Ḫarrān, one of the principal cult centers of the moon-god Sîn. After the conquest of that important Assyrian city by a coalition of Median and Babylonian forces in 610, Adad-guppi came to Babylon, where she had some (direct) access to the royal court. There, according to her "own" account of her life (which was written by her son after her death), she introduced her only son Nabonidus to the kings Nebuchadnezzar and Neriglissar, thereby, kick starting his career in Babylon's influential, administrative circles. Adad-guppi's ability to support her son in this manner suggests that she held an elevated social position in Babylon and seemingly confirms the scholarly assumption that she originated from a prominent family. At the ripe old age of 102 (although the stele states she was 104), during Nabonidus' ninth regnal year (547), she died.[27] In scholarly literature, she is sometimes referred to as a priestess of the god Sîn of Ḫarrān on account of the devotion she claims to have given to the moon-god in the stele inscription written in her name. However, this need not be the case, since it is equally as plausible that Adad-guppi was a pious, upper class lay-woman.[28] The piety expressed in her pseudo-autobiographical account of her life does not necessarily have to be interpreted as cultic obligations of a priestess.

There is no information about Nabonidus' brothers or sisters, if he indeed had siblings. According to an inscription of his from Ḫarrān, Nabonidus stated that he was an "only son who has no one" (*māru ēdu ša mamman lā īšû*).[29] This might simply be a literary topos, but, because we have no further hint in contemporary or later sources to Nabonidus' siblings, he might have indeed been the only (surviving) son of Adad-guppi.[30]

Although we have almost no information about the wife (or wives) of Nabonidus, we know that he had at least four children, three daughters and one son. All three of his known daughters might have been consecrated as priestesses. En-nigaldi-Nanna, whose (Akkadian?) birth name is not known, was appointed *ēntu*-priestess of the moon-god Sîn at Ur during his second regnal year (553),[31] and Akkabu'*unma* (exact reading uncertain) and Ina-Esagil-rīšat might have been installed as priestesses in Ebabbar, the temple of the sun-god Šamaš at Sippar.[32] Nabonidus had Egipar, the traditional residence of the *ēntu*-priestess in the Ekišnugal (Egišnugal) temple complex at Ur, rebuilt for En-nigaldi-Nanna.

Nabonidus because his father is otherwise not known as a prince or tribal leader. Schaudig also mentions Neriglissar 3 (Royal Palace Inscription), where the name of Bēl-šum-iškun is followed by the title "king of Babylon" (i 14) definitely refers to Neriglissar himself and not his father. For Schaudig, this is additional proof that the title following the father's name actually refers to the king himself. R. Da Riva (SANER 3, pp. 15–16), discussing the inscriptions of Neriglissar, has argued for an intended ambiguity in the use of this title as it could refer to both the father and the son simultaneously.

[24] Landsberger, Studies Edhem pp. 150–151; and Dandamaev, RLA 9/1–2 (1998) p. 7. There is no way to confirm with any degree of certainty that Nabû-balāssu-iqbi was an Aramean tribal chief. As H. Schaudig (Inschriften Nabonids pp. 12–13) has already pointed out, there are other possibilities: Nabonidus' father may have been either an Assyrian (military official) or related to Nabopolassar. Given the complete lack of textual evidence, Nabû-balāssu-iqbi's origins remain elusive.

[25] For the interpretation of the Akkadian form of her name as an originally Aramaic name, see Röllig, ZA 56 (1964) p. 235 n. 39; and von Soden, Orientalia NS 37 (1968) p. 271.

[26] W. Mayer (Studies Römer pp. 250–253) has suggested that Adad-guppi might have been a daughter of the Assyrian prince Aššur-etel-šamê-erṣeti-muballissu (Pempe, PNA 1/1 pp. 184–185; Novotny and Singletary, Studies Parpola pp. 170–171) and, therefore, a granddaughter of Esarhaddon, but there is no extant textual evidence to support this proposal. Nevertheless, it is remarkable that Nabonidus is the only Neo-Babylonian king who uses Assyrian royal titles in one of his inscriptions (Nabonidus 28 [Eḫulḫul Cylinder]) and who regularly mentions the Assyrian kings Esarhaddon and Ashurbanipal in inscriptions from Babylon, Sippar, and Ḫarrān.

[27] According to the Nabonidus Chronicle (ii 13), Adad-guppi died on the fifth day of the month Nisannu (I) of that year, that is, on April 6th, 547, in Dūr-karšu, which is upstream of Sippar (Grayson, Chronicles p. 107). Where she was buried is presently not recorded in extant sources. For further details on the age discrepancy of Adad-guppi, see, for example, Schaudig, Inschriften Nabonids pp. 14 and 504 n. 734 (with references to earlier scholarly literature).

[28] For this opinion, see, for example, Dhorme, RB 5 (1908) p. 131; Garelli, Dictionnaire de la Bible 6 (1960) p. 274; Funck, Das Altertum 34 (1988) p. 53; W. Mayer, Studies Römer (1998) pp. 253–256; and Jursa, Die Babylonier p. 37. Note that B. Landsberger (Studies Edhem p. 149) has long ago already argued against the idea of Adad-guppi being an *ēntu*-priestess of the moon-god at Ḫarrān and that P. Michalowski (Studies Stolper p. 207) believes that this proposal is "an unsubstantiated modern rumor."

[29] Nabonidus 47 [Ḫarrān Stele] i 8. The same image is given in an inscription of his mother, where one finds the phrase *māru ēdu* ("only son") twice (Nabonidus 2001 [Adad-guppi Stele] i 40 and ii 13).

[30] Schaudig, Inschriften Nabonids p. 14.

[31] En-nigaldi-Nanna's consecration is mentioned in Nabonidus 19 (Eigikalama Cylinder) and 34 (En-nigaldi-Nanna Cylinder), as well as in the so-called Royal Chronicle (see pp. 27–28 below). According to Nabonidus 34, the decision to appoint her to the position came as a result of an eclipse of the moon that took place on September 26th, 554, during Nabonidus' second regnal year. For the date of the eclipse, see H. Lewy, ArOr 17 (1949) p. 50 n. 105. From Nabonidus 34 and the Royal Chronicle, it is clear that the appointment was not straight forward and was met with some opposition. For details, see Beaulieu, Nabonidus pp. 127–121 (§2.3.3.1).

[32] Beaulieu, Nabonidus pp. 136–137; and Schaudig, Inschriften Nabonids pp. 12–13. Both are known from documents from Sippar.

More details about Nabonidus' son Belshazzar are known. This famous and important son appears in archival texts of his father's reign, starting in his first regnal year (555); note that Belshazzar is absent from textual sources prior to Nabonidus' tenure as king and, therefore, his rise to power came only after his father sat on the throne of Babylon. Some archival texts record Belshazzar's private economic activities and his business deals with the wealthy and influential Egibi family.[33] This parallels the early career of Neriglissar, who also belonged to the inner circle of rich Babylonian businessmen. Because Belshazzar is completely unknown from records prior to Nabonidus becoming king, it has been sometimes assumed that the property of Neriglissar's family was confiscated after the murder of his son Lâbâši-Marduk and handed over to Belshazzar, who took over the business deals of Neriglissar's family.[34]

During Nabonidus' sojourn in Arabia (see below), Belshazzar was appointed regent.[35] His regency is generally considered to have been a success because there are no hints in extant sources to unusual incidents, uprisings, or other problems in Babylonia while his father was absent. When Nabonidus returned to Babylon, probably in his thirteenth regnal year (543), power was smoothly transferred back to him. For about ten years, Belshazzar acted as the *de facto* ruler of Babylon and principal representative of his father, the divinely-appointed king. Despite his position, (a) he never commissioned an inscription in his own name, although he likely played a role in the composition of official inscriptions written in the name of his father; (b) in archival records, he was never referred to as "king" (*šarru*), the position held by his father Nabonidus, but always as "son of the king" (*mār šarri*) and, therefore, as one expects, no text is ever dated by Belshazzar's regency; and (c) he was never a surrogate for Nabonidus during an *akītu*-festival, which meant that Babylon's most important festival, the New Year's Festival, had to be cancelled while the god Marduk's earthly representative, the king, was residing on the Arabia peninsula.[36]

Nabonidus' Military Campaigns

Little is known about the military campaigns led by Nabonidus. Given the nature of Neo-Babylonian royal inscriptions, in contrast to the detailed Neo-Assyrian reports on military campaigns, we must rely on other genres of texts to find that information. Some details are provided by the Nabonidus Chronicle, the Royal Chronicle, and the Verse Account; in addition, two stele inscriptions refer to the king's military expeditions.[37]

During Nabonidus' first three years on the throne (555–553), the Babylonian army marched west three times. In his first regnal year (555), he campaigned in Cilicia, against the city Ḫumê; this may have been to complete the military operations started two years earlier (557) by Neriglissar. Despite the poor state of preservation of the account of the year 555 in the Nabonidus Chronicle, it is certain that the campaign was successful since Nabonidus placed 2,850 prisoners from Ḫumê in the service of the gods Marduk, Nabû, and Nergal during an *akītu*-festival held at the very beginning of his second regnal year (554).[38] In 554, Nabonidus' troops may have attacked Hamath, an important city located in modern day Syria.[39] Early in his third year as king (553), despite health issues, Nabonidus campaigned against the city Ammanānu, a place that reportedly had many orchards; that city might have been located in northern Beqaa or in the Anti-Lebanon.[40] Afterwards, he conquered the kingdom of Edom.[41]

---

[33] Strassmaier, Liverpool nos. Nbn 9, 50, 184, 270, and 688.

[34] Beaulieu, Nabonidus pp. 90–93.

[35] This is not mentioned in the inscriptions of Nabonidus. The part of the Nabonidus Chronicle recording the events of this year is currently not preserved, but the Verse Account explicitly states that a mercenary army was given to the crown prince Belshazzar and that he was entrusted with the "kingship" of Babylon (Verse Account ii 18′–20′). Because Belshazzar is never called "king" in contemporary and later sources, his "rule" should be referred to as a "regency," rather than a "kingship." The fact that the Verse Account refers to Belshazzar's authority by the Akkadian term *šarrūtu*, instead of *bēlūtu*, highlights the biased and negative attitude of that text towards Nabonidus.

[36] For details, see Beaulieu, Nabonidus pp. 185–203; and D'Agostino, Nabonedo pp. 27–31.

[37] Nabonidus 3 (Babylon Stele) ix 31′–41′a and 47 (Ḫarrān Stele) i 45b–ii 2. The Nabonidus Chronicle and the Royal Chronicle are translated on pp. 25–28. For the Verse Account, see Schaudig, Inschriften Nabonids pp. 563–578 P1. Note that there are significant gaps in the Nabonidus Chronicle. Accounts of the events of the accession year (556), as well as the fourth (552), fifth (551), twelfth (544), thirteenth (543), fourteenth (542), and fifteenth (541) regnal years are completely missing, and the accounts of the events of the first (555), second (554), third (553), sixth (550), eleventh (545), and sixteenth (540) regnal years are fragmentarily preserved.

[38] Nabonidus 3 (Babylon Stele) ix 31′–41′a.

[39] The account of the events of Nabonidus' second regnal year are not sufficiently preserved in the Nabonidus Chronicle to be certain that the king undertook a campaign during that year. As far as that passage is preserved, it states that it was cold in Hamath.

[40] Nabonidus Chronicle lines 9–10 and Royal Chronicle iv 24–40 (see pp. 25–28 below). R. Zadok (Rép. Géogr. 8 p. 22) places Ammanānu in the northern Beqaa region, while M. Cogan (IEJ 34 [1984] p. 259) places it in the Anti-Lebanon region. See also Bagg, Rép. Géogr. 7/1 pp. 8–9.

[41] Lemaire, Judah and the Judeans pp. 290–291. The campaign against Edom took place late in Nabonidus' third regnal year (553). It is possible that the rock relief at Sela' (Nabonidus 55 [Sela' Inscription]) commemorated Nabonidus' victory over Edom. Unfortunately, that inscription

At the beginning of his fourth year (552), immediately after his conquest of Edom, Nabonidus and his army marched south and captured the city Dadānu.[42] Tēmā and other Arabian towns in the Ḥijāz were also taken and/or destroyed early in 552.[43] Archaeological evidence supports the fact that the Babylonian army undertook military action in the region around this time.[44]

Nabonidus' Sojourn in Arabia

Near the start of his reign, most likely during his third regnal year (553), Nabonidus handed over the day-to-day management of the empire to his son Belshazzar and left Babylon, and, early in his fourth year as king (552), the Babylonian king took up residence in the Arabian oasis city Tēmā, an important caravan stop on the principal trade route linking Arabia to the Levant.[45] Exactly why Nabonidus decided to stay in Arabia for ten years is unknown,[46] but it may have been a combination of economic, political, religious, and strategic factors; many conjectures have been made about this period of Mesopotamian history, but none are entirely convincing.[47]

Little is known about Nabonidus' activities during this ten-year span of time. In his own words, he "walked the road between the cities Tēmā, Dadānu, Padakku, Ḫibrā, Yadīḫu, and (then) as far as Yatribu."[48] It is not entirely clear what that statement implies. According to the Verse Account, he set up a royal residence in Tēmā, from which he oversaw the administration of the region.[49] Archaeological and epigraphical evidence attest to Nabonidus' semi-permanent stay at Tēmā.[50] Belshazzar ruled Babylonia on Nabonidus' behalf, but, the Babylonian New Year's (*akītu*) festival could not be celebrated due to the king's absence.[51] For whatever reason, Nabonidus returned to Babylon, probably in his thirteenth (543) regnal year, and resumed direct control over Babylonia and its territorial holdings.[52]

---

is so badly weathered that most of its contents are no longer legible.

[42] Royal Chronicle v 1–24 (see pp. 27–28 below).

[43] P.-A. Beaulieu (Nabonidus p. 169) dates the conquest of Tēmā at the beginning of Nabonidus' fourth year as king (552), proposing that "the Arabian campaign began in January or February 552, the conquest of Dadanu took place in March or April, and the capture of Teima and the other Arabian cities in the first months of Nabonidus' fourth regnal year." The Verse Account ii 20′–27′ (Schaudig, Inschriften Nabonids p. 568 P1), however, states that Nabonidus took Tēmā by force at the beginning of his third regnal year (553); Nabonidus 47 (Ḫarrān Stele) i 45b–ii 2 also alludes to military action against the Arabs. Given the available, albeit limited, textual evidence (Nabonidus Chronicle, Royal Chronicle, and archival records), it seems unlikely that the Arabian campaign could have started before Nabonidus' fourth year (552) as king. The Verse Account's statement about Nabonidus handing over the reins of power to Belshazzar and setting out west in the third year likely reflects the fact that Nabonidus and his troops did not return to Babylon after the conquests of Ammanānu and Edom and before taking up residence in Tēmā.

[44] See Macdonald, PSAS 40 Suppl. pp. 10–11.

[45] As P.-A. Beaulieu (Nabonidus p. 169) has already pointed out, Nabonidus 47 (Ḫarrān Stele) "does not specifically say that Nabonidus lived ten years in Teima, but only that he 'wandered' ten years in Arabia." Therefore, the Verse Account is correct in stating that Nabonidus departed Babylon in 553 but is misleading since the text fails to report that the Babylonian army did not conquer Tēmā until his fourth year (552). Beaulieu (Nabonidus pp. 169 and 197), therefore, proposes that Nabonidus' sojourn started in his fourth year (552). H. Schaudig (Inschriften Nabonids pp. 18–19), however, suggests that it began already in his third year (553). M. Dandamayev (RLA 9/1–2 [1998] p. 8) and R. Da Riva (GMTR 4 p. 17) do not commit to a precise date and suggest that Nabonidus' sojourn could have begun anytime between his third (553) and sixth (550) regnal years and P. Michalowski (Studies Stolper p. 208) thinks that a departure between the third and the fifth is possible. For longer, more detailed studies of Nabonidus' stay in Arabia, see, for example, Beaulieu, Nabonidus pp. 149–185; and Schaudig, Inschriften Nabonids pp. 18–19.

[46] According to Nabonidus 47 (Ḫarrān Stele) i 24–26a and ii 10b–11a, Nabonidus was in Arabia for ten years. According to a later Qumran text, the Prayer of Nabonidus (Levine and Robertson, COS 1 pp. 285–286), he stayed in Tēmā for only seven years.

[47] According to Nabonidus' own account from Ḫarrān (Nabonidus 47 [Ḫarrān Stele] i 14b–27a), he left Babylon because the citizens of Babylonia's most important cult centers, including Babylon, were impious (specifically, they had neglected the cults of the moon-god Sîn) and disease and famine broke out inside them as a result. These statements cannot be confirmed from other documentary evidence and, thus, should be taken with a grain of salt. Scholars have offered various suggestions, hypothesizing that the move was politically or strategically motivated, for religious reasons (linked with his purported preference for the god Sîn, which put him in opposition with the Marduk priesthood in Babylon), or on account of a conflict with his son Belshazzar. For a summary of the various proposals, see Beaulieu, Nabonidus pp. 178–185 (§3.2.3).

[48] Nabonidus 47 (Ḫarrān Stele) i 24–26a.

[49] Schaudig, Inschriften Nabonids p. 568 P1 ii 27′.

[50] For example, see Eichmann, Schaudig, and Hausleiter, AAE 17 (2006) pp. 163–176; and Müller and al-Said, Neue Beiträge zur Semitistik pp. 105–122.

[51] For details about Belshazzar's administration during his father's stay in Tēmā, see Beaulieu, Nabonidus pp. 185–202 (§3.3). The Nabonidus Chronicle (see pp. 25–27 below) records that no *akītu*-festivals were held in Babylon while Nabonidus was living in Tēmā.

[52] Beaulieu, Nabonidus pp. 163–165 (§3.1.3); and Schaudig, Inschriften Nabonids p. 20. Note that R. Da Riva (GMTR 4 p. 18) suggests that Nabonidus returned to Babylon in 541, his fifteenth regnal year. According to Nabonidus 47 ([Ḫarrān Stele] ii 13), Nabonidus returned to Babylon on the seventeenth day of the month Tašrītu (VII).

Nabonidus' Building Activities

It is known from extant textual and archaeological sources that Nabonidus sponsored construction in no fewer than fifteen Babylonian cities (Agade, Babylon, Borsippa, Cutha, Dilbat?, Kissik, Kish, Larsa, Marad, Seleucia, Sippar, Sippar-Anunītum, Ubassu, Ur, and Uruk), one major cult center on the border of modern-day Syria and Turkey (Ḫarrān) and one important trading center in present-day Saudi Arabia (Tēmā).[53] His workmen undertook work on numerous religious (temples, shrines, ziggurats) and non-religious (palaces, city walls) structures.

General Comments

Nabonidus' inscriptions record that he sponsored the restoration, renovation, or complete rebuilding of a number of important temples and sanctuaries in Babylonia, as well as several city walls. Those self-aggrandizing sources regularly state that he instructed his workmen to carefully and painstakingly search for the original foundations of buildings in order to ensure that the buildings were constructed anew precisely on their original, divinely-sanctioned sites, thereby ensuring that structures endured for a long time and did not prematurely collapse. Some texts record that the king entrusted these important matters to his advisors, learned and experienced men (*emqūti rāš ṭēmi*) from Babylon and Borsippa.[54] Like many of his predecessors, Nabonidus frequently mentions that the temples and sanctuaries that required his attention were in a woeful, dilapidated state, sometimes because a king of the past failed to construct the building on its ancient foundations and, occasionally, on account of divine wrath. To avoid missteps in building and to guarantee success, Nabonidus regularly consulted the gods, especially the sun-god Šamaš and the storm-god Adad, the lords of divination, through extispicy, often recording the (positive as well as negative) outcomes of those haruspicial queries in his inscriptions.[55] In addition, he also claims to have initiated building projects after having been instructed to do so through a dream, one acceptable means for a king's divine patron to impart information to his/her earthy representative.[56]

Another recurring trope of Nabonidus' building reports is the boast of discovering (ancient) inscribed objects (for example, statues or foundation documents) that had been deposited within the (original) structure of the building by a(n important) former king. References to selected, famous rulers of the past not only highlighted the special relationship that the divine occupant of the temple under construction/renovation had had with important men from the (distant) past, but also gave Nabonidus' pious deeds legitimacy since his workmen were able to uncover these records of the past, especially since those relics were found together with the temple's original foundations deep in the earth.[57] Extant inscriptions record that Nabonidus discovered inscriptions of the following former Mesopotamian kings:

City	Building Project	Named King of the Past	Text No.
Agade	Eulmaš (temple of Ištar)	Narām-Sîn of Agade, Kurigalzu, Esarhaddon, Ashurbanipal, and Nebuchadnezzar II	10–12, 27
Babylon	Imgur-Enlil (inner city wall)	unnamed ruler	1
Larsa	Ebabbar (temple of Šamaš)	Ḫammu-rāpi of Babylon	16, 27
Sippar	Ebabbar (temple of Šamaš)	Narām-Sîn of Agade	26, 28–30
Sippar-Anunītu	Eulmaš (temple of Anunītu)	Šagarakti-Šuriaš	27–28
Ur	Egipar (residence of the *ēntu*-priestess)	Nebuchadnezzar I, unnamed former kings, and princess Enanedu (a former *ēntu*-priestess)	34
Ur	Elugalgalgasisa (ziggurat)	Ur-Namma and Šulgi	32–33

---

[53] For previous studies on Nabonidus' building activities, see, for example, Dandamayev, RLA 9/1–2 (1998) pp. 8–10; Da Riva, GMTR 4 p. 113; and Schaudig, Inschriften Nabonids pp. 61–65.

[54] For example, see Nabonidus 22–25.

[55] See Nabonidus 16, 21–25, 27, and 34. Twice, Nabonidus recorded the entire oracular report in his official inscriptions; see Nabonidus 3 (Babylon Stele) and 25 (Tiara Cylinder).

[56] See Nabonidus 3 (Babylon Stele), 17, 27–29, 47 (Ḫarrān Stele), and 53.

[57] See Schaudig, Studies Kienast pp. 447–497, for a study of Nabonidus actively digging up ancient foundation documents to legitimize his kingship.

Babylonia

The capital Babylon, the city of the god Marduk that Nebuchadnezzar II had transformed and expanded into a spectacle to behold, received some attention from Nabonidus. From extant sources, this king states that he renovated and reinforced (sections of) the city wall Imgur-Enlil ("Enlil Has Shown Favor"); renovated and refurbished some of the principal gateways of Esagil ("House whose Top Is High"), the temple of Marduk, and installed copper(-plated) statues of *mušḫuššu*-dragons as gateway guardians, just as they had been in the reign of Neriglissar, as well as statues of goat-fishes (*suḫurmāšū*); and rebuilt Emašdari ("House of Animal Offerings"), the temple of the goddess Ištar of Agade at Babylon, which was reported to have been in ruins for a long time.[58] Nabonidus might have also sponsored construction on a royal residence located near the Šamaš Gate, in the southwestern part of the city, assuming that the text in question actually dates to this time and records work in Babylon.[59] Bricks bearing his name discovered at Babylon confirm that Nabonidus actually had work carried out in that city.[60]

Nabonidus claims to have made generous donations to Babylon's temples and their divine residents. In addition to installing new wooden doors in Esagil, inscriptions of this king state that he made two large censers from reddish gold; had new ceremonial garments made for the deities Ea, Nabû and Tašmētu; and had a new *arattû*-throne installed for the god Ea in the Ekarzagina ("Quay of Lapis Lazuli") shrine.[61] Moreover, he provided the *akītu*-house, Esiskur ("House of the Sacrifice"), and the gods Marduk, Nabû and Nergal with a rich gift of "100 talents and 21 minas of si<lver>, 5 talents and 17 minas of gold in addition to the gifts for an entire year, which (come) from *homage-gifts*, the wealth of all of the lands, the yield of the mountain, the income from all of the settlements, the rich gifts of kings, the extensive possessions that the prince, the god Marduk had entrusted to me," as well as 2,850 prisoners of war, who were made to perform corvée labor throughout Babylonia.[62]

At Agade, the capital city of the third-millennium-BC ruler Sargon whose location is still not known today, Nabonidus had his workmen restored Eulmaš, the temple of the goddess Ištar there.[63] The precise location of the original temple in the sixth century BC, if Nabonidus' accounts are to be believed, were not easy to locate and it took a great deal of time (three years) and effort to find them;[64] the king states that not one of his predecessors — including a Kassite king (one of the Kurigalzus), the Assyrian kings Esarhaddon and Ashurbanipal, and the famous Nebuchadnezzar II — had discovered these foundations and that a few of them openly admitted to such failure.[65] So that future kings would have no problems locating the true, divine-approved, original foundations of the Eulmaš temple at Agade, Nabonidus records that he had the new temple built at ground level, on a high brick infill, constructed precisely over the Sargonic foundations "not (even) a fingerbreadth outside or inside (of them)."

Borsippa also received some attention from Nabonidus, who occasionally referred to himself as *muddiš esagil u ezida* "the one who renovates Esagil and Ezida." Few extant texts record work on Ezida ("True House"), the temple of the god Nabû there. A cylinder inscription states that the king focused his attention on the temple complex's enclosure walls. The new, reinforced walls improved the security of Ezida and the ziggurat Eurmeiminanki ("House which Gathers the Seven *Mes* of Heaven and Netherworld").[66] Nabonidus also planned

---

[58] Nabonidus 1–2 and 4 (Babylon Stele). A brick found near the bank of the Euphrates (Nabonidus 7) might have been associated with this king's work on the stretch of Imgur-Enlil that ran alongside the Euphrates river between the Ištar Gate and the Uraš Gate, a part of Babylon's city wall that regularly required renovation and reinforcing due to damage caused by the Euphrates. On the other hand, that brick might have been from another, as-of-yet unattested building enterprise of Nabonidus.

[59] Nabonidus 1001 (Palace Cylinder). The attribution to Nabonidus is not absolutely certain and the connection of the building account of that fragmentarily preserved inscriptions to Babylon is also not firmly established; Borsippa, Dilbat, Sippar, and Uruk have also been suggested as possible locations for the palace referred to in that text.

[60] Nabonidus 7–9.

[61] Nabonidus 3 (Babylon Stele) vii and ix, and 4 frgm. 13 col. ii´. A censer for Marduk is also mentioned in the fragmentary inscription written on the stele found at Tēmā (Nabonidus 56 [Tēmā Stele] line 22). It is uncertain if the two references to the censer on that stele refer to one and the same object or to two different censers given to Marduk.

[62] Nabonidus 3 (Babylon Stele) ix 3´b–41´a.

[63] For example, see Nabonidus 10–12 (Eulmaš Cylinders), 27, and 29 (Eḫulḫul Cylinder).

[64] According to Nabonidus 27, the original, third-millennium foundations were discovered through divine providence, after torrential rains created a gully in the ruins of the temple, thereby exposing the foundations of Narām-Sîn of Agade.

[65] Compare Schaudig, Studies Kienast pp. 474–478. According to Nabonidus 27, one of the Kurigalzus, perhaps the second of that name, recorded "I searched day and night for the (original) foundation(s) of Eulmaš, but I did not reach (them)"; and Esarhaddon and Ashurbanipal wrote down "I sought out the (original) foundation(s) of that Eulmaš, but I did not reach (them). I cut down poplar(s) and *maštû*-tree(s) and (then) built a replacement Eulmaš and gave (it) to the goddess Ištar of Agade, great lady, my lady." Such admissions are never included in Mesopotamian inscriptions and, therefore, it can be confidently assumed that these statements were drafted by Nabonidus' scribes.

[66] Nabonidus 13 (Ezida Cylinder). That text also records that Neriglissar started construction on that wall but never completed it. This building enterprise of Neriglissar is not known from his own inscriptions.

to renovate Ezida's processional way, but unfortunately no details about that building enterprise survive today, apart from the king's intent to carry out the work.[67] Parts of the interior of Nabû's temple were renovated.[68] Following in the footsteps of the Assyrian kings Esarhaddon and Ashurbanipal, Nabonidus had metal(-plated) statues of wild bulls (*rīmū*) set up in prominent gateway(s) of Ezida.[69] In addition, he had the wooden doors of Tašmētu's cella plated with silver.

At Cutha and Kish, this Babylonian king states that he sponsored construction on those two cities' walls, respectively Ugal-amaru ("Great Storm, (which) Is a Deluge") and Melem-kurkurra-dulla ("(Whose) Radiance Spreads over (All) Lands"), both of whose superstructures Nabonidus boasts that he had raised as high as mountains.[70] At Dilbat, Nabonidus rebuilt the *akītu*-house of the god Uraš, the patron deity of that city[71] and, at Kissik, he had Eamaškuga ("House, Pure Sheepfold"), the temple of the goddess Ningal/Nikkal, constructed anew.[72]

As he did at Sippar (see below), Nabonidus appears to have taken a deep interest in completely renovating the temple of the sun-god Šamaš at Larsa.[73] Nabonidus' inscriptions state that Larsa, the Ebabbar ("Shining House") temple, and the ziggurat Eduranna ("House, Bond of Heaven") had lain in ruins for such a long time that their original ground plans had been forgotten and that when Nebuchadnezzar II had had Šamaš' temple renovated that king (wrongly) constructed Ebabbar anew on the earliest foundations that his workmen could find, those of the Kassite king Burna-Buriaš. Because the temple fell into ruins too quickly according to Nabonidus, who was often looking for ways to discredit the pious works of some of his predecessors (Nebuchadnezzar II in particular) and to bolster his own legitimacy, the temple's 'premature' demise was attributed to the fact that Ebabbar had not been on its original foundations and this negligent act angered Šamaš, who let that earthly residence of his become dilapidated. Therefore, Nabonidus had his workmen seek out the older remains of the temple, which they eventually discovered, or so we are told. In his tenth regnal year (546), the foundations of Ebabbar that the Old Babylonian king Ḫammu-rāpi had laid were uncovered, as well as the (original) site of the ziggurat Eduranna. In rhetoric typical of Nabonidus, several inscriptions report that the king had the new temples constructed precisely over their divinely-approved, Old Babylonian foundations, "not (even) a fingerbreadth outside or inside (of them)." Despite Nabonidus' biased, ideological account of construction at Larsa, which presumably contains some factual information, it is certain that this Neo-Babylonian king actually carried out work on that Šamaš temple since bricks of his were discovered at Larsa.

Following in the footsteps of Nebuchadnezzar II, Nabonidus restored the temple of the god Lugal-Marda, Eigikalama ("House, Eye of the Land"), at Marad.[74] In addition, he states that he had an enclosure wall constructed around that holy building, something that had reportedly never been done before. Moreover, he refurbished and ornately decorated Lugal-Marda's chariot, parts of which were supposedly discovered among the ruins of the Eigikalama when the ruins of the dilapidated mudbrick superstructure were being cleared away.

Bricks discovered at Seleucia and Uruk (in the vicinity of Eanna) likely attest to Nabonidus having undertaken work in those two cities.[75] Since no textual sources record the details of projects in the former city, it is uncertain which structure(s) Nabonidus worked on in Seleucia. At Uruk, however, it is clear from the bricks themselves and archival records that he restored Eanna ("House of Heaven"), the temple of the goddess Ištar.

Of Nabonidus' numerous building activities, those at Sippar, the principal cult center of the sun-god, are perhaps the best known today. No less than ten inscriptions of his record numerous details about the long and extensive rebuilding of Ebabbar ("Shining House"), the temple of Šamaš, its cellas, and its ziggurat Ekunankuga ("House, Pure Stairway of Heaven").[76] Nabonidus' accounts of building at Sippar include information about every stage of construction, from start to finish, and, in typical Mesopotamian fashion, those texts narrate events in a manner that is more concerned with royal ideology rather than historical reality. Thus, according to these self-aggrandizing reports, Nabonidus had Ebabbar completely rebuilt anew since the temple constructed by

---

[67] Nabonidus 44.

[68] Nabonidus 4 frgm. 7.

[69] Esarhaddon had four apotropaic bull statues placed in Borsippa's main temple and Ashurbanipal set up four, and later six, wild bulls in Ezida. See, for example, Leichty, RINAP 4 p. 117 Esarhaddon 54 (Smlt.) rev. 10b–16a; and Novotny and Jeffers, RINAP 5/1 p. 216 Ashurbanipal 10 (Prism T) ii 1–6 and p. 267 Ashurbanipal 12 (Prism H) i 4′–6′.

[70] Nabonidus 19 (Eigikalama Cylinder). Both walls are also known from an explanatory temple list; see George, House Most High no. 6.

[71] Nabonidus 19 (Eigikalama Cylinder)

[72] Nabonidus 15 (Eamaškuga Cylinder).

[73] Nabonidus 16 (Larsa Cylinder) and 27.

[74] Nabonidus 19 (Eigikalama Cylinder)

[75] Respectively Nabonidus 18 and 20. It is unclear if Nabonidus actually built at Seleucia or if he sponsored construction at Opis (ancient Upî; Tulūl al-Mujaili'), which is only a short distance away from Seleucia, and those bricks were later transferred from Opis to Seleucia.

[76] Nabonidus 19, 21–26, 27–29, and 1008.

Nebuchadnezzar II forty-five years earlier had (prematurely) collapsed, something that had happened because that ruler failed to construct Šamaš' temple on its original, divinely-approved foundations.[77] After receiving divine confirmation through favorable responses to questions posed through extispicy and after much time and effort searching the ruins of the (allegedly) collapsed temple, Nabonidus' specialists from Babylon and Borsippa claim to have discovered the earliest foundation, the ones purportedly laid by the Sargonic king Narām-Sîn.[78] So not to incur the anger of the sun-god, as Nebuchadnezzar II had done, the king's workmen were instructed to lay Ebabbar's new foundations precisely over the Sargonic-period foundations, "not (even) a fingerbreadth outside or inside (of them)." Once that arduous task had been accomplished, the new mudbrick superstructure was built, 5,000 beams of cedar were stretched out as its roof, new wooden doors were hung in its prominent gateways, and the most important rooms of the temple were lavishly decorated. In addition, Nabonidus states that he rebuilt (or renovated) the ziggurat Ekunankuga; constructed Ekurra ("House of the Mountain"), the temple of the god Bunene, Šamaš' vizier; and made repairs to (parts of) the enclosure wall of the Ebabbar temple complex. Moreover, Nabonidus had a new golden crown, one apparently with something called *zarinnu*,[79] commissioned and dedicated to Šamaš; according to the inscription recording the manufacture of that sacred object, Nabonidus had a great deal of trouble obtaining divine consent to make that crown, and it was only after multiple haruspical queries that he was permitted to fashion the desired object for the sun-god.[80]

In the vicinity of Sippar, at Sippar-Anunītu, Nabonidus had Eulmaš, the temple of the goddess Anunītu, rebuilt since it was reportedly destroyed by the Assyrian king Sennacherib (704–681).[81] The temple, which shares a name with the Ištar temple at Agade (see above), was constructed anew on top of the foundations of Šagarakti-Šuriaš (1245–1233), a Kassite king of Babylon.

One inscription of Nabonidus states that the king undertook work at Ubassu, a town situated between Babylon and Borsippa. The exact nature of the project(s) there is uncertain as the passage recording the king's construction activities in that town is rather vague. Nevertheless, it seems that Nabonidus renovated/rebuilt a sanctuary of the goddess Nanāya.[82]

Lastly, Nabonidus commissioned several large-scale building projects at Ur, one of the principal cult centers of the moon-god Sîn.[83] In that important city, he made (extensive) repairs to the ziggurat Elugalgalgasisa ("House of the King who Lets Counsel Flourish"); rebuilt Enunmaḫ ("House of the Exalted Prince"), the *bīt-ḫilṣi* of the goddess Ningal/Nikkal, the consort of Sîn; and constructed Egipar, the traditional residence of the *ēntu*-priestess of the moon-god, anew for his daughter En-nigaldi-Nanna, after he had appointed her as Sîn's *ēntu*. Bricks bearing short inscriptions of Nabonidus, as well as an inscribed door socket, attest to this king actually carrying out work on these three important building at Ur. In addition, Nabonidus claims to have "made possessions (and) property copious inside Ekišnugal" and to have exempted temple personal from obligatory state service, including corvée labor, thereby, bestowing a highly coveted 'tax exempt' status upon Ur and its temples.[84]

Ḫarrān

One of the most important and extensive building projects undertaken by Nabonidus was the rebuilding of Eḫulḫul ("House which Gives Joy"), the temple of the moon-god Sîn at Ḫarrān,[85] which had been in ruins since 610, the year the Babylonian king Nabopolassar and his Median allies captured, plundered, and destroyed that city and its temples, thereby, bringing the once-great Assyrian Empire to an end once and for all.[86] Probably after

---

[77] For a study of Nabonidus criticizing Nebuchadnezzar II, in particular for failing to build temples on their original foundations, see Schaudig, Studies Ellis pp. 155–161.

[78] These ancient foundations of Ebabbar were said to have been found at a depth of eighteen cubits and to have been laid 3,200 years before Nabonidus. According to middle chronology (for example, Brinkman in Oppenheim, Ancient Mesopotamia p. 335), Narām-Sîn, who is erroneously referred to as the son of Sargon, reigned ca. 2254–2218, which is only 1,663 years from the end of that Sargonic king's reign to Nabonidus' accession to the throne. For a discussion of this passage (Nabonidus 28 [Eḫulḫul Cylinder] ii 55b–60a), including the free interchangeability of the names of Sargonic kings in Nabonidus' inscriptions, see Schaudig, Studies Ellis pp. 157–159.

[79] The meaning of the Akkadian word *zarinnu* is unclear; see the note on p. 127 of this volume for further details.

[80] Nabonidus 25 (Tiara Cylinder).

[81] Nabonidus 28–29 (Eḫulḫul Cylinders). For the rebuilding of Eulmaš, see Frame, Mesopotamia 28 (1993) pp. 21–50; and Bartelmus and Taylor, JCS 66 (2014) pp. 113–128.

[82] Nabonidus 19 (Eigikalama Cylinder) ii 5–7 records "As for the city Ubassu, (which is) between Babylon and Borsippa, I raised up its superstructure with bitumen and baked brick(s) and (then) had the goddess Nanāya, the supreme goddess, enter her cella."

[83] Nabonidus 19 (Eigikalama Cylinder) and 32–39.

[84] Nabonidus 34 (En-nigaldi-Nanna Cylinder) ii 19 and 21–28, and Nabonidus 36.

[85] Nabonidus 3 (Babylon Stele), 28–29 (Eḫulḫul Cylinders), 46–52, and 2001 (Adad-guppi Stele). For a study of earlier Assyrian building activities at Ḫarrān, see Novotny, Eḫulḫul.

[86] Grayson, Chronicles p. 95 Chronicle 3 lines 63–64. Note that Nabonidus 3 (Babylon Stele) x 14′ credits only the Medes with this sacrilege, and not the Babylonian king.

his return to Babylon, after his long sojourn in Arabia, Nabonidus started rebuilding the long-dilapidated Eḫulḫul temple and its sanctuaries. He claims to have rebuilt it directly on top of the foundations of Ashurbanipal (668–ca. 631), who is implied to have done the same since that Assyrian king had seen the earlier foundations of the ninth-century ruler Shalmaneser III (858–824).[87] As one expects from an account of construction in a Mesopotamian royal inscription, the king boasts that he completed the brick superstructure of the temple, lavishly decorated it, and returned newly-refurbished statues of its divine occupants (Sîn, Ningal/Nikkal, Nusku, and Sadarnunna) to their proper places in their home town.[88] It is unknown if construction on Sîn's temple at Ḫarrān had been completed or not by the time Cyrus captured Babylon and Nabonidus in 539.

Tēmā

Nabonidus, during his extended sojourn in Arabia, appears to have undertaken construction on a royal residence at Tēmā, as well as on other important structures in that oasis city. A few, rather vague details are recorded in the later, pro-Cyrus Verse Account. The relevant passage of that propagandistic text reads: "[He] made the city resplendent (and) buil[t a palace]. He built it (just) like the palace of Babylon, ... [... He constantly placed] the treasures of the city and l[and inside it]. He surrounded it with a garris[on ...]."[89] Recent Saudi-German excavations at Tēmā have unearthed direct proof that Nabonidus actually lived in that important Arabian city.[90]

Nabonidus' Veneration of the Moon-god Sîn

According to the now-famous Cyrus Cylinder, as well as the 'propaganda' text known as the Verse Account,[91] Nabonidus is 'accused' of **(a)** promoting the moon-god Sîn to Marduk's long-held and pre-eminent rank of "king of the gods" (Akk. *šar ilī*) and "Enlil of the gods" (Akk. *Enlil ilī*), **(b)** altering the (traditional) rites and rituals of Babylonian cults (especially those in the venerated city of Babylon), **(c)** building a temple in Ḫarrān that rivaled the most important temple at Babylon (Esagil), and **(d)** oppressing the people of Sumer and Akkad (Babylonia). These alleged sins and cruel behavior of this Babylonian king are reported to have led to his quick downfall.[92] Because the pious, downtrodden Babylonia population were ready to throw their support behind a ruler who would not only respect them, but also treat Babylonian cults with the utmost respect and venerate the god Marduk above all other deities, and because Cyrus II of Persia was seen as the savior who would restore Babylon's tutelary deity to his rightful place in the pantheon, at least according to these two biased sources, Nabonidus was effortlessly removed from power. These post-539, anti-Nabonidus sources have had a great deal of influence on modern researchers, some of whom have completely bought pro-Cyrus rhetoric. Thus, one easily finds today numerous references to Nabonidus being an unwavering, fanatical devotee of the moon-god who neglected Marduk and Babylonia's cults in his solitary quest to make Sîn the supreme god of the Empire. The full extent of the impact that the pro-Cyrus propaganda had in ancient times is uncertain, but it is clear that this anti-Nabonidus rhetoric has left its mark in modern scholarship.[93]

---

[87] According to J. Novotny (Eḫulḫul *passim*), Ashurbanipal did not necessarily rebuild Eḫulḫul precisely on earlier foundations since it is clear from several of that king's inscriptions that Eḫulḫul was substantially enlarged and that Nusku's temple Emelamana might have been built as an attached twin of the newly-enlarged Eḫulḫul temple. Based on extant textual and archaeological evidence, it is clear that Assyrian kings regularly moved and changed the plans of temples. Therefore, it was not problematic, generally speaking, for a Mesopotamian king to not build precisely on the original foundations of a temple. For some details, see Novotny, JCS 66 (2014) pp. 103–109; and Novotny, Kaskal 11 (2014) pp. 162–165.

[88] It is certain from contemporary inscriptions discovered at Ḫarrān, including numerous inscribed bricks, that work was indeed carried out on Eḫulḫul. Like Ashurbanipal, Nabonidus claims to have stationed metal(-plated) statues of wild bulls (*rīmū*) and long-haired heroes (*laḫmū*) in prominent gateways of the temple. A partially intact bowl (Nabonidus 52) and a bead (Nabonidus 53) attest to this Neo-Babylonian king dedicating some (cult) utensils to Eḫulḫul, in particular, a *kallu*-bowl, a *šulpu*-vessel, and (most likely) an ornamental dagger.

[89] Schaudig, Inschriften Nabonids p. 568 P1 ii 28′–31′.

[90] See, for example, Eichmann, Schaudig, and Hausleiter, AAE 17 (2006) pp. 163–176.

[91] Schaudig, Inschriften Nabonids pp. 550–556 and 563–578. An annotated (lemmatized) online version of the Cyrus Cylinder is also available via the 'Babylon 8' subproject of the Royal Inscriptions of Babylonia online (RIBo) project; see http://oracc.org/ribo/babylon8/Q006653/ [2020].

[92] See the section 'End of Nabonidus' Reign: Cyrus' Conquest of Babylonia' below for further details.

[93] See, for example, Beaulieu, Nabonidus pp. 43–65; Schaudig, Inschriften Nabonids p. 21; and Tadmor, Studies Landsberger pp. 362–363. H. Tadmor was the first modern scholar to propose that Nabonidus actively promoted the god Sîn over Babylon's tutelary deity Marduk, something he felt could be clearly demonstrated in Nabonidus' own texts through the study of epithets. The most detailed study of the moon-god's elevation at this time is presented by P.-A. Beaulieu in his seminal study of Nabonidus' reign. That well-researched and detailed study has had a major impact on scholarship since its publication. A new study of the god Sîn by A. Hätinen (The Theologies and the Cults of the Moon God Sîn in Neo-Assyrian and Neo-Babylonian Times) is in an advanced state of preparation and will soon appear. That book will present a comprehensive analysis of the available first-millenium-BC sources for that important god.

In more recent years, this view of Babylon's last native king has been increasingly scrutinized. A. Kuhrt was the first to re-examine the modern, perceived image of Nabonidus as a pro-Sîn adversary of the Marduk priesthood at Babylon.[94] In that study, Kuhrt convincingly demonstrated that modern explanations for Nabonidus' speedy downfall that are deeply rooted in the image of the Babylonian king presented by later pro-Cyrus sources[95] and Nabonidus' perceived elevation of the moon-god in favor of Marduk in his own inscriptions are not supported by contemporary Babylonian sources. In the latter case, she correctly notes that references to Sîn as "king of the gods" (Akk. *šar ilī*) and "Enlil of the gods" (Akk. *Enlil ilī*) are generally limited to texts and passages recording work on the Eḫulḫul ("House which Gives Joy") temple at Ḫarrān and, thus, suggests that these few pieces of contemporary evidence fail to provide a strong case for Nabonidus being a fanatic devotee of the moon-god who sought to replace Marduk with Sîn as the national god of Babylon.[96] Therefore, we should abandon the notion that this king of Babylon actively sought to promote the moon-god outside of that deity's cult centers, as the Cyrus Cylinder and the Verse Account would have us believe.[97]

End of Nabonidus' Reign: Cyrus' Conquest of Babylonia

The last native dynasty of Babylon came to a quick and abrupt end. The Persian king Cyrus II (559–530), the very man who had 'liberated' the city Ḫarrān from the Medes when he defeated Astyages shortly after Nabonidus had become king, eventually set his eyes on Babylonia, once he had successfully concluded his war with the wealthy kingdom of Lydia and its famous king Croesus.[98] In 539, Nabonidus' seventeenth regnal year, the Persian king marched on Babylonia.[99] The beginning of that year, if the Nabonidus Chronicle is to be believed, started off as normal, that is, the king held the New Year's festival. However, by the middle of the year, the Babylonian king was on the defensive and started transferring Babylonia's gods and goddesses from their home cities into the fortified walls of the capital Babylon. Not all of the deities, including the revered gods of Borsippa and Sippar, made it to Babylon before the first clash between the Babylonian and Persian armies took place.

The war, as most textual sources seem to report, was very short and lasted less than thirty days. In the month Tašrītu (VII), on an unspecified day, Nabonidus' forces fought Cyrus' troops at Opis, a city located near the eastern bank of the Tigris River, where its course is not very far from that of the Euphrates River.[100] On the 14th

---

[94] Kuhrt, Pagan Priests pp. 119–155. Note that already in 1960, P. Garelli (Dictionnaire de la Bible 6 [1960] pp. 283–284) had given a well-rounded, carefully-considered evaluation of the impact of Nabonidus' reverence of the moon-god. Garelli concluded that the elevated position of Sîn was confined to texts/passages concerning activities at Ḫarrān and, therefore, had little/no impact on Marduk's position in the pantheon, thus, Nabonidus' veneration for the moon-god was not seen as a threat to the influence of the priests in Babylon.

[95] M. Jursa (PBA 136 [2007] pp. 74–76) has stressed that Babylonian temples, including Esagil at Babylon, were probably not strong or independent enough to have played a significant role in Nabonidus' downfall. Moreover, contemporary cuneiform sources seem to show Babylonia as an internally stable country at this time. Extant sources do not support the idea that the clergy strongly opposed Nabonidus' policies or actively sought to have him removed as king; for this opinion, see Jursa, Imperien und Reiche p. 125; and Jursa, Tempel im Alten Orient p. 162.

[96] P.-A. Beaulieu (Nabonidus p. 43) has noted that no Neo-Babylonian religious text providing a theological explanation for Sîn as the supreme deity — for example, compositions comparable to the elevation of Marduk in the Babylonian myth of creation, *Enūma eliš*, or the elevation of the goddess Ištar by the kings of Agade — has yet come to light. This might simply be a coincidence or provide further proof that Nabonidus (and his mother Adad-guppi) made no attempt to elevate the moon-god outside of his well-established cult centers at Ḫarrān and Ur.

[97] For a recent study on the matter, see Da Riva, Concepts of Kingship in Antiquity pp. 45–46. In that study, Da Riva demonstrated that in Nabondus' inscriptions mentioning Sîn and Šamaš (texts mostly found at Sippar) the glorification of the moon-god never exceeds that of the sun-god. Moreover, she also notes that Šamaš is venerated in those same texts (from Sippar) as if he was the most important god in the pantheon, that is, like Marduk. Since pro-Cyrus compositions do not depict Nabonidus as a Šamaš fanatic, modern scholars have never proposed that that Babylonian king sought to supplant Marduk with Šamaš.

[98] For the translations of the primary sources dealing with the events of Cyrus' reign, see Kuhrt, Persian Empire pp. 56–103. For Cyrus' war against Astyages of Media, see op. cit. pp. 56–60 §C nos. 6–11; for his conquest of Lydia and western Asia Minor, see op. cit. pp. 60–70 §D nos. 12–20; and for the Persian conquest of Babylonia, see op. cit. pp. 70-87 §E nos. 21–28. A. Kuhrt divides the sources dealing with Cyrus' defeat of Nabonidus into three broad categories: (a) the Babylonian evidence (the Cyrus Cylinder [no. 21], the Verse Account [no. 23], the Dynastic Prophecy [no. 24], Berossus' Babyloniaca [no. 25 = FGrH 680 F10a]); (b) Old Testament writers (Isaiah 41:1–5, 25, 42:1–7, 28–45:7 [no. 26]; and Ezra 6:2–5 [no. 27]), and (c) Greek sources (Herodotus I 177–178 and 188–192). The Nabonidus Chronicle (see pp. 24–25) also records the details of the end of Nabonidus' reign. The fall of Babylon is also mentioned by Xenophon in his Cyropaedia (VII 5). For a detailed analysis of the accounts of the classical authors, see Heller, Spätzeit pp. 212–220; and Briant, From Cyrus to Alexander pp. 41–43.

[99] Hostilities between the two kings may have begun already in 540, Nabonidus' 16th regnal year, as the Nabonidus Chronicle (iii 1′–4′) might indicate. That passage in the Nabonidus Chronicle is not sufficiently preserved for scholars to be able to properly analyze its contents. For interpretations of the events of 540, see, for example, Beaulieu, Nabonidus pp. 219–220; Heller, Spätzeit p. 208; and Briant, From Cyrus to Alexander pp. 42–43. According to the Dynastic Prophecy, an Akkadian text written in the Hellenistic Period, Cyrus is portrayed as the aggressor/instigator of the war. For a translation of that text, which 'foresaw' Cyrus' victory, see, for example, Kuhrt, Persian Empire p. 80.

[100] The city of Opis is where the Assyrian king Sennacherib famously had Syrian-built ships dragged overland on rollers from the Tigris River to the Euphrates River in 694 (Grayson and Novotny, RINAP 3/1 p. 12, with n. 23). Sippar and Sippar-Anunītu are situated between the Tigris and Euphrates at the point where those two rivers are the closest.

of that same month, not far from Opis, the Persian army is reported to have captured the important city Sippar, the revered cult center of the god Šamaš, without a fight; Nabonidus is said to have fled (south).[101] Two days later, on the 16th of Tašrītu, Ugbaru, the governor of Gutium, an important ally of Cyrus, together with (part of) the Persian army, took Babylon, also allegedly without battle.[102] Nabonidus was captured, but it is unclear where this took place; the Nabonidus Chronicle states that it was in Babylon, whereas the much later account of Berossos records that the on-the-run king of Babylon surrendered near Borsippa.[103] According to Berossos, the captured Babylonian king was exiled to Carmania, in southern Iran, where Nabonidus is said to have eventually died.[104] As to the fate of Belshazzar, that is unknown since no sources record it; he might have died in battle, been executed, or been exiled together with his father. Cyrus II ruled Babylonia until his death in 530 and, as far as we can tell, there was peace throughout Babylonia during that time.

Texts Included in RINBE 2

As is evident from its title, this volume includes editions of all of the known royal inscriptions of the Neo-Babylonian kings Amēl-Marduk, Neriglissar, and Nabonidus. Since no official inscriptions of Lâbâši-Marduk have yet been discovered, no texts of his are edited in RINBE 2; this is also why his name is not included in the book's title.

In total, eighty-seven Akkadian inscriptions are included here. The majority of these texts have been carefully edited in two scholarly monographs: Da Riva, SANER 3 and Schaudig, Inschriften Nabonids. Since the publication of those books, eighteen additional inscribed objects of Nabonidus, including a badly damaged stele from Tēmā (Nabonidus 56) and a heavily weathered rock relief from Padakku (Nabonidus 54), have come to light. Five of these have already been published, while the others (Nabonidus 11–12, 21, 30, 41–42, 58–61, 1002, and 1006–1007) have not.[105] All of these new inscriptions are edited here. For further details about the inscriptions included in this volume, see the Survey of the Inscribed Objects section below.

Texts Excluded from RINBE 2

One inscription attributed to Neriglissar and edited in Da Riva, SANER 3 (VA 2659) is not included here because that text is actually a duplicate of an unpublished inscription of Nebuchadnezzar II recording his and his father's

---

101 It is difficult to know whether or not Sippar was actually seized without bloodshed since many of the extant sources recording Cyrus' conquest of Babylonia are biased, anti-Nabonidus pieces of propaganda or later works inspired or influenced by them, for example, the Cyrus Cylinder (http://oracc.org/ribo/babylon8/Q006653/ [2020]). Since those sources want their intended audience to believe that Babylonia's deities and people abandoned Nabonidus completely and allowed Cyrus, the god Marduk's new earthly representative, to take control of Babylon and all of its territory without having to resort to violence, it is difficult for modern historians to be certain which 'facts' are authentic and which are not. Therefore, even with a source such as the Nabonidus Chronicle, which is supposed to be an unbiased witness to the events that unfolded in Babylonia at that time, we cannot be absolutely certain that Sippar, and later Babylon, were taken without a fight.

102 Nabonidus Chronicle iii 15′–16′ and Cyrus Cylinder line 17 ("without a fight or battle, he (Marduk) allowed him (Cyrus) to enter Šuanna"; http://oracc.org/ribo/babylon8/Q006653/ [2020]). Herodotus (I 191) states that the city was taken without a fight because Cyrus had his army redirect the course of the Euphrates River and had his army secretly enter Babylon via the dried-out river bed. For a study of Herodotus' account, see Rollinger, Herodots Babylonischer Logos pp. 19–28.

103 Nabonidus Chronicle iii 16′ and Cyrus Cylinder line 17 ("He (Marduk) delivered Nabonidus, the king who did not revere him, into his (Cyrus') hands"). According to early third-century-BC Babylonian scholar Berossos (Babyloniaca = FGrH 680 F10a), Nabonidus surrendered to Cyrus at Borsippa, after the Persian king is said to have razed Babylon's walls. A. Kuhrt (Persian Empire p. 82 n. 4) suggests that Borsippa is a mistake for Sippar, however, this need not be the case since that city was captured by Persian forces before Nabonidus retreated. A likely scenario, if Berossos' account is correct about where Nabonidus surrendered to Cyrus, is that the Babylonian king fled south from Sippar on the 14th of Tašrītu (VII) to Babylon, but failed to reach Babylon before its capture by Ugbaru on the 16th. With nowhere to run, Nabonidus fled to the nearest city, Borsippa. Since Nabonidus was well aware that Borsippa was not as well fortified as Babylon, he chose to surrender rather than to endure a siege. The text of the Cyrus Cylinder does not record where Nabonidus was captured. Furthermore, the sources contradict one another on the order of events. The Nabonidus Chronicle states that the Babylonian king was captured in Tašrītu (sometime after the 16th and before the end of the month) and that Cyrus only entered Babylon on the 3rd of Araḫsamna (VII). The Cyrus Cylinder (line 17) and Berossos both record that the Persian king entered Babylon and then captured Nabonidus.

104 The Dynastic Prophecy (Kuhrt, Persian Empire p. 80) also reports that Cyrus had Nabonidus exiled, although the place where this Babylonian king spent his final days is not recorded in that text. U. Moortgat-Correns (SMEA 38 [1996] pp. 153–177) has argued that Nabonidus was buried in the South Palace in Babylon. As H. Schaudig (Inschriften Nabonids pp. 16–17) has already pointed out, Moortgat-Correns' proposed location for Nabonidus' grave is highly unlikely.

105 For the published texts, see Frame in Spar, CTMMA 4 no. 176; Schaudig, AAE 17 (2006) pp. 169–174; Hausleiter and Schaudig, ZOrA 9 (2016) pp. 224–240; and in Hausleiter, ATLAL 25 (2018) pp. 99–100 and pl. 2.20 figs. c–e. Some of the previously unpublished Babylonian inscriptions were mentioned in Da Riva, GMTR 4 (p. 131). Four soon-to-be-published inscriptions from Tēmā were included here courtesy of H. Schaudig (Schaudig in Eichmann and Hausleiter, Tayma 2 nos. 3–6).

reconstruction of Ekunankuga ("House, Pure Stairway of Heaven"), the ziggurat at Sippar, now in the Vorderasiatisches Museum in Berlin (VA 8410).[106] That inscription will be edited in RINBE 1/2, with the inscriptions of Nebuchadnezzar II from Sippar.

Two texts written on multi-column clay tablets attributed to Nabonidus and edited in Schaudig, Inschriften Nabonids (BM 68234 and BM 68321) are not included in the present volume since A. Bartelmus and J. Taylor have convincingly demonstrated that these two tablets are not inscribed with copies of royal inscriptions of Babylon's last native king.[107] BM 68321 joins BM 67673 + BM 71553 (+) BM 73514[108] and the new BM 67673+ is a virtually complete clay tablet inscribed with a Neo-Babylonian copy (probably dating to the time of Nabonidus) of Sumerian inscriptions of the Kassite kings Kurigalzu I and Šagarakti-Šuriaš recording their restorations of the E(ul)maš temple at Sippar-Anunītu, together with an Akkadian translation.[109] BM 68234 appears to be a Neo-Babylonian copy of the statue inscription of Šagarakti-Šuriaš that Nabonidus quotes verbatim in his inscriptions.[110] Because these two tablets do not contain inscriptions of Nabonidus, they are excluded from RINBE 2. Two cylinder fragments cited in Catalogue of the Babylonian Tablets in the British Museum 4–5 as possibly being attributed to Nabonidus, K 10066 and Sm 486, are not included in the present volume since the authors are not convinced that the inscriptions written on these two pieces were composed in the name of Nabonidus, despite the mention of Agade and Eulmaš in K 10066. Lastly, a damaged multi-column cylinder discovered at Babylon, VA Bab 611 (BE 43333), might bear an inscription of Nabonidus or Nebuchadnezzar II. Because the authors tentatively think that the text inscribed on that cylinder likely recorded Nebuchadnezzar's, not Nabonidus', restoration of Eḫursagsikilla ("House, Pure Mountain"; the temple of the goddess Ninkarrak) or Esabad ("House of the Open Ear"; the temple of Gula) at Babylon, that inscription is excluded from RINBE 2; it will be edited as a 1000-number of Nebuchadnezzar II in RINBE 1/2.

Some famous historical texts concerning Amēl-Marduk and Nabonidus are not edited in this volume since they are not royal inscriptions. These are the four 'propaganda' texts edited in Schaudig, Inschriften Nabonids (pp. 563–595 P1–P4):[111] the first two, the Verse Account (= P1) and the King of Justice [Account] (= P2), present Nabonidus in a rather negative way, while the last two, a fragmentarily preserved chronographic text (= P3) and the so-called Royal Chronicle (= P4), offer positive images of Nabonidus' seventeen-year-long reign. The style of the fourth text, the Royal Chronicle, closely resembles a royal inscription and, like texts classified as chronicles, it is written in the third person; Neo-Babylonian inscriptions are usually written in the first person. Unlike Nabonidus' own inscriptions, the Royal Chronicle records campaigns against the city Ammanānu in Syria and against cities in Arabia; accounts of military achievements are generally not found in Neo-Babylonian inscriptions.[112] That text also narrates the consecration of Nabonidus' daughter En-nigaldi-Nanna as *ēntu*-priestess of the moon-god Sîn at Ur and the rebuilding of the temple of the sun-god Šamaš at Sippar, topics known from several of Nabonidus' inscriptions. A translation of that text, however, is provided below, on pp. 27–28.

Unlike Schaudig, Inschriften Nabonids, the inscriptions of the Persian king Cyrus II, including the famous Cyrus Cylinder, a text that negatively portrays Nabonidus and that has shaped the image of that Babylonian king

---

[106] Da Riva, SANER 3 pp. 138–140.

[107] See Bartelmus and Taylor, JCS 66 (2014) pp. 113–128. BM 68234 and BM 68321 were edited respectively in Schaudig, Inschriften Nabonids as text no. 2.15[a] (p. 467) text no. 2.16 (pp. 468–469).

[108] BM 68321 does not indirectly join BM 68234, as H. Schaudig (Inschriften Nabonids pp. 467–468) had tentatively suggested.

[109] A. Bartelmus and J. Taylor (JCS 66 [2014] pp. 114 and 124) propose "that the Sumerian inscriptions [on BM 67673+] are copies of originals, that the compilation of them onto a single tablet is the work of a Neo-Babylonian scribe, and that the Akkadian version is a translation made at that same time" and conclude that "BM 67673+ is not the Šagarakti-Šuriaš text that Nabonidus claims to have found" in his inscriptions.

The temple is called Emaš, rather than Eulmaš, in these inscriptions. As already pointed out by A. Bartelmus and J. Taylor (ibid. pp. 124–125), it is unclear "whether Emaš is another name for Eulmaš or is distinct." They further state that "it is in principle possible that Emaš could be the name of a shrine within Eulmaš or even another building altogether."

[110] A. Bartelmus and J. Taylor (JSC 66 [2014] p. 124) conclude that "BM 68234 appears to give that text [=the Šagarakti-Šuriaš text that Nabonidus claims to have found], matching exactly. It is presented as a copy of an old inscription in the classical style, written in suitably archaizing characters, and in monolingual Akkadian form, no less. ... it must be either a careful copy of an original monolingual Akkadian text or a forgery in part (i.e., a translation put into archaizing characters) or in whole (i.e., a tablet created to act as a 'copy' of the inscription quoted by Nabonidus). The orthography of the text suggests that it may be a careful copy of an original. We may question whether BM 68234 was produced directly or indirectly as a consequence of Nabonidus' excavations, in exactly the same way as for BM 67673+. The information reproduced on BM 68234 was nevertheless available to, and deemed important by, Nabonidus."

[111] See also, for example, De Breucker, Political Memory pp. 75–94; and Waerzeggers, Exile and Return pp. 181–222.

[112] The Wadi Brissa inscription (and possibly the Nahr el-Kelb inscription) of Nebuchadnezzar II and an inscription of Neriglissar record campaigns; the former describes military expeditions in Lebanon, while the latter describes a campaign in Cilicia. See respectively Da Riva, Twin Inscriptions; and Neriglissar 7.

in modern scholarship for a very long time, are not included in RINBE 2 since Cyrus was not a native king of Babylon.[113]

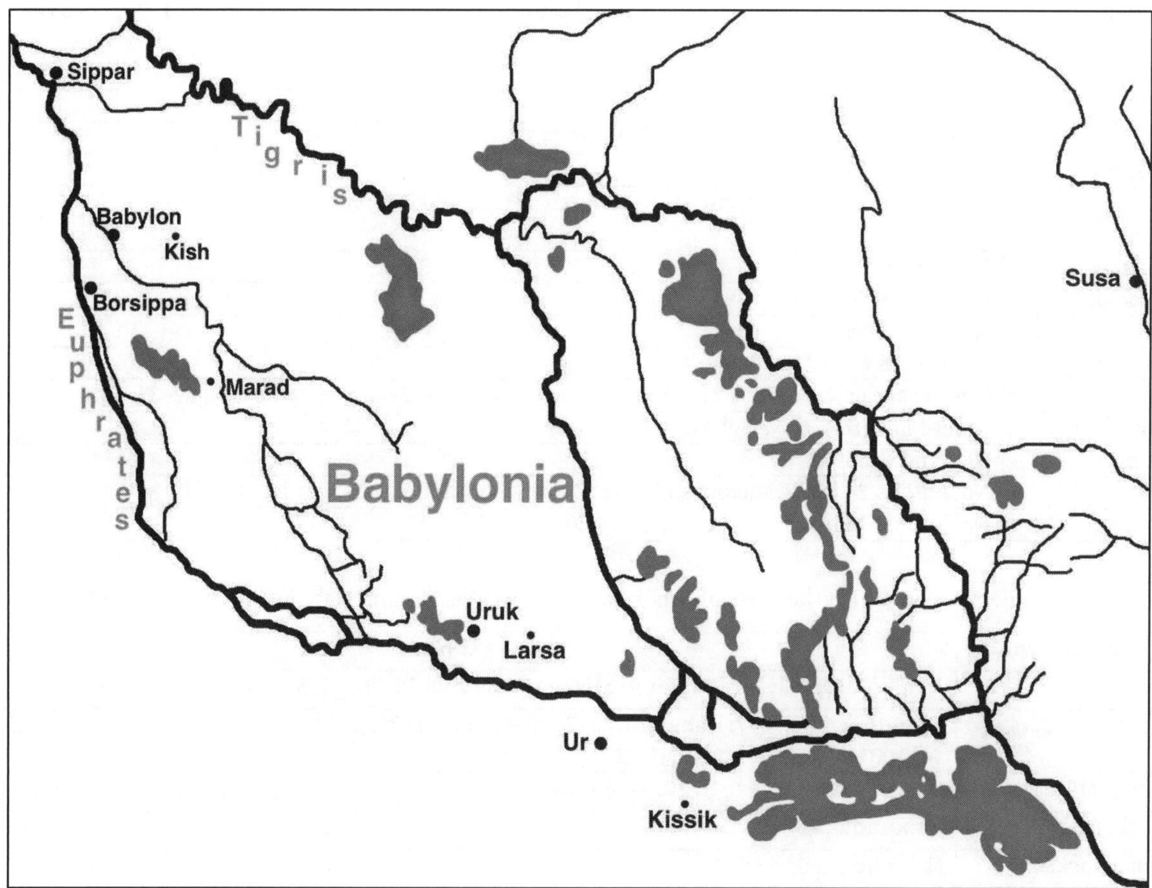

Figure 1. Map showing the most important sites in Babylonia where the inscriptions of Amēl-Marduk, Neriglissar, and Nabonidus were found.

Survey of the Inscribed Objects

Compared to the dynasty's most famous ruler Nebuchadnezzar II, relatively few inscriptions of the last four native kings of Babylon exist today; there are far fewer texts for all four rulers combined than there are for Nebuchadnezzar alone. At present, eighty-seven inscriptions for the period from 561 to 539 are known: six from the time of Amēl-Marduk, eight from the reign of Neriglissar, and seventy-three from when Nabonidus sat on the throne; unsurprisingly, not a single inscription from the short, two- to three-month reign of Lâbâši-Marduk has come to light. These Akkadian compositions,[114] which are written in the Standard Babylonian dialect and in contemporary and archaizing Neo-Babylonian script, are known from approximately 280 clay and stone objects, which originate from no less than sixteen different sites in Iran, Iraq, Jordan, Saudi Arabia, and Turkey. These objects come from archaeological excavations, as well as from antiquities markets. Many are now housed in museum collections, while some are either kept in private collections, were left in the field (or in situ), or have been lost forever. The majority of the still-accessible pieces are in the British Museum (London) and the Vorderasiatisches Museum (Berlin).

[113] New editions of Cyrus' Akkadian inscriptions from Babylon, Ur, and Uruk, with English translations, are available online via the Babylon 8 project of RIBo; see http://oracc.org/ribo/babylon8/ [2020].

[114] To date, no Sumerian or bilingual Akkadian-Sumerian texts for the Neo-Babylonian dynasty have been discovered. However, Aramaic is sometimes used on bricks; see the commentaries of Nabonidus 7 and 8 for further details. For information about the language of the inscriptions (with references to earlier literature), see, for example Da Riva, GMTR 4 pp. 89–91; and M.P. Streck, Semitic Languages pp. 381–382 (for further bibliographical references).

Provenances of the inscriptions of Amēl-Marduk, Neriglissar, and Nabonidus

Provenance	Text nos.
Babylon	Amēl-Marduk 1-3; Neriglissar 1–5; Nabonidus 1 (ex. 2), 2–4, 5, 7, 8 (exs. 1–6), 9–12, 26 (ex. 2), 28 (exs. 51–53), *43*, *1001*, *1003*
Borsippa	Nabonidus 13, *1002*
Ḫarrān	Nabonidus 46–53, 2001
Kish	Nabonidus 8 (ex. 8 [Tell Bender]), 14, 1004
Kissik	Nabonidus 15, 1005
Larsa	Nabonidus 16 (exs. 1–2 and 7), 17, 18 (exs. 1–6, 8, and 21–22)
Marad	Nabonidus 19, 1006
Nasiriyeh	Nabonidus 39 (ex. 6)
Padakku	Nabonidus 54
Sela'	Nabonidus 55
Seleucia	Nabonidus 8 (ex. 7), 20
Sippar	Neriglissar 6; Nabonidus 21–25, 26 (ex. 1), 26, 27 (exs. 2–4), 28 (exs. 1–50), 29–31, 1007–1011
Susa	Amēl-Marduk 4–6; Neriglissar 8
Tēmā	Nabonidus 56–61
Ur	Nabonidus 27 (ex. 1 and possibly exs. 2–3), 32–38, 39 (exs. 1–5 and 7–9)
Uruk	Nabonidus 16 (exs. 1–6), 18 (exs. 7, 9–20), 40

Types of objects upon which the texts of Amēl-Marduk, Neriglissar, and Nabonidus are inscribed[115]

Object Type	Text No.
Bricks	Amēl-Marduk 1; Neriglissar 4–5; Nabonidus 7–9, 18, 20, 31, 37–39, 51, 1005
Clay Cylinders	Neriglissar 1–3, 6–7; Nabonidus 1–2, 10–16, 19, 21–26, 27 (exs. 1–3), 28–29, 32–35, 41–42, 46, 1001–1002, 1004, 1006–1010
Clay Tablets	Nabonidus 5, 27 (ex. 4), 30, 44–45, 1011
Cliff Faces	Nabonidus 54–55
Door Socket	Nabonidus 36
Paving Stones	Amēl-Marduk 2
Pearl	Nabonidus 53
Pedestal	Nabonidus 57
Steles	Nabonidus 3–4, 17, 40, 43, 47, 56, 1003, 2001
Stone Fragments	Nabonidus 48–50, 58–61
Stone Vessels	Amēl-Marduk 3–6; Neriglissar 8; Nabonidus 52

Script of the inscriptions of Amēl-Marduk, Neriglissar, and Nabonidus

Script	Text no.
Contemporary Neo-Babylonian	Amēl-Marduk 3–6; Neriglissar 2–3, 6, 8; Nabonidus 1, 5, 10–12, 14–17, 19, 21–24, 26–30, 32–34, 40–61, 1002, 1004, 1006–1007, 1010–1011, 2001
Archaizing Neo-Babylonian	Amēl-Marduk 1–2; Neriglissar 4–5, 7; Nabonidus 3–4, 7–8, 13, 18, 20, 25, 31, 35–39, 1001, 1003, 1008–1009
Contemporary and Archaizing Neo-Babylonian	Neriglissar 1; Nabonidus 2

The extant texts are inscribed or stamped on eleven different types of clay and stone objects: bricks, clay cylinders, clay tablets, cliff faces, door sockets, paving stones, steles, stone beads (pearls), stone fragments (original object type uncertain), stone pedestals (for steles or anthropomorphic statues) and stone vessels (vases

[115] Da Riva discusses the different material supports of Neo-Babylonian royal inscriptions in GTMR 4; see pp. 33–43 of that book.

and bowls). Bricks and clay cylinders are the best attested media of Neo-Babylonian kings; these two object types make up approximately sixty-three percent of the corpus.[116]

Six inscriptions of Amēl-Marduk are known today. They were inscribed on a paving stone and several alabaster vases, as well as stamped on a couple of bricks. The objects were discovered at Babylon and Susa. There are slightly more official texts for his immediate successor Neriglissar. To date, eight distinct inscriptions of his have been identified. These are known from bricks, clay cylinders, and an alabaster vase. Some of the objects bearing inscriptions of Neriglissar were discovered at Babylon, during R. Koldewey's excavations, while others originate from other sites, including Sippar and Susa.

There is little surprise that more inscriptions are known for Nabonidus than for his three immediate predecessors since Babylon's last native ruler sat on the throne for seventeen years, giving his scribes ample time to write numerous texts on his behalf. Sixty-one inscriptions can be certainly attributed to Nabonidus, while another nine might have been composed in his name. In addition, one further inscription was written in his mother Adad-guppi's name. In total, seventy royal inscriptions from 555–539 are currently known. These self-aggrandizing texts were written (or stamped) on several bricks, numerous clay cylinders (of various shapes, sizes, and formats), several single- and multi-column clay tablets, two cliff faces, a door socket, a few paving stones, several steles, a pearl, and a stone bowl. Most of the objects bearing his name come from modern-day southern Iraq (Babylon, Borsippa, Kish, Kissik, Larsa, Marad, Nasiriyeh, Seleucia, Sippar, Ur, and Uruk) and a handful come from Jordan (Sela'), Saudi Arabia (Padakku, Tēmā), and Turkey (Ḫarrān).

Clay Cylinders

The clay cylinder was the most widely used medium for inscribing narrative inscriptions of Babylonian kings.[117] Although they are less numerous than inscribed or stamped bricks, inscribed cylinders are attested for most of the kings of the Neo-Babylonian Empire; five inscriptions of Neriglissar and at least thirty-two inscriptions of Nabonidus are known to have been written on this versatile medium.[118] Babylonian cylinders are generally 'barrel-shaped,' rather than being a true 'cylinder,' they vary in both size and format, and can be hollow, pierced, or solid.[119] Cylinders, depending on the length of the inscription written on them, distribute the text over one, two, three, or four columns. At present, only the two- and three-column formats are attested for Neriglissar's and Nabonidus' inscriptions.[120] Most of those texts were written in contemporary Neo-Babylonian script. A few, however, were inscribed using archaizing sign forms or using both contemporary and archaizing scripts.[121]

Some texts are known from a single exemplar, while other inscriptions are attested in several or numerous exemplars. For example, only one copy of the Tiara Cylinder of Nabonidus (text no. 25) has come to light, while

---

[116] Respectively, inscriptions written on bricks and cylinders make up approximately seventeen and forty-five percent of the known texts of Amēl-Marduk, Neriglissar, and Nabonidus.

[117] This is in contrast to late Neo-Assyrian kings (721–612), who preferred clay prisms since that medium was better suited for inscribing long, detailed accounts of their military and building activities. To date, only one prism bearing an inscription of a Neo-Babylonian king is extant. For the Nebuchadnezzar II prism, see Da Riva, ZA 103 (2013) pp. 196–229.

[118] These are Neriglissar 1–3 and 6–7; and Nabonidus 1–2, 10–16, 19, 21–26, 27 exs. 1–3, 28–29, 32–35, 41–42, and 46. In addition, five more fragmentarily preserved cylinder might preserve inscriptions of Nabonidus; these are Nabonidus 1001–1002, 1004, and 1006–1010. Ten cylinder inscriptions of Nabopolassar have been published and over fifty cylinder inscriptions of Nebuchadnezzar II have been positively identified; see Da Riva, GMTR 4 pp. 116–117 §1.2 and pp. 118–122 §2.2. No cylinder inscriptions from the reigns of Amēl-Marduk and Lâbâši-Marduk have been discovered or identified.

[119] For a summary of the various shapes and formats of cylinder, as well as the scholarly terminology for them, see Da Riva, GMTR 4 pp. 37–38; and Taylor, BBVO 26 pp. 44–59. CDLI refers to these objects as both barrels and cylinders. On the shape, R. Da Riva (GMTR 4 p. 37) states: "From a strictly geometrical point of view, the general term "cylinder" does not correspond to the physical appearance of the objects, for none of them is a cylinder. As noted above, they are rather barrel-shaped objects: symmetrical or asymmetrical ovoids with more or less flattened ends." Da Riva has pointed out (GMTR 4 p. 38) that hollow cylinders were made on a wheel and were "probably placed on wooden(?) supports inserted in a pole which was disposed horizontally, so that the cylinder could be rolled on its axis to be read"; cylinders pierced on one side were "placed on a pole disposed either vertically or horizontally"; and solid cylinders might have been "placed standing on one end, or in some other structure."

[120] All of the known cylinders of Neriglissar are of the two-column format, while Nabonidus inscriptions were written on both two- and three column cylinders. Cylinders with four columns of text are known only from the reign of Nebuchadnezzar II. The single column format is used by Nabopolassar and Nebuchadnezzar II; note that the one attested one-column cylinder of Nebuchadnezzar might have been a scribal exercise (Da Riva, GMTR 4 p. 39).

[121] Neriglissar 1 (Esagil Inscription) and Nabonidus 2 (Emašdari Cylinder) are known from copies written in both contemporary Neo-Babylonian and archaizing Neo-Babylonian scripts. It has been suggested that the Old Babylonian monumental script of the Codex Ḫammu-rāpi, even though it had been carried off to Susa by the Elamites in the twelfth century, had a strong influence on the script used for writing out Neo-Babylonian royal inscriptions; see, for example, Berger, NbK p. 95; Schaudig, Inschriften Nabonids p. 32 n. 133; and Da Riva, GMTR 4 p. 77 n. 77. As R. Da Riva has pointed out, the use of Old Babylonian sign forms is an archaism that diminishes that over the course of the Neo-Babylonian period. During the reigns of Nabopolassar and Nebuchadnezzar II, archaizing scripts was more commonly used to write out royal inscriptions than it was during the reigns of their successors.

approximately fifty-three copies of that same king's Eḫulḫul Cylinder (text no. 28) have been discovered.[122] Although cylinders could differ considerably in size and format,[123] cylinders bearing the same inscription tended to be homogeneous.[124] Given the uniformity of most Neo-Babylonian royal compositions — although numerous orthographical variants, scribal errors, omissions, additions, and other textual variations can be shared by more than one exemplar — it is difficult to determine with any degree of certainty which copy (or copies) of an inscription should be regarded as the 'principal' or 'original' version of the composition, especially when more than one exemplar was found in situ, that is, deposited within the brick structure of a building.[125] The distribution of text, the choice of individual signs, and grammatical forms vary from copy to copy. As far as we are aware, no two exemplars of any cylinder inscription are one hundred percent identical.

Cylinder inscriptions provide us with the most contemporary information about the numerous building activities of Neo-Babylonian kings (see above).[126] Without these texts, a great deal of what we know about the reigns of these rulers would be lost as that information is often not recorded in other (contemporary and later) sources. However, since reports of construction in Neo-Babylonian building inscriptions are, as one expects, more concerned with royal ideology than with historical reality, their contents should not be taken at face value. Because construction projects are always presented as a *fait accompli* and because the details provided in the texts can be ambiguous, scholars often have to make assumptions about the nature and extent of a given building activity, especially when a king's claims cannot be confirmed from the archaeological record. Thus, it is not always clear whether a ruler is simply making minor repairs to part of the building or rebuilding it in its entirety from top to bottom and whether or not a project was actually carried out in full or whether only part of the work had been finished by the end of the king's reign. Despite the inherent problems with this genre of text, cylinder inscriptions nevertheless provide information on construction enterprises of Neriglissar and Nabonidus in no less than seventeen cities, including the capital of the Empire, Babylon.[127] Bricks, paving stones, and door sockets support the claim that the former king sponsored construction at Babylon and give proof that the latter ruler undertook building at Babylon, Ḫarrān, Larsa, Seleucia (or Opis), Sippar, Ur, and Uruk, thereby giving credibility to some of the claims made by Neriglissar and Nabonidus in inscriptions written on multi-column clay cylinders.[128]

Clay Tablets

Few Neo-Babylonian inscriptions are preserved on clay tablets and all of these were either drafts of new inscriptions, models of texts to be copied on other objects (i.e., cylinders and steles), archival copies of foundation records and monuments, or scribal exercises.[129] Five or six tablets are inscribed with official inscriptions of Nabonidus.[130] A short, ten-line text recording the fashioning and dedication of an inscribed *musukkannu*-wood offering table to the goddess Ištar written on an *u'iltu*-tablet, a 'pillow-shaped' tablet, is a good example of a draft

---

[122] Respectively Nabonidus 25 (Tiara Cylinder) and 28 (Eḫulḫul Cylinder). H. Schaudig (Inschriften Nabonids pp. 412–414) catalogued seventy-five exemplars of the latter text, but that number of witnesses has been greatly reduced by joins made by the present authors (primarily Weiershäuser).

[123] The cylinders edited in the volume range in size from 9.5 cm in length and 4.7 cm in diameter (Nabonidus 32 [Elugalgalgasisa Cylinder] ex. 4) to 24.7 cm in length and 15.4 cm in diameter (Nabonidus 27 ex. 2). The thickness of the clay of hollow cylinders vary from 6 mm to more than 2 cm.

[124] As noted already by R. Da Riva (GMTR 4 p. 39).

[125] Approximately one-third of the now-extant Neo-Babylonian cylinders originate from a secure archaeological context; seventy-five percent of those come from the early-twentieth century German excavations at Babylon. Given the general lack of a find spot, it should be stressed here that not all cylinders were intended to be 'foundation documents,' that is, to be deposited in the palace, temple, or wall whose construction they commemorate. R. Da Riva (GMTR 4 pp. 38–39) has already noted that some cylinders were clearly inscribed by an inexperienced scribe or student, as can be inferred from the high number of mistakes, that some were written to serve as an archival copy, and that others cylinders might have been displayed publicly.

[126] As mentioned above, few Neo-Babylonian inscriptions record the military activities. See n. 112 above.

[127] In alphabetical order, these are Agade, Babylon, Borsippa, Cutha, Dilbat, Ḫarrān, Kissik, Kish, Larsa, Marad, Seleucia, Sippar, Sippar-Anunītum, Tēmā, Ubassu, Ur, and Uruk.

[128] For example, Nabonidus' work on the ziggurat at Ur, Elugalgalgasisa ("House of the King who Lets Counsel Flourish"), described in cylinder inscription Nabonidus 32 (Elugalgalgasisa Cylinder), can be confirmed from not only twenty-three bricks found in the structure of that building (Nabonidus 38), but also from the fact that five cylinders inscribed with that text were found in situ, buried upright in a brick capsule, in all four corners of the second tier of Ur's temple-tower. According to some scholars (for example, Da Riva, GMTR 4 p. 39), the upright orientation of these small, two-column cylinders indicates that they were intended to be read vertically.

[129] Da Riva, GTMR 4 pp. 24–25 n. 111. As R. Da Riva (ibid.) has already pointed out, these tablets were never written to function as royal inscriptions, that is, to be placed into the foundation or the structure of a building or to be displayed publicly like a monument.

[130] These are Nabonidus 6, 27 ex. 4, 30, 44–45, and 1011. Given the short duration of the reigns of Amēl-Marduk and Neriglissar, it comes as little surprise that no clay tablets bearing inscriptions of those two kings are presently known. A handful of inscriptions of Nabopolassar and Nebuchadnezzar II on clay tablets are extant.

or scribal exercise.[131] A multi-column clay tablet bearing an inscription recording Nabonidus' restoration of temples in Sippar, Larsa, Agade, and Sippar-Anunītu, a text also preserved on three clay cylinders, might have served as a model for the copies of that text written on foundation documents or was an archival copy of that inscription. The other tablets bearing Nabonidus inscriptions are not sufficiently preserved to comment on their precise nature or function.

Baked Bricks

Given the number of known building activities of Babylon's last native kings, it comes as no surprise that brick inscriptions are attested for every ruler of the 'dynasty,' with the exception of Lâbâši-Marduk, whose tenure as king lasted only two or three months. Approximately two hundred bricks bearing one inscription of Amēl-Marduk, two texts of Neriglissar, and at least ten different inscriptions of Nabonidus have been published.[132] These originate not only from the capital Babylon, but also from Ḫarrān, Kissik, Larsa, Seleucia, Sippar, Ur, and Uruk, and these objects, like door sockets and paving stones, provide physical proof of some of the construction projects recorded in inscriptions written on clay cylinders and tablets. Most of the brick inscriptions edited in this volume were written in an archaizing script; the Nabonidus bricks from Ḫarrān were stamped using contemporary Neo-Babylonian sign forms. In general, the bricks from this time are inscribed in a stamped and ruled frame; in scholarly literature, these brick inscriptions are sometimes referred to as 'stamped bricks,' which is correct with regard to the inscribed area of the brick, but wrong when referring to the inscription itself, which is written. These texts were placed on the face or on the edge of the bricks.[133]

Unlike the brick inscriptions of Nabopolassar and Nebuchadnezzar II, whose inscriptions on bricks could be quite lengthy, brick inscriptions of Amēl-Marduk, Neriglissar, and Nabonidus tended to be short, usually between three to six lines in length. In general, inscriptions on bricks during this time just contain the king's name, his titles and epithets (most often, *muddiš esagil u ezida* "the one who renovates Esagil and Ezida") and the name of his father and, therefore, provide no chronological information or details about the structure in which they were placed.[134] A few of Nabonidus' brick inscriptions from Ḫarrān and Ur, however, provide some information about the king's building activities. The Ḫarrān bricks mention the rebuilding of Eḫulḫul, while the Ur bricks state that the king worked on Egipar (the residence of the *ēntu*-priestess), Elugalgalgasisa (the ziggurat), and Enunmaḫ (a building inside the Ekišnugal complex).

Stone Paving Slabs

Very few Neo-Babylonian paving stones outside of the reign of Nebuchadnezzar II were discovered during the German excavations at Babylon.[135] At present, only one such object is presently attested and it bears a short, two-line proprietary inscription of Amēl-Marduk.[136]

Stone Door Sockets

At present, only one inscribed Neo-Babylonian door socket has come to light and it is engraved with an inscription of Nabonidus discovered at Ur.[137] This door socket commemorates the rebuilding of the Egipar temple, the age-old, traditional residence of the *ēntu*-priestess at Ur, and its discovery provides physical proof that this Neo-Babylonian king undertook construction on that building. The inscription itself is unusual since the cuneiform signs are not only written in an archaizing script, but the text is engraved on the door socket in

---

[131] Nabonidus 5. For some details on the *u'iltu*-tablet format (1:2 ratio), see Radner, Nineveh 612 BC pp. 72–73 (with fig. 8). As has been already pointed out by H. Schaudig (Inschriften Nabonids p. 476), this short text contains two scribal errors and, therefore, unlikely served as a model for the inscription that was physically engraved on the metal plating of that offering table.

[132] These are Amēl-Marduk 1; Neriglissar 4–5; Nabonidus 7–9, 18, 20, 31, 37–39, 51, and 1005. The exact number of known bricks is currently not known since the actual count of the Nabonidus bricks discovered in the debris of the Islamic settlement of Ḫarrān has never been provided; V. Donbaz (ARRIM 9 [1991] pp. 11–12) indicates that about one hundred bricks and brick fragments bearing a four-line cuneiform inscription had been found. The excavation number of only one of those bricks has been published. Many more bricks of Nabopolassar and Nebuchadnezzar II are known. For a survey of the seven Nabopolassar brick inscriptions and thirty-one brick inscriptions of Nebuchadnezzar II, see Da Riva, GTMR 4 pp. 116–117 §§1.1 and 2.1.

[133] Inscriptions on the face of the brick, unlike those on the narrow edge, were not visible after the brick had been set in place.

[134] Da Riva, GTMR 4 p. 37.

[135] Da Riva, GTMR 4 p. 124 §2.13.

[136] Amēl-Marduk 2. The authors would like to thank O. Pedersén (personal communication, September 10th and October 14th, 2019) for pointing out that the object bearing the excavation number BE 41580 is actually inscribed with a well-attested inscription of Nebuchadnezzar II, rather than a hitherto, unpublished inscription of Nabonidus. See the introduction of Nabonidus 6 for further information.

[137] Nabonidus 36. The Nebuchadnezzar door socket mentioned by R. Da Riva (GTMR 4 p. 124 §2.11) is actually a paving stone.

an archaizing orientation, that is, the lines of the inscription are written vertically from top to bottom and horizontally from right to left; this was probably inspired by the ancient monuments known to Nabonidus' literary craftsmen.[138]

Stone Steles and Pedestals for Monuments

Relatively few Neo-Babylonian steles are known today and all but one of them come from the reign of Nabonidus.[139] The ten steles firmly attributed to Nabonidus, including two written in the name of his mother Adad-guppi, as well as one fragmentarily preserved monument comprising sixteen fragments, were discovered at various sites in Babylonia (Babylon, Larsa, and Uruk), at Ḫarrān in Turkey, and at Tēmā in Saudi Arabia.[140] Nabonidus' steles, as far as we can tell, all had a rounded top and an image of the king, usually facing to the right,[141] standing before symbols of the moon (Sîn), sun (Šamaš), and the planet Venus (Ištar) engraved on the top of the obverse face.[142] Some of the monuments had curved, semi-circular backs, while others had flat backs.[143] The former type was inscribed on the flat obverse face and the curved reverse surface and the latter stele type was generally only engraved on the obverse, although text was occasionally written on the narrow sides of the monument.[144] In all instances, the inscription is divided into columns. Flat-back steles generally had three columns of text, while rounded-back monuments could have had as many as eleven columns of text. Like inscriptions written on cylinders, Nabonidus' steles usually provide information on the king's building activities; the Babylon Stele (Nabonidus 3) also gives information about historical events that took place before Nabonidus became king, starting at least in the time of the Assyrian king Sennacherib (704–681). In the case of the monuments of the king's mother, those steles give a pseudo-autobiographical account of the centenarian Adad-guppi.

Recently, two fragments of a rounded or oblong pedestal for a stele or statue were excavated at Tēmā in Saudi Arabia.[145] At present, this is the only known inscribed, royal monument base. This sandstone pedestal, on which a stele or anthropomorphic statue stood, bears a one-line inscription of Nabonidus written in contemporary Neo-Babylonian script.

Rock Reliefs

Given the short duration of the reigns of Amēl-Marduk and Neriglissar, it is not a surprise that no rock reliefs from these two kings are known. However, Nabonidus had at least two such monuments carved during his seventeen years as king: one at Padakku (mod. al-Ḥā'iṭ) in Saudi Arabia and one at Sela' in Jordan.[146] Both rock reliefs are heavily weathered and little of their original texts survive today. The monuments were presumably commissioned to commemorate Nabonidus' activities in the region and the relief at Sela' might have recorded the king's conquest of Edom, an event mentioned in the Nabonidus Chronicle. The inscriptions are both carved in a rounded-top frame (in the shape of a stele) and are accompanied by an image of the king wearing traditional Babylonian royal attire, holding a staff, and standing before symbols of the moon (Sîn), sun (Šamaš), and the planet Venus (Ištar).

---

[138] For further details on the archaizing orientation of this text, see Schaudig, Inschriften Nabonids pp. 82–83.

[139] That stele dates to the reign of Nebuchadnezzar II and most likely originates from Babylon; see Da Riva, GTMR 4 p. 124 §2.19. No steles of Nabopolassar, Amēl-Marduk and Neriglissar have been discovered.

[140] Nabonidus 3–4, 17, 40, 43, 47, 56, and 2001; Nabonidus 58–61 are probably fragments of one or more steles. It is uncertain if the fragments comprising the stele bearing Nabonidus 4 belong to one or two steles. Note that the original pieces are housed in the British Museum (London) and the Vorderasiatisches Museum (Berlin). For further information, see Schaudig, Inschriften Nabonids p. 537. The object edited in this volume as Nabonidus 1003 might have also been inscribed with a text of this Neo-Babylonian king. The text is not sufficiently preserved to assign this stele fragment to Nabonidus with any degree of certainty. It is tentatively included in this volume since it was edited in Schaudig, Inschriften Nabonids. Although the inscription written on the so-called Uruk Stele (Nabonidus 40 [Uruk Stele]) has been obliterated by a later ruler, the assignation to Nabonidus is based on the shape of the monument and the still-visible iconography.

[141] On the two steles from Ḫarrān (Nabonidus 47 [Ḫarrān Stele]), the king faces to the left.

[142] The iconography on the steles of Adad-guppi (Nabonidus 2001 [Adad-guppi Stele]) is, of course, different. The one monument whose upper portion is sufficiently preserved shows four people walking right to left, towards an alter; a similar image appears on the disk of Enḫeduana. The first two individuals are assumed to have been Nabonidus and Adad-guppi.

[143] For example, Nabonidus 3 (Babylon Stele), 4, and 40 (Uruk Stele) had rounded backs, while Nabonidus 43 (Tarif Stele), 47 (Ḫarrān Stele), and 2001 (Adad-guppi Stele) had flat backs.

[144] The Tarif Stele (Nabonidus 43) is inscribed on the right edge of the monument.

[145] Schaudig in Hausleiter, ATLAL 25 p. 81 [Arabic section], pl. 2.20 figs. c–e and pp. 99–100.

[146] Further details about the rock relief at Sela' will appear in several forthcoming publications of R. Da Riva, who examined the monument firsthand in September 2018. See Da Riva, BAR 45 (2019) pp. 25–32.

Vessels

A handful of fragmentarily preserved stone vases and bowls bearing inscriptions of Amēl-Marduk, Neriglissar and Nabonidus are known.[147] Most were discovered in the Elamite/Persian city Susa, in modern-day Iran, presumably where they were deposited after Cyrus II captured Babylon in 539,[148] while one is thought to have come from Babylon and another is believed to have come from Ḫarrān, as inferred from the text written on it. The Amēl-Marduk and Neriglissar vases are all inscribed with a short proprietary label, as well as the vessel's capacity. The Nabonidus bowl, however, is engraved with a longer, dedicatory inscription stating that the king had two vessels made for the moon-god at Ḫarrān.[149]

Beads, Eyestones, and Pearls

Few inscribed beads, eyestones, and pearls from the Neo-Babylonian period are known today and most bear inscriptions of Nebuchadnezzar II.[150] One chalcedony bead (or pearl), now in a private collection, records that the moon-god Sîn requested a dagger of Nabonidus in a dream, which the king then had made for him.[151] It is uncertain, because the provenance of the object is unknown, if the dagger, which presumably had this bead inlaid in its handle, was given to the god Sîn at Ur or the one at Ḫarrān.

Overview of Previous Editions

Individual Neo-Babylonian royal inscriptions have been edited and published as early as 1852, when G.F. Grotefend (Erläuterungen) first presented an edition of Nabonidus' Tarif Stele (Nabonidus 43); note that Grotefend's translation of that badly preserved text bears little resemblance to a modern translation of that same Akkadian text. It was not until much later in the nineteenth century that more Neo-Babylonian inscriptions, including the Babylon Stele (Nabonidus 3), began to appear in scholarly publications. The first significant publication of this group of texts was in 1890, in volume 3/2 of the then-important series Keilinschriftliche Bibliothek. C. Bezold edited the then-available inscriptions of Neriglissar and F.E. Peiser published the then-known inscriptions of Nabonidus.[152]

Twenty-two years later, in 1912, S. Langdon edited all of the Neo-Babylonian inscriptions known to him in his Die neubabylonischen Königsinschriften. That seminal work contained three texts of Neriglissar and fifteen inscriptions of Nabonidus. The transliterations were accompanied by German translations.[153] Despite the importance of Neo-Babylonian royal inscriptions, Langdon's 1912 edition was the last successful attempt to collect and publish all of the known texts of that genre and period in a single place.

P.-R. Berger, however, had planned to remedy that desideratum in the 1970s by publishing a three-volume edition (with up-to-date transliterations, translations, and studies) of the then-known corpus of texts. The first volume, Die neubabylonischen Königsinschriften: Königsinschriften des ausgehenden babylonischen Reiches (626–539 a. Chr.), which contained a catalogue and bibliographical information, appeared in 1973, but the planned second and third volumes were never published and, therefore, Langdon, NBK continued to be the discipline-standard edition of the inscriptions of Babylon's last native kings.

In 1989, P.-A. Beaulieu published a comprehensive study of the inscriptions of Nabonidus as part of his book The Reign of Nabonidus, King of Babylon 556–539 BC. Although he did not include fully-fledged editions as part of his study, Beaulieu did include transliterations and translations of key passages of Nabonidus' inscriptions, thus, updating some of the more important sections of that king's texts.

In 2001, H. Schaudig published his doctoral dissertation Die Inschriften Nabonids von Babylon und Kyros' des Großen samt den in ihrem Umfeld entstandenen Tendenzschriften: Textausgabe und Grammatik, and this

147 Amēl-Marduk 4–6, Neriglissar 8, and Nabonidus 52.

148 Da Riva, SANER 3 p. 32.

149 Interestingly, this inscription mentions a ziggurat as part of the Eḫulḫul complex, which is rather puzzling since no other extant cuneiform sources mention or refer to a temple-tower at Ḫarrān.

150 Da Riva, GMTR 4 p. 123 §§2.8–9.

151 Nabonidus 53.

152 In that same volume, H. Winckler edited the inscriptions of Nabopolassar and Nebuchadnezzar II. French translations of a few inscriptions of Neo-Babylonian kings, including a few of Neriglissar and Nabonidus did appear in Ménant, Babylone et la Chaldée, which was published in 1875. That book did not, however, include transliterations of those sources.

153 Five inscriptions of Napolassar and fifty-two texts of Nebuchadnezzar II were also included in that book. No inscriptions of Amēl-Marduk were included in Langdon, NBK. The Napolassar and Nebuchadnezzar II texts were adapted from his 1905 book Building inscriptions of the Neo-Babylonian Empire: Part 1, Nabopolassar and Nebuchadnezzar, which was based on his Ph.D. dissertation (Columbia University).

greatly improved matters. After nearly ninety years, Schaudig was the first person to undertake the publication of an up-to-date and authoritative treatment of Neo-Babylonian royal inscriptions. Not only did he provide carefully-prepared transliterations and German translations of fifty-five inscriptions of Nabonidus, but he also prepared a detailed grammatical analysis of that group of texts. R. Da Riva accurately remarked in 2008 that "Schaudig's work is the only substantial improvement over Langdon that we have today."[154] Apart from some of Da Riva's own later publications, this currently holds true.[155]

In 2008, R. Da Riva published a very informative, general study of the genre entitled The Neo-Babylonian Royal Inscriptions: An Introduction. Although that book does not include editions of the texts themselves, it does include a wealth of information about this important group of texts, including extensive bibliography and a comprehensive catalogue of inscriptions.[156] Several years later, in 2013, Da Riva performed a similar service to Assyriology by publishing up-to-date editions and studies of the known inscriptions of Nabopolassar, Amēl-Marduk, and Neriglissar. Her book The Inscriptions of Nabopolassar, Amel-Marduk and Neriglissar includes transliterations and translations of fifteen inscriptions of Nabopolassar, six inscriptions of Amēl-Marduk, and nine inscriptions of Neriglissar. Between Schaudig and Da Riva, a sizeable portion of Langdon's 1912 edition of inscriptions has been updated. New, authoritative editions of the numerous texts of the dynasty's most famous ruler, Nebuchadnezzar II, however, are yet to appear.[157]

Since 2015, the inscriptions included in Da Riva, SANER 3 have been included on the LMU Munich-based Royal Inscriptions of Babylonia online (RIBo) Project, in its "Babylon 7" sub-project, in a lemmatized (linguistically annotated) and Open Access format.[158] The texts in Schaudig, Inschriften Nabonids were made publically available in December 2018. Thus, earlier versions of the inscriptions included in this book, as well as those in the currently in preparation RINBE 1 volume, have been available for free for several years.[159]

Dating and Chronology

Unless it is stated otherwise, the dates given in this volume (excluding those in bibliographical citations) are all BC. Each ancient Mesopotamian year has been given a single Julian year equivalent even though the ancient year actually encompassed parts of two Julian years, with the ancient year beginning around the time of the vernal equinox. Thus, for example, the sixteenth regnal year of Nabonidus is indicated to be 540, although it actually ended in early 539 and, thus, events which took place late in the ancient year "540" actually took place early in the Julian year 539.

Texts edited in this volume occasionally mention contemporary dates and the charts in this section are intended to aid the reader in understanding those dates.

The Mesopotamian month names and their modern equivalents are:

I	Nisannu	March–April	VII	Tašrītu	September–October
II	Ayyāru	April–May	VIII	Araḫsamnu	October–November
III	Simānu	May–June	IX	Kislīmu	November–December
IV	Du'ūzu	June–July	X	Ṭebētu	December–January
V	Abu	July–August	XI	Šabāṭu	January–February
VI	Ulūlu	August–September	XII	Addaru	February–March
VI2	Intercalary Ulūlu		XII2	Intercalary Addaru	

The table below for the reigns of Amēl-Marduk, Neriglissar, and Nabonidus is adapted from Parker and Dubberstein, Babylonian Chronology pp. 26–27 and it attempts to precisely convert Babylonian dates to Julian ones. The dates are given as civil days, from midnight to midnight, and the dates (month/day) provided in the chart are those of the first day of each month. Intercalary months occurred in Amēl-Marduk's second (XII2) year on the throne, Neriglissar's third regnal year (XII2), and Nabonidus' first (XII2), third (XII2), sixth (XII2), tenth (VI2), twelfth (XII2), and fifteenth (XII2) years on the throne.

[154] Da Riva, GMTR 4 p. ix.
[155] Especially Da Riva, Twin Inscriptions; Da Riva, SANER 3; and Da Riva, ZA 103 (2013) pp. 196–229.
[156] Of note, Da Riva, GTMR 4 p. 131 mentions seven fragments not included in Schaudig, Inschriften Nabonids.
[157] These texts are to be edited in the first volume of this series, in two parts.
[158] http://oracc.org/ribo/babylon7/pager, as well http://oracc.org/ribo/pager [2020].
[159] The Nebuchadnezzar II inscriptions to be included in RINBE 1/1 were made public in December 2019. Note that the version included on RIBo also includes German translations.

Year	BC	Nis	Aja	Sim	Duz	Abu	Ulu	U II	Taš	Ara	Kis	Kan	Šab	Add	A II
Amēl-Marduk															
1	561	4/6	5/5	6/3	7/3	8/2	9/1		10/1	10/30	11/29	12/28	1/27	2/25	
2	560	3/26	4/24	5/24	6/22	7/22	8/21		9/20	10/20	11/18	12/18	1/16	2/15	3/16
Neriglissar (and Lâbâši-Marduk)[160]															
1	559	4/14	5/14	6/12	7/11	8/10	9/9		10/9	11/7	12/7	1/5	2/4	3/5	
2	558	4/4	5/3	6/2	7/1	7/31	8/29		9/28	10/27	11/26	12/25	1/24	2/23	
3	557	3/23	4/22	5/21	6/20	7/19	8/18		9/16	10/15	11/14	12/13	1/12	2/11	3/12
4	556	4/11	5/11	6/9	7/9	8/7	9/6		10/5	11/3	12/3	1/1	1/30	3/1	
Nabonidus															
1	555	3/31	4/30	5/30	6/28	7/28	8/26		9/25	10/24	11/22	12/22	1/20	2/19	3/20
2	554	4/19	5/19	6/17	7/17	8/15	9/14		10/14	11/12	12/11	1/10	2/8	3/9	
3	553	4/7	5/7	6/5	7/5	8/3	9/2		10/2	10/31	11/30	12/29	1/28	2/26	3/28
4	552	4/26	5/25	6/24	7/23	8/22	9/21		10/21	11/19	12/19	1/18	2/16	3/17	
5	551	4/16	5/15	6/13	7/13	8/11	9/10		10/10	11/8	12/8	1/7	2/6	3/7	
6	550	4/5	5/5	6/3	7/2	8/1	8/30		9/29	10/29	11/27	12/27	1/26	2/24	3/25
7	549	4/23	5/23	6/21	7/20	8/19	9/17		10/17	11/16	12/15	1/14	2/13	3/14	
8	548	4/13	5/12	6/11	7/10	8/8	9/7		10/6	11/5	12/5	1/3	2/2	3/3	
9	547	4/2	5/2	5/31	6/29	7/29	8/27		9/26	10/25	11/24	12/23	1/22	2/20	
10	546	3/22	4/21	5/20	6/19	7/18	8/17	9/15	10/15	11/14	12/13	1/11	2/10	3/10	
11	545	4/9	5/8	6/7	7/6	8/5	9/4		10/3	11/2	12/2	12/31	1/29	2/28	
12	544	3/29	4/27	5/27	6/25	7/25	8/24		9/23	10/23	11/21	12/21	1/19	2/17	3/19
13	543	4/17	5/16	6/15	7/14	8/13	9/12		10/12	11/11	12/10	1/9	2/7	3/8	
14	542	4/6	5/6	6/4	7/4	8/2	9/1		10/1	10/30	11/29	12/29	1/27	2/26	
15	541	3/26	4/25	5/24	6/22	7/22	8/20		9/19	10/18	11/17	12/17	1/16	2/14	3/16
16	540	4/14	5/13	6/12	7/11	8/10	9/8		10/8	11/7	12/6	1/5	2/3	3/5	
17	539	4/4	5/3	6/2	7/1	7/31	8/29		9/27	10/27	11/25	12/24	1/23	2/22	

Proposed Dates of the Texts of Nabonidus

Although Nabonidus' inscribed objects are never dated, it is possible to suggest dates of composition for many of that king's official texts, as P.-A. Beaulieu and H. Schaudig have already attempted.[161] In general, those two scholars agree in their dating,[162] but disagree significantly on their proposed dates of Nabonidus 3 (Babylon Stele), 46 (Ḫarrān Cylinder), and 53.[163] The authors of the present volume more or less agree with dates proposed by Beaulieu or Schaudig, but suggest alternatives in a few cases, in particular Nabonidus 23 (Ebabbar Cylinder), which, based on a recently-published inscription (Nabonidus 22) and a text published for the first time in this book (Nabonidus 21), likely dates to the beginning of Nabonidus' seventeen-year reign, rather than to his tenth regnal year (546).[164] The chart below is intended to aid the reader in understanding the dates proposed by Beaulieu, Schaudig, and the present authors. The text numbers in the 'this volume' column in **bold** font indicates that the present authors propose a date that differs from those suggested by both Beaulieu and Schaudig, while the text numbers in *italics* indicates the dates of texts that were published after those two scholars' books.

Proposed Date	Beaulieu	Schaudig	This volume
Beginning of the reign	—	Nabonidus 13	Nabonidus 13
Middle of year 1 (555)	Nabonidus 3	—	Nabonidus 3
Second half of year 2 (554)	Nabonidus 34, 36, 39	Nabonidus 34, 36, 39	Nabonidus *21–22*, **23**, 34, 36, 39
End of year 2 (554)	Nabonidus 24–25	Nabonidus 24–25, 1008	Nabonidus 24–25
First years of the reign	—	—	Nabonidus *41*, *1002*, *1006*
Between years 3 (553) and 10 (546), possibly before year 6 (550)	Nabonidus 19	Nabonidus 19	Nabonidus 19
Between years 4 (552) and 13 (543), possibly year 6 (550)	Nabonidus 26	Nabonidus 26	Nabonidus 26, *54*, 56, *57–61*

[160] Lâbâši-Marduk's short, two- to three-month-long reign is included with Neriglissar's 4th regnal year (556).

[161] See Beaulieu, Nabonidus pp. 1–42; and Schaudig, Inschriften Nabonids pp. 47–48 and *passim*.

[162] These two scholars differ marginally on the date of Nabonidus 27. P.-A Beaulieu proposes that that text was composed after Nabonidus' 13th regnal year (543), probably in his 16th year as king (540), while H. Schaudig (Inschriften Nabonids pp. 48 and 447) simply indicates that it was written sometime after the king's return from Arabia in 543.

[163] P.-A. Beaulieu (Nabonidus pp. 21, 42, and 240–241) suggests that Nabonidus 3 (Babylon Stele) was composed in the middle of Nabonidus' first regnal year (555) and that Nabonidus 46 (Ḫarrān Cylinder) was written sometime between the king's third (553) and thirteenth (543) years on the throne. He proposes no date for Nabonidus 53. H. Schaudig (Inschriften Nabonids pp. 48, 472, 515, and 545) dates Nabonidus 3 (Babylon Stele) and 53 to the period after Nabonidus' thirteenth regnal year (544–539) and Nabonidus 46 (Ḫarrān Cylinder) to the king's sixteenth year (540). Further details about the dating of these texts will be treated in the commentaries of those three texts.

[164] See Beaulieu, Nabonidus pp. 30–31; and Schaudig, Inschriften Nabonids p. 48.

Proposed Date	Beaulieu	Schaudig	This volume
Year 7 (549) or later	Nabonidus 10	Nabonidus 10	Nabonidus 10, *11–12*
Between years 9 (547) and 11 (545)	Nabonidus 18	Nabonidus 18	Nabonidus 18
Year 10 (546) or before			Nabonidus *42*
Year 10 (546)	Nabonidus 15–16, 23	Nabonidus 15–16, 23	Nabonidus 15–16
Between years 3 (553) and 13 (543)	Nabonidus 46	Nabonidus 55	Nabonidus 55
After year 13 (after Nabonidus' return from Arabia; 543)	Nabonidus 51	Nabonidus 3, 27, 48–53	Nabonidus 27, 51, **2001**
After year 13 (543), possibly year 14 (542) or 15 (541)	Nabonidus 43, 47	Nabonidus 43, 47, 2001	Nabonidus 43, 47–50
Between years 13 (543) and 16 (540)	Nabonidus 17	Nabonidus 17	Nabonidus 17
After year 13 (543), probably year 16 (540)	Nabonidus 27–29	Nabonidus 28–29, 40, 46	Nabonidus 28–29, *30*, 46, **52**
After year 13 (543), probably year 16 (540) or 17 (539)	Nabonidus 32, 37–38	Nabonidus 32, 37–38	Nabonidus 32–33, 37–38
No date possible	Nabonidus 1–2, 6–9, 44, 53, 1001, 1004, 1009	Nabonidus 1–2, 4–9, 14, 20, 31, 35, 44–45, 1001, 1003–1004, 1009–1011	Nabonidus 1–2, 4–9, 14, 20, 31, 35, **40**, 44–45, 53, 1001, 1003–1005, *1007*, **1008,** 1009–1010, *1011*

King Lists

Two king lists record that Amēl-Marduk, Neriglissar, Lâbâši-Marduk, and Nabonidus were kings of Babylon. For the convenience of the user of this volume, it has been thought useful to present translations of the relevant passages here. The entries immediately preceding and following those of the kings whose inscriptions are edited in this volume are also given when they are preserved.

1. *Uruk King List*

(van Dijk, UVB 18 pl. 28; Grayson, RLA 6/1–2 [1980] pp. 97–98 §3.5)

Obv. 6′)	21 year(s)	Nabopolassar
Obv. 7′)	43 [ye]ar(s)	Nebuchadnezzar (II)
Obv. 8′)	2 [ye]ar(s)	Amēl-Marduk
Obv. 9′)	3 [years], 8 month(s)	Neriglissar
Obv. 10′)	[(...)] 3 month(s)	Lâbâši-Marduk
Obv. 11′)	*17* [year(s)]	Nabonidus
Obv. 12′)	[N year(s)]	[C]yrus (II)

2. *Ptolemaic Canon*

(Wachsmuth, Alten Geschichte p. 305; Grayson, RLA 6/1–2 [1980] p. 101 §3.8)

Ναβοπολασσάρου	κα	Nabopolassaros (Nabopolassar)	21 (years)
Ναβοκολασσάρου	μγ	Nabokolassaros (Nebuchadnezzar II)	43 (years)
Ἰλλοαρουδάμου	β	Illoaroudamos (Amēl-Marduk)	2 (years)
Νηριγασολασσάρου	δ	Nerigasolassaros (Neriglissar)	4 (years)
Ναβοναδίου	ιζ	Nabonadios (Nabonidus)	17 (years)

Chronicles

Two Mesopotamian chronicles provide useful information both on the events of the reigns of Amēl-Marduk, Neriglissar, Lâbâši-Marduk, and Nabonidus and on the order of those events. The standard edition of Mesopotamian chronicles is the edition of A.K. Grayson (Grayson, Chronicles), but note also the recent edition by J.-J. Glassner (Glassner, Chronicles) and the ongoing work by I. Finkel and R.J. van der Spek (see www.livius.org/cg-cm/chronicles/chron00.html [2020]). For an excellent study dealing with classifications and provenances of Babylonian Chronicles, see Waerzeggers, JNES 71 (2012) pp. 285–298. For the convenience of the user of this volume, it has been thought useful to present translations of the relevant passages here; these translations have been adapted from the aforementioned works.

1. *Chronicle of the Third Year of Neriglissar*

(Grayson, Chronicles pp. 103–104 no. 6; Glassner, Chronicles pp. 230–233 no. 25)

1–4) The third year (557): [*On the Nth day of the month* ...] Appuašu, the king of the land Pirind[u, mus]tered h[is numerous] troops and [set ou]t to raid and plu[nder] (cities) Across the Rive[r (Syria-Palestine)]. Neriglissar muste[red his] troops [and] march[ed] to the city Ḫumê to oppose him.

5–13) Before his (Neriglissar's) (arrival), App[u]ašu placed the troops and mounted messengers whom he had conscripted in a gorge of the mountains for ambushes, but (when) Neriglissar reached them, he brought about th[eir] defeat. He killed many troops. He (Neriglissar) captured his (Appuašu's) troops and many of his horses. He pursued Appuašu for a distance of fifteen leagues of difficult mountain terrain, where the men had to walk one behind the other (lit. "man after man"), as far as the city Ura'a, his royal city. [*He capt*]*ured* him, seized the city Ura'a, and plundered it.

14) (erasure)

15–19) When he (Neriglissar) had marched from the city Ura'a to the city Kirši, his ancestors' royal city, a distance of six leagues of hard mountain terrain (and) difficult (mountain) pass(es), he seized the city Kirši, a fortified city, his (Appuašu's) royal city. He burned with fire its wall, its palace, and its people.

20–23a) By means of boats, he (Neriglissar) seized the city Pitusu, a mountain that is in the midst of the sea, and the 6,000 combat troops who had gone into hiding inside it. He *destroyed* his city. Moreover, he took its people captive.

23b–27) In that same year, he started fires from the (mountain) pass of the city Sallunê to the border of Lydia. Appuašu disappeared and (therefore) [he (Neriglissar) did] not capture him. In the month Addaru (XII), the king of Akkad returned t[o] his [land].

----

2. *Nabonidus Chronicle*

(Grayson, Chronicles pp. 104–111 no. 7; Glassner, Chronicles pp. 232–239 no. 26)[165]

i 1–8) [The *first* year (555): ...] ... [...] lifted his [...]. The king [... of] their land (whom/that) he had brought to Babylon. [...] were terrified, but he did not lift [...] their famil(ies), as many as there were [...]. The king mustered his troops and [*marched*] to (the city) Ḫumê. [...] ...

----

i 9–10) [The *second* year (554)]: It was cold in the land Hamath during the month Ṭebētu (X). [...] ...

----

i 11–22) [The *third* year (553): In the mon]th Abu (V), [*he* ...] Mount Ammanānu. [...] the fruit orchards, as many as there were, [...] in their midst, [*he brought (them)*] into Babylon. [*The king* became sic]k, but recovered. In the month Kislīmu (IX), the king [*mustered*] his troops [*and* ...] ... Moreover, [he ...] to Nabû-*tattan-uṣur* [...] ... of the land Amurru to [...] they set up [(their) camp *against* E]dom. [...] and numerous troops [... the ci]ty gate of the city Šinṭini [...] he killed him. [...] ... [... tr]oops

Lacuna[166]

ii 1–4) [he (Astyages) mu]stered [his troops] and, for conq[uest], marched against Cyrus (II), king of (the land) Anšan, and (then) [...]. (As for) Astyages (Ištumegu), his troops rebelled against him and he was captured. Th[ey *handed (him) over*] to Cyrus (II). Cyrus (II) <marched> to Ecbatana, his (Astyages') royal city, <and> took (back) to the land Anšan the silver, gold, possessions, property, [...] that he had carried off (from) Ecbatana. [He ...] the possessions (and) property of the troop[s of ...].

----

ii 5–8) The seventh year (549): The king (stayed) in the city Tēmā. The heir designate, his magnates, (and) his troops (stayed) in Akkad. [The king] did not come to Babylon [in the month Nisannu (I)]. The god Nabû did not come to Babylon. The god Bēl (Marduk) did not come out. The [*akītu*]-festi[val did not take place]. Offering(s) in Esagil and Ezida were given to the gods of Babylon and Borsippa *a*[*s in normal times*]. The *šešgallu*-priest performed a strewn offering and oversaw the temple.

----

[165] See also Waerzeggers, JNES 71 (2012) pp. 285–298; Waerzeggers, Political Memory pp. 95–124; and Zawadzki, Who Was King pp. 142–154.

[166] The lacuna between BM 35382 i 22 and ii 1 would have contained the rest of the description of the events of Nabonidus' third regnal year (553), accounts of that king's fourth (552) and fifth (551) regnal years, and the beginning of the account of the events of the sixth (550) regnal year.

ii 9) The eighth year (548): (contents left blank)

----

ii 10–12) The ninth year (547): Nabonidus, the king, (stayed) <in> the city Tēmā. The heir designate, his magnates, (and) his troops (stayed) in Akkad. The king did not come to Babylon in the month Nisannu (I). The god Nabû did not come to Babylon. The god Bēl (Marduk) did not come out. The *akītu*-festival did not take place. Offering(s) in Esagil and Ezida were given to the gods of <Babylon> and Borsippa *as in normal times.*

ii 13–15a) On the fifth day of the month Nisannu (I), the mother of the king died in (the city) Dūr-karašu, which (is on) the bank of the Euphrates River, upstream of Sippar. The heir designate and his troops *were mourning* for three days (and) an (official) mourning ceremony took place. In the month Simānu (III), an (official) mourning ceremony for the mother of the king took place in Akkad.

ii 15b–18) In the month Nisannu (I), Cyrus (II), king of the land Parsu(a), mustered his troops [a]nd crossed the Tigris River downstream of Arbela. In the month Ayyāru (II), [*he march*]*ed* to Ly[dia]. He killed its king, took its possessions, (and) stationed a garrison of his own [*(inside) it*]. Afterwards, the king (Cyrus) and his garrison (text: "his garrison and the king") were inside.

----

ii 19–21a) The tenth year (546): The king (stayed) in the city Tēmā. The heir designate, his magnates, (and) his troops (stayed) in Akkad. The king [did not come to Babylon] in [the month Nisannu (I)]. The god Nabû did not come to Babylon. The god Bēl (Marduk) did not come out. The *akītu*-festival did not take place. Offering(s) in E[sagil and Ezida were gi]ven to the gods of Babylon and Borsippa *as in normal times.*

ii 21b–22) On the twenty-first day of the month Simānu (III), [...] of Elammya in Akkad ... [...] the provincial governor [...] in Uru[k ...].

----

ii 23–25) The eleventh year (545): The king was (still) in the city Tēmā. The heir designate, his magnates, (and) his troops (stayed) in Akka[d. The king did not come to Babylon in the month Nisannu (I). The god Nabû] did not come [to Babylon]. The god Bēl (Marduk) did not come out. The *akītu*-festival did not take place. Offe[ring(s) in Esagil and Ezida] were given [to the gods of Bab]ylon and Borsippa [*as in normal tim*]*es.*

Lacuna[167]

iii 1′–4′) [...] *killed* [...]. [...] the [...] River [... *In the month*] *Addaru* (XII), [...] the goddess Ištar of Uruk [... *the troop*]s of the land *Pa*[*rsu(a)* ... *troo*]*ps* [...].

----

iii 5′–8′a) [The *seventeenth* year (539): The god N]abû [came] from Borsippa for the procession of [the god Bēl (Marduk). The god Bēl (Marduk) came out. In the month] Ṭebētu (X), the king entered Eturkalamma. In the *temple* [...] ... he made a libation of wine ... [... The god B]ēl (Marduk) came out. They performed the *akītu*-festival *as in normal times.*

iii 8′b–12′a) In the month [..., *the god Lugal-Marda and* the god]s of Marad, the god Zababa and the gods of Kish, the goddess Mullissu [and the gods of] Ḫursagkalamma entered Babylon. Until the end of the month Ulūlu (VI), the gods of Akkad [...], which are upstream and downstream of *Isin*, were entering Babylon. The gods of Borsippa, Cutha, and Sippar did not enter (Babylon).

iii 12′b–16′a) In the month Tašrītu (VII), when Cyrus (II) did battle at (the city) Opis, (which is) on the [*bank of*] the Tigris River against the troops of Akkad, the people of Akkad retreated. He pillaged (the city Opis and) killed (its) people. On the fourteenth day, Sippar was captured without a fight. Nabonidus fled. On the sixteenth day, Ugbaru, the governor of the land Gutium, and the troops of Cyrus (II) entered Babylon without a fight.

iii 16′b–18′a) Afterwards, after Nabonidus had retreated, he was captured in Babylon. Until the end of the month, the shield-(bearers) of the land Gutium surrounded the gates of Esagil. There was no interruption of any kind in Esagil or (in) the (other) temples. Moreover, no appointed (festival) time was missed.

iii 18′b–22′a) On the third day of the month Araḫsamna (VIII), Cyrus (II) entered Babylon. *(Drinking) straws* were filled up before him. There was peace in the city (and) Cyrus (II) decreed peace for Babylon, all of

[167] The lacuna between BM 35382 ii 25 and iii 1′ might have contained the rest of the description of the events of Nabonidus' eleventh regnal year (545), reports of his twelfth (544) to fifteenth (541) regnal years, and the beginning of the account of the events of the sixteenth (540) regnal year.

it. Gubaru (Ugbaru?), his governor, appointed (provincial) governors in Babylon.[168] From the month Kislīmu (IX) to the month Addaru (XII), the gods of Akkad which Nabonidus had brought down to Babylon returned to their cult centers. On the night of the eleventh day of the month Araḫsamna (VIII), Ugbaru died.

iii 22´b– 24´a) In the mon[th ...], the king's wife died.[169] From the twenty-seventh <day> of the month of Addaru (XII) to the third day of the month Nisannu (I), [there were] (official) mourning ceremon(ies) in Akkad. All of [the peo]ple bared their heads.

iii 24´b– 28´) On the fourth day, when Cambyses (II), the son of C[yrus (II)], went to Egidrikalamasumu, (and) when he arrived (lit. "came"), the person (in charge of) the *Egidri* of the god Nabû, who [...] the scepter [..., *did not let him (Cambyses) take*] the hand of the god Nabû because of (his) Elamite attire. [... sp]ears and quivers from [...] the *heir designate* [...] to the *wo*[*rk* ...] the god Nabû to Esagil ... before the god Bēl (Marduk) and the son-of-B[ēl (Nabû) ...]

Lacuna[170]

Propaganda Texts

As mentioned in the section Texts Excluded in the present volume, four 'propaganda' texts provide information about the reigns of the Neo-Babylonian kings whose inscriptions are edited in this volume. For the convenience of the user of this volume, it has been thought useful to present a translation of the Royal Chronicle. The translation has been adapted from Glassner, Chronicles.

1. *Royal Chronicle*

(Glassner, Chronicles pp. 312–317 no. 53; Schaudig, Inschriften Nabonids pp. 590–595 P4)

Col. i completely broken away

Lacuna

ii 1´–6´) [... an *ē*]*ntu*-priestess [... heaven] and earth [...] that he had requested of me [... "...] among the women of my land?" "Yes."

ii 7´–9´) "[(Is she) a ..., who] will be born through a god?" ["*Yes/No*." "(Is she) a ..., who] will be born through a god?" "No." "[...] *older* [...]?" "Yes."

ii 10´–12´) [He] wrote down [...] and [...] the god Sîn, [..., an]swered him.

Lacuna

iii 1´–5´a) [...] his face turned pale. [...] the tablets of the Series *Enūma Anu Enlil*, the scribes brought a basket (of them) from Babylon into his presence for inspection, (but) he did not heed (what the tablets said and) he did not understand anything it (*Enūma Anu Enlil*) said.

iii 5´b–12´a) A foundation document [o]f Nebuchadnezzar (I), king of Babylon, son of Ninurta-nādin-šumi, on which an image of an *ēntu*-priestess, its cultic rites, its ways, [and] its [*kid*]*udû*-rites were recorded, [*was brought* (from Ur) t]o Babylon with the tablets (of *Enūma Anu Enlil*), without knowledge [of what the god Sîn, the lord of king(s)], had wanted to place in his hand(s). [...] ... He inspected the tablets (carefully) and became af[raid].

iii 12´b–16´a) He was attentive to [the] great [command of the god Sîn] and [...]. He dedicated [En-nigald]i-Nanna, (his) daughter, [his] o[wn] offspring, [to] the god Sîn, the lord of kings, whose co[mmand] cannot be altered, [as] an *ēntu*-priestess.

iii 16´b–23´a) In the month of Ulūlu (VI), [... of th]at (same) [year], (with regard to) Ebabbar, the temple of the god Šamaš that is inside Si[ppar (and) whose original] foundation [the kin]gs who came before him had sought out (but) could not find, the places [...] of his royal majesty as the primordial residence of his happiness, he revealed the foundation(s) of Narām-Sîn, the (grand)son of Sargon, to him (Nabonidus), the servant who reveres him, the one who is assiduous towards his place (of worship).

iii 23´b–28´) In that (same) year, in a favorable month, on an auspicious day, he firmly established the foundations of Ebabbar, the temple of the god Šamaš, (precisely) on the foundation(s) of Narām-Sîn, the (grand)son of Sargon, not (even) a fingerbreadth outside or inside (of them). He discovered an

---

[168] J.-J. Glassner (Chronicles p. 239) translates this passage as "He [Cyrus] installed Gubaru as governor of (all) governors in Babylon."

[169] This is presumably Cyrus', not Nabonidus', wife.

[170] The contents of BM 35382 iv 1´–9´ are not translated here because that passage records information about the reign of Cyrus II.

inscription and returned (it) to its place without altering (it), and (then) he deposited (it) with his (own) inscription.

iii 29′–iv 5) He discovered a statue of Sargon, the (grand)father of Narām-Sîn, inside those foundation(s). Half of its head was (broken) away and it had become (so) old (that) its features were unrecognizable. Out of respect for the gods (and) esteem for kingship, he employed craftsmen who know (how to do) the work and he had the head of the statue restored and had its features made perfect (again). He did not alter the place of that statue. He made it reside inside Ebabbar (and) firmly established *taklīmu*-offering(s) for it.

iv 6–13) For the god Šamaš, the great lord, his lord, he built that Ebabbar during joyous celebrations. He had 6,000 (beams of) strong cedar stretched out for its roof. He made that temple shine like daylight and raised its superstructure like a high mountain. At each gate, he securely fastened tall doors of cedar, threshold(s) of copper, bolts, and *nukuššû*-fittings, and (thereby) completed its construction.

iv 14–18) [...] the god Šamaš, the gr[eat] lord, [...], in the temple and ... [...]. On the [Nth day] of the month [...], after the offer[ing(s)], ... [...] *taklīmu*-offering (for) the cultic rite(s) of h[is] divinity [...] he made (him) reside in the residence of [his happiness].

iv 19–26) A mounted messenger from the land Ḫatti [...] (and) he reported [(his) r]eport [to me], saying: "[...] ... [..." The] great [gods ... hear[t's con]tent [... di]stant [...], a path through [...] mountain(s), [... a p]ath of death, he don[ned] (his) weapon(s) [... the p]eople of the land Ḫatti.

iv 27–41) In the month Ayyāru (II) of the third year (553), [... Bab]ylon, he took command of his troops. [He] mustered [...] and, on the thirteenth day, they arrived at [...]. He cut off the [... (and)] heads the people living in the city Ammanānu and [...] in *heaps*. He hung [(their) king on a p]ole and divided the city [...] of the mountain(s). [...], which is inside the mountains, fruit orchards, [*all of them*, ...] their *shade* [... he had ...] to their full extent [burned with] fir[e. ...] ..., whose slope(s) are far away, [...] he turned into [ruins] until far-off days. [...] ... (mountain) passes [...] day(s), he lef[t ...] ... [...]

Lacuna

v 1–4) (No translation possible)

v 5–12) He listened to [the ... of] his [...] and his [...] struck him. [...], he spoke with him. He laid a hand on [...] and [... his cultic r]ites [... w]ith him [...].

v 13–24) [...] battle array [...] ... [h]is troops [...] he bore weapon(s) and to [..., ... lea]gues distant, difficult roads, [...], difficult [terr]ain [where access was bloc]ked (and) approach was not possible, [...] at the mention of his name [...] grass of the steppe [...] the king of Dadanu took refuge [in the] distant [...]s. He wiped clean [...] a[nd ... mi]nd ... [...] ... [...]

Lacuna

Col. vi completely broken away

1

Two bricks discovered during Koldewey's excavations at Babylon (western pillar of the Euphrates bridge) are stamped with a short, three-line inscription of Amēl-Marduk; the script is archaizing Neo-Babylonian. One of the king's titles in this text suggests that this son of Nebuchadnezzar II may have renovated Marduk's temple Esagil ("House whose Top Is High") at Babylon and Nabû's temple Ezida ("True House") at Borsippa. Because Nabopolassar, Nebuchadnezzar II, and Nabonidus all call themselves *zānin Esagil u Ezida* ("the one who provides for Esagil and Ezida"), that epithet might have simply been an honorary title in the case of Amēl-Marduk, rather than one that actually referred to him undertaking work on those two temples. This inscription is cited in previous literature as "Ewil-Merodach Brick A I, 1" or "[Amēl-Marduk] Brick Inscription (B1)."

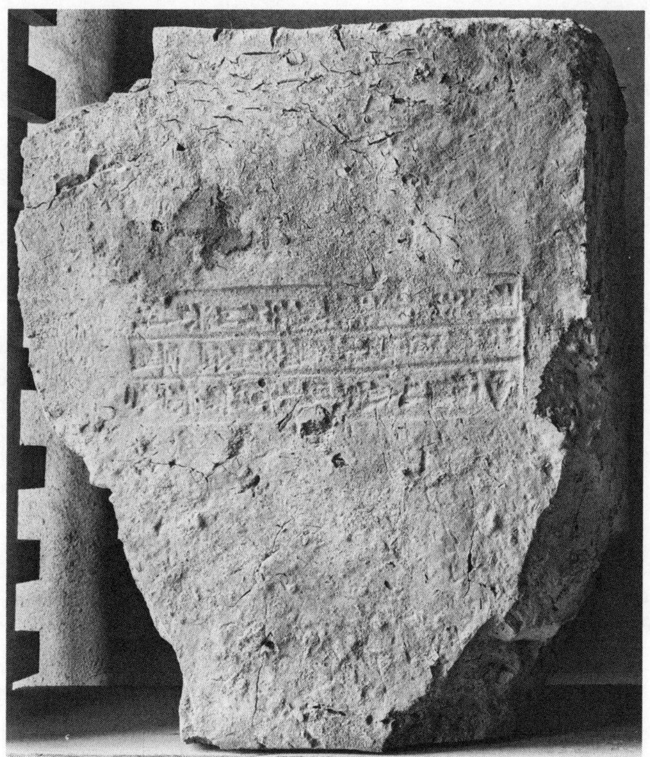

Figure 2. EŞ 9176 (BE 42296; Amēl-Marduk no. 1 ex. 2), a brick with a three-line proprietary inscription from Babylon. © Staatliche Museen zu Berlin - Vorderasiatisches Museum. Photo: Robert Koldewey, 1911.

CATALOGUE

Ex.	Museum Number	Excavation Number	Photograph Number	Provenance	Lines Preserved	cpn
1	—	BE 28999	Bab ph 1370	Babylon	1–3	p
2	EŞ 9176	BE 42296	Bab ph 2302	Babylon, near the western pillar of the Euphrates bridge	1–3	p

COMMENTARY

The present whereabouts of ex. 1 (BE 28999) are unknown, but ex. 2 (BE 42296) is in the Eşki Şark Eserleri Müzesi (Istanbul). The master text and lineation follow ex. 1. No score of this short Amēl-Marduk text is given on Oracc since scores are not provided for texts on bricks (following the model of the RIM and RINAP series).

BIBLIOGRAPHY

1911 Wetzel, MDOG 45 p. 21 (study)
1925 Koldewey, WEB[4] p. 78, with fig. 50 (photo, study)
1930 Wetzel, Stadtmauern p. 56 (study)
1973 Berger, NbK p. 330 Backstein A I, 1 (study)
1990 Koldewey, WEB[5] p. 89, with fig. 50 (photo, study)
2008 Da Riva, GMTR 4 pp. 125 and 130 (study)
2013 Da Riva, SANER 3 p. 106 no. 3.1 (B1) (edition)

TEXT

1) LÚ-^{d}AMAR.UTU LUGAL KÁ.DINGIR.RA.KI
2) GIBIL-*iš é-sag-íl ù é-zi-da*
3) DUMU ^{d}AG-*ku-dúr-ri*-ÙRU LUGAL TIN.TIR.KI

1–3) Amēl-Marduk, king of Babylon, the one who renovates Esagil and Ezida, son of Nebuchadnezzar (II), king of Babylon.

2

Two paving stones found at Babylon bear a proprietary inscription of Amēl-Marduk in an archaizing Neo-Babylonian script. This text is sometimes referred to as "Ewil-Merodach Paving Stone I" or "[Amēl-Marduk] Paving Stone (PS1)" in earlier literature.

CATALOGUE

Ex.	Museum Number	Excavation Number	Photograph Number	Provenance	Lines Preserved	cpn
1	—	BE 3162	Bab ph 1167, 2410	Babylon, Kasr, processional street, at point 3	1–2	p
2	—	BE 20461	Bab ph 1177	Babylon, Kasr 16t, Ištar Gate	1–2	p

COMMENTARY

The edition of the inscription presented here is based on the published excavation photograph in Koldewey, WEB[5] (p. 160 fig. 99) since the original objects were not available, principally as the present whereabouts of the paving stones are unknown. Note that R. Koldewey (Ischtar-Tor p. 41) wrongly states that the excavation number of ex. 2 is BE 19274, which is joined to BE 20451 and which bears an inscription of an Assyrian king (probably Sennacherib). The correct number is BE 20461, which is photographed on Bab ph 1177.

Figure 3. BE 3162 (Amēl-Marduk no. 2 ex. 1), a paving stone with a two-line proprietary inscription found at Babylon. © Staatliche Museen zu Berlin – Vorderasiatisches Museum. Photo: Robert Koldewey, 1907.

BIBLIOGRAPHY

1918 Koldewey, Ischtar-Tor p. 41 (ex. 2, study, provenance)
1925 Koldewey, WEB^{4} pp. 156–158, with fig. 99 (ex. 1, photo)
1973 Berger, NbK pp. 25 and 329 Pflasterstein I (ex. 1, study)
1990 Koldewey, WEB^{5} pp. 160–161, with fig. 99 (ex. 1, photo)
2008 Da Riva, GMTR 4 pp. 125 and 131 (ex. 1, study)
2013 Da Riva, SANER 3 pp. 110–111 no. 3.3 (PS1) (ex. 1, edition)

TEXT

1) É.GAL LÚ-^{d}AMAR.UTU LUGAL TIN.⸢TIR⸣.[KI]
2) IBILA ^{d}AG-*ku-dúr-ri*-ÙRU LUGAL TIN.⸢TIR⸣.[KI]

1–2) Palace of Amēl-Marduk, king of Bab[ylon], heir of Nebuchadnezzar (II), king of Bab[ylon].

3

Two fragments of an alabaster vase now in the Eşki Şark Eserleri Müzesi of the Arkeoloji Müzeleri (Istanbul) bear a proprietary inscription of Nebuchadnezzar II's son and immediate successor Amēl-Marduk. The text records that the vase had a capacity of one *qa* (ca. one liter). This inscription, which is written in contemporary Neo-Babylonian script, is referred to in previous studies and editions as "Ewil-Merodach Vase I, 1" or "[Amēl-Marduk] Babylon Vase (V1)."

CATALOGUE

Museum Number	Excavation Number	Provenance	cpn
EŞ —	—	Babylon	n

COMMENTARY

Because the original could not be found in the Eşki Şark Eserleri Müzesi (Istanbul), as the collection number of the piece has never been published, the edition of the Babylon Vase in this volume is based on E. Nassouhi's copy (AfO 3 p. 66).

BIBLIOGRAPHY

1926 Nassouhi, AfO 3 p. 66 (copy)
1973 Berger, NbK p. 325 Gefäß I, 1 (study)
2008 Da Riva, GMTR 4 pp. 125 and 131 (study)
2013 Da Riva, SANER 3 p. 107 no. 3.2.1 (V1) (edition)

TEXT

1) 1 *qa*
2) É.GAL LÚ-[d]⌜AMAR.UTU⌝

1) One *qa*.
2) Palace of Amēl-Marduk.

4

A fragment of a vase inscribed with a short text of Amēl-Marduk stating that the vessel once belonged to him was discovered in the ruins of the Elamite capital Susa; the script is contemporary Neo-Babylonian. The inscription records that the stone object had a capacity of one seah and six and a half *akalu*, which is about 6.64 liters. This text is cited in previous literature as "Ewil-Merodach Vase I, 2" or "[Amēl-Marduk] Susa Vase 1 (V2)."

CATALOGUE

Source	Excavation Number	Provenance	cpn
Scheil, MDP 5 p. xxiii	—	Susa	n

COMMENTARY

The present whereabouts of Susa Vase 1 is unknown and, therefore, the edition of it in this volume is based on the partial copy and transliteration given by V. Scheil in MDP 5 (p. xxiii).

BIBLIOGRAPHY

1904 Scheil, MDP 5 p. xxiii (line 1, copy; line 2, transliteration)
1973 Berger, NbK p. 326 Gefäß I, 2 (study)
2008 Da Riva, GMTR 4 pp. 125 and 131 (study)
2013 Da Riva, SANER 3 pp. 107–108 no. 3.2.2 (V2) (edition)

TEXT

1)	1 BÁN 6 1/2 NINDA *ša*	1–2) One seah, six and a half *akalu* belonging to the palace of Amēl-Marduk, the king.
2)	É.GAL LÚ-^{d}AMAR.UTU LUGAL	

5

A second vase fragment from Susa preserves part of a proprietary inscription of the Babylonian king Amēl-Marduk. It records that the stone vessel's capacity was at least two *qa* (that is, about two liters). This text, which is written in contemporary Neo-Babylonian script, is referred to as "Ewil-Merodach Vase I, 3" or "[Amēl-Marduk] Susa Vase 2 (V3)" in earlier literature.

CATALOGUE

Source	Excavation Number	Provenance	cpn
Scheil, MDP 10 p. 96	—	Susa	n

COMMENTARY

The present whereabouts of Susa Vase 2 is unknown. Like the previous text, the edition of this Amēl-Marduk inscription is based on V. Scheil's transliteration (MDP 10 p. 96).

BIBLIOGRAPHY

1908 Scheil, MDP 10 p. 96 (edition)
1973 Berger, NbK p. 327 Gefäß I, 3 (study)
2008 Da Riva, GMTR 4 pp. 125 and 131 (study)
2013 Da Riva, SANER 3 pp. 108–109 no. 3.2.3 (V3) (edition)

TEXT

1)	2 *qa* [(...)]	1) Two *qa*, [(...)].
2)	É.GAL LÚ-^{d}AMAR.UTU ⸢LUGAL⸣ [TIN.TIR.KI]	2–3) Palace of Amēl-Marduk, ki[ng of Babylon], son of Nebuchadnezzar (II), king of [Babylon].
3)	DUMU ^{d}MUATI-NÍG.DU-ÙRU LUGAL [TIN.TIR.KI]	

6

A damaged vase with a short, proprietary inscription of Nebuchadnezzar II's son and successor was discovered during the French excavations at Susa. The text, which is written in contemporary Neo-Babylonian script, states that the alabaster vessel had a capacity of three and one-third *akalu*, which is approximately one-third of a liter. The inscription is cited in previous literature as "Ewil-Merodach Vase I, 4" or "[Amēl-Marduk] Susa Vase 3 (V4)." The edition given here is based on the published photograph.

CATALOGUE

Museum Number	Excavation Number	Provenance	cpn
Sb 12042	—	Susa	p

BIBLIOGRAPHY

1912 Thureau-Dangin, RA 9 pp. 24–25 (photo, edition)
1913 Scheil, MDP 14 p. 60 (copy, edition)
1973 Berger, NbK p. 328 Gefäß I, 4 (study)
2008 Da Riva, GMTR 4 pp. 125 and 131 (study)
2013 Da Riva, SANER 3 pp. 109–110 no. 3.2.4 (V4) (edition)

TEXT

1) 3 1/3 NINDA
2) É.GAL LÚ-^{d}AMAR.UTU LUGAL TIN.TIR.KI
3) DUMU ^{d}MUATI-⸢NÍG.DU-ÙRU⸣ LUGAL TIN.TIR.KI

1) Three and one-third *akalu*.
2–3) Palace of Amēl-Marduk, king of Babylon, son of Nebuchadnezzar (II), king of Babylon.

1

Two large, two-column clay cylinders are inscribed with a text of Neriglissar recording that he made restorations to part of Marduk's temple at Babylon, Esagil ("House whose Top Is High"); the script of ex. 1 is archaizing Neo-Babylonian, while that of ex. 2 is contemporary Neo-Babylonian. The king states that he rebuilt one of the temple's enclosure walls since it had fallen into disrepair and was near collapsing; the work took place near to where the *ramku-* and *kiništu*-priests of Esagil lived. Neriglissar claims to have laid the new foundations of the wall in the exact same spot as the previous foundations. The inscription is referred to as "Neriglissar Cylinder II, 1," "[Neriglissar] Cylinder C21," or "the Esagil Inscription" in previous studies and editions.

Figure 4. BM 113233 (Neriglissar no. 1 ex. 1), a two-column clay cylinder reporting on this king's restorations to Esagil. © Trustees of the British Museum.

CATALOGUE

Ex.	Museum Number	Registration Number	Provenance	Lines Preserved	cpn
1	BM 113233	1915-12-11,1	Probably Babylon	i 1–ii 39	c
2	BM 32550	76-11-17,2293	As ex. 1	i 1–17, 30–33	c

COMMENTARY

Ex. 1 (BM 113233) was owned by Emily Ripley when it was studied and copied by E.A.W. Budge in 1888. In 1915, the cylinder was donated to the British Museum by Dr. Laurie A. Lawrence. The master text and lineation are based on ex. 1, the only near-complete witness of this inscription. A score is presented on Oracc and the minor (orthographic) variants are given in the critical apparatus at the back of the book.

BIBLIOGRAPHY

1888 Budge, PSBA 10 p. 146 and pls. 1–3 (ex. 1, copy, study)
1889 Teloni, Giorn. della Società As. Ital. 3 pp. 80–93 (ex. 1, edition)
1890 Abel and Winckler, KGV p. 39 (ex. 1 i 1–14, copy)
1890 Bezold in Schrader, KB 3/2 pp. 76–79 (ex. 1, edition)
1912 Langdon, NBK pp. 45–46 and 214–219 no. 2 (ex. 1, edition)
1921 Gadd, CT 36 pls. 17–20 (ex. 1, copy)
1922 BM Guide³ p. 141 no. 63 (study)
1925 Bezold and Delitzsch in Koldewey, WEB⁴ pp. 187–188 (ex. 1 ii 9–28, translation)
1953 von Soden, SAHG pp. 287–288 no. 34 (ex. 1 ii 29–39, translation)
1957 Borger, AfO 18 p. 88 (ex. 1 ii 9, study)
1973 Berger, NbK p. 336 Zyl. II, 1 (ex. 1, study)
2008 Da Riva, GMTR 4 pp. 103–104, 112, 125 and 131 (exs. 1–2, study)
2013 Da Riva, SANER 3 pp. 14–18, 114–120 no. 4.2.1 (C21) and CD-ROM figs. 18–19 (exs. 1–2, photo, edition)

TEXT

Col. i

1) ^{d}NÈ.ERI$_{11}$.GAL-LUGAL-*ú-ṣu-ur* LUGAL TIN.TIR.KI
2) *ru-ba-a-am na-a-da mi-gi-ir* ^{d}AMAR.UTU
3) *áš-ru ka-an-šu pa-li-iḫ* EN EN.EN
4) *e-em-qá-am mu-ut-né-en-nu-ú*
5) *mu-uš-te-e'-ú aš-ra-a-tì* ^{d}AG EN-*šu*
6) ÉNSI *za-ni-nu-um*
7) *ba-bi-il i-gi-se-e ra-bu-ù-tim*
8) *a-na é-sag-íl ù é-zi-da*
9) *mu-ṭa-aḫ-ḫi-id sa-at-tu-uk-ku*
10) *mu-uš-te-ši-ru šu-lu-úḫ-ḫi-šu-un*
11) DUMU ^{md}EN-*šu-um-iš-ku-un* NUN *e-em-qá*
12) *eṭ-lum gi-it-ma-lum na-ṣi-ir*
13) *ma-aṣ-ṣa-ar-tì é-sag-íl ù* TIN.TIR.KI
14) *ša ki-ma* BÀD *dan-nu pa-ni ma-a-tim i-di-lu a-na-ku*

i 1–14) Neriglissar, king of Babylon, pious prince, the favorite of the god Marduk, the humble (and) submissive one who reveres the lord of lords, the wise (and) pious one, the one who constantly seeks out the shrines of the god Nabû — his lord — the ruler who provides, the one who brings large gifts to Esagil and Ezida, the one who copiously supplies *sattukku*-offerings (and) ensures that their purification rites are carried out correctly, son of Bēl-šum-iškun, wise prince, the perfect warrior, the one who ensures the protection of Esagil and Babylon, the one who blocks the approach to the country like a strong wall, am I.

15) *ì-nu-um* ^{d}AMAR.UTU ^{d}EN.LÍL DINGIR.DINGIR
16) *ru-bu-ú* (erasure) *mu-uš-ta-li*
17) ABGAL *ša li-ib-bi* ^{d}*i-gi*$_{4}$*-gi*$_{4}$ *ka-la-mu mu-du-ú*
18) *i-na ni-ši-ša ra-ap-ša-a-tim iš-ta-an-ni-ma*
19) *iš-tu mé-eṣ-ḫe-ru-ti-ia i-ša-ri-iš ṣab-ta-an-ni*
20) *šu-um ṭa-a-bi lu-ú im-ba-an-ni*
21) *áš-ri šu-ul-mi ù ba-la-ṭa lu-ú ir-te-ed-dan-ni*
22) *a-na i-ša-ru-ti-ia ša qá-qá-da-a a-pá-lu-šu*

i 15–25) When the god Marduk, the Enlil of the gods, the prince who deliberates, the sage who knows the hearts of all of the Igīgū gods, sought me out among his widespread people and properly provided for me since my youth, he gave me an appropriate name (and) indeed constantly guided me in places of well-being and health. For my righteousness, with which I always answer him, (and) for my submissiveness,

i 11 NUN *e-em-qá* "wise prince": To whom the title refers, Neriglissar or his father Bēl-šum-iškun, is ambiguous. R. Da Riva (SANER 3 pp. 14–15) describes the issue as follows: "Neriglissar mentions his father by name on several occasions. According to Schaudig (2001: 12–13), both Neriglissar, and later Nabonidus, allude to their respective progenitors in an ambiguous way in their inscriptions. In fact, the mention of Bēl-šum-iškun in the inscriptions of his son always has a double meaning, due to orthographical indistinctiveness in the texts, so we do not know whether the title after the name of Bēl-šum-iškun (in genitive) refers to him or to Neriglissar (nominative). ... The repetition of the title *rubû*, albeit with a different qualification, is not common in the corpus of the inscriptions, and the second *rubû* may in fact refer to Bēl-šum-iškun, not to Neriglissar, though both solutions are syntactically possible. ... the title *rubû* is used with the apparent intention of creating ambiguity. One would not object to a Puqūdu chieftain being called 'prince.'" Compare text no. 3 (Royal Palace Inscription) i 1 and 14, where both Neriglissar and Bēl-šum-iškun are given the title *šar Bābili*, "king of Babylon." See also the on-page note to text no. 3 (Royal Palace Inscription) i 14.

i 22 *a-na i-ša-ru-ti-ia ša qá-qá-da-a a-pá-lu-šu* "For my righteousness, with which I always answer him": The interpretation of this line follows Da Riva, SANER 3 p. 119. Compare the CAD (I/J p. 227 sub *išarūtu* 1), which understands this line as *a-na i-ša-ru-ti-ia ša qá-qá-da-a a-ba-lu-šu* "on account of my righteousness, with which I constantly prayed to him."

23) *a-na ka-an-šu-ti-ia ša ka-a-a-nim*
24) *pu-lu-úḫ-tì i-lu-ti-šu aš-te-e'-ú*
25) *ša e-li-šu ṭa-a-bi e-pé-šu* u_4*-mi-ša-am a-ta-mu-ú*
26) *ip-pa-al-sa-an-ni-ma i-na ma-a-tim*
27) *šu-um da-am-qá a-na šar-ru-tim iz-ku-úr*
28) *a-na re-é-ú-tì ni-ši-ša a-na da-rí e-pé-šu*
29) GIŠ.NÍG.GIDRU *i-ša-ár-ti mu-ra-ap-pí-ša-at ma-a-tú*
30) *a-na šar-ru-ti-ia lu-ú iš-ru-kam*
31) *ši-bi-ir-ri ki-i-nu mu-ša-al-li-im ni-ši*
32) *a-na be-lu-tú lu-ú i-qí-pí-im*
33) *uš-pa-ri mu-ka-an-ni-iš za-'i-i-ru*
34) *lu-ú ú-ša-at-mi-ḫa qá-tu-ú-a*
35) *a-ga-a ki-i-nu ú-ša-aš-ša-an-ni-ma*
36) *a-na šar-ru-ti-ia ša-ni-nu ù mu-gal-li-tú ul ú-ša-ab-ši*

through which I constantly strive after respect for his divinity, I plan daily to perform that which is pleasing to him.

i 26–36) He looked upon me and declared (my) gracious name to be king in the land. In order to shepherd his people for eternity, for my kingship, he indeed gave me a just scepter that widens the land; for (my) lordship, he indeed entrusted me with a legitimate rod that protects the people, let my hands grasp a staff that subdues enemies, made me wear a legitimate crown, and he did not bring about rivals or intimidators for my kingship.

37) *a-na-ar a-a-bi aš-gi-iš za-ma-nu*

Col. ii

1) *la ma-gi-ri ka-li-šu-nu a-lu-ut*
2) *mi-ša-ri i-na ma-a-tim aš-ta-ak-ka-an*
3) *ni-ši-ia ra-ap-ša-a-tim i-na šu-ul-mi*
4) (erasure) *ar-ta-né-e'-e*

i 37–ii 4) I killed foes, slaughtered enemies, (and) suppressed all of the unsubmissive. I constantly established justice in the land (and) peacefully shepherded my widespread people.

5) *i-na* u_4*-mi-šu a-na* ^{d}AMAR.UTU DINGIR *ba-an né-me-qí*
6) *ša i-na* ^{d}*i-gi*$_4$*-gi*$_4$ *šu-úr-ba-tim a-ma-at-su*
7) *i-na* ^{d}*a-nun-na-ki šu-tu-qá-at be-lu-ut-su*
8) *pa-al-ḫi-iš at-ta-'i-id-ma*

ii 5–8) At that time, I gave reverent attention to the god Marduk, the god who creates wisdom, whose words are supreme among the Igīgū gods, whose lordship is the most outstanding among the Anunnakū gods.

9) É.GAR_8 *si-ḫi-ir-tì é-sag-íl mé-eḫ-ra-at* IM.SI.SÁ
10) *ša ra-am-ku-tim ki-ni-iš-ti é-sag-íl*
11) *ra-mu-ù qé-re-eb-ša*
12) *ša šar ma-aḫ-ri uš-ši-ša id-*⸢*du-ma*⸣
13) *la ul-lu-ú re-e-ši-*⸢*ša*⸣
14) *i-na ta-am-le-e iš-ta-ap-pí-lu-*⸢*ma*⸣
15) *i-ni-šu i-ga-ru-ša*
16) *ri-ik-sa-ti-ša la du-un-nu-nim*
17) *si-ip-pu-šu la ku-un-nu-*⸢*um*⸣

ii 9–17) (As for the section of) the enclosure wall of Esagil that faces north, (an area) in which the *ramku*- (and) *kiništu*-priests of Esagil reside, whose foundations a former king had laid but whose superstructure he had not raised, which had become progressively lower due to terracing, and whose walls had become weak, its construction was no longer very stable, (and) its door-jamb(s) were no longer secure.

18) BUR.SAG.GÁ *a-na ul-lu-lu šu-lu-uḫ-ḫu a-na* ⸢*na*⸣-[*de-e*]
19) *ta-ak-li-mu be-lí ra-bu-ú* ^{d}⸢AMAR⸣.[UTU]
20) *a-na ub-bu-bi-im-ma šu-ul-lu-mu sa-at-*⸢*tuk*⸣-[*ku*]
21) *še-eṭ-ṭim ù ḫi-ṭi-tim a-na la šu-ub-ši-*[*i*]
22) *te-em-me-en-ša la-bí-ri a-ḫi-iṭ ab-re-e-*⸢*ma*⸣
23) *e-li te-em-me-en-ni-šu la-bí-ri ú-ki-in uš-ši-šu*
24) *ú-za-aq-qí-ir mé-la-a-šu ul-la-a ḫu-úr-sa-ni-iš*
25) *si-ip-pu-šu ú-ki-in-ma i-na* KÁ*-šu*
26) *e-er-ta-a* GIŠ.IG.MEŠ

ii 18–28) To keep *bursaggû*-offerings clean, to arr[ange] purification rites, to keep *taklīmu*-offerings pure for the great lord, the god M[arduk], to properly administer *sattuk*[*ku*]-offerings, (and) to prevent act(s) of omission and cultic mistake(s) from occurr[ing], I examined (and) inspected its original foundation and (then) I secured its (new) foundations on its original foundations. I raised its high parts, making (them) as lofty as a mountain. I secured its door-jamb(s) and set up doors in its gate(s). I surrounded (it) with a strong base using bitumen and baked bricks.

---

ii 10 *ra-am-ku-tim ki-ni-iš-ti é-sag-íl* "the *ramku*- (and) *kiništu*-priests of Esagil": This interpretation follows Da Riva, SANER 3 p. 119 and CAD K p. 386 sub *kiništu* a.

ii 22 *la-bí-ri* "original": Alternatively "old" or "ancient." It is difficult to know which nuance of *labīru* is meant in this inscription since, as far as we know, Neriglissar does not appear to have been obsessed with or interested in building a structure directly over its earliest foundations, unlike his second successor Nabonidus. Because Nabonidus was very interested in rebuilding temples precisely on their original, divinely-approved plans, *labīru* is translated in this volume as "original" when it follows the word *temmēnu* ("foundation").

ii 23 *te-em-me-en-ni-šu* and *uš-ši-šu* "its foundations": Following the published volumes of the RINAP Project, as well as the CAD (T pp. 338–339 sub *temmennu* 2), both Akkadian words *temmēnu* and *uššu* are translated as "foundations." For a recent discussion of the Akkadian words *temmēnu* and *uššu*, see Tudeau, Studies Postgate pp. 634–644.

27) ⸢*ki-sa*⸣-*a* ⸢*dan-nim*⸣ *i-na* ESIR.UD.A
28) *ù* SIG$_4$.AL.ÙR.RA *ú-ša-às-ḫi-ir*
29) ^{d}AMAR.UTU EN *šu-úr-bi-i e-te-el-lu ṣi-i-ri*
30) *ka-ab-ti ši-it-ra-ḫu nu-úr ì-lí ab-bé-e-šu*
31) *li-pí-it qá-ti-ia šu-qú-ru-um*
32) *ḫa-di-iš na-ap-li-is-ma*
33) *ba-la-ṭa$_4$* UD.MEŠ *ar-ku-tim še-bé-e li-it-tu-tú*
34) *ku-un-nu* GIŠ.GU.ZA *ù la-ba-ri pa-le-e*
35) *a-na še-ri-ik-tim šu-úr-kam*
36) *i-na qí-bi-ti-ka ki-it-tim ša la na-ka-ri*
37) ^{d}NÈ.ERI$_{11}$.GAL-LUGAL-*ú-ṣur lu-ú* LUGAL *za-ni-nu*
38) *mu-uš-te-e'-ú aš-ra-ti-ka*
39) *a-na du-úr da-ra a-na-ku*

ii 29–35) O Marduk, supreme lord, the pre-eminent one, the exalted one, the venerated one, the magnificent one, the light of the gods — his fathers — look with pleasure upon my precious handiwork and grant me a life of long days, the attainment of very old age, a firmly secured throne, and a long-lasting reign!

ii 36–39) Through your firm command, which cannot be altered, may I, Neriglissar, be the king who provides (and) the one who constantly seeks out your shrines for eternity.

2

An inscription of this Neo-Babylonian king describing the restoration of the Lībil-ḫegalla canal ("May It Bring Abundance"; Babylon's eastern canal) and the strengthening of its banks is preserved on a large, two-column clay cylinder whose surface is badly damaged; the text is written in contemporary Neo-Babylonian script. Neriglissar criticizes the canal's former builder(s) for not reinforcing the banks with bitumen and baked bricks, something which he had his workmen do. The inscription is cited in previous literature as "Neriglissar Cylinder II, 2," "[Neriglissar] Cylinder C22," or "the Lībil-ḫegalla Inscription."

CATALOGUE

Museum Number	Registration Number	Provenance	cpn
BM 90913 (BM 12041)	—	Probably Babylon	c

COMMENTARY

As already noted by R. Da Riva (SANER 3 p. 120), the surface of the cylinder is very badly damaged and the inscription written on it is extremely difficult to read. The present edition, although based on collation of the original in the British Museum (London), generally follows the one given in Da Riva, SANER 3, with only a few minor changes.

1 ii 29 *e-te-el-lu ṣi-i-ri* "the pre-eminent one, the exalted one": Or possibly "the exalted lord."

BIBLIOGRAPHY

1968 Hunger, Kolophone p. 3 (left edge, study)
1973 Berger, NbK pp. 48, 69, 100 and 337 Zyl. II, 2 (study)
1990 Koldewey, WEB[5] p. 65 (i 32–37, translation [Winckler]; study)
2008 Da Riva, GMTR 4 pp. 75, 79, 103–104, 112, 125 and 131 (study)
2013 Da Riva, SANER 3 pp. 14–15, 17–18, 120–124 no. 4.2.2 (C22) and CD-ROM fig. 20 (photo, edition)

TEXT

Col. i

1) ^{d}NÈ.ERI$_{11}$.GAL-LUGAL-*ú-ṣur* LUGAL [*ba*]-⸢*bi*⸣-*lam*.KI
2) ⸢*ša*⸣ ^{d}AMAR.UTU *be-lu ra-bí-ù* DINGIR <x> ⸢*ba-nu-šu*⸣
3) ⸢*i*⸣-*na ku-un li-ib-bi-šu* ⸢*ut-tu-šu-ma*⸣
4) *ni-šim ra-ap-ša-a-ti* ⸢*iš-ru-ku-šu-ma*⸣
5) *ṣa-al-ma-at qá-qá-dam a-na* ⸢*re*⸣-[*ʾe*]-⸢*e*⸣
6) *ú-ma-al-lu-ú qá-tu-uš-šu*
7) ⸢*ša*⸣ NÍG.GIDRU *i-ša-ar-ti uš-pa-ri ki-*⸢*i*⸣-*nim*
8) ⸢*ša*⸣ ^{d}AG *pa-qí-id ki-iš-*[*ša*]-*at*
9) ⸢*ša*⸣-*mé-e ù er-*⸢*ṣe*⸣-*ti*
10) ⸢*a*⸣-*na šu-um-mu-ḫu ba-*⸢*ʾu*⸣-*ú-la-a-ti*
11) [*ú*]-*ša-at-mi-iḫ qá-tu-uš-šu*
12) [*ša za*]-*ʾi-i-ri na-a-ri a-a-bi ka-ša-dam*
13) [^{d}]*èr-ra ša-ga-pú-ru* DINGIR.DINGIR
14) [*id*]-*di-nu-šu ka-ak-ku-šu*
15) [*ša*] ⸢DINGIR⸣ GAL.GAL *i-na pu-úḫ-ri-šu-nu*
16) ⸢*za-ni-nu-ut-su-nu*⸣ *e-pé-*⸢*ša iq*⸣-[*bu*]-*šu*
17) *a-na za-na-na$_{7}$ é-sag-íl* ⸢*é-zi-da*⸣
18) ⸢*ù é-mes-lam ma-ḫa-zi ṣi-i-ru$^{?}$-ti$^{?}$*⸣
19) x x x x ⸢*ša*⸣ DINGIR.DINGIR ⸢KÁ.DINGIR.KI⸣
20) [^{d}NÈ].ERI$_{11}$.GAL-LUGAL-*ú-ṣu-úr* LUGAL ⸢KÁ.DINGIR.RA⸣.[KI] <*a-na-ku*>

i 1–20) Neriglissar, king of [Ba]bylon, whom the god Marduk — the great lord (and) the god who created him — selected in his steadfast heart and (then) granted to him a widespread people and entrusted him with shep[her]ding the black-headed (people); in whose hands the god Nabû — the overseer of the tota[li]ty of heaven and earth — [le]t grasp a just scepter (and) legitimate rod in order to make (his) subjects prosper; [to wh]om [the god] Erra — the majestic one of the gods — [ga]ve his weapon(s) to kill [ene]mies (and) conquer foes; [wh]om the great gods in their assembly prono[unced] to act as the one who provides for them by taking care of Esagil, Ezida, and Emeslam — the *exalted* cult centers — (and) ... of the gods of Babylon; [Ne]riglissar, king of Babylon, <am I>.

21) [*ì-nu-ma*$^{?}$ ^{d}]⸢AMAR.UTU *be-lu*⸣ *ra-bí-ù* KI$^{?}$ A$^{?}$ x x x x x x
22) [*mé*]-⸢*e*⸣ *nu-úḫ-*⸢*šu gap*⸣-*šu-ti ina ṭe-em$_{4}$* ^{d}*ni-in-ši-*⸢*qa*⸣
23) [*ù*] ⸢*i-na*⸣ *né-me-qí* ⸢*ša*⸣ ^{d}*é-a iš-ru-ku*
24) ⸢*i-na le*⸣-*ʾu-ú-ti ša* ^{d}AMAR.UTU *i-qí-*⸢*šu*⸣
25) ⸢*i-na*⸣ [*di*]-⸢*in*⸣ *na-as-qu ša* ⸢^{d}UTU$^{?}$⸣ *ú-ša-lam-an-ni*
26) [...] ⸢KI⸣ *ma-aḫ-ri a-na* (blank) *bár-sipa*.KI
27) ⸢*é*⸣-*zi-da* ⸢É⸣ *gur-šu* x x x x x ḪU x x
28) ⸢IGI.SÁ⸣ *šu-um-mu-ḫu ni-qu i-qí-ip-*⸢*pu*⸣ E x x NI x E
29) *é-sag-íl ù é-zi-da a-za-an-na-an*
30) *e-eš-re-e-ti* DINGIR.DINGIR *uš-te-eš-še-er*
31) ⸢*ši-ṭir* MU⸣-*ia ab-na-a qé-er-bu-uš-šú-nu* [*aš-ku*]-⸢*un*⸣

i 21–31) [*When* the god] Marduk, the great lord, ... an abundance of [wat]er in full spate, by the will of the deity Ninšiqa [and] through the wisdom granted by the god Ea, with the competence provided by the god Marduk, (and) the choice [decisi]on of the god *Šamaš, he* makes me successful; former [...], to/for Borsippa, Ezida, the *bīt-guršu*, ... very plentiful gifts (and) offerings they entrust (to me) ... I provide for Esagil and Ezida, (and) keep the shrines of the gods in good order. I made inscriptions (written) in my name (and) [plac]ed (them) inside them (the shrines).

32) ⸢*ì-nu*⸣-*mi-šu li-bi-il-ḫé-gál-la* PA$_{5}$ ^{d}UTU.⸢È⸣ KÁ.DINGIR.RA.KI
33) [*ša*] ⸢LUGAL⸣ *ma-aḫ-ri ú-ša-aḫ-ru-ma*

i 32–37) At that time, Lībil-ḫegalla, the eastern canal of Babylon, [which] a former king had had dug, but had not constructed its bank with bitumen and

i 33 ⸢LUGAL⸣ *ma-aḫ-ri* "a former king": As already pointed out by R. Da Riva (SANER 3 p. 124), the unnamed previous builder of the Lībil-ḫegalla canal was none other than Nebuchadnezzar II.

34) ⸢*i*⸣*-na ku-up-ri ù a-gur-ri la ik-ṣú-ru su-uk-ki-šu*
35) [PA$_{5}$] *ú-ša-aḫ-ri-ma su-uk-ki-šu ak-ṣu-*⸢*úr*⸣*-*[*ma*]
36) [*nu*]*-*⸢*uḫ-šu*⸣ *mé-e i-na* ⸢*la na-pa*⸣*-*[*ar-ku-ti*]
37) [*ú*]*-na-ak-ki-mu i-na ma-a-ti*

baked bricks: I had [the canal] (re)dug and I (properly re)constructed its bank [and (thereby) *I* a]massed [an abun]dance of cease[less] water in the land.

Col. ii

1) *ia-ti e-em-qá mu-ut-né-en-nu*
2) LUGAL *pa-*⸢*li-ḫu*⸣ DINGIR.DINGIR *mu-du-u'*
3) ⸢*li-bi-il-ḫé-gál-lu*⸣ *ú-ša-aḫ-ri-*⸢*ma*⸣
4) *mé-e ḫé-gal-*⸢*la*⸣ *ina ma-a-*⸢*ti*⸣ *e-re-bi-*[*ma*?]
5) *ab-na-a* ⸢*su*⸣*-*[*uk*]*-*⸢*ki-ša*⸣
6) *mé-e nu-*⸢*uḫ*⸣*-ši* ⸢*ša la*⸣ *na-pa-ar-ku-ti*
7) *ú-ki-in* ⸢*i-na*⸣ *qé-re-eb-šu*

ii 1–7) (As for) me, the wise (and) pious one, the king who knows how to revere the gods, I had Lībil-ḫegalla (re)dug so that a plentitude of water can enter the land [*and*] I (re)constructed its b[a]nk. I firmly established inside it an abundance of ceaseless water.

8) I NI? IR? TI? *x x a-ši-ib* KÁ.DINGIR.RA.KI
9) ⸢*ša*⸣ *qer-bi-šú* ⸢*aq-qá*⸣*-a mé-e nu-*⸢*uḫ-šu*⸣
10) *i-na* ⸢*li*⸣*-ib-bi-ši-na da-mi-iq-ti x* [*x* (*x*)]
11) IG TA NA *x* [(*x*)] A IG TA NA RA AB BI IS SI ⸢MA?⸣
12) E? *x* ^{d}NÈ.ERI$_{11}$.GAL-LUGAL-*ú-ṣu-úr* ⸢LUGAL⸣ *a-*⸢*kà*⸣*-*[*dè*].⸢KI⸣
13) ^{d}A-⸢É⸣ *da*?*-x-a-*⸢*šal*?⸣ *x x x* ⸢*ki*⸣*-i-num*
14) ⸢*u*$_{4}$?*-mu*?⸣ *ul-li-i li-ib-*⸢*bu*⸣*-*[*uš-šu*] *x x*
15) ⸢Ú MI? IS? DU? *x* KA? AP?⸣ *x x x x*
16) *mé-e nu-uḫ-šu* ⸢*da-rí-ú-tim*⸣
17) *ina* KI IN NA AN NA A ⸢TI⸣

ii 8–17) ... reside in Babylon, in which I poured out an abundance of water, ... goodness in their hearts ... Neriglissar, king of Aga[de], ... the god Mār-bīti ... legitimate ..., in an earlier time, [in *his*] heart ... an abundance of everlasting water, in ...

18) *i-na qí-bi-ti* ^{d}AMAR.UTU LUGAL DINGIR.DINGIR DINGIR *ba-nu-*[*ú-a*]
19) *ù* ^{d}*èr-ra qar-ra-ad* ⸢*qar*⸣*-*[*ra-de* (*x x*)]
20) [(*x*)] NA *x x* NA BI É *x* [*x x*]
21) *še-ri-šu u*$_{4}$*-um* [...]
22) LI? NA? DU *an-dul-la* BI? NA A *x* [*x* (*x*)]
23) *li-ku-*⸢*un-ma*⸣ *dam-*⸢*qá*⸣*-*[*a*]*-ti maḫ-*⸢*ri*⸣*-*[*ka*] IGI *x x x x*
24) *x x* RA? TA? PA? *x x x* LI *x x x x x*
25) LI ' *x* ⸢*re-'u-ú-ti*⸣
26) *li-na-ar a-a-bi-*⸢*šu*⸣
27) *li-na-am-ri ta-mar-ti-šu*
28) *ki-ma* ^{d}30 *a-na* ⸢*ni-ip-ḫi*⸣
29) *ki-ma* ^{d}UTU *a-na nu-*[*wu*]*-*⸢*ri*⸣*-*[*im*]
30) *ṣa-al-ma-at qá-qá-dam li-iḫ-*[*du-ù*]
31) SAG? KI? ^{d}AG? *x x* [*x*] E? *x* AN *x* [*x*]
32) A NA? *x x x* [*x x*] ŠÁ A NI ŠI NA
33) LUGAL.⸢LUGAL⸣ [*ki*]*-*⸢*ib*⸣*-ra-a-ti ša* [*ka-al*] ⸢*te*⸣*-né-še-e-ti*
34) *a-ši-ib* ⸢KAR RI⸣ *x* [*x x*] TI? *x dan-nu-ti*
35) *a-na x x x* MI? *x x x x*
36) *li-iš-ša-kin i-na pi-i-*⸢*ka*⸣
37) *a-na* ⸢UD.MEŠ⸣ *da-ra-ti*
38) KI *x x x* ŠA IB NU LI IZ MA RU

ii 18–38) By the command of the god Marduk, the king of the gods, the god who creat[ed me], and the god Erra, the warrior of war[riors, (...)] ... his morning (meal), the day of [...] ... [...] may [...] be firmly in place and ... good thi[ng]s before [you]. ... shepherdship; may he kill his enemies; may his appearance shine; may the black-headed (people) be ha[ppy (about it)] like the moon when rising (and) the sun while s[hi]nin[g]; ... *the god Nabû* ... the kin[gs of the re]gions of [the entire] inhabited world, who sit on ... strong ... for ... may (it/they) be placed in your mouth. For eternity ...

Left edge

1) IGI.TAB

Left edge 1) Collated.

---

ii 11 IG TA NA *x* [(*x*)] A IG TA NA RA AB "...": M. Worthington (personal communication) tentatively proposes reading the signs as *iq-ta-na-ab-*[*ba*]*-a ik-ta-na-ra-ab* "they were constantly spea[kin]g (and) blessing." P.-A. Beaulieu (personal communication) tentatively suggests reading the second half of the line as *ik-ta-na-ra-ab-bi is-si-*⸢*ma*?⸣ "they were constantly spea[kin]g (and) he shouted *and*."

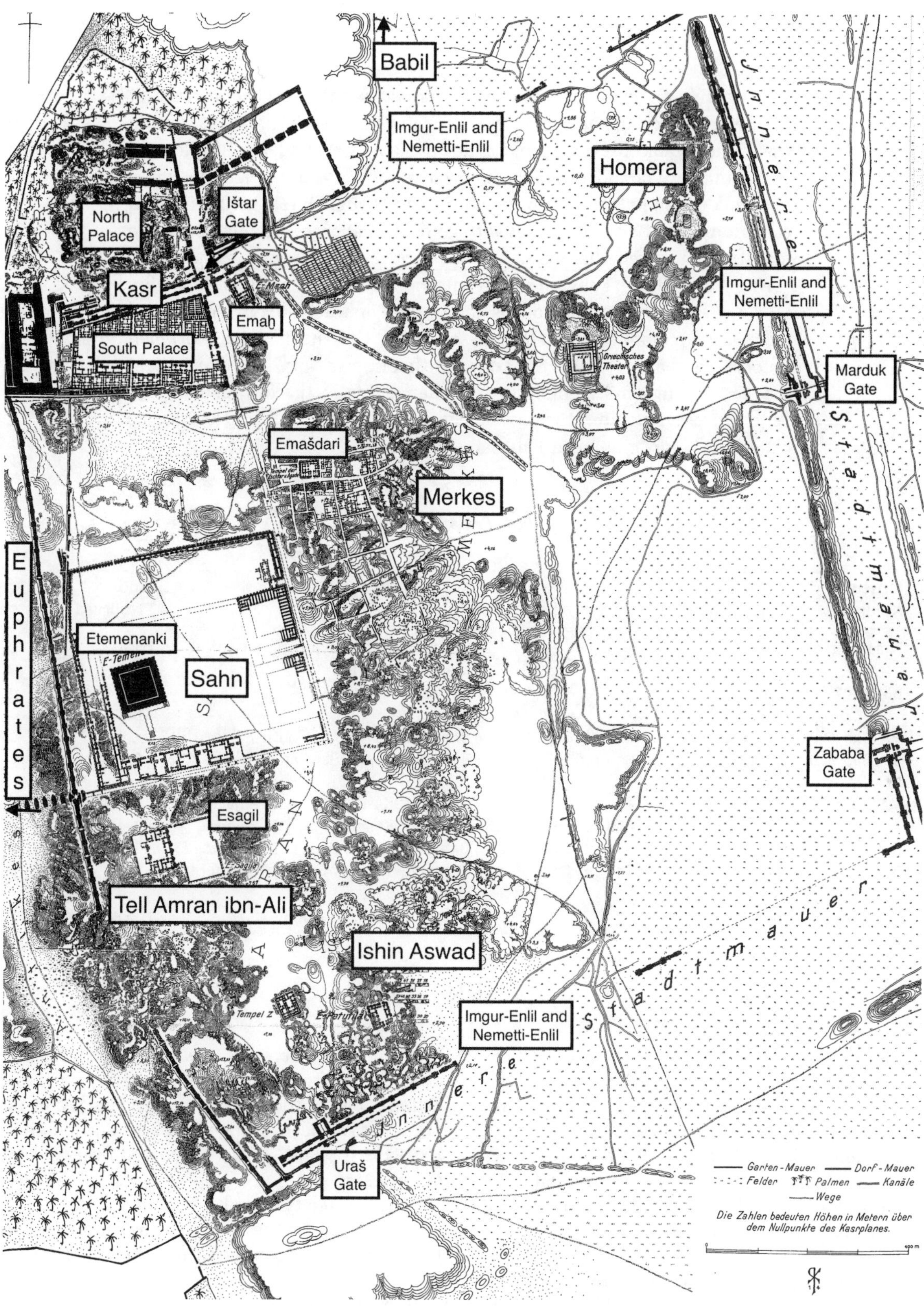

Figure 5. Annotated plan of the ruins of the inner city of Babylon. Adapted from Koldewey, WEB[5] fig. 256.

3

Nine two-column clay cylinders are inscribed with an Akkadian text of Neriglissar written in contemporary Neo-Babylonian script. The inscription records the details of several projects undertaken by this ruler at Babylon: (1) the manufacture of copper *mušḫuššu*-dragons for a few prominent gateways of Marduk's temple Esagil ("House whose Top Is High"); (2) the plating and decoration of the Dais of Destinies with gold and elaborate ornaments; (3) the renovation and strengthening of the banks of the Lībil-ḫegalla canal ("May It Bring Abundance"; Babylon's eastern canal); and (4) the repair of a wing of the royal palace that had collapsed into the Euphrates River. With regard to the last accomplishment, Neriglissar states that he had his workmen reinforce the banks of the Euphrates with bitumen and baked bricks in order to prevent similar collapses from happening in the future. This text is cited in previous literature as "Neriglissar Cylinder II, 3," "[Neriglissar] Cylinder C23," or "the Royal Palace Inscription."

CATALOGUE

Ex.	Museum Number	Excavation/ Registration No.	Photograph Number	Provenance	Lines Preserved	cpn
1	Loan Ant-43	—	—	Purchased at Babylon by Sir John Malcolm ca. 1811	i 1–ii 42	p
2	BM 40073	81-2-1,37	—	As ex. 1	i 1–14, 37–ii 9, 41–42	c
3	VA Bab 620	BE 29614	Bab ph 707	Babylon, Kasr 23m, South Palace, fill	ii 29–37	c
4	VA Bab 610	BE 29836	Bab ph 707	Babylon, Kasr 27k, South Palace, top fill	i 23–30	c
5	VA Bab 1974	BE 46942	—	Babylon, Kasr 24h, South Palace	i 38–ii 8	p
6	—	BE 47286	Bab ph 2961–2962	Babylon, Kasr 26k, South Palace	i 1–15, 41–ii 14	p
7	B 17	BE 47322	Bab ph 2741, 3059	Babylon, Kasr 26h–i, South Palace	i 1–14	p
8	B 2	BE 30220	Bab ph 873	Babylon, southern part of Homera, surface	i 1–2, 31–37	p
9	VAT 22763	BE 34065	—	Babylon, Kasr, south slope	i 7–9, ii 3–5	p

COMMENTARY

Contrary to Da Riva, SANER 3 p. 125, the collection number of ex. 1 is not ANE 39.1902, but still Loan Ant-43 (information kindly provided by J.H. Stephenson on January 29th, 2020). ANE 39.1902 is a fragment of five-column cylinder with a list of offerings of food and drink. That object appears to have been either a school exercise in which a scribe in training copied an Ur III account onto a cylinder or an ancient or modern fake; for cylinders being used as text carriers of school exercises, see Gesche, Schulunterricht pp. 194–195. According to the original, 1969 slip-book entry of Loan Ant-43 into the Fitzwilliam Museum, this cylinder of Neriglissar was purchased at Babylon around 1811 by Sir John Malcolm, thus, making the cylinder one of the first objects bearing a cuneiform text to have been brought back to Europe and the UK. Ex. 2 (BM 40073) was purchased from Spartali & Co. in 1881.

The master text and lineation follow ex. 1, the only complete witness of this inscription. A score is presented on Oracc and the minor (orthographic) variants are given in the critical apparatus at the back of the book.

BIBLIOGRAPHY

1861 Rawlinson, 1 R p. 67 (ex. 1, copy)
1863 Oppert, EM 1 p. 181 (ex. 1, partial translation)
1875 Ménant, Babylone pp. 249–251 (ex. 1, translation)
1875 Rodwell, Records of the Past 5 pp. 139–142 (ex. 1, translation)
1887 Pognon, Wadi Brissa p. 91 n. 1 (ex. 1 i 34, study [Pinches])
1886 Bezold, Literatur §76a (ex. 1, provenance)
1890 Bezold in Schrader, KB 3/2 pp. 70–75 (ex. 1, edition; variants, ex. 2)
1890 Jensen, Kosmologie p. 86 (ex. 1 i 33–36, edition)
1895 Meissner, Chrestomathie p. 41 (ex. 1 ii 15–42, copy)
1912 Langdon, NBK pp. 45 and 208–215 no. 1 (ex. 1, edition)
1913 Jensen, ThLZ 38 col. 356 (ex. 1 i 5, study)
1925 Koldewey, WEB[4] pp. 51–52 and 208 (ex. 1 i 18–30 and ii 6–11, translation [Bezold and Winckler])
1931 Güterbock, ZA 40 pp. 289–290 (exs. 1–2, 5–6, 8, partial edition)
1931 Koldewey, Königsburgen 1 p. 32 and pl. 2 (ex. 1 ii 15–30, translation [Delitzsch]; exs. 3–8, provenance)
1931 Schott, ZA 40 p. 20 (ex. 1 i 33–ii 5, study)
1938 Weissbach and Wetzel, Hauptheiligtum p. 60 (ex. 1 i 33–40, translation [Weissbach])
1973 Berger, NbK pp. 338–339 Zyl. II, 3 (exs. 1–8, study)
1990 Koldewey, WEB[5] pp. 65 and 208 (ex. 1 i 18–30 and ii 6–11, translation [Wilcke])
2008 Da Riva, GMTR 4 pp. 75, 79, 103–104, 112, 125 and 131 (study)
2013 Da Riva, SANER 3 pp. 13–15, 17, 19, 31, 124–135 no. 4.2.3 (C23) and CD-ROM figs. 21–29 (exs. 1–4, 6–8, photo; exs. 1–8, edition)

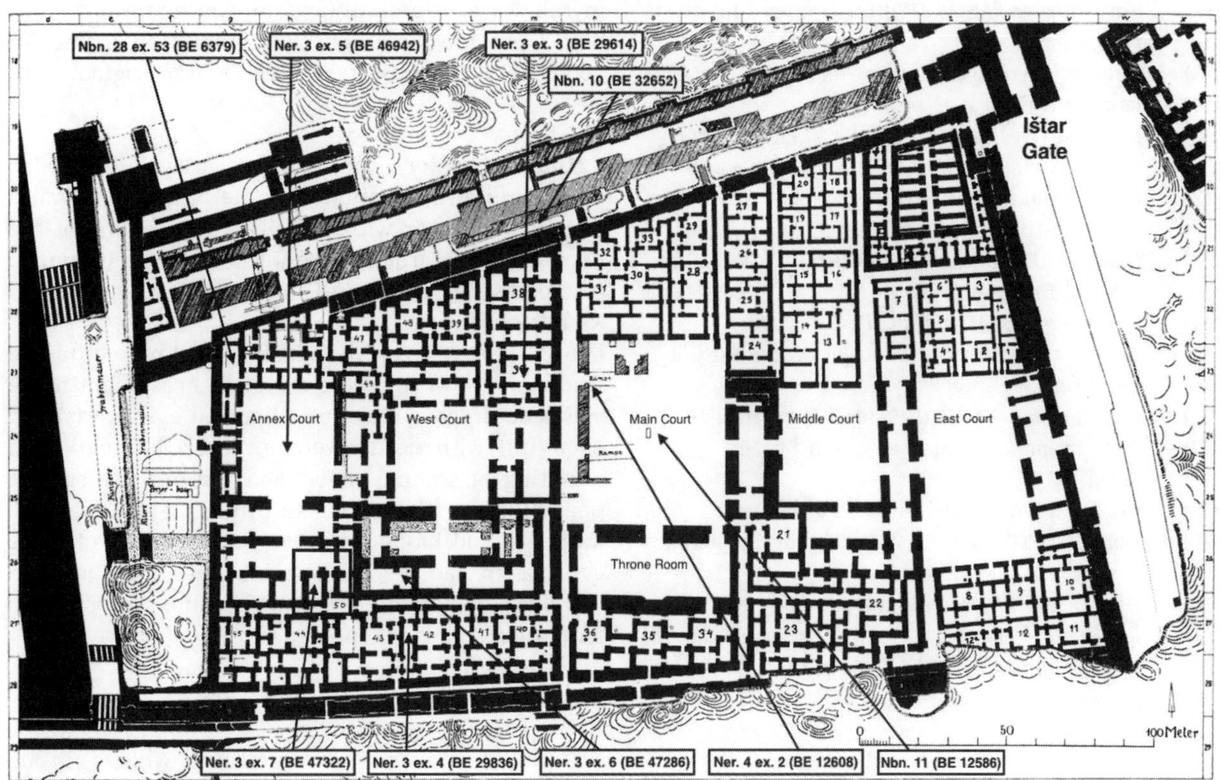

Figure 6. Annotated plan of the South Palace showing the general find spots of several clay cylinders and bricks of Neriglissar and Nabonidus, including exs. 2–7 of this text (Neriglissar no. 3). Adapted from Koldewey, WEB[5] fig. 44.

TEXT

Col. i

1) ^{d}NÈ.ERI$_{11}$.GAL-LUGAL-*ú-ṣu-úr* LUGAL KÁ.DINGIR.RA.KI
2) *mu-ud-di-iš é-sag-íl ù é-zi-da*
3) *e-pí-iš da-am-qá-a-ti*

i 1–14) Neriglissar, king of Babylon, the one who renovates Esagil and Ezida, the one who performs good deeds, about the exercise of whose everlasting kingship the great gods made a decision, whose fate

4) *ša a-na e-pe-e-šu* LUGAL-*ú-ti-šu da-ri-ti*
5) DINGIR GAL.GAL *iš-ku-nu mi-it-lu-uk-ti*
6) ^{d}AMAR.UTU *a-ša-re-du* DINGIR.DINGIR *mu-ši-im ši-ma-a-ti*
7) *a-na ki-iš-šu-ti* MA.DA.MA.DA *e-pé-e-šu*
8) *i-ši-mu ši-ma-at-su*
9) *a-na re-é-ú-ti ṣa-al-ma-at qá-qá-dam e-pé-e-šu*
10) ^{d}AG IBILA *ki-i-nim* GIŠ.NÍG.GIDRU *i-ša-ar-ti*
11) *ú-ša-at-mi-ḫu qa-tu-uš-šu*
12) *a-na e-ṭe-ri ni-šim ga-ma-lu ma-a-ti*
13) ^{d}*èr-ra ša-ga-pú-ru* DINGIR.DINGIR *id-di-nu-šu ka-ak-ku-šu*
14) DUMU ^{d}EN-MU-IN.GAR LUGAL TIN.TIR.KI *a-na-ku*

the god Marduk — the foremost of the gods, the one who determines fates — determined to exercise authority over the lands, whose hands the god Nabû — the legitimate heir — let grasp a just scepter to perform the shepherdship over the black-headed (people), to whom the god Erra — the majestic one of the gods — gave his weapon(s) to save the people (and) spare the land, son of Bēl-šum-iškun, king of Babylon, am I.

15) *ì-nu-um* ^{d}AMAR.UTU EN GAL *re-e-ši-ia ú-ul-lu-ú*
16) MA.DA *ù ni-šim a-na bé-e-lu id-di-nam*
17) *a-na-ku a-na* ^{d}AMAR.UTU EN-*ia ka-a-a-na-ak la ba-aṭ-la-ak*
18) *é-sag-íl ù é-zi-da a-za-an-na-an*
19) *uš-te-te-eš-še-er e-eš-re-e-ti*
20) *pa-ar-ṣu re-eš-tu-tu aš-te-né-e'-a ka-a-a-nam*

i 15–20) When the god Marduk, the great lord, elevated me (and) gave me the land and people to rule, I myself was ever-present (and) unstinting towards Marduk. I provide for Esagil and Ezida, keep shrines in good order, (and) constantly strive after original rites.

21) MUŠ.ḪUŠ *e-ri-i ša i-na ki-sè-e* KÁ.KÁ *é-sag-íl*
22) *it-ti ri-i-mu* KÙ.BABBAR *ša sì-ip-pe-e na-an-zu-zu ka-a-a-nam*
23) *i-na* KÁ-^{d}UTU.È KÁ-^{d}LAMMA-*a-ra-bi* KÁ-ḪÉ.GÁL *ù* KÁ-U_6.DE.BABBAR
24) *la uš-zi-zu* LUGAL *ma-aḫ-ri*

i 21–24) (As for) the copper *mušḫuššu*-dragon(s), which are always stationed at the bases of the gates of Esagil together with the silver wild bull(s) of the door-jambs, a former king did not station (them) in (the gates) Ka-Utu-e, Ka-Lamma-arabi, Ka-ḫegal, and Ka-ude-babbar.

25) *ia-ti áš-ru ša-aḫ-ṭu ša pa-la-ḫa* DINGIR.DINGIR *mu-du-ú*
26) *e-ep-ti-iq-ma* 8 MUŠ.ḪUŠ *e-ri-i še-zu-zu-ú-ti*
27) *ša le-em-nim ù a-a-bi i-za-an-nu i-ma-at mu-ú-ti*
28) *ti-i-ri* KÙ.BABBAR *e-eb-bi ú-ša-al-bi-iš-ma*
29) *i-na* KÁ-^{d}UTU.È KÁ-^{d}LAMMA-*a-ra-bi* KÁ-ḪÉ.GÁL *ù* KÁ-U_6.DE.<BABBAR>
30) *i-na ki-se-e* KÁ.KÁ *ši-na-a-ti ki-ma la-bi-ri-im-ma*
31) *it-ti ri-i-mu* KÙ.BABBAR *ša sì-ip-pe-e*
32) *ki-ma sì-ma-a-ti-šu re-eš-ta-a-ti ú-uš-zi-iz i-na ki-gal-lam*

i 25–32) (As for) me, the humble (and) respectful one who knows how to revere the gods, I cast eight fierce *mušḫuššu*-dragons of copper that coat evil doer(s) and enem(ies) with deadly venom, covered (them) with a plating of shining silver, and stationed (them) on pedestal(s) in (the gates) Ka-Utu-e, Ka-Lamma-arabi, Ka-ḫegal, and Ka-ude-<babbar>, at the bases of those gates, as (it had been) in ancient times, together with the silver wild bull(s) of the door-jambs, according to its (Esagil's) original appearance.

33) BÁRA *ši-ma-a-ti ša qé-re-eb é-zi-da*
34) *ša i-na za-am-mu-uk-ku re-e-ša ša-at-ti*
35) *i-na i-sì-in-ni a-ki-ti ta-be-e* ^{d}EN.LÍL DINGIR.DINGIR ^{d}AMAR.UTU
36) ^{d}*na-bi-um* IBILA *ki-nim i-ša-ad-di-ḫu a-na qé-re-eb šu-an-na*.KI

i 33–40) (As for) the Dais of Destinies, which is inside Ezida — which at the New Year, at the beginning of the year, during the *akītu*-festival, (during) the setting out of the Enlil of the gods, the god Marduk, the god Nabû, the legitimate heir, goes in procession into Šuanna (Babylon), (and) on the fifth (and) eleventh days, when

---

i 14 LUGAL TIN.TIR.KI "king of Babylon": To whom the title refers, Neriglissar or his father Bēl-šum-iškun, is ambiguous. R. Da Riva (SANER 3 pp. 15–16) describes the issue as follows: "The repetition of the title in I 14 is very unusual, especially as it appears after the name of Bēl-šum-iškun, apparently referring to him, not to Neriglissar. This ambiguity raises a number of questions regarding the role played by Bēl-šum-iškun in Babylonian politics and whether he had any claims to the throne. At present they remain unanswered, due to the lack of sources. Nevertheless, some observations can be made: Neriglissar did not need to forge his father's *curriculum*, since royal lineage was not a *conditio sine qua non* to ascend the Babylonian throne, and Nabopolassar was an illustrious precedent. To call a tribal leader a "prince" would not raise any suspicion, but to play with the syntax in order to introduce a double meaning and turn an Aramean chieftain into a "king of Babylon" would be a quite different matter. Tribal leaders were called kings — Esarhaddon called Šamaš-ibni "king" of the Bīt-Dakkūri, see Frame 2008 [= RLA 11/7–8]: 617 — but of their respective tribe, not of Babylon." Compare text no. 1 (Esagil Inscription) i 2 and 11 and text no. 7 i 1′ and 11′, where both Neriglissar and Bēl-šum-iškun are given the title *rubâm*, "prince." See also the on-page note to text no. 1 (Esagil Inscription) i 11.

37) UD.5.KÁM UD.11.KÁM *i-na a-la-ku ù ta-a-ri ša ba-bi-lam*.KI
38) ^{d}AG ⌜IBILA⌝ [*šit*]-⌜*lu-ṭù*⌝ *i-ra-am-mu-ú ṣe-ru-uš-šu*
39) *ša* LUGAL *ma-aḫ-ri i-na* KÙ.BABBAR *ip-ti-qu pi-ti-iq-šu*
40) KÙ.GI ⌜*nam*⌝-*ru ti-iq-nim mé-lam-mu ú-ša-al-bi-iš-šu*

going and returning from Babylon, the god Nabû, the [tri]umphant heir, takes up residence upon it — whose structure a former king had cast with silver, I covered it with shining gold (and) ornaments of brilliance.

41) ÍD.BURANUN.KI ÍD ḪÉ.GÁL-*lam ša iš-tu bi-na-a-ti-šu*
42) *i-te-e é-sag-íl šu-te-šu-ru mu-ú-šu ga-ap-šu-ti*
Col. ii
1) *i-na pa-le-e* LUGAL *ma-aḫ-ri mu-ú-šu a-na i-te-e é-sag-íl*
2) *is-su-ú i-re-e-qu a-na sa-a-bu*
3) *ia-ti a-ša-ar-šu la-bí-ri aš-te-e*ʾ*-e-ma*
4) *ma-la-ak mé-e-šu ki-ma la-bi-ri-im-ma*
5) *a-na i-te-e é-sag-íl uš-te-te-ši-ir*

i 41–ii 5) (As for) the Euphrates River, the river of abundance, whose waters since its creation have flowed in full spate directly beside Esagil, (but) whose waters had withdrawn during the reign of a former king from the side of Esagil (and) had become too distant to draw (water from it), (but as for) me, I sought out its original location and directed the course of its water beside Esagil, as (it had been) in ancient times.

6) PA$_5$ ^{d}UTU.È *ša* LUGAL *ma-aḫ-ri ú-ša-aḫ-ru-ma*
7) *la ib-na-a su-uk-ki-šu*
8) PA$_5$ *ú-ša-aḫ-ri-ma i-na ku-up-ri ù a-gur-ri*
9) *ab-na-a su-uk-ki-šu*
10) *mé-e nu-uḫ-šu la na-pa-ar-ku-ti*
11) *ú-ki-in a-na* MA.DA

ii 6–11) (As for) the eastern canal, which a former king had had dug, but without constructing its bank, I had the canal (re)dug and (properly re)constructed its bank with bitumen and baked bricks. I firmly established for the land an abundance of water that does not cease.

12) *a-na é-sag-íl ù é-zi-da la ba-aṭ-la-ak sa-at-ta-kam*
13) *ka-al ma-ḫa-zi* DINGIR.DINGIR *a-na zi-in-na-a-ti*
14) *aš-te-né-e*ʾ*-a ka-a-a-nam*

ii 12–14) I am constantly unstinting towards Esagil and Ezida, (and) I constantly strive to provision all of the cult centers of the gods.

15) *ì-nu-mi-šu* É.GAL *mu-ša-bu šar-ru-ti-ia*
16) *ša er-ṣe-tì* KÁ.DINGIR.RA.KI *ša qé-re-eb ba-bi-lam*.KI
17) *iš-tu a-a-i-bu-úr-ša-bu-um su-le-e* KÁ.DINGIR.RA.KI
18) *a-di ki-ša-du* ÍD.BURANUN.KI
19) *ša* LUGAL *ma-aḫ-ri i-pú-šu-ma ú-ra-ak-ki-su sì-ip-pu-šu*
20) *i-na li-ib-bi a-na ki-da$_4$-a-nim* É.GAL
21) *a-na mu-úḫ ki-ša-du* ÍD.BURANUN.KI
22) *i-qu-up-ma up-ta-aṭ-ṭi-ri ṣi-in-du-šu*
23) *i-ga-ru-ša qu-up-pu-tu ad-ke-e-ma*
24) *šu-pú-ul mé-e ak-šu-ud*
25) *mé-ḫe-ra-at mé-e i-na ku-up-ri ù a-gur-ri*
26) *i-ši-id-sa ú-ša-ar-ši-id-ma*
27) *e-pú-uš ú-ša-ak-li-il-ma*
28) *ú-ul-la-a re-e-ša-a-ša*
29) GIŠ.EREN *da-nu$_4$-tum a-na ši-i-pí-ša*
30) GIŠ.GAN.DU$_7$-*ša ù ṣu-lu-li-ša ú-ša-at-ri-iṣ*

ii 15–30) At that time, (as for) the palace, (which is) the residence of my royal majesty, which is in the Kadingirra district — which is in Babylon, (extending) from Ay-ibūr-šabû, the (main) street of Babylon, to the bank of the Euphrates River — which a former king had built and whose door-jamb(s) he had installed inside (it), it collapsed towards the outside of the palace onto the bank of the Euphrates river and its brickwork fell apart. I removed its collapsed walls until I reached the level of the water. With bitumen and baked bricks, I firmly secured its base against water, and (then) built (it), completed (it), and raised its superstructure. I spread out strong cedar(s) to be its *šīpu*(s), architrave(s), and roof.

31) ^{d}AMAR.UTU EN GAL ^{d}EN.LÍL DINGIR.DINGIR *šu-pu-ú*
32) *nu-úr* DINGIR.DINGIR *ab-bé-e-šu*
33) *i-na qí-bi-ti-ka ṣi-ir-ti ša la na-ak-ri*
34) É *e-pú-šu la-la-a-šu lu-uš-bu*
35) *i-na qé-er-bi-ša ši-bu-tu lu-uk-šu-ud*
36) *lu-uš-ba-a li-it-tu-ú-ti*

ii 31–42) O Marduk, the great lord, the Enlil of the gods, the resplendent one, the light of the gods — his fathers — by your exalted command, which cannot be altered, may I be sated with the charms of the palace that I built; may I reach extreme old age (and) attain very old age inside it; may I receive inside it, from the horizon to the zenith, wherever the sun

i 39 LUGAL *ma-aḫ-ri* "a former king": Or "the previous king," that is, the last ruler who worked on the Dais of Destinies before Neriglissar.

37) *iš-tu* AN.ÚR *a-di* AN.PA *e-ma* ^{d}UTU *a-ṣu-ú*
38) *ša* LUGAL.LUGAL *ki-ib-ra-a-ti ša ka-al te-né-še-e-ti*
39) *bi-la-at-su-nu ka-bi-it-ti*
40) *lu-um-ḫu-úr qé-er-bu-uš-ša*
41) *li-i-pu-ú-a i-na qé-er-bi-ša a-na da-rí-a-ti*
42) *ṣa-al-ma-at qá-qá-dam li-be-e-lu*

rises, substantial tribute from the kings of the regions of the entire inhabited world; (and) inside it may my descendants rule over the black-headed (people) forever.

4

Five bricks, including at least two discovered during the German excavations at Babylon, bear a short, proprietary inscription of Neriglissar; the script is archaizing Neo-Babylonian and the Akkadian text is stamped on at least one of them. One of the bricks (ex. 5) is also inscribed with an Aramaic docket. The king calls himself "the one who renovates Esagil and Ezida"; work on Marduk's temple at Babylon is recorded in text nos. 1 ([Esagil Inscription] ii 9–28) and 3 ([Royal Palace Inscription] i 21–40). This inscription is cited in previous literature as "Neriglissar Brick A I, 1" or "[Neriglissar] Brick Inscription B1."

CATALOGUE

Ex.	Museum Number	Excavation/ Registration No.	Photograph Number	Provenance	Lines Preserved	cpn
1	BM 201a–b, BM 227	—	—	Babylon, river bank	1–3	n
2	—	BE 12608	Bab ph 1525A	Babylon, Kasr 23n, South Palace, main courtyard, grave	1–3	n
3	—	—	—	Babylon, western annex building	1–3	n
4	Private collection (Berlin)	—	—	Babylon, picked up by a traveller in 1964	1–3	n
5	VA Bab 4619	BE 41298	—	Babylon, Merkes, street	1–3	p

COMMENTARY

Ex. 1 is now known only from the hand-drawn facsimile in Rawlinson 1 R (pl. 68 no. 5). The (composite) copy of the inscription was prepared from three squeezes (BM 201a–b and BM 227) of brick(s) found (near) the bank of the Euphrates at Babylon. It is uncertain if these squeezes are still in the British Museum (London) or if they were destroyed by S. Smith on the grounds that they had outlived their usefulness. The master text and lineation follow ex. 1. No score of the inscription is given on Oracc (a) since scores are not provided for texts on bricks (following the model of RIM and RINAP) and (b) since the contents of exs. 3–4 have never been published in any form (photograph, copy, or transliteration).

BIBLIOGRAPHY

1859 Oppert, EM 2 p. 324 (ex. 1, copy, edition)
1861 1 R pl. 8 no. 5 (ex. 1, copy)
1875 Ménant, Babylone p. 249 (ex. 1, edition [Rawlinson and Oppert])
1886 Bezold, Literatur §76b (ex. 1, provenance)
1889 de Vogüé, CIS 2 pp. 59–60 no. 58 (ex. 1, copy [Oppert])
1899 Bezold, Cat. 5 p. 2235 no. IX E 5 (ex. 1, study)
1912 Langdon, NBK pp. 46 and 218–219 no. 3 (ex. 1, edition)
1913 Koldewey, MDOG 51 pp. 17–18 (ex. 4, study)
1925 Koldewey, WEB⁴ pp. 78–79, with fig. 51g, and p. 124 (ex. 2, copy, translation, provenance)
1931 Koldewey, Königsburgen 1 pp. 32–33 and 115 (ex. 3, translation; ex. 2, provenance)
1938 Wetzel and Weissbach, Hauptheiligtum p. 37 n. 7 (ex. 2, study)
1973 Berger, NbK pp. 113 and 334 Backsteine A I, 1 (ex. 1–4, study)
1990 Koldewey, WEB⁵ pp. 89–90, with fig. 51g, and p. 132 (ex. 2, copy, translation, provenance)
2008 Da Riva, GMTR 4 pp. 103–104, 125 and 131 (study)
2010 Sass and Marzahn, WVDOG 127 p. 30 no. 12 (cat. nos. 46 and 54), p. 36 figs. 118–120, pp. 82 and 87 figs. 509–511, pp. 88 and 93 fig. 569–571 and p. 88 (exs. 1, 5, photo, copy, transliteration)
2013 Da Riva, SANER 3 pp. 13 and 112–113 no. 4.1.1 (B1) (exs. 1–2, edition; exs. 3–4, study)

TEXT

1) ᵈU.GUR-LUGAL-ÙRU LUGAL TIN.TIR.KI
2) *mu-ud-diš é-sag-íl ù é-zi-da*
3) *e-pi-iš da-am-qa-a-ti*

1–3) Neriglissar, king of Babylon, the one who renovates Esagil and Ezida, the one who performs good deeds.

5

Two bricks apparently bearing a four-line version of the previous inscription were discovered during Koldewey's excavations at Babylon. Like text no. 4, this short, proprietary inscription of Neriglissar is written in archaizing Neo-Babylonian script. Since no photograph, copy, or transliteration of this inscription has ever been published, it is not known how the text was distributed over the four lines and which cuneiform signs were used to write out the inscription. For these reasons, no edition of the inscription is provided here. This text is sometimes referred to as "Neriglissar Brick A I, 2" or "[Neriglissar] Brick Inscription B2."

CATALOGUE

Ex.	Museum Number	Excavation Number	Provenance	Lines Preserved	cpn
1	—	BE 41545	Babylon, Sahn 36y, wall north of the gate of the bridge	1–4	n
2	—	BE 41544	As ex. 1	1–4	n

BIBLIOGRAPHY

1910 Wetzel, MDOG 44 p. 26 (ex. 1, translation, study)
1930 Wetzel, Stadtmauern p. 52 (ex. 1, study)
1931 Koldewey, Königsburgen 1 pp. 32 and 115 (translation)
1938 Wetzel and Weissbach, Hauptheiligtum p. 37 n. 7 (study)
1973 Berger, NbK p. 335 Backsteine A I, 2 (study)
2008 Da Riva, GMTR 4 pp. 103–104, 125 and 131 (study)
2013 Da Riva, SANER 3 pp. 13 and 113–114 no. 4.1.2 (B2) (exs. 1–2, study)

6

An inscription of Neriglissar recording construction on Šamaš ziggurat Ekunankuga ("House, Pure Stairway of Heaven") at Sippar is written on a large, two-column clay cylinder; this Akkadian text is inscribed in contemporary Neo-Babylonian script. Work on the temple tower is reported to have been undertaken because its brick structure had been severely eroded due to heavy rains; the text also states that the previous builder never finished rebuilding it, although he did manage to have it raised to a height of twenty-two cubits. Unfortunately, the passage in which Neriglissar describes his own restorations of the ziggurat is no longer preserved. This inscription is referred to in previous studies and editions as "Neriglissar Cylinder Fragment II, 2" or "[Neriglissar] Cylinder C022." The edition given here is based on the photograph published by R. Da Riva.

CATALOGUE

Museum Number	Registration Number	Provenance	cpn
LB 2124	—	Probably Sippar	p

BIBLIOGRAPHY

1957 van Dijk, TLB 2 fig. 25 no. 22 (copy)

1973 Berger, NbK p. 341 Zyl.-Frag II, 2 (study)

2008 Da Riva, GMTR 4 pp. 79, 103–104, 112, 125 and 131 (study)

2013 Da Riva, SANER 3 pp. 13, 17 n. 59, 19, 23–24, 140–143 no. 4.2.6 (C022) and CD-ROM fig. 32 (photo, edition)

TEXT

Col. i

1) ^{d}NÈ.ERI$_{11}$.GAL-LUGAL-*ú-ṣu-úr* LUGAL KÁ.DINGIR.RA.KI
2) *ru-ba-a-am na-a-dam*
3) *bi-ib-il li-ib-bi* ^{d}AMAR.UTU
4) *iš-ša-ak-ku ṣi-i-ri*
5) *na-ra-am* ^{d}*na-bi-um*
6) *mu-uš-ta-lam a-ḫi-iz né-me-qí*
7) *ša a-na zi-in-na-a-ti é-sag-íl*
8) *é-zi-da*
9) ⸢*ù é*$^{?}$-<<*x*>>-*mes*$^{?}$-*lam*$^{?}$⸣ *ma-ḫa-zi* DINGIR GAL.GAL
10) [*ti-iṣ-mu-ru-um-ma*] ⸢*la na*⸣-*pa-ar-ka-a*
11) [...] ŠU KU
12) [...] *x-nim*
13) [...] *x*

Lacuna

1′) *x x x* ⸢$^{d?}$UTU$^{?}$⸣ *x* [...]
2′) *ṣu-lu-ul-šu* ⸢*ṭa*$^{?}$⸣-[*a-bu*]
3′) *e-li um-ma-ni-ia* ⸢*it*$^{?}$⸣-[*ru-uṣ*$^{?}$]

i 1–13) Neriglissar, king of Babylon, pious prince, the desire of the god Marduk's heart, exalted ruler, beloved of the god Nabû, the one who deliberates and acquires wisdom, the one who [is] unceasingly [mindful] of provisioning Esagil, Ezida, and *Emeslam* — the cult centers of the great gods — [...] ... [...] ... [...]

Lacuna

i 1′–6′) ... *the god Šamaš* [...] *ex*[*tended*] his *fa*[*vorable*] protection over my army. Through pronouncement and divination, the god [*Šamaš* (...)] spoke unequiv-

4′) *i-na di-i-nim ù bi-ri* ⸢^{d}⸣[UTU$^{?}$ (*x*)]
5′) *i-ša-ri-iš i-dá-ab-bu-*⸢*bu*⸣ [*x x*]
6′) *pa-al-ḫi-iš at-ta-ʾi-*⸢*id*⸣*-*[*ma*]
7′) *i-na šu-ru-ti* LUGAL*-ú-ti-ia ṭa-ab-ti*
Col. ii
1) *zi-qú-ra-at* ⸢ZIMBIR⸣.[KI]
2) *ša* LUGAL *ma-aḫ-ri i-*⸢*pú*⸣*-*[*šu-ma*]
3) *zu-un-nu ù ra-a-*[*du*]
4) *ú-na-as-su-ú li-bi-it-*⸢*tu*⸣*-*[*ša*]
5) LUGAL *pa-nim ik-ši-ru-*⸢*ma*⸣
6) *li-bi-it-ta-ša ú-uš-te-*[*ši-ir-ma*]
7) *ma-qí-it-ta-šu ú-uš-*[*zi-iz-ma*]
8) 22 KÙŠ *i-pú-šu-ma la* ⸢*ú*⸣*-*[*šak-li-lu*]
9) *re-e-ša-*[*a-ša*]
10) *ia-ti e-*[*em-qa mu-ut-né-en-nu-ú*]
11) *ša pa-la-ḫa* DINGIR.⸢DINGIR⸣ [*mu-du-ú*]
12) *i-na né-me-qí ša* ⸢^{d}⸣[*é-a*]
13) *iš-ru-*⸢*ka*⸣*-*[*am* (*x*)]
14) [*a*$^{?}$]*-*⸢*na* ^{d}UTU⸣ [...]
Lacuna
1′) *x* [...]
2′) *i-na* ⸢*di-i-nim*⸣ [...]

ocally [...] I gave reverent attention.

i 7′–ii 9) At the beginning of my gracious kingship, the ziggurat of Sip[par], which a former king had b[uilt and whose] brickwor[k] rains and downpo[urs] had carried away, (which) a king of the past had restored, had put its brickwork in goo[d order], had reb[uilt] its collapsed section(s), had constructed (it to a height of) twenty-two cubits, but [had] not co[mplete its] superstructu[re]:

ii 10–14) (As for) me, the w[ise (and) pious one] who [knows how] to revere the god[s], through the wisdom that the god [Ea] granted to [me, f]or the god Šamaš [...]

Lacuna
ii 1′–2′) [...] through a pronouncement [...].

7

A fragment of a large, two-column clay cylinder preserves a small portion of an inscription of Neriglissar that records a military expedition in detail, something that is not typical of official Babylonian inscriptions; the script is archaizing Neo-Babylonian. The campaign in question might have been the one against Cilicia (Ḫumê and Pirindu), which took place during his third regnal year (557). The attribution of the text is certain since Neriglissar's father Bēl-šum-iškun is mentioned. This inscription, which might have been composed after the events of 557, is cited in previous literature as "[Neriglissar] Cylinder C011." The edition given here is based on the photograph published by R. Da Riva.

CATALOGUE

Museum Number	Registration Number	Provenance	cpn
SPL W 2/8	Grolier 9	Possibly Borsippa	p

6 i 7′ *šu-ru-ti* LUGAL*-ú-ti-ia* "the beginning of my kingship": Intentional wordplay.

BIBLIOGRAPHY

1976 Brinkman, Studies Kramer pp. 48–50 (copy, study)

2008 Da Riva, GMTR 4 pp. 78, 103–104, 125 and 131 (study)

2013 Da Riva, SANER 3 pp. 14–16, 19–20, 135–138 no. 4.2.4 (C011) and CD-ROM figs. 30a–e (photo, edition)

TEXT

Col. i

Lacuna

1′) ⸢ru⸣-ba-a-am ⸢em⸣-[qá-am (x)]
2′) ša i-na ⸢tu⸣-[kul-ti DINGIR.MEŠ-šú]
3′) u_4-mi-ša-am pu-[luḫ-ti ^{d}AMAR.UTU EN GAL]
4′) ù ^{d}AG IBILA-šu ⸢ki⸣-[i-nim]
5′) ⸢iš⸣-te-né-eʾ-ú ⸢ka⸣-[a-a-nam]
6′) a-na é-sag-íl ù é-zi-⸢da⸣
7′) ṭú-úḫ-ḫu-du sa-at-tu-[uk-ki (x)]
8′) ša e-li ^{d}AG ù ^{d}AMAR.UTU EN.MEŠ-[šú? ṭa-a-bu]
9′) u_4-mi-ša-am e-pé-šu iš-te-⸢né⸣-[eʾ-ú]
10′) ⸢ú⸣-ša-al-la-mu qí-bi-⸢it⸣-[su-nu]
11′) ⸢DUMU⸣ ^{d}EN-šu-um-⸢iš-ku-un⸣ ru-ba-a-⸢am⸣ [e-em-qá? (x)]
12′) ⸢eṭ-lu⸣ gi-it-ma-lu e-⸢ṭe-el?⸣ qá?-⸢ár?⸣-[du (x)]
13′) ⸢i⸣-nu-ma ^{d}AG su-uk-kal-lu ⸢ṣi⸣-[i-ri]
14′) mu-ta-mu-ú da-am-⸢qá⸣-[ti-ia]
15′) ⸢a⸣-ma-a-ti da-mi-iq-ti-ia i-⸢ta⸣-[ma-a]
16′) re-eš LUGAL-ú-⸢ti⸣-ia ú-ul-lu-[ú]
17′) ⸢i⸣-na pa-ni-šu dam-qú-ti ip-pal-sa-an-ni-⸢ma⸣
18′) šar-ru-ti mi-ša-ri ia-ti ⸢iš-ru-kam⸣ [(x)]
19′) i-na qí-bi-ti-šu ṣi-ir-⸢tim⸣ [(x)]
20′) ḫar-ra-an na-ki-ri ⸢er⸣-te-⸢ed-de⸣-[e-ma (x)]
21′) ú-ru-uḫ ša-di x [...]
22′) ⸢ma-ta-a-ti⸣ [...]
23′) [x] x I DI TA ⸢MA?⸣ [...]
24′) ⸢na?⸣-ak-ru-⸢ti⸣ [...]
25′) [x] x ⸢KA⸣ AN [...]
26′) [x (x)] ⸢LUGAL⸣ [...]

Lacuna

Col. ii

Completely missing

Lacuna

i 1′–12′) w[is]e prince, the one who daily through the su[pport of his gods] const[antly] strives after re[spect for the god Marduk — the great lord] — and the god Nabû — his t[rue] heir — the one who st[rives] to copiously supply *sattu*[*kku*-offerings (...)] to Esagil and Ezida (and) to perform daily that [which is pleasing] to the gods Nabû and Marduk, [*his*] lords, the one who fulfills [their] comman[d], son of Bēl-šum-iškun, [*wise*] prince [(...)], the perfect warrior, *the vali*[*ant*] *warrior*, [(...)].

i 13′–18′) When the god Nabû, the e[xalted] vizier, the one who speaks about [*my*] *good de*[*eds*], spr[ead] word of my good deeds (and) elevated the head of my royal majesty, he looked upon me with his gracious face an[d] granted me a just reign.

i 19′–26′) At his exalted command, I travel[led] enemy road(s), [...] mountain path(s), [...] lands [...] ... [... h]ostil[e ...] ... [... k]i[ng ...]

Lacuna

Completely missing

8

A fragment of a vase inscribed with a short text of Neriglissar stating that the vessel once belonged to him was discovered in the ruins of the Elamite capital Susa; the script is contemporary Neo-Babylonian. The inscription records that the stone object had a capacity of two *qa* and one half *akalu*, which is slightly over two liters. This text is cited in previous literature as “Neriglissar Vase I” or “[Neriglissar] Vase V1.”

CATALOGUE

Source	Excavation Number	Provenance	cpn
Scheil, MDP 10 p. 96	—	Susa	n

COMMENTARY

The present whereabouts of Vase V1 is unknown, so the edition of this short inscription is based on V. Scheil's transliteration (MDP 10 p. 96).

BIBLIOGRAPHY

1908 Scheil, MDP 10 p. 96 (edition)
1927 Scheil, RA 24 p. 47 (study)
1973 Berger, NbK p. 333 Gefäß I (study)
2008 Da Riva, GMTR 4 p. 104, 125 and 131 (study)
2013 Da Riva, SANER 3 pp. 13 and 143–144 no. 4.3 (V1) (edition)

TEXT

1) 2 *qa* 1/2 NINDA
2) ^{d}U$^{?}$.GUR$^{?}$-LUGAL-ÙRU LUGAL TIN.TIR.KI

1) Two *qa*, one half *akalu*.
2) (Palace of) Neriglissar, king of Babylon.

1

Two almost completely preserved, barrel-shaped clay cylinders, as well as a small fragment of a third cylinder, bear an inscription of Nabonidus recording renovations made to Babylon's inner wall Imgur-Enlil ("The God Enlil Showed Favor"); the text is written in two columns. One cylinder (ex. 1) was purchased in Istanbul sometime before 1900, while the other (ex. 2) was discovered in situ by Iraqi archaeologists in 1978, in the brick structure of Imgur-Enlil, near the Ištar Gate, in a clay box together with two clay cylinders of Nabopolassar (also recording work on Babylon's inner wall); the fragment (ex. 3) is registered as coming from Sippar. The text, which is written in contemporary Neo-Babylonian script, states that Nabonidus rebuilt the dilapidated sections of Imgur-Enlil and raised the superstructure as high as a mountain. In addition, Nabonidus reports that he had inscriptions of an unnamed previous king of Babylon (undoubtedly Nabopolassar) placed in the brick structure of that wall alongside his own inscriptions; this claim can be confirmed from the archaeological record (see commentary below). Interestingly, the length of Imgur-Enlil is recorded in this text: 20 UŠ, which is approximately 7,200 m long (see the on-page note to i 22); according to A. George (BTT pp. 135–136), the actual length of the wall was 8,015 m. This text is referred to as "Nabonidus Cylinder II, 1," "[Nabonidus] Inscription A," and "the Imgur-Enlil Cylinder" in previous studies and editions.

CATALOGUE

Ex.	Museum Number	Excavation/ Registration No.	Provenance	Lines Preserved	cpn
1	CBS 16108	—	Probably Babylon; purchased in Istanbul before 1900	i 1–ii 25	p
2	A Babylon 10	—	Babylon, Kasr, in the middle of the first tower east of the Ištar Gate	i 1–ii 25	n
3	BM 40578	AH 81-4-2,122	Registered as coming from Sippar	i 12–22, ii 16–25	c

COMMENTARY

Interestingly, the distribution of text on all three exemplars is identical. Although ex. 2 is fully intact and the ends of ii 4–16 of ex. 1 are missing, the master text is a conflation of exs. 1 and 2; preference is generally given to ex. 1. A score is presented on Oracc and the minor (orthographic) variants are given in the critical apparatus at the back of the book. The major variant in i 18, however, is provided in the on-page note to that line.

Nabonidus' description of Babylon's inner wall is very reminiscent of that of Nabopolassar, which is presently recorded on clay cylinder A Babylon 11; compare i 25–ii 4 to A Babylon 11 ii 6–iii 10, especially ii 8–12 (Da Riva, SANER 3 pp. 94–95). That passage in that text of Nabopolassar evidently served as inspiration for the description of Imgur-Enlil in this text. It is clear from Iraqi excavations at Babylon in 1978 and 1979 that Nabonidus' scribes had consulted foundation documents of Nabopolassar discovered in the brick structure of Babylon's wall (between the Ištar and Zababa Gates). Nabonidus had clay cylinders of his deposited with those of his predecessor in clay boxes. A Babylon 10 (ex. 2) was found in such a box together with two cylinders of Nabopolassar, A Babylon 11 (the aforementioned text) and A Babylon 12 (Da Riva, SANER 3 pp. 50–54 ex. 2).

BIBLIOGRAPHY

1923 Legrain, MJ 14 pp. 282–287 (ex. 1, copy, edition)
1926 Legrain, PBS 15 pp. 46–47 and pls. 33–34 no. 80 (ex. 1, copy, edition)
1928 Poebel, OLZ 31 cols. 701–702 (ex. 1 i 5–6, 9, 14, 17, 19, 20, ii 4, 12, study)
1929 Landsberger, ZA 38 p. 115 (ex. 1 i 14–16, 20, 22, study)
1929 Langdon, JRAS 1929 pp. 379–382 (ex. 1 i 2, 6–9, 14–16, 19–20, 23–ii 2, 4, 8, 10, 12–13, 18–19, 21, study)
1965 Tadmor, Studies Landsberger p. 360 no. 21 (study)
1973 Berger, NbK p. 354 Nbn. Zyl. II, 1 (study)
1979 Abdul-Razaq, Sumer 35 p. 116 (ex. 2, study)
1985 Al-Rawi, Iraq 47 p. 2 and pl. 1 (ex. 2, photo, study)
1985 Al-Rawi, Sumer 41 p. 23 (ex. 2, study)
1989 Beaulieu, Nabonidus pp. 38–39 Inscription A (study)
1991 Al-Rawi, ARRIM 9 pp. 5 and 7–8 (ex. 2, copy, transliteration, study)
1992 George, BTT pp. 348–349 (i 17–ii 4, edition; study)
2001 Schaudig, Inschriften Nabonids pp. 345–350 no. 2.1 (edition)
2010 Heller, Spätzeit p. 178 (study)
2011 Heinsch, Kuntner and Rollinger, CLeO 3 pp. 518–520 (ex. 2, study)

TEXT

Col. i

1) ^{d}AG-*na-ʾi-id* LUGAL TIN.TIR.KI NUN *na-a-du*
2) *re-é-a-am za-ni-nu šá a-na* $ṭe_4$*-em* DINGIR.MEŠ *pu-tuq-qu*
3) *e-em-qá mu-ut-né-en-nu-ú mu-uš-te-né-eʾ-ú aš-ra-a-tì* DINGIR.MEŠ GAL.MEŠ
4) *eṭ-lu šu-us-su-mu bi-nu-ut* ABGAL DINGIR.MEŠ ^{d}AMAR.UTU
5) *na-ab-ni-it* ${}^{d}E_4$.RU_6 *ba-na-a-ta gi-mir ma-al-ku*
6) *i-ti-it* ^{d}MU.Ú.A.TI *a-pil é-sag-íl sa-niq mit-ḫur-tú*
7) *bi-nu-tu* ^{d}*nin-ši-kù mu-du-ú ba-nu-ú ka-la-ma*
8) *ni-bi-it* ^{d}ŠEŠ.KI-*ri be-lu a-gi-i mu-kal-li-im ṣa-ad-du*
9) *ša* u_4*-mi-šam-ma iš-te-né-eʾ-ú pu-luḫ-*tu_4 DINGIR.MEŠ GAL.MEŠ
10) *a-na zi-in-na-a-ti é-sag-íl ù é-zi-da*
11) *ba-ša-a uz-na-a-šu*
12) DUMU ^{md}*na-bi-um-ba-lat-su-iq-bi* NUN *e-em-qá a-na-ku*

i 1–12) Nabonidus, king of Babylon, attentive prince, the shepherd who provides, the one who is constantly attentive to the will of the gods, the wise (and) pious one, the one who constantly seeks out the shrines of the great gods, most befitting warrior, creation of the sage of the gods — the god Marduk — product of the goddess Erua — creator of all rulers — selected by the god Nabû — the heir of Esagil who controls (cosmic) harmony — creation of the god Ninšiku — the (all-)knowing creator of everything — chosen by the god Nannāru — the lord of the crown who makes astrological signs known — the one who strives every day (to show) devotion to the great gods (and) whose mind is focused on provisioning Esagil and Ezida, son of Nabû-balāssu-iqbi, wise prince, am I.

13) URU KÁ.DINGIR.RA.KI *a-na dam-qa-a-ti aš-te-né-eʾ-e*
14) *a-na é-sag-íl* É.GAL DINGIR.MEŠ GAL.MEŠ *šu-tú-ra-ku* IGI.SÁ-*e*
15) *a-na é-zi-da šá-ad ba-la-ṭu mim-ma šum-šu du-uš-šá-ku*
16) *šá é-mes-lam* É *qar-ra-du* DINGIR.MEŠ *ṭú-uḫ-ḫu-da-ak ḫi-iṣ-bi*

i 13–16) I constantly seek out the city of Babylon for good deeds. I increase gifts to Esagil, the palace of the great gods; I abundantly supply everything to Ezida, the mountain of life; (and) I lavishly provide abundance to Emeslam, the temple of the hero of the gods.

17) *ì-nu-šu im-gur-*^{d}EN.LÍL BÀD KÁ.DINGIR.RA.KI
18) *iš-da-a-šu i-nu-šu-ma i-qu-pu i-ga-ru-šu*
19) *re-e-ši-šu it-ru-ur-ma né-mé-et-ta la i-ši*

i 17–19) At that time, (with regard to) Imgur-Enlil, the wall of Babylon, its foundations had become shaky, its walls had buckled, its superstructure was tottering,

---

i 6 *i-ti-it* "selected by": The expected form is *itût*, not *itīt*. For other references to the vowel change of *u* to *i* in the inscriptions of Nabonidus, see Schaudig, Inschriften Nabonids p. 129. *sa-niq mit-ḫur-tú* "who controls (cosmic) harmony": Ex. 1 (collation from the photograph on CDLI) clearly has *sa-niq*, not ÍL (as copied in Legrain, PBS 15 pl. 33 no. 80). It is unclear if ex. 2 (Al-Rawi, ARRIM 9 [1991] pp. 5–8 and fig. 4) has ÍL or *sa-niq* since there is a discrepancy between F.N.H. Al-Rawi's copy and transliteration; the copy, which has ÍL, is tentatively assumed here to be wrong.

i 18 *iš-da-a-šu i-nu-šu-ma i-qu-pu i-ga-ru-šu* "its foundations had become shaky, its walls had buckled": Ex. 2 has DAL.BA.AN.NA KÁ.GAL ^{d}AMAR.UTU *ù* KÁ.GAL ^{d}*za-*ba_4*-*ba_4 "between the Gate of the god Marduk and the Gate of the god Zababa." Based on this variant, H. Schaudig (Inschriften Nabonids p. 76 §I.7.d) thinks that this might refer to an earlier phase of the restoration of Babylon's wall, which was carried out only between the Marduk and Zababa Gates. Ex. 3 has [DAL.BA.AN.NA KÁ.GAL ^{d}AMAR.UTU] ⸢*ù*⸣ KÁ.GAL ^{d}*za-*ba_4*-*ba_4 / [*iš-da-a-šu i-nu-šu-ma*] ⸢*i*⸣*-qu-up-pu i-ga-ru-šu* "[between the Gate of the god Marduk] and the Gate of the god Zababa, its foundations had become shaky, its walls had buckled" and, thus, is likely an intermediary version of the text.

and it had no support.

20) BÀD *šu-a-ti* <*ana*> *du-un-nu-nim-ma né-mé-et-ta šu-úr-ši-i*
21) *i-ga-ru-šu qu-up-pu-tim ad-ke-e-ma*
22) BÀD.*im-gur*-^{d}EN.LÍL BÀD KÁ.DINGIR.RA.KI *ku-du-ur-ru* UŠ.20.TA.A
23) *pu-lu-uk-ku da-ru-ú ú-ṣur-tì ki-na-a-ta*
24) *mi-ṣi-ir šu-úr-šu-du ki-sur-ra-a šu-un-du-lu*
25) *tu-uk-šu da-núm e-di-il pa-ni a-a-bi*

Col. ii

1) *ma-ḫa-za re-eš-tu-ú tuk-la-tu*$_{4}$ *ba-ú-la-a-ti i-ši-id-su*
2) *ú-da-an-ni-in ki-ma kin-né-e ú-pat-tin-ma*
3) *ša-da-ni-iš ú-zaq-qí-ir mé-la-a-šu*
4) *úḫu-mi-iš ú-šar-ši-id-su** *a-na tab-ra-a-tú aš-ták-kan-šu*

i 20–ii 4) <In order to> strengthen that wall and give (it) support, I removed the buckled sections of its wall (lit. "its buckled walls"). (As for) Imgur-Enlil, the wall of Babylon, the boundary (with a length) of 20 UŠ (7,200 m), the eternal boundary marker, the plan of stability, the firmly-founded border, the wide-stretching ground plan, the strong shield that bolts (Babylon) before enemies, the foremost cult center on which people rely, I strengthened its foundation(s), made (them) firm like mountains, and (then) I raised its high parts up like mountain(s), (and) made it as secure as a great mountain. I established it as an object of wonder.

5) *ši-ṭi-ir šu-mi šá* LUGAL *maḫ-ri šá qé-reb-šu ap-pal-su*
6) *it-ti ši-ṭi-ir šu-mi-ia qer-ba-šu ú-ki-in a-na ṣa-a-tú*

ii 5–6) (As for) an inscription bearing the name of a former king that I had discovered inside (it), I firmly placed (it) inside it (Imgur-Enlil) forever with an inscription bearing my name.

7) ^{d}EN.LÍL DINGIR.MEŠ ^{d}AMAR.UTU *šá qí-bit-su ki-na-at*
8) *be-lu ap-kal-lu*$_{4}$ DINGIR.MEŠ *šu-úr-bu-ú qu-ra-du*
9) *ši-ip-ri šu-a-ti ḫa-di-iš nap-lis-ma*
10) *mi-im-mu-ú e-te-ep-pu-šu li-bur-ma*
11) *li-ku-un ma-ḫa-ar-ka*

ii 7–11) O Enlil of the gods, Marduk, whose command is reliable, (divine) lord, sage of the gods, supreme hero, look with pleasure upon this work (of mine) so that whatever I have built stays in good repair and endures in your presence.

12) *šu-ri-ik* UD.MEŠ *ba-la-ṭi-ia lu-uš-ba-a lit-tu-tu*
13) *a-a ar-šá-a šá-ni-na šu-um-qí-it a-a-bi-ia*
14) *lu-pu-uš re-é-ú-si-na šá ka-li-iš kib-ra-a-ti*
15) *nap-ḫar ṣal-mat* SAG.DU *gi-mir te-né-še-e-ti*
16) *lu-be-el a-na da-rí-a-ti lu-re-ʾe-e na-gab-šu-un*

ii 12–16) Prolong the days of my life so that I may be sated with old age. May I have no rival. Cut down my enemies so that I may exercise the shepherdship of all (four) quarters (of the world and) rule over the entirety of the black-headed (people), all humankind; may I shepherd all of them for eternity.

17) LUGAL.MEŠ *a-ši-ib pa-rak-ku*
18) *ša iš**-*ta**-*na-at-tu-ú mé-e nag-bi*
19) *e-li-šu-nu lu-ki-in* GIŠ.NÍG.GIDRU *lu-pu-uš*

ii 17–19) (As for) the kings who sit on (royal) dais(es), *wherever* they drink spring water, may I impose (my) scepter upon them (and) exercise dominion over them.

---

i 22–ii 4 Compare the description of Nabopolassar's renovation of Babylon's inner wall Imgur-Enlil, which is known from A Babylon 11 ii 6–iii 10 (Da Riva, SANER 3 pp. 94–95), especially ii 8–12, which have *im-gur*-^{d}EN.LÍL BÀD *ra-ba-a šá ba-bi-lim*.KI ⸢BULUG⸣ *reš-ta-a šá iš-tu ṣa-a-tim šu-pu-ú ki-sur-ra-a šu-úr-šu-du ša la-bar du-úr* UD.MEŠ *ki-in-na-a zaq-ru šá šit-nu-nu šá-ma-mi tuk-šu dan-nu e-di-il pi-i* KUR *a-a-bi* "Imgur-Enlil — the great wall of Babylon, the original boundary marker which has been manifest since the distant past, the firmly-founded ground plan that has endured for all eternity, the high mountain that rivals the heavens, the strong shield that bolts the entrance to the land of enemies."

i 22 UŠ.20.TA.A "20 UŠ (7,200 m)": UŠ is a unit measuring length, but its precise linguistic interpretation is uncertain since the sections of the lexical series Ea (Tablet VI) and Aa dealing with UŠ are missing. According to M. Powell (RLA 7/5–6 [1989] pp. 459 and 465–467 § I.2k), one UŠ equals 6 ropes, 12 *ṣuppu*, 60 *nindan*-rods, 120 reeds, and 720 cubits, that is, approximately 360 m. According to this inscription of Nabonidus, Imgur-Enlil measured UŠ.20.TA.A "20 UŠ," which would be approximately 7,200 m (= 360 m × 20). A. George (BTT pp. 135–136) has demonstrated that the actual length of Imgur-Enlil in the Neo-Babylonian period was 8,015 m.

i 23 *ki-na-a-ta* "stability": The reading of the first sign as KI, rather than TE, is confirmed from collation of ex. 1 (CBS 16108); note that Al-Rawi's copy of ex. 2 (A Babylon 10) also clearly has KI. The confusion in scholarly literature stems from Legrain's copy of CBS 16108 in PBS 15 (pl. 33 no. 80), where the sign could be read as either TE or KI; this misreading is followed by the CAD (see CAD U p. 291b), despite the correct reading in Schaudig, Inschriften Nabonids (p. 347).

i 25 *tu-uk-šu da-núm e-di-il pa-ni a-a-bi* "the strong shield that bolts (Babylon) before enemies": Compare A Babylon 11 ii 12 (Da Riva, SANER 3 pp. 94–95), which has *tuk-šu dan-nu e-di-il pi-i* KUR *a-a-bi* "the strong shield that bolts the entrance to the land of enemies."

ii 5–6 LUGAL *maḫ-ri* "a former king": It is certain that the unnamed former king is none other than Nabopolassar. The identification is based on the fact that ex. 2 (A Babylon 10) was discovered in a clay foundation box together with two cylinders of Nabopolassar: A Babylon 11 and A Babylon 12. For details on the discovery, see Abdul-Razak, Sumer 35 (1979) p. 116 and Al-Rawi, Iraq 47 (1985) p. 8; and, for editions of the two Nabopolassar inscriptions, see Da Riva, SANER 3 pp. 50–54 (ex. 2) and 93–104.

ii 18 *ša iš**-*ta**-*na-at-tu-ú mé-e nag-bi* "*wherever* they drink spring water": Literally "who drink spring water." The translation provided here tentatively follows H. Schaudig (Inschriften Nabonids p. 350 "wo immer sie ihr Wasser trinken mögen"). This passage seems to imply that (remote) minor rulers, men who drank from (distant) fresh water springs, were subordinate to Nabonidus.

be-lu-su-un
20) *be-lu pa-li-iḫ-ka i-lab-bi-ir a-na da-rí-a-ti*
21) *uṣ-ṣa-ab ba-la-ṭu*
22) *i-ba-ʾi-il šu-um-šu*
23) *a-na-ku lu-ú* LUGAL *za-nin-ku*
24) *mu-uš-te-ʾu-ú*
25) *aš-ri-ka a-na da-rí-a-ti*

ii 20–22) The lord who reveres you will live for eternity (and) he will increase (his) vigor; his name will be important.

ii 23–25) May I be the king who provides for you (and) the one who constantly seeks out your place (of worship) for eternity.

2

Four barrel-shaped clay cylinders are inscribed with an inscription recording Nabonidus' rebuilding of Emašdari ("House of Animal Offerings"), the temple of the goddess Ištar of Agade at Babylon; three of the cylinders were found in situ, in the brick structure of the temple. The text is written in two columns and the script of two of the exemplars (exs. 1–2) is archaizing Neo-Babylonian, while the script of the two other exemplars (exs. 3–4) is contemporary Neo-Babylonian. The text includes (1) a hymnic list of Ištar's titles and epithets that emphasize her warlike aspects; (2) a passage in which Nabonidus portrays himself as a pious ruler who humbly and submissively follows the will of his divine patrons and who abundantly provides for their temples and shrines; (3) a building report recording the renovation of the Emašdari temple, which Nabonidus claims was in such bad repair that alkali had eroded its brickwork and that little remained standing; and (4) a prayer to the goddess Ištar, asking for her blessing and for her to speak well of Nabonidus in the presence of Marduk. This text is referred to as "Nabonidus Cylinder II, 3," "[Nabonidus] Inscription B," and the "Emašdari Cylinder" in previous editions and studies.

Figure 7. VA Bab 2971 (Nabonidus no. 2 ex. 1), a two-column clay cylinder with an inscription recording the rebuilding of Emašdari, temple of the goddess Ištar of Agade at Babylon. © Staatliche Museen zu Berlin – Vorderasiatisches Museum. Photo: Olaf M. Teßmer.

Figure 8. Annotated plan of the Merkes showing the ruins of Emašdari and the find spot of VA Bab 2971 (Nabonidus no. 2 ex. 1). Adapted from Koldewey, WEB[5] fig. 256.

CATALOGUE

Ex.	Museum Number	Excavation Number	Photograph Number	Provenance	Lines Preserved	cpn
1	VA Bab 2971	BE 43242	Bab ph 2413, 2478a–f	Babylon, Merkes, Emašdari, in the northern enclosure wall, +7.8 m	i 1–ii 31	c
2	IM 95927 (formerly A Babylon 201)	79-B-91	—	Babylon, Merkes, Emašdari	i 1–ii 18, 20–31	c
3	IM 95335	79-B-2:35	—	As ex. 1	i 1–13, 16–ii 31	n
4	IM 95926	79-B-22	—	As ex. 2	i 1–13, 16–ii 31	c

COMMENTARY

All of the extant exemplars were excavated at Babylon, in the Emašdari temple. This inscription of Nabonidus is unusual as it is the only known text of this Neo-Babylonian king with copies written in both archaizing Neo-Babylonian (exs. 1–2) and contemporary Neo-Babylonian (exs. 3–4) script; most are written in one or the other only. The master text and lineation follow ex. 1. A score is presented on Oracc and the minor (orthographic) variants are given in the critical apparatus at the back of the book. The major variants between the archaizing Neo-Babylonian and the Neo-Babylonian copies of the inscription are provided in the on-page notes.

The excavation number of ex. 2 is 79-B-91, despite the fact that "97-B-22" is erroneously written on it. The object is now housed in the Iraq Museum (Baghdad) and bears the collection number IM 95927. The cylinder was formerly in the Nebuchadnezzar Museum (Babylon), where it had it been assigned the museum number A Babylon 201.

BIBLIOGRAPHY

1911 Koldewey, MDOG 47 pp. 22–23 (ex. 1, study)
1911 Reuther, MDOG 47 pp. 23–24 (ex. 1, study)
1925 S. Smith, RA 22 pp. 57–70 (ex. 1, copy, edition)
1926 Reuther, Merkes pp. 135–139 and pl. 42 (ex. 1, photo, edition [Ehelolf], study)
1952–53 Weidner, AfO 16 p. 71 (study)
1953 von Soden, SAHG p. 290 no. 36 (ii 16–31, translation)
1965 Tadmor, Studies Landsberger p. 360 no. 20 (study)
1968 Ellis, Foundation Deposits p. 112 (ex. 1, study)
1973 Berger, NbK p. 360 Nbn. Zyl. II, 3 (study)
1979 Nasir, Sumer 35 pp. 66–81 and fig. 3 (ex. 3, photo; exs. 2–3, study)
1985 Al-Rawi, Sumer 41 pp. 23–24, 41 and 44 (exs. 2–3, photo, study)
1985 Al-Suba'ai, Sumer 41 p. 63 (ex. 4, study)
1989 Beaulieu, Nabonidus p. 39 Inscription B (study)
1990 Koldewey, WEB[5] pp. 289–290 (study)
1991 Al-Rawi, ARRIM 9 pp. 7 and 9–10 with fig. 5a–b and pl. 2 (ex. 2, photo; ex. 3, copy, transliteration; exs. 2–3, study)
1999 Seipel and Wieczorek, Von Babylon bis Jerusalem 2 pp. 100 and 102–103 (ex. 1, photo, translation, study)
2001 Schaudig, Inschriften Nabonids pp. 353–358 no. 2.3[a] (edition)
2019 Radner, Short History of Babylon p. 116 fig. 7.4 and pp. 118–116 (ex. 2, photo; translation)

TEXT

Col. i

1) *a-na* ^{d}*iš-tar šu-úr-bu-tim*
2) *ru-um-tì ì-lí qá-ri-it-tim*
3) ^{d}IN.NIN *i-la-at ta-am-ḫa-ru*
4) *e-pí-ša-at tu-qu-un-tim*
5) *na-mi-ir-ti be-le-et da-ad-mi*
6) *ša-qu-tì i-gi$_4$-gi$_4$*
7) *ru-ba-a-tì* ^{d}*a-nun-na-ki*
8) *na-ša-a-at pu-lu-úḫ-tim*
9) *be-el-tim ša mé-lam-mu-šu*
10) *ša-mu-ù ka-at-mu*
11) *nam-ri-ir-ru-šu* KI-*tim* DAGAL-*tim sa-aḫ-pu*
12) ^{d}INANNA *a-kà-dè*.KI *be-let ta-ḫa-za*
13) *ša-ki-na-at ṣu-la-a-ti*
14) *a-ši-ba-at é-máš-da-ri*
15) *ša qé-re-eb* KÁ.DINGIR.RA.KI GAŠAN-*ia*

i 1–15) For the goddess Ištar, supreme (lady), beloved of the gods, most valiant, the goddess Innin(ni), goddess of battle, the one who wages war, radiant lady of (all of the) settlements, most exalted of the Igīgū gods, princess of the Anunnakū gods, bearer of fear, lady whose brilliance covers the heavens (and whose) awe-inspiring radiance overwhelms the wide earth, the goddess Ištar of Agade, the lady of battle who incites fighting, who dwells in Emašdari — which is inside Babylon — my lady:

16) ^{d}AG-*na-'i-id* LUGAL TIN.TIR.KI
17) *ti-ri-iṣ qá-ti* ^{d}*tu-tu*
18) *à-aš-ru ka-an-šu pa-li-iḫ* DINGIR GAL.GAL
19) *re-é-a-am za-ni-nu-um*
20) *ša a-na ṭè-mi* DINGIR.MEŠ *pu-tuq-qú*
21) GÌR.NÍTA *ša-aḫ-ṭa mur-te-ed-du-ú ú-si iš-tar*
22) *mu-ṭa-aḫ-ḫi-id sa-at-tu-uk-ku*
23) *mu-ki-in ni-id-bé-e*
24) *ša ud-da-kam iš-te-né-e'-ú*
25) *du-mu-uq ma-ḫa-zi* DINGIR.MEŠ

i 16–32) Nabonidus, king of Babylon, protégé of the god Tutu, the humble (and) submissive one who reveres the great gods, the shepherd who provides, the one who is attentive to the will of the gods, the respectful governor who constantly follows the way(s) of the goddess Ištar, the one who makes *sattukku*-offering(s) abundant (and) (re)confirms *nindabû*-offerings, (the one) who strives all day long to improve the cult centers of the gods, (the one who) in Esagil — the palace of the gods — makes splendid gifts enter

---

i 11b–12a Exs. 3 and 4, the copies of this inscription written in contemporary Neo-Babylonian script, add *ka-ši-da-at a-a-bi mu-ḫal-li-qá-at za-ma-nu* "the one who conquers enem(ies) (and) destroys adversar(ies)" between *nam-ri-ir-ru-šu er-ṣe-tim ra-pa-aš-tim sa-aḫ-pu* "whose awe-inspiring radiance overwhelms the wide earth" and ^{d}INANNA *a-kà-dè*.KI "the goddess Ištar of Agade." The exemplars of this text written in archaizing Neo-Babylonian script (exs. 1–2) do not include this epithet of Ištar.

i 14–15 *a-ši-ba-at é-máš-da-ri ša qé-re-eb* KÁ.DINGIR.RA.KI GAŠAN-*ia* "who dwells in Emašdari — which is inside Babylon — my lady": These two lines are omitted in ex. 3.

i 17 *ti-ri-iṣ qá-ti* ^{d}*tu-tu* "protégé of the god Tutu": Literally "the one to whom the god Tutu stretches out his hand." As P.-A. Beaulieu (Representations of Political Power p. 159) points out, Tutu is a name that is used for both Marduk and Nabû and, thus, unclear as to whom the mention of Tutu refers in this inscription. Moreover, Beaulieu notes that only Nabopolassar and Nabonidus use the epithet *tiriṣ qātī* DN in their inscriptions; for example, Nabonidus refers to himself as [*ti*]*-ri-iṣ* ŠU.II $^{d⸢}$*nisaba*⸣ "[pr]otégé of the goddess Nisaba" in text no. 44 obv. 1.

i 23 *mu-ki-in ni-id-bé-e* "the one who (re)confirms *nindabû*-offerings": Exs. 3 and 4, the copies of this inscription written in contemporary Neo-Babylonian script, have *mu-šar-ri-iḫ ni-id-bé-e* "the one who makes *nindabû*-offerings splendid."

26) *i-na é-sag-íl* É.GAL DINGIR.DINGIR
27) *i-gi-sa-a šu-ur-ru-ḫu*
28) *ú-še-er-re-bu qé-re-eb-šu*
29) *a-na eš-re-e-ti* DINGIR.DINGIR *ka-li-ši-na*
30) *sa-ad-ru šu-ul-ma-nu*
31) DUMU ^{md}AG-*ba-lat-su-iq-bi*
32) *ru-bu-ù e-em-qa a-na-ku*

inside it, (and who ensures that) present(s) are regularly provided to all of the sanctuaries of the gods, son of Nabû-balāssu-iqbi, wise prince, am I.

33) *ì-nu-šu é-máš-da-ri* É ^{d}INANNA *a-kà-dè*.KI
34) *ša uš-šu-šu in-na-mu-ú*
Col. ii
1) *i-mu-ú ka-ar-mi-iš*
2) *li-ib-na-as-su id-ra-num*
3) *iq-mu-ú di-ta-al-li-iš*
4) *a-šar-šu šu-ud-du-ú*
5) *la ba-aš-mu sa-gu-šu*
6) *na-du-ú si-ma-ak-ki-šu*
7) *na-pa-ar-ku-ú qú-ut-re-nu*
8) *e-pe-eš* É *ša-a-tim lìb-bi i-ta-mi-ma*
9) *ka-ba-at-tì ḫa-áš-ḫa-tuš*

i 33–ii 9) At that time, (with regard to) Emašdari, the temple of the goddess Ištar of Agade, whose foundation(s) had fallen to pieces (and) turned into ruins, whose brickwork alkali burned to ashes, whose site remained desolate, whose shrine was not standing (lit. "built"), whose cella was in ruins, (and where) incense(-offerings) had ceased, my heart pondered (re)building this temple and my mind desired (to carry) it (out).

10) *a-šar* É *šu-a-tim aš-te-e'-e-ma*
11) *a-ḫi-iṭ te-em-mé-en-šu*
12) *i-ši-id-su ab-re-e-ma*
13) *ú-ki-in li-ib-na-as-su*
14) *é-máš-da-ri in qé-reb* KÁ.DINGIR.RA.KI
15) *e-eš-ši-iš e-pú-uš*

ii 10–15) I sought out the (original) site of this temple, examined its foundation platform, (and) checked its foundation(s), and (thereby) secured its brickwork. I built Emašdari anew inside Babylon.

16) *a-na šu-a-tim* ^{d}INANNA *a-kà-dè*.KI
17) *i-la-at ta-am-ḫa-ru*
18) É *ša-a-tim*
19) *šu-ba-at na-ra-mi-ki*
20) *ḫa-di*-iš na-ap-li-si-ma*
21) *qí-bi-i ba-la-ṭa*$_4$
22) *ša úr-ru-ku u*$_4$*-mi-ia*
23) *šu-um-ú-da*$_4$ *ša-na-ti-ia*
24) *ma-ḫa-ar* ^{d}AMAR.UTU LUGAL DINGIR.DINGIR
25) *at-mi-i ud-da-kam*

ii 16–25) On account of this, O Ištar of Agade, goddess of battle, look with pleasure upon this temple, your beloved residence, and (then) proclaim good health for me. In the presence of the god Marduk, king of the gods, speak all day long about the prolongation of my days (and) the increasing of my years.

26) *a-ša-ar qá-ab-lum*
27) *ù ta-ḫa-zi-im*
28) *i-da-a-a al-ki*
29) *lu-na-ar a-a-bi-ia*
30) *lu-ša-am-qí-it*
31) *na-ki-ri-ia*

ii 26–31) March at my side (in) the place of battle and war so that I can kill my foes (and) cut down my enemies.

---

i 26 The copies of the inscription written in contemporary Neo-Babylonian script (exs. 3–4) add the epithet "surpassing in provisioning" after *in é-sag-íl* É.GAL DINGIR.DINGIR "in Esagil, the palace of the gods." Ex. 3 adds *šu-tu-ru zi-in-na-a-tim* in an additional line while, ex. 4 adds *šu-tu-ru zi-in-na-a-ti* in the same line after *i-na é-sag-íl* É.GAL *ì-lí*.

i 33 Exs. 2–4 add *ša qé-er-bi* KÁ.DINGIR.MEŠ.KI, "which (is situated) in Babylon" after É ^{d}INANNA *a-kà-dè*.KI, "the temple of the goddess Ištar of Agade." Only the one archaizing Neo-Babylonian ex. 1 does not include this statement about the location of Emašdari. As H. Schaudig (Inschriften Nabonids p. 355) has already pointed out, one expects the mention of the temple's location in this spot.

ii 2–3 *li-ib-na-as-su id-ra-num iq-mu-ú di-ta-al-li-iš* "whose brickwork alkali burned to ashes": These two lines are omitted in ex. 4.

ii 15 After *e-eš-ši-iš e-pú-uš* "I built anew," exs. 3 and 4, the contemporary Neo-Babylonian exemplars, add *uš-ši-šu uš-te-ši-ir ú-ki-in te-em-mé-en-šu* "I realigned its foundation(s and) thereby secured its (new) foundation(s)."

ii 17 *i-la-at ta-am-ḫa-ru* "goddess of battle": Exs. 2-4 have *i-la-at ta-am-ḫa-ri*.

ii 19 *šu-ba-at na-ra-mi-ki* "your beloved residence": Ex. 2 omits this line.

ii 20 *ḫa-di*-iš* "with pleasure": All four exemplars write *ḫa*-MI-*iš*, which may suggest that the word is an otherwise unattested adverb *hamiš* (meaning "trusting") rather than the expected *hadîš* "with pleasure"; for details, see Schaudig, Inschriften Nabonids p. 356.

ii 26 *qá-ab-lum* "battle": Ex. 3 has *qá-ab-li*.

3

This long, Akkadian inscription written in archaizing Neo-Babylonian script is known from a broken basalt stele that was discovered at Babylon before 1896; it has been suggested (Schaudig, Inschriften Nabonids p. 514) that the monument might have originally stood beside the Processional Street, before the Ištar Gate. The text, which is inscribed in eleven columns on its flat front side and its rounded reverse face, includes: (1) a detailed historical prologue of events that took place from Sennacherib' destruction of Babylon and abduction of the god Marduk in 689 to the deposing of Lâbâši-Marduk in 556; (2) an account of Nabonidus' elevation to kingship; (3) a passage recording several dreams and visions that Nabonidus had after becoming king and his subsequent visits to sanctuaries of the gods Nabû and Marduk seeking their approval of him being king; (4) an account of the adornment and support of temples in Babylon, which included giving sumptuous gifts to the gods Marduk, Nabû, and Nergal during an *akītu*-festival and dedicating 2,850 prisoners from the land Ḫumê (Cilicia) to Nabû and Nergal; (5) reports about Nabonidus visiting important temples in Keš, Larsa, Ur, and Uruk; (6) a passage in which Marduk commissions Nabonidus to rebuild Eḫulḫul ("House which Gives Joy"), the temple of the moon-god Sîn at Ḫarrān, a venerated temple that had been destroyed fifty-four years earlier; (7) a statement reporting that a jasper seal inscribed by Assyria's last great king Ashurbanipal was restored to its rightful place in Esagil ("House whose Head Is High") in Babylon; and (8) quotations of selected haruspical omens. As for the historical prologue, the section detailing events before Nabonidus took power from Neriglissar's son and successor Lâbâši-Marduk records the murder of Sennacherib by one of his sons (likely Urdu-Mullissu), the fall of Assyria, and the restoration of temples in Uruk and Sippar-Anunītu by Nebuchadnezzar II and Neriglissar. Because the stele is not dated, there is no scholarly consensus on its date of composition; for example, P.-A. Beaulieu (Nabonidus pp. 20–22 and 42) suggests that it was written in the middle of Nabonidus' first regnal year (555), while H. Schaudig (Inschriften Nabonids p. 515) proposes that it was written after his thirteenth year (543) as king (see below). In scholarly literature, the text is referred to as "Nabonid Stele Fragment XI", "[Nabonidus] Inscription 1," and the "Babylon Stele."

CATALOGUE

Museum Number	Excavation Number	Provenance	cpn
EŞ 1327	—	Babylon, Kasr, North Palace, northeast corner	p

COMMENTARY

This inscription is one of the few texts of Nabonidus for which P.-A. Beaulieu (Nabonidus pp. 20–22 and 42) and H. Schaudig (Inschriften Nabonids p. 515) disagree about the date of composition. The former suggests that the text on the Babylon Stele was composed in the middle of the king's first regnal year (555), while the latter thinks that this text was written much later, sometime after Nabonidus' thirteenth year (543), when he returned from his sojourn in Arabia and undertook construction on Eḫulḫul, the temple of Sîn at Ḫarrān. Because the inscription is not fully preserved, it is extremely difficult to propose a convincing and universally-accepted date of composition. The lengthy description of events prior to Nabonidus ascending the throne (i 1′–iv 42′) and of his accession and first regnal years (v 1′–x 51) likely suggest that the text was composed near the beginning of Nabonidus' seventeen-year reign, as early as the middle of his first regnal year (555), as Beaulieu has already proposed. An early date of composition might be confirmed by the facts that only the king's intent to rebuild the temple of the moon-god is mentioned, with no reference at all to the building program itself, and that the Persian king Cyrus II's defeat of the Median ruler Astyages (Ištumegu) and his driving off the Ummān-manda hordes near Ḫarrān in Nabonidus' third year are not recorded, as they are in several later inscriptions commemorating the rebuilding of Eḫulḫul; compare text nos. 28 (Eḫulḫul Cylinder) and 46 (Ḫarrān Cylinder). Therefore, an early date of composition for this inscription, sometime between mid-555 and early 553, is preferred here. Of course, this cannot be proven since the text is not fully preserved.

It is unclear if the Babylon Stele was a standalone monument, like most Assyrian and Babylonian steles, or if it was part of a pair of monuments on which a complete text was written. Since the upper portions of all eleven columns are missing, it is impossible to precisely determine what principal achievement(s) of the king the inscription commemorated, especially as key passages in cols. i and xi are completely missing. Because the final lines of the stele (xi 1′–42′) contain a long list of favorable omens that the king's diviners had observed in an extispicy, it seems unlikely that these lines represent the actual end of the inscription, as one would expect the inscription to have ended in a more traditional fashion with the king petitioning his tutelary deities to grant him a long and prosperous reign. Therefore, it seems likely that the inscription continued on a second stele, which is no longer extant, unless some of the fragments of text nos. 4 or 1003 are parts of that now-missing monument. Evidence in support of this proposal comes from a comparison of the structure and contents of text no. 25 (Tiara Cylinder), which also includes lists of auspicious omens related to haruspical queries of Nabonidus to the lords of divination Šamaš and Adad. The fact that one inscription of Esarhaddon appears to have been written on a pair of steles erected in Babylon, at least according to the subscript of an archival copy of the "stele on the left, the first excerpt" (Leichty, RINAP 4 p. 109 Esarhaddon 48 lines 109–110); and that inscriptions of Sargon II and Sennacherib were often written on pairs of human-headed bull colossi (respectively Frame, RINAP 2 Sargon II 9; and Grayson and Novotny, RINAP 3/1 pp. 38–97 Sennacherib 40–43, 46, and probably 49–50) further supports this proposal.

In text no. 25 (Tiara Cylinder), the lists of omens are included between statements about the king requesting answers and him carrying out the action for which Šamaš and Adad had placed a "firm 'yes'" in his extispicies. That text, like all of this king's other cylinder inscriptions, ends with Nabonidus addressing the god(s) to act on his behalf, and not with a list of favorable omens that finally permitted Nabonidus to fashion the crown he wished to make for the sun-god at Sippar. The inscription written on the Babylon Stele and its partner monument, assuming the text was indeed written on two steles and not just one, therefore, might have included such list(s) halfway through its narrative, at the point where the inscribed surface of one monument ended and that of the second began. One possible occasion for the divination in question might have been the appointment of Nabonidus' daughter as the *ēntu*-priestess of Sîn at Ur. It is well-known from other sources (for example, text no. 34 [En-nigaldi-Nanna Cylinder]) that Nabonidus appointed his daughter for this position during his second regnal year (554) and that he had multiple extispicies performed regarding that appointment. It is possible that xi 1′–42′ lists the favorable omens observed by his diviners in the extispicy confirming Sîn's request for a new priestess at Ur or those endorsing his nomination of En-nigaldi-Nanna as the new *ēntu*. Alternatively, just like text no. 25 (Tiara Cylinder), these lines could record the gods' approval of Nabonidus' desire to make a crown with *zarinnu* (meaning uncertain) for Šamaš at Sippar, a deed of the king generally thought to have also taken place in 554. Should the Babylon Stele be the first of a pair of monuments and should the litany of omens inscribed on the final column of that stele (xi 1′–42′) be associated with En-nigaldi-Nanna's appointment as *ēntu*-priestess or Nabonidus' fashioning of a crown for Šamaš, then the earliest possible date of composition for the inscription would be 554, Nabonidus' second regnal year. Given the current state of preservation of the known stele fragments from Babylon, the suggestions tentatively given here cannot be proven, at least not until further pieces of the monument(s) are identified. Despite the meagerness of the Babylonian evidence for inscriptions being written across pairs of monuments, a two-stele, rather than a single-stele, inscription is preferred here.

The inscription was collated from several legible, high-resolution images found on the internet taken by Osama Shukir Muhammed Amin in the Eşki Şark Eserleri Müzesi (Istanbul), in September 2013. The present edition has greatly benefitted from access to these images.

BIBLIOGRAPHY

1896 Messerschmidt, MVAG 1/1 pp. 1–70 and 73–83 (copy, edition)
1896 Winckler, MVAG 1/1 pp. 71–72 (study)
1896 Scheil, RT 18 pp. 15–29 and pls. I–III (photo, edition)
1899 Ball, Light pp. 212–216 (photo, study)
1904 Harper, Literature pp. 158–163 (translation)
1905 Boissier, Choix 1 pp. 52–56 (xi, copy, edition)
1909 Langdon, ZA 23 pp. 217–220 (iii 11′–39′, translation, study)
1912 Jastrow, Religion 2 pp. 265–271 (xi 1′–42′, translation, study)
1912 Langdon, NBK pp. 53–57 and 270–289 Nbd. no. 8 (edition)
1912 Meissner, DLZ 33 col. 1697 (vii 32′, viii 10′, ix 16′, study)
1913 Jensen, ThLZ 38 pp. 356–357 (iii 20', vii 22′, xi 35′, study)
1913 Thureau-Dangin, RA 10 p. 95 n. 2 (ix 13′, 29′, study)
1922 Weidner, RSO 9 p. 299 (vi 31′–35′, study)
1923 Boutflower, Book of Daniel pp. 108 and 116 (v 1′–24′, translation, study)
1923 Schwenzner, Klio 18 p. 56 n. 1 (iv 37′–39′, study)
1924 S. Smith, BHT p. 49 (vi 3′–36′, translation)
1925 Lewy, MVAG 29/2 pp. 80–81 and 86 (ii 1′–ii 42′, edition)
1926 Ebeling in Gressman, ATAT^{2} p. 361 (i–ii, translation)
1926 Landsberger and Bauer, ZA 37 p. 83 n. 2 (ii 32′–41′, translation)
1927 Thureau-Dangin, RA 24 p. 203 (iii 11′–15′, edition)
1927 Unger, ABK p. 139 fig. 102 (photo)
1931 Meissner, BAW 1 pp. 52–53 (ii 39′, study)
1932 Meissner, SPAW 12 p. 254 (iv, 38′–39′, study)
1932–33 Meissner, AfO 8 pp. 224–225 (v 8′–13′, edition)
1938 Schott, ZA 44 p. 208 (vi 32′, study)
1941–44 Ungnad, AfO 14 p. 271 (ii 34′–35′, ix 32′, study)
1945–46 Nougayrol, RA 40 pp. 64, 77, 86 and 93 (xi 2′–3′, 23′–24′, 26′, 33′–34′, 37′, study)
1947 Landsberger, Studies Edhem p. 147 (study)
1949 Lewy, ArOr 17/2 pp. 42–43, 51–53 and 70 (vii 1′–22′, edition; vi 4′–36′, vii 45′–56′, translation, study)
1949 Oppenheim, JNES 8 pp. 172–173 (viii 1′–15′, translation, study)
1950 Albright, BASOR 120 p. 23 (ix 31′–41′, translation, study)
1955 Oppenheim, ANET^{2} pp. 309–311 (i 1′–x 51′, translation)
1956 Oppenheim, Dream-book p. 250 (vi 4′–36′, translation, study)
1958 von Soden, Orientalia NS 27 p. 259 (ii 29′–31′, edition)
1959 Moran, Orientalia NS 28 p. 140 III 27–28 (viii 52′–54′, study)
1960 Reiner, JNES 19 p. 24 n. 2 (vii 4′–5′, 22′, transliteration; vii 1′–37′, study)
1964 Galling, Studien pp. 4, 10 and 12 (study)
1965 Tadmor, Studies Landsberger p. 355 (x 12′–31′, transcription, study)
1966 Aro, CRRA 14 p. 115 (xi 11′–15′, 18′–21′, edition)
1971 von Soden, UF 3 pp. 255–256 (iii 11′–29′, study)
1972 Lambert, Arabian Studies 2 p. 58 (study)
1973 Berger, NbK pp. 384–386 Nbn. Stelen-Fragment XI (study)
1983 Starr, BibMes 12 pp. 129–131 (xi, edition)
1984–85 Borger, TUAT I/4 p. 407 (i, translation)
1989 Beaulieu, Nabonidus pp. 20–22, 47–50, 74, 88–89, 104–107, 110–114, 117, 145, and 227–228 Inscription 1 (ii 32′–41′, iv 14′–23′, v 1′–7′, 14′–vi 36′, vii 38′–56′, ix 11′–22′, x 1′–31′, edition; study)
1990 Koldewey, WEB^{5} pp. 167–168 (study)
1992 George, BTT pp. 414–415 (viii 31′–60′, edition; study)
1993 Beaulieu, Studies Hallo p. 45 (iii 11′–43′, translation, study)
1993 Berger, Rolle der Astronomie pp. 279–280 (vi 1′–5′, translation, study)
1993 Lee, RA 87 pp. 133–136 (ii 1′–41′, x 22′–51′, edition; study)
1994 D'Agostino, Nabonedo pp. 32–37 (iv 34′–42′, v 1′–vi 3′, edition; study)
1996 Gallagher, WZKM 86 pp. 119–126 (study)
1998 Butler, Dreams pp. 233–234 (vii 1′–15′, study)
1999 D'Agostino, ISIMU 2 pp. 75–78 (iv 34′–42′, v 1′–vi 3′, edition; study)
2000 Seidl, OBO 175 p. 99 (x 32′–51′, translation, study)
2001 Beaulieu, CRRA 45/1 pp. 32–34 (iii 11′–39′, edition; study)
2001 Schaudig, Inschriften Nabonids pp. 514–529 no. 3.3^{a} (edition)
2007 Beaulieu, Representations of Political Power pp. 141, 143, 148, 155 and 159 (vii 22′–56′, study)
2007 Ehring, Rückkehr JHWHs pp. 99–111 (i 1′–3′, ii 8′–10′, edition; x 12′–31′, translation, study)
2009 Winter, On Art in the Ancient Near East 2 pp. 468–469 (study)
2010 Fried, Studies Ellis p. 322 (iv 14′–33′, x 12′–24′, translation)
2010 Heller, Spätzeit pp. 119, 168, 172, 175–179, 190, 193, 196, 241 and 259 (iv 37′–42′, vii 22′–29′, edition; study)

TEXT

Col. i

Lacuna

1′) *[ik]-ta-pu-ud* ḪUL-*tim*
2′) ⸢*ta*⸣-*ri* UN *lìb-ba-šú*
3′) *i-ta-ma-a* ⸢*ḫi-ṭi-ti*⸣
4′) *ni-še-e ma-*[*at*-URI].⸢KI⸣

Lacuna

i 1′–19′) [(who) pl]otted evil [to t]ake away the people, his (Sennacherib's) heart thought about sin. [He did] not [have] mercy on the people of the la[nd of Akkad. He approach]ed Babylon with evil [int]ent,

5′) *ta-a-a-ru* ⸢*ul*⸣ [*ir-ši*]
6′) *le-em-*[*ni*]*-*⸢*iš*⸣
7′) *a-na* TIN.TIR.[KI *is-ni*]*-*⸢*iq*⸣
8′) *ú-na-am-mi*
9′) *eš-re-e-ti-iš*
10′) *ú-sa-aḫ-ḫi*
11′) *ú-ṣu-ra-a-ti*
12′) *pel-lu-de-e*
13′) *ú-ša-al*-pi-it*
14′) *qá-ti* NUN ^{d}AMAR.UTU
15′) *iṣ-ba-at-ma*
16′) *ú-še-ri-ib*
17′) *qé-reb bal-ti-la*.KI
18′) *ki-ma uz-zi* DINGIR*-ma*
19′) *i-te-pu-uš* KUR

laid waste to its sanctuaries, made its ground plans unrecognizable, destroyed (its) rituals, took the prince, the god Marduk, by the hand, and had (him) enter inside Baltil (Aššur). He treated the land like the wrath of a god.

20′) *ul ip-šu-ur*
21′) ⸢*ki*⸣*-mil-ta-šu*
22′) NUN ^{d}AMAR.UTU
23′) 21 MU.MEŠ
24′) *qé-reb bal-ti-la*.KI
25′) ⸢*ir*⸣*-ta-me šu-bat-su*
26′) ⸢*im*⸣*-lu-ú* UD.MEŠ
27′) *ik-šu-da a-dan-nu*
28′) *i-nu-úḫ-ma*
29′) *uz-za-šu*
30′) *šá* LUGAL DINGIR.DINGIR EN EN.ME
31′) *é-sag-íl*
32′) *ù* KÁ.DINGIR.RA.KI
33′) *iḫ-su-us*
34′) *šu-bat be-lu-ti-šú*

i 20′–34′) The prince, the god Marduk, did not assuage his divine wrath (and) for twenty-one years he took up residence inside Baltil (Aššur). The days elapsed (and) the appointed time arrived. The wrath of the king of the gods, the lord of lords, relented and he remembered Esagil and Babylon, the residence of his lordly majesty.

35′) LUGAL SU.BIR$_4$.KI
36′) *šá i-na uz-za* ^{d}AMAR.UTU
37′) *ša-al-pu-ut-tì*
38′) KUR *iš-ku-nu*
39′) DUMU *ṣi-it lìb-bi-šú*
40′) *i-na* GIŠ.TUKUL
41′) *ú-ra-as-si-ib-šú*

i 35′–41′) (As for) the king of Subartu (Assyria), who had brought about the ruination of the land through the wrath of the god Marduk, a son (that was) his own offspring, cut him down with the sword.

Col. ii
Lacuna
1′) *re-ṣu id-din-*⸢*šum*⸣
2′) *tap-pa-a ú-šar-ši-iš*
3′) LUGAL *um-man-ma-an-da*
4′) *šá ma-ḫi-ri la i-šu-u*
5′) *ú-šak-ni-iš*
6′) *qí-bi-tu-uš-šu*
7′) *ú-šá-lik re-ṣu-ut-su*
8′) ⸢*e*⸣*-li-iš u šap-liš*
9′) ⸢*im-nu*⸣ *ù šu-me-lu*
10′) ⸢*a-bu*⸣*-ba-niš is-pu-un*
11′) *ú-ter gi-mil-lu*
12′) TIN.TIR.KI
13′) *i-ri-ba tuk-te-e*

Lacuna
ii 1′–13′) He (Marduk) gave him (Nabopolassar) support (and) allowed him to find an ally. He made a king of a barbarian horde (the Medes), who had no opponents, submit to his command and made him come to his aid. Above and below, right and left, he overwhelmed (Subartu) like the Deluge. He avenged Babylon, he exacted vengeance.

14′) LUGAL *um-man-ma-an-da*
15′) *la a-di-ru*
16′) *ú-šá-al-pi-it*

ii 14′–31′) The fearless king of a barbarian horde (the Medes) destroyed the sanctuaries of the gods of the land of Subartu (Assyria), all of them. Moreover, (as

17′) *eš-re-et-su-un*
18′) *šá* DINGIR KUR SU.BIR$_4$.KI
19′) *ka-la-šu-nù*
20′) *u* URU.MEŠ *pa-aṭ* KUR-KI.URI
21′) *šá it-ti* LUGAL KUR-KI.URI
22′) *na-ak-ru-ma*
23′) *la il-li-ku*
24′) *re-ṣu-ut-sú*
25′) *ú-šá-al-pi-it-ma*
26′) *mé-e-si-šu-un*
27′) *ma-na-ma la e-zib*
28′) *ú-šaḫ-ri-ib*
29′) *ma-ḫa-zi-šu-un*
30′) *ú-ša-ti-ir*
31′) *a-bu-bi-iš*

for) the cities on the border of the land of Akkad that had become hostile towards the king of the land of Akkad and that had not come to his aid, he destroyed their cultic rites, spared no one, (and) laid waste to their cult centers even more severely than the Deluge.

32′) LUGAL TIN.TIR.KI
33′) *ši-pi-ir* ^{d}AMAR.UTU
34′) *ša ši-il-la-ti*
35′) *ik-kib-šu*
36′) *la ú-bil* ŠU.II-*sú*
37′) *a-na pel-lu-de-e*
38′) DINGIR.MEŠ *ka-la-ma*
39′) *iš-ši ma-la-a*
40′) *ma-a-a-al qaq-qar*
41′) *i-na-al*

ii 32′–41′) The king of Babylon (Nabopolassar), envoy of the god Marduk, to whom blasphemy is a taboo, did not lay his hand(s) upon any of the rituals of the gods, wore matted hair (as if in mourning), laid down on a bed on the ground,

Col. iii
Lacuna
1′) [*x*] *x* DINGIR.MEŠ-[*šú*]-*nu*
2′) [*mu-šá*]-⌜*ak*⌝-*li-il*
3′) ⌜*šu*⌝-[*luḫ*]-*ḫi-šu-un*
4′) *ša* ^{d}AMAR.UTU
5′) *a-na šu-šu-bu ma-ḫa-za*
6′) DINGIR.MEŠ *ḫar-bu-tú*
7′) *im-bu-ú ni-bit*-si*
8′) DU$_6$.MEŠ *na-du-ti*
9′) *eš-re-e-ti* DINGIR.MEŠ
10′) *iš-ku-nu qa-tu-uš-šú*

Lacuna
iii 1′–10′) ... of [the]ir deities, [the one who carries] out their puri[fication] rites to perfection, whose name the god Marduk called to (re)settle the desolate cult center(s) of the gods, (and) in whose hands he placed the abandoned mounds (that were) the sanctuaries of the gods.

11′) ^{d}INANNA* UNUG*.KI
12′) *ru-ba-a-ti ṣir-ti*
13′) *a-ši-bat at-ma-nu* KÙ.GI
14′) *ša ṣa-an-da-ti*
15′) 7 *la-ab-bu*
16′) *ša i-na* BALA-*e*
17′) ^{m}*eri-ba*-^{d}AMAR.UTU LUGAL
18′) LÚ.UNUG.KI-*a-a*
19′) *šu-luḫ-ḫi-šu*
20′) *uš-pe-el-lu*
21′) *at-ma-an-šú id-ku-ma*
22′) *ip-ṭu-ru ṣi-mi-it-tuš*
23′) *i-na uz-zi*
24′) *iš-tu qé-reb é*-an-na*
25′) *tu-ṣu-ma*
26′) *tu-ši-bu la šu-bat-su*
27′) ^{d}LAMMA *la si-mat é*-an-na*

iii 11′–29′) (As for) the goddess Ištar of Uruk, the exalted princess who resides in an inner sanctum (which is clad) in gold, who harnesses seven lions, whose purification rites the people of Uruk had overturned, whose inner sanctum they had removed, and whose yoked team they had dismantled during the reign of the king Erība-Marduk, who in anger had gone out from Eanna and who had dwelt (in a place) that was not her residence, (and) in whose shrine they had made a protective goddess who did not befit Eanna dwell —

iii 11′ UNUG*.KI "Uruk": The stele has visually similar ÈŠ×BAR.KI.

28′) *ú-še-ši-bu*
29′) *i-na si-ma-ak-ki-šú*
30′) ^{d}15 *ú-šal-lim at-man-šú*
31′) *ú-kin-šu* 7 *la-ab-ba*
32′) *si-mat i-lu-ti-šu*
33′) *iṣ-mi-id-su*
34′) ^{d}15 *la si-ma-a-tú*
35′) *iš-tu qé-reb é*-an-na*
36′) *ú-še-ṣi-ma*
37′) ^{d}IN.NIN$_9$.NA
38′) *ú-ter a-na é*-an-na*
39′) *ki-iṣ-ṣi-šu*

iii 30′–39′) he (Nebuchadnezzar II) brought the goddess Ištar (back) safely, firmly (re)established (her) in her inner sanctum, (re)harnessed for her (her) seven lions, the insignia of her divinity, drove the unbefitting goddess out of Eanna, and returned the goddess Innina (Ištar) to Eanna, her cella.

40′) ^{d}*iš-tar*
41′) *be-let* ELAM.MA.KI
42′) *ru-ba-a-tim*
43′) *a-ši-bat šu-ši*.KI

iii 40′–43′) (As for) the goddess Ištar, the lady of Elam, the princess who resides in Susa,

Col. iv
Lacuna
1′) *za-*[...]
2′) *kaš-*[*kaš* DINGIR.MEŠ]
3′) *a-šib* [...]
4′) *ša* ⸢*qé*⸣-[*reb x x*]
5′) *ša iš-tu u$_4$-mu*
6′) *ru-qu-ú-ti*
7′) *ma-am-ma-an*
8′) *la ip-pal-su-uš*
9′) *i-na* NA$_4$.GIŠ.NU$_{11}$.GAL
10′) *ša ki-ma u$_4$-mi*
11′) ⸢*it*⸣*-ta-na-an-bi-ṭu*
12′) *ù* KÙ.GI ḪUŠ.A
13′) *ú-kin šu-bat-sa*

Lacuna
iv 1′–13′) [...], the most overpo[wering one of the gods], the one who resides in [...], which is ins[ide ...], whom no one had seen since distant days — he firmly established his residence (for him) with alabaster, which is always as radiant as daylight, and reddish gold.

14′) ^{d}*a-nu-ni-tum*
15′) *a-ši-bat* ZIMBIR.KI-
16′) -^{d}*a-nu-ni-tum*
17′) *ša i-na pa-ni* LÚ.⸢KÚR⸣
18′) *šu-bat-sú a-na qé-reb*
19′) *ar-ra-ap-ḫa*.KI
20′) *ú-na-ak-ki-ru-ma*
21′) *gu-tu-um*.KI
22′) *ú-šá-al-pi-tu*
23′) *me-e-si-šu*
24′) ^{d}U.GUR-LUGAL-ÙRU
25′) *ud-di-iš-ma*
26′) *te-di-iq* DINGIR-*ú-ti*
27′) *ud-di-iq-šu*
28′) É-*su na-mi-ma*
29′) *ina qé-reb* ZIMBIR.KI-
30′) -^{d}*am-na-nu*
31′) *šu-ub-*⸢*ti*⸣
32′) *ú-šar-mi-šu-*⸢*ma*⸣
33′) *ú-kin ni-id-ba-*⸢*šu*⸣

iv 14′–33′) (As for) the goddess Anunītu who resides in Sippar-Anunītu, whose residence in the time of the enemy had been transferred into Arrapḫa and whose cultic rites the Gutian had destroyed — Neriglissar renovated (her cult statue) and clad her in a ceremonial garment (befitting her) divinity. Her temple was in ruins, so he had her take up residence in Sippar-Amnānu and (re)confirmed her *nindabû*-offering(s in that city).

34′) *iš-tu u$_4$-um*

iv 34′–42′) After (his) day(s) had elapsed (and) he

iv 2′ The epithet *kaškaš ilī* ("most overpowering one of the gods") is also attested in an inscription of Ashurbanipal (Frame, RIMB 2 p. 229 B.6.32.22 line 1) and in an inscription of his brother Šamaš-šuma-ukīn (Frame, RIMB 2 p. 259 B.6.33.2001 line 18). In both instances *kaškaš ilī* is associated with the god Nergal.

35′) *im-lu-ú iṣ-ba-*⸢*tú*⸣
36′) *ú-ru-uḫ ši-im-ti*
37′) ^{m}*la-a-ba-ši-*^{d}AMAR.[UTU]
38′) DUMU-*šu ṣa-aḫ-*⸢*ri*⸣
39′) *la a-ḫi-iz ri-id-di*
40′) GIM *la* ŠÀ DINGIR-*ma*
41′) *ina* GIŠ.GU.ZA LUGAL-⸢*ti*⸣
42′) *ú-ši-im-ma*

had taken the road to (his) fate, Lâbâši-Mar[duk], his you[ng] son who was untutored in proper behavior, ascended the royal throne against the will of the gods and

Col. v
Lacuna
1′) *a-na qé-*⸢*reb* É.GAL⸣
2′) *ub-lu-ʾi-in-ni-ma*
3′) *kul-lat-sú-nu a-na* GÌR-*ía*
4′) ⸢*iš*⸣*-šap-ku-nim-ma*
5′) *ú-na*-áš-ši-qu še-pa-a-a*
6′) *ik-ta-na-ar-ra-bu*
7′) LUGAL-*ú-ti*

Lacuna
v 1′–7′) they brought me inside the palace, and all of them fell limp at my feet and (then) kissed my feet. They constantly blessed my being king.

8′) *i-na a-mat* ^{d}AMAR.UTU EN-*ía*
9′) *a-na be-lu-ti* KUR
10′) *an-na-ši-ma*
11′) *e-ma ú-ṣa-am-ma-ru*
12′) *a-kaš-šad-ma*
13′) *ša-ni-ni ul i-ši*

v 8′–13′) By the word of the god Marduk, my lord, I was raised up to rule over the land and (thus) I achieve whatever I desire and have no rivals.

14′) *šá* ^{md}AG-*ku-dúr-ri*-ÙRU
15′) *ù* ^{md}U.GUR-LUGAL-ÙRU
16′) LUGAL.MEŠ *a-lik maḫ-ri-ia*
17′) *na-áš-pa-ar-šu-nu*
18′) *dan-nu a-na-ku*
19′) *um-ma-na-ti-šu-nu*
20′) *qá-tu-ú-a paq-da*
21′) *a-na qí-*É**-šu-nu*
22′) *la e-ga-ku-ma*
23′) *ka-bat-ta-šu-nu*
24′) *šu-ṭu-ub-ba-ak*

v 14′–24′) I am the strong envoy of Nebuchadnezzar (II) and Neriglissar, the kings who came before me. Their troops are entrusted to my hand. By their command(s), I am not negligent and I please them.

25′) ⸢^{m}⸣LÚ-^{d}AMAR.UTU
26′) DUMU ^{md}AG-NÍG.GUB-ÙRU
27′) *u* ^{m}*la-a-*⸢*ba*⸣*-ši-*^{d}AMAR.UTU
28′) DUMU ^{md}[U.GUR]-LUGAL-ÙRU
29′) [...] AD-*šú-nu*
30′) [...]-*ma*
31′) [...]-*ti*
32′) [...]-⸢*e*⸣*-šu-nu*
33′) ⸢*ú*⸣*-pa-aṭ-ṭi-ru*
34′) [*a*]*-ma-a-ti-šu-nu*

v 25′–34′) Amēl-Marduk, son of Nebuchadnezzar (II), and Lâbâši-Marduk, son of [Nerigl]issar, [...] their fathers [...] and [...] their [...] they *made void*. Their [w]ords

Col. vi
Lacuna
1′) [*da-am-qí*]*-iš*
2′) [*ap-pa-lis-šú*]-⸢*nu*⸣*-ti-ma*
3′) ⸢*ú*⸣*-sal-li-šú-nu-ti*
4′) *a-na ṭe-ḫu-ti* MUL ⸢GAL⸣
5′) *u* ^{d}30 *a-ta-me ina* ŠÀ-*ia*
6′) 1-*en eṭ-lu ina* Á-*ia*

Lacuna
vi 1′–11′) [I looked at t]hem [pious]ly and prayed to them. I was concerned (lit. "spoke with my heart") about the close approach of the Great Star (Jupiter) and the moon (Sîn). A young man stood by my side and spoke to me, saying: "(As for) the close approach (of the celestial bodies), there are no inauspicious signs."

---

v 5′ *ú-na*-áš-ši-qu* "they kissed": The text has *ú-*ŠÁ*-áš-ši-qu*.
vi 6′–11′ The literary topos of a young man appearing in a dream and reassuring the dreamer is also found in Ludlul Bēl Nēmeqi Tablet III lines 9–28; see Lambert, BWL pp. 48–49 and Beaulieu, Nabonidus p. 112.

7′) *iz-ziz-ma i-ta-ma-a*
8′) *a-na ia-a-ti*
9′) *um-ma ṭe-ḫu-ti mim-ma*
10′) *i-da-ti lum-ni*
11′) *ul i-ba-áš-ši*
12′) *i-na* MÁŠ.GI$_6$*-im-ma*
13′) *šu-a-ti* ^{md}AG-NÍG.GUB-ÙRU
14′) LUGAL *pa-ni maḫ-ra-a*
15′) *u* 1*-en* LÚ.GÌR.SÌ.GA
16′) *ina* GIŠ.GIGIR *ú-zu-uz-zu*
17′) LÚ.GÌR.SÌ.GA*-ú*
18′) *a-na* ^{md}AG-NÍG.GUB-ÙRU
19′) *i-ta-me um-ma*
20′) KI ^{md}AG-NÍ.TUKU
21′) *du-bu-ub-ma* MÁŠ.GI$_6$
22′) *ši-i šá iṭ-ṭu-lu*
23′) *lu-šá-an-ni-ka ka-a-šú*

vi 12′–23′) In that same dream, Nebuchadnezzar (II), a former king of the past, and a palace attendant were standing in a chariot. The palace attendant spoke to Nebuchadnezzar (II), saying: "Speak with Nabonidus and he will report to you this dream (of his) that he had seen."

24′) ^{md}AG-NÍG.GUB-ÙRU
25′) *iš-me-e-šu-ma*
26′) *i-ta-me it-ti-ía*
27′) *um-ma mi-na-a dum-qí*
28′) *šá ta-aṭ-ṭu-lu qí-ba-a*

vi 24′–29′a) Nebuchadnezzar (II) heard him and said to me, saying: "Tell me, what are the good things that you have seen?"

29′) *ia-a-ši a-pul*-šu-ma*
30′) *aq-bi-iš um-ma*
31′) *i-na* MÁŠ.GI$_6$*-ia*
32′) MUL GAL ^{d}30 *u* ^{d}AMAR.UTU
33′) *ina qé-reb šá-ma-me šu-lu-tú*
34′) *da-am-qí-iš*
35′) *ap-pa-lis-šú-nu-ti*
36′) *ina* MU*-ía il-sa-an-ni-me*

vi 29′b–36′) I answered him and said to him, saying: "In my dream, the Great Star (Jupiter), the moon (Sîn), and the god Marduk were risen high in the heavens. (As) I looked piously at them, he called out to me by my name."

Col. vii
Lacuna

1′) [*x x* MUL].*dil-bat* ^{d}UDU.IDIM.SAG.UŠ
2′) [*x x*] MUL.ŠU.PA MUL.AB×ḪAL
3′) [MUL] GAL *a-ši-ib ša-ma-me*
4′) [*sur*]*-⸢qin⸣-nu ra-ab-bu-tim*
5′) *áš-tak-kan-šu-nu-ti-ma*
6′) *a-na* TIN UD.MEŠ *ru-qu-ti*
7′) *kun$_8$-nu* GIŠ.GU.ZA *la-bar* BALA*-e*
8′) *du-um-mu-qa a-ma-tu-ú-a*
9′) *ina ma-ḫar* ^{d}AMAR.UTU *be-lí-ia*
10′) *ú-sa-al-li-šú-nu-ti*

Lacuna

vii 1′–10′) [...], Venus, Saturn, [...], Boötes, ..., the great star(s) who reside in heaven, I established a large amount of strewn offerings for them and I prayed to them for a long life (lit. "a life of long days"), a firmly secured throne, a long reign, (and) making my words gain favor in the presence of the god Marduk, my lord.

11′) *a-na-al-ma ina šat mu-ši*
12′) ^{d}*nin$_9$-<tin>-ug$_5$-ga be-el*-ti*
13′) *mu-bal-li-ṭa-at mi-i-tú*
14′) SUM*-at* ZI*-tim ru-uq-tú*
15′) *ap-pa-li-is-ma*
16′) *a-na* TIN ZI.MEŠ*-ia da-ra-a*

vii 11′–21′) I laid down and, during the night, I saw the goddess Nin<tin>ugga, the lady who brings the dead (back) to life (and) who gives distant life, and I prayed to her for preserving my life forever (and) showing (me) favor, and (then) she turned her attention towards me and looked steadfastly at me

vi 29′ *a-pul*-šu-ma* "I answered him and": The stele has visually similar *a*-LAGAB×MAN*-šu-ma*.

vii 2′ The meaning of the signs MUL.AB×ḪAL is as unclear, as is their correct/exact reading in this context. H. Lewy (ArOr 17 [1949] pp. 51–52) read ^{kakkab}*erû* and identified the star as Vindemiatrix, a star in the constellation virgo. S.A.L. Butler (Dreams p. 233) read $^{MUL\ d}$ŠÀM ("the ŠÀM-star"), and H. Schaudig (Inschriften Nabonids p. 519) suggested reading MUL.ÙZ as a star called "goat," which is also attested in the *mīs pî* ritual for animating a divine statue. That star appears together with the other stars mentioned in this passage in the Babylon Stele Inscription (= this text).

vii 12′ *be-el*-ti* "the lady": The text has visually similar *be*-NIN$_9$*-ti*.

17′) *a-na sú-uḫ-ḫu*-ru pa-ni-šu*
18′) *ú-sa-al*-li-šu-ma*
19′) *pa-ni-šu tu-saḫ*-ḫi-⸢ram⸣-ma*
20′) *ina bu-ni-šú nam-ru-ti*
21′) *ki-niš tap-pal-sa-an-ni-ma*
22′) *ur-ri im-mi-ra-am-ma*
23′) *a-na é*-níg-gidru-kalam-ma-sum-ma*
24′) *e-ru-ub ina ma-ḫar* ^{d}AG
25′) *mu-šá-rik pa-le-e-a*
26′) GIŠ.NÍG.GIDRU *i-šar-ti*
27′) *uš-pa-ru ki-i-ni*
28′) *mu-⸢rap⸣-pi-šá-at* KUR
29′) *ú-šat-mi-ḫu* ŠU.II-*ú-a*
30′) *šu-bat* ^{d}*taš-me-tum*
31′) ^{d}*gu-la qa-i-šat* TIN
32′) *ap-pa-lis-ma ur-ri-ku* TIN
33′) UD.MEŠ *ru-qu-tu*
34′) *šum-qut* LUGAL.LUGAL-*ú-tú*
35′) *ina ma-ḫar* ^{d}AMAR.UTU EN
36′) *tu-dam-mi-iq*
37′) *a-ma-tu-ú-a*
38′) *i-nu-šú ⸢a⸣-na* ^{d}AMAR.UTU EN-*ía*
39′) *pa-al-ḫi-iš*
40′) *at-ta-ʾi-id-ma*
41′) *ina te-me-qí u ut-nen*$_{9}$*-ni*
42′) *áš-te-eʾ-a áš-ri-šu*
43′) *aṣ-bat-ma su-pe-e-šu*
44′) *a-mat lìb-bi-ia aq-bi-iš*
45′) *um-ma lu-ú a-na-ku-ma*
46′) LUGAL *mi-⸢gir⸣ lìb-bi-⸢ka⸣*
47′) *šá* LUGAL-*ú-tú ina* ŠÀ-*ia*
48′) *la ⸢tab*⸣-šu-ú ia-a-ti*
49′) *la mu-da-a-ka*
50′) *šá at-ta* EN EN.EN
51′) *tu-⸢mál-lu⸣-ú* ŠU.II-*ú-a*
52′) UGU LUGAL.MEŠ *šá tam-bu-ma*
53′) *iš-tu ul-lu i-pú-šu*
54′) *be-⸢lu-tú⸣ šu-ri-ku* UD.MEŠ-*ia*
55′) *⸢lil-bi⸣-ra šá-na-ti-ia*
56′) *lu-⸢pú⸣-uš-ma ⸢za⸣-ni-nu-tú*

Col. viii
Lacuna
1′) [...]-⸢*bi-šu*⸣
2′) [*x x*]-*nu* DINGIR-*ú-tú*
3′) [*šu-lu*]-*ka-at*
4′) [*ina*] ⸢*ni*⸣-*siq*-ti* NA$_{4}$ *u* KÙ.GI
5′) *nu-um-mu-ru zi-mu-šú*
6′) *a-na* ^{d}*é-a be-lí*
7′) *mu-šar*-bu-u* LUGAL-*ti-ía*
8′) ^{d}AG *pa-qid* kiš-šat*
9′) AN-*e ù* KI-*tim*
10′) *mu-šá-rik* UD.ME TIN-*ia*

with her bright countenance.

vii 22′–37′) The day became bright and I entered Eniggidrukalamasuma. In the presence of the god Nabû, the one who prolongs my reign (and) who lets my hands grasp a just scepter (and) legitimate rod that widen the land, I saw the seat(s) of the goddesses Tašmētu (and) Gula, the one who gives life, and, for lengthening (my) life (to) distant days (and) cutting down would-be kings, she (Nintinugga) made my words gain favor in the presence of the god Marduk, (my) lord.

vii 38′–42′) At that time, I was reverently attentive towards the god Marduk, my lord, and, with prayer(s) and supplication(s), I frequently visited his places (of worship).

vii 43′–56′) I began a prayer to him and told him my thought(s) (lit. "the word of my heart"), saying: "May I be the king who is the favorite of your heart, (although the thought) of being king was not (originally) in my heart. (As for) me, I did not know that you, O lord of lords, would place (kingship) into my hand(s and elevate me) more than (all of the other) kings that you have called (to be king) and who have exercised lordship since the distant past. Prolong my days so that my years are long (and) that I perform the role of (your) provider."

Lacuna

viii 1′–15′) [...] ... [... befit]ting (his) divinity, whose appearance is brightened [with a se]lection of stones and gold — For the god Ea, (my) lord, the one who makes my kingship surpassing, the god Nabû, the overseer of the totality of heaven and earth and the one who prolongs the days of my life, (and) the goddess Tašmētu, the lady who safeguards my life, I made (these garments) fitting as ceremonial garment(s) for their great divinity.

---

vii 17′ *sú-uḫ-ḫu*-ru* "turning": The stele has visually similar *sú-uḫ*-RI-*ru*.
vii 18′ *ú-sa-al*-li-šu-ma* "I prayed to her": The stele has visually similar *ú-sa*-BUR-*li-šu-ma*.
vii 19′ *tu-saḫ*-ḫi-⸢ram⸣-ma* "she turned": The stele has visually similar *tu*-IŠ-*ḫi-⸢ram⸣-ma*.

11′) ^{d}*taš-me-tum* GAŠAN *na-ṣi-rat**
12′) *na-piš-ti-ia*
13′) *a-na te-di-qu*
14′) DINGIR-*ú-ti-šú-nu* GAL-*ti*
15′) *as-mi-iš ú-šá-lik*

16′) *áš-ni-ma a-na* ^{d}*é-a*
17′) *be-lí-ia a-rat-te-e*
18′) KÙ.GI *ḫu-uš-ša-a*
19′) *ša* LUGAL *maḫ-ri*
20′) *la i-pu-šu-uš*
21′) *ki-ma šá* u_4*-mu maḫ-ri*
22′) *e-pu-uš-ma*
23′) *ina é-⸢kar-za⸣-gìn-na*
24′) *ina si-ma-ak-⸢ki⸣-šú ú-kin*
25′) *a-na mu-šá-bi-šu*

viii 16′–25′) As a second (gift) for the god Ea, my lord, I made an *arattû*-throne of reddish gold, (something) that no king of the past had ever built, (just) like one in the past and I firmly established (it) as his seat in Ekarzagina, in his shrine.

26′) LUGAL *šá a-na za-ni-nu-ti*
27′) *é-sag-íl u é-zi-da*
28′) *qá-qá-da-a pu-tuq-qú-ma*
29′) u_4*-mi-ša-am*
30′) *la na-par-ku-ú a-na-ku*

viii 26′–30′) I am the king who is constantly attentive to the provisioning of Esagil and Ezida, and who never stops (even for a) single day.

31′) GIŠ.IG.MEŠ *iṣ-ṣi šá ina*
32′) É.MEŠ *é-ḫal*-an-ki*
33′) É *pi-riš-ti* ^{d}AMAR.UTU
34′) *ù* ^{d}*⸢zar⸣-pa-ni-tum*
35′) *ù* GIŠ.IG.MEŠ du_6**-ki-sikil**$^{?}$
36′) *ki-la-⸢at⸣-ta-an*
37′) *ša* É KISAL.MAḪ
38′) *ù* KÁ ^{d}GAŠAN-*ia*
39′) *šá maš-da-ḫu* ^{d}*zar-pa-ni-tum*
40′) *na-ra-am-ti* ^{d}AMAR.UTU
41′) *mu-šar-ši-da-at* SUḪUŠ
42′) GIŠ.GU.ZA *šar-ru-ti-ia*
43′) KÙ.BABBAR *eb-ba* ú-šal-biš*

viii 31′–43′) (As for) the wooden doors that are in the rooms of Eḫalanki, the room of secret(s) of the god Marduk and the goddess Zarpanītu, as well as both doors of Dukisikil, (those) of the chapel(s) of the main courtyard, and (those of) the Gate of the goddess Bēltīya, on the procession street of the goddess Zarpānītu, the beloved of the god Marduk who made the foundation(s) of the throne of my royal majesty secure, I had (them) clad in shiny silver.

44′) *ká-gu-la* KÁ KISAL.MAḪ
45′) *ša* GIŠ.IG.MEŠ-*šú* GIŠ.IG
46′) *lu-bu-uš-ti ina iṣ-ṣi*
47′) *ba-aš-mu* GIŠ.IG-*ši-na*
48′) GIŠ.IG.MEŠ *lu-li-mu*
49′) *šá* GIŠ.EREN *eš-šiš ab-ni*
50′) *eš-ma-ra-a uḫ-ḫi-iz*
51′) *ú-nam-mir* u_4*-mi-iš*
52′) *lu-bu-uš-ti*
53′) *ki-ma si-ma-ti-ši-na*
54′) *re-eš-ta-a-tú ú-lab-⸢biš*$^{?}$⸣
55′) *ina* KI.UŠ ^{d}*namma ú-⸢rat⸣-ta-a*
56′) *áš-ru-uš-ši-in*

viii 44′–56′) (As for) Kagula, the gate (leading to) the main courtyard, whose doors, doors with cover(s), were made with (just ordinary) wood, I built anew its doors, magnificent doors of cedar. I inlaid (them) with *ešmarû*-metal (and thereby) made (them) as bright as daylight. I clad (them) with a covering according to their original appearance(s). I installed (them back) on the track(s) of the goddess Namma, in their (proper) place(s).

57′) MUŠ.ḪUŠ *e-ri-i*
58′) *šá ina ki-se-e* KISAL.MAḪ
59′) *ù* SUḪUR*.MÁŠ URUDU
60′) *⸢ú⸣-[...]*

viii 57′–60′) (As for) the copper *mušḫuššu*-dragon(s), which are (stationed) at the bases of the main courtyard, and the copper goat-fish [...]

Col. ix
Lacuna

Lacuna

viii 32′ *é-ḫal*-an-ki* "Eḫalanki": The stele has visually similar *é*-AN-*an-ki*.
viii 35′ du_6**-ki-sikil**$^{?}$ "Dukisikil": The text has visually similar SIKIL-*ki-sikil**$^{?}$.
viii 43′ *eb-ba** "shiny": The object has *eb*-UD.

1′) *za-ni-nu ba-bil* IGI.SÁ
2′) GAL.MEŠ *a-na* DINGIR GAL.⸢MEŠ⸣
3′) *a-na-ku ina* ITI.BÁRA
4′) UD.10.KAM *e-nu-ma*
5′) LUGAL DINGIR.MEŠ ^{d}AMAR.UTU
6′) *u* DINGIR.MEŠ *šu-ut* AN KI
7′) *i-na é*-⸢sískur⸣*
8′) É *ik-ri-bi*
9′) É* *a-ki-ti* ^{d}EN.LÍL-*tú*
10′) *ra-mu-ú šu-ub-ti*
11′) 1 ME GUN 21 MA.NA
12′) KÙ.<BABBAR> 5 GUN 17 MA.NA
13′) KÙ.GI *e-li* ⸢*kad*$_{4}$⸣-*re-e*
14′) *ša ka-al* MU.1.KAM
15′) *šá ina šu-kin-né-e*
16′) *i-na i-pat ma-ti-tan*
17′) *ḫi-ṣi-ib* KUR.MEŠ
18′) *er-bi kal* da-ad-me*
19′) *ku-bu-ut-te-e* LUGAL.MEŠ
20′) *bu-še-e šá-ad-lu-ti*
21′) *ša* NUN ^{d}AMAR.UTU
22′) *i-qí-pa-an-ni*
23′) *ia-⸢a⸣-ti a-na* ^{d}EN*
24′) ^{d}AG *u* ^{d}NÈ.ERI$_{11}$*.GAL
25′) DINGIR.MEŠ *ra-bu-ti*
26′) *ra-ʾi-im* BALA*-*e-a*
27′) *na-ṣir na-⸢piš⸣-ti-ia*
28′) *a-na da-rí-a-ti*
29′) ⸢*kad*$_{4}$⸣-*re-e bi-bil* ŠÀ
30′) *ú-še-rib-šú-nu-ti*
31′) 2 LIM ⸢8⸣ ME 50 *i-na* ERIM-*ni*
32′) *ši-⸢il⸣-la-ti* KUR*.*ḫu-me-e*
33′) *ša* EN ^{d}AMAR.UTU
34′) *e-li* LUGAL.MEŠ
35′) *a-lik maḫ-ri-ia*
36′) *ú-šá-tir-an-ni-ma*
37′) *ú-mál-la-a* ŠU.II-*ú-a*
38′) *a-na za-ba-lu* tup-šik*-ku*
39′) *a-na* ^{d}EN ^{d}AG *u* ^{d}U.GUR
40′) DINGIR.MEŠ-*e-a a-lik i-di-ia*
41′) *áš-ru-uk* TA *e-pu-šú*
42′) *i-sin-nu* É* *a-ki-ti*
43′) ^{d}EN *ù* DUMU ^{d}EN
44′) *ú-šar-mu-ú*
45′) *šu-bat-su-nu ṭa-ab-ti*
46′) *i-gi-se-e šur-ru-ḫu-*<*tú*?>
47′) *ú-še-rib qé-reb-šú-un*
48′) *ina ma-ḫa-zi* GAL.MEŠ
49′) *a-ba-lu* DINGIR *u* ^{d}EŠ$_{18}$.TÁR*
50′) *a-na* UNUG*.KI *larsa**.KI
51′) *u úri**.⸢KI⸣ *al-lik-ma*

ix 1′–3′a) I am the provider who brings large gifts to the great gods.

ix 3′b–30′) In the month Nisannu (I), (on) the tenth day, when the king of the gods, the god Marduk, and the gods of heaven and earth take up residence in Esiskur, the house of blessing, the *akītu*-house of supreme power — (as for) me, as voluntary gifts, I had 100 talents and 21 minas of si<lver>, 5 talents and 17 minas of gold in addition to the gifts for an entire year, which (come) from *homage-gifts*, the wealth of all of the lands, the yield of the mountain, the income from all of the settlements, the rich gifts of kings, the extensive possessions that the prince, the god Marduk had entrusted to me, brought in(to Esiskur) for the gods Bēl (Marduk), Nabû, and Nergal, the great gods who love my reign (and) protect my life, for eternity.

ix 31′–41′a) To carry basket(s), I gave to the gods Bēl (Marduk), Nabû, and Nergal, the gods who march at my side, 2,850 (people) from an (enemy) army, booty from the land Ḫumê, which the lord, the god Marduk, had placed in my hands (and thereby) made me surpass the kings who came before me.

ix 41′b–47′) After I had performed the *akītu*-festival (and) had made the gods Bēl (Marduk) and Son-of-Bēl (Nabû) occupy their pleasant residence(s), I had splendid gifts brought inside them.

ix 48′–59′) In the great cult centers, I prayed to the god(s) and goddess(es). I went to Uruk, Larsa, and Ur and had silver, gold, (and) selected stone(s) brought in before the deities Sîn, Šamaš, and Ištar. In Keš, the

ix 18′ *kal** "all": The stele has visually similar GUR.
ix 24′ ^{d}NÈ.ERI$_{11}$*.GAL "the god Nergal": The stele has visually similar ^{d}NÈ.AD.GAL.
ix 38′ *za-ba-lu** "carry": The stele has visually similar *za-ba*-KU.
ix 50′ UNUG*.KI *larsa**.KI "Uruk, Larsa": The text has visually similar ÈŠ×PA.KI UD.ÈŠ×BAR.KI.
ix 51′ *úri**.⸢KI⸣ "Ur": The stele has visually similar ŠEŠ.ÈŠ×BAR.⸢KI⸣.

52′) KÙ.BABBAR KÙ.GI NA$_4$ ni-siq*-ti
53′) a-na ma-ḫar* ^{d}30
54′) ^{d}UTU u ^{d}iš-tar
55′) ú-še-ri-ib
56′) ina kèš*.KI URU DINGIR.MAḪ
57′) ina i-te-et-tu-qí-ia
58′) ⸢UDU.SÍSKUR⸣ [taš]-ri-⸢iḫ⸣-ti
59′) ⸢le⸣-e ⸢ma⸣-ru-ti

city of (the goddess) Bēlet-ilī, when I was passing by, [...] sumptuous offerings, fattened bulls,

Col. x

Lacuna

1′) šá iš-[ša-al-lu]
2′) i-ši-it-⸢ta-šu-un⸣
3′) la ir-mu-ú šu-bat-⸢su⸣-nu
4′) ^{d}AMAR.UTU be-lí ia-ti
5′) ú-qá-ʾa-an-ni-ma
6′) ú-te-ed-du-šú me-si DINGIR
7′) ú-šá-áš-kin ŠU.II-ú-a
8′) sú-ul-lu*-mu DINGIR.MEŠ ze-nu-tú
9′) šu-ur-ma-a šu-bat-sú-un
10′) ina pi-i-šú el*-lu i-ta-me
11′) a-na pa-le-e-a

Lacuna

x 1′–11′) whose treasure(s) had be[en carried off] (and who) could no longer occupy their residence(s), the god Marduk, my lord, waited for me and he had the constant renewal of the cultic rite(s) of the god(s) placed in my hands. With his pure mouth, he ordered the reconciliation of the angry gods (and) the (re)occupation of their residence to (take place during) my reign.

12′) ⸢ḫar⸣-ra-nu.KI é*-ḫúl-ḫúl
13′) šá in-na-du-u 54 MU.MEŠ
14′) ina šal-pu-ut-ti ERIM-man-du
15′) uš-taḫ-ri-bi eš-re-ti
16′) i-te-ek-pu-uš
17′) it-ti DINGIR.MEŠ
18′) a-dan-nu sa-li-mu
19′) 54 MU.AN.NA.MEŠ
20′) e-nu-ma ^{d}30
21′) i-tu-ru áš-ru-uš-šú

x 12′–21′) (With regard to the city) Ḫarrān (and) Eḫulḫul, which have been in ruins for fifty-four years, (whose) sanctuaries had been laid to waste by the desecration wrought by a barbarian horde (the Medes), with (the consent of) the gods, the appointed time for (divine) reconciliation drew near, the fifty-four years, when the god Sîn would return to his place.

22′) i-na-an-na
23′) a-na aš-ri-šu
24′) i-tu-ra-am-ma
25′) ^{d}30 EN a-gi-i
26′) iḫ-su-su šu-bat-su
27′) ṣir-ti u DINGIR.MEŠ
28′) ma-la it-ti-šú
29′) ú-ṣu-ú* <ina> ku-um-mi-šú
30′) ^{d}AMAR.UTU-ma LUGAL DINGIR.MEŠ
31′) iq-ta-bi pa-ḫar-šú-un

x 22′–31′) Now, he returned to his place and the god Sîn, the lord of the crown, remembered his exalted residence. Moreover, (as for) the gods, as many as had gone out <of> his cella with him, it was the god Marduk, king of the gods, who had commanded that they be assembled (together).

32′) NA$_4$.KIŠIB NA$_4$.aš-pú-u
33′) šu-qu-ru NA$_4$ LUGAL-tú
34′) šá ^{m}AN.ŠÁR*-DÙ-IBILA
35′) LUGAL KUR-aš-šur ṣa-lam ^{d}30
36′) a-na zi-ki-ir MU-šú
37′) ú-ṣa-ab-bu-ú-ma
38′) ib-nu-ú ṣe-ru-uš-šú
39′) ta-nit-ti ^{d}30
40′) ina NA$_4$.KIŠIB šu-a-ti

x 32′–51′) (As for) a seal (made) of valuable jasper, the stone of kingship, upon which Ashurbanipal, king of Assyria, had an image of the god Sîn conceived and made for his (own) fame, which he had the praise of the god Sîn written on that seal, and which he had firmly placed around the neck of the god Sîn, whose (Sîn's) features had been revealed in distant days, (about which) his (Sîn's) oracular decisions had not ceased on account of the desecration by the enemy,

ix 53′ ma-ḫar* "before": The text has visually similar ma-AḪ.
ix 56′ kèš*.KI "Keš": The stele has visually similar ÉN.ŠÁR×ÁŠ.KI.
x 8′ sú-ul-lu*-mu "the reconciliation of": The stele has visually similar sú-ul-KU-mu.
x 10′ el*-lu "pure": The text has visually similar NIN$_9$×MIN-lu.
x 29′ ú-ṣu-ú* "had gone out": The text has ú-ṣu-ÁŠ.
x 34′ ^{m}AN.ŠÁR*-DÙ-IBILA "Ashurbanipal": The stele has visually similar ^{m}AN.ŠÁ×EŠ$_5$-DÙ-IBILA.

41′) *iš-ṭù-ur-ru-ú-ma*
42′) *ina* GÚ ^{d}30 *ú-kin-nu*
43′) *šá ina* UD.MEŠ *ul-lu-ti*
44′) ⌜*kul*$^{?}$⌝*-lu-mu bu-un-na-*
45′) *-an-né-e-šú*
46′) *ina šal*-pu-ut-ti* LÚ.KÚR
47′) *a-na la ba-ṭa-lu*
48′) *te-re-e-ti-šu*
49′) *ina é-sag-íl*
50′) É *na-ṣi-ir*
51′) *na-piš-ti* DINGIR ⌜GAL.MEŠ⌝

in Esagil, the temple that protects the life of the great gods,

Col. xi

Lacuna

1′) [*x*] ⌜GÌR⌝ KA ⌜DIŠ⌝ *x* [*x x*]
2′) [BE] ŠU.SI *šá-lim*
3′) EN ⌜SÍSKUR⌝ *i-šá-lim*
4′) UD.MEŠ-*šú* GÍD.DA.MEŠ

Lacuna

xi 1′–4′) [... f]oot ... [... If] the 'Finger' (*ubānu*) is intact, (then) the lord of the sacrifice will prosper (and) his days will be long.

5′) BE SILIM* MÁŠ 2.30 MÁŠ *x*
6′) *ina* SU LÚ.KÚR *mim-ma* TI-*a*
7′) BE MÁŠ DAGAL DÙG *lìb-bi*

xi 5′–7′) If the 'Well-Being' (*šulmu*) of the 'Increment' (*ṣibtu*) ... the left side of the 'Increment' (*ṣibtu*), (then) I will take something from the body of (my) enemy. If the 'Increment' (*ṣibtu*) is wide, (then) there will be happiness.

8′) BE GIŠ.TUKUL MÁŠ *ana* 2.30 *te-bi*
9′) ERIM-*ni ḫi-im-ṣa-ta*
10′) ERIM-*ni* LÚ.KÚR *ik-kal*
11′) BE *ina* IGI *gi-ip-ši šá* 15
12′) 2 GIŠ.TUKUL *na-an-du-ru-ti*
13′) GAR *per-níq-qu** MU-*šú-nu*
14′) *mu-ze-er-ri*
15′) *ir-ta-a-mu*
16′) *ina qaq-qar nu-kúr-ti*
17′) *sú-lum-ma-a* GÁL-*ši*
18′) ^{d}30 *u* ^{d}UTU *i-di** ERIM-⌜*ia*$_{5}$⌝
19′) DU.MEŠ-*ma* LÚ.KÚR KUR-⌜*ád*⌝
20′) DINGIR.MEŠ *ze-nu-ti*
21′) *it-ti* LÚ SILIM-*mu*

xi 8′–21′) If the 'Weapon'-Mark (*kakku*) of the 'Increment' (*ṣibtu*) is raised on the left side, (then) my army will enjoy (a share) of the plundered goods of the army of the enemy. If there are two intertwined 'Weapon'-Marks (*kakku*) in front of the right 'Thickening' (*gipšu*), (then) their name is '*Perniqqu*' (and) those (who) hate each other will come to love each other, there will be peace in hostile territory, the gods Sîn and Šamaš will march at the side of my army, I will conquer (my) enemy, (and) the angry gods will become reconciled with the man (with whom they are angry).

22′) BE ZÍ IGI.MEŠ-*šú ana* 15 GAR.⌜MEŠ⌝

xi 22′) If the 'eyes' of the Gall Bladder (*martu*) are on the right side, (then ...).

23′) SI.LÁ BE *ina* SAG NA GIŠ.TUKUL
24′) GAR-*ma* NA UŠ-*di*

xi 23′–24′) Check: If the 'Weapon'-Mark (*kakku*) is placed in front of the 'Station' (*mazzāzu*) (and) *abuts* the 'Station' (*mazzāzu*), (then ...).

25′) BE *gi-ip-šú* 15 ZÍ ⌜U$_{5}$*⌝

xi 25′) If the 'Thickening' (*gipšu*) straddles the right side of the Gall Bladder (*martu*), (then ...).

26′) BE *ina bi-rit* SAGŠU MUR
27′) *u* MU SAG MUR MUN$^{?}$ GÚ

xi 26′–27′) If ... is between the 'Cap' (*kubšu*) of the lung and the 'Head Lifter' (*mukīl rēši*) of the lung, (then ...).

28′) BE AN.TA DU GÌR ⌜*uš*⌝-
29′) *-šu-uš-ti* ERIM-*ni* ⌜SILIM-*lim*⌝
30′) *šum*$_{4}$*-ma* LÚ *ina di-i-ni*
31′) UGU *ge-ri-šú* GUB-*az*
32′) BE AN.TA EDIN MUR *ša* 15 *i-*[*bir*]
33′) *u* ⌜UZU⌝.GAG.ZAG.GA *ina* ⌜MURUB$_{4}$⌝-[*šú*]

xi 28′–37′) If the 'Upper Part' (*elītu*) moves (and) a 'Foot'-Mark (*šēpu*) (indicating) *abandonment*, (then) my military forces will be intact. If (the same result), (then) a man will prevail against his adversary in a legal decision. If the 'Upper Part' (*elītu*) cr[osses over] the back of the right lung and the breast-bone is

xi 5′ SILIM* "'Well-Being' (*šulmu*)": The stele has visually similar KI.
xi 18′ *i-di** "the side of": The text has visually similar *i*-KI.
xi 22′, 23′–24′, 25′, 26′–27′, 36′–37′, and 42′ There are no apodoses included for these omen protases.
xi 25′ ⌜U$_{5}$*⌝ "straddles": The scribe wrote ⌜MÁŠ⌝.

34′)	GAM-*iš mu-sa-ri-ir** ERIM KÚR*	pierced in [its] mid[dle], (then) there is a deceiver (in) the army of the enemy (and) its main body will fall.
35′)	ERIM KÚR *ina* DUGUD-*šú* ŠUB-*ut*	
36′)	BE AN.TA DU-*ik*	If the 'Upper Part' (*elītu*) moves and the 'Cap' (*kubšu*) *straddles* the 'Outside' (*kīdītu*), (then ...)
37′)	*u* <<*u*>> SAGŠU UGU *ki-di**-*tú x*	
38′)	BE MU SAG MUR 15 *ul-lu-uṣ*	xi 38′–39′) If the 'Head Lifter' (*mukīl rēši*) of the right side of the lung is swollen, (then) rejoicing for the heart of the army.
39′)	*ul-lu-uṣ* ŠÀ ERIM-*ni*	
40′)	BE SILIM *um-mat* MUR 15 GAR-*at*	xi 40′–41′) If the 'Well-Being' (*šulmu*) of the main part of the lung at the right side is present, (then) there is well-being for a (whole) year.
41′)	SILIM MU.1.KAM	
42′)	BE ŠU.SI LÁ*-*ṣa*-[*at*]	xi 42′) If the 'Finger' (*ubānu*) is exten[ded], (then ...).
11 uninscribed lines		11 uninscribed lines

4

Sixteen fragments of (a) semi-cylindrical diorite stele(s) discovered in 1899 by R. Koldewey at various spots in Babylon are inscribed with one or more inscriptions written in archaizing Neo-Babylonian script. The pieces, which probably originally come from more than one monument, are known from the original fragments, which are housed in the British Museum (London) and the Vorderasiatisches Museum (Berlin). The attribution of the fragments to Nabonidus is not entirely certain, apart from ex. 4 (BE 2728), which bears his name. Due to the fragmentary state of preservation of the pieces, it is uncertain from how many monuments these sixteen fragments stem and how many actually bear (an) inscription(s) of Nabonidus. In addition, it is unknown if any of these fragments belong to the same monuments as text nos. 3 (Babylon Stele) and 1003. The inscription(s) are not sufficiently preserved to be able to propose a date of composition. Following the edition of H. Schaudig (Inschriften Nabonids pp. 537–543), all sixteen stele pieces are edited together, despite the fact that they do not necessarily all come from one and the same object or all bear inscription(s) of Nabonidus.

CATALOGUE

Ex.	Museum Number	Excavation Number	Provenance	Lines Preserved	cpn
1	VA Bab 4177	BE 548	Babylon, Kasr, processional street, at point 2, east wall	frgm. 1	n
2	VA Bab 4177	BE 651	As ex. 1	frgm. 2	c
3	VA Bab 4177	BE 680	Babylon, Kasr, processional street, between point 2 and 3, east wall	frgm. 3	c
4	BM 119298	BE 2728	Babylon, Kasr, processional street, northwest of point 3	frgm. 4	c
5	VA Bab 4760	BE 3346	Babylon, Kasr, processional street, at point 3, near the northwest wall block	frgm. 5	c
6	VA —	BE 3351	As ex. 5	frgm. 6	n
7	BM 119298	BE 3379	Babylon, Kasr, processional street, at point 3	frgm. 7	c

3 xi 34′ *mu-sa-ri-ir** "a deceiver" and KÚR* "enemy": The stele has *mu-sa-ri*-MU and NI respectively.
3 xi 37′ *ki-di**-*tú* "the 'Outside' (*kīdītu*)": The object has *ki*-KI-*tú*.

8	VA Bab 4761	BE 3401	As ex. 7	frgm. 8	c
9	VA —	BE 3409	Babylon, Kasr, processional street, at point 3, near the east end of the north wall of the North Palace	frgm. 9	n
10	BM 119298	BE 3419	As ex. 9	frgm. 10	c
11	VA Bab 4177	BE 3420	As ex. 7	frgm. 11	c
12	VA Bab 4762	BE 3471	As ex. 7	frgm. 12	c
13	VA Bab 4763	BE 3684	Babylon, Kasr, processional street, at point 3, on the inner wall	frgm. 13	c
14	VA Bab 4177	BE 4655	Babylon, Kasr, North Palace, near the North-South wall	frgm. 14	c
15	VA Bab 4764	BE 46262	Babylon, Kasr 4s, surface	frgm. 15	c
16	VA Bab 4177	BE 47320	Babylon, Kasr, North Palace, near the lion	frgm. 16	c

COMMENTARY

The fragments were discovered in various spots in Babylon, between May and November 1899; see the catalogue and Schaudig, Inschriften Nabonids pp. 537–538 for further details. The excavators attributed all of the pieces to Nabonidus and assumed that they belonged to the same stele as EŞ 1327 (text no. 3 [Babylon Stele]). It should be stressed here that not all of these pieces necessarily bear inscription(s) of Nabonidus and that not all of the fragments belong to one and the same monument, as is clear from the distribution of the find spots and from the varying line heights on the individual fragments (see below). Although some pieces could belong to the same monuments as text nos. 3 (Babylon Stele; EŞ 1327) and 1003 (VA 3217), provisionally, all sixteen pieces are edited here, following Schaudig's edition. The 'exemplars' (= fragments) are arranged sequentially by excavation number, in ascending order. According to H. Schaudig (Inschriften Nabonids p. 539, quoting J. Marzahn), exs. 15 (VA Bab 4764; BE 46262) and 16 (VA Bab 4177; BE 47320) do not form part of a Nabonidus stele but rather belong to one of the lion statues of the procession street. A.R. Gallagher (AfO 48/49 [2001–02] p. 106) repeated this information about ex. 15. This information, however, is inaccurate since the two pieces most likely come from (a) Nabonidus stele(s) and, thus, they are included here with the other fourteen stele fragments.

According to Koldewey, Königsburgen 2 pp. 22–23, exs. 4, 8, and 12–13 were sent back to Berlin; ex. 13 was reported to have been stolen from the dig house in Babylon and recovered from the antiquities market in 1927. Exs. 4, 7, and 10 — all of which have been assigned the museum number BM 119298 (1928-2-11,1; 1928-2-11,1a; 1928-2-11,1b) — are now in the British Museum (London); see Reade, NABU 2000 no. 81. The remaining fragments — exs. 1–3, 5–6, 8–9, and 11–16 — are housed in the Vorderasiatisches Museum (Berlin) and these have been given the collection numbers VA Bab 4177, VA Bab 4760, VA Bab 4761, VA Bab 4762, VA Bab 4763, and VA Bab 4764. In addition, the fragments are also known from watercolor facsimiles (probably made by W. Andrae) and squeezes made by Koldewey in 1899; Schaudig's published copies (Inschriften Nabonids pp. 761–765 figs. 44–57) are drawn from the squeezes, which are in the Vorderasiatisches Museum.

Frgms. 1 and 11–12 come from the edge of the stele(s). Small portions of two columns are preserved on all three fragments, one from the flat obverse face and one from the curved side and reverse of the monument(s). Frgms. 2–10 are all from the curved, reverse face(s) of the stele(s). The heights of the lines vary on the individual pieces, which suggests that the fourteen fragments might not all belong to one and the same monument. The line heights are as follows: ca. 1.1 cm on ex. 10; ca. 1.1–1.4 cm on ex. 6; ca. 1.2 cm on exs. 5, 8–9, and 14; 1.2–1.9 cm on ex. 12; ca. 1.3–1.4 cm on exs. 2–3 and 7; ca. 1.5–1.7 cm on ex. 11; and ca. 1.7 cm on ex. 13. Exs. 2 and 3 might (indirectly) join, as might exs. 7 and 8. Because there is no apparent overlap between the fragments, no score is provided on Oracc and no minor (orthographic) variants are given at the back of the book.

BIBLIOGRAPHY

1932 Koldewey, Königsburgen 2 pp. 22–23 nos. 19 a–p (study)

1990 Koldewey, WEB[5] pp. 167–168 (study)

2000 Reade, NABU 2000 no. 81 (ex. 7, study)

2001 Schaudig, Inschriften Nabonids pp. 537–543 no. 3.8[a] and 761–765 figs. 44–57 (exs. 1–14, copy, edition; exs. 15–16, study)

2001–02 Gallagher, AfO 48/49 pp. 105–106 (exs. 5, 8, 12–13, 15, copy, study)

2008 Da Riva, GMTR 4, p. 127 (study)

Figure 9. VA Bab 4763 (Nabonidus no. 4 ex. 13), a fragment of a semi-cylindrical diorite stele discovered by R. Koldewey in 1899 at Babylon. Photo: Olaf M. Teßmer.

TEXT

Fragment 1 (BE 548)

Col. i′	Lacuna
Lacuna	
1′) [...] (blank)	Frgm. 1 i′ 1′–4′) (No translation possible)
2′) [...] *x*	
3′) [...] *x*	
4′) [...]-⸢*ú*⸣	
Lacuna	Lacuna
Col. ii′	
Lacuna	Lacuna
1′) *x* [...]	Frgm. 1 ii′ 1′–4′) [...] *not* [...] *the seed* [...]
2′) *la* [...]	
3′) NUMUN [...]	
4′) *x* [...]	
Lacuna	Lacuna

Fragment 2 (BE 651)

Lacuna
1′) [...] (blank) [...]
2′) [...] *x ad-*⸢*da*⸣ [...]
3′) [...]*-an-ni-šú-nu* [...]
4′) [*x* (*šá*) *mu*$^{?}$*-dam*]*-*⸢*mi*⸣*-qu* ⸢*te*⸣*-*[*re-ti-ia x x*]
5′) [...]*-*⸢*tum*⸣ [...]
Lacuna

Lacuna
Frgm. 2 1′–5′) [...] ... [...] their ... [... (*the one who*) *makes* my ome]ns [fav]orable [...]
Lacuna

Fragment 3 (BE 680)

Lacuna
1′) [...] *x* [...]
2′) [...] *x x* [...]
3′) [...] ⸢^{d}⸣DUMU-É *šá* [...]
4′) [...] ID [...]
5′) [...] *x* [...]
Lacuna

Lacuna
Frgm. 3 1′–5′) [...] ... [...] the god Mār-bīti, who [...]
Lacuna

Fragment 4 (BE 2728)

Lacuna
1′) [...] *x-a* URU-⸢*ia*⸣ [...]
2′) [...] *ar*$^{?}$ *a a x* [...]
3′) [*a-a*] *ar*$^{?}$*-šá-a šá-ni-*[*na* ...]
4′) [^{m}]^{d}AG-NÍ.TUKU ⸢LUGAL⸣
5′) ⸢*šá*⸣ <*ana*> DINGIR.DINGIR GAL.⸢GAL⸣
6′) ⸢*na*⸣*-a-du a-na-*[*ku*]
7′) ⸢*a*⸣*-na* DINGIR.MEŠ *u* ^{d}[EŠ$_{18}$.TÁR]
8′) *pu-tuq-qá-ku* KUR UB$^{?}$ *x* [*x x*]
9′) ⸢^{d}⸣*mi-*⸢*šar*⸣*-ru* ^{d}⸢GAŠAN⸣-NI-*x*
10′) [*a*]*-šib é-al-ti-la*
11′) [*šá*] *qé-reb é-sag-*⸢*íl*⸣
12′) [*šá i*]*-*⸢*na*$^{?}$⸣ *pa-ni iz-nu-*[*ú*]
Lacuna

Lacuna
Frgm. 4 1′–3′) [...] ... my city [...] ... [... may] *I* have [no] riv[al(s) ...].

Frgm. 4 4′–6′) Nabonidus, the ki[ng] who reveres the gre[at] gods, am I.

Frgm. 4 7′–8′) I am attentive to the gods and [goddess(es)] ... [...]
Frgm. 4 9′–12′) (As for) the god Mīšaru (and) the goddess Šarrat-..., [who re]side in Ealtila — [which] is inside Esagi[l — who] had been angry in the past,
Lacuna

Fragment 5 (BE 3346)

Lacuna
1′) [...] ⸢TA⸣ [...]
2′) [...] ^{d}AG [...]
3′) [...] *šá ina x* [...]
4′) [...] *iš-te-*⸢*né*⸣*-*[*eʾ-ú* ...]
5′) [...] *x* ⸢AN⸣ *x* [...]
Lacuna

Lacuna
Frgm. 5 1′–5′) [...] the god Nabû [...] *who* in [...] he sought [out ...] ... [...]
Lacuna

Fragment 6 (BE 3351)

Col. i′
Lacuna
1′) [...]*-*⸢*ti*⸣
2′) [...] *x-da*
3′) [...] ḪÉ.GÁL
4′) [... *mu*]*-kin-ni*

Lacuna
Frgm. 6 i′ 1′–6′) [...] ... [...] abundance [... the one who (re)con]firmed their [...] ...

Frgm. 2′ 4′ [*mu*$^{?}$*-dam*]*-*⸢*mi*⸣*-qu* "[(*the one who*) *makes* fav]orable": It is uncertain if this line originally had the participle *mudammiqu* or the finite verb *udammiqu* ([*ú*$^{?}$*-dam*]*-*⸢*mi*⸣*-qu* "[*who made fav*]*orable*"). The former is tentatively restored here.

Frgm. 4 4′–6′ [^{m}]^{d}AG-NÍ.TUKU ⸢LUGAL *šá*⸣ <*ana*> DINGIR.DINGIR GAL.⸢GAL *na*⸣*-a-du a-na-*[*ku*] "Nabonidus, the ki[ng] who reveres the gre[at] gods, am I": H. Schaudig (Inschriften Nabonids p. 540) suggests that these three lines should be read as [^{m}]^{d}AG-NÍ.TUKU ⸢LUGAL⸣ [*pa-liḫ*] / ⸢*šá*⸣ DINGIR.DINGIR GAL.⸢GAL⸣ [NUN] / ⸢*na*⸣*-a-du a-na-*[*ku*] "Nabonidus, the ki[ng *who reveres*] the gre[at] gods, attent[ive prince], am I." The space available in each line, however, does not support Schaudig's reading, as there is not sufficient space at the end of lines 4′ and 5′ to restore *pa-liḫ* and NUN respectively.

5′) [...]-⸢*ti*⸣-*šú-nu*
6′) [...]-⸢*ki-in*⸣
Lacuna

Lacuna

Col. ii′
Lacuna
1′) ⸢*gu*⸣-[...]
2′) *ul i*-[...]
3′) *ki-ma šá x* [...]
4′) *ak*-⸢*šu*⸣-[*ud*? ...]
5′) *i*-⸢*da*⸣-[...]
6′) KU *x* [...]
7′) *x x* [...]
Lacuna

Lacuna
Frgm. 6 ii′ 1′–7′) [...] *he* [did] not [...] just as [...] I *reac*[*hed* ...] ... [...] ... [...] ... [...]
Lacuna

Fragment 7 (BE 3379)

Col. i′
Lacuna
1′) [...] *x*
2′) [...] UD
3′) [...]-⸢*tum*⸣
4′) [...]-*ni*
5′) [...] *x*
Lacuna

Lacuna
Frgm. 7 i′ 1′–5′) (No translation possible)
Lacuna

Col. ii′
Lacuna
1′) [...] *x*
2′) [...]-*ma*
3′) [GIŠ.IG].⸢MEŠ⸣ KÙ.BABBAR
4′) [*ú*]-⸢*ra*⸣-*at-tu-ši-na-tú*
5′) [*iš*]-⸢*tu*⸣ *i-ta-at* AM.AM
6′) ⸢*šú*⸣-*nu-ti a-di* SIG$_{7}$.IGI.KÙ
7′) *u* GIŠ.IG.MEŠ *iṣ-ṣi šá* KÁ
8′) *pa-pa-ḫi* ^{d}*taš-me-tum*
9′) *iḫ-zu* KÙ.BABBAR *eb-ba uḫ-ḫi-iz*
10′) 2 AM.MEŠ URUDU *ek-du-ti*
11′) ⸢*šá a-na é-lagab-gíd*⸣
Lacuna

Lacuna
Frgm. 7 ii′ 1′–11′) [...] and [in]stalled [door]s (plated with bands of) silver in them. [Af]ter I had inlaid the sides of [th]ese bulls as far as the *vault* and the wooden doors of the gate of the cella of the goddess Tašmētu with mounting(s) of shining silver, [I had] two fierce wild bulls of copper, which [...] *to* [...] Elagabgid, [...]
Lacuna

Col. iii′
Lacuna
1′) (blank) [...]
2′) ⸢*ú*⸣-[...]
3′) *i-x* [...]
4′) ⸢*ú*⸣-[...]
5′) *te*-[...]
6′) *x* [...]
7′) *i*-[...]
8′) ⸢LUGAL⸣ [...]
9′) *pa*-[...]
10′) ⸢^{d}EN⸣ [...]
11′) *ú*-[...]
Lacuna

Lacuna
Frgm. 7 iii′ 1′–7′) (No translation possible)
Frgm. 7 iii′ 8′–11′) ki[ng ...] *the god Bēl* (*Marduk*) [...]
Lacuna

Frgm. 7 ii′ 3′–11′ This passage presumably records work on Ezida ("True House"), temple of the god Nabû at Borsippa, as suggested by similar passages in inscriptions of the Assyrian kings Esarhaddon and Ashurbanipal recording the decoration of this temple. See, for example, Leichty, RINAP 4 p. 117 Esarhaddon 54 rev. 10–12 (esp. 11), [... KÙ].GI 2 AM.MEŠ KÙ.BABBAR 2 AM.MEŠ ZABAR 2 SUḪUR.MÁŠ.KU$_{6}$ ZABAR "[go]ld [...], two wild bulls of silver, two wild bulls of bronze, two goat-fish of bronze"; and Novotny and Jeffers, RINAP 5/1 p. 216 Ashurbanipal 10 (Prism T) ii 1–6 (esp. ii 1), 4 AM.MEŠ KÙ.BABBAR *ek-du-u-ti ... ul-ziz* "I stationed four fierce wild bulls of silver."

Frgm. 7 ii′ 6′ SIG$_{7}$.IGI.KÙ "*vault*": It is uncertain if this word is to be read as *mat(i)gigu* or *kur(i)gigu*. This rarely-attested Akkadian word also appears in the inscriptions of Esarhaddon (Leichty, RINAP 4 p. 24 Esarhaddon 1 vi 25) and Nebuchadnezzar II (CT 37 pl. 10 ii 5; and Legrain, PBS 15 no. 79 i 71) and is used to designate part of a gate, perhaps the vaulted, glazed-brick archway (Schaudig, Inschriften Nabonids p. 541).

Frgm. 7 ii′ 11′ ⸢*é-lagab-gíd*⸣ "Elagabgid": This Sumerian ceremonial name, which means "House, Long Block," is not otherwise attested and H. Schaudig (Inschriften Nabonids p. 541 n. 854) tentatively suggests that it could be the name of a temple magazine.

Fragment 8 (BE 3401)

Col. i′

Lacuna

1′) [...] (blank)
2′) [...]-⸢*sú*⸣
3′) [...]-⸢IG⸣
4′) [...] *x*
5′) [...]-⸢*ma*⸣
6′) [...]-⸢*šu*?⸣
7′) [...] (blank)

Lacuna

Col. ii′

Lacuna

1′) *x* [...]
2′) ⸢*ma*⸣-[...]
3′) *ina* ⸢É⸣ [...]
4′) GIŠ *x* [...]
5′) *lu-du-x* [...]
6′) *ul ú*-⸢*nak*?-*kìr*⸣ [...]
7′) *ku-ul-li-šú-nu-*[*ti* ...]
8′) ⸢*ú*⸣-*x x x* [...]

Lacuna

Lacuna

Frgm. 8 i′ 1′–7′) (No translation possible)

Lacuna

Lacuna

Frgm. 8 ii′ 1′–8′) [...] in the *temple* (of) [...] ... [...] ... [...] *did not alter* [...] the[ir] holding [...] ... [...]

Lacuna

Fragment 9 (BE 3409)

Col. i′

Lacuna

1′) [...] ⸢MI⸣

Lacuna

Col. ii′

Lacuna

1′) [*x*] ⸢*ú*⸣-[...]
2′) ⸢*iṣ*⸣-*ṣu-riš ip-*[*par-šú-ma*]
3′) *i-lu-ú* ⸢*ša*⸣-[*ma-míš*]
4′) *šá i-na* ⸢*ba*⸣-[...]
5′) *ù ta-*[...]
6′) *i-ši-ru* ⸢*a*⸣-[*na* ...]
7′) *it-ti* [...]
8′) *šil-lat* KUR [...]
9′) *qé-reb* ⸢URU⸣.[...]
10′) *ú-še-*⸢*rib*⸣ [...]
11′) ⸢GÌR.NÍTA⸣ [...]

Lacuna

Lacuna

Frgm. 9 i′ 1′) (No translation possible)

Lacuna

Lacuna

Frgm. 9 ii′ 1′–11′) [...] ... [...] (the gods) fl[ew] up to the hea[vens] like birds, who in [...] and [...] thrived, t[o ...] together with [...] booty of the land [...] I made enter the city [...]. The governor [...]

Lacuna

Fragment 10 (BE 3419)

Col. i′

Lacuna

1′) [...] *x* [*x*]
2′) [...] *x-ti ú-*⸢*kin*⸣
3′) [...] *x-na*
4′) [...] NUMUN

Lacuna

Col. ii′

Lacuna

Frgm. 10 i′ 1′–4′) [...] firmly established [...] (my) ... [...] ... [...] seed

Lacuna

Frgm. 9 ii′ 2′–3′ ⸢*iṣ*⸣-*ṣu-riš ip-*[*par-šú-ma*] *i-lu-ú* ⸢*ša*⸣-[*ma-míš*] "(the gods) fl[ew] up to the hea[vens] like birds": This exact wording appears in several inscriptions of Esarhaddon describing the divine abandonment of Babylon; see Leichty, RINAP 4 p. 196 Esarhaddon 104 i 44–46, pp. 203–204 Esarhaddon 105 ii 10–11, and p. 245 Esarhaddon 116 obv. 15′.

Lacuna
1′) (blank) [...]
2′) *pa-ni x* [...]
3′) *šá* KISAL.MAḪ *é-zi-*⸢*da*⸣ [...]
4′) ⸢*ú-kin*⸣ *a-na* ^{d}30 [...]
5′) [*x x*] *x* [...]
Lacuna

Lacuna
Frgm. 10 ii′ 1′–5′) [...] *before* [...] of the main courtyard of Ezid[a ...] I installed. For the god Sîn [...]
Lacuna

Fragment 11 (BE 3420)

Col. i′
Lacuna
1′) [...] (blank)
2′) [...] *x*
3′) [...] *x*
4′) [...] *x*
5′) [...] *x*
Lacuna

Lacuna
Frgm. 11 i′ 1′–5′) (No translation possible)
Lacuna

Col. ii′
Lacuna
1′) *x* [...]
2′) *x* [...]
3′) *i-*[...]
4′) ^{d}[...]
5′) *x* [...]
6′) [...]
Lacuna

Lacuna
Frgm. 11 ii′ 1′–6′) (No translation possible)
Lacuna

Fragment 12 (BE 3471)

Col. i′
Lacuna
1′) [...]-⸢*sú*$^{?}$⸣
2′) [...] *x*.MEŠ
3′) [...]-⸢*zi*⸣
4′) [...] ⸢AN$^{?}$⸣
Lacuna

Lacuna
Frgm. 12 i′ 1′–4′) (No translation possible)
Lacuna

Col. ii′
Lacuna
1′) [...] *x* [...]
2′) [...] *x* [...]
3′) [...] ⸢*ra*⸣ [...]
4′) [...] ⸢LÚ⸣ [...]
5′) [*x* (*x*)]-⸢*ta*⸣-*nu* ⸢*šá*$^{?}$⸣ [...]
6′) *x*-⸢*ga*⸣-[...]
Lacuna

Lacuna
Frgm. 12 ii′ 1′–6′) (No translation possible)
Lacuna

Fragment 13 (BE 3684)

Col. i′
Lacuna
1′) [*x x uḫ*]-⸢*ḫi*$^{?}$⸣-*iz*
2′) [...] *x* A KU *x*
3′) [...]-⸢*ta*$^{?}$⸣-*šú-nu*
4′) [...] *x-bir*
5′) [...] ⸢LÚ⸣.KÚR
6′) [...] *x* KI
7′) [...] *x*
8′) [...] (blank)

Lacuna
Frgm. 13 i′ 1′–5′) [... I inla]id [...] ... [...] ... [...] enemy
Frgm. 13 i′ 6′–10′) (No translation possible)

9′) [...]-⸢*ma*⸣
10′) [...] (blank)
Lacuna

Lacuna

Col. ii′
Lacuna
1′) ⸢^{d}⸣AMAR.⸢UTU⸣ *u*$^{?}$ ^{d}⸢*zar*$^{?}$-*pa*$^{?}$⸣-[*ni-tum*$^{?}$]
2′) EN.MEŠ-*e-a ú-še-pa*
3′) 2 NÍG.NA ⸢KÙ.GI⸣ ḪUŠ.A
4′) *šá* MIN$_6$ GUN 2 MA.NA
5′) ⸢*ki*⸣-*ma si-ma-ti-šú-nu*
6′) *reš-ta-a-ti*
7′) *ú-še-pi-iš*
8′) ⸢*ṣa*⸣-*lam*$^{?}$ ⸢*šá-ru*⸣-*ti*-⸢*ia*⸣
9′) ⸢*mu*⸣-*ut-nen-nu-ú*
10′) x x x x x
Lacuna

Lacuna
Frgm. 13 ii′ 1′–10′) I made [the ... of] the god Marduk *and* the goddess *Zarpa*[*nītu*], my lords, glorious. I had two censers of reddish gold, whose (weight is) two talents (and) two minas, (re)made according to their original appearance(s). [*A stat*]*ue of my royal majesty*, (shown as) a pious person, ...
Lacuna

Col. iii′
Lacuna
1′) *u* x [...]
2′) É [...]
3′) *ša* ⸢*im*⸣ [...]
4′) *a-di* x [...]
5′) x x [...]
6′) ⸢KÁ⸣ [...]
7′) (blank) [...]
Lacuna

Lacuna
Frgm. 13 iii′ 1′–7′) and [...] *temple* (*of*) [...], which [...] *up to* [...] ... [...] gate (of) [...]
Lacuna

Fragment 14 (BE 4655)

Lacuna
1′) [...] (blank) [...]
2′) [...] x [...]
3′) [...] x [...]
4′) [...] x [...]
5′) [...] x [...]
Lacuna

Lacuna
Frgm. 14 1′–5′) (No translation possible)
Lacuna

Fragment 15 (BE 46262)

Col. i′
Lacuna
1′) [...]-⸢*ba*$^{?}$⸣
2′) [...] (blank)
3′) [...] x
Lacuna

Lacuna
Frgm. 15 i′ 1′–3′) (No translation possible)
Lacuna

Col. ii′
Lacuna
1′) x x [...]
2′) x-*ma* [...]
3′) ⸢*i-na*⸣ [...]

Lacuna
Frgm. 15 ii′ 1′–8′) (No translation possible)

Frgm. 13 ii′ 2′ *ú-še-pa* "I made glorious": W.R. Gallagher (AfO 48/49 [2001–02] p. 105) suggests reading this word as *ú-še-reb* "I had (them) enter." If that proposal proves correct, then the KAL sign is defectively written: it is missing a vertical wedge.
Frgm. 13 ii′ 5′–6′ ⸢*ki*⸣-*ma si-ma-ti-šú-nu reš-ta-a-ti* "according to their original appearance(s)": A similar statement is made by Neriglissar in a passage in an inscription recording the creation of eight copper *mušḫuššu*-dragons for four prominent gateways in Esagil; compare Neriglissar 3 (Royal Palace Inscription) i 32, *ki-ma sì-ma-a-ti-šu re-eš-ta-a-ti* "according to its original appearance."
Frgm. 13 ii′ 8′ ⸢*ṣa*⸣-*lam*$^{?}$ ⸢*šá-ru*⸣-*ti*-⸢*ia*⸣ "[*a stat*]*ue of my royal majesty*": The reading of the line tentatively follows Gallagher, AfO 48/49 (2001–02) p. 106. The interpretation of the second sign, however, is not entirely certain. H. Schaudig (Inschriften Nabonids p. 543) suggested that last four signs of the line could be read either as *šá šub-ti*-⸢*ia*⸣ "of my dwelling" or *šá-ru-ti*-⸢*ia*⸣ "of my kingship." The latter proposal is preferred here based on the preceding and following words, respectively *ṣalmu* and *mutnennû*.

4′) ⌜*ú*?-*ra*?⌝-[...]
5′) ⌜UG⌝-[...]
6′) *ú*-[...]
7′) *i*-[...]
8′) *x* [...]
Lacuna

Lacuna

Fragment 16 (BE 47320)

Col. i′
Lacuna
1′) [...] *x*
2′) [...] *x*
3′) [...] *x*
4′) [...] *x*
5′) [...] *x*
Lacuna

Lacuna
Frgm. 16 i′ 1′–5′) (No translation possible)
Lacuna

Col. ii′
Lacuna
1′) *x* [...]
2′) *x* [...]
3′) *x* [...]
4′) *x* [...]
5′) *x* [...]
6′) *x* [...]
Lacuna

Lacuna
Frgm. 16 ii′ 1′–6′) (No translation possible)
Lacuna

5

This draft or archival copy of an Akkadian inscription recording the dedication of an offering table to the goddess Ištar is inscribed on a small, rectangular clay tablet. According to this text, Nabonidus had the table constructed from *musukkannu*-wood, a valuable hard wood (possibly *Dalbergia sissoo*) and had it plated with silver and gold. The tablet is not dated and there is not enough information in the inscription to suggest a date of composition.

CATALOGUE

Museum Number	Registration Number	Provenance	cpn
BM 38770	80-11-12,645	Possibly Babylon	c

COMMENTARY

BM 38770 is a crudely-fashioned *u'iltu*-tablet, a horizontal, 'pillow-shaped' tablet (1:2 ratio); for details of this format, see Radner, Nineveh 612 BC pp. 72–73 (with fig. 8). In the Neo-Assyrian period, such tablets could be inscribed with first or early drafts of inscriptions, not all of which were approved by the king (or by his chief scribe, who likely vetted compositions in advance); see the comments in Grayson and Novotny, RINAP 3/2 pp. 5–7. The fact that the tablet is badly made and that the text includes mistakes suggests that BM 38770 was not a model used to directly copy its contents onto the metal plating of the *musukkannu*-wood table presented to Ištar and was not an archival copy of that inscription since those types of texts were commonly written on well-fashioned tablets. T.G. Lee (JAC 10 [1995] p. 69) suggests that BM 38770 was either an archival copy or a later copy, while H. Schaudig (Inschriften Nabonids p. 476) proposes that it might have served as a draft for the model of the final, approved inscription. While it is likely that this small tablet might have contained an early draft of a Nabonidus inscription, one should not rule out the possibility that BM 38770 and its text is a scribal exercise made by a student or a copy prepared by an inexperienced scribe.

BIBLIOGRAPHY

1995 Lee, JAC 10 pp. 65–69 (copy, edition)

2001 Schaudig, Inschriften Nabonids p. 476 no. 2.21 (edition)

TEXT

Obv.
1) *a-na* ^{d}INANNA ⸢GAŠAN⸣ [...]
2) *ru-ba-a-ti* ⸢*ru-uṣ-ṣu*⸣-[*un-ti* GAŠAN-*ia*]
3) ^{d}AG-*na-'i-id* LUGAL TIN.[TIR.KI]
4) *za-ni-in é-sag-íl u* [*é-zi-da*]
5) *mu-uš-te-e'-ú aš-ra-a-*[*ti-šá ana-ku*]
6) GIŠ.BANŠUR MES.MÁ.KAN.NA *iṣ-*[*ṣi da-rí-a*]
7) *i-na* KÙ.BABBAR *eb-bi ù* KÙ.⸢GI⸣ [*nam-ri*]
8) ⸢*uḫ*⸣-*ḫi-iz-ma ú-ki-in* [*ma-ḫar-šá*]
Bottom
9) ^{d}INANNA* GAŠAN *dam-qá-*[*a-tu-ú-a*]
Rev.
10) *a-ta-mi**-*i ud-*[*da-kam*]

1–5) For the goddess Ištar, [(...)] la[dy (of) ...], splend[id] princess, [my lady]: Nabonidus, king of Ba[bylon], the one who provides for Esagil and [Ezida], the one who constantly seeks out [her] shrin[es, am I].

6–8) [I i]nlaid a table of *musukkannu*-wood, a [durable wo]od, with shiny silver and [bright] gold and placed (it) firmly be[fore her].

9–10) O Ištar, (my) lady, say good [things about me] all [day long].

6

A paving stone discovered near Tower 2 of the Euphrates embankment wall of Babylon is reported by F. Wetzel (Stadtmauern p. 51) to have been inscribed with a text already known from paving stones found in the processional street ("bekannte Inschrift der Pflasterplatten der Prozessionsstraße"). Because the object originated from the vicinity of the so-called 'Nabonidus Wall' and because Wetzel did not explicitly state the name of the royal author of the text, P.-R. Berger (NbK p. 345) assumed that the inscription on that paving stone (BE 41580) belonged to Nabonidus. P.-A. Beaulieu (Nabonidus p. 40) and H. Schaudig (Inschriften Nabonids p. 343) followed Berger's assignment of the text since no on-the-spot copy

("Fundkopie"), excavation photograph, transliteration, or translation of this alleged text of Nabonidus had been published. O. Pedersén, having carefully re-examined the German Excavation field journals, excavation photographs, and resulting publications, has pointed out (via personal communication) that BE 41580 (Bab ph 2154–2155) actually bears an inscription of Nebuchadnezzar II (Lb1 2), rather than a hitherto, unpublished inscription of Nabonidus. Thus, the text referred to as "Nabonidus Paving Stone U" and "[Nabonidus] Inscription H" in scholarly literature does not exist, so no edition of it is presented here.

BIBLIOGRAPHY

1930 Wetzel, Stadtmauern p. 51 and pl. 46 (study, provenance)
1973 Berger, NbK p. 345 Nbn. Pflasterstein U (study)
1989 Beaulieu, Nabonidus p. 40 Inscription H (study)
2001 Schaudig, Inschriften Nabonids p. 343 no. 1.11 (study)

7–9

Reports of the German excavations at Babylon record that bricks inscribed with either a three-, four-, or six-line 'Nabonidus stamp' were found in various locations in Babylon, including the so-called 'Nabonidus Wall' and the Emaḫ temple. To date, only the three- and six-line texts have been published; the four-line text, however, remains unpublished. The known three-, four-, or six-line inscriptions are edited in this volume as text nos. 8, 9, and 7 respectively. There are undoubtedly more Nabonidus bricks than the ones included in the catalogues of text nos. 7–9, but they are not included in this volume since (a) their contents and arrangement of the inscription are unknown and (b) since their excavation (and museum) numbers are not recorded. Some might be duplicates of text nos. 7–9, while others might bear hitherto, unique inscription(s) of this king of Babylon.

BIBLIOGRAPHY

1908 Koldewey, MDOG 38 pp. 19–20 (study)
1911 Koldewey, Tempel pp. 8 and 10 (study)
1930 Wetzel, Stadtmauern p. 52 (study)
1973 Berger, NbK p. 353 Nbn. Backsteine U (study)
1989 Beaulieu, Nabonidus p. 40 Inscription E (study)
1990 Koldewey, WEB[5] pp. 76, 89 and 234 (study)
2001 Schaudig, Inschriften Nabonids p. 343 no. 1.10 (study)

7

Several bricks bear a short Akkadian inscription of Nabonidus; the script, which is written in a stamped frame, is archaizing Neo-Babylonian. One of the bricks was found in Babylon at the banks of the Euphrates. The six-line text mentions Nabonidus' name, title, and filiation. This inscription is sometimes referred to as "Nabonidus Brick A I, 1" and "[Nabonidus] Inscription C" in scholarly literature.

CATALOGUE

Ex.	Museum Number	Excavation/ Registration No.	Provenance	Lines Preserved	cpn
1	BM 236a–c	—	Babylon, Euphrates embankment	1–6	n
2	VA Bab 4743	BE 66113	Babylon, Babil	1–6	p
3	—	BE 41546	Babylon, Sahn 36y, wall north of the gate of the bridge	1–6	n

COMMENTARY

Ex. 1 is now known only from the hand-drawn facsimile in Rawlinson 1 R (pl. 68 no. 3). The (composite) copy of the inscription was prepared from three squeezes (BM 236a–c) of brick(s) found in situ in the Euphrates embankment wall at Babylon. It is uncertain if these squeezes are still in the British Museum (London) or if they were destroyed by S. Smith on the grounds that they had outlived their usefulness. The size of the bricks has not been previously published and, therefore, that information remains unknown.

Ex. 2 (VA Bab 4743) has a short, two-word Aramaic text impressed beneath the six-line Akkadian inscription: *byt'l lwny*, meaning "Bethel has accompanied me" or "Bethel, accompany me!" (see Sass and Marzahn, WVDOG 127 pp. 34, 48 and 166). For further information on Aramaic impressions on bricks, see the commentary to text no. 8 and Sass and Marzahn, WVDOG 127.

The master text and lineation follow ex. 1. No score of the inscription is given on Oracc since scores are not provided for texts on bricks (following the model of RIM and RINAP). In addition, no minor (orthographic) variants are given in the critical apparatus at the back of the book, as no such variants occur in exs. 2–3.

BIBLIOGRAPHY

1859 Oppert, EM 2 pp. 325–326 (ex. 1, copy, edition)
1861 Rawlinson, 1 R pl. 68 no. 3 (ex. 1, copy)
1863 Oppert, EM 1 p. 184 (ex. 1, translation, study)
1875 Ménant, Babylone p. 253 (ex. 1, translation)
1890 Peiser in Schrader, KB 3/2 pp. 118–119 (ex. 1, edition)
1899 Bezold, Cat. 5 2235 no. 236a–236c (ex. 1, study)
1912 Langdon, NBK pp. 58 and 294–295 Nbd. no. 11 (ex. 1, edition)
1973 Berger, NbK p. 346 Nbn. Backsteine A I, 1 (ex. 1, study)
1989 Beaulieu, Nabonidus p. 39 Inscription C (ex. 1, study)
2001 Schaudig, Inschriften Nabonids p. 335 no. 1.2[a] (ex. 1, edition)
2010 Sass and Marzahn, WVDOG 127 p. 34 no. 14 (cat. no. 14) and p. 37 figs. 127–128 (ex. 2, photo, copy, transliteration)

TEXT

1) ^{d}*na-bi-um-na-'i-id*
2) LUGAL KÁ.DINGIR.RA.KI
3) *mu-ud-di-iš*
4) *é-sag-íl ù é-zi-da*
5) IBILA ^{d}AG-TIN-*su-iq-bi*
6) *ru-bu-u e-em-qá*

1–6) Nabonidus, king of Babylon, the one who renovates Esagil and Ezida, heir of Nabû-balāssu-iqbi, wise prince.

8

Six bricks from Babylon, one brick from Kish, and one brick from Seleucia-on-the-Tigris bear a short, three-line Akkadian inscription. The text, which was placed on either the face of the brick or on its edge, is written inside a stamped frame, in archaizing Neo-Babylonian script. The inscription, which is called "Nabonidus Brick Ap I, 1" and "[Nabonidus] Inscription D" in previous editions and studies, comprises only the king's name, title, and filiation.

CATALOGUE

Ex.	Museum Number	Excavation/ Registration No.	Provenance	Lines Preserved	cpn
1	BM 235	—	Babylon, Euphrates embankment	1–3	n
2	VA Bab 4727	BE 36837	Babylon, Merkes 28m1, +7.4 m	1–3	p
3	VA Bab 4728	BE 36837	As ex. 2	1–3	p
4	VA Bab 4729	BE 36837	As ex. 2	1–3	p
5	EŞ 9071	BE 36837	As ex. 2	1–3	n
6	VA Bab 4072	BE 36838	As ex. 2	1–3	n
7	—	S 6784	Seleucia	1–3	n
8	VA Bab 4072	BE 3868 (Bab ph 1525A)	Kish, Tell Bender	1–3	n

COMMENTARY

Ex. 1 is now known only from the hand-drawn facsimile in Rawlinson 1 R (pl. 68 no. 2). The copy of this short Nabonidus text was prepared from a squeeze (BM 235) of a brick seen in the Euphrates embankment wall at Babylon. The present fate of the nineteenth-century squeeze is unknown. It might have been destroyed by S. Smith with other squeezes or it might still exist somewhere in the storerooms of the British Museum (London). The size of the bricks has not been previously published and, therefore, that information remains unknown. The rectangular-stamped area of ex. 7 (S 6784), as far as it is preserved, is 6.5 cm high and 10 cm wide.

The master text and lineation follow ex. 1. Like other brick inscriptions included in RINBE 2, no score of this inscription is given on Oracc. Moreover, as no minor (orthographic) variants occur in exs. 2–8, no variants are given in the critical apparatus at the back of the book.

Exs. 2–5 have a one-word Aramaic text *nbwntn* ("Nabû-natan," which means "the god Nabû has given") stamped on them. During the Neo-Babylonian Period, bricks stamped with Aramaic texts almost exclusively come from Babylon. The function of these auxiliary inscriptions is still a matter of discussion, but according to B. Sass and J. Marzahn (WVDOG 127 pp. 193–194), they could designate the place where the bricks were created or the destinations of the bricks, rather than being the names of people. Moreover, the people named in these Aramaic labels are otherwise unknown and the impression of a personal name beside the name of the king in the cuneiform Akkadian text, even if it were the name of a(n important) high official, might be viewed as problematic.

R. Koldewey (MDOG 38 [1908] p. 19; and WEB[5] pp. 89 and 234) stated that bricks with both a three- or four-line cuneiform (Akkadian) inscription of Nabonidus and an impressed-Aramaic label reading *nbwn'd* ("Nabonidus") were discovered in the floor of a house in the Merkes. P.-R. Berger (NbK pp. 23, 25 and 353) and H. Schaudig (Inschriften Nabonids p. 9 n. 14 and p. 343 no. 1.10 [ex. 2]) repeated this information, without having seen the bricks. Sass and Marzahn (WVDOG 127 p. 30 n. 37 and p. 80 [with n. 74]), in their careful and detailed examination of the Aramaic impression of Neo-Babylonian bricks available to them, were unable to verify Koldewey's claim that Nabonidus' bricks bore both an Akkadian and an Aramaic inscription, stating "Nabonidus four-liners with auxiliary Aramaic impressions are unknown to us among the bricks in Berlin and the published ones elsewhere." They tentatively suggest that Koldewey might have been "influenced by the royal name in the cuneiform impressions" and "read the Aramaic name *nbwn'd* instead of *nbwntn*"; see Sass and Marzahn, WVDOG 127 p. 80 n. 74. An individual with the name Nabonidus (*nbwn'd*), however, did have his name impressed on a brick from Babylon, but that brick clearly dates to the reign of Nebuchadnezzar II (Sass and Marzahn, WVDOG 127 p. 20 no. 3).

BIBLIOGRAPHY

1859 Oppert, EM 2 p. 326 (ex. 1, copy, edition)
1861 Rawlinson, 1 R pl. 68 no. 2 (ex. 1, copy)
1863 Oppert, EM 1 p. 185 (ex. 1, translation, study)
1875 Ménant, Babylone p. 253 (ex. 1, translation)
1890 Peiser in Schrader, KB 3/2 pp. 118–119 (ex. 1, edition)
1899 Bezold, Cat. 5 p. 2235 no. 235 (ex. 1, study)
1912 Langdon, NBK pp. 58 and 294–295 Nbd. no. 10 (ex. 1, edition)
1990 Koldewey, WEB[4] p. 79 fig. 51h (ex. 2, copy)
1931 Koldewey, Königsburgen 1 p. 32 (translation)
1970–71 Pettinato, Mesopotamia 5–6 pp. 54 and 61 no. 25 fig. 46 (ex. 7, photo, edition)
1973 Berger, NbK p. 347 Nbn. Backsteine Ap I, 1 (exs. 1–2, study)
1989 Beaulieu, Nabonidus pp. 39–40 Inscription D (exs. 1–2, study)
1990 Koldewey, WEB[5] p. 90 fig. 51h (ex. 2, copy)
2001 Schaudig, Inschriften Nabonids pp. 336–337 no. 1.4[a] (exs. 1–2, 7, edition)
2010 Sass and Marzahn, WVDOG 127 p. 30 no. 13 (cat. nos. 43.1–3) and pp. 36–37 figs. 122–125 (exs. 2–6, photo, copy, transliteration)

TEXT

1) [d]AG-*na-'i-id* LUGAL KÁ.DINGIR.RA.KI
2) *ni-bi-it* [d]*na-bi-um ù* [d]AMAR.UTU
3) IBILA [d]AG-TIN-*su-iq-bi* NUN *em-qá a-na-ku*

1–3) Nabonidus, king of Babylon, the one nominated by the gods Nabû and Marduk, heir of Nabû-balāssu-iqbi, wise prince, am I.

9

At least one brick in the Vorderasiatisches Museum (Berlin) bears an inscription of Nabonidus written in four lines of text. That brick may be one of the four-line bricks of this king mentioned in the Babylon excavation reports with a four-line 'Nabonidus stamp.' Since that brick has never been published and since it was not available to the authors of this volume, no edition is presented here. This still unpublished text is sometimes referred to in scholarly publications as "Nabonidus Brick U" and "[Nabonidus] Inscription E."

CATALOGUE

Museum Number	Excavation Number	Provenance	cpn
VA —	BE 36862	Babylon, Sahn 21u–x, +0.9 m	n

BIBLIOGRAPHY

1973 Berger, NbK p. 353 Nbn. Backsteine U (study)
1989 Beaulieu, Nabonidus p. 40 Inscription E (study)
2001 Schaudig, Inschriften Nabonids p. 343 no. 1.10 (study)

10–12

Three clay cylinder fragments unearthed at Babylon each bear part of an Akkadian inscription describing Nabonidus' rebuilding of Eulmaš, the temple of the goddess Ištar at Agade. All three pieces most likely come from the middle column of a large, three-column cylinder; this is certainly the case for BE 32652 (text no. 10 [Eulmaš Cylinder]) and BE 12586 (text no. 11), but not necessarily for BE 40133 (text no. 12) since only the middle part of one column is preserved. The inscription(s) written on these fragments might have been similar to text nos. 27, 28 (Eḫulḫul Cylinder), and 29 (Eḫulḫul Cylinder) and, thus, might have included reports of three, or possibly four, building projects. Since each fragment preserves only a small portion of the original inscription, it is unclear what the other building activities of Nabonidus might have been. Because the pieces all come from Babylon, one could suggest that the inscription(s) likely recorded one of Nabonidus' building projects in that city. Given the small, fragmentary state of preservation of BE 32652, BE 12586, and for BE 40133, it is not yet possible to determine if the inscription written on them belong to one and the same text or to two or three different inscriptions. Since it is not yet possible to determine the relationship between the text(s) inscribed on these three pieces, it is best to edit the texts written on them separately. Therefore, BE 32652, BE 12586, and BE 40133 are edited respectively as text nos. 10 (Eulmaš Cylinder), 11, and 12 in the present volume.

10

A fragment of a three-column clay cylinder unearthed at Babylon preserves part of an Akkadian inscription that records the restoration of Eulmaš, the temple of the goddess Ištar at Agade; the piece comes from the middle column (col. ii). This text, which is written in Neo-Babylonian script, describes Nabonidus' painstaking efforts to find the temple's original foundations, an undertaking that he claims previous rulers (namely, Esarhaddon, Ashurbanipal, and Nebuchadnezzar II) were unsuccessful in; the composer(s) of this inscription (falsely) state that seventh-century Assyrian kings recorded their failure to find the original foundations in their inscriptions commemorating the rebuilding of this ancient temple. The text, which H. Schaudig refers to as the "Eulmaš Cylinder," was written during or after Nabonidus' seventh regnal year (549).

CATALOGUE

Museum Number	Excavation Number	Photograph Number	Provenance	cpn
B 16	BE 32652	Bab ph 1153	Babylon, Kasr 20m, in brick debris, east of the crossing brick wall between the inner city wall and the wall of the South Palace	p

COMMENTARY

Because the original was not available for study in the Eşki Şark Eserleri Müzesi (Istanbul), the present edition of BE 32652 is based on the published excavation photograph (Bab ph 1153), as well as on G. Frame's hand-drawn facsimile of that photograph.

For a complete account of Nabonidus' rebuilding of the Eulmaš temple at Agade, from which the present text has been restored, see text no. 27 ii 28–iii 25.

BIBLIOGRAPHY

1930 Wetzel, Stadtmauern pls. 14 and 16 (provenance)
1931 Koldewey, Königsburgen 1 pl. 14 (provenance)
1948 Goossens, RA 42 p. 154 nos. 3–4 (study)
1989 Beaulieu, Nabonidus pp. 141 n. 43 and 239 Frgm. 4 (study)
1993 Frame, Mesopotamia 28 pp. 29–37 (copy, edition)
2001 Schaudig, Inschriften Nabonids pp. 469–470 no. 2.17 (edition)
2003 Schaudig, Studies Kienast pp. 475, 477 and 490 (study)
2009 Winter, On Art in the Ancient Near East 2 pp. 463–466 (study)

TEXT

Col. i
Completely missing
Col. ii
Lacuna
1′) *[la ik-šu-du]* ⸢*iš*⸣-*ṭù-ru-ma [iš-ku-nu]*
2′) ⸢*um*⸣-*ma te-me-en-na é-ul-*⸢*maš*⸣ *[ú-ba-ʾi-i-ma la ak-šu-ud]*
3′) GIŠ.ÁSAL *ù* GIŠ.*maš-tu-*⸢*ú*⸣ *[ak-šiṭ-ma]*
4′) *te-né-e é-ul-maš e-pu-uš-ma* <*a-na*> ^{d}INANNA *a-*⸢*kà*⸣*-[dè*.KI *ad-din]*
5′) ^{md}AG-NÍG.GUB-ÙRU LUGAL TIN.TIR.KI DUMU ^{md}AG-IBILA-⸢ÙRU⸣
6′) LUGAL *a-lik maḫ-ri-ia e-peš* É *šu-a-tim lìb-ba-šú ub-[lam-ma]*
7′) *te-me-en-šú la-bi-ri ú-ba-ʾi-i-ma la i-mu-ur la i-*⸢*pu*⸣*-[uš]*
8′) *ia-ti* ^{d}AG-NÍ.TUKU LUGAL TIN.TIR.KI *e-peš* É *šu-a-tim áš-te-eʾ-e-ma*
9′) *i-na qé-reb a-kà-dè*.KI *pa-ni qaq-qa-ru ú-pat-ti-ma*

Completely missing

Lacuna
ii 1′–4′) [they (Esarhaddon and Ashurbanipal) sought out the (original) foundation(s) of Eulmaš, but did not reach (them)]. They put down in writing, saying: "[I sought out] the (original) foundation(s) of Eulma[š, but I did not reach (them). I cut down] poplar(s) and *martû*-tree(s) and (then) built a replacement Eulmaš and [gave (it)] <to> the goddess Ištar of Ag[ade]."
ii 5′–7′) (As for) Nebuchadnezzar (II), king of Babylon, son of Nabopolass[ar], a king who came before me, his heart pro[mpted (him)] to (re)build that temple [and] he sought out the original foundation(s), but did not find (them) and (therefore) did not (re)bu[ild (Eulmaš)].
ii 8′–10′a) (But as for) me, Nabonidus, king of Babylon, I continuously strove to (re)build that temple. Inside Agade, I opened up the surface of (its former) location and (then) sought out (its) foundation(s).

Lacuna before ii 1′ The translation assumes that the line now-missing before ii 1′ contained *te-me-en-na é-ul-maš ú-ba-ʾu-ú* "they sought out the (original) foundation(s) of Eulmaš"; compare the parallel passage in text no. 27 ii 39.
ii 5′–7′ Compare the passage in text no. 27 (ii 45b–49) describing Nebuchadnezzar II's unsuccessful search for Eulmaš' original foundation.
ii 8′–13′ Compare text no. 27 ii 50–56, which contains a similar, but not identical, account of Nabonidus' successful search for the original foundations of Eulmaš.

10′) *áš-te-e*ʾ*-a te-me-en-na i-na* MU.7.KAM *i-na pa-le-e-a ki-i-nim*
11′) *i-na na-ra-am* LUGAL-*ú-ti-ia* ^{d}INANNA *a-kà-dè*.KI GAŠAN GAL-*ti*
12′) *šu-ba-at-su da-rí-ti iḫ-ta-as-sa-as-ma*
13′) *a-na* É *šu-a-tim* ⸢*is*⸣-[*li*]-⸢*im*⸣-*ma ip-pa-šìr ka-bat-tu-uš*

ii 10′b–13′) During the seventh year of my legitimate reign, the goddess Ištar of Agade, the great lady, through (her) love for my royal majesty, remembered her eternal dwelling, beca[me reco]nciled towards this temple, and her mood relaxed.

14′) ⸢^{d}IŠKUR GÚ.GAL⸣ [AN-*e u* KI-*tim x x*] *x x x*-⸢*di-ma*⸣

ii 14′) The god Adad, canal inspector of [heaven and earth ...] ... *and*

Lacuna

Col. iii

Completely missing

11

A second fragment of a three-column clay cylinder found at Babylon (BE 12586; B 39 [formerly D 274]) preserves part of an Akkadian inscription recording Nabonidus' restoration of the temple of the goddess Ištar at Agade, Eulmaš; the script is contemporary Neo-Babylonian. The extant text records that the Neo-Babylonian king's workmen, after much effort, discovered the foundations of Eulmaš laid by the Sargonic king Narām-Sîn (2254–2218), the grandson of Sargon of Agade. Like text no. 10 (Eulmaš Cylinder), this inscription was probably also written during or after Nabonidus' seventh regnal year (549).

CATALOGUE

Museum Number	Excavation Number	Photograph Number	Provenance	cpn
B 39	BE 12586	Bab ph 559	Babylon, Kasr, South Palace, main courtyard	p

TEXT

Col. i

Completely missing

Col. ii

Lacuna

1′) [...] *x x x x x x x x x*
2′) [... *ú-ṣu*]-*ra-ti-šá la ut-tu-ú ši-kin*-⸢*šu*⸣
3′) [...]-⸢*ra-am*?⸣-*mu-ú* (*x*)-*qa-am pa-ni-ia*
4′) [... *i-na ḫi-da*]-⸢*a*⸣-*ti ù ri-ša-a-ti*

ii 1′–5′a) [...] ... [...] its ground plan could not be found, i[ts] structure [...] ... before me [... during joy]ous celebrations.

5′) [... *é*]-⸢*ul*⸣-*maš šu-a-tim ul-tu pa-ni qaq-qa-ru*
6′) [... *ú-šap*?]-⸢*pil*⸣-*ma te-me-en-na* ^{m}*na-ra-am*-^{d}EN.ZU
7′) [...] *x-ma* ši-ṭir šu-mi*-⸢*šu*⸣ *ap-pa-lis-ma*
8′) [... *šu-a*]-*tim la ka-ṣi-ir ši-pí*-⸢*ir*⸣-*šu*
9′) [...] ^{m}⸢*na-ram*⸣-^{d}30 3 ⸢KÙŠ⸣ *ú-šap-pil-ma*
10′) [... *a*]-⸢*di*⸣ 2.TA ⸢*ziq*⸣-*qur*-⸢*re*⸣-[*e-ti-šú*]

ii 5′b–11′) [... (of)] that Eulmaš, from the surface of the ground, [*I dug do*]*wn* [...] and the (original) foundation(s) of Narām-Sîn [...]. Then, I saw an inscription bearing his name and the work of [th]at [...] was not (well) constructed. [... (of)] Narām-Sîn, I dug down (a further) three cubits and [... togeth]er with (those of) [its] two ziggur[ats, ...] ... [...]

11′) [...] *x x* [(*x*)] *x* [...]	
Lacuna	Lacuna
Col. iii	
Lacuna	Lacuna
1′) *x* [...]	iii 1′–4′) (No translation possible)
2′) *x* [...]	
3′) *man*?-[*nu*? ...]	
4′) *x* [...]	
Lacuna	Lacuna

12

A small piece of a multi-column clay cylinder discovered at Babylon preserves part of an Akkadian inscription recording the rebuilding of Eulmaš, the temple of the goddess Ištar at Agade; the script is contemporary Neo-Babylonian. Because the extant text describes the discovery of the (original) foundations of the temple laid by Narām-Sîn of Agade (2254–2218), the inscription was almost certainly composed in the name of Nabonidus, rather than in that of some other Neo-Babylonian king. The proposed attribution is further supported by the fact that the king claims to have become distressed upon discovering the ancient foundations of Eulmaš; the wording *aplaḫ akkud naqutti aršêma* ("I became frightened, worried, (and) anxious") is presently known only from inscriptions of Nabonidus. For these reasons, the inscription written on BE 40133 is included in the present volume as a certain text of Nabonidus. Like text no. 10 (Eulmaš Cylinder), this inscription was probably also written during or after Nabonidus' seventh regnal year (549).

CATALOGUE

Museum Number	Excavation Number	Photograph Number	Provenance	cpn
B 29	BE 40133	Bab ph 2074	Babylon, Merkes 22q2	p

COMMENTARY

The authors would like to thank G. Frame for bringing this inscription to their attention and to O. Pedersén for providing them with information about the piece. BE 40133 (B 29; former D 264) was collated from Bab ph 2074.

TEXT

Col. i

Completely missing

Completely missing

Col. ii

Lacuna

1′) [...] *x* [...]

2′) [...] *x* ⸢*te*⸣-*me-en*-⸢*na*⸣ [...]

3′) [...] *x-ma ši-ṭir šu*-[*mi-šu*$^{?}$ ...]

4′) [...] ⸢*šu*⸣-*a-tim la ka*-⸢*ṣi*⸣-[*ir*$^{?}$ ...]

5′) [...] ⸢*te*⸣-*me-en-na* ^{m}*na-ram*-⸢^{d}⸣[30 ...]

6′) [...] ⸢LUGAL⸣ *a-lik maḫ-ri-šú x* [...]

7′) [...] *a-mur-ma iḫ-di lìb-bi* ⸢*im*$^{?}$⸣-[*mi-ru zi-mu-ú-a*]

8′) [... ^{m}]⸢*na*⸣-*ram*-^{d}30 AD AB *x* [(*x*)] *x* [...]

9′) [...] *x e-em-qá mu-ut-né**-*en**-⸢*nu-ú*⸣ *x* [...]

10′) [...] (*x*) *x te-me-en-na šu-a-tim ap-la*-⸢*aḫ*⸣ [*ak-ku-ud*]

11′) [*na-qut*]-⸢*ti ar*⸣-*še-e-ma** *áš-ši* ⸢*qá*$^{?}$⸣-[*ti-ia*$^{?}$]

12′) [...] (*x*) *x x x* (*x*) [...]

Lacuna

Lacuna

ii 1′–8′) [...] foundatio[n(s) ...] and [...] an inscription bearing [*his*] *na*[*me* ... t]hat [...] was not (*well*) *const*[*ructed* ... f]oundation(s) of Narām-[Sîn ... a k]ing who came before him [...] I discovered. Then, my heart was happy (and) [my face] *b*[*eamed*. ... N]arām-Sîn ... [...].

ii 9′–12′) [...], the wise (and) pious one, [...] ... that foundation, I became frighten[ed, worried, (and) anxi]ous, and (then) I raised [*my*] *h*[*ands* ...] ... [...]

Lacuna

Col. iii

Completely missing

Completely missing

13

A purchased, damaged two-column cylinder, probably from Borsippa, is inscribed with an Akkadian text of Nabonidus recording the rebuilding of the walls surrounding Nabû's temple and ziggurat, Ezida ("True House") and Eurmeiminanki ("House which Gathers the Seven *Mes* of Heaven and Netherworld"). The text, which is written in archaizing Neo-Babylonian script, records that construction on these walls was started during the reign of Nabonidus' predecessor Neriglissar, but that the work remained unfinished. In typical Mesopotamian fashion, Nabonidus boasts that he completed the work and made those walls more impressive than the previous ones. H. Schaudig called this inscription the "Ezida Cylinder."

CATALOGUE

Museum Number	Excavation Number	Photograph Number	Provenance	cpn
VA 5273	BE 21200B	Bab ph 556, 1642–1645	Probably Borsippa	c

12 i′ 9′ *mu-ut-né**-*en**-⸢*nu-ú*⸣ "pious one": The text has *mu-ut-en-né*-⸢*nu-ú*⸣.

BIBLIOGRAPHY

1982 Klengel-Brandt, Turm p. 130 fig. 53 and p. 187 no. 53 (photo, study)

1989 Jakob-Rost, FuB 27 pp. 80–85 no. 24 and copy 4 (photo, copy, edition)

1995 Schaudig, AoF 22 pp. 247–264 (copy, edition)

2001 Schaudig, Inschriften Nabonids pp. 395–397 no. 2.10[a] and 755 fig. 19 (copy, edition)

2005–06 George, AfO 51 p. 88 n. 18 (i 9′–13′, edition)

Figure 10. VA 5273 (Nabonidus no. 13), a damaged two-column cylinder inscribed with a text recording this king's work on the enclosure walls of the Ezida complex at Borsippa. © Staatliche Museen zu Berlin – Vorderasiatisches Museum. Photo: Olaf M. Teßmer.

TEXT

Col. i

1) [ᵈ*na-bi*]-⸢*um*⸣-*na-ʾi-id* LUGAL TIN.TIR.KI
2) [*ru-bu-ú*] ⸢*mi*⸣-*gi-ir* ᵈAMAR.UTU
3) [*re-é-a-um*] ⸢*ni-bi-it* ᵈ⸣AG
4) [*x x za-ni-in é*]-*sag-íl*
5) [*ù é-zi-da x x*] *x-šu*

i 1–5) [Nab]onidus, king of Babylon, [prince] who is the favorite of the god Marduk, [shepherd] chosen by the god Nabû, [... who provides for E]sagil [and Ezida, ...] ...

Lacuna

1′) [*x x*] *x* ⸢*li-ib-bi*⸣
2′) [*a-na*] *ša-a-ṭi se-er-de-šu-un*
3′) ⸢*ka*⸣-*an-šu ki-ša-ad-su*
4′) ⸢*i*⸣-*ša-ad-da-du sa-ar-ma-šu-un*
5′) *a-na ša e-li-šu-nu ṭa-a-bi e-pé-šu*
6′) *gi-na-a ú-sa-al-lu-ù* DINGIR.DINGIR GAL.GAL
7′) DUMU ᵐᵈ*na-bi-um-ba-la-at-su-iq-bi*
8′) *ru-bu-ú e-em-qu a-na-ku*

Lacuna

i 1′–8′) [...] heart, whose neck is bowed down to pull their (the gods') chariot pole, (the one) who drags their *yoke*, (the one who) constantly prays to the great gods to do what(ever) is pleasing to them, son of Nabû-balāssu-iqbi, wise prince, am I.

9′) *e-nu-ma ši-pí-ir é-zi-da*
10′) *a-na šu-ul-lu-mu aš-te-eʾ-ú*
11′) *i-ga-ra-ti si-ḫi-ir-ti é-ur*$_4$*-me-imin-an-ki*
12′) *uš-ši ad-di-ma ú-kin te-me-en-ši-in*
13′) *e-eš-šiš e-pú-uš-ma a-na ta-na-da-a-ti aš-ták-kan*

i 9′–13′) When I strove to finish off the work on Ezida, I laid the foundations of the enclosure walls of Eurmeiminanki and (thereby) secured their foundation(s). I built (them) anew and made (each) worthy of (high) praise.

---

i 4′ *sa-ar-ma-šu-un* "their *yoke*": According to the CAD (S p. 177), the meaning of *sarmāʾu* is uncertain, but, according to the AHw (p. 1019), the *sarmānu* should be translated as "Handgriffe (der Sänftentragstange)." As a *sarmāʾu* appears to be an object that one can drag, H. Schaudig (Inschriften Nabonids pp. 666–667) proposed translating that Akkadian word as "yoke"; his interpretation is tentatively followed here.

Col. ii

1) *a-na ta-ab-ra-a-ti ki-iš-ša-at ni-ši*
2) *lu-le-e uš-ma-al-li*
3) *i-ga-ra-a-ti si-ḫi-ir-ti é-zi-da*
4) *iš-tu* KÁ *né-re-bi* ^{d}*na-na-a a-di* ÍD
5) [*mé*]-⌜*eḫ*⌝-*ra-at* IM.SI.SÁ *ù mé-eḫ-re-et* IM.MAR.TU
6) [*ki-lal*]-*la-šu i-di* ÍD.*ga-at-tim*
7) [*ša*] ⌜^{d}⌝NÈ.ERI$_{11}$.GAL-LUGAL-ÙRU LUGAL *pa-ni-*⌜*i*⌝
8) [*i-pú-šu-ma*] ⌜*la*⌝ *ú-šak-li-lu ši-pí-*⌜*ir*⌝-[*šu*]
9) [*a-šar-šu ul ú*]-⌜*na*⌝-*ak-ki-ir-*⌜*ma*⌝
10) [*ú-ul-la-a re*]-*e-ši-šu*
11) [*a*?]-⌜*ab*⌝-*ni-*⌜*ma e-li*⌝ *ša pa-ni ú-ša-tir*

ii 1–11) To be an object of wonder for all of the people, I had (it) filled with splendor. (As for) the enclosure walls Ezida from the entrance gate of the goddess Nanāya to the river, (those) [f]acing north and (those) facing west, [bo]th of which are adjacent to the Gattu River (Euphrates), (walls) [that] Neriglissar, a king (who came) before me, [had built but whose] construction he had not completed — I [did not ch]ange [its (original) emplacement], but (only) [raised] its [su]perstructure. [I] (re)built (it) and made (it) surpass the previous one.

12) [*aš-ša*]-⌜*at*⌝-*tim* ^{d}AG IBILA *ki-i-num*
13) [*ša*]-*qu-ú ši-it-ra-ḫu*
14) *nu-úr* DINGIR.MEŠ *ab-bé-e-šu*
15) *mi-im-mu-ú e-te-ep-pu-šu*
16) *ḫa-di-iš na-ap-*⌜*li*⌝-*is-ma*
17) *ba-la-ṭa*$_4$ UD.MEŠ *ar-ku-ti*
18) *še-bé-e li-it-tu-ti*
19) *šar-ru-ti ki-iš-šu-ti be-lu-ti ba-ú-la-a-ti*
20) GIŠ.GU.ZA *šu-úr-šu-du pa-la-a ar-ki*
21) *a-na* UD.MEŠ *da-rí-ú-ti*
22) *a-na ši-ri-ik-tim šu-úr-ka-am*

ii 12–22) On account of this, O Nabû, true heir, [exa]lted one, splendid one, light of the gods — his fathers — look with pleasure upon everything that I have done and grant me a long life (lit. "a life of long days"), the attainment of very old age, kingship over the world, dominion over (all) people, a firmly secured throne, (and) a long reign (that lasts) for ever.

23) *i-na* GIŠ.LE.É.UM-*ka ki-i-nim*
24) *mu-kin pu-lu-uk ša-mé-e ù er-ṣe-tim*
25) *ša a-ra-ku* UD.MEŠ-*ia šu-uš-ṭi-ir qá-tuk-ka*

ii 23–25) Upon your reliable writing board, which firmly establishes the boundary of heaven and earth, have (an entry concerning) the lengthening of my days written out by your (own) hand.

26) *at-ta lu-ú še-e-du du-um-qí-ia-ma*
27) *ma-ḫa-ar* ^{d}AMAR.UTU *ù* ^{d}E$_4$.RU$_6$
28) *šu-ri-ib a-ma-a-at du-um-qí-ia*

ii 26–28) May you be the *šēdu* of my good fortune (and) send good words about me into the presence of the god Marduk and the goddess Erua.

14

Two clay cylinders discovered at Kish preserve a small portion of an inscription of Nabonidus written in contemporary Neo-Babylonian script; both pieces come from the first column of what are presumed to have originally been two-column cylinders. The extant text contains the end of the section recording the king's epithets and filiation and the beginning of a passage recording Marduk's nomination and support of Nabonidus as the legitimate king of Babylon. H. Schaudig refers to this badly preserved text as the "Kish Cylinder."

CATALOGUE

Ex.	Museum Number	Excavation Number	Provenance	Lines Preserved	cpn
1	Ash 1969-582	—	Kish	i 1′–13′	c
2	Ash 1969-585	1657	Kish, Mound W	i 6′–17′	c

COMMENTARY

The master text and lineation is a conflation of exs. 1 and 2. Ex. 1 is the main source for i 1′–8′ and ex. 2 is the principal exemplar used for i 12′–17′. Col. i 9′–11′, however, is a conflation of both exemplars. A score is presented on Oracc and the one minor (orthographic) variant is given in the critical apparatus at the back of the book.

BIBLIOGRAPHY

1977 Gurney, Studies Finkelstein pp. 95–96 and 100 (copy, edition)

2001 Schaudig, Inschriften Nabonids pp. 471–472 no. 2.18 (edition)

TEXT

Col. i

Lacuna

1′) [...] x NU DU *qá-⸢qá⸣-[da-a]*

2′) *[šá a-na é-sag]-⸢íl⸣ ù é-zi-[da]*

3′) *[la ip-pa]-⸢ra⸣-ak-ku-ú ka-a-[a-na]*

4′) *[a]-⸢na⸣* DINGIR GAL.GAL *su-ud-du-ru i-[x x]*

5′) *ud-du-šu ma-ḫa-zi* DINGIR.MEŠ *iš-te-né-e'-[ú]*

6′) DUMU ^{md}*na-bi-um-ba-la-at-su-[iq-bi]*

7′) *ru-bu-ú e-em-qá [a-na-ku]*

8′) *i-nu-um* ^{d}AMAR.UTU *be-el ra-[bí-ù]*

9′) *a-na be-lu-ut ma-a-ti ib-bu-ú [ni-bi-tì]*

10′) *i-na na-ap-ḫa-ar ṣa-al-ma-at qá-⸢qá⸣-[du]*

11′) *⸢ú-šar⸣-bu-ú zi-ik-⸢ra⸣* [LUGAL-*ú-ti-ia*]

12′) *⸢ni⸣-ši ki-ib-⸢ra⸣-a-ti er-bé-⸢et⸣-[ti]*

13′) *[a]-na re-⸢é⸣-ú-ti id-di-na [x]*

14′) [...] *ba-ú-la-a-ti-⸢šu⸣* [...] *i-x [x x]*

15′) [...] ⸢AL TE KI ŠÚ⸣ [...]

16′) [x x] x x ⸢MU⸣ x x [...]

17′) *[ki]-⸢ib⸣-ra-at er-⸢bet⸣-[ti ...]*

Lacuna

Col. ii

Completely missing

Lacuna

i 1′–7′) [who] con[stantly ...] ..., [(the one) who] never cea[ses (provisioning) Esag]il and Ezi[da], (the one who) regularly [... fo]r the great gods, (the one) who constantly strives to renovate the cult centers of the gods, son of Nabû-balāssu-[iqbi], wise prince, [am I].

i 8′–17′) When the god Marduk, the gre[at] lord, called [my name] for ruling over the land, made the fame of [my royal majesty] great among all of the black-hea[ded] (people), gave [me] the people of the fo[ur] quarters (of the world) to shepherd, [...] ... [... of hi]s people, [...] ... [...] ... [... the fo]ur quarters (of the world),

Lacuna

Completely missing

15

This Akkadian inscription is presently known from a single, damaged double-column clay cylinder discovered at Tell el-Laḥm (probably to be identified with ancient Kissik). The text, which is written in contemporary Neo-Babylonian script, commemorates Nabonidus' rebuilding of the temple of the goddess Ningal at Kissik, Eamaškuga ("House, Pure Sheepfold"); a portion of the building account is completely destroyed. Scholars often suggest that this still-incomplete text was composed during Nabonidus' tenth regnal year (546); for this opinion, see Beaulieu, Nabonidus p. 42 and Schaudig, Inschriften Nabonids p. 48. In previous editions and studies, the inscription is referred to as "Nabonidus Cylinder II, 6," "[Nabonidus] Inscription 10," and the "Eamaškuga Cylinder."

CATALOGUE

Museum Number	Excavation Number	Provenance	cpn
IM 55296	—	Kissik, northeastern part of the main mound, Trench 7, Room 8, on the floor, in the east corner	n

COMMENTARY

IM 55296 was not available for collation in the Iraq Museum (November 2018) and, therefore, the present edition is based on H.W.F. Saggs' published copy (Sumer 13 [1957] pls. 1–2).

BIBLIOGRAPHY

1949 Safar, Sumer 5 p. 159 and pl. vii (photo)
1957 Saggs, Sumer 13 pp. 190–195 and pls. 1–2 (copy, edition)
1960 Jacobsen, Iraq 22 p. 183 (i 36–41, edition)
1965 Tadmor, Studies Landsberger p. 360 (i 21–23, study)
1966 Falkenstein, AfO 21 pp. 50–51 (study)
1966 Sollberger, TCS 1 p. 107 (study)
1973 Berger, NbK p. 363 Nbn. Zyl. II, 6 (study)
1989 Beaulieu, Nabonidus pp. 28–30 Inscription 10 (i 8–25, edition; study)
1993 George, House Most High pp. 32–33 (i 36–39, study)
2001 Schaudig, Inschriften Nabonids pp. 370–372 no. 2.6 (edition)
2010 Heller, Spätzeit pp. 35 and 227–228 (i 1–16, 28–35, edition)

TEXT

Col. i

1) ^{d}*na-bi-um-na-'i-id* LUGAL TIN.TIR.KI
2) *ru-bu-ú na-a-du ni-bi-it* ^{d}AMAR.UTU
3) *za-ni-in é-sag-íl ù é-zi-da*
4) *mu-ṭa-aḫ-ḫi-du sa-at-tuk-ki*
5) *iš-šak-ku ṣi-i-ri pa-qid gi-mir* É.KUR
6) *ša-ak-ka-na-ak-ka za-ni-nu*
7) *mu-uš-pa-ar-zi-ḫu* ⸢*eš-re-e-ti*⸣
8) *re-é-a-am* [*mu-uš-ta-lu*]
9) *mu-uš-te-ši-ru ni-*⸢*ši*⸣ [*ma-a-ti*]

i 1–9) Nabonidus, king of Babylon, the attentive prince chosen by the god Marduk, the one who provides for Esagil and Ezida, the one who makes *sattukku*-offering(s) abundant, the exalted ruler who is entrusted with (the care of) all of the temple(s), the governor who provides, the one who abundantly provides for sanctuaries, the shepherd [who deliberates] (and) sets the people of [(his) land] on the right path,

10) *ša* ^{d}AMAR.UTU IGI.GÁL DINGIR.MEŠ ⸢*mu*⸣-[...]
11) *na-ap-ḫa-ar* ⸢KUR⸣.KUR ⸢*ka*⸣-[*li-ši-na*]
12) *šu-um-šu ki-ni-iš* ⸢*iz*⸣-[*ku-ru a-na* LUGAL-*ú-ti*]
13) ^{d}*na-bi-um pa-qí*-⸢*du*⸣ [*ki-iš-ša-at*]
14) *ša-mé-e* [*ù er-ṣe-tim*]
15) *i-na ku-ul-la-at* ⸢*a*⸣-[*šib* BÁRA.MEŠ]
16) *ú-ša-áš-qu-ú* [*be-lu-ut-su*]
17) ^{d}NÈ.ERI$_{11}$.GAL *da*-⸢*an*⸣-[*da-an-nu*]
18) ^{d}EN.LÍL *er-ṣe-tum* ⸢*mu*⸣-[*un-dal-ku*]
19) ⸢*i*⸣-*na ša-aš-mu da*-⸢*an*⸣-[*ni*]
20) ⸢*il*⸣-*li-ku* ⸢*i*⸣-*da*-⸢*a-šú*⸣
21) ^{d}EN.ZU *ù* ^{d}*nin-gal*
22) ⸢*a*⸣-*ge-e du**-*úr* UD.MEŠ
23) ⸢*i*⸣-*pi-ri ra-šu-uš-šu*
24) ^{d}UTU *ù* ^{d}*a-a*
25) *ṭu-da-at mi-ša-ri ú-pa-at-tu-šu*

i 10–25) the one whose name the god Marduk — the wisest of the gods, the one who [...] the entirety of a[ll of] the lands — steadfastly ca[lled for kingship], (the one) [whose lordship] the god Nabû — the overseer of the [totality of] heaven [and earth] — made supreme among all (of the kings) who si[t upon (royal) daises], (the one) at whose side the god Nergal — the alm[ighty], the cir[cumspect] Enlil of the netherworld — marches into fie[rce] war, on whose head the god Sîn and the goddess Ningal placed an eternal crown, (and) for whom the god Šamaš and the goddess Aya opened the ways of justice,

26) DINGIR.MEŠ GAL.GAL *i-na ku-ú-nu lìb-bi-šú-nu*
27) *ra-bí-iš ik-ru-bu-šu*
28) *i-na ki-ib-ra-a-ta er-bé-et-ti*
29) *ú-ša-ar-bu-ú be-lu-ut-su*
30) *ku-ul-la-at da-ád-me*
31) *a-na qí-bi-ti-šu ú-še-ši-bu*
32) ⸢*za*⸣-*na-nu ma-ḫa-zi*
33) ⸢*ù*⸣ *ud-du-šú eš-re-e-ti i-ši-mu ši-mat-su*
34) DUMU ^{md}*na-bi-um-ba-la-at-su-iq-bi*
35) *ru-bu-ú e-em-qu a-na-ku*

i 26–35) whom the great gods magnificently blessed in their steadfast heart(s), whose lordship they made great in the four quarters (of the world), by whose command they made all of the settlements reside (in peace), whose fate they determined to provision the cult centers and renew (their) sanctuaries, son of Nabû-balāssu-iqbi, wise prince, am I.

36) *i-nu-šu é*-⸢*amaš*⸣-*kù-ga*
37) É ^{d}*nin-gal be-let gi-mi-ir el-le-ti*
38) *su-pu-ru e*-⸢*el*⸣-*li*
39) *ša qé-er-ba* URU.KISIG*.KI
40) *ša i-na la-ba-ri i-ni-šu*
41) *i-qu-pu i-ga-ru-šu*

Col. ii

1) *i-ga-ru*-⸢*šu*⸣ [*qa-a-a-pu-ti*]
2) *ša i-ni*-⸢*šu*⸣ [*ad-ka-a-ma*]
3) *te-em-me*-⸢*en*⸣-[*šu la-bi-ra*]
4) *a-ḫi*-⸢*iṭ*⸣ [*ab-re-e-ma*]
5) *e*-⸢*li*⸣ [*te-em-me-ni-šu la-bi-ri*]
6) *ú*-⸢*ki*⸣-[*in li-ib-na-at-su*]

i 36–ii 6) At that time, (with regard to) Eamaškuga, the temple of the goddess Ningal — the pure lady of everything — the pure sheepfold that is inside the city Kissik, which a long time ago had become weak (and) whose walls had buckled, [I removed] its [buckled] walls that had become weak [and (then)] I examined (and) [checked its original] foundation(s) and (thereby) secu[red its brickwork] on top of [its original foundation(s).

Lacuna

1′) *šu*-⸢*um*?⸣ [...]

ii 1′) *nam*[*e* ...].

2′) *i-nu*-[*šú* ...]
3′) *ú*-⸢*qá*⸣-[*a-an-ni-ma* ...]
4′) *i-na* [...]
5′) PAT ⸢TE⸣ [...]

ii 2′–5′) At that [time, ...] wai[ted for me and ...] in [...] ... [...].

6′) ^{d}[*nin-gal* ...]
7′) ⸢*be*⸣-[*let gi-mi-ir*? *el-le-tú*?]
8′) [...]
9′) x [...]
10′) *i-na é*-[*amaš-kù-ga*]
11′) *ša qé-er-ba* [URU.KISIG.KI]
12′) *e-el-ṣi*-⸢*iš*⸣ [*i-na a-šá-bi-ki*]
13′) ⸢*dam*⸣-*qa-a-ta* ⸢^{d}⸣[*na-bi-um-na-ʾi-id*]
14′) *šar**-*ri* [*za-ni-ni-ki*]

ii 6′–22′) [O Ningal, ...], *the* [*pure*] *l*[*ady of everything*, ... when you are] joyous[ly dwelling] in E[maškuga], which is inside [the city Kissik], speak good things about [Nabonidus], the king [who provides for you] (and) built [your cella], all day long. Daily, make [my] de[eds] find acceptance [in the presence of] the god Sîn [..., your] belov[ed], (and) speak go[od (words) about me].

i 22 *du**-*úr* "eternal": The text has GI-*úr*.

15′) *e-pí*-iš* [*ku-um-mi-ki*]
16′) *at-mé-e* [*ud-da-kam*]
17′) u_4*-me-šam-ma* [*ma-ḫa-ar*]
18′) ^{d}EN.ZU [...]
19′) *na-ar-*[*mi-ki*]
20′) *e-ép-še-*[*ti-ia*]
21′) ⸢*šu*⸣*-um-*[*gi-ri*]
22′) *qí-bi* ⸢*du*⸣-[*um-qí-ia*]

16

One complete, large, three-column clay cylinder and several fragmentarily preserved cylinders are all inscribed with a lengthy Akkadian inscription of Nabonidus commemorating the restoration of Ebabbar ("Shining House") and Eduranna ("House, Bond of Heaven"), the temple and ziggurat of the sun-god Šamaš at Larsa. Despite the text's Larsa-centric contents, the majority of the copies of this inscription were found at Uruk (exs. 3–6), and not at Larsa (ex. 7) as one would expect. The script of all seven exemplars is contemporary Neo-Babylonian script. The inscription contains: (1) a long introduction enumerating how various gods and goddesses supported Nabonidus; (2) an account of the state of affairs at Larsa prior to Nabonidus' tenth regnal year (546); (3) a passage recording how Nabonidus came to find Ebabbar's original foundations with the help of the god Marduk; (4) a description of how the king confirmed the gods' will through extispicy, not once but twice; (5) a report of the rebuilding of Ebabbar and Eduranna on their original foundations; and (6) concluding formulae, which contain Nabonidus' petitions to Larsa's tutelary deities to look favorably upon him. According to this inscription, Nebuchadnezzar II (wrongly) rebuilt Šamaš' temple on the foundations of a Kassite king by the name of Burna-Buriaš, as he was unable to find Ebabbar's original ground plan; the site of that building was deemed (by Nabonidus) to be too small for its divine occupant. Nabonidus, on the other hand, was able to find Ebabbar's original foundations, which he states had been laid "700 years before Burna-Buriaš" by the famous Old Babylonian king Ḫammu-rāpi; Marduk is said to have sent strong winds that removed the debris covering Larsa's holy buildings and thereby revealed the original ground plans of Šamaš' temple and ziggurat. The inscription, which was composed during Nabonidus' tenth year as king (546) or slightly later, is referred to as "Nabonidus Cylinder III, 1," "[Nabonidus] Inscription 9," and the "Larsa Cylinder" in previous editions and studies.

CATALOGUE

Ex.	Museum Number	Excavation/ Registration No.	Provenance	Lines Preserved	cpn
1	BM 91143	85-4-30,2	Larsa or Uruk; purchased in 1885 from J.M. Shemtob	i 1–iii 54	c
2	—	K 6364	Larsa or Uruk	i 28–34	c
3	NBC 2508 + VA 10971	W 3610	Uruk, Qc XV 1, between the door of Room 14 and Staircase 16, south of Archive K	ii 1–16, 52–iii 54	(c)
4	IM 58186	W 18060	Uruk	i 1–22, 38–47, ii 47–53	c
5	IM 58183	W 18025	As ex. 4	ii 6–15	c
6	IM 59824	W 18418	Uruk, Qa XIV, under the floor	iii 16–43	c
7	IM —	L 70.17	Larsa	i 33–38	n

COMMENTARY

The line arrangement follows ex. 1, the only more-or-less complete copy of this inscription. The master text is generally ex. 1, but with help from the other exemplars where that copy of the text is damaged. A score is presented on Oracc and the minor (orthographic) variants are given in the critical apparatus at the back of the book.

As already pointed out by H. Schaudig (Inschriften Nabonids p. 42) and R. Da Riva (GMTR 4 p. 39), the exemplars of the inscription discovered at Uruk (exs. 3–6) were archival copies, that is, they were never intended to be deposited in the structure of the Ebabbar temple at Larsa, unlike ex. 1 (assuming it actually originates from Larsa, and not Uruk). In the Neo-Babylonian Period, Larsa was part of the territory of Uruk; see, for example, Beaulieu, RA 87 (1993) pp. 137–152.

BIBLIOGRAPHY

1889 Bezold, PSBA 11 pp. 84–88, 92–103 and pls. 3–5 (ex. 1, copy, edition)
1890 Peiser in Schrader, KB 3/2 pp. 88–93 (ex. 1 i 31–iii 32, edition)
1912 Langdon, NBK pp. 47 and 234–243 Nbd. no. 3 (ex. 1, edition)
1913 Jensen, ThLZ 38 p. 357 (ex. 1 ii 40, study)
1920 Keiser, BIN 2 p. 47 and pl. 20 no. 29 (ex. 3a, copy, study)
1921 Bezold, Studies Lehmann-Haupt p. 116 no. 8 (ex. 2 i 29–34, variants, study)
1923 Langdon, OECT 1 p. 32 n. 2 (ex. 1 ii 5, study)
1926 Thureau-Dangin, RA 23 p. 31 (ex. 1 ii 53, study)
1923 Boutflower, Book of Daniel p. 100 (study)
1930 Schott, UVB 1 pp. 62–63, pls. 9 and 30 no. 30 (ex. 3b, copy, study)
1948 Goossens, RA 42 nos. 3–4 pp. 154–155 (study)
1955 Gurney, AnSt 5 p. 108 n. 15 (ex. 1 ii 45, study [quoting Lambert])
1956 von Soden, Orientalia NS 25 p. 246 n. 1 (ex. 1 ii 51, study)
1964 Galling, Studien pp. 11, 16, 24–25, 131 and 142 (study)
1968 Ellis, Foundation Deposits pp. 96 and 181 (iii 27–31, edition; study)
1970 Berger, ZA 60 pp. 128–133 (exs. 1–3 ii 14, 55–56, study)
1971 Arnaud, Syria 48 p. 293 (ex. 7, study)
1973 Berger, NbK pp. 369–370 Nbn. Zyl. III, 1 (exs. 1–3, study)
1976 Arnaud, Syria 53 pp. 48 and 80 no. 8 (ex. 7, copy, study)
1982 Kessler, Bagh. Mitt. 13 pp. 16–17 and pls. 2a–c and 3a–b (ex. 5, copy; exs. 4, 6, photo, study)
1989 Beaulieu, Nabonidus pp. 27–29 and 51–53 Inscription 9 (i 13–15, 54–55, ii 10–13, 34–40, 48–49, edition; study)
1994 Beaulieu, BCSMS 28 p. 41 (ii 20–21, study)
2001 Schaudig, Inschriften Nabonids pp. 397–409 no. 2.11 and 756 fig. 20 (ex. 2, copy; exs. 1–7, edition)
2003 Schaudig, Studies Kienast pp. 463–465, 491 and 494 (iii 27–31, edition; study)
2009 Winter, On Art in the Ancient Near East 2 p. 463 (study)

Figure 11. BM 91143 (Nabonidus no. 16 ex. 1), a three-column clay cylinder inscribed with a text commemorating the restoration of Ebabbar and Eduranna, the temple and ziggurat of the sun-god Šamaš at Larsa. © Trustees of the British Museum.

TEXT

Col. i

1) [^{md}]*na-bi-um-na-ʾi-id* LUGAL KÁ.DINGIR.RA.KI
2) [*re*]-⸢*é*⸣-*a-um ni-bi-it* ^{d}AMAR.UTU
3) [*za*]-⸢*ni*⸣-*in é-sag-íl ù é-zi-da*
4) *mu-ṭa-aḫ-ḫi-id sa-at-tu-uk-ku*
5) *mu-ud-di-iš ma-ḫa-zi* DINGIR.MEŠ GAL.MEŠ
6) *i-da-an za-ni-na-a-ti*
7) *mu-ṭaḫ-ḫi-id gi-mi-ir* É.KUR
8) *za-ni-in eš-re-e-tim mu-šar-ri-iḫ i-gi-se-e*
9) *na-áš-pa-ri la a-ne-ḫi*
10) *ka-ši-du ša-di-i e-lu-tim*
11) *re-é-a-am mu-uš-ta-lu*
12) *mu-uš-te-ši-ir ni-ši ma-a-tim*
13) ⸢*ša*⸣ ^{d}AMAR.UTU ^{d}EN.LÍL DINGIR.DINGIR *a-na za-na-nu ma-ḫa-zi*
14) *ù ud-du-šu eš-re-e-ti*
15) *šu-um-šu ki-ni-iš iz-ku-ru a-na šar-ru-ti*
16) ^{d}*na-bi-um pa-qid kiš-šat* AN-*e ù* KI-*tim*
17) *i-na nap-ḫa-ar a-ši-ib* BÁRA
18) *ú-šar-bu-ú be-lu-ut-su*
19) ^{d}NÈ.ERI$_{11}$.GAL *dan-dan-ni*
20) ^{d}EN.LÍL *er-ṣe-tim mu-ut-tal-ku*
21) *i-na qá-ab-lu ù ta-ḫa-zi*
22) *il-li-ki i-da-a-šu* ^{d}EN.ZU *ù* ^{d}*nin-gal*
23) *a-ge-e du-úr* UD.MEŠ *i-pi-ir ra-šu-uš-šú*
24) ^{d}UTU *ù* ^{d}*a-a ṭu-da-at mi-ša-*⸢*ru*⸣
25) *ú-pa-at-tu-šu* DINGIR.MEŠ GAL.MEŠ
26) *i-na ku-*⸢*un*⸣ [*lìb-bi*]*-šú-nu ra-bi-iš ut-*⸢*tu*⸣*-šu*

i 1–12) Nabonidus, king of Babylon, shepherd chosen by the god Marduk, the one who provides for Esagil and Ezida, the one who makes *sattukku*-offering(s) abundant, the one who renovates the cult centers of the great gods, (the one who has) generously providing hands, the one who provides abundantly for all temples, the one who provides for the sanctuaries, the one who makes gifts splendid, the indefatigable envoy who (succeeds) in reaching high mountains, the shepherd who deliberates (and) sets the people of (his) land on the right path,

i 13–30) the one whose name the god Marduk — the Enlil of the gods — steadfastly called for kingship to provision the cult centers and renew (their) sanctuaries, (the one) whose lordship the god Nabû — the overseer of the totality of heaven and earth — made the greatest among all (of the kings) who sit upon (royal) daises, (the one) at whose side the god Nergal — the almighty, the circumspect Enlil of the netherworld — marches into battle and war, (on) whose head the god Sîn and the goddess Ningal placed an eternal crown, (and) for whom the god Šamaš and the goddess Aya opened the ways of justice, whom the great gods magnificently choose in their steadfast [heart(s)], whose name they made import[ant], (and) whose [lord]ship they made great, son of Nab[û-

27) *ú-ba-⸢'i⸣-[lu] šu-um-šu*
28) *ú-šar-bu-⸢ú⸣ [be]-⸢lu⸣-ut-su*
29) DUMU ^{md}*na-bi-⸢um⸣-[ba-lat]-⸢su⸣-iq-bi*
30) *ru-ba-a-am ⸢e-em⸣-qá a-na-ku*

balāss]u-iqbi, wise prince, am I.

31) *ì-nu-um* ^{d}UTU *be-lu* ⸢GAL⸣-*ú šá* AN-*e ù* KI-*tim*
32) *re-'u-ú ṣal-mat* SAG.DU *be-lu te-né-še-e-tim*
33) *larsa*.KI *a-lu na-ar-mi-šu é-babbar-ra*
34) *⸢šu⸣-ba-at ṭú-ub lìb-bi-šú šá ul-tu* UD.MEŠ *ul-lu-tim*
35) *in-na-mu-ú e-mu-ú kar-mi-iš*
36) *ba-aṣ-ṣa ù tu-ru-ba ši-pi-ik e-pe-ru*
37) *ra-bu-tim e-li-šu iš-ša-ap-ku-ma*
38) *la uṣ-ṣa-ab-bu-ú ki-su-úr-šu*
39) *la in-⸢na⸣-aṭ-ṭa-la ú-ṣu-ra-ti-ša*

i 31–39) When the god Šamaš, the great lord of heaven and earth, shepherd of the black-headed (people), lord of humankind, (with regard to) Larsa, his beloved city, (and) Ebabbar, the seat of his happiness, which had fallen to pieces (and) turned into ruins in distant days, (and) over which sand dune(s) and dust heap(s), (as well as) massive pile(s) of earth, were heaped, so that its ground plan could not be determined (and) its design could not be seen,

40) *i-na* BALA-*e* ^{md}MUATI-NÍG.GUB-ÙRU LUGAL *maḫ-ri*
41) DUMU ^{md}MUATI-*ap-lu-ú-ṣur ba-aṣ-ṣa ši-pi-ik e-pe-ri*
42) *⸢ša⸣ e-li* URU *ù* É *šu-a-tim*
43) *ša-ap-ku in-na-ši-ir-ma te-me-en-na é-babbar-ra*
44) *ša* ^{m}*bur-na-bur-ia-áš* LUGAL *pa-na-a a-li-ik maḫ-ri*
45) *i-mu-ur-ma te-me-en-na* LUGAL *la-bi-ri šá la-am*
46) ^{m}*bur-na-bur-ia-áš ú-ba-'i-i-ma la i-mu-ur*

i 40–46) during the reign of Nebuchadnezzar (II), a former king, son of Nabopolassar, the sand dune(s and) pile(s) of earth that were heaped over the city and that temple were removed and he discovered the foundation(s) of the Ebabbar of Burna-Buriaš, a former king who had come before (him). He then sought out the foundation(s) of an ancient king (who came) before Burna-Buriaš, but did not find (them).

47) *e-li te-me-en-na* ^{m}*bur-na-bur-ia-áš*
48) *ša qé-re-eb-ša ip-pa-al-sa é-babbar-ra i-pu-uš-ma*
49) ^{d}UTU *be-lu* GAL-*ú ú-šar-mi qé-re-eb-šu*

i 47–49) On top of the foundation(s) of Burna-Buriaš that he had seen inside it, he (re)built Ebabbar and had the god Šamaš, the great lord, dwell therein.

50) É *šu-a-tim a-na mu-ša-ab* ^{d}UTU EN GAL-*ú*
51) *ù* ^{d}*a-a kal-la-tim na-ra-am-ti-šu*
52) *⸢ta⸣-al-la-ak-tu-šu i-ṣa-at-ma*
53) *[ṣu]-uḫ-ḫu-ru ši-pi-ir-šu*

i 50–53) (As for) that temple, its processional way was (too) tiny for the residence of the god Šamaš, the great lord, and the goddess Aya, his beloved bride, and its construction was (too) small.

54) *[i]-na-an-na i-na* MU.10.KAM *i-na* *u*$_4$*-mu* BALA-*e-a*
55) *⸢da⸣-am-qa i-na šar-ru-ti-ia da-rí-tim*
Col. ii
1) *ša* ^{d}UTU *i-ra-am-mu-šu*$_{14}$
2) ^{d}UTU *be-lu* GAL-*ú iḫ-su-su šu-bat-⸢sa⸣ reš*-ti-tim*

i 54–ii 2) [N]ow, during (my) tenth year, in the days of my favorable reign, during my eternal kingship, which the god Šamaš loves, the god Šamaš, the great lord, remembered his original residence.

3) *ša zi-qu-ra-tim ⸢ge⸣-gu-<na>-a-šu*
4) *re-e-ši-ša e-⸢li ša⸣ pa-nim ul-li-ma*
5) *li-ib-ba-⸢šu ḫa-di-iš⸣ ub-lam-ma*
6) *a-na ia-tim* ^{d}MUATI-NÍ.TUKU LUGAL *za-ni-ni-šu*
7) *é-babbar-ra a-na aš-ri-šu ⸢tu⸣-úr-ru*
8) *ki-ma šá* UD.MEŠ *ul-lu-tim šu-ba-at ṭu-ub lìb-bi-šú*
9) *e-pe-šu ú-qa-a-⸢wa*$_6$*⸣-an-ni*

ii 3–9) With regard to the ziggurat, his (Šamaš') sacred building, his heart joyfully prompted (him) to raise up its superstructure higher than the one in the past and (then) he waited for me, Nabonidus, the king who provides for him, to return Ebabbar to its (original) place (and) to (re)build the seat of his happiness like (it was) in distant days.

10) *i-na qí-bi-it* ^{d}AMAR.UTU *be-lu* GAL-*⸢ú it⸣-bu-nim-ma*
11) *ša-a-ri er-bet-ti-šu-nu me-ḫe-[e ra-bu]-tim*
12) *ba-aṣ-ṣa ša e-⸢li⸣* URU *ù ⸢*É *ša⸣-a-šu*
13) *ka-at-ma in-na-si-iḫ-ma é-babbar-ra*
14) *ki-iṣ-ṣi ra-áš-ba ú-ra-⸢ša⸣ [za]-⸢ma⸣-ri*
15) *mu-ša-ab* ^{d}UTU *ù* ^{d}*[a]-a*

ii 10–19) By the command of the god Marduk, the great lord, their four winds, the [great] stor[ms], rose up, (and) the sand dune(s) that were covering the city and that temple were removed and the foundation(s) of Ebabbar, the awe-inspiring shrine, the *urāšu*-building of [si]nging, the residence of the god Šamaš and the goddess [A]ya, and the ziggurat, his

---

ii 3–5 For the topos of raising up a ziggurat higher than before, see Frayne, RIME 4 pp. 376–377 Samsu-iluna E4.3.7.3 Akkadian version lines 13–16 and 83–85.

16) *ù zi-qú-ra-ti ge-gu-na-a-šu ṣi-*[*i*]*-*⸢*ri*⸣
17) *ku-um-mu da-*⸢*ru*⸣*-ú maš-ta-*[*ku*] ⸢*la-le*⸣*-*[*šu-un*]
18) *te-mé-en-šu-un in-na-mi-ir-ma*
19) *in-na-aṭ-ṭa-la ú-ṣu-ra-ti-*⸢*šu*⸣*-un*

(Šamaš') exalted sacred building, the eternal cella, the chamb[er of their] desire, their foundation(s) became visible and their ground plans could be seen.

20) *ši-ṭi-ir šu-um ša* ^{m}*ḫa-am-mu-ra-pí*
21) LUGAL *la-bí-ri ša* 7 ME MU.AN.NA.MEŠ
22) *la-am* ^{m}*bur-na-bur-ia-áš*
23) *é-babbar-ra ù zi-qu-ra-ti*
24) *e-li te-me-en-na la-bi-ri*
25) *a-na* ^{d}UTU *ib-nu-ù*
26) *qé-er-ba-*⸢*šu*⸣ *ap-pa-li-is-ma ap-la-*[*aḫ*]
27) *ak-ku-ud-ma ar-ša-a ni-iq-*⸢*it-ti*⸣

ii 20–27) Inside of it (Ebabbar), I discovered an inscription bearing the name of Ḫammu-rāpi, an ancient king who had built Ebabbar and (its) ziggurat for the god Šamaš on top of the original foundation(s) 700 years before Burna-Buriaš. I became frightened, worried, and anxious.

28) *ki-a-am aq-bi a-na li-*⸢*ib*⸣*-*[*bi-ia*]
29) *um-ma* ⸢LUGAL *a-li*⸣*-ku ma-*⸢*aḫ-ri-ia*⸣
30) É *i-pu-uš-ma* ^{d}UTU *be-*⸢*lu ra-bu-ú*⸣
31) *ú-ša-ar-mi* ⸢*qé-re-eb-šu*⸣

ii 28–31) I spoke to m[y heart] as follows, saying: "A king who came before me built (this) temple and had Šamaš, the great lord, dwell therein."

32) *ia-ti* É *šu-a-tim* [*mu-ša-ab* ^{d}UTU *ù* ^{d}*a-a*]
33) *i-na a-šar šu-*⸢*us*?⸣*-*[*su-mu a-na e-pé-šu*]
34) *áš-ši qá-ti ú-ṣal-*[*la-a* EN EN.EN *um-ma*]
35) ^{d}EN.LÍL* DINGIR.DINGIR *ru-bu-um* ^{d}AMAR.UTU
36) *ba-lu-uk-ka ul in-na-an-da šu-ub-ti*
37) *ul ib-ba-áš-ši-mu ki-su-ur-šu*
38) *ša la ka-a-šú ma-an-ni mi-na-a ip-pu-uš*
39) *be-lu i-na qí-bi-ti-ka ṣi-ir-ti*
40) *ša e-li-ka ṭa-a-bi lu-*⸢*še-ep-pe*⸣*-eš*

ii 32–40) (But as for) me, I raised (my) hands (and) bes[eeched the lord of lords to build] that temple, [the residence of the god Šamaš and the goddess Aya], in the *most befi*[*tting*] place, [saying]: "O Enlil of the gods, prince Marduk, without you no site can be laid out (and) its ground plan(s) cannot be created. Who can do anything without you? O lord, at your exalted command, I will have what(ever) pleases you done."

41) *áš-ra-a-ti* ^{d}UTU ^{d}IŠKUR *ù* ^{d}U.⸢GUR⸣
42) *a-na e-pé-šu* É *šu-a-tim aš-te-e'-*[*e*]*-*⸢*ma*⸣
43) UZU *dum-qí ša a-ra-ku* ⸢u_{4}*-mi-ia*⸣
44) *ù e-pe-eš* É *iš-ṭu-ru i-na* ⸢*lìb*⸣*-*[*bi*]*-*⸢*šu*⸣

ii 41–44) I frequently visit[ed] the shrines of the gods Šamaš, Adad, and Nergal with regard to (re)building that temple and they (the gods) wrote out in[side] it (a lamb) an auspicious omen concerning the lengthening of my days and the building of (that) temple.

45) *áš-ni-ma al-pu-ut pu-*[*ḫa-da*]
46) *an-na ki-i-ni ša šá-*⸢*la*⸣*-mu* ⸢*ši*⸣*-*[*ip-ri-ia*]
47) *ú-šá-áš-ki-ni i-na* ⸢*ter-ti-ia*⸣

ii 45–47) For a second time, I performed an exti[spicy] (lit. "I touched the la[mb]"). They (the gods) made sure that a firm 'yes' regarding the success of m[y work] was present in my extispicy.

48) *a-na a-mat* ^{d}AMAR.UTU *be-lu šu-úr-bi-ia ù a-na a-mat*
49) ^{d}UTU *ù* ^{d}IŠKUR EN.MEŠ *bi-ri at-ka-al-ma*
50) *i-li-iṣ lìb-bi ka-ba-*⸢*at*⸣*-ta ip-pa-ar-da*
51) *iḫ-di ra-ma-ni im-mi-ru zi-*⸢*mu*⸣*-ú-a*

ii 48–51) I trusted in the word of the god Marduk, my supreme lord, and in the word(s) of the gods Šamaš and Adad, the lords of divination, and my heart rejoiced, (my) liver cheered up, I myself was happy, (and) my face beamed.

52) *ad-ka-am-ma um-ma-na-a-ti* ^{d}UTU *ù* ^{d}AMAR.UTU
53) *ṣa-bi-it al-lu na-áš* GIŠ.MAR *za-bi-il* ⸢GIŠ.DUSU⸣
54) *a-na e-pé-eš é-babbar-ra ki-iṣ-*⸢*ṣi*⸣ [*ra-áš-ba ù zi-qú*]*-*⸢*ra*⸣*-tim*
55) BÁRA*-ša ṣi-i-ri ra-bi-iš ú-*[*ma*]*-*⸢*'e*⸣*-er-ma*
56) *um-man-nu mu-du-ú a-šar-ša uš-ta-*[*am*]*-*⸢*ḫir*⸣
57) *te-me-en-na i-ḫi-ṭu-ma ú-ṣa-ab-bu-ú si-ma-a-tim*

ii 52–57) I mustered the workmen of the gods Šamaš and Marduk — those who wield hoes, hold spade(s), (and) carry basket(s) — and I [laid] a great commission (on them) to (re)build Ebabbar, the [awe-inspiring] shrine, [and the ziggu]rat, the exalted dais. I then made expert craftsmen [con]front its (Ebabbar's) site. They examined (its) foundation (and) surveyed (its) (original) appearance.

58) *i-na* ITI *ša-al-ma i-na* UD ŠE.GA *ša é-babbar-ra*
59) É *na-ra-am* ^{d}UTU *ù* ^{d}*a-a pa-pa-ḫi šu-ba-at*
60) *i-lu-ti-šu-un maš-ta-ku la-le-šu-un*

Col. iii

1) *ki-ma* ⸢*si-ma*⸣*-ti-*⸢*šu*⸣*-*[*un*] *re-eš-ta-a-tim*
2) *e-*⸢*li*⸣ [*te-me-en-na ša*] ^{m}*ḫa-am-*[*mu*]*-ra-pí* LUGAL *la-bi-ri*

ii 58–iii 7a) In a favorable month, on an auspicious day, with regard to Ebabbar, the beloved temple of the god Šamaš and the goddess Aya, the cella (and) seat of their divinity, the chamber of their desire, I (re)laid their brickwork according to the[ir] original appearances, over [the foundation(s) of] Ḫam[mu]-rāpi, an ancient king, and put their foundation(s back)

3) li-ib-na-⸢at⸣-su-un ad-di-ma
4) uš-te-ši-ir te-mé-en-šu-un
5) É šu-a-tim ki-ma la-bi-ri-im-ma
6) e-eš-ši-iš e-pú-uš-ma

in the(ir) correct position(s). I built that temple anew as (it had been) in ancient times and appropriately adorned its structure.

7) us-si-mi ši-ki-in-šu é-dur-an-na
8) É na-ra-mi-šu ki-ma šá UD.MEŠ ul-lu-tim
9) ul-la-a re-e-ši-šu
10) é-babbar-ra a-na ^{d}UTU ù ^{d}a-a
11) e-pu-uš ú-ša-ak-li-il-ma
12) ú-ba-an-na-a ta-al-la-ak-tu-uš

iii 7b–12) (As for) Eduranna, his beloved temple, I raised its superstructure just like the one of the distant past (lit. "distant days"). I built (and) completed Ebabbar for the god Šamaš and the goddess Aya and (then) made its processional way beautiful.

13) pa-pa-ḫi šu-ba-at i-lu-ti-šu-un ṣir-tim
14) ša i-te-e zi-qu-ra-tim re-tu-ú te-me-en-šú
15) a-na si-ma-at i-lu-ti-šu-num
16) ra-bi-tim šu-lu-ku
17) a-na ^{d}UTU ù ^{d}a-a EN.MEŠ-e-a
18) u$_{4}$-mi-iš ú-na-am-mi-ir-ma
19) ú-za-aq-qí-ir ḫur-sa-ni-iš

iii 13–19) (As for) the cella, the seat of their exalted divinity, whose foundation(s) were set in place at the side of the ziggurat, to make (it) befit their great divinity, I made (it) as bright as day for the god Šamaš and the goddess Aya, my lords, and raised (it) as high as a mountain.

20) ša a-na LUGAL ma-na-ma la im-gu-ru
21) ^{d}UTU be-lu GAL-ú ia-tim LUGAL pa-li-iḫ-šú
22) im-gu-ur-an-ni-ma i-ir-a-am qá-tu-ú-a

iii 20–22) That which the god Šamaš, the great lord, had never granted any king, he granted to me, the king who reveres him, and he presented (it) into my hands.

23) é-babbar-ra a-na ^{d}UTU ù ^{d}a-a
24) EN.MEŠ-e-a ki-ma la-bi-ri-im-ma
25) da-am-qí-iš e-pú-uš-ma
26) a-na áš-ri-ša ú-te-er

iii 23–26) I piously built Ebabbar for the god Šamaš and the goddess Aya, my lords, as (it had been) in ancient times and returned (it) to its (original) place.

27) ⸢ṭup⸣-pi NA$_{4}$.GIŠ.NU$_{11}$.GAL ši-ṭi-ir šu-mi
28) ⸢ša⸣ ^{m}ḫa-am-mu-ra-pí LUGAL la-bi-ri
29) ša qé-re-eb-šu ap-pa-al-sa
30) ⸢it⸣-ti ši-ṭi-ir šu-mi-ia áš-ku-un-ma
31) ú-ki-in [ana] du-úr u$_{4}$-mi

iii 27–31) (As for) the alabaster tablet bearing the name of Ḫammu-rāpi, an ancient king, that I had discovered inside of it, I placed (it) with an inscription bearing my name and firmly established (it there) [for] ever.

32) a-na ša-at-ti ^{d}UTU be-lu šu-úr-bu-ú
33) ša-qu-ú be-lu gim-ri
34) LUGAL AN-e ù KI-tim
35) nu-úr KUR.KUR É šu-a-tim ḫa-di-iš nap-lis-ma
36) ⸢ba⸣-la-ṭa$_{4}$ u$_{4}$-mu ru-[qu-ú]-ti
37) še-bé-e lit-tu-tu ku-⸢un⸣-nu GIŠ.GU.ZA
38) ù la-ba-ra pa-le-e a-na ši-rik-ti šur-kam

iii 32–38) On this account, O Šamaš, supreme lord, exalted one, lord of everything, king of heaven and earth, light of the lands, look with pleasure upon this temple and grant me a l[on]g life (lit. "a life of l[on]g days"), the attainment of very old age, a firmly secured throne, (and) a long reign.

39) i-na qí-bi-ti-ka ṣi-ir-ti
40) ^{d}UTU be-lu ra-bu-ú É šu-a-tim
41) ma-ḫa-ar-ka lu-la-ab-bi-ir
42) a-na da-rí-a-ti
43) ni-ši ṣa-al-ma-at qaq-qa-du
44) ma-la i-ba-ar-ra-a nu-úr-ka nam-ri
45) šu-uk-ši-da qá-tu-ú-a
46) šu-uk-ni-šu še-e-pu-ú-a

iii 39–46) By your exalted command, O Šamaš, great lord, may this temple grow old in your presence for eternity. Make my hands conquer the black-headed (people), as many as see your bright light, (and) make (them) bow down at my feet.

47) ^{d}a-a kal-la-ti ra-bi-tim
48) i-na ku-um-mi-ka ṣi-i-ri
49) ka-a-a-na li-ta-mi-ka
50) da-am-qa-a-ti

iii 47–50) May the goddess Aya, the great bride, constantly say good thing about me to you in your exalted cella.

51) ^{d}bu-ne-ne su-uk-kal-lum
52) mi-it-lu-uk-ti-ka u$_{4}$-mi-ša-am-ma
53) li-ka-al-li-mu
54) i-da-a-ti du-um-qí-ia

iii 51–54) May the god Bunene, the vizier with whom you deliberate, reveal favorable signs for me daily.

17

A fragment from the upper part of a round-topped, stone stele discovered in Ebabbar ("Shining House"), the temple the god Šamaš at Larsa, preserves a small portion of an inscription of Nabonidus written in contemporary Babylonian script. The extant text is on the rounded back side of the stele, which was broken in antiquity and reused as a door socket in the Hellenistic Period. On the stele's flat front side, only part of the relief (an image of the king) remains; none of the inscription is preserved on that side of the object, assuming it was also inscribed. The surviving thirty-five lines of text duplicate passages in the well-known "Ḫarrān Stele" (text no. 47). Because the inscription mentions Nabonidus' return to Babylon from his ten-year sojourn in Tēmā, it is certain that the text was composed after this king's thirteenth regnal year (543); H. Schaudig suggests an approximate date of composition between 543 and 540 (Nabonidus' sixteenth year as king). This inscription is referred to as "[Nabonidus] Fragment 1" and the "Larsa Stele" in scholarly literature.

CATALOGUE

Museum Number	Excavation Number	Provenance	cpn
IM —	L 83.50	Larsa, Ebabbar, Room 24, door socket 37	n

COMMENTARY

The present edition is based on D. Arnaud's published copy of the stele fragment (Sumer 44 [1985–86] p. 52), since the original in the Iraq Museum was not available for study (because the museum number of the object is not presently known) and since the published photograph is not sufficiently legible. The restorations are based on parallel passages in text no. 47 (Ḫarrān Stele).

BIBLIOGRAPHY

1985 Arnaud and Huot, Akkadica 44 pp. 14–20 (study)
1985–86 Arnaud, Sumer 44 pp. 45 (figs. 41–42), 48–49 and 51–52 (photo, copy, edition)
1985–86 Huot et al., Sumer 44 pp. 26–46 (study)
1989 Beaulieu, Nabonidus p. 239 Frgm. 1 (study)
1997 Moortgat-Correns, SMEA 39 pp. 116–118 (photo, study)
2001 Schaudig, Inschriften Nabonids pp. 532–534 no. 3.5 (edition)

TEXT

Lacuna

Col. i′

1) [*a-dan-nu*] ⸢*im*⸣-*lu-ú* u_4-*mu*

2) [*šá iq-bu*]-⸢*ú*⸣ ^{d}*na-an-na-ri*

3) [*ina* ITI.DU$_6$] UD.17.KAM u_4-*mu* ^{d}30

Lacuna

i′ 1–11) The appointed time [arrived and] the days [that] the god Nannāru [had command]ed had elapsed. [In the month Tašrītu (VII)], (on) the seventeenth

Lacuna before i′ 1 The translation assumes that the now-lost final line of the completely-missing column that preceded col. i′ ended with *ik-šu-dam-ma* "arrived and."

i′ 1–11 The restorations are based on text no. 47 (Ḫarrān Stele) ii 11b–18.

4) [*i-ma-ag*]-⸢*gàr*⸣ *pi-ši-ir-šú*
5) [^{d}30 EN DINGIR].⸢MEŠ⸣ *šá i*-na* UD.1.KAM.MA
6) [TUKUL ^{d}*a-nim*] ⸢*zi*⸣-*kir-šu** AN-*e*
7) [*ta-lap-pa*]-⸢*tu*$_4$⸣ [*u*] KI-*tim*
8) [*ta-ḫe-ep*]-⸢*pu*⸣-*ú ḫa-mi-im*
9) [*pa-ra-aṣ* ^{d}]*a-nu-ú*-⸢*tim*⸣
10) [*mu-gam-mi-ir pa-ra*]-*aṣ* ^{d}EN.LÍL-*ú*-[*tú*]
11) [*le-qu-u pa*]-⸢*ra*⸣-*aṣ* ^{d}IDIM-*ú*-[*ti*]

day, whose interpretation is "the day the god Sîn [is favor]able," [the god Sîn, the lord of the god]s, whose [n]ame on the first day is ["the *weapon* of the god Anu," you (who) touc]h the sky [and bre]ak the earth, the one who has gathered (to himself all of) [the divine offices of hi]ghest rank, [the one who has collected (all of) the divine offi]ces of supreme pow[er, the one who has taken (for himself all of) the div]ine offices of the ro[le of] the god Ea,

Lacuna

Lacuna

Col. ii′

1) *it-ti* LÚ.⸢ḪAL⸣ [*u*] ⸢LÚ$^{?}$⸣.[*šá*]-⸢*ʾi*$^{?}$⸣-*lim*
2) *a*-⸢*lak*⸣-[*tú ul par-sa*]-*at*
3) *at-til-ma* [(*ina šat mu-ši*$^{?}$) MÁŠ.GI$_6$] *pár-da-at*
4) *a*-⸢*di*⸣ [*a-mat* ...] ⸢*im*⸣-*li* MU
5) ⸢*ik*⸣-[*šu-du a-da*]-⸢*an*⸣-*na*
6) [*šá iq-bu-ú* ^{d}*na-an*]-⸢*na*⸣-*ri*
7) [*ul-tu* URU.*te-ma-a ú-x*]-x [x]

ii′ 1–7) (my) pa[th did not sto]p with the divi[ner or the *dream-inte*]*rpreter*. I laid down [and, (during the night,) (my) dream] was frightening, *until* [the word of the god ...]. The year [elap]sed. [(When) the appoint]ed time [that the god Nann]āru [had command]ed ar[rived, ... from the city Tēmā].

8) [TIN.TIR.KI] ⸢URU⸣ *be-lu-ti*-[*ia*]
9) [...]-⸢*ú*⸣-*a i-mu-ru*-⸢*ma*⸣
10) [...]-*ši-na*

ii′ 8–10) [Babylon, my] capital [ci]ty, they saw my [...] a[nd ...] their [...]

11) [...]
12) [...]
13) [...]
14) [...] x x

ii′ 11–14) (No translation possible)

15) [LUGAL.MEŠ *qer-bu-tú il-lu*]-*nim-ma*
16) [...] x

ii′ 15–16) [the kings (living) close by came up to me] and [...]

Lacuna

Lacuna

Col. iii′

Lacuna

Lacuna

1′) [*man-nu at*]-⸢*ta*⸣ *šá* [^{d}30 *u* ^{d}UTU *a-na* LUGAL-*u-ti*]
2′) *i-na-am-bu-ka* [DUMU-*ú-ia-a-ma*]
3′) [*i*]-*qab-bu-nik*-[*ku aš-rat* ^{d}30]
4′) [*a*]-*ši-ib šá-ma*-⸢*mi*⸣ [...] x
5′) [...] ⸢2-*šu**⸣ [...] x

iii′ 1′–5′) [Whoever y]ou are, whom [the gods Sîn and Šamaš] name [for kingship] (and) call ["my son," (when) the sanctuary of the god Sîn, the one who res]ides in the heav[ens, *whose command cannot be revoked and whose word(s) are not said*] twice, [...]

6′) [...] x
7′) [...]-⸢*ti*⸣
8′) [...] x

iii′ 6′–8′) (No translation possible)

Lacuna

Lacuna

---

i′ 6 [TUKUL ^{d}*a-nim*] "the *weapon* of the god Anu": The interpretation of the logogram TUKUL is problematic. For further details, see the on-page note to text no. 47 (Ḫarrān Stele) ii 25 and Schaudig, Inschriften Nabonids pp. 491–492 n. 700. ⸢*zi*⸣-*kir-šu** "whose [n]ame": The text has ⸢*zi*⸣-*kir*-IŠ*.

i′ 1–8 The restorations are based on text 47 (Ḫarrān Stele) iii 0–6 and 8.

ii′ 2 *a*-⸢*lak*⸣-[*tú*] "(my) pa[th]": The restoration given here is based on text no. 47 (Ḫarrān Stele) iii 1. H. Schaudig (Inschriften Nabonids p. 533) restores this word as *a*-⸢*lak*⸣-[*ti*], which is also possible; compare Ludlul Bēl Nēmeqi Tablet I line 52.

iii′ 1′–5′ The restorations are based on text no. 47 (Ḫarrān Stele) iii 34–38. It is clear from the preserved contents of this column that col. iii′ is the last column of this stele.

iii′ 4′b–5′ The translation assumes that these lines contained [*šá qí-bit-su la in-nen-nu-ú u a-mat-su la ta-qab-bu-u*] 2-*šú* "[*whose command cannot be revoked and whose word(s) are not said*] twice."

18

Numerous bricks discovered at Larsa and Uruk bear a short, three-line inscription that includes Nabonidus' name, title, and filiation. The text is stamped in archaizing Neo-Babylonian script on the bricks' faces. As proposed by P.-A. Beaulieu (Nabonidus p. 32), theses bricks were likely made between Nabonidus' ninth (547) and eleventh (545) regnal years since Ebabbar ("Shining House"), the temple of the god Šamaš at Larsa, was restored during his tenth year as king (546) and since Eanna ("House of Heaven"), the temple of the goddess Ištar at Uruk, was renovated between Nabonidus' ninth and eleventh regnal years; H. Schaudig (Inschriften Nabonids p. 48) espouses Beaulieu's suggested date. In scholarly literature, this text is referred to as "Nabonidus Brick Ap I, 2" and "[Nabonidus] Inscription 12."

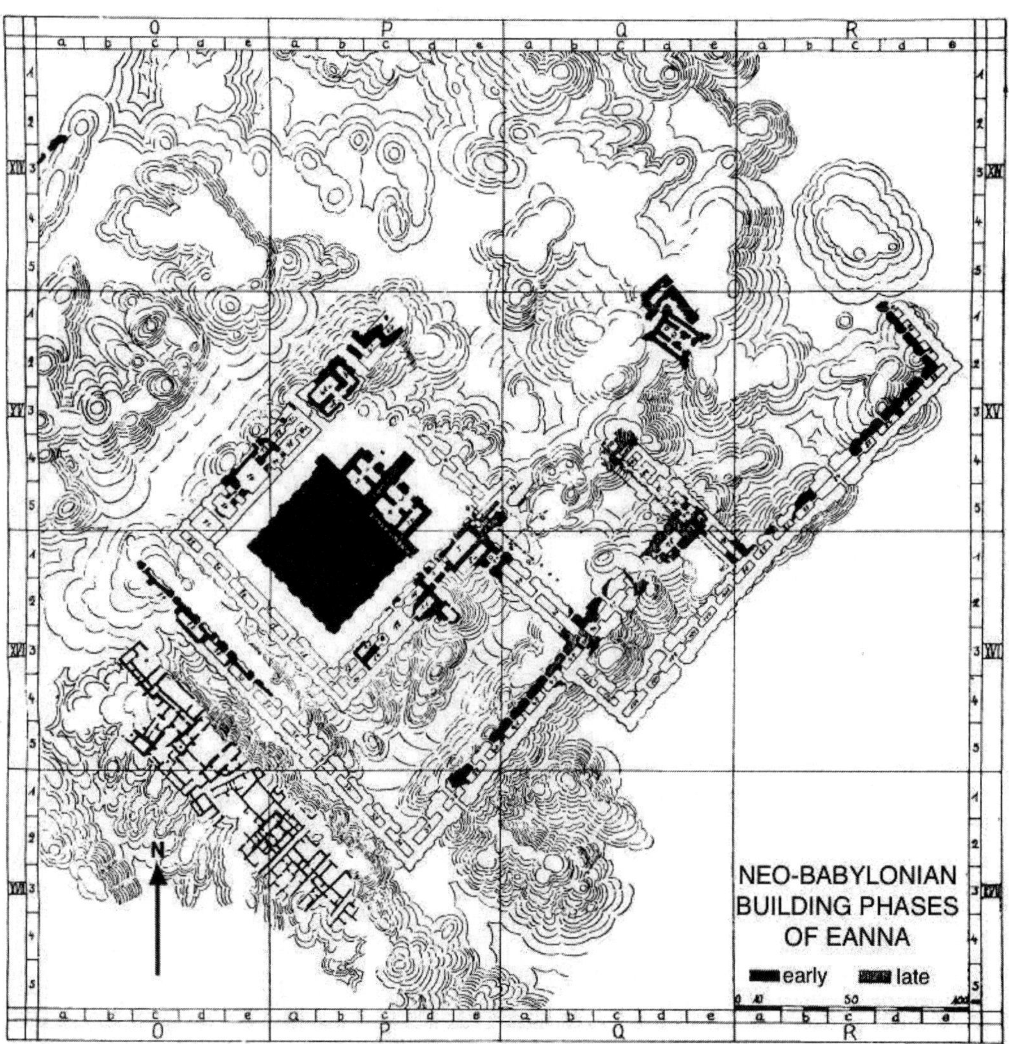

Figure 12. Plan of the Eanna temple complex in the Neo-Babylonian Period. Adapted from Lenzen, UVB 10 pl. 5.

CATALOGUE

Ex.	Museum Number	Excavation/ Registration No.	Provenance	Lines Preserved	cpn
1	BM 90143	1979-12-20,66	Larsa	1–3	p
2	BM 90144	1979-12-20,67	As ex. 1	1–3	p
3	BM 90145	1979-12-20,68	As ex. 1	1–3	p
4	BM 90146	1979-12-20,69	As ex. 1	1–3	p
5	BM 90147	1979-12-20,70	As ex. 1	1–3	p
6	BM 90159	1979-12-20,76	As ex. 1	1–3	p
7	BM 90160	55-1-1,280	Uruk	1–3	p
8	BM 90284	1979-12-20,175	As ex. 1	1–3	p
9	—	W 4404a	Uruk, Eanna, Qc XIV 5 (east corner of Court A²)	1–3	n
10	—	W 4404b	As ex. 9	—	n
11	—	W 4595a	Uruk, Eanna, Qc XIV 5	—	n
12	—	W 4595b	As ex. 11	—	n
13	—	W 67	Uruk, Eanna, southeast, near the east corner, in the upper floor (floor of the east corner of of Court A²)	1–3	n
14	—	W 601a	Uruk, Eanna, Qb XVI 2 (south corner of Court A¹)	—	n
15	—	W 601b	As ex. 14	—	n
16	—	W 1873	Uruk, Eanna, Ob XVI 3	—	n
17	—	W 4233	Uruk, Eanna, northeast of the Ištar Temple	—	n
18	—	W 4596	As ex. 14	—	n
19	—	W —	Uruk, Eanna, flooring of Temple F3, in the wall between Court A¹ and A⁴ (Qd/e XV 5)	—	n
20	—	W —	Uruk, Eanna, floor of the east corner of Court A²	—	n
21	IM —	L 69.85	Larsa, near Ebabbar	—	n
22	IM —	L 70.85	As ex. 21	—	n

COMMENTARY

Because an identical inscription was stamped on bricks incorporated in the superstructures of both the Ebabbar temple at Larsa and the Eanna temple at Uruk, the Larsa and Uruk bricks are edited here as a single text, as they were by H. Schaudig (Inschriften Nabonids pp. 337–338), rather than as two separate inscriptions. Following Schaudig (ibid.), the master text of the inscription is based on ex. 9, even though it is presently only known from A. Schott's hand-drawn facsimile of W 4404a. No score of the inscription is given on Oracc since scores are not provided for texts on bricks.

The square-shaped bricks vary marginally in size. The largest and smallest bricks measure 34.5×33.5×10 cm and 32.5×32.5×8 cm respectively. The stamped area in which the inscriptions are written measure between 21 and 22.7 cm in length and 6.5 and 6.8 cm in height. Three different stamps were used to impress the catalogued bricks; for further details, see Schaudig, Inschriften Nabonids p. 338. On BM 90284, there is a deep imprint of a right foot across the inscription; the text is completely destroyed in that spot.

BIBLIOGRAPHY

1863 Oppert, EM 1 p. 269 (translation, study)
1875 Ménant, Babylon p. 253 (ex. 1, translation)
1884 Rawlinson, 1 R pl. 68 no. 4 (ex. 1, copy)
1890 Peiser in Schrader, KB 3/2 pp. 120–121 (edition)
1899 Bezold, Cat. 5 p. 2235 (study)
1912 Langdon, NBK pp. 58 and 294–295 Nbd. no. 12 (ex. 1, edition)
1928 Jordan, Uruk-Warka pl. 107a (ex. 3, photo)
1930 Schott, UVB 1 p. 61 and pl. 30 nos. 28–29 (exs. 9–10, copy, edition)
1939 Lenzen, UVB 10 p. 12 and pl. 18a (exs. 9–13, photo, study)
1956 Lenzen UVB 12/13 pp. 17 and 30 (ex. 20, study)
1958 Lenzen, UVB 14 pl. 5 (exs. 9–20, provenance)
1968 Birot, Syria 45 pp. 242–243 (exs. 21–22, study)
1971 Arnaud, Syria 48 p. 292 (exs. 21–22, study)
1973 Berger, NbK pp. 348–349 Nbn. Backsteine Ap I, 2 (exs. 1–22, study)
1981 Walker, CBI pp. 91–92 no. 110 Nabonidus 12 (exs. 1–8, study)

1989 Beaulieu, Nabonidus pp. 31–32 Inscription 12 (exs. 1–22, study)

2001 Schaudig, Inschriften Nabonids pp. 337–338 no. 1.5^{a} (exs. 1–22, edition; collations)

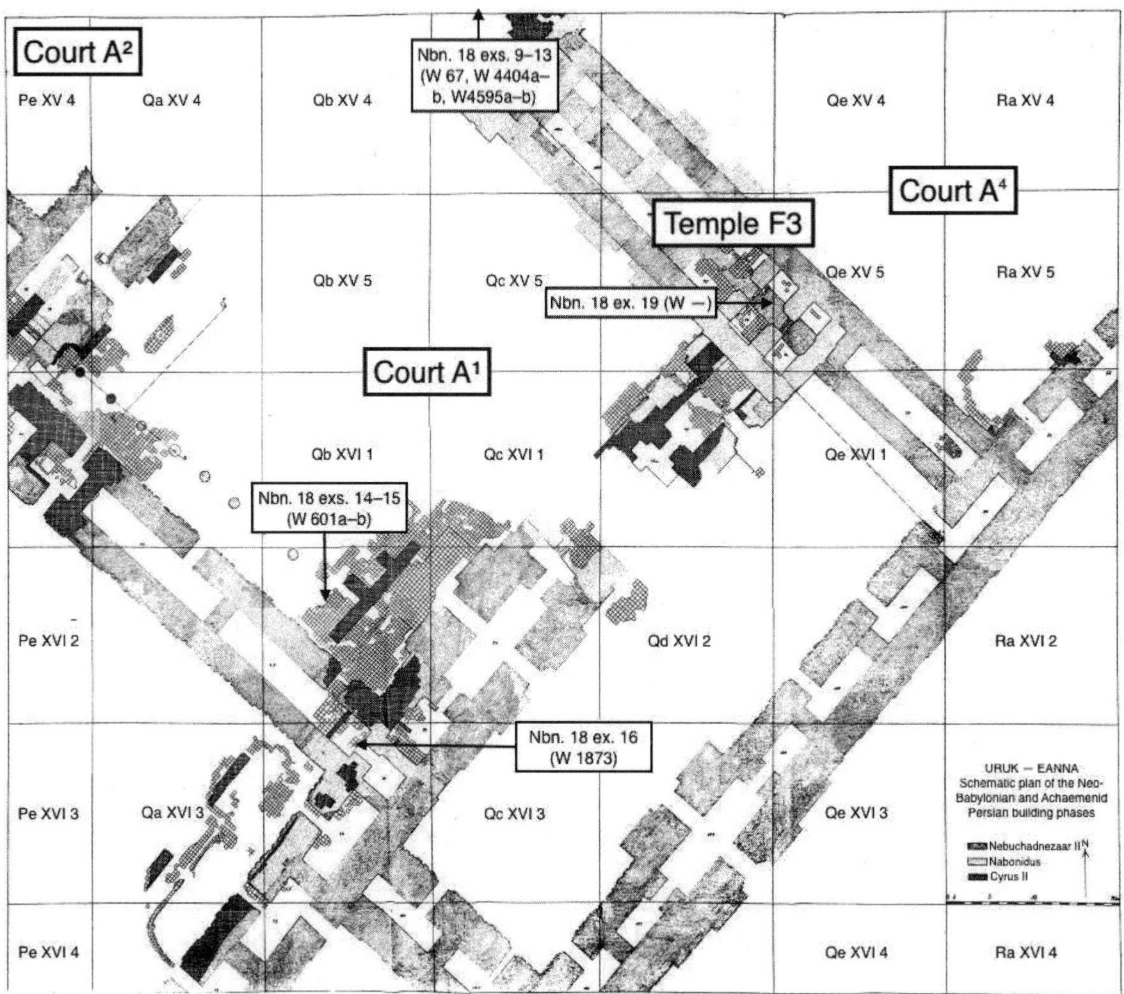

Figure 13. Annotated plan of the Eanna showing the general find spots of some bricks of Nabonidus discovered in the ruins of Court A^1, Court A^2, and Temple F3. Adapted from Lenzen, UVB 10 pl. 2.

TEXT

1) ^{d}*na-bi-um-na-ʾi-id* LUGAL TIN.TIR.KI
2) *za-nin é-sag-íl u é-zi-da e-piš* SIG$_5$.MEŠ
3) DUMU ^{md}AG-TIN-*su-iq-bi* NUN *gít-ma-lu ana-ku*

1–3) Nabonidus, king of Babylon, the one who provides for Esagil and Ezida, the one who performs good deeds, son of Nabû-balāssu-iqbi, perfect prince, am I.

19

Two nearly complete, double-column clay cylinders bear an Akkadian inscription commemorating various building activities of Nabonidus in Babylonia, as well as the installation of his daughter En-nigaldi-Nanna as *ēntu-*

priestess of the moon-god Sîn at Ur. The text, which is written in contemporary Neo-Babylonian script, records that Nabonidus: (1) rebuilt Ebabbar ("Shining House"), the temple of the god Šamaš at Sippar; (2) raised up the superstructures of Ugal-amaru ("Great Storm, (which is) a Deluge") and Melem-kurkurra-dulla ("(Whose) Radiance Spreads over (All) Lands"), the city walls of Cutha and Kish respectively; (3) built the *akītu*-house of the god Uraš according to its original appearance; (4) undertook construction at the town Ubassu, a cult center of the goddess Nanāya, that was located between Babylon and Borsippa; (5) increased the offerings of Ekišnugal, the temple of the god Sîn at Ur, and installed his daughter as *ēntu*-priestess there; (6) reconstructed a ceremonial chariot of the god Lugal-Marda; and (7) completely rebuilt Eigikalama ("House, Eye of the Land"), the temple of Lugal-Marda at Marad. Based on the inscription's main building report, both cylinders are thought to have come from Marad, although there is no absolute proof of this. Although the inscription is not dated, its date of composition is generally thought to have been between Nabonidus' third (553) and tenth (546) regnal years, possibly before his sixth year (550) as king; for this opinion, see Beaulieu, Nabonidus pp. 26–27 and Schaudig, Inschriften Nabonids p. 363. In previous editions and studies, this text is referred to as "Nabonidus Cylinder II, 5," "[Nabonidus] Inscription 7," and the "Eigikalama Cylinder."

CATALOGUE

Ex.	Museum Number	Registration Number	Provenance	Lines Preserved	cpn
1	AO 6444	—	Probably Marad	i 1–ii 37	(p)
2	BM 108981	1914-4-8,1	Purchased from J.J. Naaman	i 1–ii 37	c

COMMENTARY

The line arrangement and master text follow ex. 1. A score is presented on Oracc and the minor (orthographic) variants are given in the critical apparatus at the back of the book.

Both exemplars were purchased and are assumed to have originated from Marad (mod. Wannat es-Sadum) based on their contents. According to the online British Museum Collection database (March 2020), ex. 2 (BM 108981) was purchased in 1914 from J.J. Naaman.

BIBLIOGRAPHY

1914 Dhorme, RA 11 pp. 105–117 (ex. 1, copy, edition)
1921 Gadd, CT 36 pls. 21–23 (ex. 2, copy)
1931 Landsberger, OLZ 34 p. 129 (ex. 1 ii 13, study)
1936 Rutten, Encyclopédie photographique de l'art 2 pl. 42a (ex. 1, photo)
1947 Landsberger, Studies Edhem p. 131 (ex. 1 i 29, transliteration, study)
1953 Böhl, OpMin p. 174 (study)
1968 Ellis, Foundation Deposits pp. 157 and 182 (i 19, edition; study)
1973 Berger, NbK p. 362 Nbn. Zyl. II, 5 (study)
1989 Beaulieu, Nabonidus pp. 26–27 and 50–51 Inscription 7 (i 1–5, i 24–32, ii 33–35, edition; study)
1994 Beaulieu, BCSMS 28 pp. 39–40 (study)
1995 Boulanger, Naissance de l'écriture p. 235 (ex. 1, photo)
2001 Schaudig, Inschriften Nabonids pp. 362–370 no. 2.5 (edition)
2008 Finkel, Babylon: Myth and Reality p. 162 and fig. 147 (photo, study)
2010 Heller, Spätzeit p. 178 (study)
2010 Schaudig, Studies Ellis pp. 145–146 (ii 23–24, study)

TEXT

Col. i

1) *ì-nu-um* ^{d}AMAR.UTU ^{d}EN.LÍL DINGIR.MEŠ *ša-qu-ú* EN *gi-im-ra*
2) *ú-ša-pu-ú ma-al-ku a-na e-pé-eš e-nu-tim*
3) ^{d}*na-bi-um-na-ʾi-id šar-ri a-na za-ni-nu-tim im-bu-ù*
4) *ú-ul-lu-ú re-e-ši-šu e-li ka-li-šu-nu* LUGAL.MEŠ
5) *qí-bi-tu-uš-šu* DINGIR.DINGIR GAL.GAL *iḫ-du-ú a-na šar-ru-ti-šu*

i 1–5) When the god Marduk, the Enlil of the gods, the exalted one, the lord of everything, proclaimed a ruler to exercise lordship, named Nabonidus, the king, as the one who provides (for the gods), (and) elevated him above all of the (other) kings, the great gods were happy about his command(s) regarding his (Nabonidus') kingship.

6) ^{d}*a-num ù* ^{d}EN.LÍL GIŠ.GU.ZA *a-gu-ú* GIŠ.NÍG.GIDRU *ù ši-bir-ri*
7) *pa-ra-aṣ šar-ru-tim a-na du-ur* u_4*-mu i-qí-šu-šum*
8) ^{d}*é-a ba-an ka-la-mu né-me-qí ú-šá-ag-mi-ir-šu*
9) ^{d}*be-let-ì-lí ba-na-at gi-im-ra ú-šá-ak-li-lu bu-na-an-né-e-šu*
10) ^{d}*na-bi-um pa-qid ki-iš-šá-ti iš-ru-uk-šu šu-ka-ma*
11) ^{d}ŠEŠ.KI-*ri* DUMU *ru-bé-e ú-ṣa-ab-ba-a nab-ni-it-su*

i 6–11) The gods Anu and Enlil gave him a throne, crown, scepter, and staff, the eternal insignia of kingship; the god Ea, the creator of all (things), gave him every (type of) wisdom; the goddess Bēlet-ilī, the creator of everything, perfected his features; the god Nabû, the overseer of the totality (of heaven and earth), gave him (knowledge of) scribal skills; the god Nannāru, the son of the prince, inspected his form;

12) ^{d}UTU-*ši nu-úr ì-lí ir-i-am re-é-ut-su*
13) *ba-ʾu-la-a-ti ú-še-ši-ib qí-bi-tu-uš-šu*
14) ^{d}*èr-ra-gal ga-aš-ru* DINGIR.DINGIR *iš-ru-uk-šu du-un-num*
15) ^{d}*za-ba*$_4$*-ba*$_4$ *mu-ut-ta-al-lum ú-ma-ša ú-ša-ag-mi-ir-šu*
16) ^{d}*nusku da-pi-nu ú-za-ʾi-in-šu me-lam-mi* LUGAL-*ú-tu*
17) *a-na ú-ʾu-úr ṭè-e-mu ša-ka-ni*$_7$ *ši-tul-tum ù pa-ra-as ár-kát i-tur še-du-uš-šu*
18) *a-na mu-er-ru-ti-šu e-pé-šu* DINGIR.DINGIR GAL.GAL *ú-šá-li-ku re-ṣu-su*

i 12–18) the god Šamaš, the light of the gods, loved his shepherdship (and) allowed (Nabonidus) to settle people through his (Nabonidus') command; the god Erragal, the (most) powerful one among the gods, gave him power; the god Zababa, the noble one, made him supremely powerful; the god Nusku, the martial one, decorated him with the brilliance of kingship, became his *šēdu* in order to give orders, hold counsel, and investigate matters, (and) sent the great gods to his aid so that (he) could exercise his leadership.

19) *i-nu-šu* ^{d}*na-bi-um-na-ʾi-id* LUGAL TIN.TIR.KI *ru-bu-um na-a-dam*
20) *re-é-a-am it-pe-šu pa-li-iḫ* DINGIR.DINGIR GAL.GAL
21) GÌR.NÍTA *za-ni-nu ša a-na ṭè-e-mu* DINGIR.DINGIR *pu-tuq-qu*
22) *ša* u_4*-mi-ša-am-ma iš-te-né-eʾ-ú aš-rat* DINGIR.MEŠ *ù* ^{d}IŠ.TAR
23) DUMU ^{md}*na-bi-um-*TIN-*su-iq-bi* NUN *e-em-qá a-na-ku*

i 19–23) At that time, Nabonidus, king of Babylon, attentive prince, the capable shepherd who reveres the great gods, the governor who provides, the one who is attentive to the will of the gods, (the one) who is constantly seeks out the sanctuaries of the gods and goddesses daily, son of Nabû-balāssu-iqbi, wise prince, am I.

24) *e-nu-ma* ^{d}AMAR.UTU EN GAL-*ú a-na be-lu-tì ma-a-ti im-bu-ù ni-bi-tì*
25) *mar ru-bé-e* ^{d}*na-bi-um zi-ik-ru šar-ru-ti-ia ú-šar-bu-ù*
26) u_4*-mi-ša-am-ma a-ta-mi pu-lu-úḫ-tì i-lu-ti-šu-un*
27) *ka-a-a-nam aš-te-né-e ša e-li-šu-nu ṭa-a-bu*

i 24–27) When the god Marduk, the great lord, called my name for ruling over the land (and) the son of the prince — the god Nabû — made the fame of my kingship surpassing, I spoke daily, (showing) devotion to their divinity, (and) I constantly strove (to do) what(ever) was pleasing to them.

28) *a-na é-sag-íl ù é-zi-da šu-tu-ra-ku zi-in-na-a-tim*
29) *re-eš mi*-im*-ma-a-a dam-qa ú-še-er-re-eb*

i 28–32) I am foremost in provisioning Esagil and Ezida: I send the best of everything into their (Marduk and Nabû's) presence. Constantly (and) without inter-

i 29 *mi*-im*-ma-a-a* "everything": Both exemplars have *im-mi-a-a*, with the MI and IM signs written in inverted order.

ma-ḫa-ar-šu-un
30) *gi-na-a la na-par-ka-a aš-te-né-e'-a aš-ri-šu-un*
31) *ma-ḫa-zi-šu-nu ra-bu-tim a-na ta-na-da-a-ta aš-ták-ka-an*
32) *ú-šar-bi zi-ik-ra-<šú>-nu in a-pa*$_{12}$*-ta-áš da-ád-me*

ruption, I constantly seek out their places (of worship). I make their great cult centers worthy of (high) praise (and) make their fame great among the people of the inhabited world.

33) *a-na* ^{d}UTU DI.KU$_5$.GAL DINGIR *ša-qu-ú* EN ZIMBIR.KI *é-babbar-ra ki-iṣ-ṣi** KÙ
34) *šu-bat-sa reš-ti-ti ša ma-na-ma šar-ri maḫ-ri la ú-kal-li-mu te-me-en-šú*
35) *e-pé-eš-su* ^{d}UTU EN GAL-*ú ú-qá-an-ni-ma*
36) *e-li te-me-en-na šá na-ra-am-*^{d}EN.ZU *ú-ki-in uš-šu-šu*

i 33–36) For the god Šamaš, the great judge of the gods, the exalted one, lord of Sippar: (As for) Ebabbar, the pure cella, his original dwelling whose (ancient) foundation(s) he had never revealed to any former king, the god Šamaš, the great lord, waited for me to build it and I secured its (new) foundation(s) on top of the (original) foundation(s) of Narām-Sîn.

Col. ii
1) *ša* BÀD *u*$_4$*-gal-a-má-ru*$_{10}$ BÀD GÚ.DU$_8$.A.KI *ul-la-a re*-ši-šu**
2) BÀD *me-lem*$_4$*-kur-kur-ra-dul-la* BÀD *kiš*.KI *ú-za-aq-qí-ir ḫur-sa-ni-iš*

ii 1–2) As for the wall Ugal-amaru, the wall of Cutha, I raised up its superstructure. (As for) the wall Melem-kurkurra-dulla, the wall of Kish, I raised (it) as high as a mountain.

3) *a-na* ^{d}*uraš* EN *ga-aš-ru* É *á-ki-tu*$_4$ *ta-ap-šu-uḫ-ti-šu*
4) *ki-ma la-bi-ri-im-ma e-eš-ši-iš e-pú-uš*

ii 3–4) For the god Uraš, the (most) powerful lord, I built the *akītu*-house of his rest anew as (it had been) in ancient times.

5) *ša* URU.*ú-ba-as-si* DAL.BA.AN.NA KÁ.DINGIR.RA.KI *ù bár-sipa*.KI
6) *i-na* ESIR.UD.DU.A *ù a-gur-ru re-e-ši-šu ul-li-ma*
7) ^{d}*na-na-a* ^{d}IŠ.TAR *šu-úr-bi-tum ú-še-ri-ib ki-iṣ-ṣu-uš-šu*

ii 5–7) As for the city Ubassu, (which is) between Babylon and Borsippa, I raised up its superstructure with bitumen and baked brick(s) and (then) had the goddess Nanāya, the supreme goddess, enter her cella.

8) *a-na* ^{d}30 EN GAL-*ú a-ši-ib é-kiš-nu-gál šá qé-reb úri*.KI
9) *sa-at-tuk-ki-šu ú-ṭa-aḫ-ḫi-id-ma ú-šar-ri-ḫu ni-id-bé-e-šú*
10) *aš-te-né-e'-e-ma aš-ri-šu a-ba-lu be-lu-ut-su*

ii 8–10) For the god Sîn, the great lord, the one who resides in Ekišnugal, which is inside Ur, I lavishly provided his *sattukku*-offerings and made his *nindabû*-offerings plentiful. I constantly sought out his places (of worship) and beseeched his lordship.

11) *a-na e-ri-iš-ti i-ri-ša-an-ni ap-làḫ at-ta-'i-id-ma*
12) *e-ri-iš-ta-šu la ak-la-am-ma am-gu-ru qí-bit-su*
13) DUMU.MUNUS *ṣi-it lìb-bi-ia a-na e-nu-tim áš-ši-ma en-níg-al-di-*^{d}*nanna šum-šú am-bé-e-ma*

ii 11–14a) At the request that he (Sîn) made of me, I became frightened, (but) I was attentive and did not deny his request and consented to his command. I elevated (my) daughter, my own offspring, to the office of *ēntu*-priestess and (then) I named (her) Ennigaldi-Nanna, as her (new, official) name, and had (her) enter the Egipar.

14) *a-na é-gi*$_6$*-pàr ú-še-ri-ib a-na ma-ḫa-zi* DINGIR.DINGIR GAL.GAL
15) *ka-li-šu-nu za-na-nu na-ša-an-ni lìb-bi*

ii 14b–15) My heart dearly wanted me to provide for all of the cult centers of the great gods.

16) *i-nu-šu a-na* ^{d}*lugal-már-da qar-ra-du mu-ut-ta-al-lum*
17) *eṭ-lu-um mu-ut-le-él-lu-ú šá da-na-num šu-uk-lu-lu*
18) *u*$_4$*-um ez-zi šá la im-maḫ-ḫa-ru qá-bal-šu*
19) *ra-ḫi-iṣ* KUR *nu-kúr-ti ša-lil* KUR *a-a-bi a-ši-ib é-igi-kalam-ma*

ii 16–20a) At that time, I was attentive to the god Lugal-Marda, the noble warrior, the exalted warrior who is perfect in strength, the fierce storm whose onslaught cannot be withstood, the one who storms over hostile land(s) (and) plunders the land(s) of his foe(s), the one who resides in Eigikalama, my lord.

20) *be-lí-ia at-ta-'i-id-ma* GIŠ.GIGIR *ru-ku-bu i-lu-ti-šu*
21) *sì-ma-at qar-ra-du-ti-šu ša-li-la-at* KUR *a-a-bi*
22) *<ša> a-na ta-ḫa-zi šu-lu-ka-at ša iš-tu* UD.MEŠ *ru-qu-tú*

ii 20b–26) (As for) the chariot, the vehicle of his divinity, the insignia of his heroism that plunders the land(s) of (his) foe(s), <which> is (well) suited for battle, which no former king had built since distant days, its stone ornaments and its equipment became

i 33 *ki-iṣ-ṣi** "cella": Both exemplars have visually similar *ki-iṣ*-AD.

23) *šar-ri maḫ-ri la i-pú-šu i-na te-me-en é-igi-kalam-ma*
24) NA$_{4}$.MEŠ *ti-iq-ni-šu ù ú-nu-ut-su in-na-mir-ma* GIŠ.GIGIR *šu-a-ti*
25) *e-eš-ši-iš ab-ni i-na* KÙ.BABBAR *eb-bi* KÙ.GI *nam-ri ù ni-sì-iq-tu*$_{4}$ NA$_{4}$.MEŠ
26) *ra-biš ú-za-ʾi-in-šu-ma a-na maḫ-ri-šu ú-še-ri-ib*
27) *é-igi-kalam-ma* É-*su šá* LUGAL *maḫ-ri i-pú-šu-ma ul-lu-ú re-e-ši-šu*
28) *i-ga-ri ki-di-šú la ú-šá-as-ḫi-ru-ma la ú-dan-ni-in ma-aṣ-ṣar-tu-uš*
29) *a-šar-šu na-di-ma la ru-uk-ku-su sip-pe-e-šu e-pe-ri-šu*
30) *qa-a-a-pu-ti ad-ka te-me-en-šu la-bí-ra a-ḫi-iṭ ab-re-e-ma*
31) *e-li te-me-en-ni-šu ú-kin uš-šu-šu* BÀD-*šu ab-ni-ma*
32) *ma-aṣ-ṣar-ta-ša ú-dan-ni-in e-eš-ši-iš e-pú-uš-ma ul-la-a re-e-ši-šu*
33) ^{d}*lugal-már-da* EN *šur-bu-ú* UR.SAG *mug-da-aš-ri a-na* É *šu-a-ti*
34) *ḫa-di-iš i-na e-re-bi-ka mim-mu-ú e-te-ep-pu-uš ḫa-diš in nap-lu-si-ka*
35) *in ma-ḫa-ar* ^{d}AMAR.UTU LUGAL AN *ù* KI *u*$_{4}$*-mi-šam-ma at-ma-a* SIG$_{5}$-*tì*
36) *li-ri-ku* UD.MEŠ TIN-*ia lu-uš-ba-a lit-tu-tu i-na* GIŠ.TUKUL.MEŠ-*ka ez-zu-tim*
37) *šu-um-qí-tu a-a-bi-ia ḫu-ul-li-iq gim-ra-at ga-ri-ia*

visible in the foundation(s) of Eigikalama. I (then) built that chariot anew with shiny silver, bright gold, and precious stones. I magnificently decorated it and had (it) sent into his presence.

ii 27–32) (As for) Eigikalama, his temple, which a former king had built and had raised up its superstructure, (but) without surrounding (it) with its (own) outside wall and (thereby) failing to strengthen its protection — its site was in ruins (and) its door-jamb(s) were not joined (together). I removed its buckled (piles of) earth. I examined (and) checked its original foundation(s) and (then) I laid its (new) foundation(s) on top of the (original) foundation(s). I built its (outer) wall and (thereby) strengthened its protection. I built (the outer wall) anew and raised up its superstructure.

ii 33–37) O Lugal-Marda, supreme lord, mighty warrior, when you joyfully enter this temple (and) look with pleasure upon everything that I have done (for you), speak good thing(s) about me in the presence of the god Marduk, king of heaven and earth, daily so that the days of my life are long (and) I am sated with old age. With your fierce weapons, cut down my enemies (and) destroy all of my foes.

20

A brick fragment unearthed at Seleucia preserves the final two lines of a short Akkadian inscription of Nabonidus written in archaizing Neo-Babylonian script. The text is inscribed inside a frame that is stamped on the face of the brick. The edition is based on the published photograph of the brick since the present whereabouts of the object are not known.

CATALOGUE

Museum Number	Excavation Number	Provenance	cpn
—	—	Seleucia	n

19 ii 27 LUGAL *maḫ-ri* "a former king": This presumably refers to Nebuchadnezzar II, who also records that he renovated Lugal-Marda's temple at Marad (Eigikalama); see Da Riva, GMTR 4 pp. 120–121 no. C32.

BIBLIOGRAPHY

1933 Waterman, Tel Umar 2 p. 78 and pl. 25 fig. 2 (photo, study)
1968 Brinkman, PKB pp. 205–206 and 351 no. 26.2.1 (study)
1970–71 Pettinato, Mesopotamia 5–6 p. 54 n. 20 (line 2′, study)
1987–90 Brinkman, RLA 7 p. 376 (study)
1995 Frame, RIMB 2 p. 109 (study)
2001 Schaudig, Inschriften Nabonids p. 336 no. 1.3[a] (edition)

TEXT

Lacuna
1′) *x x* ⸢*ša*? ^{d}30⸣ *x x x*
2′) ^{d}AG-TIN-*su-iq-bi* NUN ⸢*em*$_4$⸣-*qá*

Lacuna
1′–2′) ... *of* the god Sîn, ..., (son of) Nabû-balāssu-iqbi, wise prince.

21

This Akkadian inscription of Nabonidus recording the rebuilding of Šamaš' temple at Sippar, Ebabbar ("Shining House"), is known only from a small fragment of a two-column clay cylinder, which presumably comes from Sippar. The inscription, which is written in contemporary Neo-Babylonian script, is a shorter version of text nos. 22–23 (Ebabbar Cylinder). Like those two inscriptions, this text was probably also composed near the beginning of Nabonidus' reign, perhaps during his second regnal year (554); for details, see the commentary to text no. 23 (Ebabbar Cylinder).

CATALOGUE

Museum Number	Registration Number	Provenance	cpn
BM 46600	81-8-30,66	Probably Sippar	c

BIBLIOGRAPHY

2008 Da Riva, GMTR 4 p. 131 sub 1a (study)

TEXT

Col. i
1) [*ì*]-⸢*nu-ma* ^{d}*a-nu*⸣ *ù* ^{d}⸢EN.LÍL⸣ *ša* ⸢ZIMBIR.KI⸣

Lacuna
1′) [(...) *i-na ki-iṣ-ṣi da-am*]-⸢*qu aš-ri*⸣ [*šu-us-su-mu*]
2′) [*ú-še-ši-bu*] ⸢*a*⸣-*ta-mi* <<*mi*>> *a-na* [*ni-ši* KUR ...]
3′) [... *an-ni*]-*ta i-ta-mu-nim ul* ⸢*bu*⸣-[*ʾa-a*]
4′) [*a-šar-šu e*]-*li šu-ub-ti-šu ki-it-tim* ⸢*ul*⸣ [*e-pú-uš*]
5′) ^{d}UTU *be-el ra-bí-ù* (erasure) *é-babbar*-⸢*ra*⸣ [...]

i 1) [W]hen the gods Anu and Enlil [had commanded the renovation of] Sippar
Lacuna
i 1′–2′a) [(...) they had (them) reside in a go]od [shrine], a [suitable] place.
i 2′b–3′a) I spoke to [the people of (my) land, ...].
i 3′b–5′) [Th]is is what they said me: "[Its (original) emplacement] had not [been sought out. It was] not [(re)built o]n its true site. The god Šamaš, the great

lord, [...] Ebabbar."

6′) *a-na da-ke-e* É *šu-a-ti* ⸢ŠÀ?⸣ [*pa-li-iḫ ra-šá-a-ku ni-qí-it-ti*]
7′) *i-na ma-a-a-al* GE$_6$ *ul ú-qa-at-ta-*[*a ši-it-tim ṭa-ab-tim*]
8′) *áš-ši qá-ti-ia ú-ṣa-al-la-a* ^{d}EN.[LÍL DINGIR.MEŠ ^{d}AMAR.UTU]

i 6′–8′) [*My*] *he*[*art* was afraid (at the thought of)] removing that temple; [I was worried]. In (my) night bed, I did not get enoug[h good sleep]. I raised my hands (and) beseeched the En[lil of the gods, the god Marduk].

9′) *a-na e-pe-eš é-babbar-ra áš-ra-a-tì* ^{d}UTU *ù* ⸢^{d}⸣[IŠKUR EN.MEŠ *bi-ri aš-te-e-ma*]
10′) ^{d}UTU *ù* ^{d}IŠKUR *an-na ki-i-nu i-ta-*[*ap-pa-lu-in* ...]
11′) *a x x x du un taḫ ú-ša-aš-ṭi-ru i-*⸢*na*?⸣ [...]

i 9′–11′) With regard to (re)building Ebabbar, [I frequently visited] the shrines of the gods Šamaš and [Adad, the lords of divination, and] the gods Šamaš and Adad ans[wered me] with a firm 'yes.' [...] they had ... written *i*[*n* ....]

Col. ii
Completely missing

Completely missing

22

A fragment of a three-column clay cylinder preserves part of an Akkadian inscription recording Nabonidus' rebuilding of Ebabbar ("Shining House"), the temple of Šamaš at Sippar. The text, which is written in contemporary Neo-Babylonian script, is similar, but not identical, to text no. 23 (Ebabbar Cylinder). As far as it is preserved, this inscription appears to be a shorter version of the following inscription and, therefore, was likely composed before text no. 23. If that proves true, then this text also dates towards the beginning of Nabonidus' reign, perhaps during his second regnal year (554); for details, see the commentary to text no. 23. The piece was purchased by the Metropolitan Museum of Art (New York) from Rev. W.H. Ward in 1886.

CATALOGUE

Museum Number	Registration Number	Provenance	cpn
MMA 86.11.52	—	Probably Sippar	c

BIBLIOGRAPHY

2014 Frame in Spar, CTMMA 4 pp. 304–306 no. 176 (edition)

TEXT

Col. i
Lacuna

1′) [*mu-ṭaḫ*]-⸢*ḫi-id sa-at-tuk-ka*⸣
2′) [*mu*]-⸢*šar-ri*⸣-*iḫ ni-id-bé-e*
3′) ⸢DUMU⸣ ^{d}AG-*ba-la-at-su-iq-bi*
4′) ⸢*ru*⸣-*ba-a-am e-em-qá a-na-ku*

Lacuna

i 1′–4′) [the one who makes] *sattukku*-offerings [abun]dant (and) *nindabû*-offerings [spl]endid, [so]n of Nabû-balāssu-iqbi, wise [p]rince, am I.

5′) [*i*]-⸢*nu*⸣-*ma* ^{d}AMAR.UTU ^{d}EN.LÍL DINGIR.DINGIR

i 5′–14′) [Wh]en the god Marduk, the Enlil of the gods,

6′) ⸢*be*⸣-*lu-ut ma-ti-šu i-qí-pa-an-ni*
7′) ⸢*gi*⸣-*na-a aš-te-né-e*ʾ-*a*
8′) ⸢*pu*⸣-*lu-úḫ-ti i-lu-ti-šu*
9′) *ša e-li-šu ṭa-a-bu e-pe-šu*
10′) u_4-*mi-ša-am a*-⸢*ta-mi*⸣
11′) *aš-šum la ba-še-e* ⸢*ḫi*⸣-[*ṭi-tì*]
12′) *ka-a-a-nam šu-tu*-⸢*ra*⸣-[*ku*]
13′) *a-na* DINGIR.DINGIR GAL.GAL *qá*-[*qá-da-a*]
14′) *šu-te-mu-qá-ak-šu*-⸢*nu*⸣-[*ti*]
15′) *i-nu-šu é-babbar-ra ki-iṣ-ṣi ra-aš-bu*
16′) *šu-ba-at* ^{d}UTU *da-a-a-na*
17′) <*ša*> *i-na qé*-⸢*re*⸣-*eb* ZIMBIR.KI
18′) ⸢LUGAL⸣ *pa-ni i-pú-uš-ma ul-lu-ú re-e-ši-šú*
19′) 45 MU.AN.NA.MEŠ *la im-la-ma*
20′) ⸢*i*⸣-*qu-pu i-ga-ru-šu*
21′) [*ra*]-⸢*am*⸣-*ku-ut é-babbar-ra i*-⸢*ta-mu*⸣-[*nim*]
22′) [*i-qu*]-⸢*up*⸣ [É]
23′) [*qí-bi-it-su-nu*] ⸢*la*⸣ *a-qí-ip-ma* ⸢*ra*⸣-[*šá-a-ku* <*ni-qí-it-ti*>]
24′) [*ú-ma-*ʾ*e-er*]-⸢*ma*⸣ DUMU.MEŠ TIN.⸢TIR⸣.[KI]
25′) [*ù bár-sipa*.KI] ⸢*e*?-*em*?⸣-[*qu-tu*]

Lacuna

Col. ii

Lacuna

1′) *ú*-⸢*ša*⸣-[*ad-gi-il pa-ni-ka*]
2′) *a-na* ⸢*da*⸣-[*ke-e é-babbar-ra*]
3′) *lìb-bi* [*pa-li-iḫ ra-šá-a-ku ni-qí-it-ti*]
4′) *i-na* ⸢*ma*⸣-[*a-a-al mu-ši-im ul ú-qa-at-ta-a*]
5′) *ši-it*-[*ti ṭa-ab-tim* (...)]
6′) *áš-ši* ⸢*qa*⸣-[*ti-ia ú-ṣa-al-la-a*]
7′) ^{d}⸢EN⸣.[LÍL DINGIR.MEŠ ^{d}AMAR.UTU]
8′) *aš*-⸢*šum*?⸣ [*e-pé-eš é-babbar-ra*]
9′) *áš*-⸢*ra*⸣-[*a-ti* ^{d}UTU *ù* ^{d}IŠKUR]
10′) EN.[MEŠ *bi-ri aš-te-e-ma*]
11′) *x* [...]
12′) [...]
13′) [...]
14′) [...]
15′) ⸢*ša*⸣ [...]
16′) GIŠ.AL [...]
17′) *al-x* [...]
18′) *uš-te-x* [...]
19′) *i-na* ITI ⸢*šal*⸣-[*ma* ...]
20′) *ad*-⸢*ka*⸣ [...]
21′) ⸢*ad-kam-ma*⸣ [...]

Lacuna

Col. iii

Completely missing

entrusted me [(to) r]ule over his land, I constantly strove (to show) devotion to his divinity (and) I was speaking daily about doing what(ever) is pleasing to him. So that there would be no cu[ltic mistake(s), I was] constantly forem[ost] (in everything I did and) I was co[nstantly] praying devoutly to the great gods.

i 15′–20′) At that time, (with regard to) Ebabbar, the awe-inspiring shrine, the residence of the god Šamaš, the judge, <which> is inside Sippar, (which) a king of the past had built (and) raised its superstructure, forty-five years had not (yet) elapsed and its walls had buckled.

i 21′–23′) [The *ra*]*mku*-priests of Ebabbar tol[d me: "The temple had buck]led." I did [no]t believe [their report], but (nevertheless) I w[as <worried>].

i 24′–25′) [I sent] citizens of Baby[lon and Borsippa], *skill*[*ed men*]

Lacuna

Lacuna

ii 1′) "He has en[trusted you with building it on its true site]."

ii 2′–7′) My heart [was afraid (at the thought of)] re[moving Ebabbar; I was worried]. In (my) [night] b[ed, I did not get enough good] sle[ep. (...)] I raised [my] h[ands (and) beseeched] the E[nlil of the gods, the god Marduk].

ii 8′–11′) *With re*[*gard to* (re)building Ebabbar, I frequently visited] the shri[nes of the gods Šamaš and Adad], the lord[s of divination, and ...]

ii 12′–15′) (No translation possible)

ii 16′–21′) hoe(s) [...] I ... [...] I ... [...] In a fav[orable] month, [...] I *tore dow*[*n* ...] I mustered [the workmen of the gods Šamaš and Marduk] and

Lacuna

Completely Missing

Lacuna before ii 1′ The translation assumes that the now-missing line immediately before ii 1′ contained *i-na aš-ri-šu ki-nim e-pé-eš-su* "with building it on its true site."

23

This Akkadian inscription commemorating Nabonidus' rebuilding of Ebabbar ("Shining House"), the temple of the sun-god at Sippar, is known from a large, but damaged, three-column clay cylinder; the script is contemporary Neo-Babylonian. The text is reported to have come from Larsa, which also has a temple of Šamaš called Ebabbar, but given the description of the work undertaken on the sun-god's temple in this inscription (compare text no. 24 [Ebabbar Cylinder]), it is more probable that the object originates in Sippar; the confusion seems to have stemmed from the fact that Nabonidus worked on not one, but two different Ebabbar temples, the one at Sippar and the one at Larsa. Like the following inscription (text no. 24), this text records many of the details of how Nabonidus, his advisors, and his master builders expertly renovated the Ebabbar temple on the foundations laid in the distant past by the famous Narām-Sîn of Agade; here, Nabonidus states that he did not deviate even a finger's length from the ancient, divinely-sanction plan of the temple. As one expects, no date is inscribed on the cylinders. In contrast to text no. 24, which, as scholars agree, dates to the end of Nabonidus' second regnal year (554), the proposed date of composition of this inscription is still a matter of scholarly debate. P.-R. Berger suggests that it was written in 554, while P.-A. Beaulieu and H. Schaudig argue that the inscription was written in 546, Nabonidus' tenth regnal year; see the commentary for further details. In scholarly literature, this text is referred to as "Nabonidus Cylinder III, 3," "[Nabonidus] Inscription 11," and the "Ebabbar Cylinder."

CATALOGUE

Museum Number	Registration Number	Provenance	cpn
Ash 1922-201	W-B 5	Reportedly Larsa, but possibly Sippar	c

COMMENTARY

According to P.-A. Beaulieu (Nabonidus pp. 30–31), the inscription on Ash 1922-201 commemorated the restoration of Sippar's ziggurat Ekunankuga ("House, Pure Stairway of Heaven"), because that temple-tower of Šamaš is mentioned in i 6 and so the text must date to Nabonidus' tenth regnal year (546); this date of composition was followed by H. Schaudig (Inschriften Nabonids p. 48). Beaulieu rejected Berger's suggestion (NbK p. 111) that the central focus of the inscription was on the rebuilding of Ebabbar and that the text was composed during the king's second year as king (554), on the grounds that he saw "no apparent reason why two distinct building inscriptions recorded on clay cylinders (inscriptions 5 and 11) should have been commissioned in the second year to commemorate the restoration of the Ebabbar, especially as inscription 11 [= this text] by and large repeats the account found in inscription 5 [= text no. 24]." Since the publication of Beaulieu's study of Nabonidus' reign in 1989, two new inscriptions closely related to the one written on Ash 1922-201 have come to light: BM 46600 (text no. 21) and MMA 86.11.52 (text no. 22). Both seem to be earlier, shorter versions of this text and it is very likely that all three were inscribed around the same time, with text no. 21 being the earliest and text no. 23 being the latest of the group. The language and contents of these three inscriptions are very similar to those of text no. 24 (Ebabbar Cylinder), which most scholars generally date to 554, Nabonidus' second regnal year.

In fact, it is not impossible that text nos. 21–23 are earlier in date than text no. 24, as inferred from their lengthy descriptions of the rebuilding of the sun-god's temple. If this proves true, despite the fact that the inscription written on Ash 1922-201 mentions the ziggurat in i 6, then Nabonidus appears to have had at least four different inscriptions commemorating the rebuilding of Ebabbar at Sippar composed during 554: BM 46600 (text no. 21), MMA 86.11.52 (text no. 22), Ash 1922-201 (this text), and BM 91140 and duplicates (text no. 24). An early date of composition for this inscription, following Berger, is preferred here since this text does not appear to have recorded work on Ekunankuga and since the description of construction on Ebabbar is more closely related to text no. 24 (Ebabbar Cylinder) than to accounts of that temple's rebuilding in inscriptions clearly composed later in Nabonidus' reign, such as text no. 28 (Eḫulḫul Cylinder).

As for the provenance of Ash 1922-201, Berger (NbK p. 376) suggests that the piece came from Larsa. As Beaulieu (Nabonidus pp. 30–31) has already correctly noted, it is "impossible to determine if this information is reliable." He later notes, assuming that the inscription written on this cylinder dates to Nabonidus' tenth year (546), that the damaged cylinder could have come from Larsa, stating: "It is not overly hazardous to assume that this copy of inscription 11 was inserted in the structure of the Ebabbar of Larsa to commemorate the fact that the two building works were contemporaneous." Schaudig (Inschriften Nabonids p. 440), on the other hand, suggests that the confusion of Larsa and Sippar arose because both cities had an Ebabbar temple. Based on the early date of composition proposed for this text in this volume, Sippar is tentatively suggested as the provenance of Ash 1922-20, although this cannot be proven.

BIBLIOGRAPHY

1923 Langdon, OECT 1 pp. 32–37 and pls. 23–28 (copy, edition)
1937 Meissner, MAOG 11 p. 44 no. 40.1 (iii 27–28, study)
1953 von Soden, SAHG p. 288 no. 35a (iii 43–61, translation)
1960 Lambert, BWL p. 320 no. 96 (ii 12, study)
1965 Gurney and Hulin apud Tadmor, Studies Landsberger p. 360 n. 48 (i 50, study)
1973 Berger, NbK pp. 111–112 and 376 Nbn. Zyl. III, 3 (study)
1977 Gurney, Studies Finkelstein p. 96 (study)
1989 Beaulieu, Nabonidus pp. 7 and 30–31 Inscription 11 (i 1–8, 14′–16′, edition; study)
1991 Powell, ZA 81 pp. 24–25 (ii 4′–8′ translation, study)
1994 Beaulieu, BCSMS 28 pp. 37–42 (study)
2001 Schaudig, Inschriften Nabonids pp. 440–445 no. 2.13 (edition)
2003 Schaudig, Studies Kienast pp. 456–461 and 491–495 (ii 1′–15′, edition; study)
2009 Winter, On Art in the Ancient Near East 2 p. 466 (study)
2010 Schaudig, Studies Ellis pp. 146, 156–161 and 469 no. 6.4 (ii 11–12, 1′–12′ edition; study)

TEXT

Col. i

1) *ì-nu-um* AN-*num ù* ^{d}EN.LÍL
2) *ša* URU ZIMBIR.KI *iq-bu-ú e-de-eš-su*
3) *a-da-an-šu-num ki-i-ni ik-šu-dam*
4) *a-na e-pé-eš é-babbar-ra* ^{d}UTU *be-el ra-bí-ù*
5) *i-iḫ-su-sa šu-bat-sa re-eš-ti-tú*
6) *ša zi-qú-ra-at ge-gu-na-šu*
7) *re-ši-šu e-li ša pa-ni ul-lu-ù*
8) *lib-ba-šu-ni ḫa-di-iš ub-lam-ma*
9) ^{d}*na-bi-um-na-ʾi-id* LUGAL *za-ni-nu*
10) *mu-ṭi-ib lib-bi-šu-nu ib-bu-ú*
11) *re-é-a-am ka-an-šu*
12) *muš-te-*⸢*e*⸣*-ú aš-ra-a-ti* DINGIR.DINGIR GAL.GAL
13) GÌR.NÍTA *it-pé-šu*
14) *ša a-na ṭè-em* DINGIR.MEŠ *pu-tuq-qu*
15) *za-ni-in é-sag-íl ù é-zi-da*
16) *mu-ud-di-iš eš-re-e-ti* DINGIR.MEŠ *ù* EŠ$_{18}$.TÁR
17) *mu-ṭaḫ-ḫi-id sa-at-tuk-ku*
18) *mu-šar-ri-iḫ ni-id-bé-e*
19) DUMU ^{md}*na-bi-um-ba-la-at-su-iq-bi*

i 1–5) When the gods Anu and Enlil had commanded the renovation of the city, Sippar, (and) their firmly appointed time to (re)build Ebabbar had arrived, the god Šamaš, the great lord, remembered his original residence.

i 6–10) Their hearts prompted (them) with pleasure to raise the superstructure of the ziggurat, his raised temple, higher than the previous one and they nominated Nabonidus, the king who provides for (and) pleases their heart(s).

i 11–20) The submissive shepherd who constantly seeks out the shrines of the great gods, the capable governor who is constantly attentive to the will of the gods, the one who provides for Esagil and Ezida, the one who renovates the shrines of the gods and goddesses, the one who makes *sattukku*-offerings abundant (and) *nindabû*-offerings splendid, son of Nabû-balāssu-iqbi, wise prince, am I.

20) *ru-bu-ú e-em-qá a-na-ku*
21) [*ì-nu-um* ^{d}AMAR.UTU *be-lu*]-⸢*ut*⸣ KUR$^{?}$⸣-*šú* *i-qí-pa-*⸢*ni*$^{*?}$⸣
22) [...] ^{d}*na-bi-um*
23) [... *im*]-*ba-an-ni*

i 21–23) [When the god Marduk] entrusted me [(to) rule ov]er his *land* [...] the god Nabû [... nom]inated me

Lacuna

Lacuna

1′) [...] *ḫi-ṭi-tì*
2′) [...] x x *su-pe-e-šu-un*
3′) [...] x ⸢GAL⸣ (erasure) *qá-qá-da-a*
4′) [x x *šu-te*]-*mu-qá-ku*$_{13}$-*šu-nu-ti*

i 1′–4′) [So that there would be no] cultic mistake(s), [...] ... praying to them [(and) I was] constantly [praying de]voutly [to the gr]eat [gods].

5′) ⸢*i*⸣-*nu-šu é-babbar-ra ki-iṣ-ṣi** *ra-áš-bu*
6′) *šu-ba-at* ^{d}UTU *ù* ^{d}*a-a*
7′) *ša i-na qé-re-eb* ZIMBIR.KI
8′) *ša* LUGAL *ma-ḫar i-pu-šu-ma ul-la-a re-e-ši-šu*
9′) 45 MU.AN.NA.MEŠ *la im-la-ma i-qu-pu* *i-ga-ru-šu*

i 5′–9′) At that time, (with regard to) Ebabbar, the awe-inspiring shrine, the residence of the god Šamaš and the goddess Aya that is inside Sippar, which a king of the past had built (and) raised its superstructure, forty-five years had not (yet) elapsed and its walls had buckled.

10′) *ra-am-ku-tì é-babbar-ra i-ta-mu-nim*
11′) *i-qu-pu* É
12′) *qí-bi-it-su-nu la a-qí-ip-ma*
13′) *ra-šá-a-ku** *ni-qí-it-ti*

i 10′–13′) The *ramku*-priests of Ebabbar told me: "The temple had buckled." I did not believe their report, but (nevertheless) I was worried.

14′) *ú-ma-ʾe-er-ma* DUMU.MEŠ TIN.TIR.KI *ù* *bár-sipa*.KI
15′) *em-qu-tu mu-de-e ši-ip-ri*
16′) *a-na qé-re-eb é-babbar-ra* ⸢*ú-še*⸣-*rib-ma*
17′) *ip-pa-al-*⸢*su*⸣-*ma*
18′) É *šu-a-ti i-ga-ru-šu qu-up-pu-ma*
19′) *pu-uṭ-ṭu-ru ri-ki-is* KÁ.KÁ

Col. ii

1) GIŠ.ÙR *ṣú-lu-li-šu šu-uḫ-ḫu-ṭu*
2) *a-ṣú-ú qé-re-eb* É
3) *ip-pal-su-ma ú-ša-am-lu-in-ni pu-lu-ùḫ-tú*

i 14′–ii 3) I sent citizens of Babylon and Borsippa, skilled men who know (every) task, (to Sippar) and had (them) enter Ebabbar. Then, they saw that the walls of that temple had buckled, that the structure of (its) gates were falling apart, (and) that the beam(s) of its roof were stripped away (and) protruding inside the temple. They saw (this) and they filled me with fear.

4) *iš-tu* É *šu-a-ti*
5) *qá-at* ^{d}UTU *ù* ^{d}*a-a iṣ-ba-tu-ma*
6) *i-na ki-iṣ-ṣi da-am-qu*
7) *aš-ri šu-us-su-mu ú-še-ši-bu*

ii 4–7) They led the god Šamaš and the goddess Aya out of that temple by the hand and had (them) reside in a good shrine, a suitable place.

8) *a-ta-*⸢*mi*⸣ [*a*]-⸢*na*⸣ *ni-ši ma-a-ti*
9) *mi-na-a i-ši-ir-šum-ma i-qu-up-ma*

ii 8–9) I spoke [t]o the people of (my) land, (saying): "What has happened to it so that it buckled?"

10) *an-ni-ta i-ta-mu-nim*
11) *ul bu-ʾa-a a-šar-šu*
12) *e-li šu-ub-ti-šú kit-ti ul e-pú-uš-ma e-ni* *qá-qá-ar-šu*
13) ^{d}UTU *be-el ra-bí-ù*
14) *e-pé-eš é-babbar-ra ú-qa-a re-eš-ka*
15) *ši-pí-ir-šu bu-un-ni-i*
16) *i-na aš-ri-šu ki-nim e-pé-eš-su*
17) *ú-ša-ad-gi-il pa-ni-ka*

ii 10–17) This is what they said me: "Its (original) emplacement had not been sought out. It was not (re)built on its true site and its location was changed. The god Šamaš, the great lord, has waited for you to (re)build Ebabbar. (Therefore,) make its construction beautiful! He has entrusted you with building it on its true site."

18) *a-na da-ke-e é-babbar-ra* ŠÀ *pa-li-iḫ*
19) *ra-šá-a-ku ni-qí-it-ti*
20) *i-na ma-a-a-al* (erasure) *mu-ši-im*
21) *ul ú-qa-at-ta-a ši-it-tim ṭa-ab-tim*
22) *áš-ši qa-*[*ti-ia ú-ṣa*]-⸢*al-la*⸣-*a*

ii 18–23) My heart was afraid (at the thought of) removing Ebabbar; I was worried. In (my) night bed, I did not get enough good sleep. I raised [my] ha[nds (and) bese]eched the Enlil of the gods, the god Marduk.

---

i 20 The subject of this phrase are the gods, who appoint Nabonidus, but after the list of epithets of the king the scribe added *anāku* as if Nabonidus were the subject of the phrase and as one finds it in other inscriptions.
i 21 *i-qí-pa-*⸢*ni*$^{*?}$⸣ "he entrusted me": The scribe appears to have written *i-qí-pa-*⸢MEŠ⸣.
i 5′ *ki-iṣ-ṣi** "shrine": The text has visually similar *ki-iṣ*-AD.
i 13′ *ra-šá-a-ku** "I had": The cylinder has *ra-šá-a*-RA.

23) ^{d}EN.LÍL ⌈DINGIR.MEŠ⌉ ^{d}AMAR.UTU
24) *[aš]-⌈šum⌉ e-⌈pé⌉-[eš] é-babbar-ra*
25) *[aš-ra-a-ti* ^{d}]UTU *ù* ^{d}IŠKUR
26) [EN.MEŠ *bi-ri*] *aš-te-e-ma*
27) *[bi-ri ab-re-e-ma* ^{d}UTU *ù*] ^{d}IŠKUR
28) *[an-na ki-i-nu i-tap-pa]-⌈lu⌉-in*

ii 24–28) [With reg]ard to (re)buil[ding] Ebabbar, I frequently visited [the shrines of] the gods Šamaš and Adad, [the lords of divination], and [I performed extispicies. The gods Šamaš and] Adad [always answer]ed me [with a firm 'yes].'

29) *[áš-né-e-ma te-er-tum ap-qid]-⌈ma⌉*
30) [...]-*e*?

ii 29–30) [I repeated (and) checked the extispicy] and

Lacuna

Lacuna

1′) *⌈za-bi-il⌉ [tu]-⌈up⌉-ši-ik-ku*

ii 1′) [I mustered the workmen of the gods Šamaš and Marduk — those who wield hoes, hold spade(s)], (and) carry [bas]ket(s).

2′) *iš-tu pa-ni* (erasure) *⌈qá⌉-qá-ri-im*
3′) 18 KÙŠ *ú-ša-ap-pí-lu-ma*
4′) *te-me-en la-bi-ri-im*
5′) *ša na-ra-am-*^{d}EN.ZU LUGAL *ma-ḫar*
6′) *ap-pa-li-is-ma*
7′) *ṭup-pí* KÙ.GI NA$_4$.ZA.GÌN *ù* NA$_4$.GUG
8′) *ša e-pé-eš é-babbar-ra a-mu-ur-ma*
9′) *a-šar-šu-nu la ú-na-ak-ki-ir-ma*
10′) *ú-te-er aš-ru-uš-šu-*<*un*>
11′) *ši-ṭi-ir šu-mi-ia it-ti-šu-un*
12′) *ú-ki-in a-na* (erasure) *ṣa-a-ti*

ii 2′–12′) From the surface of the ground, they dug down eighteen cubits and I saw the original foundation(s) of Narām-Sîn, a king of the past, and (then) found tablet(s) of gold, lapis lazuli, and carnelian concerning the construction of Ebabbar. I did not alter their (original) place(s) and I returned (them) to their (proper) place(s). I firmly placed my (own) inscription(s) with them forever.

13′) *e-li te-em-mé-ni-šú la-bi-ri*
14′) ŠU.SI *a-na la a-ṣe-e ù la e-re-bi*
15′) *pu-lu-uk-ka-šu lu-ú ú-ki-in*

ii 13′–15′) I indeed firmly established its boundary marker(s precisely) on its original foundation(s), not (even) a fingerbreadth outside or inside (of them).

16′) *mi-im-ma ḫi-ši-iḫ-tum e-pé-eš* É *šu-a-tú*
17′) *la ak-la-am-ma ú-še-ri-ib qé-re-eb-šu*

ii 16′–17′) I did not withhold anything needed to (re)build that temple, but had (all of those things) brought inside it.

18′) *ša* LUGAL *ma-ḫar i-na* GIŠ.ÙR GIŠ.GIŠIMMAR
29′) *ib-nu-ú ṣú-lu-ul-šu*
20′) GIŠ.EREN.MEŠ *da-an-nu-ti*

Col. iii

1) *iš-tu la-ab-na-nu*
2) GIŠ.TIR *el-le-ti*
3) *ú-bi-il-lam-ma*
4) 1 LIM 50 GIŠ.EREN.MEŠ *a-na e-pé-eš é-babbar-ra*
5) *lu-ú ú-še-ri*-ib**

ii 18′–iii 5) (For the temple,) whose roof a king of the past had built with beam(s) of date palm(s), I carried strong cedars from Mount Lebanon, the bright forest, and indeed had 1,050 cedars for (re)building Ebabbar brought inside.

6) *a-na ši-i-pí-šu* GIŠ.EREN.MEŠ* KÙ.MEŠ *aš-tak-ka-an*
7) GIŠ.DAL GIŠ.GAN.DU$_7$ *giš-ká-na-ku*
8) GIŠ.SAG.KUL LÁL *šá* GIŠ.EREN *el-lu-tim*
9) *e-ma* KÁ.MEŠ *ù* É.MEŠ *ú-šar-ši-id*

iii 6–9) For its *šīpu*, I set bright cedars in place. At each gate and room, I securely fastened crossbeam(s), architrave(s), *giškanakku*(s), (and) *sikkūru šāqilu* lock(s) of bright cedar.

10) *ki-ma ša iš-tu* KUR-*i* GIŠ.EREN
11) ^{d}UTU EN *šur-bu-ú i-na na-pa-ḫi-šú*
12) *i-na* GIŠ.EREN *da-an-nu-tu*
13) *e-li-šu ṣú-lu-lu ab-ni*

iii 10–13) Just like when the god Šamaš, the supreme lord, rises up from the Cedar Mountain, I built a roof over it with strong cedar(s).

14) *a-šar mu-ša-bi-šu ki-ma* GIŠ.TIR ḪA.ŠUR

iii 14–15) I made the scent of the place where he

Lacuna before ii 1′ Following H. Schaudig (Inschriften Nabonids p. 441), the translation assumes that the two now-missing lines before ii 1′ contained *ad-ka-am-ma um-ma-na-a-ti* ^{d}UTU *ù* ^{d}AMAR.UTU / *ṣa-bi-it al-lu na-áš* GIŠ.MAR "I mustered the workmen of the gods Šamaš and Marduk — those who wield hoes, hold spade(s)."

iii 6 *ši-i-pí-šu* "its *šīpu*": *šīpu* designates a part of the roof.

iii 7 *giš-ká-na-ku* "*giškanakku*(s)": It is not entirely clear which part of the door the *giškanakku* designates. In the dictionaries it is referred to as a "part of the doorframe," but without going into any detail.

iii 14 ḪA.ŠUR "*ḫašūru*-tree(s)": *ḫašūru-*/*ḫašurru*-tree designates a kind of cypress or cedar (see CAD Ḫ p. 147, which designates this word as a kind of cedar). It is difficult to distinguish if the *ḫašurru*-tree was a type of cypress or cedar tree, especially as both belong to the same botanic order of Coniferales.

15) *i-ri-iš-su uš-ṭi-ib*

(Šamaš) resides as pleasing as a forest of *ḫašūru*-tree(s).

16) GIŠ.⸢IG⸣.MEŠ GIŠ.EREN.MEŠ *ù* GIŠ.MES.MÁ.KAN.NA
17) *e-ma* KÁ.MEŠ-*šu ú-šar-ši-id*
18) <É.MEŠ$^{?}$> *si-ḫi-ir-ti é*-babbar*-ra**
19) *i-na* GIŠ.Ù.<SUḪ$_5$>.MEŠ *pa-ag-lu-tim*
20) *ṣú-lu-ul-ši-na ab-ni*

iii 16–20) At each of its gates, I securely fastened doors of cedar and *musukkannu*-wood. (As for) <*the temples*> in the vicinity of Ebabbar, I built their roof(s) with (beams of) thick pine-tree(s).

21) *aš-šum ug-ga-tú ar-ra-tim ù ḫi-ṭi-tì*
22) *qé-er-ba-šu la šu-ub-ši-i*
23) *i-na pi-i um-ma-na-a-ti e-pé-eš šip-ri-šú*
24) *la ša-ka-nim-ma*
25) *ik-ri-ib da-mi-iq-tim*
26) *i-na pi-i-ši-na šá-ka-na-am*
27) NINDA.ḪI.A KAŠ.SAG UZU.ḪI.A *ù* GEŠTIN *ṭù-úḫ-ḫu-du*
28) *ú*-da-áš-ši-šú-nu-ti piš-šá-tú* Ì.GIŠ *el-lu*
29) *zu-mur-šú-un ú-ṭaḫ-ḫi-id nar-qí-ti* Ì.GIŠ DÙG.GA
30) *mu-uḫ-ḫa-šu-nu ú-šá-áš-qí*

iii 21–30) So that anger, curse, (and) cultic mistake are not brought into existence inside it (nor) placed in the mouth(s) of the workmen executing its construction, but (instead) that blessing(s) of good fortune are placed in their mouths, I copiously supplied them with bread, beer, meat, and an abundance of wine, lavishly anointed their bod(ies) with (ritually-)pure oil, (and) had their heads drenched with a perfume of sweet-smelling oil.

31) [*el*]-⸢*ṣi*⸣-*iš* ⸢*lìb-ba-šú-nu*⸣ *uš-par-di*
32) [... *li*]-*ib-ba-šu-nu-ma*
33) [...]-*a-ri*
34) [...] *aš-ru-uš-šu*
35) [...]-*an-ni-ma*

iii 31–35) [Jo]yously, I cheered up their heart(s). [...] their [h]earts and [...] ... [...] in his place [...] me.

36) [*a-na* ^{d}UTU EN GAL *mu*]-⸢*dam*⸣-*mi-iq*
37) [*it-ta-ti-ia* É *šá*] *ma-*[*na-ma*] ⸢LUGAL⸣ *i-na* LUGAL
38) [*ki-ma*] *ia-a-ti-ma la ib-nu-ú*
39) [*ia-a-ti*] *a-na* ^{d}UTU [*ù*] ^{d}*a-a*
40) [EN.MEŠ]-⸢*e*⸣-*a dam-*[*qí-iš*] *e-pú-šu*
41) [*ra*]-⸢*bi*⸣-*iš ab-ni-šu-ma*
42) *ú-ša-ak-li-il ši-pí-ir-šu*

iii 36–42) [For the god Šamaš, the great lord, the one who] makes [my signs] favorable, I magnificently built for him [a temple — (one) that] n[one] of the king(s) among the king(s of the past) had built [like] me, (but as for) me, (the one that) I had (it) built well for the god Šamaš and the goddess Aya, my [lor]ds — and completed its construction.

43) ^{d}UTU EN GAL *ša* AN-*e ù* KI-*tim*
44) *a-na* É *šu-a-ti*
45) *ḫa-di-iš i-na e-re-bi-ka*
46) *šu-bat-ka* el-le-ti re-eš-ti-tú*
47) *ṭa-bi-iš i-na ra-mé-e-ka*
48) *a-na* ^{d}AG-*na-ʾi-id* LUGAL *za-ni-nu*
49) *ik-ri-bi da-mi-iq-tú ku-úr-ba*
50) *šu-úr-ka-am-ma* TIN UD.MEŠ *ru-qu-tim*
51) *lu-bu-úr a-na da-rí-a-tim* (over erasure)
52) *id-na be-lu-tì ṣal-mat qá-qá-du*
53) *lu-úr-a-am na-gab-šu-un*

iii 43–53) O Šamaš, great lord of heaven and earth, when you enter this temple with pleasure (and) gladly occupy your pure, original residence, bless me, Nabonidus, the king who provides, with blessings of good fortune (and) grant me a long life (lit. "a life of long days") so that I stay in good health for eternity. Give me dominion over the black-headed (people) so that I may shepherd all of them.

54) ^{d}*a-a ḫi-ir-ti na-ra-*<*am*>*-ta-ka*
55) *li-ta-mi-ka da-mi-iq-tì*

iii 54–55) May the goddess Aya, your beloved spouse, say good thing(s) about me to you.

56) *i-na di-nim ù bi-ri*
57) *e-ma qa-ti a-na-áš-šu-ka*
58) *i-ša-ri-iš ap-la-an-ni*
59) *ma-ḫa-ar* ^{d}AMAR.UTU LUGAL AN *ù* KI
60) *ka-a-a-na šu-um-gi-ra*
61) *ep-še-tu-ú-a*

iii 56–58) In (divine) pronouncement(s) and extispicy, whenever I raise up (my) hands to you, answer me unequivocally. Make my (good) deeds constantly find acceptance in the presence of the god Marduk, king of heaven and earth.

---

iii 18 <É.MEŠ$^{?}$> *si-ḫi-ir-ti é*-babbar*-ra** "<*the temples*> in the vicinity of Ebabbar": The cylinder has *si-ḫi-ir-ti* É.MEŠ "the entirety of the temples." The corrected reading of the line follows Schaudig, Inschriften Nabonids p. 442.
iii 28 *ú*-da-áš-ši-šú-nu-ti* "I copiously supplied them": The cylinder has visually similar GI-*da-áš-ši-šú-nu-ti*.
iii 46 *šu-bat-ka** "your residence": The scribe wrote *šu-bat*-IŠ.

24

An Akkadian inscription recording Nabonidus' rebuilding of Ebabbar ("Shining House"), the temple of the sun-god Šamaš at Sippar, is known from two complete and three fragmentarily preserved, double-column clay cylinders. The text's two principal exemplars were both discovered in Ebabbar, near the main cella; the other three pieces are presumed to have come from Sippar. The inscription, which is written in contemporary Neo-Babylonian script, includes a lengthy and detailed description of the rebuilding of Ebabbar, which Nabonidus claims was in an abysmal state when he ascended the throne. The temple's deplorable state of being is blamed on the fact that an unnamed previous builder (undoubtedly Nebuchadnezzar II) did not build Šamaš' earthly abode on its original foundations, so that the temple had not been constructed according to divine will. In contrast to his predecessor, Nabonidus records that he, his advisors, and his master builders painstakingly ensured that Ebabbar was renovated in exact accordance with its original and divinely-sanctioned plan: the gods Šamaš and Adad confirmed the undertaking's success via favorable haruspical queries and the new temple was built directly on top of the foundations laid by the Sargonid king Narām-Sîn (2254–2218). In addition, the inscription records that Nabonidus had the temple, especially its cella, suitably outfitted and lavishly decorated. The text ends with a long petition to Ebabbar's tutelary deities (Šamaš, Aya, and Bunene) to act beneficently towards the king. Although none of the cylinders bear a date, some scholars have suggested that the text was composed at the end of Nabonidus' second regnal year (554); see Beaulieu, Nabonidus p. 25 and Schaudig, Inschriften Nabonids p. 385. This text is referred to as "Nabonidus Cylinder II, 9," "[Nabonidus] Inscription 5," and the "Ebabbar Cylinder" in previous editions and studies.

CATALOGUE

Ex.	Museum Number	Registration Number	Provenance	Lines Preserved	cpn
1	BM 91140	AH 81-4-28,3A	Sippar, Ebabbar, Room 170, near the main cella	i 1–ii 52	c
2	EŞ —	(formerly AH 81-4-28, 4)	As ex. 1	i 1–ii 52	(p)
3	BM 91088	82-5-22,794 + 82-5-22,795 + 82-5-22,812 + 82-5-22,847	Probably Sippar	i 1–ii 52	c
4	BM 50814	82-3-23,1807	As ex. 3	i 32–39	c
5	BM 48234	81-11-3,944	As ex. 3	ii 19?–29	c

COMMENTARY

Ex. 2 (formerly AH 81-4-28, 4) was sent to Istanbul, perhaps along with a cylinder of Sennacherib (formerly 80-7-19,3; Grayson and Novotny, RINAP 3/1 p. 56 Sennacherib 4 ex. 5). The cylinder is presently on display in the Eşki Şark Eserleri Müzesi (Istanbul), as is evident from photographs of tourist(s) posted online. The museum number of that fully intact cylinder is unfortunately still not known. As for ex. 5, BM 48234, not BM 48232 (as cited in Da Riva, GMTR 4 p. 131), is the correct collection number; BM 48232 is an exemplar of Nebuchadnezzar II's cylinder inscription C41 (ibid. p. 121).

The line arrangement follows ex. 1. The distribution of text varies greatly between the copies of the inscription. Col. i of ex. 2 ended with ex. 1 ii 10a and col. ii of ex. 3 began with ex. 1 ii 6. The master text is generally ex. 1, but with help from the other four exemplars where that copy of the text has scribal errors. A score is presented on Oracc and the minor (orthographic) variants are given in the critical apparatus at the back of the book. Exs. 1 and 3–5 were collated from the originals in the British Museum, while ex. 2 was partially collated from photographs posted of it by (a) tourist(s) visiting the Eşki Şark Eserleri Müzesi. The orthographic variants noted in Rawlinson and Norris, 5 R pl. 65 and in Strassmaier, Liverpool no. 109 are included in both the score and critical apparatus for the lines of ex. 2 that were not visible or legible in the photographs of the cylinder found online (March 2020). The paleographic variants, following the practice of RIM and RINAP, are not noted.

BIBLIOGRAPHY

1883–85 Rassam, TSBA 8 p. 176 (exs. 1–2, study)
1884 Rawlinson and Pinches, 5 R pl. 65 (ex. 1, copy; ex. 2, variants)
1885 Strassmaier, Liverpool no. 109 (ex. 1, copy; ex. 2, variants)
1885 Latrille, ZK 2 p. 239 (ex. 1 i 27, study)
1886 Latrille, ZA 1 pp. 27–35 (ex. 1 i 1–40, edition)
1888 Teloni, ZA 3 pp. 159–173 and 293–310 (ex. 1 ii 1–52, edition)
1890 Peiser in Schrader, KB 3/2 pp. 108–112 (ex. 1 i 16–ii 15, edition)
1895 Meissner, Chrestomathie pp. 43–44 (ex. 1 i 16–ii 15, copy)
1899 Bezold, Cat. 5 p. 2235 no. 2244b (study)
1912 Langdon, NBK pp. 49–50 and 252–261 Nbd. no. 6 (edition)
1913 Jensen, ThLZ 38 pp. 356–357 (i 36, ii 7, 11, 20, 31, 41, 44, study)
1929 Langdon, JRAS 1929 p. 381 (ii 7, study)
1941–44 Ungnad, AfO 14 p. 271 (ii 41, study)
1947 Kraus, Orientalia NS 16 p. 184 (ii 45, study)
1948 Goossens, RA 42 nos. 3–4 pp. 155 and 157 (study)
1953 von Soden, SAHG pp. 288–290 no. 35b (ii 15–52, translation)
1958 Landsberger, MSL 6 pp. 133–134 (ex. 1 ii 4–5, 25, study)
1964 Galling, Studien p. 7 (study)
1967–74 Sollberger, JEOL 20–23 p. 53 n. 22 (exs. 1–2, study)
1968 Ellis, Foundation Deposits pp. 14 and 181 (i 16, 19–22, edition; study)
1968–69 Lambert, AfO 22 p. 8 (ex. 1 ii 6, study)
1973 Berger, NbK pp. 367–368 Nbn. Zyl. II, 9 (exs. 1–2, study)
1989 Beaulieu, Nabonidus pp. 7, 25, 47–50, 133 and 144–145 Inscription 5 (i 6, 26–30, 30–37, ii 9–10, 22–23, 39–46, 48–52, edition; study)
1991 Powell, ZA 81 pp. 23–24 (study)
1994 Beaulieu, BCSMS 28 pp. 37–42 (study)
2001 Schaudig, Inschriften Nabonids pp. 384–394 no. 2.9 and 754 figs. 14–18 (edition; i 35, ii 5, 6, 15, 25, collations)
2008 Da Riva, GMTR 4 p. 131 sub 1a (ex. 5, study)
2010 Schaudig, Studies Ellis pp. 156–161 and 469 no. 6.3 (i 19–22, 31–32, edition; study)

TEXT

Col. i

1) ^{d}*na-bi-um-na-ʾi-id* LUGAL KÁ.DINGIR.RA.KI *eṭ-⸢lam ki-num ša a-na ṭè-me* DINGIR.MEŠ *pu-ú-qu⸣*
2) *aš-ri ka-an-šu pa-li-iḫ* DINGIR.MEŠ GAL.MEŠ
3) NUN *e-em-qá ḫa-sis mim-ma šum-šu* ÉNSI *ṣi-i-ri mu-ud-di-iš kal ma-ḫa-zu*
4) *ma-al-ku it-pe-šu mu-šak-lil eš-re-e-ti mu-ṭaḫ-ḫi-id sat-tuk-ku*

i 1–4) Nabonidus, king of Babylon, the reliable warrior who is attentive towards the will of the gods, the humble (and) submissive one who reveres the great gods, the wise prince who understands everything there is, the exalted ruler who renovates all of the cult centers, the capable ruler who completes sanctuaries (and) makes *sattukku*-offerings abundant,

5) SIPA *ni-ši* DAGAL.MEŠ *ra-ʾi-im mi-ša-ri mu-kin kit-ti*
6) *lu-li-mu šu-pu-ú e-tel-lu* LUGAL.MEŠ *bi-nu-tu qá-at šá* ^{d}AG *u* ^{d}AMAR.UTU
7) *mu-uṣ-ṣir ú-ṣu-ra-a-ti* É.MEŠ DINGIR.MEŠ *mu-šar-šid giš-ḫur-ri*
8) *na-áš-pa-ri ḫa-an-ṭu ša* DINGIR.MEŠ GAL.MEŠ *mu-šal-lim kal šip-ri mu-ṭi-ib lìb-bi-šú-un*
9) DUMU ^{md}AG-TIN-*su-iq-bi* GÌR.NÍTA *qit-ru-du pa-li-iḫ* DINGIR.DINGIR *u* ^{d}15 *a-na-ku*

i 5–9) the shepherd of a widespread people, the one who loves justice (and) establishes truth, the splendid stag, the (most) pre-eminent one of kings, the creature of the hand(s) of the gods Nabû and Marduk, the one who draws out the design(s) of the temples of the gods (and) firmly establishes their ground plans, the quick messenger of the great gods, the one who fully carries out every task, the one who pleases their heart(s), son of Nabû-balāssu-iqbi, the brave governor who reveres gods and goddesses, I am.

10) *a-na* ^{d}UTU EN AN.TA.MEŠ *ù* KI.TA.MEŠ

i 10–15) To the god Šamaš, lord of the upper and

DI.KU$_5$.GAL AN-*e u* KI-*tim*
11) *da-a-a-nu ṣi-i-ri šá* DINGIR.MEŠ GAL.⸢MEŠ⸣ *pa-ri-is pu-ri-se-e*
12) *ḫa-ʾi-iṭ lìb-ba* UN.MEŠ *ba-ru-ú te-re-e-ti ra-ʾi-im* LUGAL-*ú-ti-ia*
13) *na-ṣir na-piš-ti-ia ka-šid a-a-bi-ia mu-ḫal-liq za-ʾi-i-ri-ia*
14) *a-ši-ib é-babbar-ra ša qé-reb* ZIMBIR.KI EN GAL EN-*ia ina mi-gir lìb-bi-ía ki-nim*
15) *pal-ḫi-iš uš-te-mi-iq-ma áš-ra-a-ti* DINGIR-*ú-ti-šú* GAL-*ti áš-te-eʾ-e-ma*
16) *é-babbar-ra* É-*su ša qé-reb* ZIMBIR.KI *at-ma-nu ṣi-i-ri si-mat* DINGIR-*ú-ti-šú*
17) *ki-iṣ-ṣi el-lu šu-bat tap-šu-uḫ-ti mu-šab be-lu-ti-šú*
18) *ša* u$_4$-*mi ma-aʾ-du-tu ub-bu-tu te-me-en-šú su-uḫ-ḫa-a ú-ṣu-ra-tu-šú*
19) LUGAL *ma-aḫ-ri te-me-en la-bi-ri ú-ba-ʾi-i-ma la i-mu-ru*
20) *i-na ra-man-ni-šú* É *eš-šú a-na* ^{d}UTU *ú-še-piš-ma la šu-pu-šu a-na be-lu-ti-šú*
21) *la šu-lu-ku a-na si-ma-at* DINGIR-*ú-ti-šú*
22) *i-na la a-dan-ni-šú ša* É *šu-a-ti re-ša-a-šu iq-du-du ut-tab-bi-ka mé-la-šú*
23) *ia-a-ti ap-pa-lis-su-ma ma-aʾ-diš ap-làḫ-ma ni-qit-ti ar-ši*
24) *a-na šu-ur-šu-du te-me-en ú-ṣu-ra-at* É-*šu šu-ul-lu-mu*
25) *pa-pa-ḫu ù* DU$_6$.MEŠ *a-na si-mat* DINGIR-*ú-ti-šú e-pe-ša*
26) u$_4$-*mi-šam-ma ut-nen-šum-ma a-na ša-at-ti ni-qa-a aq-qí-šum-ma* EŠ.BAR-*a ap-ru-us-su*
27) ^{d}UTU EN *ṣi-ri ul-tu* UD.ME *ru-qu-tu ia-a-ši ú-qa-wa$_6$-an-ni*
28) *an-na šá-lim-ti* EŠ.BAR-*a ki-nim ša ša-la-mu šip-ri-ía u kun-nu eš-re-e-ti*
29) ^{d}UTU *ù* ^{d}IŠKUR *ú-šá-áš-ki-nu i-na te-er-ti-ia*
30) *a-na* EŠ.BAR-*šu-nu ki-nim šá la in-nen-nu-ú ma-gal at-kal-ma qa-ti* ^{d}UTU EN-*ia aṣ-bat-ma*
31) *i-na* É UD.1.KAM *šá-na-at ú-še-šib-šú im-nu u šu-me-lu pa-ni u ár-ku ša pa-pa-ḫu u lìb-bi* DU$_6$.MEŠ
32) *ḫi-iṭ-ṭa-tú aṭ-ṭu-uṭ-ma ú-pa-aḫ-ḫi-ir-*⸢*ma*⸣ *ši-bu-ut* URU DUMU.MEŠ TIN.TIR.KI DUB.SAR *mi-na-a-ti*
33) *en-qu-ú-tu a-ši-ib* É *mu-um-mu na-ṣir pi-riš-ti* DINGIR.MEŠ GAL.MEŠ *mu-kin* GARZA LUGAL-*ú-tu*
34) *a-na mi-it-lu-uk-ti áš-pur-šu-nu-ti-ma ki-a-am az-kur-šu-nu-ti um-ma te-me-en la-bi-ri*

lower worlds, chief judge of heaven and earth, the exalted judge of the great gods who render decisions, inspects the hearts of people who perform extispicies, the one who loves my royal majesty, the one who protects my life, the conqueror of my enemies, the destroyer of my foes, the one who resides in Ebabbar, which is in Sippar, the great lord, my lord: In the contentedness of my steadfast heart, I reverently and devoutly prayed, and constantly sought out the shrines of his great divinity.

i 16–18) (With regard to) Ebabbar, his temple which is in Sippar, the exalted inner sanctum, the embodiment of his divinity, the pure cella, the dwelling of rest, the residence of his lordly majesty, whose foundation(s) were thoroughly destroyed for a long time (and) whose ground plans were in ruins —

i 19–21) a king of the past looked for (its) original foundation(s), but he did not find (them). On his own, he had a new temple for the god Šamaš built, but it was not splendid (enough) for his lordly majesty, nor was it befitting (enough) to be the embodiment of his divinity.

i 22–23) Prematurely (lit. "out of its appointed time"), the superstructure of that temple sagged down (and) its high parts crumbled. (As for) me, I looked at it and (then) became frightened and worried.

i 24–26) With regard to firmly securing the foundation(s), perfectly executing the designs of his (Šamaš') temple, (re)building the cella and throne platforms as the embodiment of his divinity, I prayed to him daily and, on account of this, I made an offering to him and (then) I made a decision about it.

i 27) The god Šamaš, the exalted lord, had waited for me since distant days.

i 28–29) The gods Šamaš and Adad had a favorable 'yes,' a firm decision about the completion of my work and making (those) sanctuaries endure, placed in my extispicy.

i 30–31a) I completely trusted in their firm decision, which cannot be changed, and took the god Šamaš by the hand and had him reside in the "House of the First Day" for a(n entire) year.

i 31b–34a) I dug pits to the right and left, in front of and behind the cella, as well as inside the throne platforms and (then) I gathered city elders, citizens of Babylon, architects, (and) skilled men who reside in the *bīt-mummu*, protect the secret lore of the great gods, (and) maintain the rite(s) of kingship, and I sent them (a message) about (making) a decision.

i 34b–35) I spoke to them as follows: "Search for the original foundation(s) and look for the cella of the god

i 31 É UD.1.KAM "'House of the First Day'": According to H. Schaudig (Inschriften Nabonids p. 386 and 601), the É UD.1.KAM designates the *akītu*-house, an idea refuted already by G.J.P. McEwan (Iraq 43 [1981] p. 135).

ši-te-ʾe-ma

35) *pa-pa-ḫu* ^{d}UTU *da-a-a-nu na-pa-li-sa-ma* É *da-rí-a a-na* ^{d}UTU *u* ^{d}*a-a* EN.MEŠ-*a* ⸢*lu*⸣-*pu-uš*

36) *ina te-me$_{5}$-qu* ^{d}UTU EN-*ia ina su-pe-e-šu šá* DINGIR GAL.GAL UKKIN DUMU.MEŠ UM.ME.A *te-me-en la-bi-ri*

37) *ip-pal-su-ma pa-pa-ḫi u* DU$_{6}$.MEŠ *i-ḫi-ṭu-ma za-mar i-tu-ru-nim ia-a-ti iq-bu-nu*

38) *ap-pa-lis-ma te-me-en la-bi-ri šá na-ram-*^{d}30 LUGAL *ul-lu pa-pa-ḫi* ^{d}UTU *ka-a-a-nu mu-šab* DINGIR-*ú-ti-šú*

39) *lìb-bi iḫ-de-e-ma im-me-ri pa-nu-ú-a pa-pa-ḫi be-lu-ti-šú u* DU$_{6}$.MEŠ *ú-ṣa-ab-bi-ma*

40) *ina ḫi-da-a-ti u ri-šá-a-ti* UGU *te-me-en la-bi-ri ad-da uš-šu-ša*

Col. ii

1) *i-šid-su ú-dan-nin-ma ki-ma* KUR-*i zaq-ru ul-la-a re-šá-a-šú é-babbar-ra* É-*su šá šu-pu-šu*

2) *a-na be-lu-ti-šú šu-lu-ku a-na si-mat* DINGIR-*ú-ti-šú a-na* ^{d}UTU EN-*ía eš-ši-iš ú-še-piš-ma*

3) *ki-ma šu-ú u$_{4}$-mi-*<*iš*> *ú-nam-mir-šú* 1 LIM 50 GIŠ.EREN *pa-ag-lu-tú la mi-nu* GIŠ.Ù.SUḪ$_{5}$ *ši-ḫu-*⸢*ti*⸣

4) GIŠ.*šur-i-ni iṣ-ṣi dam-qu-tu* GIŠ.MES.MÁ.KAN.NA *iṣ-ṣi da-rí-a ana ši-i-pu* GIŠ.*tal-lu*

5) GIŠ.GAN.DU$_{7}$ *giš-šà-ká-na-ku u ṣu-lul-tu$_{4}$* É *ú-šat-mi-iḫ-ma ki-ma* GIŠ.TIR ḪA.ŠUR *i-ri-is-su uš-ṭi-ib*

6) GIŠ.IG.MEŠ GIŠ.EREN.MEŠ MAḪ.MEŠ NU.KÚŠ.Ù URUDU *dan-nu-tu me-de-lu šu-pu-tu e-ma* KÁ.MEŠ-*šú ú-rat-ti-ma*

7) *ki-ma né-re-bi kin-né-e ú-dan-nin ri-kis* É *pa-pa-ḫi be-lu-ti-šú a-na mu-ša-bu* DINGIR-*ú-ti-šú*

8) *ša-lum-ma-at ú-šal-biš ú-nu-tu* É *ina* KÙ.BABBAR *u* KÙ.GI *ú-za-ʾi-in-ma*

9) *a-na tab-rat ni-ši la-la-a uš-ma-al-la-a ši-ṭir šu-mi-ia u ṣa-lam* LUGAL-*ú-ti-ia*

10) DA.RÍ.A *ú-kin qé-reb-šú maš-ta-ku la-le-šú pa-pa-ḫi*.MEŠ *ù* DU$_{6}$.MEŠ *ina ši-ip-ri*

11) ^{d}*kulla ud-di-iš-ma zi-i-me nam-ru-tu ú-šá-áš-ši-ma šu-bat* DI.KU$_{5}$.GAL DINGIR.DINGIR *da-ri-ti*

Šamaš, the judge, so that I can build a lasting temple for the god Šamaš and the goddess Aya, my lords."

i 36–37) Through prayer(s) to the god Šamaš, my lord, (and) through supplications to the great gods, the assembly of craftsmen saw the original foundation(s) and examined the (old) cella and throne platforms. They immediately returned (and) spoke with me.

i 38–40) I indeed saw the original foundation(s) of Narām-Sîn, a king of the distant past, the cella of the god Šamaš, the permanent residence of his divinity. My heart rejoiced and my face lit up. I inspected the cella of his lordly majesty and the throne platforms, and (then) during joyous celebrations, I laid its foundations on top of (its) original foundation(s).

ii 1–3a) I strengthened its foundation(s) and I raised its superstructure up like a high mountain. (As for) Ebabbar, his (Šamaš') temple that had been built for his lordly majesty to be the embodiment of his divinity, I had (it) built anew for the god Šamaš, my lord, and I made it shine like daylight, just like (its) name.

ii 3b–5) For the *šīpu*(s), crossbeam(s), the architrave(s), the *giššakanakku*(s), and the roof of the temple, I put in place 1,050 thick cedars, without number, tall pine-tree(s), cypress-tree(s), beautiful trees, (and) *musukkannu*-tree(s), a hard-(wood) tree, and I made its scent as pleasing as a forest of *ḫašūru*-tree(s).

ii 6–7a) At each of its gates, I installed immense doors of cedar (with) strong copper *nukuššû*-fittings (and) splendid bolts and I reinforced the structure of the temple like a mountain pass.

ii 7b–10a) For the residence of his divinity, I clad the cella of his lordly majesty with an awesome radiance. I decorated the utensil(s) of the temple with silver and gold and filled (it) with splendor to be an object of wonder for the people. I securely placed an inscription of mine and an image of my royal majesty inside it for eternity.

ii 10b–12) Through the craft of the god Kulla, I renovated the bed chamber of his desire(s), the cellas, and throne platforms and provided (it) with a shining façade. Then, I firmly established inside it an eternal residence for the great judge of the gods. For the god

i 35 ⸢*lu*⸣-*pu-uš* "so that I can build": Ex. 2 has visually similar *ep-pu-uš** (copy: RI) "I will build."

ii 3 *šu-ú* "it": The translation follows exs. 2–3, which have *šu-mi-šu-ma** (text: ŠU) and *šu-mi-šu* respectively; ex. 1, on which the master line is based, has *šu-ú*. 1 LIM 50 GIŠ.EREN *pa-ag-lu-tú la mi-nu* GIŠ.Ù.SUḪ$_{5}$ *ši-ḫu-*⸢*ti*⸣ "1,050 thick cedars, without number, tall pine-tree(s)": The CAD (M/2 p. 96 sub *mīnu* 1.c.1′) translates this contradictory passage as "1,050 thick cedars, tall pine-tree(s) without number." As noted by H. Schaudig (Inschriften Nabonids p. 393 n. 488), *lā mīni* ("without number") generally follows the noun it modifies, rather than preceding it and, therefore, his interpretation is followed here. M. Worthington (personal communication) tentatively suggests that a word might have been omitted between *pa-ag-lu-tú* and *la mi-nu*. This, however, seems unlikely since this proposed omission would have occurred in three different exemplars (exs. 1, 2, and 3).

ii 5 GIŠ.TIR "a forest of": Ex. 1 has GIŠ.LI (*burāšu*) "juniper."

12) *ú-kin qé-reb-šú a-na* ^{d}UTU *u* ^{d}*a-a* EN-*ú-a* É *ta-na-da-a-tú ú-še-piš*

Šamaš and the goddess Aya, my lords, I had a glorious house built.

13) *sip-pu ši-ga-ri me-de-lu u* GIŠ.IG.MEŠ *ì-gu-la-a ú-ṭaḫ-ḫi-id-ma ana né-re-bi* DINGIR-*ú-ti-šu-nu*
14) *ṣi-ir-ti si-mat* É *ú-mál-la-a i-ri-šu ṭa-a-bi* É *a-na e-re-bi* ^{d}UTU EN-*ia*

ii 13–15a) I lavishly provided the finest oil for the door-jamb(s), door bolt(s), bolts, and doors and, in the entryway(s) of their exalted divinity, I filled the appurtenance(s) of the temple with a sweet scent. When the god Šamaš, my lord, enters the temple, its gates are thrown wide open (and) filled with joy.

15) *šu-pal-ka-a* KÁ*.MEŠ-*šu ma-li ri-ša-a-ti* ^{d}UTU EN *ṣi-i-ri ana é-babbar-ra šu-bat*
16) *tap-šu-uḫ-ti-ka ina e-re-bi-ka* KÁ.MEŠ *né-re-bi*.MEŠ *pa-pa-ḫi u* DU$_6$.MEŠ
17) *liḫ-du-ú pa-nu-uk-ku ki-ma a-a-ri li-ri-šu-ku ina pa-pa-ḫi be-lu-ti-ka*

ii 15b–17a) O Šamaš, exalted lord, when you enter Ebabbar, the residence where you rest, may the gates, entrances, cellas, and throne platforms be happy in your presence. May they exult over you as (over) an *ayyaru*.

18) *šu-bat da-a-a-nu-ti-ka ina a-šá-bi-ku* DINGIR.MEŠ URU-*ka u* É-*ka li-šap-ši-ḫu*
19) *kab-ta-at-ka* DINGIR.MEŠ GAL.MEŠ *lìb-ba-ka li-ṭi-ib-bi* ^{d}*a-a* É.GI$_4$.A GAL-*ti*
20) *a-ši-bat é-ki-nú ka-a-a-nam-ma pa-nu-ka liš-nam-mir u$_4$-mi-šam da-mi-<iq>-ta-a liq-bi-*⌜*ku*⌝

ii 17b–20) When you are sitting in the cella of your lordly majesty, the residence where you preside as judge, may the gods of your city and temple appease your mind (and) may the great gods please your heart. May the goddess Aya, the great bride who resides in Ekinu, constantly make your face shine (and) say good thing(s) about me to you.

21) *i-na bu-ni-ka nam-ru-tu ḫi-du-tu pa-ni-ka li-pit qá-ti-ía šu-qu-ru*
22) *e-ep-še-tu-ú-a dam-qa-a-ta ši-ṭir šu-mi-ia u ṣa-lam* LUGAL-*ú-ti-ia*
23) *ḫa-di-iš na-ap-li-sa-a-ma* SIG$_5$.MEŠ-*ú-a liš-šá-kin šap-tuk-ku i-bi šu-mi ana du-ru* UD.MEŠ
24) É *e-pu-uš-šu lu-bi-ir ina qé-re-bi-šu li-ku-un šu-bat-ka*

ii 21–24) With your bright countenance, your happy face, look with pleasure upon my precious handiwork, my good deeds, my inscription(s), and image(s) of my royal majesty, and may good things about me be set upon your lips. Call my name for eternity. Make the temple that I have built for him last for a long time so that your residence endures inside it.

25) DINGIR É *ú-ṣu-rat* É *tal-lu* GIŠ.GAN.DU$_7$ *giš-šà-ká-na-ku sip-pu ši-ga-ri* KUN$_4$ É.⌜ME⌝ *u* GIŠ.IG.MEŠ
26) *ki-ib-su li-iṣ-ṣi-ru liš-te-ši-ru tal-la-ak-ka*
27) *i-na maḫ-ri-ka li-ša-qí-ri e-ep-še-tu-ú-a*
28) *ur-ra ù mu-šu lit-taz-ka-ar dum-qu-ú-a*

ii 25–28) May the god(s) of the temple, the utensils of the temple, the crossbeam(s), the architrave(s), the *giššakanakku*(s), the door-jamb(s), door bolt(s), the threshold(s) of the temples, and the doors guard the route(s and) keep the accessway in good repair. In your presence, may they hold my good deeds in high esteem (and) speak good things about me day and night.

29) ^{d}*kit-tum* ^{d}*mi-šá-ri ù* ^{d}*da-a-a-nu* DINGIR.MEŠ *a-šib maḫ-ri-ka*
30) *ina qí-bi-ti-ka ṣi-ir-ti šá la ut-tak-ka-ri ina a-mat* DINGIR-*ti-ka* GAL-*ti*
31) *ša la uš-te-pe-lu* KASKAL *šul-lum u meš-re-e ur-ru-uḫ kit-ti ù mi-ša-ri*

ii 29–32a) By your exalted command, which cannot be changed, (and) the word of your great divinity, which cannot be overturned, may the deities Kittu, Mišāru and Dayyānu, the gods who sit in your presence, have the path of well-being and riches (and) the road of truth and justice placed at my feet.

32) *li-šá-áš-ki-na a-na še-pi-ia suk-kal-la-ku* MAḪ

ii 32b–38) May your exalted vizier, the one who

---

ii 13 *sip-pu ši-ga-ri me-de-lu u* GIŠ.IG.MEŠ "door-jamb(s), door bolt(s), bolts, and doors": Compare the parts of the gate mentioned in Ludlul Bēl Nēmiqi Tablet IV line 99 (Lambert, BWL p. 61; and Foster, Before the Muses 1 p. 321 Frgm. B 59′). DINGIR-*ú-ti-šu-nu* "their divinity": Ex. 3 has DINGIR-*ú-ti-šú* "his divinity."

ii 17 *a-a-ri* "*ayyaru*": The meaning of *ayyaru* in this passage is uncertain. According to the CAD (A/1 pp 229–230 sub *ajaru* A–E), there are five different *ayyarus*. This passage is cited under *ajaru* B (mng. uncert.), together with a citation from a damaged text mentioning Ashurbanipal (Bauer, Asb. pl. 53 DT 229 line 5′); this corresponds to CDA p. 32 sub *ayyaru* III (mng. uncl. jB; in comparsions). Compare AHw p. 24 sub *ajjaru* I ("Blüte; Rosette"), where this passage as translated as "wie B.n(?) mögen sie dir zujauchzen." This interpretation is followed by H. Schaudig (Inschriften Nabonids p. 393).

ii 29 ^{d}*kit-tum* ^{d}*mi-šá-ri ù* ^{d}*da-a-a-nu* "the deities Kittu, Mišāru and Dayyānu": Literally "truth," "justice," and "judge." These attributes of the sun-god Šamaš' role as judge are to be regarded here as deities, as indicated from context, as well as the use of the divine determinative.

ii 30 *qí-bi-ti-ka ṣi-ir-ti* "your exalted command" and DINGIR-*ti-ka* GAL-*ti* "your great divinity": Ex. 3 has *qí-bi-ti-ka* GAL-*ti* "your great command" and <DINGIR>-*ti-ka ṣi-ir-ti* "your exalted <divin>ity."

mu-uz-zi-iz maḫ-ri-ku
33) *^{d}bu-ne-ne šá mi-lik-šu dam-qa ra-kib* GIŠ.GIGIR *a-šib sa-as-si šá la im-maḫ-ḫa-ri*
34) *qa-bal-šu ṣa-mi-id pa-re-e qar-du-tu ša la in-na-ḫu bir-ka-šu-un*
35) *ina a-la-ku u ta-a-ri ša i-ša-ad-di-ḫu a-na maḫ-ri-ka*
36) *ina su-ú-qu u su-la-a' li-da-am-mi-qu e-ger-ra-a-a*
37) *a-ra-ku* UD.ME LUGAL-*ú-ti-ia lim-ta-al-lik-ka ka-a-šu*
38) *i-na ši-ip-ri-ka šu-qu-ru lil-lik-ki re-ṣu-ú-tu*

stands before you, the god Bunene, whose advice is good, the one who rides in a chariot (and) sits on (its) floor-boards, whose onslaught cannot be opposed, the one who harnesses valiant mules, whose knees do not become tried while marching and returning, (and) who goes out in procession before you, make (people) speak well of me in every street. May he constantly advise you about the prolongation of the days of my kingship. May he assist you in your precious work.

39) *me-lam-mu bir-bir-ru-ka zi-i-me be-lu-tu šá-lum-ma-at* LUGAL-*ú-tu*
40) *a-na ša-la-la* KUR LÚ.KÚR-*ia šu-lik-ki i-da-a-a lu-ur-ḫi-iṣ* KUR *a-a-bi-ia*
41) *lu-nar za-'i-ri-ia šil-lat na-ki-ri-ia lu-ku*-ul bu-še-e ma-ti-tan*

ii 39–42a) Make the fearsome brilliance of your luminosity, the appearance of lordship, (and) the awesome radiance of kingship march at my side to plunder the land(s) of my enem(ies) so that I can devastate the land of my foe(s), kill those hostile to me, consume the booty of my enemies, (and) bring the possessions of all lands into my land.

42) *lu-še-ri-bi a-na qé-reb ma-ti-ia a-na-ku lu-ú* LUGAL *za-ni-in*
43) *mu-diš ma-ḫa-zu mu-šak-lil eš-re-e-ti a-na* UD.MEŠ *da-ru-tu*

ii 42b–43) May I be the king who provides, renovates cult center(s), and completes sanctuaries forever.

44) *a-na zi-kir šu-mi-ia kab-tu kul-lat na-ki-ri lit-tar-ri li-nu-šu*
45) *lik-ni-šu a-na še-e-pi-ia a-na* UD.ME *ṣa-a-ti liš-du-du ni-i-ri*
46) *bi-lat-su-nu ka-bit-ti a-na qé-reb* URU-*ia* TIN.TIR.KI *li-bil-lu-nu ana maḫ-ri-ía*

ii 44–46) May all of (my) enemies quiver (and) quake at the (mere) mention of my important name. May they bow down at my feet, pull my yoke until far-off days, (and) bring their heavy tribute into my city, Babylon, into my presence.

47) *ina qé-reb* TIN.TIR.KI *li-kun šu-ub-ti ina su-le-e-šu a-tál-lu-ku lu-uš-bu*
48) *i-na é-sag-íl u é-zi-da šá a-ram-mu lu-lab-bi-ir man-za-za*

ii 47–48) May my residence be firmly inside Babylon (and) may I be sated walking about in its streets. May I grow old standing in Esagil and Ezida, which I love.

49) *i-na maḫ-ri be-lum ^{d}na-bi-um u ^{d}*NÈ.ERI$_{11}$.GAL
50) DINGIR.MEŠ-*e-a u* DINGIR.MEŠ *si-ḫi-ir-ti á-ki-it šá ^{d}*EN.LÍL DINGIR.MEŠ ^{d}ŠÚ
51) *a-na ni-qí-i ma-aṣ-ḫa-ti pa-qa-du é-da-di-ḫé-gál ù ut-nen-ni* EN EN.EN
52) *lu-ú sa-ad-ra-ak tal-lak-ti a-na da-rí-a-ti*

ii 49–52) In the presence of the gods Bēl, Nabû, and Nergal, my gods, and the gods of the perimeter of the *akītu*(-house) of the Enlil of the gods, Marduk, may I be constantly concerned with the proper procedure(s) for (sacrificial) offering(s and) *maṣḫatu*-flour (offerings), providing for Edadiḫegal, and praying to the lord of lords (Marduk) for eternity.

25

This Akkadian inscription of Nabonidus is known from a single, double-column clay cylinder found at Sippar, in Šamaš' temple Ebabbar ("Shining House"); the script is archaizing Neo-Babylonian. The text records that

24 ii 39 *šá-lum-ma-at* "awesome radiance": Ex. 2 has *šá mi-na-ta* "of (perfect) proportions."

24 ii 41 *lu-ku*-ul* "so that I can consume": Exs. 2–3 have respectively *lu*-uš-lu*-ul* and *⌜lu⌝-uš-lu-ul* "so that I can carry off."

24 ii 51 *a-na ni-qí-i ma-aṣ-ḫa-ti* "for (sacrificial) offering(s and) *maṣḫatu*-flour (offerings)": The interpretation follows CAD N/2 p. 258 sub *niqû* b.11′ and Schaudig, Inschriften Nabonids p. 394. M. Worthington (personal communication) notes that *ni-qí-i ma-aṣ-ḫa-ti* could be an error for *na-qí-i ma-aṣ-ḫa-ti* "to pour out *maṣḫatu*-flour (offerings)."

Nabonidus renovated Ebabbar and made a new, ornately decorated crown for its principal occupant, Šamaš, but only after divine permission was obtained through extispicy; Šamaš and Adad, the gods of divination, are said to have given their approval after the fourth divinatory query, having refused to give the king a 'firm yes' the first three times. To commemorate the occasion, Nabonidus had his scribe(s) record in this inscription the favorable omens that his diviners had observed in the liver that resulted in the positive response to the king's request about fashioning a new crown for Šamaš, as well as those of a fifth query that was performed in order to reconfirm the positive outcome of the fourth query. The crown, following the will of the gods, is reported to have been fashioned exactly as in ancient times: made of alabaster, decorated with *ḫusīgu*-stones and other precious stones, and with *zarinnu* (meaning uncertain). The inscription on this undated cylinder is generally thought to have been composed at the end of Nabonidus' second regnal year (554). The text is referred to as "Nabonidus Cylinder II, 8," "[Nabonidus] Inscription 6," and the "Tiara Cylinder" in earlier scholarly literature.

CATALOGUE

Museum Number	Registration Number	Provenance	cpn
BM 42269	81-7-1,28	Sippar, Ebabbar, Room 50	c

BIBLIOGRAPHY

1864 Rawlinson and Pinches, 5 R p. 63 (copy)
1899 Bezold, Cat. 5 p. 2244b (study)
1905 Boissier, Choix 1 pp. 48–52 (ii 10–19, 23–31, copy, edition)
1912 Jastrow, Religion 2 pp. 247 and 252–257 (ii 10–19, study)
1912 Langdon, NBK pp. 50–53 and 262–271 Nbd. no. 7 (edition)
1912 Langdon, RA 9 p. 161 (ii 5, study)
1912 Meissner, DLZ 33 col. 1697 (i 20–21, ii 16, study)
1913 Jensen, ThLZ 38 p. 356 (ii 30, study)
1914 Boissier, Seconde note pp. 19–20 (ii 12, 16, 18, 25, 28, study)
1924 S. Smith, BHT pp. 58–61 (i 41–ii 9, 20–23a, 32–38, translation, study)
1931 Denner, AfO 7 pp. 186–187 (i 41–ii 9, 20–23, 32–36, edition)
1939 Stamm, Namengebung p. 204 (i 9, study)
1942–44 Thureau-Dangin, RA 39 p. 16 (i 34–37, edition)
1957 Goetze, JCS 11 p. 104 (ii 29, edition)
1964 Galling, Studien p. 7 (study)
1968 Ellis, Foundation Deposits pp. 157 and 183 (i 30–33, edition; study)
1973 Berger, NbK pp. 365–366 Nbn. Zyl. II, 8 (study)
1974 Berger, ZA 64 p. 206 (i 44–47, ii 3, 5, 7, 9, study)
1983 Starr, BibMes 12 pp. 126–129 (ii 10–19, 23–31, edition)
1989 Beaulieu, Nabonidus pp. 9–11, 25–26, 48–50 and 145 Inscription 6 (i 17–23, 47–ii 1, 6–8, 34–38, 44–47, edition; study)
2001 Hecker, TUAT Erg. pp. 17–20 (translation)
2001 Schaudig, Inschriften Nabonids pp. 378–384 no. 2.8[a] (edition)

TEXT

Col. i

1) ^{d}AG-*na-'i-id* LUGAL TIN.TIR.KI *za-[nin é-sag]-*⸢*íl*⸣ *ù é-zi-da*

2) NUN *na-a-du mu-uš-te-e'-ú* ⸢*aš*⸣*-[ra]-*⸢*a*⸣*-ti* DINGIR GAL.GAL

3) *i-dan za-ni-na-tú šá* u_4*-mi-šá-am* ⸢*a-na*⸣ *pa-làḫ* DINGIR.MEŠ *ba-šá-a* GEŠTU.II*-šú*

4) *lib-ba pa-al-ḫu ša a-na a-*⸢*mat*⸣ DINGIR *ù*

i 1–16) Nabonidus, king of Babylon, the one who pr[ovides for Esagi]l and Ezida, the attentive prince who constantly seeks out the sh[rin]es of the great gods, (the one who has) generously providing hands (and) whose mind is focused daily on revering the gods, (the one who has) a reverent heart that is constantly (and) greatly attentive to the word(s) of the

Figure 14. BM 42269 (Nabonidus no. 25), the Tiara Cylinder, which describes the creation of an ornately decorated crown for the sun-god at Sippar. © Trustees of the British Museum.

EŠ$_{18}$.TÁR *ra-bi-iš pu-tuq-qú*
5) *áš-ru ka-an-šu* ⸢*šá*⸣ *ra-šu-ú pu-lu-úḫ-tim*
6) *a-na* DINGIR.MEŠ *ù* ^{d}EŠ$_{18}$.⸢TÁR⸣ *gi-na-a ú-sa-ap-pu-ú*
7) *a-na la ra-še-*⸢*e*⸣ *ḫi-ṭi-tì*
8) *ṣa-ab-tu si-is-si-*⸢*ik-ti*⸣ DINGIR.MEŠ *iš-te-né-e*ʾ*-ú ba-la-ṭi*
9) *lib-bu-uš pa-al-ḫu-*⸢*ma*⸣ *a-mat* DINGIR.MEŠ *na-aṣ-ru*
10) *aš-šum i-na pa-ra-aṣ* DINGIR.MEŠ ⸢*la*⸣ *šá-la-ṭi ú-sal-lu-ú* DINGIR GAL.GAL
11) *mim-mu-ú ip-pu-šu iš-te-né-*⸢*e*ʾ*-ú*⸣ *ar-ka-at-su ḫi-i-ṭa*
12) *a-na su-pe-e ù te-mi-qí ar-*⸢*ki* DINGIR⸣.MEŠ *re-du-ú*
13) *in lìb-bi-šu ga-am-ru ú-sal-lu-ú* ^{d}EN *ù* DUMU ^{d}EN
14) *a-na šá-a-ṭi se-er-de-e-šu-nu ku-un-nu-šu ki-šad-su*
15) *a-na šu-mi-šu-nu šu-qu-ru pa-al-ḫu* DINGIR.DINGIR GAL.GAL
16) DUMU ^{md}AG-TIN-*su-iq-bi* NUN *em-qa a-na-ku*

god(s) and goddess(es), the humble (and) submissive one who shows reverence (and) constantly beseeches the gods and goddess(es), who takes hold of the hem of the gods to avoid cultic mistake(s) (and thereby) constantly strives after life, whose heart is reverent and honors the word(s) of the gods, who prays to the great gods in order to avoid *deviating from* the rite(s) of the gods, who checks (through expisticy) the circumstances of everything he does (or) strives to do, who serves the gods with supplication(s) and prayer(s), who prays wholeheartedly to the gods Bēl (Marduk) and the Son-of-Bēl (Nabû), whose neck is bent down to pull their chariot pole(s), who holds their names in high esteem, the one who shows reverence for the great gods, son of Nabû-balāssu-iqbi, wise prince, am I.

17) *e-nu-ma* ^{d}AMAR.UTU EN GAL *be-lu-ut* KUR-*šú i-qí-pa-an-ni*
18) *za-na-nu-ut ma-ḫa-za ud-du-šu eš-re-e-ti ú-mál-lu-ú qa-tu-ú-a*
19) *a-na zi-in-na-a-ti é-sag*-íl ù é-zi-da*
20) *ul ap-pa-ra-ak-ka-a ka-a-a-na*
21) *re-eš mim-ma-a-a dam-qá ú-še-er-reb qé-reb-šu-un*
22) *i-gi-se-e šu-qu-ru-ti at-ta-nab-bal-šú-nu-ši*

i 17–25a) When the god Marduk, the great lord, entrusted me (to) rule over his land, placed in my hands (the responsibility of) providing for the cult centers (and) renovating sanctuaries, I have never ceased provisioning Esagil and Ezida. I (constantly) send the best of everything into them, constantly bring them precious gifts, (and) copiously supply every lavish thing there is into their midst, together with the (normal) provisioning of Esagil, Ezida, and the

i 10 ⸢*la*⸣ *šá-la-ṭi* "avoid *deviating from*": The meaning of the verb *šalāṭu* is uncertain, as already pointed out by the CAD (CAD Š/1 p. 240) and H. Schaudig (Inschriften Nabonids p. 380). The translation here tentatively follows CAD S p. 367 sub *sullû* A 1a-2′; also compare Schaudig, Inschriften Nabonids p. 380, where *šalāṭu* is translated as "(eigenmächtig) eingreifen." Note that E. Robson translates ⸢*la*⸣ *šá-la-ṭi* as "not to inadvertently overrule"; see http://oracc.org/cams/tlab/X800003 [2020].

23) *mim-ma šum-šu ṭù-uḫ-ḫu-du ú-da-aš-ši i-na qé-er-bi-šu-un*
24) *it-ti zi-in-na-a-ti é-sag-íl é-zi-da*
25) *ù eš-re-e-ti* DINGIR GAL.GAL *é-babbar-ra* É ^{d}UTU *šá qé-reb* ZIMBIR.KI
26) *ša* LUGAL *maḫ-ri i-*⸢*pú*⸣*-šu-ma la in-nen-du i-ga-ru-šu*
27) É *šu-a-ti i-qu-up-ma it-ru-ra re-e-šá-a-šu*
28) *aš-šum* É *šu-a-ti e-pe-šu* EN GAL ^{d}AMAR.UTU *ú-qá-a-an-ni*
29) *i-ga-ru-šu qá-a-a-pú-tim ad-ke*
30) *e-pe-ri qer-bi-šu as-su-uḫ-ma* 18 KÙŠ *qaq-qar ú-šá-ap-pil*
31) *te-em-mé-en-na la-bi-ru ša na-ra-am-*^{d}30
32) LUGAL *ma-aḫ-ri ap-pa-li-is-ma*
33) *e-li te-me-en-na la-bi-ru ad-da-a* SIG$_4$*-su*
34) *ša iš-tu* UD.MEŠ *ṣa-a-ti* LUGAL *i-na* LUGAL *la ib-nu-ú*
35) *ma-na-ma i-na* LUGAL *ma-aḫ-ri* É *ša ki-a-am*
36) *bu-un-nu-ú a-na* ^{d}UTU *la i-pú-šu*
37) *é-babbar-ra a-na* ^{d}UTU *be-lí-ia ra-bi-iš e-pú-uš*
38) *mim-ma ḫi-ši-iḫ-ti é-babbar-ra la ak-la-am-ma ú-še-rib qé-reb-šu*
39) GIŠ.EREN.MEŠ *da-nu*$_4$*-tim* GIŠ.Ù.SUḪ$_5$.MEŠ *pa-ag-lu-ti*
40) GIŠ.MES.MÁ.KAN.NA GAL.MEŠ *qer-ba-šu ú-še-ri-ib*
41) *ì-nu-šu ša* ^{d}UTU EN GAL DI.KU$_5$ *ṣi-rim ša* AN*-e ù* KI*-tim*
42) *a-ši-ib é-babbar-ra ša qé-reb* ZIMBIR.KI EN*-ia*
43) AGA KÙ.GI *si-mat i-lu-ti-šu ša ap-ru ra-šu-uš-šu*
44) *ti-iq-nu tu-uq-qù-nu bu-un-nu-ú za-ri-nu*
45) *šat-ti-ša-am-ma šu-úr-šu-du la i-ba-aš-šu-ú te-na-a-šu*
46) *ma-na-ma* LUGAL *a-lik maḫ-ri-ia te-né-e* AGA *šu-a-ti* ⸢*la i-pú-šú*⸣
47) *a-na e-peš* AGA KÙ.GI ŠÀ *pa-li-iḫ ra-ša-ku* ⸢*pu*⸣*-[lu-úḫ]-*⸢*ti*⸣
48) *ú-pa-aḫ-ḫi-ir-ma* DUMU.MEŠ TIN.TIR.KI *ù* ⸢*bár*⸣*-[sipa]*.KI

Col. ii
1) *en-qu-ti ra-áš ṭè-mi ki-ma la-bi-ri-im-ma li-in-né-pu-uš iq-bu-ni*
2) *aš-ra-a-ti* ^{d}UTU *ù* ^{d}IŠKUR EN.MEŠ *bi-ri aš-te-e'-e-ma*
3) *ša e-peš* AGA *ša la za-ri-ni* ^{d}UTU *ù* ^{d}IŠKUR
4) *i-na te-er-ti-šu-nu ul-li i-tap-pa-lu-in-ni*
5) *ap-qid-ma ul-li ú-šal-liš-ma* UZU *lum-nu iš-šak-na in ter-ti-ia*

sanctuaries of the great gods.

i 25b–28) (With regard to) Ebabbar, the temple of the god Šamaš that is inside Sippar, which a king of the past had built, but whose wall(s) had not been (properly) supported, that temple buckled and its superstructure was tottering. With regard to (re)building that temple, the great lord, the god Marduk, had waited for me.

i 29–33) I removed its buckled walls, cleared away the rubble from its interior, and (then) dug down eighteen cubits into the earth. I saw the original foundation(s) of Narām-Sîn, a king of the past, and laid its brickwork (directly) on (its) original foundation(s).

i 34–37) That which no king among the king(s of the past) had built since distant days (and which) no king of the past had built a temple for the god Šamaš so beautifully decorated, I magnificently (re)built Ebabbar for the god Šamaš, my lord.

i 38–40) I did not withhold anything needed for Ebabbar, but had (all of those things) brought inside it. I had (beams of) strong cedars, thick pine-tree(s), (and) large *musukkannu*-tree(s) brought inside it.

i 41–47) At that time, as for the god Šamaš, the great lord, the exalted judge of heaven and earth, the one who resides in Ebabbar that is inside Sippar, my lord — (as for) a crown of gold, the embodiment of his divinity that he wears on his head, that is adorned with (his) insignia, (and) that is beautifully decorated with *zarinnu*, that is securely attached every year, for which there is no replacement, no king who came before me had made a replacement for that crown. My heart was afraid (at the thought of) making a (new) crown of gold; I was ter[rifi]ed.

i 48–ii 1) I gathered the citizens of Babylon and Bor[sippa], skilled men who have (sufficient) experience, and they said to me "Let it be made (exactly) as (it had been) in ancient times."

ii 2–5) I frequently visited the shrines of the gods Šamaš and Adad, the lords of divination, and the gods Šamaš and Adad repeatedly answered me 'no' in their extispicies regarding the making of a crown without *zarinnu*. I double checked and (they answered me) with a 'no.' I did (it) a third time and an unfavorable omen was placed in my extispicy.

i 44 *za-ri-nu* "*zarinnu*": The meaning of the word and its precise reading (*zarīnu* or *zarinnu*) are uncertain. The CAD (Z p. 68 sub *zarinnu* B) suggests "(a decorated stand or support for precious objects)", the AHw (p. 1515 sub *z/ṣarīnu*) proposes "ein Ständer?," and the CDA (p. 445 sub *zarīnu*) offers "(a stand for precious objects)." H. Schaudig (Inschriften Nabonids pp. 381–382 n. 459) discusses the matter in detail and argues that *za-ri-nu* here and elsewhere in this inscription designates a special material, as well as an object, that was used to decorate the gold crown of Šamaš. Schaudig's interpretation is tentatively followed here.

6) *áš-ni-ma aš-šum e-peš* AGA *ša la za-ri-ni aš-ra-a-ti* ^{d}UTU
7) *ù* ^{d}IŠKUR *aš-te-e'-e-ma šum-ma ša e-li i-lu-ti-šu-nu ṭa-a-bu*
8) *ù e-li* ^{d}AMAR.UTU *a-šib é-sag-íl* EN-*ia*
9) ^{d}UTU *ù* ^{d}IŠKUR *an-na ki-nu ú-šá-aš-ki-nu in ter-ti-ia*

ii 6–9) I performed (an extispicy) again regarding the making of a crown without *zarinnu* and frequently visited the shrines of the gods Šamaš and Adad. (In response to) if it was pleasing to their divinity and to the god Marduk, the one who resides in Esagil, my lord, the gods Šamaš and Adad had a firm 'yes' placed in my extispicy:

10) BE NA GÍD.DA UD.MEŠ NUN GÍD.MEŠ BE GÍR KI.TUŠ.MEŠ-*šú ka-šid*
11) *ki-bi-is* GÌR LÚ KI DINGIR *šu-*⌜*šur*⌝ DINGIR *ana* LÚ NINDA SUM *ú-lu me-e uṣ-ṣab*
12) BE SILIM GAR SILIM ZI-*tim* BE ZÍ SUḪUŠ.MEŠ-*šú* 15 GI 2.30 ZI
13) <<BE>> SUḪUŠ ERIM-*ia*$_5$ GI SUḪUŠ ERIM KÚR ZI

ii 10–13) If the 'Station' (*mazzāzu*) is long, (then) the days of the ruler will be long. If the 'Path' (*padānu*) reaches its 'dwellings,' (then) the way(s) of man are in harmony with the god (and) the god will give food to the man or increase (his) water. If the 'Well-Being' (*šulmu*) is present, (then) there is well-being of life. If the base of the Gall Bladder (*martu*) is firm on the right (and) torn out on the left, (then) the foundation of my army is firm (and) the foundation of (my) enemy is torn out.

14) BE 2.30 ZÍ *šá-ti-iq* KÚR ILLAT*-*su i-šal-liṭ-su* ERIM NUN ḪA.LA GU$_7$
15) BE ŠU.SI <*šá-lim*> EN SÍSKUR *i-šal-lim* UD.MEŠ-*šú* GÍD.MEŠ BE MÁŠ DAGAL DÙG-*ub* ŠÀ
16) BE AN.TA DU GÌR *uš-šur-ti šum-ma* LÚ *in di-ni* UGU *ga-ri-šú* GUB-*az*

ii 14–16) If the left side of the Gall Bladder (*martu*) is split, (then) he will separate (his) enemy from his forces (and) the army of the ruler will enjoy a share (of the booty). If the 'Finger' (*ubānu*) <is intact>, (then) the lord of the sacrifice will prosper (and) his days will be long. If the 'Increment' (*ṣibtu*) is wide, (then) there will be happiness. If the 'Upper Part' (*elītu*) moves (and) 'Foot'-Mark (*šēpu*) (indicating) *abandonment*. If (the same result, then) a man will prevail against his adversary in a legal decision.

17) BE ŠU.SI MUR MURUB$_4$ SUḪUŠ-*su uš-šur* ERIM-*ni* ḪA.LA GU$_7$
18) BE ŠÀ.NIGIN 14 *ina* SILIM-*tim ki-šit-ti* ŠU.II-*ia*$_5$ ŠÀ.SÈ.SÈ.KE ERIM-*ia*$_5$ KUR.MEŠ
19) ERIM-*ni ina* KASKAL DU-*ku* ḪA.LA GU$_7$

ii 17–19) If the base of the 'Middle Finger' (*ubān ḫašî qablītu*) of the lung is loose, (then) my troops will enjoy a share (of the booty). If the Coils of the Colon are fourteen (and) are on the favorable side of the exta, (then) conquest by my hand, the aims of my army will be achieved, (and my) troops (who) go on campaign will enjoy a share (of the booty).

20) *du-um-qu te-er-ti an-ni-ti u*$_4$*-mi maḫ-ra-a a-mur-ma*
21) *aš-šum ša e-li* ^{d}AMAR.UTU EN-*ia ṭa-bu áš-né-e ter-ti ap-qid*
22) UZU SIG$_5$ *šá e-peš* AGA *šu-a-ti ki-ma la-bi-ri-im-ma*
23) *iš-šak-na in te-er-ti-ia* BE NA GÍD.DA UD.MEŠ NUN GÍD.MEŠ
24) BE GÍR 2-*ma ina* 15 GAR.MEŠ DINGIR.MEŠ *ina* Á DU.MEŠ
25) BE SILIM *uš-te-eš-ni* SUḪUŠ GI.MEŠ KI.TUŠ *né-eḫ-tim*
26) BE GÍR 15 ZÍ *pa-šiṭ* ZÍ GAR ERIM-*ka* SAG A.ŠÀ-*šú* KUR-*ad* SILIM-*su* GUR-*ra*

ii 20–23a) I recognized the auspicious meaning of this omen on the first day and concerning what was pleasing to the god Marduk, my lord, I repeated (and) checked the extispicy. A favorable omen regarding the making of that crown (exactly) as (it had been) in ancient times was placed into my extispicy:

ii 23b–26) If the 'Station' (*mazzāzu*) is long, (then) the days of the ruler will be long. If the 'Path' (*padānu*) is two (in number) and they are placed on the right, (then) the gods will go at (my) side. If the 'Well-Being' (*šulmu*) is doubled, (then there will be) firm foundation(s and) peaceful abode(s in the land). If the 'Path' (*padānu*) on the right side of the Gall Bladder (*martu*) is obliterated, (but) the Gall Bladder is (nonetheless) there, (then) your army will reach its destination (and) turn safely.

27) BE ZÍ GÍD.DA UD.MEŠ NUN GÍD.MEŠ
28) BE 2.30 ZÍ *ṣa-mi-id* GÌR *ka-sa-at* KÚR
29) BE *ina* MURUB$_4$ EDIN ŠU.SI MURUB$_4$*-i* GIŠ.TUKUL GAR-*ma* KI.TA IGI GIŠ.TUKUL ^{d}15 Á.TAḪ-*ia*$_5$ ZI KÚR *suḫ-ḫur šá-niš* GIŠ.TUKUL *de-e-pi* MU-*šú*

ii 27–29) If the Gall Bladder (*martu*) is long, (then) the days of the ruler will be long. If the left side of the Gall Bladder is bound (and) 'Foot'-Mark (*šēpu*) of the (magical) constraint of the enemy. If there is a 'Weapon'-Mark (*kakku*) placed in the middle of the back of the 'Middle Finger' (*ubānu qablītu*) and it faces downwards, (then) the weapon of the goddess Ištar is my helper (and) the onslaught of the enemy will be repelled; alternatively, the name of the weapon is "my thruster."

30) BE AN.TA EDIN MUR 15 *i-bir ù ka-as-ka-su ina* MURUB$_4$-*šú pa-liš mu-sar-ri-ir* ERIM KÚR *ina* DUGUD-*šú* ŠUB-*ut*
31) BE <SAGŠU> UGU *ki-di-tum ir-kab* GIŠ.MI DINGIR UGU LÚ GÁL DINGIR *ze-nu-ú* KI LÚ SILIM-*im*

ii 30–31) If the 'Upper Part' (*elītu*) crosses over the back of the right lung and the breast-bone is pierced in its middle, (then) there is a deceiver (in) the army of the enemy (and) its main body will fall. If <the 'Cap'> (*kubšu*) rides on the exterior part, (then) there will be divine protection over man (and) an angry god will become reconciled with the man (with whom he is angry).

32) *ter-ti šu-a-ti ap-pa-lis-ma a-na a-mat* ^{d}UTU
33) *ù* ^{d}IŠKUR EN.MEŠ *bi-ri at-kal-ma*
34) AGA KÙ.GI *ki-ma la-bi-ri-im-ma šá za-ri-ni in* NA$_4$.GIŠ.NU$_{11}$.GAL
35) *ù* NA$_4$.UGU.AŠ.GÌ.GÌ *šu-šu-bu in* NA$_4$.MEŠ *ni-siq-tim šuk-lu-lu*
36) *in ši-pir* ^{d}*kù-si$_{22}$-bàn-da u* ^{d}*nin-za-dím eš-ši-iš ab-ni*
37) *u$_4$-mi-iš ú-na-am-mi-ir-ma*
38) *ma-ḫa-ar* ^{d}UTU *be-lí-ia ú-ki-in*

ii 32–38) I saw this extispicy and (immediately) trusted in the word(s) of the gods Šamaš and Adad, the lords of divination. Then, through the craft of the deities Kusibanda and Ninzadim, I created anew the crown of gold (exactly) as (it had been) in ancient times with *zarinnu* in (which) alabaster and *ḫusīgu*-stone have been set (and) perfected with precious stones. I made (it) shine like daylight and firmly placed (it) in the presence of the god Šamaš, my lord.

39) ^{d}UTU EN GAL *mim-mu-ú e-te-ep-pu-šu*
40) *ḫa-di-iš na-ap-li-is-ma*
41) *a-na ia-ti* ^{d}AG-*na-ʾi-id* LUGAL *za-ni-ni-ka*
42) *ba-la-ṭa$_4$* UD.MEŠ GÍD.DA.MEŠ *še-bé-e lit-tu-tu*
43) *a-na še-ri-ik-tim šu-úr-kam*

ii 39–43) O Šamaš, great lord, look with pleasure upon everything that I have done and grant me, Nabonidus, the king who provides for you, a long life (lit. "a life of long days") (and) the attainment of very old age.

44) *i-pa-at ki-ib-ra-at er-bé-et-tim*
45) *nu-ḫu-uš ta-ma-a-ti ḫi-ṣi-ib ša-di-i*
46) *ù ma-ti-ta-an ša-ti-ša-am-ma*
47) *a-na é-sag-íl* É.GAL AN-*e ù* KI-*tim lu-še-*⸢*rib*⸣

ii 44–47) Annually, may I have the wealth of the four quarters (of the world), the abundance of the sea(s), (and) the yield of the mountain(s) and of all lands brought into Esagil, the palace of heaven and earth.

48) *a-na-ku lu* LUGAL *za-ni-nu mu-ud-di-iš* [(*x*)]
49) *eš-re-e-ti* DINGIR.DINGIR GAL.GAL *a-na da-rí-a-ti*

ii 48–49) May I be the king who provides for (and) renovates the sanctuaries of the great gods forever.

26

Two double-column clay cylinders, one from Sippar and another from Babylon, bear an Akkadian inscription of Nabonidus written in contemporary Neo-Babylonian script. The text records several building activities at Sippar: (1) the rebuilding of Ebabbar ("Shining House"), the temple of the god Šamaš, on top of the foundations laid by the Sargonic ruler Narām-Sîn (2254–2218); (2) the renovation of Ekurra ("House of the Mountain"), the temple of Šamaš' vizier Bunene; and (3) the reinforcing of the enclosure wall of the Ebabbar temple complex at the outer gate. The second half of the inscription is devoted to Nabonidus' petition to Sippar's patron deities. Although the cylinders are not dated, scholars generally think that this text was composed between Nabonidus' fourth (552) and thirteenth (543) regnal years, perhaps during his sixth (550) year as king; see Beaulieu, Nabonidus pp. 27 and 42 and Schaudig, Inschriften Nabonids p. 358. Previous editions and studies refer to this inscription as "Nabonidus Cylinder II, 4," "[Nabonidus] Inscription 8," and the "Ebabbar-Ekurra Cylinder."

CATALOGUE

Ex.	Museum Number	Excavation/ Registration No.	Provenance	Lines Preserved	cpn
1	BM 42267	81-7-1,9	Probably Sippar, Ebabbar, Room 50	i 1–ii 35	c
2	B 33	BE 62068	Babylon, Kasr 10t, processional street, east wall	—	n

COMMENTARY

The present edition is based solely on ex. 1, which is now in the British Museum (London), since ex. 2, which remains unpublished to this day, was not available for study. No on-the-spot copy ("Fundkopie"), excavation photograph, transliteration, or translation of that piece from Babylon has ever been published. BE 62068 is now in the Eşki Şark Eserleri Müzesi (Istanbul), as H. Schaudig (Inschriften Nabonids p. 385) has suggested. Because only the contents of ex. 1 (BM 42267) are currently known, no score is given on Oracc and no minor (orthographic) variants are given in the critical apparatus at the back of the book.

BIBLIOGRAPHY

1889 Bezold, PSBA 11 pp. 84–92, 101–102 and pls. 1–2 (ex. 1, copy, edition)
1890 Peiser in Schrader, KB 3/2 pp. 106–109 (i 14–ii 1, edition)
1912 Langdon, NBK pp. 47 and 230–235 Nbd. no. 2 (ex. 1, edition)
1928 Ungnad, ZA 38 p. 80 (i 13, study)
1931 Unger, Babylon p. 225 no. 22 (study)
1932 Koldewey, Königsburgen 2 p. 24 (study)
1957 Borger, AfO 18 p. 88 (i 33, ii 29, study)
1965 Tadmor, Studies Landsberger pp. 358–359 (ii 29–32, study)
1967 Seux, ERAS p. 277 (study)
1968 Ellis, Foundation Deposits pp. 157 and 182 (i 17–19, 27–28, edition; study)
1973 Berger, NbK p. 361 Nbn. Zyl. II, 4 (exs. 1–2, study)
1989 Beaulieu, Nabonidus pp. 11, 27 and 134–135 Inscription 8 (i 30–32, 34–ii 1, edition; study)
1990 Koldewey, WEB[5] p. 169 (study)
2001 Schaudig, Inschriften Nabonids pp. 358–362 no. 2.4 and 753–754 figs. 2–13 (edition; i 7, 31, ii 11, 14, 18–19, 21, 24, 27, 34–35, collations)

TEXT

Col. i

1) ^{d}*na-bi-um-na-ʾi-*⸢*id*⸣ LUGAL KÁ.DINGIR.RA.<KI>
2) SIPA *ki-num li-pit* ŠU.II ^{d}*é-a*
3) GURUŠ *šu-pú-ú bi-nu-tu* ^{d}*nin-men-na*
4) LUGAL *la šá-na*-an* mi-gir* ^{d}EN *ù* ^{d}AMAR.UTU
5) *ma-al-ka it-pe-šu ni-bit* ^{d}30 *u* ^{d}UTU
6) NUN *mu-un-dal-ka pa-li-iḫ* DINGIR *ù* ^{d}15
7) GÌR*.NÍTA* *la-ni-i-ḫu mu-ṭi-ib* ŠÀ DINGIR GAL.GAL
8) *za-ni-in é-sag-íl ù é-zi-da*
9) *mu-ud-diš ma-ḫa-zu mu-šak-lil eš-re-e-ti*
10) ÉNSI *ṣi-i-ri mu-ṭah-ḫi-id sat-tuk-ku*
11) *šá a-na pa-la-aḫ* DINGIR.MEŠ *pi-it-qu-du*
12) *la ig-gu-ú mu-ši ù ur-ra*
13) DUMU ^{md}AG-TIN-*su-iq-bi* ⸢NUN⸣ *em$_4$-qá a-na-ku*

i 1–6) Nabonidus, king of Babylon, the true shepherd who is the handiwork of the god Ea, the resplendent warrior who is the creation of the goddess Ninmena, the king without rival (who is) the favorite of the gods Bēl and Marduk, the capable ruler chosen by the gods Sîn and Šamaš, the circumspect prince who reveres the god(s) and goddess(es),

i 7–13) the indefatigable governor who pleases the heart(s) of the great gods, the one who provides for Esagil and Ezida, the one who renovates the cult centers (and) completes sanctuaries, the exalted ruler who makes *sattukku*-offerings abundant, (the one) who is always concerned about revering the gods (and) who is not negligent night or day, son of Nabû-balāssu-iqbi, wise prince, am I.

i 4 *la šá-na*-an** "without rival": Ex. 1 has *la šá-an-na*.
i 7 GÌR*.NÍTA* "governor": Ex. 1 has NÍTA.GÌR. *la-ni-i-ḫu* "indefatigable": The form *lânīhu* is a plene-writing of *lā anīhu*.

14) *a-na* ^{d}UTU EN ⸢*ra*⸣-[*bu*]-*ú be-li-ia*
15) *ù* ^{d}*a-a kal*-⸢*la*⸣-[*tum*] *be-el-tum* GAL-*tum*
16) *be-el-<ti>-ia* uš-te-mi-iq-ma*
17) *é-babbar-ra* É-*su-un ina qé-reb* ZIMBIR.KI
18) *e-li te-me-en na-ram*-^{d}30 LUGAL *ul-la*
19) *e-eš-ši-iš ú-še-pi-iš-ma*
20) *a-na ta-na-da-a-ti áš-tak-ka-an*

i 14–20) I devoutly prayed to the god Šamaš, the gr[ea]t lord, my lord, and to the goddess Aya, (his) bri[de], the great lady, my lad<y>, and I had Ebabbar, their temple (that) is inside of Sippar, (re)built anew on the foundation(s) of Narām-Sîn, a king of the distant past, and made (it) worthy of (high) praise.

21) *a-na* ⸢*ši-pu-šú*⸣ GIŠ.GIŠIMMAR *dan-nu-tu ú-šar-ši-id*
22) GIŠ.EREN *pa-ag-lu-tu tar-bit* KUR.*ḫa-ma-ni*
23) *ù* KUR.*lab-<na>-ni* a-na ṣu-lu-li-šu*
24) *u* GIŠ.IG.MEŠ KÁ.MEŠ-*šu ú-šat-mi-iḫ*

i 21–24) I securely fastened strong date palm(s) for its *šīpu*. I put in place thick cedars, (which were) grown on Mount Amanus and Mount Leb<an>on, for its roof and the doors of its gates.

25) *ú-nu-tu-šu ina* KÙ.BABBAR *u* KÙ.GI *ú-za-ʾi-in-ma*
26) *a-na tab-ra-a-tú la-la-a uš-mál-la*
27) *ši-ṭir* MU-*ia* KI *ši-ṭir šu-mu šá na-ram*-^{d}30
28) LUGAL *maḫ-ru áš-tak-kan qé-er-bi-uš-šu*

i 25–26) I decorated its utensil(s) with silver and gold and filled (it) with splendor to be an object of wonder. I placed an inscription of mine, together with an inscription of Narām-Sîn, a former king, inside it.

29) É *šá* ^{d}UTU *u* ^{d}*a-a* EN.MEŠ-*a ina im-na u* ⸢*šú-me-lu*⸣ *ki-ma* u_4-*me*

i 29–30a) (As for) the temple of the god Šamaš and the goddess Aya, my lords, I made (it) shine like daylight on the right and left.

30) *uš*-⸢*nam-mir*⸣-*ma é-kur-ra* É ^{d}*bu-ne-ne šá* ⸢*qé-reb*⸣ *si-par*
31) *ana* ^{d}*bu-ne-ne* EN-*ía eš-šiš e-pú-uš*-ma* te-bi-ib-ti-šú*
32) *ú-qa-ad-diš-ma us-si-ma ana* É.KUR DINGIR-*ú-ti-šú ki-ma* u_4-*me zi-mu-šu ú-šá-an-na-bi-iṭ*

i 30b–32) Then, for the god Bunene, my lord, I (re)built anew Ekurra, the temple of Bunene that is inside Sippar, purified it with purification ritual, made (it) suitable as a temple of his divinity, (and) made its façade radiant as daylight.

33) É.GAR_8.MEŠ *šá si-ḫir-tú é-babbar-ra šá* KÁ AŠ.ÀM
34) *ú-še-piš-ma* UGU *šá* IGI *ú-dan-nin ši-ṭir šu-mi-ía*
35) *u ṣa-lam* LUGAL-*ú-ti-ía ma-ḫar* ^{d}UTU *ù* ^{d}*a-a* EN.MEŠ-*ú-a*

Col. ii

1) *ú-ki-in a-na du-ur* u_4-*mi*

i 33–ii 1) I had the perimeter walls of Ebabbar, at the outer gate, (re)built and reinforced more than the previous one(s). I securely placed an inscription of mine and an image of my royal majesty in the presence of the god Šamaš and the goddess Aya, my lords, for eternity.

2) ^{d}UTU EN *ṣi-i-ri ra-ʾi-im na-piš-tú*
3) *a-na é-babbar-ra* É-*ka na-am-ra*
4) *ina a-ṣe-e-ka ù e-re-bi-ka*
5) *ép-še-tu-ú-a* SIG_5-*a-tú ši-ṭir šu-mi-ia*
6) *ù ṣa-lam* LUGAL-*ú-ti-ia ḫa-di-iš*
7) *na-pa-lis-ma* SIG_5-*tu-ú-a ana du-ur da-rí*
8) *lib-ša-aʾ-ma a-na maḫ-ri-ka*
9) *a-ra-ku* UD.ME LUGAL-*ú-ti-ia liš-šá-kin ina pi-i-ka*
10) *ina nu-ú-ri-ka na-am*-⸢*ri*⸣ *lu-la-ab-bi-ir*
11) *tal*-lak-ka a-na* ⸢*da*⸣-*ra*-⸢*a*⸣-*ti**
12) *li-ku-un* BALA-*lu-ú-a* ^{d}*a-a*

ii 2–12a) O Šamaš, the exalted lord who loves (my) life, when you exit and enter Ebabbar, your bright temple, look with pleasure upon my good deeds, my inscription, and the image of my royal majesty so that good thing(s) about me are present before you forever and (a command about) the prolongation of the days of my kingship is placed in your mouth (so that) I may grow old walking in your bright light (and that) my reign may be firmly established for eternity.

13) *kal-la-tum* GAL-*tum na-ram-mat* ^{d}UTU-*ši*
14) *ina é-ki-nú* É-*ka nam-ri ḫa-diš ina a-šá-bi-ka*
15) *ma-ḫar* ^{d}UTU *nu-úr* DINGIR *sú-pi-ia* SIG_5.MEŠ

ii 12b–16) O Aya, great bride, beloved of the god Šamaš, when you are sitting with pleasure in Ekinu, your shining temple, *make my prayers gain favor* in the presence of the god Šamaš, the light of the gods, (and)

---

i 16 *be-el-<ti>-ia** "my lad<y>": Ex. 1 has *be-el-<ti>*-E.
i 21 ⸢*ši-pu-šú*⸣ "its *šīpu*": The Akkadian word *šīpu* designates a part of the roof.
i 23 KUR.*lab-<na>-ni** "Mount Leb<an>on": The scribe of ex. 1 wrote visually similar KUR.*lab-<na>*-DÙ.
i 31 *e-pú-uš*-ma** "I (re)built": In ex. 1, the word is written *e-pú+uš-ma*; see Schaudig, Inschriften Nabonids p. 753 fig. 3.
ii 15 *sú-pi-ia* SIG_5.MEŠ "*make my prayers gain favor*": The interpretation, which tentatively follows H. Schaudig (Inschriften Nabonids p. 361), is uncertain. SIG_5.MEŠ is understood here as a D-Stem imperative of the verb *damāqu* (*dummiqī*). Alternatively, one could understand *sú-pi-ia* as a D-Stem imperative of the verb *suppû* and SIG_5.MEŠ as a feminine plural nominal form of *damiqtu* (*damqātu*), with the meaning "*beseech good things for me.*" For a discussion of the issues, see Schaudig, Inschriften Nabonids pp. 105–106.

16) *šu-ri-ka u$_{4}$-mi ba-la-ṭi-ia*
17) *suk-kal-lum mit-lu-ku ^{d}am-na ^{d}bu-ne-ne*
18) *šá mi-lik-šu dam-qa ma-ḫar* ^{d}UTU *u ^{d}a-a x x-⸢ka⸣*
19) *a-ṣú-ka šu-lu-lu el-ṣi-iš ina x x x*
20) *ma-ḫar* ^{d}UTU EN *gim-ri šal-ṭiš ina ⸢ú-zu-zi-ka⸣*
21) *e-gér-⸢re*⸣-e* SIG$_{5}$*-ti-⸢ía lu⸣ sa-⸢dir ina* KA⸣*-ku*
22) *ina lìb*-bi-šu* MAḪ *šal-mi-iš it-tal-lak*

23) GIŠ.GU.ZA LUGAL*-ú-ti-ía lu-lab-bir a-di še-bé lit-tu-tu*
24) DINGIR.⸢MEŠ⸣ (over erasure) *sip-par*.KI *u é-babbar-ra ma-ḫar* ^{d}UTU
25) *u ^{d}a-a li-dam-qa ép-še-tu-ú-a*
26) *a-na-ku lu-ú* LUGAL *da-ru-ú za-ni-in*

27) *⸢lu-pu⸣-uš bi-lat-⸢si⸣-nu šá ka-liš kib-rat ma-ḫar* ^{d}ŠÚ
28) *u ^{d}zar-pa-ni-tum* ^{d}AG *u* ^{d}U.GUR DINGIR.MEŠ*-ú-a u* DINGIR *gi-mir-šú-nu*
29) *a-šib si-ḫir-tú á-ki-it šá* LUGAL DINGIR *šá-qu-ú*
30) EN EN.EN ZAG.MUK *re-eš šat-ti i-sin-nu á-ki-it*
31) *ana ni-qé-e ma-aṣ-ḫa-tú u pa-qa-du é-⸢da-di⸣-ḫé-gál*
32) *ù ut-né-en-na* EN EN.EN
33) *lu sa-ad-ra-ak tal-lak-tum*
34) *a-na da-rí-a-tú ⸢li-ir-a-šu⸣* BALA*-lu-ú-a*
35) *li-x-x lik-tar-rab a-na* LUGAL*-ú-ti-ia*

prolong the days of my life.

ii 17–22) O Vizier (who) advises the god Amna (Šamaš), the god Bunene, (and) whose advice is good, in the presence of the god Šamaš and the goddess Aya, ... when you joyously ... (and) exit (*in*) *exultation*, when you stand triumphantly in the presence of the god Šamaš, the lord of everything, may favorable words about me be continually (placed) in your mouth. Walk about safely in its (Ekurra's) exalted interior.

ii 23–27a) May I keep the throne of my royal majesty for a long time, until the attainment of very old age. O gods of Sippar and Ebabbar, *make* my deeds *pleasing* in the presence of the god Šamaš and the goddess Aya. May I be the eternal king who provides so that I *can offer* tribute to them from all (four) quarters (of the world).

ii 27b–35) In the presence of the deities Marduk, Zarpanītu, Nabû, and Nergal, my gods, and all of the gods who reside in the perimeter of the *akītu*(-house) of the king of the god(s), the exalted one, the lord of lords (Marduk), may I be constantly concerned with the proper procedure(s) (for) the *zagmukku*-festival (at) the beginning of the year, (for) the *akītu*-festival, for offerings, for (sacrificial) offering(s and) *maṣḫatu*-flour (offerings), providing for Edadiḫegal, and praying to the lord of lords (Marduk) for eternity. May they exult my reign, ..., and constantly bless my kingship.

27

This long, Akkadian inscription comprises four different texts, which are said to have originally been inscribed on steles erected in Agade, Larsa, Sippar, and Sippar-Anunītu. The final lines of the text state that it was composed so that people of later generations could hear about the deeds of Nabonidus' patron deity, the moon-god Sîn. The inscription, which is known from four exemplars (including a damaged three-column clay cylinder and a fragment of a multi-column clay tablet), was, despite the fact that the text does not record work on any holy building in that city, likely compiled for cylinders deposited in the structure of a building at Ur since ex. 1 was

26 ii 17 *mit-lu-ku* "(who) advises": The word *mitluku* is regarded as a Gt-Stem infinitive, following H. Schaudig (Inschriften Nabonids pp. 361–362 n. 402), who discusses this form in detail and argues against the dictionaries (AHw p. 663 and CAD M/2 p. 139), where *mitluku* is regarded as adjective, meaning "considerate, full of good advice." If *mitluku* were an adjective here, one would expect the determinative pronoun *ša* after *mitluku*. *^{d}am-na* "the god Amna": According to the god-list An-Anum III line 98 (Litke, Assyro-Babylonian God-lists p. 128), Amna is one of the names of the god Šamaš.

26 ii 22 *it-tal-lak* "walk": One expects *a-tal-lak*; see Schaudig, Inschriften Nabonids p. 220 §IV.7.1.a. For other instances of irregular consonantal doubling in the inscriptions of Nabonidus see Schaudig, Inschriften Nabonids p. 110 §II.2.13.a.

26 ii 25 *li-dam-qa "may they make pleasing"*: One expects *li-dam-mi-qu*, not *li-dam-qa* (or *li-dam-mi-qa*), since the subject of the verbal form is the gods of Sippar and Ebabbar, not Nabonidus' deeds. For further information on this word, see Schaudig, Inschriften Nabonids p. 135 §III.4.4. and p. 360 n. 393.

26 ii 27 *⸢lu-pu⸣-uš bi-lat-⸢si⸣-nu* "so that I *can offer* tribute to them": The exact meaning of the form *lūpuš*, which literally means "may I do," is unclear in this passage and is tentatively understood here as "to *offer* tribute." Compare Schaudig, Inschriften Nabonids p. 362, where this passage is tentatively interpreted as "*receiving* tribute" ("*empfangen* den Tribut").

discovered in the ruins of Ur's ziggurat and since the concluding lines (iii 79–81) record that the inscription was intended to proclaim the deeds of Sîn, Ur's patron deity, to future generations. The four inscriptions record that Nabonidus renovated two temples for the god Šamaš, the Ebabbar ("Shining House") temples at Sippar and Larsa, and two temples for the goddess Ištar, the Eulmaš temples at Agade and Sippar-Anunītu. The king boasts in all four instances to have discovered ancient inscriptions and to have rebuilt the temples directly on their original foundations. Moreover, he criticizes his predecessors (Nebuchadnezzar II, as well as the Assyrian kings Esarhaddon and Ashurbanipal) for their inability to discover the original, divinely-sanctioned foundations of those temples. All four copies of this text are written in contemporary Neo-Babylonian script. The inscription was compiled after Nabonidus' return to Babylon, in Tašrītu (VII) of his thirteenth (543) regnal year, perhaps between the end of that year and his sixteenth (640) year as king; for details, see Beaulieu, Nabonidus p. 35 and Schaudig, Inschriften Nabonids p. 447. In scholarly literature, this inscription is referred to as "Nabonidus Cylinder III, 4" and "[Nabonidus] Inscription 16."

CATALOGUE

Ex.	Museum Number	Excavation/ Registration No.	Provenance	Lines Preserved	cpn
1	BM 91124	K 1688 + 1924-9-20,243 + 1924-9-20,244; U 1560, U 1560a	Ur, ziggurat, in debris northeast and northwest of the central staircase	i 1, 10–61, ii 1–66, iii 28–81	c
2	BM 104738	1912-7-6,2	Sippar or Ur	i 1–16, 31–iii 81	c
3	—	K 2746	As ex. 2	i 62–ii 1	c
4	BM 63713	82-9-18,3680	Sippar	i 1–21, 41–66, iii 51–66, 80–81	c

COMMENTARY

P.-A. Beaulieu (Nabonidus p. 35) suggests that the text was composed for objects deposited in the Eulmaš temple at Sippar-Anunītu since ex. 4, the copy of the text written on a clay tablet, was discovered at Sippar and, therefore, he argues that the 'main object' of the text was the restoration of that temple of Ištar in that city. He concludes "that copies of inscription 16 were found not only at Ur, in the remains of the ziggurat, but also at Sippar (find-spot unrecorded), can only be explained if one accepts the hypothesis that the inscription was written for the rebuilding of the temple of Anunītu at Sippar (together with inscription 15), and then placed also in the restored structure of the ziggurat of Ur, the rebuilding of which would have been undertaken at the same time." Although this might be true, given the fact that the final account of construction in this text is concerned with the renovation of the Eulmaš temple at Sippar-Anunītu (just like text no. 28 [Eḫulḫul Cylinder]), the possibility that this inscription was originally compiled for Ur, not for Sippar, should not be dismissed, especially since the final three lines state that the text was to promote the deeds of the moon-god. Given the facts that ex. 1 was found in the debris of the ziggurat at Ur and that the exact purpose of ex. 4 is unknown, it is unclear whether Nabonidus originally had this inscription compiled for Ur, Sippar, or both cities.

The line arrangement and master text are a conflation of all four exemplars. When possible, preference is given to ex. 2 and then ex. 1. The column divisions given in this edition follow ex. 2 since the beginning and end of all three columns are preserved in that copy of the text. A score is presented on Oracc and the minor (orthographic) variants are given in the critical apparatus at the back of the book. Ex. 1 was collated by G. Frame. The authors were unable to personally examine that cylinder during the preparation of this volume since it is on display in Gallery 1 of the British Museum.

BIBLIOGRAPHY

1855 Taylor, JRAS 15 pp. 262–263 and 265 (ex. 1, study)
1861 Rawlinson, 1 R pl. 69 (ex. 1, copy)
1863 Oppert, EM 1 pp. 272–275 (ex. 1, translation)
1875 Ménant, Babylone pp. 255–258 (ex. 1, translation)
1886 Latrille, ZA 1 p. 36 (ex. 1 i 49, collations [Delitzsch])
1889 Bezold, Cat. 1 p. 333 (ex. 1, study)
1890 Peiser in Schrader, KB 3/2 pp. 80–89 no. 1 (ex. 1, edition)
1912 Langdon, NBK pp. 48 and 242–251 Nbd. no. 4 (ex. 1, edition)
1912 Meissner, DLZ 33 col. 1696 (ex. 1 iii 53, study)
1914 King, CT 34 pls. 23–37 (exs. 2, 4, copy)
1916 Langdon, AJSL 32 pp. 116–117 (exs. 1, 4, study, collations)
1922 Fossey, JA 11/19 pp. 1–18 (exs. 1–2, 4, edition)
1923 Boutflower, Book of Daniel p. 100 (study)
1939 Woolley, UE 5 pp. XI, 103 and 133 (ex. 1, study)
1951 Gadd, Iraq 13 p. 36 (i 53, study)
1953 von Soden, SAHG pp. 290–291 no. 37 (iii 70–77, translation)
1964 Galling, Studien pp. 11–12, 16, 24–25, 130–131 and 142 (study)
1965 Sollberger, UET 8 p. 37 no. 50 (ex. 1, study)
1968 Ellis, Foundation Deposits pp. 156–157 and 181–182 (i 12–15, ii 28–32, 69–71, 74–iii 2, edition; study)
1973 Berger, NbK pp. 377–378 Nbn. Zyl. III, 4 and p. 387 Nbd. Tfl-Frgm. VI, 1 (exs. 1–4, study)
1989 Beaulieu, Nabonidus pp. 17–18, 34–35, 55–57, 64 and 214 Inscription 16 (i 1–2, 38–52, ii 37–38, iii 26–29, 33–35, 70–81, edition; study)
2001 Schaudig, Inschriften Nabonids pp. 445–466 no. 2.14 and 757–758 figs. 28–34 (ex. 1 ii 14′–22′, iii 11′–24′, copy; exs. 1–4, edition; ex. 1 i 1, 10′–18′, 20′, ii 17′–18′, 58′, iii 59′, collations)
2003 Schaudig, Studies Kienast pp. 465–478 and 494–497 (ii 32–49, 76–iii 6, 38–65 edition; study)
2009 Winter, On Art in the Ancient Near East 2 pp. 464–465 (study)
2010 Heller, Spätzeit p. 244 (study)
2010 Schaudig, Studies Ellis pp. 144, 147 and 155–156 (ex. 2 ii 76–iii 5, edition; ex. 2 iii 44–63, study)

TEXT

Col. i

1) *é-babbar-ra* É ^{d}UTU *šá* ZIMBIR.KI
2) *šá* ^{md}AG-NÍG.GUB-ÙRU LUGAL TIN.TIR.KI LUGAL *maḫ-ri*
3) É *šu-a-tim id-ku-ʾi-i-ma*
4) *te-me-en-šú la-bi-ri la ik-šu-du*
5) *é-babbar-ra šu-a-tim i-pu-uš-ma*
6) *a-na* ^{d}UTU *be-lí-šú id-di-in*
7) *i-na* 52 MU.MEŠ *šá* É *šu-a-tum i-ga-ra-tu-šú*
8) *i-qu-pa-a-ma il-li-ku la-ba-ri-iš*

i 1–8) (With regard to) Ebabbar, the temple of the god Šamaš of Sippar, which Nebuchadnezzar (II), king of Babylon, a king of the past, had removed and whose original foundation(s) he did not reach, he (re)built that Ebabbar (anyway) and gave (it) to the god Šamaš, his lord. In (only) fifty-two years, the walls of that temple buckled and became old.

9) *ia-a-ti* ^{md}AG-NÍ.TUKU LUGAL TIN.TIR.KI
10) *za-ni-in é-sag-íl ù é-zi-da ina* BALA-*e-a ki-nim*
11) *šá* ^{d}30 *ù* ^{d}UTU *i-ram-mu é-babbar-ra šu-a-ti*
12) *ad-ke-e-ma ḫi-iṭ-ṭa-at-su aḫ-ṭu-uṭ te-me-en-šú la-bi-ri*
13) *šá* ^{m}LUGAL-GIN LUGAL *maḫ-ri i-pu-šu a-mu-ur-ma e-li te-me-en-na*
14) ^{m}LUGAL-GIN *i-pu-uš-šu* ŠU.SI *la a-ṣe-e* ŠU.SI *la e-re-bi*
15) *uš-*⸢*šú-šú*⸣ *ad-di-ma ú-kin* ⸢*li-ib*⸣*-na-at-su*

i 9–15) (As for) me, Nabonidus, the king of Babylon who provides for Esagil and Ezida, during my legitimate reign that the gods Sîn and Šamaš love, I removed that Ebabbar and dug pits in it. I found its original foundation(s) that Sargon (of Agade), a king of the past, had made, and I laid its foundations (precisely) on the foundation(s) that Sargon had made, not (even) a fingerbreadth outside or inside (of them), and (thereby) secured its brickwork.

16) GIŠ.ÙR.MEŠ [GIŠ].⸢EREN⸣ *ṣi-ru-tum tar-bit* KUR.*ḫa-ma-nu*
17) [*a-na ṣu*]-⸢*lu*⸣*-li-šú ú-šat-ri-iṣ* [GIŠ.IG.MEŠ] ⸢GIŠ⸣.EREN.BABBAR
18) *šá i-ri-is-si-na* ⸢*ṭa-a-bi i-na*⸣ KÙ.BABBAR *eb-bi*
19) *ù* URUDU *nam-ru ú-šá-al-bi-iš-ma*
20) *e-ma* KÁ.MEŠ-*šú ú-ra-at-ta é-babbar-ra šu-a-tim*

i 16–20a) I had immense beams of cedar, (which were) grown on Mount Amanus, stretched out [for] its roof. I had [doors] of white cedar, whose scent is sweet, clad with pure silver and bright copper and installed at each of its gates.

21) *ši-pir-šú ú-šak-lil-ma* É *ki-ma* u$_{4}$*-mu ú-nam-mir-ma*

i 20b–23a) I completed the construction of that Ebabbar and made (it) shine like daylight. For the preservation of my life (and) to overwhelm my enem(ies), I

i 3 *id-ku-ʾi-i-ma* "he had it removed and": As H. Schaudig (Inschriften Nabonids p. 310 §VII.2.3.e) has pointed out, the verbal form appears to exhibit an Aramaic suffix and, therefore, should probably be understood as *idkûhēma*, instead of the expected Akkadian *idkûšuma*.

22) *a-na* TIN ZI.MEŠ-*ia sa-ka-pu* LÚ.KÚR-*ia*
23) *a-na* ^{d}UTU EN-*ia lu-ú a-qí-iš* ^{d}UTU EN GAL-*ú*
24) *u_4-mi-šam-mu la na-par-ka-a' i-na ma-ḫar* ^{d}30
25) AD *a-li-di-ka dam-qa-a-ti é-sag-íl*
26) *é-zi-da é-giš-nu_{11}-gal é-babbar-ra é-an-na*
27) *é-ul-maš šu-bat* DINGIR-*ú-ti-ku-nu* GAL-*ti*
28) *liš-šá-kin šap-tuk-ka ki-ma* AN-*e* ⌜SUḪUŠ⌝.MEŠ-*šú-nu li-ku-nu*
29) *ù pu-luḫ-ti* ^{d}30 EN DINGIR.MEŠ *ù* ^{d}IŠ.TAR
30) *i-na šá-ma-mu lìb-bi* UN.MEŠ-*šú šu-uš-ki-na-a-ma*
31) *a-a ir-šá-a_4 ḫi-ṭi-ti iš-da-šú-nu li-kunu^{nu}*
32) *ia-a-ti* ^{md}AG-NÍ.TUKU LUGAL TIN.TIR.KI
33) *pa-liḫ* DINGIR-*ú-ti-ku-nu ra-bi-ti*
34) *la-le-e ba-la-ṭu lu-uš-bi*
35) *ù šá* ^{md}EN-LUGAL-ÙRU DUMU *reš-tu-ú ṣi-it lìb-bi-ia*
36) *šu-ri-ku* UD.MEŠ-*šú a-a ir-šá-a' ḫi-ṭi-tum*
37) *šá* UGU NA_4.*a-su-mit-tum šá* ZIMBIR.KI
38) *é-babbar-ra* É ^{d}UTU *šá larsa*.KI *šá u_4-mu ru-qu-ú-ti*
39) ^{d}30 LUGAL *šá* DINGIR.MEŠ EN DINGIR.MEŠ *ù* ^{d}IŠ.TAR
40) *a-ši-bu-tú šá* AN-*e ù* KI-*tim e-li* URU
41) *ù* É *šá-a-šu is-bu-su-ma ši-pik ba-aṣ-ṣi* GAL.MEŠ
42) *e-li-šú iš-šap-ku-ma la in-nam-ru*
43) *ki-iṣ-ṣi-šú i-na* BALA-*e* ^{md}AG-NÍG.GUB-ÙRU
44) LUGAL TIN.TIR.KI LUGAL *maḫ-ri a-lik maḫ-ri-ia*
45) DUMU ^{md}AG-IBILA-ÙRU LUGAL TIN.TIR.KI
46) *i-na qí-bi* ^{d}30 *ù* ^{d}UTU EN.MEŠ-*šú*
47) *it-bu-nim-ma šá-a-ri er-bet-ti me-ḫe-e* GAL.MEŠ
48) *ba-aṣ-ṣi šá e-li* URU *ù* É *šu-a-tim kát-mu*
49) *in-na-si-iḫ-ma ḫi-iṭ-ṭa-tum iḫ-ṭu-uṭ-ma*
50) *te-me-en-na é-babbar-ra šá* ^{m}*bur-na-bur-ía-àš*
51) LUGAL *pa-na-a a-lik maḫ-ri-šú i-pu-šu*
52) *i-mur-ma e-li te-me-en-na* ^{m}*bur-na-bur-ía-àš*
53) ŠU.SI *la a-ṣe-e* ŠU.SI *la e-re-bi*
54) *uš-šú é-babbar-ra šu-a-ti id-di a-na mu-šab*
55) ^{d}UTU EN GAL-*ú ù* ^{d}*a-a kal-lat na-ram-ti-šú*
56) É *i-pu-uš-ma ú-šak-lil ši-pir-šú*
57) ^{d}UTU *be-lum ra-bu-ú*
58) *qer-ba-šú ú-šar-ma-a šub-tum*
59) *ia-a-ti* ^{md}AG-NÍ.TUKU LUGAL TIN.TIR.KI
60) *za-nin é-sag-íl ù é-zi-da*
61) *i-na-an-na i-na* MU.10.KAM *ina* BALA-*e-a ki-nim*
62) *šá* ^{d}30 *ù* ^{d}UTU *i-ram-mu* ^{d}UTU EN GAL-*ú*
63) *iḫ-su-us-ma šu-bat-su re-eš-ti-ti*
64) *i-na šu-ut-ti šá a-mu-ru ù* UN.MEŠ *i-tam-ma-ru-ni*
65) *a-na* UGU *te-me-en-na é-babbar-ra la-bi-ri šu-a-tú*
66) *é-babbar-ra a-na áš-ri-šú tur-ru šu-bat ṭu-ub*

indeed gave (it) to the god Šamaš, my lord.

i 23b–31) O Šamaš, great lord, may good things about Esagil, Ezida, Ekišnugal, Ebabbar, Eanna, (and) Eulmaš, the residence(s) of your great divinity, be placed on your lips daily (and) without ceasing in the presence of the god Sîn, the father who engendered you. May their foundations be as firm as (those of) the heavens. Moreover, have reverence for the god Sîn, lord of the gods and goddesses, placed from the heavens (in) the hearts of his (Nabonidus') people so that they do not commit a(ny) sin. May their foundations be firm.

i 32–36) (As for) me, Nabonidus, the king of Babylon who reveres your great divinity, may I be sated with happiness in life. Moreover, with regard to Belshazzar, (my) first-born son, my own offspring, prolong his days. May he not commit a(ny) sin.

i 37) That which is (written) upon on a monument from Sippar.

i 38–49a) (With regard to) Ebabbar, the temple of the god Šamaš of Larsa — which in distant days the god Sîn, king of the gods, lord of the gods and goddess(es) who reside in heaven and on earth, had become angry with the city and that temple and over which massive sand dune(s) were heaped so that its cellas could not be seen — during the reign of Nebuchadnezzar (II), king of Babylon, a king of the past who came before me, son of Nabopolassar, king of Babylon, by the command of the gods Sîn and Šamaš, his lords, the four winds, the great storms, rose up (and) the sand dune(s) that were covering the city and that temple were removed.

i 49b–58) He (Nebuchadnezzar) dug pits and saw the foundation(s) of Ebabbar that Burna-Buriaš, a former king who had come before him, had made and (then) he laid the (new) foundation(s) of that Ebabbar (precisely) on the foundation(s) of Burna-Buriaš, not (even) a fingerbreadth outside or inside (of them). For the residence of the god Šamaš, the great lord, and the goddess Aya, his beloved bride, he built the temple and completed its construction. He made the god Šamaš, the great lord, take up residence inside it.

i 59–63) (As for) me, Nabonidus, the king of Babylon who provides for Esagil and Ezida — now, during the tenth year of my legitimate reign, which the gods Sîn and Šamaš love, the god Šamaš, the great lord, remembered his original residence.

i 64–67a) In dream(s) that I had seen and that the people had seen *about* me, with regard to the original foundation(s) of that Ebabbar, he (Šamaš) commissioned me to restore Ebabbar, the seat of his happiness, to its (original) place.

---

i 46 *qí-bi* "the command of": Possibly a scribal error for *qí-bi-it*.

i 52 *te-me-en-na* ^{m}*bur-na-bur-ía-àš* "the foundation(s) of Burna-Buriaš": Exs. 1 and 3 add *šá* between *te-me-en-na* and ^{m}*bur-na-bur-ía-àš*.

lìb-bi-šú
67) *ú-ma-ʾe-er-an-ni ia-a-ši na-aḫ-lap-tu*$_4$ *ziq-qur-rat*
68) *e-li-tú ap-pa-lis-ma ú-šad-kam-ma* UN.MEŠ *ma-du-tum*
69) *li-mi-tu*$_4$ É *ziq-qur-rat šu-a-tum* 15 2.30
70) *pa-ni ù* EGIR *aḫ-ṭu-uṭ-ma é-babbar-ra*
71) *a-di si-ḫir-ti-šú a-mur-ma ši-ṭir šu-um*
Col. ii
1) *šá* ^{m}*ḫa-am-mu-ra-pí* LUGAL *maḫ-ri a-lik maḫ-ri-ia*
2) *<<qé-reb-šú ap-pa-lis-ma>> <šá>* 7 ME MU.MEŠ *la-am* ^{m}*bur-na-bur-ía-àš*
3) *é-babbar-ra ù ziq-qur-ra-tum e-li te-me-en-na*
4) *la-bi-ri <<é-babbar-ra>> a-na* ^{d}UTU *i-pu-šú*
5) *qer-ba-šú ap-pa-lis-ma iḫ-di lìb-bi*
6) *im-mi-ru zi-mu-ú-a*

i 67b–ii 6) I discovered the upper facing of the ziggurat and (then) I had many people mustered. I dug up the environs of that ziggurat, on the right (and) left, before and behind (it), and I (eventually) found (the original) Ebabbar, as far as its perimeter. I discovered inside it an inscription of Ḫammu-rāpi, a king of the past who came before me, <who> for the god Šamaš had built Ebabbar and the ziggurat (precisely) on the original foundation(s) 700 years before Burna-Buriaš. Then, my heart was happy (and) my face beamed.

7) *é-babbar-ra e-li te-me-en-na* ^{m}*ḫa-am-mu-ra-pí*
8) LUGAL *maḫ-ri* ŠU.SI *la a-ṣe-e* ŠU.SI *la e-re-bi*
9) *uš-šú-šú ad-di-ma ú-kin li-ib-na-at-su*
10) *é-babbar-ra eš-šiš e-pu-uš-ma ú-šak-lil ši-pir-šú*

ii 7–10) I laid the foundations of Ebabbar (precisely) on the foundation(s) of Ḫammu-rāpi, a king of the past, not (even) a fingerbreadth outside or inside (of them), and (thereby) secured its brickwork. I built Ebabbar anew and completed its construction.

11) GIŠ.ÙR.MEŠ GIŠ.EREN *ṣi-ru-tum tar-bit* KUR.*ḫa-ma-nu*
12) *a-na ṣu-lu-li-šú ú-šat-ri-iṣ* GIŠ.IG.MEŠ GIŠ.EREN.BABBAR
13) *šá i-ri-is-si-na ṭa-a-bi e-ma* KÁ.MEŠ-*šú ú-rat-ti*

ii 11–13) I had immense beams of cedar, (which were) grown on Mount Amanus, stretched out for its roof. I had doors of white cedar, whose scent is sweet, installed at each of its gates.

14) É *šu-a-tum e-pu-uš-ma ki-ma u*$_4$-*mu ú-nam-mir-ma*
15) *a-na* ^{d}UTU EN GAL-*ú* EN-*ia a-na* TIN ZI.MEŠ-*ia*

ii 14–16a) I (re)built that temple and made (it) shine like daylight. For the preservation of my life (and) to overwhelm my enem(ies), I indeed built (it) for the god Šamaš, the great lord, my lord.

16) *sa-kap* LÚ.KÚR-*ia lu e-pu-uš* ^{d}UTU EN *ra-bu-ú*
17) ⸢*u*$_4$⸣-*mi-šam-ma la na-par-ka-aʾ i-na ma-ḫar* ^{d}30
18) [*a*]-⸢*bi*⸣ *a-li-di-ka i-na ni-ip-ḫi ù ri-bi*
19) ⸢*dam*⸣-*qa-a-ti é-sag-íl é-zi-da*
20) *é-giš-nu*$_{11}$-*gal é-babbar-ra é-an-na é-ul-maš*
21) *šu-bat* DINGIR-*ú-ti-ku-nu* GAL.MEŠ *liš-šá-kin šap-tuk-ka*
22) *ki-ma* AN-*e iš-da-šú-nu li-kunu*^{nu}

ii 16b–22) O Šamaš, great lord, may good things about Esagil, Ezida, Ekišnugal, Ebabbar, Eanna, (and) Eulmaš, the residence(s) of your great divinity, be placed on your lips daily, at sunrise and sunset, (and) without ceasing, in the presence of the god Sîn, [the fath]er who engendered you. May their foundations be as firm as (those of) the heavens.

23) *ia-a-ti* ^{md}AG-I LUGAL TIN.TIR.KI *pa-liḫ* DINGIR-*ú-ti-ku-nu* GAL-*tú*
24) *la-le-e* TIN *lu-uš-bi ù šá* ^{md}EN-LUGAL-ÙRU
25) DUMU *reš-tu-ú ṣi-it lìb-bi-ia*
26) *šu-ri-ku* UD.MEŠ-*šú a-a ir-šá-aʾ ḫi-ṭi-ti*

ii 23–26) (As for) me, Nabonidus, the king of Babylon who reveres your great divinity, may I be sated with happiness in life. Moreover, with regard to Belshazzar, (my) first-born son, my own offspring, prolong his days. May he not commit a(ny) sin.

27) *šá* UGU NA$_4$.*a-su-mit-tum šá larsa*.KI

ii 27) That which is (written) upon on a monument from Larsa.

28) *te-me-en-na é-ul-maš šá a-kà-dè*.KI
29) *šá ul-tu pa-ni* ^{m}LUGAL-GIN LUGAL TIN.TIR.KI
30) *ù* ^{m}*na-ram*-^{d}30 DUMU-*šú* LUGAL *šu-ut maḫ-ri*
31) *ù a-di pa-le-e* ^{md}AG-I LUGAL TIN.TIR.KI

ii 28–36) (With regard to) the foundation(s) Eulmaš of Agade — which had not been seen from the time of Sargon, king of Babylon, and Narām-Sîn, his (grand)son, kings of the past, up to the reign

i 68 UN.MEŠ *ma-du-tum* "many people": Ex. 3 has ⸢LÚ.ERIM.ḪI.A-*ia*⸣ [*ma-du-tum*] "[many] of m[y] people."
ii 4 *<<é-babbar-ra>>* "<<Ebabbar>>": On the basis of ex. 1 ii 5′–6′, the addition of *é-babbar-ra* after *te-me-en-na la-bi-ri* in ex. 2 (ii 4) is assumed here, and in the edition of H. Schaudig (Inschriften Nabonids p. 452), to be a scribal error.
ii 21 DINGIR-*ú-ti-ku-nu* "your (pl.) divinity": Ex. 1 has ⸢DINGIR⸣-*ú-ti-ka* "your (sg.) divinity."
ii 23 DINGIR-*ú-ti-ku-nu* GAL-*tú* "your (pl.) great divinity": Ex. 1 has [DINGIR-*ú-ti*]-*ka* GAL-*ti* "your (sg.) great [divinity]."

32) *la in-nam-ru* ^{m}*ku-ri-gal-zu* LUGAL TIN.TIR.KI
33) LUGAL *šu-ut maḫ-ri ú-ba-ʾi-i-ma*
34) *te-me-en-na é-ul-maš la ik-šu-ud*
35) *ki-a-am iš-ṭur-ma iš-kun um-ma te-me-en-na*
36) *é-ul-maš ú-ba-ʾi-i-ma ad-lip-ma la ak-šu-ud*

of Nabonidus, king of Babylon — Kurigalzu, king of Babylon, a king of the past, had sought (them) out, but he did not reach the (original) foundation(s) of Eulmaš. Thus, he put down in writing, saying: "I searched day and night for the (original) foundation(s) of Eulmaš, but I did not reach (them)."

37) ^{m}AN.ŠÁR-ŠEŠ-MU LUGAL KUR-*aš-šur u* ^{m}AN.ŠÁR-DÙ-A DUMU-*šú*
38) *šá* ^{d}30 LUGAL DINGIR.MEŠ *kiš-šat* KUR.KUR *ú-šat-li-mu-šú-nu-ti-ma*
39) *te-me-en-na é-ul-maš ú-ba-ʾu-ú la ik-šu-du-uʾ*
40) *iš-ṭu-ru-ma iš-ku-nu um-ma te-me-en-na*
41) *é-ul-maš šu-a-ti ú-ba-ʾi-i-ma*
42) *la ak-šu-ud* GIŠ.*ṣar-ba-tum ù* GIŠ.*maš-tu-ú*
43) *ak-šiṭ-ma te-né*-e é-ul-maš*
44) *lu-ú e-pu-uš-ma a-na* ^{d}INANNA *a-kà-dè*.KI GAŠAN GAL-*tú* GAŠAN-*ia*
45) *lu-ú ad-di-in* ^{md}AG-NÍG.GUB-ÙRU LUGAL TIN.TIR.KI

ii 37–45a) Esarhaddon, king of Assyria, and Ashurbanipal, his son, to whom the god Sîn, king of the gods, granted the totality of (all) lands, sought out the (original) foundation(s) of Eulmaš, but did not reach (them). They put down in writing, saying: "I sought out the (original) foundation(s) of that Eulmaš, but I did not reach (them). I cut down poplar(s) and *maštû*-tree(s) and (then) built a replacement Eulmaš and gave (it) to the goddess Ištar of Agade, great lady, my lady."

46) DUMU ^{md}AG-A-ÙRU LUGAL *maḫ-ri um-ma-ni-šú*
47) *ma-du-tum id-kam-ma te-me-en é-ul-maš šu-a-tú*
48) *ú-ba-ʾi-i-ma id-lip-ma iḫ-ṭu-uṭ-ma*
49) *iš-pil-ma te-me-en-na é-ul-maš la ik-šu-ud*

ii 45b–49) Nebuchadnezzar (II), king of Babylon, son of Nabopolassar, a king of the past, mustered his numerous workmen, sought out the (original) foundation(s) of that Eulmaš day and night, although he had dug deep, he (still) did not reach the (original) foundation(s) of Eulmaš.

50) *ia-a-ti* ^{md}AG-NÍ.TUKU LUGAL TIN.TIR.KI
51) *za-nin é-sag-íl ù é-zi-da*
52) *i-na* BALA-*e-a ki-nim ina pu-luḫ-tú šá* ^{d}INANNA *a-kà-dè*.KI GAŠAN-*ia*
53) *bi-ri ab-re-e-ma* ^{d}UTU *ù* ^{d}IŠKUR
54) *i-pu-lu-ʾi-in-ni an-na ki-i-ni*
55) *šá ka-šá-du te-me-en-na é-ul-maš šu-a-ti*
56) UZU *dum-qí i-na* UZU.KIN-*ia iš-kunu*

ii 50–56) (But as for) me, Nabonidus, the king of Babylon who provides for Esagil and Ezida, during my legitimate reign, out of reverence for the goddess Ištar of Agade, my lady, I performed extispicies and the gods Šamaš and Adad answered me with a firm 'yes,' with regard to reaching the (original) foundation(s) of that Eulmaš, they placed a favorable omen in my extispicy.

57) LÚ.UN.MEŠ-*ia ma-du-tum ú-ma-ʾe-er-ma*
58) *a-na bu-ʾi-i te-me-en-na é-ul-maš šu-a-ti*
59) 3.TA MU.MEŠ *ina ḫi-iṭ-ṭa-tum šá* ^{md}AG-NÍG.GUB-ÙRU
60) LUGAL TIN.TIR.KI *aḫ-ṭu-uṭ-ma im-nu šu-me-lu pa-ni*
61) *ù ár-ku ú-ba-ʾi-i-ma la ak-šu-ud*

ii 57–61) I instructed many of my people to search for the (original) foundation(s) of that Eulmaš. For three years, I dug out the pits of Nebuchadnezzar (II), king of Babylon, and I sought (them) out on the right (and) left, before and behind (them), but I did not reach (the original foundations).

62) *ki-a-am iq-bu-ni um-ma te-me-en-na šu-a-tú*
63) *nu-ú-ba-ʾi-i-ma la ni-mur ra-a-du šá* A.MEŠ ŠÈG
64) *ib-ba-ši-ma ḫi-pi iš-kun-ma ni-mur-ma*
65) *ki-a-am aq-bi-šú-nu-ti*
66) *um-ma ḫi-iṭ-ṭa-tum ina ḫi-pi šu-a-ti*
67) *ḫu-uṭ-ṭa-a-ma a-di te-me-en-na* <*ina*> *ḫi-pi*
68) *šu-a-ti ta-ta-ma-ra-aʾ*

ii 62–68) Thus, they spoke to me, saying: "We sought out those foundation(s), but we did not find (them). There was a downpour of heavy rain and we saw the gully that it had made." Then, I said to them, saying: "Dig a pit in that gully until you find the (original) foundation(s) <in> that gully."

69) *ḫi-pi šu-a-ti iḫ-ṭu-ṭu-ma*
70) *te-me-en-na é-ul-maš šá* ^{m}*na-ram*-^{d}30
71) LUGAL *maḫ-ri mu-šab* ^{d}INANNA *a-kà-dè*.KI
72) ^{d}*na-na-a* ^{d}*a-nu-ni-tum*
73) *ù* DINGIR.MEŠ *šu-ut é-ul-maš*
74) *ik-šu-du-ma iq-bu-ni*

ii 69–74) They dug (in) that gully and they reached the (original) foundation(s) of Eulmaš of Narām-Sîn — a king of the past — the residence of the goddesses Ištar of Agade, Nanāya, (and) Anunītu, and the gods of (that) Eulmaš and they told me (about it).

75) *iḫ-di lìb-bi im-mi-ru pa-nu-ú-a*
76) UGU *te-me-en-na é-ul-maš šu-a-ti*

ii 75–iii 2) My heart was happy (and) my face beamed. I laid these (new) foundation(s of Eulmaš), (those of its)

ii 57 LÚ.UN.MEŠ-*ia* "my people": Ex. 1 has LÚ.ERIM.ḪI.A-*ia* "my workmen."

77) ŠU.SI *la a-ṣe-e* ŠU.SI *la e-re-bi*
78) *te-me-en-na šu-a-ti di-ʾu-um* BÁRA
Col. iii
1) *a-di* 2.TA *ziq-qur-re-e-ti-šú*
2) *ad-di-ma ú-kin li-ib-na-at-su*
3) *ta-am-la-aʾ ú-mál-li-šu-ma*
4) *e-li pa-ni qaq-qar áš-kun-šú*
5) *áš-šú la ma-še-e te-me-en-na é-ul-maš*
6) *é-ul-maš e-pu-uš-ma ú-šak-lil ši-pir-šú*
7) GIŠ.ÙR.MEŠ GIŠ.EREN *ṣi-ru-tum tar-bit* KUR.*ḫa-ma-nu*
8) *a-na ṣu-lu-li-šú ú-šat-ri-iṣ* GIŠ.IG.MEŠ GIŠ.EREN.BABBAR
9) *šá i-ri-is-si-na ṭa-a-bi ina* KÁ.MEŠ-*šú*
10) *lu uš-ziz* É *šu-a-ti ki-ma* u_4-*mu*
11) *ú-nam-mir-ma a-na* ^{d}INANNA *a-kà-dè*.KI
12) GAŠAN GAL-*ti* GAŠAN-*ia a-na* TIN ZI.MEŠ-*ia*
13) *sa-kap* LÚ.KÚR-*ia lu-ú e-pu-uš*
14) ^{d}INANNA *a-kà-dè*.KI GAŠAN GAL-*tum* GAŠAN-*ia*
15) *i-na ma-ḫar* ^{d}30 *a-bi a-li-di-ka*
16) *dam-qa-a-ti é-sag-íl é-zi-da*
17) *é-giš-*nu_{11}*-gal é-babbar-ra é-an-na é-ul-maš*
18) *šu-bat* DINGIR-*ú-ti-ku-nu* GAL.MEŠ *liš-šá-kin šap-tuk-ka*
19) *ki-ma* AN-*e iš-da-šu-nu li-kunu*^{nu}
20) *ia-a-ti* ^{md}AG-NÍ.TUKU LUGAL TIN.TIR.KI
21) *pa-liḫ* DINGIR-*ú-ti-ku-nu* GAL-*ti*
22) *la-le-e* <TIN> *lu-uš-bi šá* ^{md}EN-LUGAL-ÙRU DUMU *reš-tu-u*
23) *ṣi-it lìb-bi-ia šu-ri-ku* UD.MEŠ-*šú*
24) *a-a ir-šá-aʾ ḫi-ṭi-ti*
25) *šá* UGU NA_4.*a-su-mit-tum šá a-kà-dè*.KI
26) *é-ul-maš šá* ZIMBIR.KI-^{d}*a-nu-ni-tum*
27) *šá* ^{d}30 LUGAL DINGIR.MEŠ UGU URU *ù* É *šá-a-šu*
28) *is-bu-su ú-šad-kam-ma* ^{md}30-ŠEŠ.MEŠ-SU LUGAL KUR-*aš-šur*
29) LÚ.KÚR *za-ma-nu-ú* URU *ù* É *šá-a-šú ú-šá-lik kar-mu-tú*
30) *i-na-an-ni ia-a-ti* ^{md}AG-NÍ.TUKU LUGAL TIN.TIR.KI
31) *za-nin é-sag-íl ù é-zi-da*
32) *ina* BALA-*e-a ki-nim šá* ^{d}30 *ù* ^{d}UTU *i-ram-mu-uš*
33) ^{d}*a-nu-ni-tum* GAŠAN GAL-*tum* GAŠAN-*ia a-ši-bat é-ul-maš*
34) *i-na qí-bit* ^{d}30 LUGAL DINGIR.MEŠ AD *a-li-di-šú*
35) ⌜*a*⌝-*na* URU *ù* É *šu-a-tum tar-šu-ú sa-li-mu*
36) *ina* MÁŠ.GI_6 *i-na šat mu-ši a-na e-peš é-ul-maš*
37) *tu-šab-ra-an-ni šu-ut-ti iḫ-di lìb-bi*
38) *im-mi-ru zi-mu-ú-a ú-šad-kam-ma*
39) LÚ.ERIM.ḪI.A *ma-du-tum te-me-en é-ul-maš šu-a-ti*
40) *aḫ-ṭu-uṭ-ma ṣal-mu ši-ṭir* MU *šá* ^{m}*šá-ga-rak-ti-šur-ia-áš*

throne platform(s and) dais(es), together with (those of) its two ziggurats, (precisely) on the (original) foundation(s) of that Eulmaš, not (even) a fingerbreadth outside or inside (of them), and (thereby) secured its brickwork.

iii 3–6) I filled it in with an infill and placed it (the new temple) at ground level so that the (original) foundation(s) of Eulmaš will never be forgotten. I (re)built Eulmaš and completed its construction.

iii 7–10a) I had immense beams of cedar, (which were) grown on Mount Amanus, stretched out for its roof. I indeed had doors of white cedar, whose scent is sweet, erected in its gates.

iii 10b–13) I made that temple shine like daylight. For the preservation of my life (and) to overwhelm my enem(ies), I indeed built (it) for the goddess Ištar of Agade, the great lady, my lady.

iii 14–19) O Ištar of Agade, great lady, my lady, may good things about Esagil, Ezida, Ekišnugal, Ebabbar, Eanna, (and) Eulmaš, the residence(s) of your great divinity, be placed on your lips in the presence of the god Sîn, the father who engendered you. May their foundations be as firm as (those of) the heavens.

iii 20–24) (As for) me, Nabonidus, the king of Babylon who reveres your great divinity, may I be sated with happiness <in life>. With regard to Belshazzar, (my) first-born son, my own offspring, prolong his days. May he not commit a(ny) sin.

iii 25) That which is (written) upon on a monument from Agade.

iii 26–29) (With regard to) Eulmaš of Sippar-Anunītu — which the god Sîn, king of the gods, had become angry with the city and that temple and (then) he incited Sennacherib, king of Assyria, the bitter enemy, so that he (Sennacherib) turned the city and that temple into ruins —

iii 30–37a) Now, (as for) me, Nabonidus, the king of Babylon who provides for Esagil and Ezida — during my legitimate reign that gods Sîn and Šamaš love, the goddess Anunītu, the great lady, my lady, the one who resides in Eulmaš, by the command of the god Sîn, king of the gods, the father who engendered her, became reconciled with the city and that temple. In a dream during the night, she made me see a dream regarding the (re)building of Eulmaš.

iii 37b–42a) My heart was happy (and) my face beamed. I had many workmen mustered. I dug out the foundation(s) of that Eulmaš and I found an image (with) an inscription of Šagarakti-Šuriaš, king of Babylon, a king of the past, in that pit.

iii 39 LÚ.ERIM.ḪI.A "workmen": Ex. 1 has LÚ.UN.MEŠ-*ia* "my people."

41) LUGAL TIN.TIR.KI LUGAL *maḫ-ri ina ḫi-iṭ-ṭa-tum šu-a-ti*
42) *a-mur-ma ki-i an-na-a'*
43) *ina* UGU *ṣal-mu ši-ṭir* MU-*šú šá-ṭir*
44) *um-ma* ^{m}*ša-ga-rak-ti-šur-ia-áš* SIPA *ki-num*
45) NUN *na-a-du mi-gir* ^{d}UTU *ù* ^{d}*a-nu-ni-tum a-na-ku*

iii 42b–45) This is what his inscription written over the image says: "Šagarakti-Šuriaš, true shepherd, the attentive prince who is the favorite of the god Šamaš and the goddess Anunītu, am I."

46) *i-nu* ^{d}UTU *ù* ^{d}*a-nu-ni-tum a-na be-lu-ut ma-a-ti*
47) *šu-um im-bu-ú ṣer-ret ka-la* UN.MEŠ ŠU.II-*ú-a*
48) *uš-ma-al-lu-ú i-nu-šú é-babbar-ra*
49) É ^{d}UTU *šá* ZIMBIR.KI EN-*ia ù é-ul-maš*
50) É ^{d}*a-nu-ni-tum šá* ZIMBIR.KI-^{d}*a-nu-ni-tum* GAŠAN-*ia*
51) *šá iš-tu* ^{m}*sà-bu-um ina la-bar u$_4$-mu i-ga-ru-šú-nu*
52) *i-qu-up-ma i-ga-ri-šú-nu aq-qur*
53) *uš-ši-šú-nu e-ep-tú e-pe-ri-šú-nu as-suḫ*
54) BÁRA-*šú-nu aṣ-ṣur ú-ṣu-ra-ti-šú-nu ú-šal-lim*
55) *uš-mál-lu uš-ši-šú-nu e-pe-ri ki-di ú-ter*
56) *i-ga-ri-šú-nu a-na áš-ri-šú-nu ú-nam-mir*
57) *ši-kit-ta-šú-nu e-li šá pa-ni ú-šá-tir*

iii 46–57) "When the god Šamaš and the goddess Anunītu called (my) name for ruling over the land (and) placed the lead-rope of all of the people in my hands — at that time, I tore down the wall(s) of Ebabbar, the temple of the god Šamaš of Sippar, my lord, and Eulmaš, the temple of the goddess Anunītu of Sippar-Anunītu, my lady, whose wall(s) had buckled owing to the long time (that had elapsed) since (the time of) Sabûm. I opened up their foundation pits (and) removed their earth. I kept their dais(es) safe (and) kept their ground plans intact. I had their foundation pits filled in (and) I returned the earth from outside. I made their wall(s) shine in their (original) places, (and) made their structure(s) larger than before."

58) *a-na šá-at-ti* ^{d}UTU *u* ^{d}*a-nu-ni-tum a-na ep-še-ti-ia*
59) *šu-qu-ra-a-ti lìb-ba-ku-nu li-iḫ-du-ma li-ri-ku* UD.MEŠ-*ía*
60) *li-id-di-šú* TIN *u$_4$-mu ri-šá-a-tú* ITI *ta-ši-la-a-ti*
61) MU.AN.NA.MEŠ ḪÉ.GÁL-*la a-na ši-rik-ti liš-ru-ku-nu*
62) *di-in kit-ti mi-šá-ri liq-ba-a ù sa-li-mu*
63) *li-šab-šu-ma ma-ti-ma an-na-a ši-ṭir* MU *šá* ^{m}*ša-ga-rak-ti-šur-ia-áš*
64) LUGAL TIN.TIR.KI LUGAL *maḫ-ri šá é-ul-maš šá* ZIMBIR.KI-
65) -^{d}*a-nu-ni-tum i-pu-šú te-me-en-šú la-bi-ri ap-pa-lis-ma*

iii 58–63a) On account of this, O Šamaš and Anunītu, may your heart(s) be happy with my precious deeds so that my days are long. May they renew (my) life and grant me day(s) of joy, month(s) of delight, (and) years of abundance. May they command for me true and just decision(s). May they always allow peace to exist."

iii 63b–65a) This is (the wording of) the inscription of Šagarakti-Šuriaš, king of Babylon, a king of the past who had built Eulmaš of Sippar-Anunītu.

66) ŠU.SI *la a-ṣe-e* ŠU.SI *la e-re-bi* UGU *te-me-en-na la-bi-ri*
67) *uš-šú-šú ad-di-ma ú-kin* SIG$_4$-*at-su é-ul-maš ši-pir-šú ú-šak-lil-ma*
68) *ki-ma u$_4$-mu ú-nam-mir-ma a-na* ^{d}*a-nu-ni-tum* GAŠAN GAL-*ti* GAŠAN-*ía*
69) *a-na* TIN ZI.MEŠ-*ia sa-kap* LÚ.KÚR-*ia lu-ú e-pu-uš*

iii 65b–69) I discovered its original foundation(s) and (then) I laid its foundations (precisely) on the original foundation(s), not (even) a fingerbreadth outside or inside (of them), and (thereby) secured its brickwork. (As for) Eulmaš, I completed its construction and made (it) shine like daylight. For the preservation of my life (and) to overwhelm my enem(ies), I indeed built (it) for the goddess Anunītu, the great lady, my lady.

70) ^{d}*a-nu-ni-tum* GAŠAN GAL-*tú ina ma-ḫar* ^{d}30 AD *a-li-di-ka*
71) SIG$_5$.MEŠ *é-sag-íl é-zi-da é-giš-nu$_{11}$-gal é-babbar-ra é-an-na*
72) *é-ul-maš šu-bat* DINGIR-*ti-ku-nu* GAL.MEŠ *liš-šá-kin šap-tuk-ka ki-ma* AN-*e*
73) SUḪUŠ.MEŠ-*šú-nu li-kunu*^{nu} *u pu-luḫ-ti* ^{d}30 EN DINGIR.MEŠ *ina šá-ma-mu*
74) *lìb-bi* UN.MEŠ-*šú šu-uš-ki-na-a-ma a-a ir-šá-a'*

iii 70–75a) O Anunītu, great lady, may good things about Esagil, Ezida, Ekišnugal, Ebabbar, Eanna, (and) Eulmaš, the residence(s) of your great divinity, be placed on your lips in the presence of the god Sîn, the father who engendered you. May their foundations be as firm as (those of) the heavens. Moreover, have reverence for the god Sîn, lord of the gods and goddesses, placed from the heavens (in) the hearts of his (Nabonidus') people so that they do not commit

iii 72 DINGIR-*ú-ti-ku-nu* "your (pl.) divinity": Ex. 1 has DINGIR-*ú-ti-ka* "your (sg.) divinity."

ḫi-ṭi-ti SUḪUŠ.MEŠ-*šú-nu*
75) *li-ku-nu ia-a-ti* ^{md}AG-I LUGAL TIN.TIR.KI *pa-liḫ* DINGIR-*ú-ti-ku-nu* GAL-*tú*
76) *la-le-e* TIN *lu-uš-bi ù šá* ^{md}EN-LUGAL-ÙRU DUMU *reš-tu-u*
77) *ṣi-it lìb-bi-ia šu-ri-ku* UD.MEŠ-*šú a-a ir-šá-a' ḫi-ṭi-ti*
78) *šá* UGU NA$_4$.*a-su-mit-tum šá sip-par-*^{d}*a-nu-ni-tum*
79) *e-piš-tú* ^{d}30 EN DINGIR.MEŠ *ù* ^{d}IŠ.TAR *a-ši-bu-tú*
80) *šá* AN-*e u* KI-*tim šá ina* UGU NA$_4$.*a-su-mi-né-e-tú*
81) *šá ga-la-la áš-ṭu-ru-ma a-na šá-me-e šá* UN.MEŠ *ár-ku-tum*

a(ny) sin. May their foundations be firm.
iii 75b–77) (As for) me, Nabonidus, the king of Babylon who reveres your great divinity, may I enjoy happiness in life. Moreover, with regard to Belshazzar, (my) first-born son, my own offspring, prolong his days. May he not commit a(ny) sin.

iii 78) That which is (written) upon on a monument from Sippar-Anunītu.
iii 79–81) (These are) the deed(s) of the Sîn, lord of the gods and goddesses who reside in heaven and on earth, that I had written on monuments of stone so that people of a later generation can hear (about them).

28

Numerous clay cylinders and cylinder fragments discovered at Sippar, as well as at Babylon, bear a lengthy Akkadian inscription of Nabonidus commemorating the rebuilding of Eḫulḫul ("House which Gives Joy"), the temple of the god Sîn at Ḫarrān, Ebabbar ("Shining House"), the temple of the god Šamaš at Sippar, and Eulmaš, the temple of the goddess Ištar-Anunītu at Sippar-Anunītu. The inscription, which was probably composed for objects deposited in Eulmaš, is distributed over three columns and the script of all of the extant copies of the text is contemporary Neo-Babylonian. For each building project, Nabonidus narrates the circumstances in which he came to rebuild the old and dilapidated temple. For example, with regard to construction at Ḫarrān, Nabonidus reports that the moon-god became angry with his temple Eḫulḫul, allowed it to be destroyed and turned into a mound of ruins by the Ummān-manda (the Medes), and, after a fifty-four-year period of abandonment, the gods Marduk and Sîn permitted him to rebuild that venerated temple, which he states that he was able to do because Persian king Cyrus II had defeated the Median ruler Astyages (Ištumegu) and driven off the Ummān-manda hordes near Ḫarrān; Nabonidus also states that his commission to renovate the temple was revealed to him in a dream by Marduk. In all three building accounts, Nabonidus states that he rebuilt the temples on the (original) foundations; the new Eḫulḫul temple was built on the foundations laid by the Assyrian king Ashurbanipal (668–ca. 631), the renovated Ebabbar temple was constructed anew on top of the foundations laid by the Sargonic king Narām-Sîn (2254–2218), and the restored Eulmaš was built on top of the foundations of the Kassite ruler Šagarakti-Šuriaš (1245–1233). Two unusual features of this inscription are Nabonidus' Assyrian-style self-presentation and his address to future rulers who discover inscribed objects of his to respect them and return them to where they were found; the later feature is presently attested also in text nos. 17 (Larsa Stele), 29 (Eḫulḫul Cylinder), and 47 (Ḫarrān Stele). Although the cylinders inscribed with this text do not bear a date, scholars generally date this text to after Nabonidus' thirteenth (543) regnal year, perhaps

27 iii 75 DINGIR-*ú-ti-ku-nu* GAL-*tú* "your (pl.) great divinity": Ex. 1 has [DINGIR-*ú*]-⸢*ti*⸣-*ka* GAL-*ti* "your (sg.) great [divinit]y."

his sixteenth year (540); for this opinion, see Beaulieu, Nabonidus p. 42 and Schaudig, Inschriften Nabonids p. 48. The inscription is referred to as "Nabonidus Cylinder III, 2," "[Nabonidus] Inscription 15," and the "Eḫulḫul Cylinder" in previous editions and studies.

CATALOGUE

Ex.	Museum Number	Excavation/ Registration No.	Provenance	Lines Preserved	cpn
1	BM 91109	82-7-14,1025	Sippar, Ebabbar, possibly Room 5	i 1–iii 51	c
2	BM 54532 + BM 66728 + BM 83027 + BM 91110	82-5-22,846 + 82-9-18,6722 + 83-1-21,190 + 82-7-14,1029	As ex. 1	i 1–22, 28–43, ii 7–iii 51	c
3	BM 56638	82-7-14,1036	As ex. 1	ii 1–35, 55–iii 51	c
4	BM 56632	82-7-14,1026	As ex. 1	i 24–42, ii 29–55, iii 32–39	c
5	BM 56636	82-7-14,1034	As ex. 1	i 1–19, ii 1–19	c
6	BM 12046 + BM 28370 + BM 28381 + BM 55432 + BM 82539	Bu 91-5-9,2545 + 98-10-11,6 + 98-10-11,17 + 82-5-22,1782	As ex. 1	i 42–ii 13, 58–iii 12, 21–51	c
7	BM 56635	82-7-14,1033	As ex. 1	i 10–21	c
8	BM 56637	82-7-14,1035	As ex. 1	i 1–3, 41–ii 4, 62–iii 2	c
9	BM 56626	82-7-14,1007	As ex. 1	ii 19–26	c
10	BM 28372 + BM 54365 + BM 54386 + BM 54398 + BM 54408 + BM 54462 + BM 54491 + BM 54510 + BM 54553 + BM 56627 + BM 141850 (frgm. 8) (+)? BM 141850 (frgm. 9)	98-10-11,8 + 82-5-22,640 + 82-5-22,671 + 82-5-22,684 + 82-5-22,697 + 82-5-22,756 + 82-5-22,793 + 82-5-22,817 + 82-5-22,819 + 82-5-22,872 + 82-7-14,1009	As ex. 1	i 8–24, ii 1–34, 62–iii 31, 46–51	c
11	VA 2536	—	Probably Sippar, Ebabbar	i 1–iii 51	c
12	BM 28377 + BM 28388 + BM 28394 + BM 54529 + BM 68646 + VA 2537 + VA 2539	98-10-11,13 + 98-10-11,24 + 98-10-11,30 + 82-5-22,843 + 82-9-18,8645	Probably as ex. 1	i 1–18, 36–ii 20, 56–iii 7, 24–51	c
13	VA 2538	—	Probably as ex. 1	ii 39–59, iii 32–51	c
14	VA 2540 + BM 54360 + BM 54428 (+) VA 2541	82-5-22,635 + 82-5-22,718	Probably as ex. 1	i 21–28, ii 16–40, iii 20–22	c
15	BM 50271	82-3-23,1262	Probably as ex. 1	iii 4–12	c
16	BM 54334 + BM 54338 + BM 54368 + BM 54383 + BM 54401 + BM 54410 + BM 54436 + BM 54440 + BM 54454 + BM 54463 + BM 54505 + BM 54507 + BM 54508 + BM 54534 + BM 54535 + BM 54538	82-5-22,607 + 82-5-22,611 + 82-5-22,619 + 82-5-22,643 + 82-5-22,664 + 82-5-22,690 + 82-5-22,700 + 82-5-22,726 + 82-5-22,730 + 82-5-22,738 + 82-5-22,748 + 82-5-22,757 + 82-5-22,764 + 82-5-22,811 + 82-5-22,815 + 82-5-22,816 + 82-5-22,849 + 82-5-22,850 + 82-5-22,853	Sippar	i 1–iii 51	c

17	BM 22408 + BM 28378 + BM 28380 + BM 28385 + BM 28386 + BM 54335 + BM 54380 + BM 54393 + BM 54420 + BM 54426 + BM 54439 + BM 54448 + BM 54451 + BM 54455 + BM 54467 + BM 54468 + BM 54518 + BM 141850 (frgm. 4)	96-4-9,513 + 98-10-11,14 + 98-10-11,16 + 98-10-11,21 + 98-10-11,22 + 82-5-22,608 + 82-5-22,659 + 82-5-22,678 + 82-5-22,710 + 82-5-22,716 + 82-5-22,729 + 82-5-22,742 + 82-5-22,745 + 82-5-22,749 + 82-5-22,761 + 82-5-22,762 + 82-5-22,769 + 82-5-22,778 + 82-5-22,788 + 82-5-22,799 + 82-5-22,829 + 82-5-22,855 + 82-5-22,858 + 82-5-22,873	As ex. 16	i 1–iii 51	c
18	BM 54329 + BM 54336 + BM 54348 + BM 54351 + BM 54366 + BM 54400 + BM 54412 + BM 54422 + BM 54433 + BM 54458 + BM 54469 + BM 54485 + BM 54513 + BM 54524 + BM 54528 + BM 54545	82-5-22,599 + 82-5-22,609 + 82-5-22,623 + 82-5-22,626 + 82-5-22,641 + 82-5-22,688 + 82-5-22,702 + 82-5-22,712 + 82-5-22,723 + 82-5-22,752 + 82-5-22,765 + 82-5-22,784 + 82-5-22,823 + 82-5-22,836 + 82-5-22,842 + 82-5-22,863 + 82-5-22,1792	As ex. 16	i 1–iii 51	c
19	BM 54330 + BM 54339 + BM 54340 + BM 54350 + BM 54352 + BM 54354 + BM 54359 + BM 54384 + BM 54388 + BM 54389 + BM 54407 + BM 54427 + BM 54452 + BM 54456 + BM 54459 + BM 54475 + BM 54476 + BM 54482 + BM 54483 + BM 54486 + BM 54492 + BM 54531 + BM 54542 + BM 54546	82-5-22,600 + 82-5-22,612 + 82-5-22,613 + 82-5-22,625 + 82-5-22,627 + 82-5-22,629 + 82-5-22,634 + 82-5-22,667 + 82-5-22,673 + 82-5-22,674 + 82-5-22,696 + 82-5-22,717 + 82-5-22,741 + 82-5-22,746 + 82-5-22,750 + 82-5-22,753 + 82-5-22,772 + 82-5-22,773 + 82-5-22,781 + 82-5-22,782 + 82-5-22,785 + 82-5-22,796 + 82-5-22,839 + 82-5-22,845 + 82-5-22,860 + 82-5-22,864	As ex. 16	i 1–14, 35–ii 15, 33–iii 51	c
20	BM 54349 + BM 54353 + BM 54372 + BM 54381 + BM 54394 + BM 54399 + BM 54409 + BM 54414 + BM 54415 + BM 54423 + BM 54429 + BM 54432 + BM 54457 + BM 54473 + BM 54481 + BM 54499 + BM 54501 + BM 54506 + BM 54516 + BM 54525 + BM 54530 + BM 54533 + BM 54547 + BM 54551 + BM 141850 (frgms. 1, 3, 7)	82-5-22,624 + 82-5-22,628 + 82-5-22,649 + 82-5-22,661 + 82-5-22,662 + 82-5-22,669 + 82-5-22,679 + 82-5-22,680 + 82-5-22,685 + 82-5-22,698 + 82-5-22,699 + 82-5-22,704 + 82-5-22,705 + 82-5-22,713 + 82-5-22,719 + 82-5-22,722 + 82-5-22,751 + 82-5-22,770 + 82-5-22,780 + 82-5-22,787 + 82-5-22,804 + 82-5-22,806 + 82-5-22,809 + 82-5-22,813 + 82-5-22,820 + 82-5-22,827 + 82-5-22,837 + 82-5-22,838 + 82-5-22,844 + 82-5-22,848 + 82-5-22,854 + 82-5-22,865 + 82-5-22,868 + 82-5-22,870	As ex. 16	i 1–ii 21, 26–iii 51	c
21	BM 54331 + BM 54370 + BM 54379 + BM 54387 + BM 54413 + BM 54430 + BM 54438 + BM 54461 + BM 54497 + BM 54509 + BM 54521 + BM 141850 (frgm. 10)	82-5-22,601 + 82-5-22,645 + 82-5-22,657 + 82-5-22,672 + 82-5-22,703 + 82-5-22,720 + 82-5-22,728 + 82-5-22,755 + 82-5-22,802 + 82-5-22,818 + 82-5-22,832	As ex. 16	i 1–ii 11, 23–29	c
22	BM 54332	82-5-22,602	As ex. 16	i 28–41, ii 40–53	c
23	BM 54333 + BM 54356 + BM 54363 + BM 54402 + BM 54404 + BM 54406 + BM 54424 + BM 54442 + BM 54444 + BM 54450 + BM 54464 + BM 54474 + BM 54494 + BM 54496 + BM 54502 + BM 54517 + BM 28387	82-5-22,603 + 82-5-22,631 + 82-5-22,638 + 82-5-22,691 + 82-5-22,693 + 82-5-22,695 + 82-5-22,714 + 82-5-22,732 + 82-5-22,735 + 82-5-22,744 + 82-5-22,758 + 82-5-22,771 + 82-5-22,798 + 82-5-22,801 + 82-5-22,807 + 82-5-22,828 + 98-10-11,23	As ex. 16	i 1–14, 40–ii 17, 26–iii 27, 39–51	c

24	BM 54337 + BM 54421 + BM 54465	82-5-22,610 + 82-5-22,711 + 82-5-22,759	As ex. 16	i 26–41	c
25	BM 54341 + BM 54344 + BM 54345 + BM 54347 + BM 54355 + BM 54357 + BM 54367 + BM 54371 + BM 54374 + BM 54375 + BM 54397 + BM 54405 + BM 54411 + BM 54425 + BM 54435 + BM 54441 + BM 54449 + BM 54466 + BM 54470 + BM 54479 + BM 54500 + BM 54512 + BM 54520 + BM 54537 + BM 141850 (frgm. 11)	82-5-22,614 + 82-5-22,617 + 82-5-22,618 + 82-5-22,621 + 82-5-22,630 + 82-5-22,632 + 82-5-22,642 + 82-5-22,648 + 82-5-22,651 + 82-5-22,652 + 82-5-22,683 + 82-5-22,694 + 82-5-22,701 + 82-5-22,715 + 82-5-22,725 + 82-5-22,731 + 82-5-22,743 + 82-5-22,760 + 82-5-22,766 + 82-5-22,777 + 82-5-22,805 + 82-5-22,822 + 82-5-22,831 + 82-5-22,852	As ex. 16	i 6–29, 32–40, 42–iii 51	c
26	BM 54342 + BM 54362 + BM 54391 + BM 54418 + BM 54453 + BM 54478 + BM 54489 + BM 54504 + BM 54511 + BM 54514 + BM 54527	82-5-22,615 + 82-5-22,637 + 82-5-22,676 + 82-5-22,708 + 82-5-22,747 + 82-5-22,776 + 82-5-22,791 + 82-5-22,810 + 82-5-22,821 + 82-5-22,825 + 82-5-22,841	As ex. 16	i 1–ii 4	c
27	BM 54343 + BM 54361 + BM 54419	82-5-22,616 + 82-5-22,636 + 82-5-22,709	As ex. 16	ii 36–55	c
28	BM 54358	82-5-22,633	As ex. 16	ii 46–54	c
29	BM 54346 + BM 54364 + BM 54376 + BM 54390 + BM 54403 + BM 54416 + BM 54431 + BM 54437 + BM 54445 + BM 54480 + BM 54484 + BM 54487 + BM 54488 + BM 54503 + BM 54522 + BM 54526 + BM 54540 + BM 54541 + BM 54543 + BM 28371 + BM 28383 + BM 141850 (frgm. 2)	82-5-22,620 + 82-5-22,639 + 82-5-22,653 + 82-5-22,675 + 82-5-22,692 + 82-5-22,706 + 82-5-22,721 + 82-5-22,727 + 82-5-22,736 + 82-5-22,779 + 82-5-22,783 + 82-5-22,786 + 82-5-22,789 + 82-5-22,790 + 82-5-22,808 + 82-5-22,833 + 82-5-22,834 + 82-5-22,840 + 82-5-22,857 + 82-5-22,859 + 82-5-22,861 + 98-10-11,7 + 98-10-11,19	As ex. 16	i 1–9, 24–ii 24, 27–iii 51	c
30	BM 54369	82-5-22,644	As ex. 16	i 25–29	c
31	BM 54373 + BM 54396 + BM 54434 + BM 54443 + BM 54447 + BM 54472 + BM 54515 + BM 54552	82-5-22,650 + 82-5-22,682 + 82-5-22,724 + 82-5-22,734 + 82-5-22,740 + 82-5-22,768 + 82-5-22,826 + 82-5-22,871	As ex. 16	i 1–20, 42–ii 30	c
32	BM 54377 + BM 54495 + BM 141850 (frgm. 5)	82-5-22,654 + 82-5-22,660 + 82-5-22,687 + 82-5-22,689 + 82-5-22,733 + 82-5-22,763 + 82-5-22,774 + 82-5-22,800 + 82-5-22,814 + 82-5-22,824	As ex. 16	ii 4–21, 57–iii 51	c
33	BM 54378 + BM 54417	82-5-22,656 + 82-5-22,707	As ex. 16	iii 28–38	c
34	BM 54382	82-5-22,663	As ex. 16	i 9–16, ii 11–23	c
35	BM 54385	82-5-22,668	As ex. 16	i 37–41, ii 58–63	c
36	BM 54392	82-5-22,677	As ex. 16	ii 38–48	c
37	BM 54395	82-5-22,681	As ex. 16	ii 35–43	c
38	BM 54446 + BM 54471	82-5-22,737 + 82-5-22,767	As ex. 16	ii 41–62, iii 27–51	c
39	BM 54460 + BM 54550	82-5-22,754 + 82-5-22,869	As ex. 16	i 17–35	c
40	BM 54477	82-5-22,775	As ex. 16	iii 21–42	c
41	BM 54490	82-5-22,792	As ex. 16	i 29–42?	c
42	BM 28374 + BM 54493 + BM 54498	82-5-22,797 + 98-10-11,10 + 82-5-22,803	As ex. 16	i 20–41, ii 34–50	c
43	BM 141850 (frgms. 6, 12, 13)	—	As ex. 16	—	c
44	BM 28392 (+) BM 54544 + BM 54549	82-5-22,862 + 98-10-11,28 (+) 82-5-22,867	As ex. 16	i 17–28, ii 27–38	c

45	BM 28376 + BM 28393 + BM 54548 + BM 70901	82-5-22,866 + 82-9-18,10902 + 98-10-11,12 + 98-10-11,29	As ex. 16	i 17–23, ii 15–36	c
46	BM 137316	82-5-22,1790	As ex. 16	—	n
47	BM 68570 + BM 72481	82-9-18,8568 + 82-9-18,12487	As ex. 16	i 42–ii 5	c
48	BM 28368 + BM 28373 + BM 28379 + BM 28395	98-10-11,4 + 98-10-11,9 + 98-10-11,15 + 98-10-11,31	As ex. 16	i 16–37, ii 6–45, iii 10–24	c
49	BM 28375	98-10-11,11	As ex. 16	ii 30–56	c
50	MMA 86.11.281	—	Probably Sippar; purchased in 1886 from W.H. Ward	ii 27–30, 38–39, 60–iii 51	(p)
51	VA Bab 624	BE 30113	Babylon, Kasr, north, surface	iii 5–20	c
52	B 25	BE 21242	Babylon, Kasr 15t, Ištar Gate	i 14–23	p
53	B 37	BE 6379	Babylon, Kasr, South Palace, northwest corner	i 14–23	p

COMMENTARY

Between June and October 2019, the authors (in particular Weiershäuser) discovered numerous joins between the seventy-five exemplars catalogued by H. Schaudig (Inschriften Nabonids pp. 412–414). The following pieces are now known to belong to one and the same cylinder: BM 91110+, BM 54532, and BM 66728 (ex. 2 = Schaudig's exs. 2, 53, and 60); BM 82539+, BM 55432, and BM 28370+ (ex. 6 = Schaudig's exs. 6, 58, and 65); BM 54365+ and BM 28372 (ex. 10 = Schaudig's exs. 10 and 66); VA 2537, VA 2539, BM 54529+, BM 28377, and BM 28388+ (ex. 12 = Schaudig's exs. 12, 14, 52, 70, and 74); VA 2540, VA 2541, and BM 54360+ (ex. 14 = Schaudig's exs. 15a–b and 32); BM 54335+, BM 28378+, BM 28380, and BM 28386 (ex. 17 = Schaudig's exs. 18 and 71–73); BM 54329 and BM 54433 (ex. 18 = Schaudig's exs. 20 and 43); BM 54346+, BM 54364+, BM 54431, and BM 54437 (ex. 29 = Schaudig's exs. 30, 33, 42, and 44); BM 54446 and BM 54471 (ex. 38 = Schaudig's exs. 45 and 47); BM 54460 and BM 54550 (ex. 39 = Schaudig's exs. 46 and 57); BM 54493, BM 54498, and BM 28374 (ex. 42 = Schaudig's exs. 50, 51, and 67); BM 54544, BM 54549, and BM 28392 (ex. 44 = Schaudig's exs. 54, 56, and 75); BM 54548, BM 70901, and BM 28376+ (ex. 45 = Schaudig's exs. 55, 62, and 69); and BM 68570 and BM 72481 (ex. 47 = Schaudig's exs. 61 and 63).

Since the publication of Schaudig, Inschriften Nabonids in 2001, a few additional copies of the Eḫulḫul Cylinder Inscription have come to light: MMA 86.11.281 (ex. 50), VA Bab 624 (ex. 51), B 25 (ex. 52; Bab ph 559); B 37 (ex. 53; Bab ph 559); and BM 141850 (ex. 43). It is likely that MMA 86.11.281 and VA 2540+ (ex. 14) belong to one and the same cylinder. VA 2540+ ii′ 1′–3′ appear to join MMA 86.11.28 ii′ 27–29. Since the authors were unable to confirm the proposed join because the Metropolitan Museum of Art (New York) did not have suitable photographs, it is best to edit the two pieces separately. It was G. Frame (RIMB 2 p. 197 Ashurbanipal B.6.32.1) who identified VA Bab 624 (BE 30113; Bab ph 707) as an inscription of Nabonidus; E. Unger (in Wetzel, Stadtmauern p. 80) had mistakenly attributed this small fragment as an exemplar of an inscription of Ashurbanipal. O. Pedersén (personal communication, October 18th, 2019) has pointed out that it is BE 21242 (ex. 52), not VA 2536 (ex. 11), that is the cylinder of Nabonidus discovered at the Ištar Gate mentioned by R. Koldewey (Ischtar-Tor p. 41 and WEB[5] p. 169) and E. Unger (Babylon p. 225 no. 21). The authors have been able to personally verify this information from Bab ph 559, thus confirming that BE 21242 is the copy of the Eḫulḫul Cylinder discovered by Koldewey at Babylon. As for VA 2536, that near-complete cylinder was acquired by the Vorderasiatisches Museum (Berlin) in the 1880s, together with VA 2537 (ex. 12), VA 2538 (ex. 13), VA 2539 (ex. 12), VA 2540 (ex. 14), and VA 2541 (ex. 14). This is evident from the fact that the first hand-drawn facsimile and edition of the text on that cylinder appeared in 1890; see Abel and Winckler, KGV pp. 40–43; and Peiser in Schrader, KB 3/2 pp. 96–107. Because some of the aforementioned Vorderasiatisches Museum cylinder fragments almost certainly join pieces in the British Museum (London) excavated by H. Rassam at Sippar (as verified from numerous digital photographs taken by the authors for personal use), VA 2536 and the other Berlin exemplars of the Eḫulḫul Cylinder are presumed to have come from the ruins of Ebbabar at Sippar, and not from Babylon, as previously reported in earlier scholarly literature (see, for example, Beaulieu, Nabonidus p. 34; and Schaudig, Inschriften Nabonids pp. 46 and 412). In late October 2019, C.B.F. Walker kindly informed the authors that BM 141850 might be of interest. Indeed it was, since BM 141850 (ex. 43) comprised thirteen unnumbered clay cylinder fragments of Nabonidus. At present, nine, possibly ten, of those small pieces can be joined to better preserved exemplars of the Eḫulḫul Cylinder Inscription. Frgms. 1, 3, and 7 join BM 54349+ (ex. 20); frgm. 2 belongs to BM 54346+ (ex. 29); frgm. 4 is part of BM 22408+ (ex. 17); frgm. 5 joins BM 54377+ (ex. 32); frgm. 8 and possibly frgm. 9. belong to BM 28372+ (ex. 10); frgm. 10 is part of BM 54331+ (ex. 21); and frgm. 11 joins BM 54341+ (ex. 25). Frgm. 6 is from the side of a cylinder and no join to the other known exemplars is yet possible and frgms. 12 and 13 are not sufficiently preserved, so the authors have not been able to join them to other cylinders in the British Museum (London). In the score, ex. 43 is not included.

The line arrangement follows ex. 1 (BM 91109). The distribution of text varies greatly between the copies of the inscription. The distribution of the inscription between the three columns is as follows for exs. 2–53, as far as they are preserved: ex. 2 col. ii starts with ii 8b and ends with ii 63; ex. 3 col. ii begins with ii 1 and concludes with ii 64; ex. 4 cols. i and ii end with i 42 and ii 56a respectively; ex. 6 cols. ii and iii start respectively with i 42 and ii 58b; ex. 8 col. i ends with ii 4; ex. 10 col. ii starts with ii 1 and col. iii begins with ii 62; cols. i and ii of ex. 11 end with ii 5a and ii 65 (just like ex. 1); ex. 12 col. ii starts with ii 4 and finishes with ii 63; ex. 13 col. iii begins with ii 58b; cols. i and ii of ex. 16 conclude with ii 5a and ii 61 respectively; ex. 17 col. ii starts with ii 8b and ends with iii 3; ex. 18 cols. ii and iii begin ii 3 and ii 59; cols. i and ii of ex. 19 conclude with i 43 and ii 62; ex. 20 col. i ends with i 40 and col. iii starts with ii 53b; ex. 21 col. i ends with ii 11a; col. ii of ex. 23 starts and ends respectively with ii 1 and ii 64; ex. 25 col. i finishes with i 41 and col. iii begins with ii 61; ex. 26 col. ii starts with ii 5; ex. 29 col. i ends with i 42 and col. iii starts with ii 60b; col. ii of ex. 31 begins with ii 2b; ex. 32 cols. ii start respectively with ii 4 and iii 4; ex. 47 col. ii begins with i 42; and ex. 50 col. iii starts with ii 60b. The master text is generally ex. 1, but with help from ex. 11 (VA 2536) and the other more-or-less complete copies of this inscription. A score is presented on Oracc and the minor (orthographic) variants are given in the critical apparatus at the back of the book.

Ex. 46 (BM 137316) comprises twenty-six small, unjoined fragments. Due to the poor and fragile state of preservation of this cylinder, the authors were unable to examine this copy of the Eḫulḫul Cylinder Inscription during the preparation of this volume. The orthographic variants provided by Schaudig (Inschriften Nabonids pp. 426–535 [ex. 59a–w]), however, are given in the online score and in the critical apparatus.

BIBLIOGRAPHY

1882–83 Pinches, PSBA 5 pp. 6–10 and pl. after p. 12 (ex. 1 i 15–29, copy, study)
1884 Rawlinson, 5 R pl. 64 (ex. 1, copy)
1895 Meissner, Chrestomathie pp. 42–43 (ex. 1 i–ii 46, copy)
1885 Latrille, ZK 2 pp. 231–262 (ex. 1, edition)
1885 Rassam, TSBA 8 p. 177 (ex. 1, study)
1886 Latrille, ZA 1 pp. 25–27 and 35–38 (ex. 1 ii 49–iii 51, edition)
1887 Winckler, ZA 2 p. 311 (ex. 1 iii 28–29, study)
1890 Abel and Winckler, KGV pp. 40–43 (ex. 11, copy)
1890 Peiser in Schrader, KB 3/2 pp. 96–107 (exs. 1, 11, edition)
1899 Ball, Light pp. 208–211 (ex. 1, translation)
1899 Bezold, Cat. 5 no. 2244b (ex. 1, study)
1903 Hilprecht, Explorations pp. 272–273 (study)
1904 Harper, Literature pp. 163–168 (translation)
1905 Prince, SSS 5 pp. 1–40 (ex. 1, copy, study)
1907 Delitzsch, VAS 1 no. 53 (ex. 11, copy [Ungnad])
1908 BM Guide[2] p. 196 and pl. XLI (ex. 1, photo; i 16–25, translation, study)
1912 Langdon, NBK pp. 46–47 and 218–229 Nbd. no. 1 (exs. 1, 11–15, edition)
1913 Jensen, ThLZ 38 p. 356 (exs. 1, 11–15 ii 14, study)
1915 Rogers, History II pl. before p. 551 (ex. 1, photo)
1918 Koldewey, Ischtar-Tor p. 41 (ex. 52, study, provenance)
1921 Unger, Babylonisches Schrifttum p. 18 fig. 29 (ex. 11, photo)
1922 BM Guide[3] pp. 142–143 and pl. XXXIX (ex. 1, photo; i 16–25, translation, study)
1923 Boutflower, Book of Daniel pp. 100 and 107 (study)
1924 S. Smith, BHT pp. 44–45 (ex. 1, 11–15 i 1–45, translation)
1931 Unger, Babylon p. 225 no. 21 (ex. 52, study)
1932 Koldewey, Königsburgen 2 p. 24 (ex. 52, study)
1945–46 Lewy, HUCA 19 pp. 434–435 (exs. 1, 11–15 i 15, 26, 34, 36, study)
1947 Landsberger, Studies Edhem pp. 147–148 (ex. 1, 11–15 i 27–29, 33–37, study)
1948 Schmidtke, WO 1 pp. 51–56 (ii 57–58, study)
1951 Gadd, Iraq 13 p. 36 (ii 65, study)
1955 Poebel, AS 15 pp. 35–36 (exs. 1, 11–15 iii 27–32, edition; study)
1956 Oppenheim, Dream-book p. 250 (ex. 1 i 12–30, translation)
1964 Galling, Studien pp. 4, 7, 10–16 and 141 (exs. 1, 11–15 i 34–39, translation; i 18–29, study)
1965 Tadmor, Studies Landsberger pp. 351–363 (i 12–31, translation; study)
1968 Ellis, Foundation Deposits pp. 7, 30, 157 and 183 (i 31–33, ii 5–6, 56–60, 64–65, edition; study)

1969 Seux, RB 76 pp. 228–229 (i 24–28, edition; study)
1972 Lambert, Arabian Studies 2 pp. 58–59 (study)
1973 Baltzer, WO 7 pp. 91–95 (i 15, 24–33, study)
1973 Berger, NbK pp. 371–375 Nbn. Zyl. III, 2 (exs. 1–14, study)
1980 de Meyer (ed.), Tell ed-Dēr 3 fig. 3b (ex. 1, provenance)
1988 Hecker, TUAT 2/4 pp. 493–496 (ex. 1 i 1-ii 46, translation)
1989 Beaulieu, Nabonidus pp. 34, 57–59, 107–109 and 113 Inscription 15 (i 4–5, 10–12, 15–32, 36–38, ii 26–27, 30–31, 38–41, iii 43, edition; study)
1990 Koldewey, WEB^{5} p. 169 (ex. 52, study)
1991 Powell, ZA 81 pp. 25–26 (study)
1993 Berger, Rolle der Astronomie pp. 284–285 (i 21–29, translation, study)
1994 D'Agostino, Nabonedo pp. 55–58 (i 16–29, edition; study)
1994 Beaulieu, BCSMS 28 p. 41 (ii 27–28, 57–58, study)
1999 Rollinger, ZA 89 pp. 128–132 (i 24–29, edition; study)
2000 Beaulieu, COS 2 pp. 310–313 (translation)
2001 Hecker, TUAT Erg. pp. 16–17 (ex. 1 ii 47–iii 51, translation)
2001 Schaudig, Inschriften Nabonids pp. 409–440 no. 2.12 and 756 fig. 21 (edition)
2003 Schaudig, Studies Kienast pp. 465–468, 473, 488–489 and 494 (iii 48–51, edition; study)
2008 Beaulieu, Babylone p. 188 no. 110 (ex. 1, photo; i 1–3, 15–29, ii 47–50, 54–58, translation; study)
2008 Beaulieu, Babylon: Wahrheit p. 163 fig. 97 and p. 164 no. 81 (ex. 1, photo; i 1–3, 15–29, ii 47–50, 54–58, translation; study)
2009 Winter, On Art in the Ancient Near East 2 p. 466 (study)
2010 Heller, Spätzeit pp. 180, 192–194, 196, 228 and 259 (study)
2010 Schaudig, Studies Ellis pp. 155–156 and 160 (ii 56–60, edition; study)
2014 Frame in Spar, CTMMA 4 pp. 299–303 no. 175 (ex. 50, edition)
2018 Taylor, BBVO 26 p. 45 fig. 9a (ex. 1, photo)

Figure 15. VA 2536 (Nabonidus no. 28 ex. 11), a copy of the Eḫulḫul Cylinder, which bears an Akkadian inscription commemorating the rebuilding of Eḫulḫul at Ḫarrān, Ebabbar at Sippar, and Eulmaš at Sippar-Anunītu.

TEXT

Col. i

1) *a-na-ku* ^{d}*na-bi-um-na-ʾi-id* LUGAL *ra-bu-ú* LUGAL *dan-nu*
2) LUGAL *kiš-šá-ti* LUGAL TIN.TIR.KI LUGAL *kib-ra-a-ti er-bet-ti*
3) *za-ni-in é-sag-íl ù é-zi-da*

i 1–6) I am Nabonidus, great king, strong king, king of the world, king of Babylon, king of the four quarters (of the world), the one who provides for Esagil and Ezida, whose fate the god Sîn and the goddess Ningal determined as a royal lot (while he was still) in his

i 1–2 LUGAL *ra-bu-ú* LUGAL *dan-nu* LUGAL *kiš-šá-ti* ... LUGAL *kib-ra-a-ti er-bet-ti* "great king, strong king, king of the world, ..., king of the four quarters (of the world)": Nabonidus is the only Neo-Babylonian king who uses these Assyrian royal titles; see Schaudig, Studies Kienast pp. 476 and 489.

4) *ša* ^{d}EN.ZU *ù* ^{d}*nin-gal i-na* ŠÀ *um-mi-šu*
5) *a-na ši-ma-at* LUGAL-*ú-tu i-ši-mu ši-ma-at-su*
6) DUMU ^{md}AG-TIN-*su-iq-bi* NUN *e-em-qu pa-li-iḫ* DINGIR GAL.GAL *a-na-ku*

mother's womb, son of Nabû-balāssu-iqbi, wise prince, the one who reveres the great gods, am I.

7) *é-ḫúl-ḫúl* É ^{d}EN.ZU *ša qé-reb* URU.*ḫar-ra-nu*
8) *ša ul-tu* u_4*-mu ṣa-a-ti* ^{d}EN.ZU EN *ra-bu-ú*
9) *šu-ba-at ṭu-ub lìb-bi-šu ra-mu-ú qé-re-eb-šú*
10) *e-li* URU *ù* É *šá-a-šu lìb-bu-uš i-zu-uz-ma*
11) LÚ.ERIM-*man-da ú-šat-ba-am-ma* É *šu-a-tim ub-bi-it-ma*

i 7–12a) (With regard to) Eḫulḫul, the temple of the god Sîn, which is inside the city Ḫarrān, in which the god Sîn, the great lord, has occupied the residence of his happiness since distant days: His (Sîn's) heart became angry with the city and that temple and he raised up a barbarian horde (the Medes), and it destroyed that temple and turned it into ruins.

12) *ú-ša-lik-šu kar-mu-tu i-na pa-le-e-a ki-i-nim*
13) ^{d}EN.ZU EN GAL-*ú i-na na-ra-am* LUGAL-*ú-ti-ia*
14) *a-na* URU *ù* É *šá-a-šu is-li-mu ir-šu-ú ta-a-a-ri*
15) *i-na re-eš* LUGAL-*ú-ti-ia da-rí-ti ú-šab-ru-ʾi-in-ni šu-ut-ti*
16) ^{d}AMAR.UTU EN GAL *ù* ^{d}EN.ZU *na-an-na-ri* AN-*e ù* KI-*tim*
17) *iz-zi-zu ki-lal-la-an* ^{d}AMAR.UTU *i-ta-ma-a it-ti-ia*
18) ^{d}AG-NÍ.TUKU LUGAL TIN.TIR.KI *i-na* ANŠE.KUR.RA *ru-ku-bi-ka*
19) *i-ši* SIG_4.ḪI.A *é-ḫúl-ḫúl e-pu-uš-ma* ^{d}EN.ZU EN GAL-*ú*
20) *i-na qé-er-bi-šu šu-ur-ma-a šu-ba-at-su*

i 12b–20) During my legitimate reign, the god Sîn, the great lord, out of love for my royal majesty, became reconciled towards the city and that temple (and) had mercy. At the beginning of my eternal kingship, he showed me a dream. The god Marduk, the great lord, and the god Sîn, the light of heaven and earth, were both standing (and) the god Marduk spoke with me, (saying): "Nabonidus, king of Babylon, carry bricks using the horse(s) of your (royal) vehicle, (re)build Eḫulḫul, and enable the god Sîn, the great lord, to take up residence in his dwelling place inside it."

21) *pa-al-ḫi-iš a-ta-ma-a a-na* ^{d}EN.LÍL DINGIR.MEŠ ^{d}AMAR.UTU
22) É *šu-a-tim ša taq-bu-ú e-pe-šu*
23) LÚ.ERIM-*man-da sa-ḫi-ir-šum-ma pu-ug-gu-lu e-mu-qá-a-šu*
24) ^{d}AMAR.UTU-*ma i-ta-ma-a it-ti-ia* LÚ.ERIM-*man-da šá taq-bu-ú*
25) *ša-a-šu* KUR-*šu ù* LUGAL.MEŠ *a-lik i-di-šu ul i-ba-áš-ši*

i 21–25) I spoke reverently to the Enlil of the gods, the god Marduk: "(As for) that temple whose (re)building you have commanded, a barbarian horde (the Medes) is all around it and its forces are powerful." The god Marduk spoke with me, (saying): "(As for) the barbarian horde (the Medes) that you spoke of, it, its land, and the kings who march at its side will not exist."

26) *i-na ša-lu-ul-ti* MU.AN.NA *i-na ka-šá-du*
27) *ú-šat-bu-niš-šum-ma* ^{m}*ku-ra-áš* LUGAL KUR.*an-za-an* ARAD-*su ṣa-aḫ-ri*
28) *i-na um-ma-ni-šu i-ṣu-tu* LÚ.ERIM-*man-da rap-šá-a-ti ú-sap-pi-iḫ*
29) ^{m}*iš-tu-me-gu* LUGAL LÚ.ERIM-*man-da iṣ-bat-ma ka-mu-ut-su a-na* KUR-*šu il-qé*

i 26–29) When (my) third year arrived, they had Cyrus (II), king of the land Anšan, a young servant of his (Astyages'), rise up against him (Astyages), and he (Cyrus) scattered the extensive barbarian horde (the Medes) with his small body of troops. He seized Astyages (Ištumegu), king of the barbarian horde (the Medes), and took him to his land as a captive.

30) *a-mat* ^{d}EN GAL-*ú* ^{d}AMAR.UTU *ù* ^{d}EN.ZU *na-an-na-ri* AN-*e ù* KI-*tim*
31) *šá qí-bi-it-su-nu la in-nen-nu-ú a-na qí-bi-ti-šú-nu ṣir-ti*
32) *ap-la-aḫ ak-ku-ud na-qut-ti ar-še-e-ma dul-lu-ḫu pa-nu-ú-a*

i 30–32) The word of the great divine lord, the god Marduk, and the god Sîn, the light of heaven and earth, whose command(s) cannot be changed — by their exalted command, I became frightened, worried, (and) anxious, and my face was haggard.

---

i 1–6 The inscriptions prologue — the king's name, titles, and filiation — is framed by a double *anāku* ("I"). For details on this Assyrian-style feature, see Schaudig, Inschriften Nabonids pp. 141–142.

i 14–15 The plural verbal forms in these two lines (*is-li-mu*, *ir-šu-ú*, and *ú-šab-ru-ʾi-in-ni*) are the remnants of a revision of an earlier version of this passage. For details, see Schaudig, Inschriften Nabonids pp. 77–78 §I.7.f.

i 14 *is-li-mu* "became reconciled": Exs. 7, 20, 21, and 25 have *is-si-li-mu*.

i 22 *e-pe-šu* "(re)building": Exs. 16–18, 20–21, 26, and 44 have *e-pé-eš*$_{15}$*-su*, *e-pé-eš-su*, or *e-pe-eš*$_{15}$*-su* "its (re)building."

i 28 *um-ma-ni-šu* "his troops": Ex. 16 has *ni-ši-šu* "his people."

i 32 *na-qut-ti ar-še-e-ma* "I was anxious and": The reading of the second sign as *qut*, rather than *kut*, is preferred here and in i 52, following AHw p. 745 sub *naquttu* and CDA p. 241. The RINAP Project, however, prefers *kut*, following the CAD (K pp. 198–199 sub *nakuttu*), Tadmor, Tigl. III, and Borger, BIWA; see, for example, Novotny and Jeffers, RINAP 5/1 p. 252 Ashurbanipal 11 (Prism A) viii 31, and Tadmor and Yamada, RINAP 1 p. 127 Tiglath-pileser III 48 line 21′.

33) *la e-gi la a-še-et a-ḫi la ad-da ú-šat-ba-am-ma*
34) *um-ma-ni-ia rap-šá-a-ti ul-tu* KUR.*ḫa-az-za-ti pa-aṭ* KUR.*mi-ṣir*
35) *tam-tim e-li-ti a-bar-ti* ÍD.BURANUN.KI *a-di tam-tim šap-li-ti*
36) LUGAL.MEŠ NUN.MEŠ GÌR.NÍTA.MEŠ *ù um-ma-ni-ia rap-šá-a-ti*
37) *ša* ^{d}EN.ZU ^{d}UTU *ù* ^{d}*iš-tar* EN.MEŠ-*e-a ia-ti i-qí-pu-nu*
38) *a-na e-pe-šu é-ḫúl-ḫúl* É ^{d}EN.ZU EN-*ia a-lik i-di-ia*
39) *ša qé-reb* URU.*ḫar-ra-nu šá* ^{m}AN.ŠÁR-*ba-an*-IBILA LUGAL KUR-*aš-šur*.KI
40) DUMU ^{m}AN.ŠÁR-ŠEŠ-MU LUGAL KUR-*aš-šur*.KI NUN *a-lik maḫ-ri-ia i-pú-šu*

i 33–40) I was not lazy, negligent, (or) careless. I raised up my extensive troops from the land (of the city) Gaza (on) the border of Egypt (and) the Upper Sea on the other bank of the Euphrates River to the Lower Sea — kings, nobles, governors, and my extensive troops, whom the deities Sîn, Šamaš, and Ištar, my lords, had entrusted to me — to (re)build Eḫulḫul, the temple of the god Sîn, my lord, the one who marches at my side, which is inside the city Ḫarrān, which Ashurbanipal, king of Assyria, son of Esarhaddon, king of Assyria, a ruler who came before me, had built.

41) *i-na* ITI *šá-al-mu i-na* u$_4$-*mu še-mi-i šá i-na bi-ri ú-ad-du-ni* ^{d}UTU *ù* ^{d}IŠKUR
42) *i-na né-me-qu* ^{d}*é-a ù* ^{d}*asal-lú-ḫi i-na ka-kù-gál-ú-tu*
43) *i-na ši-ip-ri* ^{d}*kulla* EN *uš-šu ù* SIG$_4$.ḪI.A

Col. ii

1) *i-na* KÙ.BABBAR KÙ.GI NA$_4$ *ni-siq-ti šu-qu-ru-tu ḫi-biš-ti* GIŠ.TIR
2) ŠIM.ḪI.A GIŠ.EREN *i-na ḫi-da-a-ti ù ri-šá-a-ti*
3) *e-li te-me-en-na ša* ^{m}AN.ŠÁR-*ba-an*-IBILA LUGAL KUR-*aš-šur*.KI
4) *ša te-me-en-na* ^{m}*šul-man*-SAG.KAL DUMU ^{m}AN.ŠÁR-*na-ṣir*-IBILA *i-mu-ru*
5) *uš-šu-šu ad-di-ma ú-kin lib-na-at-su i-na* KAŠ GEŠTIN Ì.GIŠ LÀL

i 41–ii 5a) In a favorable month, on an auspicious day that the gods Šamaš and Adad had revealed to me through divination, using the wisdom of the gods Ea and Asalluḫi, through the craft of the incantation priest, (and) with the craft of the god Kulla, the lord of foundation(s) and brickwork, during joyous celebrations, I laid its foundations in silver, gold, a selection of precious stones, (and) crushed pieces of wood (and) cedar aromatics, (precisely) on the foundation(s) of Ashurbanipal, king of Assyria, who had seen the foundation(s) of Shalmaneser (III), son of Ashurnasirpal (II), and (thereby) I secured its brickwork.

6) *šal-la-ar-šú am-ḫa-aṣ-ma ab-lu-ul ta-ra-aḫ-ḫu-uš*
7) *e-li šá* LUGAL.MEŠ *ab-bé-e-a ép-še-ti-šu ú-dan-nin-ma*
8) *ú-nak-ki-lu ši-pí-ir-šú* É.KUR *šu-a-tim ul-tu te-me-en-ni-šu*
9) *a-di gaba-dib-bi-šú e-eš-ši-iš ab-ni-ma ú-šak-lil ši-pir-šu*

ii 5b–9) I blended its *šallaru*-plaster with beer, wine, oil, (and) honey, and mixed (it into) its revetment. I made its structure stronger than that of the kings, my ancestors, and had its construction more expertly executed. I built that temple anew from its foundation(s) to its crenellations and completed its construction.

10) GIŠ.ÙR GIŠ.EREN *ṣi-ru-tu ta-ar-bi-it* KUR.*ḫa-ma-nu*
11) *ú-ša-at-ri-iṣ ṣe-ru-uš-šu* GIŠ.IG.MEŠ GIŠ.EREN
12) *ša i-ri-is-si-na ṭa-a-bi ú-ra-at-ta-a i-na* KÁ.MEŠ-*šú*
13) KÙ.BABBAR *ù* KÙ.GI É.GAR$_8$.MEŠ-*šu ú-šal-biš-ma ú-šá-an-bi-iṭ šá-áš-šá-ni-iš*

ii 10–13) I had immense beams of cedar, (which were) grown on Mount Amanus, stretched out over it (for its roof). I had doors of cedar, whose scent is sweet, installed in its gates. I had its walls clad with silver and gold and made (them) radiate like the sun.

14) *ri-i-mu za-ḫa-le-e eb-bi mu-nak-kip ga-ri-ia*
15) *ka-ad-ri-iš uš-zi-iz i-na at-ma-ni-šu*
16) 2 ^{d}*làḫ-mu eš-ma-ru-ú sa-pi-in a-a-bi-ia*
17) *i-na* KÁ *ṣi-it* ^{d}UTU-*ši* ZAG *ù* GÙB *ú-šar-ši-id*

ii 14–17) I stationed a wild bull of shiny *zaḫalû*-metal, which aggressively gores my foes (to death), in his (Sîn's) inner sanctum. I firmly planted two long-haired heroes of *ešmarû*-metal, who overwhelm my enem(ies), in the Gate of the Rising Sun, (on) the right and left.

18) *qá-tì* ^{d}30 ^{d}*nin-gal* ^{d}*nusku ù* ^{d}*sa-dàr-nun-na*
19) EN.MEŠ-*e-a ul-tu šu-an-na*.KI URU LUGAL-*ú-ti-ia*

ii 18–21) I took the deities Sîn, Ningal, Nusku, and Sadarnunna, my lords, by the hand, (leading them

---

ii 5 KAŠ "beer": Exs. 11–12, 19, 23, 29, and 31 have KAŠ.SAG.

ii 17 ZAG "right": Exs. 1–2, 10–12, 14, 17–18, 23, 29, 31, and 45 have ZAG, while ex. 16 has *i-mit-ti* and exs. 20 and 25 have *im-ni*.

ii 19 *šu-an-na*.KI "Šuanna (Babylon)": Exs. 16 and 17 have *ba-bi-lam*.KI and TIN.TIR.KI "Babylon."

20) *aṣ-ba-at-ma i-na ḫi-da-a-ti ù ri-šá-a-ti*
21) *šu-ba-at ṭu-ub lìb-bi qé-er-ba-šu ú-še-ši-ib*

out) of Šuanna (Babylon), the city of my royal majesty, and I had (them) reside inside the residence of (their) happiness during joyous celebrations.

22) UDU.SÍSKUR *taš-ri-iḫ-ti eb-bi ma-ḫar-šú-nu aq-qí-ma*
23) *ú-šam-ḫi-ir kád-ra-a-a é-ḫúl-ḫúl re-eš-tum ú-mál-li-ma*
24) URU.*ḫar-ra-an a-na pa-aṭ gi-im-ri-šu*
25) *ki-ma ṣe-et* ITI *ú-nam-mi-ir ša-ru-ru-šu*

ii 22–25) I offered pure, sumptuous offerings before them (and) presented (them) with my gifts. I filled Eḫulḫul with joy and (then) made the radiance of the city Ḫarrān, to its full extent, shine like the appearance of the moon.

26) ^{d}EN.ZU LUGAL DINGIR.MEŠ *šá* AN-*e ù* KI-*tim šá ul-la-nu-uš-šu*
27) URU *ù* KUR *la in-nam-du-ú la i-tur-ru áš-ru-uš-šu*
28) *a-na é-ḫúl-ḫúl* É *šu-bat la-le-e-ka i-na e-re-bi-ka*
29) SIG$_5$-*tì* URU *ù* É *šá-a-šu liš-šá-ki-in šap-tu-uk-ka*

ii 26–29) O Sîn, king of the gods of heaven and earth, without whom no city or land can be founded or restored (lit. "returned to its place"), when you enter Eḫulḫul, the temple (that is) the residence you desired, may good thing(s) about the city and that temple be placed on your lips.

30) DINGIR.MEŠ *a-ši-bu-tu ša* AN-*e ù* KI-*tim*
31) *li-ik-ta-ra-bu* É ^{d}EN.ZU *a-bi ba-ni-šu-un*

ii 30–31) May the gods who reside in heaven and on earth constantly bless the temple of the god Sîn, the father who created them.

32) *ia-ti* ^{d}AG-NÍ.TUKU LUGAL TIN.TIR.KI *mu-šak-lil* É *šu-a-tim*
33) ^{d}EN.ZU LUGAL DINGIR.MEŠ *šá* AN-*e ù* KI-*tim i-na ni-iš i-ni-šú* SIG$_5$.MEŠ
34) *ḫa-di-iš lip-pal-sa-an-ni-ma ár-ḫi-šam-ma i-na ni-ip-ḫi ù ri-ba*
35) *li-dam-mi-iq it-ta-tu-ú-a* UD.MEŠ-*ia li-šá-ri-ik*
36) MU.AN.NA.MEŠ-*ia li-šá-an-di-il lu-ki-in pa-lu-ú-a*
37) LÚ.*na-ak-ru-ti-ia lik-šu-ud* LÚ.*za-ma-ni-ia li-šá-am-qit*
38) *li-is-pu-un ga-ri-ia* ^{d}*nin-gal* AMA DINGIR GAL.GAL
39) *i-na ma-ḫar* ^{d}EN.ZU *na-ra-mi-šú li-iq-ba-a ba-ni-ti*

ii 32–38a) (As for) me, Nabonidus, king of Babylon, the one who completed this temple, may the god Sîn, king of the gods of heaven and earth, look with pleasure upon me with his favorable glance and monthly, at sunrise and sunset, make my signs auspicious. May he lengthen my days, increase my years, (and) make my reign endure. May he conquer my enemies, cut down those hostile to me, (and) flatten my foes.

ii 38b–39) May the goddess Ningal, mother of the great gods, speak laudatory word(s) about me in the presence of the god Sîn, her beloved.

40) ^{d}UTU *ù* ^{d}*iš-tar ṣi-it* ŠÀ-*šú na-am-ra*
41) *a-na* ^{d}EN.ZU *a-bi ba-ni-šu-nu li-iq-bu-ú* SIG$_5$-*tì*
42) ^{d}*nusku* SUKKAL *ṣi-i-ri su-pe-e-a li-iš-me-e-ma*

ii 40–43a) May the god Šamaš and the goddess Ištar, his bright offspring, say good thing(s) about me to the god Sîn, the father who created them. May the god Nusku, the exalted vizier, hear my prayers and intercede (on my behalf).

43) *li-iṣ-ba-at a-bu-tu mu-sa-ru-ú ši-ṭi-ir šu-um*
44) *šá* ^{m}AN.ŠÁR-*ba-an*-IBILA LUGAL KUR-*aš-šur*.KI *a-mu-ur-ma*
45) *la ú-nak-ki-ir* Ì.GIŠ *ap-šu-uš* UDU.SÍSKUR *aq-qí*
46) *it-ti mu-sa-re-e-a áš-kun-ma ú-te-er áš-ru-uš-šu*

ii 43b–46) I found an inscribed object bearing the name of Ashurbanipal, king of Assyria, and I did not change (its position). I anointed (it) with oil, made an offering, placed (it) with my (own) inscribed object, and returned (it) to its place.

47) *a-na* ^{d}UTU *da-a-a-nu ša* AN-*e ù* KI-*tim*
48) *é-babbar-ra* É-*su šá qé-reb* ZIMBIR.KI
49) *šá* ^{md}AG-NÍG.GUB-ÙRU LUGAL *maḫ-ri i-pu-šu-ma*
50) *te-me-en-šu la-bi-ri ú-ba-ʾu-ú la i-mu-ru*
51) É *šu-a-tim i-pu-uš-ma i-na* 45 MU.AN.NA.MEŠ

ii 47–52a) For the god Šamaš, judge of heaven and earth: (With regard to) Ebabbar, his temple that is inside Sippar, which Nebuchadnezzar (II), a king of the past had built and whose original foundation(s) he had sought out but did not find — he (Nebuchadnezzar) built (it anyway) and, in (only) forty-five years, the walls of that temple buckled.

52) *ša* É *šu-a-tim i-qu-pu i-ga-ru-šu ak-ku-ud áš-ḫu-ut*
53) *na-qut-ti ar-še-e-ma dul-lu-ḫu pa-nu-ú-a*
54) *a-di* ^{d}UTU *ul-tu qé-er-bi-šu ú-še-ṣu-ú*
55) *ú-še-ši-bu i-na* É *šá-nim-ma* É *šu-a-tim*

ii 52b–60a) I became worried, afraid, (and) anxious, and my face was haggard. While I had the god Šamaš brought out of it (Ebabbar and) had (him) reside in another temple, I removed that temple and sought out its original foundation(s). Then, I dug down eighteen

ad-ke-e-ma
56) *te-me-en-šu la-bi-ri ú-ba-ʾi-ma* 18 KÙŠ *qá-qá-ri*
57) *ú-šap-pi-il-ma te-me-en-na* ^{m}*na-ram-*^{d}30 DUMU ^{m}LUGAL-GI.NA
58) *ša* 3 LIM 2 ME MU.AN.NA.MEŠ *ma-na-ma* LUGAL *a-lik maḫ-ri-ia la i-mu-ru*
59) ^{d}UTU EN GAL-*ú é-babbar-ra* É *šu-bat ṭu-ub* ŠÀ-*šú*

cubits into the earth and the foundation(s) of Narām-Sîn, (grand)son of Sargon, which (for) 3,200 years none of the king(s) who came before me had found — the god Šamaš, the great lord, revealed to me (the original) Ebabbar, the temple (that is) the residence of his happiness.

60) *ú-kal-lim-an-ni ia-a-ši i-na* ITI.DU$_6$ *i-na* ITI *šal-mu i-na* UD ŠE.GA
61) *ša i-na bi-ri ú-ad-du-ni* ^{d}UTU *ù* ^{d}IŠKUR
62) *i-na* KÙ.BABBAR KÙ.GI NA$_4$ *ni-siq-ti šu-qu-ru-tu ḫi-biš-ti* GIŠ.TIR
63) ŠIM.ḪI.A GIŠ.EREN *i-na ḫi-da-a-ti ù ri-šá-a-ti*
64) *e-li te-me-en-na* ^{m}*na-ra-am-*^{d}EN.ZU DUMU ^{m}LUGAL-GI.NA
65) ŠU.SI *la a-ṣe-e* ŠU.SI *la e-re-bi ú-kin lib-na-at-su*

ii 60b–65) In the month Tašrītu (VII), in a favorable month, on an auspicious day that the gods Šamaš and Adad had revealed to me through divination, during joyous celebrations, I secured its brickwork in silver, gold, a selection of precious stones, (and) crushed pieces of wood (and) cedar aromatics, (precisely) on the foundation(s) of Narām-Sîn, (grand)son of Sargon, not (even) a fingerbreadth outside or inside (of them).

Col. iii
1) 5 LIM GIŠ.EREN *dan-nu-tu a-na ṣu-lu-li-šú ú-šat-ri-iṣ*
2) GIŠ.IG.MEŠ GIŠ.EREN *ṣi-ra-a-ti as-kup-pu ù nu-ku-še-e*
3) *i-na* KÁ.MEŠ-*šu ú-ra-at-ti*

iii 1–3) I had 5,000 strong cedar(s) stretched out for its roof. I installed immense doors of cedar, (threshold) slab(s), (and) *nukuššû*-fittings in its gates.

4) *é-babbar-ra a-di é-kun*$_4$*-an-kù-ga ziq-qur-ra-ti-šú*
5) *eš-ši-iš e-pu-uš-ma ú-šak-lil ši-pí-ir-šu*
6) *qá-at* ^{d}UTU EN-*ia aṣ-bat-ma i-na ḫi-da-a-ti ù ri-šá-a-ti*
7) *šu-ba-at ṭu-ub lìb-bi qé-er-ba-šu ú-še-ši-ib*

iii 4–7) I built anew Ebabbar, together with Ekunankuga, its ziggurat, and completed its construction. I took the god Šamaš, my lord, by the hand and had (him) reside inside it, the residence of (his) happiness, during joyous celebrations.

8) *ši-ṭi-ir šu-um šá* ^{m}*na-ra-am-*^{d}30 DUMU ^{m}LUGAL-GI.NA *a-mu-ur-ma*
9) *la ú-nak-ki-ir* Ì.GIŠ *ap-šu-uš* UDU.SÍSKUR *aq-qí*
10) *it-ti mu-sa-re-e-a áš-ku-un-ma ú-te-er áš-ru-uš-šu*

iii 8–10) I found an inscription of Narām-Sîn, (grand)-son of Sargon, and I did not change (its position). I anointed (it) with oil, made an offering, placed (it) with my (own) inscribed object, and returned (it) to its place.

11) ^{d}UTU EN GAL-*ú šá* AN-*e ù* KI-*tim nu-úr* DINGIR.MEŠ *ab-bé-e-šu*
12) *ṣi-it lìb-bi ša* ^{d}EN.ZU *ù* ^{d}*nin-gal*
13) *a-na é-babbar-ra* É *na-ra-mi-ka i-na e-re-bi-ka*
14) BÁRA-*ka da-ru-ú i-na ra-mé-e-ka*
15) *ia-ti* ^{d}AG-NÍ.TUKU LUGAL TIN.TIR.KI NUN *za-ni-in-ka*
16) *mu-ṭi-ib lìb-bi-ka e-pí-iš ku-um-mi-ka ṣi-i-ri*
17) *ép-še-tu-ú-a* SIG$_5$.MEŠ *ḫa-di-iš na-ap-li-is-ma*
18) *u*$_4$*-mi-šam-ma i-na ni-ip-ḫi ù ri-ba i-na šá-ma-mi ù qá-qá-ri*
19) *du-um-mi-iq it-ta-tu-ú-a un-nin-ni-ia le-qé-e-ma*
20) *mu-gu-ur ta-aṣ-li-ti* GIŠ.NÍG.GIDRU *ù ši-bir-ri ki-i-nim*
21) *šá tu-šat-mi-ḫu qa-tu-ú-a lu-bé-el a-na du-ú-ri da-a-ri*

iii 11–21) O Šamaš, great lord of heaven and earth, light of the gods, his fathers, offspring of the god Sîn and the goddess Ningal, when you enter Ebabbar, your beloved temple, (and) when you occupy your eternal dais — (as for) me, Nabonidus, king of Babylon, the prince who provides for you, the one who pleases your heart, the one who built your exalted cella — look with pleasure upon my good deeds and daily, at sunrise and sunset, make my signs auspicious in heaven and (on) earth. Receive my prayers (and) accept my petition(s) so that I may rule forever (with) the scepter and legitimate rod that you had let my hands grasp.

22) *a-na* ^{d}*a-nu-ni-tum* GAŠAN MÈ *na-šá-ta* GIŠ.PAN *ù iš-pa-ti*

iii 22–26) For the goddess Anunītu, the lady of battle who carries bow and quiver, the one who fully carries

---

ii 59 É "the temple": Exs. 2 and 17 have É-*su* "his (Šamaš') temple."
ii 60 *ia-a-ši* (dat.) "to me": Ex. 25 has *ia-a-ti* (acc.) "me." ŠE.GA (=*šemê*) "auspicious (lit. 'hearing')": Ex. 16 has *ma-ag-ru* "favorable."
iii 5 *e-pu-uš-ma* "I built and": Exs. 25 and 32 have *ab-ni-ma* "I built and."

23) *mu-šal-li-ma-at qí-bi-it* ^{d}EN.LÍL *a-bi-šu*
24) *sa-pi-na-at* LÚ.*na-ak-ru mu-ḫal-li-qa-at ra-ag-gu*
25) *a-li-ka-at maḫ-ri ša* DINGIR.DINGIR
26) *ša i-na* ^{d}UTU.È *ù* ^{d}UTU.ŠÚ.A *ú-dam-ma-qu it-ta-tu-ú-a*
27) *é-ul-maš* É-*su šá i-na* ZIMBIR.KI-^{d}*a-nu-ni-tum šá* 8 ME MU.AN.NA.MEŠ
28) *ul-tu pa-ni* ^{m}*šà-ga-rak-ti-šur*-ia-áš* LUGAL TIN.TIR.KI
29) DUMU ^{m}NÍG.GUB-^{d}EN.LÍL LUGAL *ma-na-ma la i-pu-šu*
30) *te-me-en-šu la-bi-ri aḫ-ṭu-uṭ-ma a-ḫi-iṭ ab-re-e-ma*
31) *e-li te-me-en-na* ^{m}*šà-ga-rak-ti-šur*-ia-áš* DUMU ^{m}NÍG.GUB-^{d}EN.LÍL
32) *uš-šu-šu ad-di-ma ú-ki-in lib-na-at-su*
33) É *šá-a-šu eš-šiš e-pu-uš-ma ú-šak-lil ši-pí-ir-šú*

out the command(s) of the god Enlil, her father, the one who overwhelms enem(ies and) destroys the wicked, the one who marches at front of the gods, (and) who make my signs auspicious at sunrise and sunset —

iii 27–33) (With regard to) Eulmaš, her temple that is in Sippar-Anunītu, which no king had built in 800 years, from the time of Šagarakti-Šuriaš, king of Babylon, son of Kudur-Enlil, I dug out its original foundation(s), examined (and) checked (them), and (then) I laid its foundations (precisely) on the foundation(s) of Šagarakti-Šuriaš, son of Kudur-Enlil, and (thereby) I secured its brickwork. I built that temple anew and completed its construction.

34) ^{d}*a-nu-ni-tum* GAŠAN MÈ *mu-šal-li-mat qí-bit* ^{d}EN.LÍL *a-bi-šu*
35) *sa-pi-na-at* LÚ.*na-ak-ru mu-ḫal-li-qa-at rag-gu*
36) *a-li-ka-at maḫ-ri šá* DINGIR.MEŠ *ú-šar-ma-a šu-ba-at-su*
37) *sat-tuk-ku ù nin-da-bé-e e-li šá maḫ-ri ú-šá-te-er-ma*
38) *ú-kin ma-ḫar-šú at-ta* ^{d}*a-nu-ni-tum* GAŠAN GAL-*ti*
39) *a-na* É *šu-a-tim ḫa-di-iš i-na e-re-bi-ka*
40) *ép-še-tu-ú-a* SIG$_{5}$.MEŠ *ḫa-di-iš na-ap-li-si-ma*
41) *ár-ḫi-šam-ma i-na* ^{d}UTU.È *ù* ^{d}UTU.ŠÚ.A
42) *a-na* ^{d}EN.ZU *a-bi a-li-di-ka šu-uq-ri-ba* SIG$_{5}$-*tì*

iii 34–38a) I had the goddess Anunītu, the lady of battle who fully carries out the command(s) of the god Enlil, her father, the one who overwhelms enem(ies and) destroys the wicked, (and) the one who marches at front of the gods, dwell in her residence. I made *sattukku*-offerings and *nindabû*-offerings more plentiful than before and (re)confirmed (them) in her presence.

iii 38b–42) You, O Anunītu, great lady, when you enter this temple with pleasure, look with pleasure upon my good deeds and, monthly, at sunrise and sunset, petition the god Sîn, the father who engendered you, about good thing(s) for me.

43) *man-nu at-ta šá* ^{d}30 *ù* ^{d}UTU *a-na* LUGAL-*ú-tu i-nam-bu-šu-ma*
44) *i-na pa-le-e-šú* É *šu-a-tim in-na-ḫu-ma eš-šiš ip-pu-šu*
45) *mu-sa-ru-ú ši-ṭir šu-mi-ia li-mur-ma la ú-nak-ka-ar*
46) Ì.GIŠ *lip-šu-uš* UDU.SÍSKUR *li-iq-qí*
47) *it-ti mu-sa-ru-ú ši-ṭir šu-mi-šú liš-kun-ma lu-ter áš-ru-uš-šu*

iii 43–47) Whoever you are, whom the gods Sîn and Šamaš name to be king and during whose reign that temple becomes dilapidated and who builds (it) anew, may he find an inscribed object bearing my name and not change (its position). May he anoint (it) with oil, make an offering, place (it) with an inscribed object bearing his (own) name, and return (it) to its place.

48) ^{d}UTU *ù* ^{d}*a-nu-ni-tum su-pu-ú-šu li-iš-mu-ú*
49) *li-im-gu-ra qí-bit-su i-da-a-šú lil-li-ku*
50) *li-šá-am-qí-ta ga-ri-šú* u$_{4}$-*mi-šam-ma a-na* ^{d}EN.ZU
51) *a-bi ba-ni-šu-un da-mi-iq-ta-šú li-iq-bu-ú*

iii 48–51) (Then,) may the god Šamaš and the goddess Anunītu hear his prayer(s), accept his request(s), march at his side, cut down his foe(s), and say good things about him daily to the god Sîn, the father who created them.

---

iii 28 and 31 ^{m}*šà-ga-rak-ti-šur*-ia-áš* "Šagarakti-Šuriaš": Most copies of this inscription write the ŠUR sign in this Kassite king's name with the BUR sign. As already pointed out by H. Schaudig (Inschriften Nabonids p. 119) and M. Worthington (Textual Criticism p. 77), the scribes who wrote out these manuscripts likely did not know the name of the Kassite king and, therefore, did not know how to write his name and, thus, hypercorrected *šur* to *bur*. Schaudig described the issue as follows: "Der anscheinend nicht mehr verstandene kassitische Königsname *Šagarakti-Šuriaš* (s. Index) gibt Gelegenheit zu vielerlei Irrtümern, die sich zum Teil durch leicht zu verwechselnde Zeichen(verbindungen) erklären lassen, wie: *-šur*$^{!}$(bur)-, *-àš*$^{!}$(iá) oder *-ga*$^{!}$(bi)-<*rak*>-. ... Die in den Textvertretern von (2.12) fast ausnahmslos durchgehende Fehlschreibung *-bur-* für *-šur-* wird auf einen Schreibfehler in der Vorlage zurückgehen, der aber von den damaligen Abschreibern nicht berichtigt wurde. Der Grund dafür wird darin liegen, daß ihnen weder der König, noch der kassitische Göttername ausreichend bekannt war. Dies ist wohl auch durch die Verwechselung des Götternamens Šuriaš mit Buriaš, der im Königsnamen Burna-Buriaš (s. Index) erscheint, begünstigt worden."

29

This three-column clay cylinder from Sippar bears an inscription that is similar to text no. 28 (Eḫulḫul Cylinder). In lieu of the report commemorating work on the temple of the goddess Ištar-Anunītu at Sippar-Anunītu, this inscription records the rebuilding of the Eulmaš temple at Agade, the earthly abode of the Ištar of Agade. It also describes the rebuilding of Eḫulḫul ("House which Gives Joy"), the temple of the god Sîn at Ḫarrān, and Ebabbar ("Shining House"), the temple of the god Šamaš at Sippar. This inscription was probably composed after Nabonidus' thirteenth (543) regnal year, perhaps during in his sixteenth year (540), when the temple of the moon-god at Ḫarrān was being renovated.

CATALOGUE

Museum Number	Registration Number	Provenance	cpn
BM 91087	82-5-22,604 + 82-5-22,605 + 82-5-22,606 + 82-5-22,622 + 82-5-22,646 + 82-5-22,647 + 82-5-22,655 + 82-5-22,658 + 82-5-22,665 + 82-5-22,666 + 82-5-22,670 + 82-5-22,686 + 82-5-22,739	Sippar	c

BIBLIOGRAPHY

2001 Schaudig, Inschriften Nabonids pp. 413, 426–436 and 756 figs. 22–27 (iii 20–48, edition; variants [to text no. 28]; iii 20, 29, 34, 41, 46, 57, collations)

TEXT

Col. i

Lacuna

1′) [*šu-ba-at ṭu-ub lìb-bi-šu ra-mu-ú*] ⸢*qé-reb-šu*$^{?}$⸣

2′) [*e-li* URU *ù* É *šá-a-šu lìb-bu-uš*] ⸢*i-zu-uz-ma*⸣

3′) [LÚ.ERIM-*man-da ú-šat-ba-am-ma* É *šu-a-tim ub*]-⸢*bi*⸣-*it-ma*

4′) [*ú-ša-lik-šu kar-mu-tu i*]-⸢*na pa*⸣-[*le-e*]-⸢*a ki-i-nim*⸣

5′) [^{d}EN.ZU EN GAL-*ú i-na*] ⸢*na-ra-am* LUGAL-*ti*⸣-*ia*

6′) [*a-na* URU *ù* É *šá-a-šu*] ⸢*is-li-mu*⸣ *ir-šu*-⸢*ú ta*⸣-*a-ri*

7′) [*i-na re-eš* LUGAL-*ú-ti*]-⸢*ia da-rí-ti ú-šab-ru-ʾi-in-ni šu-ut-ti*⸣

Lacuna

Lacuna

i 1′–4′a) [has occupied the residence of his happiness: His (Sîn's) heart] became angry [with the city and that temple] and [he raised up a barbarian horde (the Medes), and it dest]royed [that temple] and [turned it into ruins].

i 4′b–7′) [D]uring my legitimate r[eign, the god Sîn, the great lord, out of] love for my royal majesty, became reconciled [towards the city and that temple] (and) had mercy. [At the beginning of] my eternal [kingship], he showed me a dream.

Lacuna

1″) [...] (traces)

2″) [LÚ.ERIM-*man-da sa-ḫi-ir-šum-ma*] ⸢*pu-ug-gu-lu e-mu-qa-a-šu*⸣

3″) [^{d}AMAR.UTU-*ma i-ta-ma-a it*]-⸢*ti-ia*

Lacuna

i 1″–4″) [...] ... [a barbarian horde (the Medes) is all around it and] its forces are powerful." [The god Marduk spoke with] me, (saying): "(As for) the barbarian horde (the Medes) [that you spoke of, it, its

i 6′–7′ See the on-page note to text no. 28 (Eḫulḫul Cylinder) i 14–15 and Schaudig, Inschriften Nabonids pp. 77–78 §I.7.f.

um-man-ma-an-du⸣
4″) [*šá taq-bu-ú ša-a-šu* KUR-*šu*] ⸢*ù* LUGAL.MEŠ *a-lik i-di-šu ul i-ba-áš-ši*⸣
5″) [*i-na ša-lu-ul-ti* MU.AN.NA *i-na*] ⸢*ka-šá-du ú-šat-bu-niš-šum-ma*⸣
6″) [^{m}*ku-ra-áš* LUGAL KUR.*an-za-an* ARAD]-⸢*su ṣa-aḫ-ri*⸣
7″) [*i-na um-ma-ni-šu i-ṣu-tu*] ⸢*um-man-ma-an-du rap-šá-a-ti ú-sap-pi-iḫ*⸣
8″) [^{m}*iš-tu-me-gu* LUGAL *um-man-ma*]-⸢*an-du iṣ-bat-ma ka-mu-ut-su a-na* KUR-*šu il-qé*⸣
9″) [*a-mat* ^{d}EN GAL-*ú* ^{d}AMAR.UTU *ù* ^{d}]⸢EN⸣.ZU ⸢*na-an-na-ri* AN-*e ù* KI-*tim*⸣
10″) [*šá qí-bi-it-su-nu la in-nen-nu*]-⸢*ú a-na qí-bi-ti-šú-nu ṣir-ti*⸣
11″) [*ap-la-aḫ ak-ku-ud na-qut*]-⸢*ti ar-še-e*⸣-[*ma*]
12″) [*dul-lu-ḫu pa-nu-ú-a la e-gi*] ⸢*la a-še-et a-ḫa la ad-du ú-šat-ba-am-ma*⸣
13″) [*um-ma-ni-ia rap*]-⸢*šá-a-ti ul-tu* KUR.*ḫa-az-za-ti*⸣
14″) [*pa-aṭ* KUR.*mi-ṣir tam-tim e*]-⸢*li-ti a-bar-tu*$_4$ ÍD.BURANUN.KI⸣
15″) [*a-di tam-tim šap-li-ti*] ⸢LUGAL.MEŠ NUN.MEŠ GÌR.NÍTA.MEŠ⸣
16″) [*ù um-ma-ni-ia rap-šá-a*]-⸢*ti*⸣ *ša* ⸢^{d}EN.ZU ^{d}UTU *ù* ^{d}*iš-tar*⸣
17″) [EN.MEŠ-*e-a ia-ti*] ⸢*i-qí-pu-nu a-na e-pe-šu é-ḫúl-ḫúl*⸣
18″) [É ^{d}EN.ZU EN-*ia a-lik*] ⸢*i-di-ia šá qé-re-eb* URU.*ḫar-ra-nu*⸣
19″) [*šá* ^{m}AN.ŠÁR-*ba-an*-IBILA LUGAL KUR-*aš*]-⸢*šur*.KI DUMU ^{m}AN.ŠÁR-ŠEŠ-MU LUGAL KUR-*aš-šur*.KI⸣
20″) [NUN *a-lik maḫ-ri-ia i-pú-šu*] ⸢*i-na* ITI *šá-al-mu*⸣ [*i*]-⸢*na u*$_4$*-mu še-mi-i*⸣
21″) [*šá i-na bi-ri ú-ad-du-ni* ^{d}UTU] ⸢*ù* ^{d}IŠKUR⸣
22″) [*i-na né-me-qu* ^{d}*é-a ù* ^{d}*asal-lú-ḫi i*]-⸢*na ka-kù-gál-ú-tu*⸣
23″) [*i-na ši-ip-ri* ^{d}*kulla* EN *uš-šu*] ⸢*ù* SIG$_4$.ḪI.A⸣
24″) [*i-na* KÙ.BABBAR KÙ.GI NA$_4$ *ni-siq-ti šu-qu-ru-tu ḫi-biš*]-⸢*ti* GIŠ.TIR⸣
25″) [ŠIM.ḪI.A GIŠ.EREN *i-na ḫi-da-a-ti ù ri-šá-a-ti*]

Col. ii

1) [*e-li te-me-en*]-⸢*na šá* ^{m}AN.ŠÁR-*ba-an*-IBILA LUGAL KUR-*aš-šur*.KI⸣
2) [*ša te-me-en-na* ^{m}*šul*]-⸢*ma-an-a-šá-red*⸣ DUMU ^{m}AN.⸢ŠÁR-*na-ṣir*-IBILA⸣
3) [*i-mu-ru uš-šu*]-⸢*šu ad-di-ma ú-kin lib-na-at-su*⸣
4) [*i-na* KAŠ GEŠTIN Ì].⸢GIŠ LÀL *šal-la-ar-šu am-ḫa-aṣ-ma*⸣
5) [*ab-lu-ul ta-ra*]-⸢*aḫ-ḫu-uš*⸣ *e-li šá* LUGAL *ab-bé-e-a*
6) [*ép-še-ti-šu*] ⸢*ú*⸣-*dan-nin*-⸢*ma*⸣ *ú-na-ak-ki-lu* ⸢*ši-pí-ir-šu*⸣
7) [É.KUR *šu-a-tim*] ⸢*ul-tu te-me-en-<ni>-šu a-di gaba-dib-bi-šu*⸣
8) [*e-eš-ši-iš*] ⸢*ab-ni-ma ú-šak-lil ši-pí-ir-šu*⸣

land], and the kings who march at its side will not exist."

i 5″–8″) [When (my) third year] arrived, they had [Cyrus (II), king of the land Anšan, a] young [servant of] his (Astyages'), rise up against him (Astyages), and he (Cyrus) scattered the extensive barbarian horde (the Medes) [with his small body of troops]. He seized [Astyages (Ištumegu), king of the barbarian] horde (the Medes), and took him to his land as a captive.

i 9″–12″a) [The word of the great divine lord, the god Marduk, and the god] Sîn, the light of heaven and earth, [whose command(s) cannot be chang]ed — by their exalted command, [I became frightened, worried, (and) an]xious, [and my face was haggard].

i 12″b–19″) [I was not lazy], negligent, (or) careless. I raised up [my ex]tensive [troops] from the land (of the city) Gaza [(on) the border of Egypt (and) the U]pper [Sea] on the other bank of the Euphrates River [to the Lower Sea] — kings, nobles, governors, [and my extens]ive [troops], whom the deities Sîn, Šamaš, and Ištar, [my lords], had entrusted [to me] — to (re)build Eḫulḫul, [the temple of the god Sîn, my lord, the one who marches] at my side, which is inside the city Ḫarrān, [which Ashurbanipal, king of As]syria, son of Esarhaddon, king of Assyria, [a ruler who came before me, had built].

i 20″–ii 3) In a favorable month, [o]n an auspicious day [that the gods Šamaš] and Adad [had revealed to me through divination, using the wisdom of the gods Ea and Asalluḫi, th]rough the craft of the incantation priest, [(and) with the craft of the god Kulla, the lord of foundation(s)] and brickwork, [during joyous celebrations], I laid its [foundations in silver, gold, a selection of precious stones, (and) crushed piec]es of wood [(and) cedar aromatics, (precisely) on the founda]tion(s) of Ashurbanipal, king of Assyria, [who had seen the foundation(s) of Shal]maneser (III), son of Ashurnasirpal (II), and (thereby) I secured its brickwork.

ii 4–8) I blended its *šallaru*-plaster [with beer, wine, o]il, (and) honey, and [mixed (it into)] its [revet]ment. I made [its structure] stronger than that of the kings, my ancestors, and had its construction more expertly executed. I built [that temple anew] from its foundat<ion>(s) to its crenellations and completed its construction.

9) [GIŠ.ÙR GIŠ].⸢EREN⸣ ṣi-ru-⸢tu ta-ar-bi-it URU.ḫa-ma-nu⸣
10) ú-ša-at-ri-iṣ ṣe-ru-uš-šu GIŠ.IG.MEŠ GIŠ.EREN
11) ⸢ša⸣ i-ri-is-si-na ṭa-a-⸢bi ú-ra-at-ta-a i-na KÁ.MEŠ-šu⸣
12) ⸢KÙ⸣.BABBAR ù KÙ.GI É.GAR$_8$.MEŠ-šu ⸢ú-ša-al-bi-iš-ma⸣
13) ⸢ú-ša⸣-an-bi-iṭ ⸢ša-aš-ša-ni-iš⸣

ii 9–13) I had immense [beams of c]edar, (which were) grown on Mount Amanus, stretched out over it (for its roof). I had doors of cedar, whose scent is sweet, installed in its gates. I had its walls clad with silver and gold and made (them) radiate like the sun.

14) ⸢ri-i-mu za-ḫa-le⸣-e eb-bi ⸢mu-nak-kip ga-ri-ia⸣
15) ⸢ka-ad-ri-iš uš-zi-iz i⸣-na at-ma-ni-šu
16) ⸢2⸣ ^{d}làḫ-mu ⸢eš-ma-ru-ú sa-pi-in⸣ a-a-bi-⸢ia⸣
17) ⸢i⸣-na KÁ ṣi-⸢it ^{d}UTU-ši ZAG ù GÙB⸣ [ú-šar]-⸢ši-id⸣

ii 14–17) I stationed a wild bull of shiny *zaḫalû*-metal, which aggressively gores my foes (to death), in his (Sîn's) inner sanctum. [I firmly plan]ted two long-haired heroes of *ešmarû*-metal, who overwhelm my enem(ies), in the Gate of the Rising Sun, (on) the right and left.

18) ⸢qá⸣-at ^{d}EN.ZU ⸢^{d}nin-gal ^{d}nusku ù ^{d}sa⸣-[dàr-nun]-⸢na⸣
19) EN.⸢MEŠ⸣-e-a ⸢ul-tu šu-an-na.KI URU LUGAL-ú-ti-ia⸣
20) aṣ-⸢ba⸣-at-ma ⸢i⸣-[na ḫi]-⸢da-a-ti ù ri-šá-a-ti⸣
21) ⸢šu-ba⸣-at ṭu-⸢ub⸣ [lìb-bi] ⸢qé-er-ba-šu ú-še-ši-ib⸣

ii 18–21) I took the deities Sîn, Ningal, Nusku, and Sa[darnun]na, my lords, by the hand, (leading them out) of Šuanna (Babylon), the city of my royal majesty, and I had (them) reside inside the residence of (their) hap[pines] du[ring jo]yous celebrations.

22) UDU.SÍSKUR taš-⸢ri-iḫ-ti eb⸣-bi ma-ḫar-šu-nu aq-[qí]-⸢ma⸣
23) ⸢ú⸣-šá-am-ḫi-ir kad-ra-a-⸢a é⸣-ḫúl-ḫúl re-⸢eš-ti ú⸣-[mál]-⸢li-ma⸣
24) ⸢URU⸣.ḫar-ra-nu a-na ⸢pa-aṭ gi-im-ri-šu⸣
25) ⸢ki⸣-ma ṣe-et ⸢ITI ú-nam-mi-ir ša-ru-ru-šu⸣

ii 22–25) I offe[red] pure, sumptuous offerings before them (and) presented (them) with my gifts. I f[ill]ed Eḫulḫul with joy and (then) made the radiance of the city Ḫarrān, to its full extent, shine like the appearance of the moon.

26) [^{d}]⸢EN⸣.ZU ⸢LUGAL DINGIR.MEŠ⸣ šá ⸢AN-e⸣ ù KI-⸢tim šá ul-la-nu-uš-šu⸣
27) ⸢URU ù KUR la in-nam-du-ú la i-tur-ru áš-ru-uš-šu⸣
28) (traces)
29) SIG$_5$.MEŠ URU ù É šá-⸢a⸣-šu (traces) [...]

ii 26–29) O Sîn, king of the gods of heaven and earth, without whom no city or land can be founded or restored (lit. "returned to its place"), *when you enter Eḫulḫul, the temple* (*that is*) *the residence you desired*, may good thing(s) about the city and that temple *be placed* [*on your lips*].

30) DINGIR.MEŠ a-ši-⸢bu-tu šá AN⸣-[e ù KI-tim]
31) li-ik-ta-ra-⸢bu É ^{d}EN.ZU a-bi ba⸣-[ni-šu]-⸢un⸣

ii 30–31) May the gods who reside in heaven [and on earth] constantly bless the temple of the god Sîn, the father who crea[ted th]em.

32) ia-a-ti ⸢^{d}AG-NÍ.TUKU LUGAL TIN.TIR.KI mu-šak⸣-[lil É šu-a]-⸢tim⸣
33) ^{d}EN.ZU LUGAL DINGIR.MEŠ šá ⸢AN⸣-e ù ⸢KI-tim i-na ni-iš i-ni-šu SIG$_5$.MEŠ⸣
34) ḫa-di-iš lip-⸢pal⸣-sa-⸢an-ni-ma ár-ḫi-šá-am-ma i⸣-[na ni-ip-ḫi ù ri-ba]
35) li-dam-mi-⸢iq⸣ it-ta-tu-ú-⸢a UD.MEŠ-ia li-šá-ri-ik⸣
36) MU.AN.NA.MEŠ-⸢ia⸣ li-šá-an-di-⸢il li-ki-in pa-lu-ú-a⸣
37) na-ak-ru-ti-ia ⸢lik-šu-ud za-ma-ni-ia li-šá-am-qí-it⸣

ii 32–38a) (As for) me, Nabonidus, king of Babylon, the one who compl[eted th]is [temple], may the god Sîn, king of the gods of heaven and earth, look with pleasure upon me with his favorable glance and monthly, a[t sunrise and sunset], make my signs auspicious. May he lengthen my days, increase my years, (and) make my reign endure. May he conquer my enemies, cut down those hostile to me, (and) flatten my foes.

38) ⸢li-is-pu-un⸣ ga-ri-⸢ia ^{d}nin-gal AMA DINGIR GAL.GAL⸣
39) i-na ma-⸢ḫar ^{d}⸣EN.ZU ⸢na-ar-mi-šu li-iq-ba-a ba-ni-ti⸣

ii 38b–39) May the goddess Ningal, mother of the great gods, speak laudatory word(s) about me in the presence of the god Sîn, her beloved.

40) ^{d}UTU ù ⸢^{d}⸣iš-tar ⸢ṣi-it lìb-bi-šú na-am-ra⸣
41) a-na ^{d}EN.⸢ZU a-bi ba-ni-šu-un li-iq-bu-ú SIG$_5$⸣-[ti]
42) ⸢^{d}nusku⸣ [su-uk-kal]-⸢lum ṣi-i-ri su-pe-e-a li-iš-me⸣-[e-ma]

ii 40–43a) May the god Šamaš and the goddess Ištar, his bright offspring, say good thing(s) abo[ut me] to the god Sîn, the father who created them. May the god Nusku, [the] exalted [vizi]er, hea[r] my prayers [and] intercede (on my behalf).

43) ⸢*li*⸣-[*iṣ-ba-at*] ⸢*a-bu-tu mu-sa-ru-ú ši-ṭi-ir*⸣ [*šu-um*]
44) ⸢*ša*⸣ mAN.ŠÁR-*ba-an*-IBILA LUGAL KUR-*aš-šur*.KI *a*-⸢*mu*⸣-[*ur-ma*]
45) *la ú-nak-ki-ir* Ì.⸢GIŠ *ap*⸣-*šu-uš* UDU.⸢SÍSKUR⸣ [*aq-qí*]
46) *it-ti mu-sa*-⸢*re*⸣-*e*-⸢*a*⸣ *áš-ku*-⸢*un*⸣-[*ma ú-te-er áš-ru-uš-šu*]
47) *a-na* dUTU ⸢*da*⸣-*a-a-nu* ⸢*šá* AN-*e ù* KI-*tim é-babbar-ra* É-*su*⸣
48) *šá qé-re-eb* ⸢ZIMBIR.KI *šá* mdAG-NÍG.GUB-ÙRU LUGAL *maḫ-ri i-pu-šu-ma*⸣
49) *te-me-en-šu la*-⸢*bi-ri ú-ba-ʾu-ú-ma la i-mu-ru*⸣
50) É *šu-a-tim i*-⸢*pu-uš-ma i-na* 45 MU.AN.NA.MEŠ⸣
51) *ša* É *šu-a-tim i*-⸢*qu-pu i-ga-ru-šu ak-ku-ud áš-ḫu-ut*⸣
52) *na-qú-ut-ti* ⸢*ar-še-e-ma dul-lu-ḫu pa-nu-ú-a*⸣
53) *a-di* dUTU ⸢*ul-tu qé-re-bi-šu ú-še-ṣu-ú*⸣
54) *ú-še-ši-bu* ⸢*i-na* É *ša-nim-ma*⸣
55) É ⸢*šu-a-tim ad-ke-e-ma te-me-en-šu la-bi-ri*⸣
56) ⸢*ú*⸣-*ba-ʾi*-⸢*ma* 18 KÙŠ *qaq-qa-ri ú-šap-pil-ma*⸣
57) *te-me-en-na* m*na-ra*-⸢*am*-dEN.ZU DUMU mLUGAL-GI.NA⸣
58) ⸢*ša*⸣ 3 LIM 2 ME MU.AN.⸢NA.MEŠ *ma-na-ma* LUGAL *a-lik maḫ-ri-ia*⸣
59) *la i-mu-ru* dUTU ⸢EN GAL-*ú é-babbar-ra* É *šu-bat ṭu-ub lìb-bi-šu*⸣
60) *ú-kal-lim-an-ni ia-a*-⸢*ši i-na* ITI.DU$_6$ *i-na* ITI *šal-mu i-na* UD ŠE.GA⸣
61) *ša i-na bi-ri* ⸢*ú-ad-du-ni* dUTU *ù* dIŠKUR⸣
62) *i-na* KÙ.BABBAR KÙ.GI* ⸢NA$_4$ *ni-siq-ti šu-qu-ru-tu ḫi-biš-ti* GIŠ.TIR⸣
63) ŠIM.ḪI.A GIŠ.⸢EREN⸣ *i*-⸢*na ḫi-da-a-ti ù ri-šá-a-ti*⸣
64) *e-li* ⸢*te-me*⸣-*en-na* m*na-ra*-⸢*am*-dEN.ZU DUMU mLUGAL-GI.NA⸣
65) ŠU.SI ⸢*la*⸣ [*a*]-*ṣe-e* ⸢ŠU.SI *la e-re-<bi> ú-ki-in lib-na-at-su*⸣
66) 5 LIM GIŠ.⸢EREN *dan-nu-tu a-na ṣu-lu-li-šú ú-šat-ri-iṣ*⸣
67) [*x x* (*x*)] *x* GIŠ.EREN *ṣi-ra-a-ti* ⸢*as-kup-pu ù nu-ku-še-e*⸣

Col. iii

1) ⸢*i-na* KÁ.KÁ-*šu ú-ra-at-ti*⸣
2) ⸢*é-babbar-ra a-di é-kun$_4$-an-kù-ga ziq-qur-ra-ti*⸣-[*šú*]
3) ⸢*eš-ši-iš e-pu-uš-ma ú-šak-lil ši-pí-ir*⸣-[*šu*]
4) *qa-at* dUTU EN-⸢*ia aṣ-bat-ma i-na ḫi-da-a-ti ù ri-šá*⸣-[*a-ti*]
5) *šu-ba-at ṭu-<ub> lìb-bi* ⸢*qé-er-ba-šu ú-še-ši*⸣-[*ib*]
6) *ši-ṭi-ir* ⸢*šu-um šá* m*na-ra-am*-d30 DUMU mLUGAL-GI.NA *a-mu*⸣-[*ur-ma*]
7) *la ú-nak*-⸢*ki-ir* Ì.GIŠ *ap-šu-uš* UDU.SÍSKUR⸣ [*aq-qí*]
8) ⸢*it*⸣-*ti mu-sa*-⸢*re-e-a áš-ku-un-ma ú-te-er*⸣

ii 43b–46) I fou[nd] an inscribed object bearing [the name of] Ashurbanipal, king of Assyria, [and] I did not change (its position). I anointed (it) with oil, [made] an offering, placed (it) with my (own) inscribed object, [and returned (it) to its place].

ii 47–51a) For the god Šamaš, judge of heaven and earth: (With regard to) Ebabbar, his temple that is inside Sippar, which Nebuchadnezzar (II), a king of the past had built and whose original foundation(s) he had sought out but did not find — he (Nebuchadnezzar) built (it anyway) and, in (only) forty-five years, the walls of that temple buckled.

ii 51b–60a) I became worried, afraid, (and) anxious, and my face was haggard. While I had the god Šamaš brought out of it (Ebabbar) (and) had (him) reside in another temple, I removed that temple and sought out its original foundation(s). Then, I dug down eighteen cubits into the earth and the foundation(s) of Narām-Sîn, (grand)son of Sargon, which (for) 3,200 years none of the king(s) who came before me had found — the god Šamaš, the great lord, revealed to me (the original) Ebabbar, the temple (that is) the residence of his happiness.

ii 60b–65) In the month Tašrītu (VII), in a favorable month, on an auspicious day that the gods Šamaš and Adad had revealed to me through divination, during joyous celebrations, I secured its brickwork in silver, gold, a selection of precious stones, (and) crushed pieces of wood (and) cedar aromatics, (precisely) on the foundation(s) of Narām-Sîn, (grand)son of Sargon, not (even) a fingerbreadth [o]utside or insi<de> (of them).

ii 66–iii 1) I had 5,000 strong cedar(s) stretched out for its roof. I installed immense [*doors*] *of* cedar, (threshold) slab(s), (and) *nukuššû*-fittings in its gates.

iii 2–5) I built anew Ebabbar, together with Ekunankuga, [its] ziggurat, and completed [its] construction. I took the god Šamaš, my lord, by the hand and had (him) resi[de] inside it, the residence of (his) happiness, during joyous celeb[rations].

iii 6–8) I fo[und] an inscription of Narām-Sîn, (grand)-son of Sargon, [and] I did not change (its position). I anointed (it) with oil, [made] an offering, placed (it) with my (own) inscribed object, and returned (it) to [its place].

[áš-ru-uš-šu]
9) ^{d}UTU EN GAL *šá* AN-*e* ⸢*ù* KI⸣-*ṭim nu-ú-[úr* DINGIR].MEŠ *ab-bé-*⸢*e-šu*⸣
10) *ṣi-it lìb-bi* ⸢*ša* ^{d}EN.ZU *ù* ^{d}*nin-gal*⸣
11) *a-na é-babbar-ra* É *na-*⸢*ra*⸣*-[mi]-*⸢*ka i-na e-re-bi-ka*⸣
12) BÁRA-*ka da-ru-*⸢*ú*⸣ *[i-na ra-mé]-*⸢*e-ka ia-ti* ^{d}AG-NÍ.TUKU LUGAL TIN.TIR.KI⸣
13) NUN *za-nin-*⸢*ka mu-ṭi-ib lìb-bi-ka e-pí-iš ku-um-mi-ka ṣi-i-ri*⸣
14) ⸢*e-ep-še-tu-ú-a dam-qa-a-ti ḫa-di-iš na-ap-li-is-ma*⸣
15) ⸢*u*$_{4}$⸣*-mi-ša-am* ⸢*i-na ni-ip-ḫu ù ri-bi i-na šá-ma-mi ù qaq-qa-ri*⸣
16) *du-um-mi-iq* ⸢*it-ta-tu-ú*⸣*-[a]*
17) *un-nin-ni-*⸢*ia le-qé-e-ma mu-gu-ur ta-aṣ-li-ti*⸣
18) ⸢GIŠ.NÍG.GIDRU *ù ši-bir-ri ki-i-nim šá tu-šat-mi-ḫu qa-tu-ú-a*⸣
19) ⸢*lu-bé-el a-na du-ur da-a-ri*⸣
20) ⸢*a-na* ^{d}INANNA *a-kà-dè*.KI *be-let* DINGIR.DINGIR⸣ x x x x x
21) ⸢*be-let ta-ḫa-za mu-šal-li*$^{?}$*-ma*$^{?}$*-at*$^{?}$ *qí-bi-it* ^{d}EN.LÍL *a-bi*⸣*-[šu]*
22) ⸢*sa-pi-na-at na-ak-ru mu-ḫal-li-qa-at ra-ag*⸣*-[gu]*
23) ⸢*a-li-ka-at maḫ-ri ša* DINGIR.MEŠ *šá i-na*⸣ x x x [x x]
24) x x x x x [x] x x x
25) x x x x x [x] ⸢I LI⸣ [x] x x x
26) x x x x x [x x] x x x
27) x x x x x [x x] x x x
28) ⸢*te-me-en-šu la-bí-ri*⸣ x x x [x x] x x x
29) x x x x ⸢*te-me-en-na* ^{m}*na-ra-am*⸣-[^{d}EN].⸢ZU⸣ [x]
30) ⸢*te-me-en-šu la*⸣*-bi-ri* ⸢*da-rí-a a-mu-ur*⸣*-[ma]*
31) ŠU.SI ⸢*la*⸣ *a-*⸢*ṣe-e* ŠU.SI *la e-re-bi*⸣
32) *e-li te-me-en-na* ⸢*ša-a-šu uš*$^{?}$⸣*-x* [x] x x x
33) ⸢É *šu-a-tim e-eš-ši-iš e*⸣*-x* x x [x] x x x
34) [^{d}]⸢INANNA$^{?}$ *a-kà-dè*.KI GAŠAN *ra-bi-ti* GAŠAN *ta-ḫa-zi*⸣
35) ⸢*mu-šal-li-ma-at qí-bi-ti* ^{d}EN.LÍL *a-bi-šu*⸣
36) ⸢*sa*⸣*-[pi]-*⸢*na-at na-ak-ru mu-ḫal-li-qa-at rag-gu*$^{?}$⸣
37) *[a-li]-*⸢*ka-at maḫ*⸣*-[ri]* ⸢*ša*⸣ DINGIR.⸢DINGIR⸣
38) *[ú-šar]-*⸢*ma*$^{?}$⸣*-a [šu]-*⸢*bat*$^{?}$*-su*$^{?}$⸣
39) *[sat-tuk-ku ù nin-da-bé]-e e-li šá maḫ-ri*
40) *[ú-šá-te-er-ma ú]-*⸢*ki-in ma-ḫar-ša*$^{?}$⸣
41) *[at-ta* ^{d}INANNA] ⸢*a-kà-dè*.KI GAŠAN *ra-bi-ti*⸣
42) *[a-na* É *šu-a]-*⸢*tim ḫa-di-iš i-na e-<re>-bi-ka*⸣
43) *[ép-še-tu]-*⸢*ú-a* SIG$_{5}$.MEŠ *ḫa-di-iš na-ap-li-si*⸣*-[ma]*
44) ⸢*ár-ḫi-šam-ma i-na*⸣ ^{d}UTU.È *ù* ^{d}UTU.⸢ŠÚ.A⸣
45) ⸢*a-na* ^{d}30 *a-bi a-li-di-ka šu*⸣*-[uq]-ri-*⸢*bi* SIG$_{5}$*-tì*⸣
46) ⸢^{d}*a-nu-ni-tum*⸣ *be-el-*⸢*ti ṣir-tum*⸣
47) ⸢*u*$_{4}$*-mi-šam*$^{?}$*-ma i-na maḫ-ri* ^{d}EN⸣.[LÍL]
48) x x x x x ⸢*da-mi-iq-ti*⸣
49) ⸢*man-nu at-ta ša* ^{d}30 *ù* ^{d}UTU⸣
50) ⸢*a-na* LUGAL*-ú-tu i-nam-bu-šu-ma*⸣

iii 9–19) O Šamaš, great lord of heaven and earth, ligh[t of the god]s, his fathers, offspring of the god Sîn and the goddess Ningal, when you enter Ebabbar, your belo[ved] temple, (and) [when] you [occup]y your eternal dais — (as for) me, Nabonidus, king of Babylon, the prince who provides for you, the one who pleases your heart, the one who built your exalted cella — look with pleasure upon my good deeds and daily, at sunrise and sunset, make [my] signs auspicious in heaven and (on) earth. Receive my prayers (and) accept my petition(s) so that I may rule forever (with) the scepter and legitimate rod that you had let my hands grasp.

iii 20–23) For the goddess Ištar of Agade, lady of the gods, ... the lady of battle who fully carries out the command(s) of the god Enlil, [her] father, the one who overwhelms enemies (and) destroys the wick[ed], the one who marches at front of the gods, (the one) *during/in* ... [...]

iii 24–27) (No translation possible)

iii 28–33) its original foundation(s) ... [...] ... I saw the foundation(s) of Narām-[Sî]n, [(...)], its original, eternal foundation, [and] ... (precisely) on th(ose) foundation(s), not (even) a fingerbreadth outside or inside (of them). I *(re)built* that temple anew (and) ...

iii 34–40) *[I had]* the goddess Ištar of Agade, great lady, the lady of battle who fully carries out the command(s) of the god Enlil, her father, the one who ov[erwh]elms enemies (and) destroys the *wicked*, [the one who ma]rches at fr[ont] of the gods, *[dwe]ll* in *her [resi]dence.* [I made *sattukku*-offerings and *nindab*]*û*-offerings [more plentiful] than before [and] (re)confirmed (them) in *her* presence.

iii 41–45) [You, O Ištar of] Agade, great lady, when you e<n>ter [th]is [temple] with pleasure, look with pleasure upon my [good deed]s [and], monthly, at sunrise and sunset, p[eti]tion the god Sîn, the father who engendered you, about good things for me.

iii 46–48) O Anunītu, exalted lady, *speak* good things about me in the presence of the god En[lil] daily.

iii 49–56) Whoever you are, whom the gods Sîn and Šamaš name to be king and during whose reign that

51) ⸢*i-na pa-le-e-šu* É *šu-a-tim*⸣
52) ⸢*in-na-ḫu e-eš-ši-iš ip-pu-šu*⸣
53) ⸢*mu-sa-ru-ú ši-ṭi-ir šu-mi-ia li-mur-ma*⸣
54) ⸢*la ú-nak-ka-ar* Ì.GIŠ *lip-šu-uš* UDU.SÍSKUR *li*⸣-[*iq-qí*]
55) ⸢*it-ti mu-sa-re-e ši-ṭi-ir šu-mi-šu*⸣
56) ⸢*li-iš-ku-un-ma lu-te-er áš-ru-uš-šu*⸣
57) ⸢^{d}INANNA *a-kà-dè*.KI *ù* ^{d}*a-nu-ni-tum*⸣
58) ⸢*su-pu-ú-šu li-iš-mu-ú*⸣
59) ⸢*li-im-gu-ra qí-bi-it-su*⸣
60) ⸢*i-da-a-šu li-il-li-ka*⸣
61) ⸢*u*$_4$*-mi-šam-ma a-na* ^{d}30 *a-bi ba-ni-šu-un*⸣
62) ⸢*da-mi-iq-ta-šu li-iq-ba-a*'⸣

temple becomes dilapidated and who builds (it) anew, may he find an inscribed object bearing my name and not change (its position). May he anoint (it) with oil, [make] an offering, place (it) with an inscribed object bearing his (own) name, and return (it) to its place.

iii 57–62) (Then,) may the goddesses Ištar of Agade and Anunītu hear his prayer(s), accept his request(s), march at his side, and say good things about him daily to the god Sîn, the father who created them.

30

A fragment from the lower left corner of a clay tablet preserves part of an Akkadian inscription of a Babylonian king, almost certainly Nabonidus, recording work undertaken on Ebabbar ("Shining House"), the temple of the god Šamaš at Sippar. Although Nabonidus' name does not appear on this damaged tablet, the attribution to him is fairly certain since the text states that Ebabbar was built anew directly on top of the foundations laid by the Sargonic king Narām-Sîn (2254–2218); Nabonidus is the only Neo-Babylonian king to make this claim. Moreover, the language of the inscriptions duplicates (with variation) other inscriptions of his from Sippar.

CATALOGUE

Museum Number	Registration Number	Provenance	cpn
BM 76825	AH 83-1-18,2197	Sippar	c

COMMENTARY

The attribution to Nabonidus, rather than some other Neo-Babylonian king, is based on the mention of Narām-Sîn of Agade as a previous builder of the Ebbabar temple at Sippar in obv. 4′ and on parallels with other inscriptions of Nabonidus from Sippar (and Marad). For obv. 2′, compare text no. 19 (Eigikalama Cylinder) ii 16–20; for obv. 6′–7′a, compare text no. 28 (Eḫulḫul Cylinder) iii 1; for obv. 7′b–rev. 2, compare text no. 23 (Ebabbar Cylinder) iii 7–9; and, for rev. 4–7, compare text no. 28 iii 39–40. The proposed restorations are generally based on those inscriptions.

BIBLIOGRAPHY

1988 Leichty, Sippar 3 p. 72 (study)

TEXT

Obv.
Lacuna
1′) [...] *x x* [...]

2′) ⸢*a-na* ^{d}UTU EN⸣ GAL EN-*ia at*-⸢*ta*$^{?}$⸣-[*ʾi-id-ma*$^{?}$]
3′) *é-babbar-ra* É-*su ša qé-reb* [ZIMBIR.KI]
4′) *e-li te-me-en-na na-ra-am*-[^{d}30]
5′) LUGAL *ma-aḫ-ri e-eš-ši-iš* ⸢*e*⸣-[*pu-uš*]
6′) GIŠ.EREN.MEŠ *dan-nu-tu a-na* ⸢*ṣu*⸣-[*lu-li-šú*]
Bottom
7′) *ú-šat-ri-iṣ x* [...]
Rev.
1) GIŠ.GAN.DU$_{7}$ *giš-ká*-⸢*na-ku ù*$^{?}$⸣ [GIŠ.IG.MEŠ$^{?}$]
2) GIŠ.EREN *ṣi-ra-a-tim e*-⸢*ma*⸣ [É.MEŠ$^{?}$-(*šú*$^{?}$)]
3) *ù* KÁ.MEŠ-*šu ú-šar-ši*-[*id*]
4) [^{d}]⸢UTU⸣ EN *ṣi-i-ri a*-⸢*na*⸣ [É *šu-a-ti*]
5) [*ḫa*]-⸢*di*⸣-*iš i-na e*-⸢*re*⸣-[*bi-ka*]
6) [*ép-še*]-⸢*tu*⸣-*ú-a da**-⸢*am*⸣-[*qa-a-ta*$^{?}$]
7) [*ḫa-di-iš*] ⸢*na*⸣-*ap-li*-[*is-ma*]
8) [...] *x e x* [...]
Lacuna

Lacuna
Obv. 1′) [...] ... [...]

Obv. 2′–Rev. 3) *I was at*[*tentive*] to the god Šamaš, the great lord, my lord, [*and*] I [built] anew Ebabbar, his temple that is inside [Sippar], on the (original) foundation(s) of Narām-[Sîn], a king of the past. I had strong cedar(s) stretched out for [its] r[oof]. At eac[h of (*its*) *rooms*] and its gates, I securely fastened [...], architrave(s), *giškanakku*(s), a[*nd doors*] of immense cedar(s).

Rev. 4–8) [O Ša]maš, exalted lord, when [you] ent[er this temple with ple]asure, loo[k with pleasure upon] my g[ood de]eds [and ...] ... [...]

Lacuna

31

Two bricks found in the temple of the god Šamaš at Sippar, Ebabbar (“Shining House”), bear a short, Akkadian inscription of Nabonidus. The inscription, which is in archaizing Neo-Babylonian script, is stamped on the face of the two bricks. The three-line text gives only the king’s name and titulary.

CATALOGUE

Ex.	Museum Number	Excavation Number	Provenance	Lines Preserved	cpn
1	—	1652/4	Sippar, Ebabbar	1–3	(p)
2	—	—	As ex. 1	1–3	p

30 rev. 8 Possibly read this line as [*še*]-⸢*bé*⸣-*e* ⸢*li*⸣-[*it-tu-ti*] “[the attainm]ent of v[ery old age].”

COMMENTARY

The master text is a conflation of both exemplars. Following RINBE editorial practices, no score of this brick inscription is given on Oracc. No minor (orthographic) variants are attested and, therefore, no variants are given in the critical apparatus at the back of the book. Although the present whereabouts of the bricks are not known, both bricks could be (fully or partially) collated from photographs published in Sumer 46 (1989–90).

BIBLIOGRAPHY

1989–90 Al-Ǧādir and ʿAbd-Allāh, Sumer 46 pp. 87–88, 90 [Arabic section] and pl. 28 (exs. 1–2, photo, study)

2001 Schaudig, Inschriften Nabonids p. 335 no. 1.1[a] (exs. 1–2, edition)

TEXT

1) ᵈAG-I LUGAL ⸢TIN.TIR⸣.KI
2) *za-nin é-*⸢*sag*⸣*-íl*
3) ⸢*ù*⸣ *é-zi-da*

1–3) Nabonidus, king of Babylon, the one who provides for Esagil and Ezida.

32

Numerous double-column clay cylinders discovered at Ur bear an Akkadian inscription of Nabonidus recording his restoration of the ziggurat of the moon-god Sîn in that city, Elugalgalgasisa ("House of the King who Lets Counsel Flourish"). The text, which on all known copies is written in contemporary Neo-Babylonian script, states that Nabonidus had Ur's ziggurat rebuilt according to its ancient plan, the one established by the founder of the Ur III Dynasty, Ur-Namma (2112–2095), and his son, Šulgi (2094–2047). Although none of the cylinders bear a date, scholars generally date this text after Nabonidus' thirteenth (543) regnal year, perhaps at the very end of his reign, in either his sixteenth (540) or seventeenth (539) year as king; see Beaulieu, Nabonidus p. 42 and Schaudig, Inschriften Nabonids p. 48. In scholarly literature, this text is referred to as "Nabonidus Cylinder II, I," "[Nabonidus] Inscription 17," and the "Elugalgalgasisa Cylinder."

CATALOGUE

Ex.	Museum Number	Excavation/ Registration No.	Provenance	Lines Preserved	cpn
1	BM 91125	K 1689	Ur, ziggurat, second tier, corner, in a brick capsule	i 1–ii 26	c
2	BM 91126	K 1690	As ex. 1	i 1–ii 26	c
3	BM 91127	K 1691	As ex. 1	i 1–ii 26	c
4	BM 91128	K 1692	As ex. 1	i 1–ii 26	c
5	Bod AB 239	W-B 4	Ur, ziggurat	—	c
6	IM 63999	—	Ur, ziggurat, second tier, near the middle staircase, in a brick capsule	i 1–ii 26	c
7	IM 66417	—	Ur, ziggurat, second tier, in debris	i 1–ii 26	(p)

8	IM 66418	—	Ur, ziggurat, first tier, in debris	i 1–ii 26	(p)
9	IM 65869	—	As ex. 7	i 1–ii 26	c
10	IM 65870	—	As ex. 7	i 1–ii 26	c
11	IM 65871	—	As ex. 7	i 1–ii 26	c
12	IM 73984	—	Probably Ur, ziggurat	i 1–ii 26	p
13	MS 1846/3	—	As ex. 12	i 1–ii 26	p
14	CBS 15618	U 1154	As ex. 12	ii 10–26	p

Figure 16. BM 91128 (Nabonidus no. 32 ex. 4), double-column clay cylinder inscribed with a text referred to as the Elugalgalgasisa Cylinder Inscription, which records the renovation of the ziggurat of the moon-god at Ur. © Trustees of the British Museum.

COMMENTARY

In Schaudig, Inschriften Nabonids (pp. 351–352), ex. 1 (BM 91125) is used as the master text. However, because the line arrangement of ex. 1 diverges significantly from most of the other catalogued exemplars (see below), the authors have decided to base the master text and lineation of the edition presented here on ex. 2 (BM 91126). The arrangement of text varies between the copies of the inscription. The distribution of the text in cols. i and ii in exs. 1, 3–5 and 7–13 is identical to that of ex. 2, but that of ex. 6 (IM 63999) differs from the other known exemplars: col. i of this copy of the Elugalgalgasisa Cylinder Inscription ends with ex. 2 i 24a. A score is presented on Oracc and the minor (orthographic) variants are given in the critical apparatus at the back of the book. Because exs. 7 and 8 were not available for firsthand study in the Iraq Museum (Baghdad) and because no complete copy, photograph, or transliteration of these two exemplars have even been published, the partial transliterations of IM 66417 and IM 66418 given in the score are based on the lines visible in the published photographs (As-Siwani, Sumer 20 [1973] unnumbered plate after p. 76).

Two fingernail marks are impressed in the middle of the left sides of exs. 4 (BM 91128), 12 (IM 73984), and 13 (MS 1846/3); the base is oriented towards the uninscribed space dividing the first and final lines of cols. i and ii. These impressions form a crescent moon, which, as Schaudig (Inschriften Nabonids p. 350) has already suggested, might have served as a visual representation of the inscribed objects' consecration to the moon-god Sîn, the divine owner of Elugalgalgasisa, in whose structure these three cylinders were deposited. These three exemplars are not only nearly identical in size (9.3–9.5 cm long with a diameter of 4.5–4.9 cm), but also distribute text in the exact same manner. In general, the orthographies of exs. 4, 12, and 13 match that of ex. 2; a handful of minor variants are attested. Based on orthography and palaeography, all three cylinders were probably inscribed by one and the same person. It is possible that ex. 8 (IM 66418) was also prepared by this same scribe since its size and orthography are nearly identical to those of exs. 4, 12, and 13. Because the object was not available for firsthand study in the Iraq Museum (Baghdad), the authors cannot prove that IM 66418 was inscribed by the scribe who wrote out the inscription on BM 91128, IM 73984, and MS 1846/3. The orthographies of exs. 5 (Bod AB 239), 9 (IM 65869), and 10 (IM 65870) are nearly identical to those of the aforementioned copies of the Elugalgalgasisa Cylinder Inscription, however, it is clear from their palaeography, size, and oblong shape that they were written by a different scribe; ex. 5 is 12.2 cm long with a diameter of 4.2–4.9 cm and exs. 9 and 10 are 13.6–13.8 cm long with diameters of 6–6.2 cm. It is fairly certain that IM 65869 and IM 65870 were inscribed by the same scribe. Since Bod AB 239 was not available for study during the preparation of RINBE 2, it is not known if it was inscribed by the same scribe as exs. 9 and 10. Thus, it is fairly certain that approximately half of the known exemplars of this inscription were written by two different scribes: 'Scribe A' wrote out exs. 4, 8?, 12, and 13, and 'Scribe B' inscribed exs. 5?, 9, and 10.

Exs. 1 (BM 91125), 6 (IM 63999), and 11 (IM 65871) deviate significantly from the other known exemplars. Ex. 1 distributes the inscription in two columns of thirty-one lines each; the other copies generally arrange the text with twenty-six lines per column. Exs. 6 and 11 contain the most orthographic variants; for example, both write Šulgi's name without the divine determinative (d). It is clear from the palaeography of IM 63999 and IM 65871, despite their orthographic similarities, that the two cylinders were inscribed by different scribes. Thus, at least five different scribes were used to write out copies of this text.

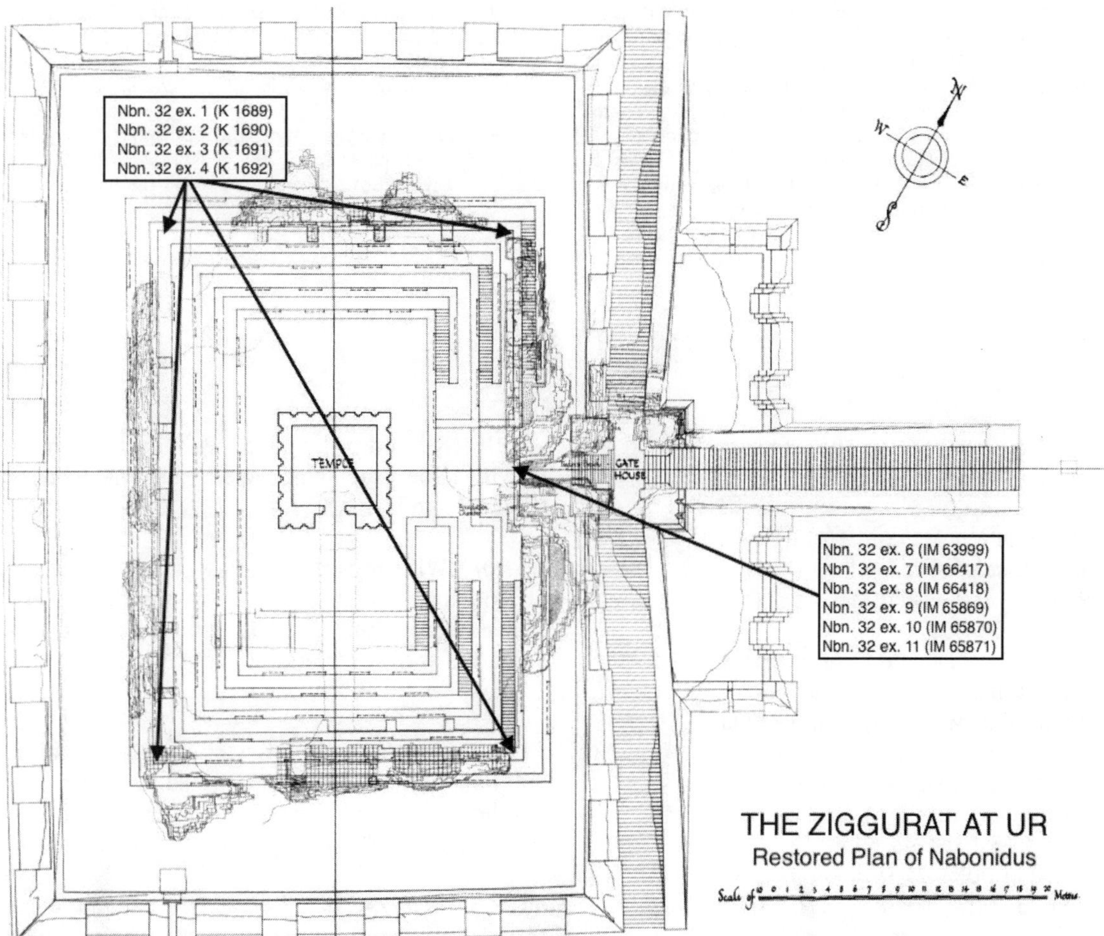

Figure 17. Annotated plan of the Elugalgalgasisa, the ziggurat at Ur, showing the general areas in which some cylinders of Nabonidus are reported to have been discovered. Adapted from Wolley, UE 5 pl. 87.

BIBLIOGRAPHY

1855 Taylor, JRAS 15 pp. 263–264 (ex. 1-4, study, provenance)

1861 Rawlinson, 1 R pl. 68 no. 1 (ex. 1, copy, with variants of exs. 2–4)

1862 Talbot, JRAS 19 pp. 193–198 (exs. 1–4, edition)

1863 Oppert, EM 1 pp. 262–263 (exs. 1–4, translation)

1875 Talbot, Records of the Past 5 pp. 143–148 (exs. 1–4, translation, study)

1875 Ménant, Babylone p. 254 (exs. 1–4 i 1–11, 19–ii 31, translation)

1880 Ménant, Manuel pp. 286–291 (ex. 1, copy, edition)

1887 Teloni, Crestomazia pp. 64–68 and 106–109 no. 7 (ex. 1, copy, study)

1889 Bezold, Cat. 1 pp. 333–334 (exs. 1–4, study)

1890 Abel and Winckler, KGV p. 43 (ex. 1, copy)

1890 Peiser in Schrader, KB 3/2 pp. 94–97 no. 2 (exs. 1–4, edition)

1895 Meissner, Chrestomathie p. 45 no. 3 (ex. 1, copy)

1899 Ball, Light pp. 207–208 (exs. 1–4, photo, translation)

1904 Harper, Literature pp. 157–158 (translation)

1908 BM Guide^{2} pp. 194–195 and pl. XL (ex. 1, photo; exs. 1–4 ii 3–31, translation, study)

1912 Langdon, NBK pp. 49 and 250–253 Nbd. no. 5 (exs. 1–4, edition)

1915 Rogers, History II pl. before p. 551 (ex. 1, photo)

1922 BM Guide^{3} p. 142 and pl. XXXVIII (ex. 1, photo; exs. 1–4 ii 3–31, translation, study)

1923 Boutflower, Book of Daniel p. 114 (ex. 1, photo)

1925 Budge, Rise and Progress fig. after p. 110 (ex. 2, photo)

1927 Contenau, Manuel 1 p. 167 fig. 102 (ex. 1, photo)

1927 Thompson, Bodleian p. 27 (ex. 5, study)

1938 Weißbach, ZA 44 p. 166 (exs. 1–4 i 23–24, study)

1941 Naster, Chrestomathie p. 77 (ex. 1, copy)

1945–46 Lewy, HUCA 19 pp. 440–441 (exs. 1–4 i 28–29, ii 5, study)

1949 Robert et al., Dictionnaire de la bible col. 399 (ex. 1, photo)

1950 Lewy, ArOr 18/3 pp. 347–348 (exs. 1–4 i 23–24, ii 5, study)

1959 Beek, An Babels Strömen fig. 52 after p. 166 (ex. 1, photo)

1964 As-Siwani, Sumer 20 pp. 69–76 and unnumbered plate after p. 76 (exs. 6–8, photo; ex. 6, copy; exs. 6–11, edition)

1968 Ellis, Foundation Deposits p. 112 (exs. 1–10, study)

1973 Berger, NbK pp. 355–359 Nbn. Zyl. II, 2 (exs. 1–11, study)

1977 Gurney, Studies Finkelstein p. 96 (ex. 5, study)

1984–05 Borger, TUAT I/4 p. 406 (ii 18–26, translation)

1989 Beaulieu, Nabonidus pp. 35–37, 61–62 and 64 Inscription 17 (ii 3–12, 13–17, 23–26, edition; study)

2000 Beaulieu, COS 2 pp. 313–314 (translation)

2001 Schaudig, Inschriften Nabonids pp. 350–353 no. 2.2 (edition)

2003 Schaudig, Studies Kienast pp. 478–482 (i 5–23, edition; study)

2008 Finkel, Babylon: Myth and Reality p. 170 fig. 160 (ex. 1, photo)

2018 Taylor, BBVO 26 pp. 45–46 with fig. 9e and p. 52 (ex. 1, photo; ex. 2, study)

TEXT

Col. i

1) ^{md}AG-NÍ.TUKU LUGAL TIN.TIR.KI
2) *za-ni-in é-sag-íl*
3) *ù é-zi-da*
4) *pa-liḫ* DINGIR.MEŠ GAL.MEŠ *a-na-ku*

i 1–4) Nabonidus, king of Babylon, the one who provides for Esagil and Ezida, the one who reveres the great gods, am I.

5) *é-lugal-galga-si-sá*
6) *ziq-qur-rat é-giš-nu_{11}-gal*
7) *šá qé-reb úri*.KI
8) *šá ^{m}ur-^{d}namma* LUGAL *šu-ut maḫ-ri*
9) *i-pu-šu-ma la ú-šak-li-lu-uš*
10) *^{md}šul-gi* DUMU-*šú ši-pir-šú ú-šak-lil*

i 5–10) (With regard to) Elugalgalgasisa, the ziggurat of Ekišnugal, which is inside Ur, which Ur-Namma, a king of former times, had built, but had not completed, Šulgi, his son, completed its construction.

11) *i-na mu-sa-re-e šá ^{m}ur-^{d}namma*
12) *ù ^{md}šul-gi* DUMU-*šú a-mur-ma*
13) *šá ziq-qur-rat šu-a-ti ^{m}ur-^{d}namma*
14) *i-pu-šu-ma la ú-šak-li-lu-uš*
15) *^{md}šul-gi* DUMU-*šú ši-pir-šú ú-šak-lil*

i 11–15) I read in the inscriptions of Ur-Namma and Šulgi, his son, that Ur-Namma had built that ziggurat, but had not completed it, (and that) Šulgi, his son, completed its (Elugalgalgasisa's) construction.

16) *i-na-an-ni ziq-qur-rat šu-a-ti*
17) *la-ba-ri-iš il-li-ik-ma*
18) *e-li te-me-en-na la-bi-ri*
19) *šá ^{m}ur-^{d}namma ù ^{md}šul-gi* DUMU-*šú*
20) *i-pu-šu ziq-qur-rat šu-a-ti*
21) *ki-ma la-bi-ri-im-ma*
22) *i-na ku-up-ri ù a-gur-ri*
23) *ba-ta-aq-šú aṣ-bat-ma a-na* ^{d}30 EN DINGIR.MEŠ
24) *šá* AN-*e u* KI-*tim* LUGAL DINGIR.MEŠ DINGIR.MEŠ

i 16–23a) Now, that ziggurat had become old so, on top of the original foundation(s) that Ur-Namma and Šulgi, his son, had built, I repaired the damage of that ziggurat with bitumen and baked bricks, as (it had been) in ancient times.

i 23b–ii 2) For the god Sîn, lord of the gods of heaven and earth, king of the gods, god of the gods, the one

i 24 and ii 5 DINGIR.MEŠ *šá* DINGIR.MEŠ "god of the gods": Literally "gods of the gods." Because this epithet refers only to the moon-god Sîn, one expects here DINGIR *šá* DINGIR.MEŠ, as it is in text no. 33 (variant of the Elugalgalgasisa Cylinder) ii 8. For other examples of redundant, plural forms used in lieu of a singular form, see Schaudig, Inschriften Nabonids pp. 158–159 §IV.2.1.j. M. Worthington (Textual Criticism pp. 284–285 §5.4.7), however, suggests that the MEŠ sign "sometimes appears in cases where grammar or idiom suggests that a sumerogram conceals a singular word" and that "the unexpected MEŠ should probably be understood as an aid to reading: it indicates to the reader that the preceding sign or group of signs is to be read sumerographically." This passage might be one of those instances.

šá DINGIR.MEŠ
25) *a-ši-ib* AN-*e* GAL.MEŠ EN *é-giš-nu*$_{11}$*-gal*
26) *šá qé-reb úri*.KI EN-*ia*
Col. ii
1) *uš-ši-iš-ma*
2) *e-pu-uš*

who resides in the great heavens, lord of Ekišnugal — which is inside Ur — my lord, I renovated and (re)built (it).

3) ^{d}30 *be-lí* DINGIR.MEŠ
4) LUGAL DINGIR.MEŠ *šá* AN-*e ù* KI-*tim*
5) DINGIR.MEŠ *šá* DINGIR.MEŠ
6) *a-ši-ib* AN-*e* GAL.MEŠ
7) *a-na* É *šu-a-ti*
8) *ḫa-di-iš i-na e-re-bi-ka*
9) SIG$_{5}$.MEŠ *é-sag-íl*
10) *é-zi-da é-giš-nu*$_{11}$*-gal*
11) É.MEŠ DINGIR-*ú-ti-ka* GAL-*ti*
12) *liš-šá-ki-in šap-tuk-ka*
13) *ù pu-luḫ-ti* DINGIR-*ú-ti-ka*
14) GAL-*ti lìb-bi* UN.MEŠ-*šú*
15) *šu-uš-kin-ma la i-ḫaṭ-ṭu-ú*
16) *a-na* DINGIR-*ú-ti-ka* GAL-*ti*

ii 3–16) O Sîn, lord of the gods, king of the gods of heaven and earth, god of the gods, the one who resides in the great heavens, when you joyfully enter this temple, may good things about Esagil, Ezida, (and) Ekišnugal, the temples of your great divinity, be set upon your lips. Moreover, have the fear of your great divinity placed in the heart(s) of his people so that they do not sin against your great divinity.

17) *ki-ma* AN-*e iš-da-šú-nu li-ku-nu*

ii 17) May their (the temples') foundations be as firm as (those of) the heavens.

18) *ia-ti* ^{md}AG-I LUGAL TIN.TIR.KI
19) *i-na ḫi-ṭu* DINGIR-*ú-ti-ka* GAL-*ti*
20) *šu-zib-an-ni-ma*
21) *ba-la-ṭu u*$_{4}$*-mu ru-qu-ti*
22) *a-na ši-rik-ti šur-kam*

ii 18–22) (As for) me, Nabonidus, king of Babylon, save me from sinning against your great divinity and grant me a long life (lit. "a life of long days").

23) *ù šá* ^{md}EN-LUGAL-ÙRU DUMU *reš-tu-ú*
24) *ṣi-it lìb-bi-ia pu-luḫ-ti* DINGIR-*ú-ti-ka*
25) GAL-*ti lìb-bu-uš šu-uš-kin-ma*
26) *a-a ir-šá-a ḫi-ṭi-ti la-le-e* TIN *liš-bi*

ii 23–26) Moreover, with regard to Belshazzar, (my) first-born son, my own offspring, have the fear of your great divinity placed in his heart so that he does not commit a(ny) sin. May he be sated with happiness in life.

33

A longer version of the previous inscription is known from a single double-column clay cylinder discovered at Ur. This text, which records the king's restoration of Elugalgalgasisa ("House of the King who Lets Counsel Flourish"), the ziggurat of the moon-god Sîn at Ur, is written in contemporary Neo-Babylonian script. The inscription was probably composed shortly after text no. 32 (Elugalgalgasisa Cylinder), perhaps after Nabonidus' thirteenth (543) regnal year, likely at the very end of his reign, in either his sixteenth (540) or seventeenth (539) year as king.

---

32 i 25 *é-giš-nu*$_{11}$*-gal* "Ekišnugal": Ex. 3 writes the ceremonial name of the temple as *é-giš-nu-gál*.

32 ii 6 *a-ši-ib* AN-*e* GAL.MEŠ "the one who resides in the great heavens": Ex. 11 has *a-ši-ib é-giš-nu*$_{11}$*-gal* "the one who resides in Ekišnugal."

32 ii 14 UN.MEŠ-*šú* "his people": As H. Schaudig (Inschriften Nabonids p. 353 n. 362) has already pointed out, this appears to have been a scribal error for UN.MEŠ-*ka* ("your people"); Nabonidus is directly addressing the god Sîn in this passage, so one expects a second person, not third person, possessive suffix.

CATALOGUE

Museum Number	Excavation Number	Provenance	cpn
CBS 15617	U 1151	Probably Ur, ziggurat	p

TEXT

Col. i

1) ^{md}AG-NÍ.TUKU LUGAL TIN.TIR.KI
2) *za-ni-in é-sag-íl u é-zi-da*
3) *pa-liḫ* DINGIR.MEŠ GAL.MEŠ *a-na-ku*
4) *é-lugal-galga-si-sá ziq-qur-rat*
5) *é-giš-nu*$_{11}$*-gal šá qé-reb úri*.KI
6) *šá* ^{m}*ur-*^{d}*namma* LUGAL *šu-ut maḫ-ri*
7) *i-pu-šu-ma la ú-šak-li-lu-uš*
8) ^{m}*šul-gi* DUMU-*šú ši-pir-šú ú-šak-lil*
9) *i-na mu-sa-re-e šá* ^{m}*ur-*^{d}*namma u* ^{m}*šul-gi* DUMU-*šú*
10) *a-mu-ur-ma šá ziq-qur-rat šu-a-tú*
11) ^{m}*ur-*^{d}*namma i-pu-šu-*⸢*ma la ú-šak-li-lu-uš*⸣

Lacuna

1′) [...] x
2′) [...] x-*šú*
3′) [...] x ⸢*ú*⸣*-šat-ri-iṣ*
4′) [...] ⸢É$^{?}$ *šu*⸣*-a-tim*
5′) [*ki-ma u*$_4$]-⸢*mu*⸣ *ú-nam-*⸢*mir*⸣*-ma*
6′) [*a*]-⸢*na*⸣ ^{d}30 EN DINGIR.⸢MEŠ⸣
7′) ⸢*šá*⸣ AN-*e ù* KI-*tim*

Col. ii

1) LUGAL ⸢DINGIR.MEŠ⸣ *ù* ^{d}15
2) *šá* AN-⸢*e*⸣ *ù* KI-*tim*
3) *a-šib* AN-*e* GAL.MEŠ EN *é-giš-nu*$_{11}$*-gal*
4) *šá qé-reb úri*.KI EN-*ia*
5) *uš-še-eš*$_{15}$*-ma e-pu-uš*
6) ^{d}30 EN DINGIR.MEŠ LUGAL DINGIR.MEŠ
7) *šá* AN-*e ù* KI-*tim*
8) DINGIR *šá* DINGIR.MEŠ *ù* ^{d}15.MEŠ
9) *a-šib* AN-⸢*e*⸣ GAL.⸢MEŠ⸣
10) *a-na* É ⸢*šu-a-ti ḫa-di*⸣-[*iš*]
11) ⸢*i*$^{?}$⸣-[*na e-re-bi-ka* SIG$_5$.MEŠ *é-sag-íl*]

Lacuna

1′) ⸢*ṣi-it*⸣ [*lìb-bi-ia*]
2′) *pu-luḫ-ti* ⸢DINGIR-*ú-ti-ka* GAL-*ti*⸣
3′) *lìb-bu-uš šu-uš-kin-ma*
4′) *a-a ir-šá-a* ⸢*ḫi*⸣*-ṭi-ti*
5′) *la-le-e ba-la-ṭu liš-bi*

i 1–3) Nabonidus, king of Babylon, the one who provides for Esagil and Ezida, the one who reveres the great gods, am I.

i 4–8) (With regard to) Elugalgalgasisa, the ziggurat of Ekišnugal, which is inside Ur, which Ur-Namma, a king of former times, had built, but had not completed, Šulgi, his son, completed its construction.

i 9–11) I read in the inscriptions of Ur-Namma and Šulgi, his son, that Ur-Namma had built that ziggurat, but had not completed it,

Lacuna

i 1′–5′) [...] its [...] I [...] stretched out [...] I made that *temple* shine [like day]light.

i 6′–ii 5) For the god Sîn, lord of the gods of heaven and earth, king of the gods and goddesses of heaven and earth, the one who resides in the great heavens, lord of Ekišnugal — which is inside Ur — my lord, I renovated and (re)built (it).

ii 6–11) O Sîn, lord of the gods, king of the gods of heaven and earth, god of the gods and goddesses, the one who resides in the great heavens, *w*[*hen* you] joyful[ly *enter*] this temple, [may good things about Esagil],

Lacuna

ii 1′–5′) [Moreover, with regard to Belshazzar, (my) first-born son], my own offspring, have the fear of your great divinity placed in his heart so that he does not commit a(ny) sin. May he be sated with happiness in life.

Lacuna before ii 1′ Based on text 32 (Elugalgalgasisa Cylinder) ii 23, the translation assumes that *ù šá* ^{md}EN-LUGAL-ÙRU DUMU *reš-tu-ú* ("moreover, with regard to Bēl-šarra-uṣur, (my) first-born son") appeared in the now-missing line(s) immediately before ii 1′.

34

This Akkadian text is known only from a single clay cylinder, which, based on its contents, is generally believed to have come from Ur. The two-column inscription, which is written in contemporary Neo-Babylonian script, records that Nabonidus consecrated his daughter En-nigaldi-Nanna as the *ēntu*-priestess of the moon-god Sîn at Ur, completely renovated and decorated Egipar (*gipāru*-house), his daughter's new residence in the Ekišnugal temple complex at Ur, and exempted the priests and personnel of that holy structure from paying taxes and performing corvée labor. The text narrates in detail the process by which En-nigaldi-Nanna became high-priestess. Nabonidus claims that he had his expert diviners examine the entrails of sheep three times: The first yielded a positive result and confirmed that the lunar eclipse observed on the thirteenth day of the month Ulūlu (VI) was indeed the mon-god's message to the king that he desired a new high-priestess; the second was negative and rejected Nabonidus' request to appoint any female member of his family to the post; and the third was again positive and fully endorsed the king's nomination of his own daughter to be the moon-god's new priestess. To commemorate the occasion, Nabonidus gave his daughter the Sumerian ceremonial name En-nigaldi-Nanna; her (Akkadian) birth name is not recorded in extant cuneiform sources. This inscription is generally thought to have been composed during the second half of Nabonidus' second regnal year (554) since scholars date the lunar eclipse recorded in this text to September 26th, 554; on the date of the eclipse, see H. Lewy, ArOr 17 p. 50. Moreover, a text called the "Royal Chronicle" records that En-nigaldi-Nanna was installed in her post later that same year. In scholarly literature, this text is referred to as "Nabonidus Cylinder II, 7," "[Nabonidus] Inscription 2," and the "En-nigaldi-Nanna Cylinder." The inscription was collated from high-resolution photographs kindly provided by K. Wagensonner.

CATALOGUE

Museum Number	Registration Number	Provenance	cpn
YBC 2182	—	Probably Ur	p

BIBLIOGRAPHY

1912 Scheil, CRAIB 56 pp. 680–681 (study)
1915 Clay, YOS 1 pp. 66–75 no. 45 and pl. LIV (photo, copy, edition)
1917 Koschaker, Rechtsvergleichende Studien pp. 232–233 (study)
1924 S. Smith, BHT pp. 54–57 (i 1–ii 8, translation, study)
1929 Gadd, History and Monuments pp. 237–239 (study)
1938 Böhl, JEOL 5 pp. 357–360 (translation, study)
1939 Böhl, Studies Koschaker pp. 151–178 (edition)
1945–46 Nougayrol, RA 40 p. 74 (i 1–24, translation)
1947 Böhl, Chrestomathy 1 pp. 50–52 no. 34 (i 1–ii 8, copy)
1951 Gadd, Iraq 13 pp. 28–29, 34 and 36–37 (ii 3, 4, 9, study)
1953 Böhl, OpMin pp. 174–187 (translation, study)
1950 Oppenheim, JAOS Suppl. 10 p. 40 (ii 22, study)
1967 Renger, ZA 58 pp. 123–126 (study)
1968 Brinkman, PKB p. 114 (study)
1969 Brinkman, Orientalia NS 38 pp. 333–334 (i 28–29, study)
1973 Berger, NbK p. 364 Nbn. Zyl. II, 7 (study)
1975 Weadock, Iraq 37 pp. 112–114 (study)
1985 Reiner, Your Thwarts in Pieces pp. 1–16 (translation, study)
1989 Beaulieu, Nabonidus pp. 22–23, 48–50 and 127–132 Inscription 2 (i 7–10, 26–38, ii 15–28, edition; study)
1991 Powell, ZA 81 p. 30 (study)

1994 Beaulieu, BCSMS 28 pp. 39–40 (i 26–38, translation, study)

1995 Reiner, Astral Magic pp. 76–77 (i 1–17, translation, study)

2001 Schaudig, Inschriften Nabonids pp. 373–377 no. 2.7 (edition)

2003 Schaudig, Studies Kienast pp. 482–488 and 494–495 (i 29–38, ii 1–5, edition; study)

2007 Beaulieu, Representations of Political Power p. 150 (i 9, 41, study)

2008 Finkel, Babylon: Myth and Reality p. 162 (i 8–10, 26–38, translation)

2010 Heller, Spätzeit p. 179 (study)

2019 Frazer, Ancient Mesopotamia Speaks pp. 174–175 (photo, study)

Figure 18. YBC 2182 (Nabonidus no. 34), the En-nigaldi-Nanna Cylinder, which celebrates the consecration of the king's daughter En-nigaldi-Nanna as a priestess at Ur and the rebuilding of her residence in the Egipar. Courtesy of the Yale Babylonian Collection; photography by Klaus Wagensonner.

TEXT

Col. i

1) *ì-nu* ^{d}ŠEŠ.KI-*ri i-ri-šu* NIN.DINGIR.RA

2) DUMU *ru-bé-e gi-is-ki-im-ma-šu ú-kal-li-im ad-na-a-tim*

3) ^{d}*nam-ra-ṣi-it ú-ša-pi pu-ru-us-sa-šu ki-i-nu*

4) *a-na* ^{d}*na-bi-um-na-ʾi-id* LUGAL TIN.TIR.KI *za-ni-in é-sag-íl ù é-zi-da*

5) *re-é-a-am pa-al-ḫu mu-uš-te-eʾ-ú aš-ra-a-ti* DINGIR.MEŠ GAL.MEŠ

6) ^{d}ŠEŠ.KI-*ri* EN *a-gi-i na-áš ṣa-ad-du a-na da-ad-mi*

7) *ú-ad-di it-ta-šu aš-šum e-re-eš* NIN.DINGIR.RA

8) *i-na* ITI.KIN-^{d}INANNA UD.13.KAM ITI *ši-pí-ir* ^{d}IŠ.TAR.MEŠ

9) ^{d}*in-bi in-na-di-ir-ma i-na na-aʾ-du-ri-šu ir-bi*

10) ^{d}EN.ZU NIN.DINGIR.RA *i-ri-iš ki-a-am it-ta-šu ù pu-ru-us-su-šú*

11) *a-na-ku* ^{md}*na-bi-um-na-ʾi-id re-é-a-am pa-li-iḫ i-lu-ti-šú*

i 1–3) When the god Nannāru desired an *ēntu*-priestess, the son of the prince (the god Marduk) revealed his sign to the world (and) the god Namra-Ṣīt made his firm decision manifest.

i 4–7) The god Nannāru, the lord of the crown who bears portent(s) for settlements, made his sign regarding (his) desire for an *ēntu*-priestess known to Nabonidus, king of Babylon, the one who provides for Esagil and Ezida, the reverent shepherd who constantly seeks out the shrines of the great gods.

i 8–10) "The Fruit" (the god Sîn) became eclipsed in the month Ulūlu (VI), (on) the thirteenth day (of) the month of "the work of the goddesses" and set while he was eclipsed. "The god Sîn desired an *ēntu*-priestess," such was his sign and his decision.

i 11–13) I, Nabonidus, the shepherd who reveres his divinity, was frightened by his firm command. I was

i 9 ^{d}*in-bi* "The Fruit": This epithet of the moon-god is used here instead of the name of the god Sîn. It is also found in inscriptions of the Assyrian king Ashurbanipal and in Babylonian hemerologies. See, for example, CAD I–J p. 146 sub *inbu* 1.d; Linssen, Cults of Uruk and Babylon p. 4 n. 7 (with references to earlier scholarly literature); and Novotny and Jeffers, RINAP 5/1 p. 68 Ashurbanipal 2 (Prism B) v 10.

12) *qí-bi-it-su ki-it-tim ap-la-aḫ at-ta-ʾi-id-ma*
13) *aš-šum e-re-eš* NIN.DINGIR.RA ⸢*ra-ša-ku ni-qí-it*⸣*-tì*

attentive, but was worried about (his) desire for an *ēntu*-priestess.

14) *aš-ra-a-ti* ^{d}UTU *ù* ^{d}IŠKUR EN.MEŠ *bi-ri aš-te-eʾ-e-ma*
15) ^{d}UTU *ù* ^{d}IŠKUR *an-na ki-i-nu i-tap-pa-lu-in-ni*
16) *i-na bi-ri-ia iš-ṭu-ru* UZU *da-mi-iq-tum*
17) UZU *e-ri-iš-ti na-da-a-ti e-ri-iš-ti* DINGIR.MEŠ *a-na* LÚ

i 14–17) I frequently visited the shrines of the gods Šamaš and Adad, the lords of divination, and the gods Šamaš and Adad answered me with a firm 'yes.' In my divination, they wrote out an auspicious omen, an omen indicating the desire for *nadītu*-priestesses, the desire of the gods to a man.

18) *áš-ni-ma te-er-tum ap-qí-id-ma* UZU SIG$_5$ *e-li šá maḫ-ri i-tap-pa-lu-ni*

i 18) I repeated and checked the extispicy and they answered me with an omen more auspicious than the previous one.

19) *áš-šú* DUMU.MUNUS.MEŠ *ki-im-ti-ia te-er-tum e-pú-uš-ma ul-la i-tap-pa-lu-ni*

i 19) I performed an extispicy (to ask) about (the suitability of) a daughter from my extended family, but they answered me 'no.'

20) *áš-lu-uš-ma áš-šú* DUMU.MUNUS *ṣi-it lib-bi-ia*
21) *te-er-tum e-pú-uš-ma* UZU SIG$_5$ *i-tap-pa-lu-in-ni*

i 20–21) I performed an extispicy a third time (to ask) about (the suitability of my) daughter, my own offspring, and they answered me (this time) with an auspicious omen.

22) *a-ma-at* ^{d}EN.ZU EN *šu-ur-bu-ú* DINGIR *ba-a-ni-ia*
23) *qí-bi-it* ^{d}UTU *ù* ^{d}IŠKUR EN.MEŠ *bi-ri at-ta-ʾi-id-ma*
24) DUMU.MUNUS *ṣi-it lib-bi-ia a-na e-nu-ti áš-ši-ma*
25) *en-níg-al-di-*^{d}*nanna šu-um-šá am-bi*

i 22–25) I was attentive towards the word of the god Sîn, the supreme lord, the god who created me, (and) the command(s) of the gods Šamaš and Adad, the lords of divination, and elevated (my) daughter, my own offspring, to the office of *ēntu*-priestess and (then) I named (her) En-nigaldi-Nanna, as her (new, official) name.

26) *áš-šú iš-tu* UD.MEŠ *ru-qu-tim pa-ra-aṣ en-ti ma-šu-ú-ma*
27) *la ud-du-ú ši-ki-in-šu u*$_4$*-mi-ša-am uš-ta-ad-da-an*

i 26–27) Because the rite(s) of the *ēntu*-priestess had been forgotten since distant days and its (the Egipar's) structure was no (longer) known, I deliberated (these matters) daily.

28) *a-da-an-nu ik-šu-da-am-ma up-ta-at-ta-a-ni* KÁ.MEŠ
29) *ap-pa-li-is-ma* NA$_4$.NA.RÚ.A *la-bi-ri ša* ^{d}*na-bi-um-ku-dúr-ri-ú-ṣur*
30) DUMU ^{md}*nin-urta-na-din-šu-mi* LUGAL *pa-na ma-aḫ-ra-a*
31) *ša ṣa-lam* NIN.DINGIR.RA *ba-áš-mu ṣe-ru-uš-šu*
32) *si-ma-a-ti-šu lu-ub-uš-ta-šu ù ti-iq-ni-šu*
33) *it-ti-i iš-ṭu-ru-ma a-na é-gi*$_6$*-pàr ú-še-ri-bu*

i 28–33) The appointed time arrived and the gates were opened for me: I discovered an ancient foundation inscription of Nebuchadnezzar (I), son of Ninurta-nādin-šumi, a previous, former king, that had an image of an *ēntu*-priestess depicted on it, whose appurtenances, attire, and insignia he had also written down, and (that) he had had brought into Egipar.

34) *ṭup-pa-nu ù* GIŠ.LE.U$_5$.UM.MEŠ LIBIR.RA.MEŠ *at-ta-aṭ*-ṭa-al-ma*
35) *ki-ma la-bi-ri-im-ma e-pú-uš*

i 34–35) I carefully inspected the ancient tablets and writing boards and made (it) as (it had been) in ancient times.

36) NA$_4$.NA.RÚ.A *si-ma-ti-šu ù ú-na-a-at* É*-šu*
37) *e-eš-ši-iš ab-ni ṣe-ru-uš-šu áš-ṭu-ur-ma*
38) *ma-ḫa-ar* ^{d}EN.ZU *ù* ^{d}*nin-gal* EN.MEŠ*-e-a ú-ki-in*

i 36–38) I created anew a foundation inscription (recording) her appurtenances and the utensils of her house, wrote down (this information) on it, and firmly established (it) before the god Sîn and the goddess Ningal, my lords.

39) *i-nu-šu é-gi*$_6$*-pàr ku-um-mi el-lu a-šar pa-ra-aṣ e-nu-tim uš-tak-la-lu qé-re-eb-šu*
40) *a-šar-šu na-di-ma e-mi kar-mi-iš*
41) GIŠ*.a-la-mi-it-tì in-bi ṣi-ip-pa-a-tim a-ṣu-ú qer-bu-uš-šu*

i 39–41) At that time, (with regard to) Egipar, the pure cella, the site wherein the rite(s) of the *ēntu*-priestess are performed to perfection, its site was in ruins and had turned into rubble. Date palms and fruit orchards were growing inside it.

---

i 18 *e-li šá maḫ-ri* "than the previous one": For a study of the Akkadian expressions *eli maḫrê* and *eli ša maḫri*, see Worthington, Textual Criticism pp. 151–152 §3.5.6.
i 34 *at-ta-aṭ*-ṭa-al-ma* "I carefully inspected and": The scribe wrote *at-ta-*ṢI*-ṭa-al-ma*.

42) *ak-ši-iṭ-ma iṣ-ṣi e-pe-ri ka-ar-mi-šu as-su-uḫ*
43) É *ap-pa-li-is-ma ud-da-a te-me-en-šu*

i 42–43) I cut down the trees and cleared away the rubble from its ruin(s). I (then) discovered (that) temple and (clearly) identified its foundation(s).

44) *ši-ṭi-ir šu-mi ša* LUGAL.MEŠ *maḫ-ri la-bi-ru-tim ap-pa-li-is qer-bu-uš-šú*

Col. ii

1) MU.SAR-*ú la-bi-ri šá en-an-e-du*$_{7}$ NIN.DINGIR.RA *úri*.KI
2) DUMU.MUNUS *ku-du-ur-ma-bu-uk a-ḫa-at ri-im-*^{d}EN.ZU LUGAL *úri*.KI
3) *ša é-gi*$_{6}$*-pàr uš-ši-šu-ma a-na áš-ri-šu ú-te-er-ru*
4) *a-na i-te-e é-gi*$_{6}$*-pàr* BÀD *e-li ma-a-a-al* NIN.DINGIR.RA.MEŠ LIBIR.RA.MEŠ *il-mu-ú*
5) *ap-pa-li-is-ma é-gi*$_{6}$*-pàr ki-ma la-bi-ri-im-ma e-eš-ši-iš e-pú-uš*

i 44–ii 5) I discovered inside it inscription(s) of ancient kings of the past. I (also) discovered an ancient inscribed object of Enanedu, *ēntu*-priestess of Ur, daughter of Kudur-mabuk, sister of Rīm-Sîn, king of Ur, who had renewed Egipar and restored it ("lit. "returned (it) to place"), (and who) surrounded the burial ground of the ancient *ēntu*-priestesses near the boundary of Egipar with a wall. Then, I built Egipar anew as (it had been) in ancient times.

6) BÁRA.MEŠ-*šu ù* GIŠ.ḪUR.MEŠ-*šu ki-ma la-bi-ri-im-ma e-eš-ši-iš ab-ni*
7) *a-na i-te-e é-gi*$_{6}$*-pàr* É *en-níg-al-di-*^{d}*nanna* DUMU.MUNUS-*ia* NIN.DINGIR.RA ^{d}30 *e-eš-ši-iš e-pú-uš*

ii 6–7) I built its daises and ground plans anew as (they had been) in ancient times. Near the boundary of Egipar I built anew the house of En-nigaldi-Nanna, my daughter, the *ēntu*-priestess of the god Sîn.

8) DUMU.MUNUS *ul-li-il-ma a-na* ^{d}30 *ù* ^{d}*nin-gal* EN.MEŠ-*e-a áš-ru-uk*
9) *i-na ši-pí-ir ka-kù-gál-ú-tim i-ši-ip-pu-ut-su e-pú-uš-ma a-na é-gi*$_{6}$*-pàr ú-še-ri-ib*

ii 8–9) I purified (my) daughter and (then) dedicated (her) to the god Sîn and the goddess Ningal. I purified it with an exorcistic ritual and had (her) enter into Egipar.

10) *sa-at-tuk-ki é-gi*$_{6}$*-pàr ú-ṭa-aḫ-ḫi-id*
11) A.ŠÀ.MEŠ GIŠ.KIRI$_{6}$.MEŠ SAG.GÉME.ARAD ÁB.GU$_{4}$.ḪI.A *ù* US$_{5}$.UDU.ḪI.A *ú-da-aš-ši-šu*

ii 10–11) I made the *sattukku*-offering(s) of Egipar abundant. I copiously supplied it with fields, orchards, domestic staff, cattle, and sheep and goats.

12) BÀD *ma-a-a-al* NIN.DINGIR.RA.MEŠ LIBIR.RA.MEŠ
13) ⸢*ki-ma la-bi-ri*⸣*-im-ma e-eš-ši-iš al-mi*
14) É *šu-a-ti a-na ma-aṣ-ṣa-ar-tim dan-na-tim aš-ku-un-šu*

ii 12–14) As (it had been) in the (distant) past, I surrounded the burial ground of the ancient *ēntu*-priestesses anew with a wall. (As for) that temple, I established it as a strong fortress.

15) *ì-nu-šu ša* ^{d}EN.ZU *ù* ^{d}*nin-gal* EN.MEŠ-*e-a*
16) *sa-at-tuk-ki-šu-nu e-li ša pa-na ú-ṭa-aḫ-ḫi-id*
17) *mi-im-ma šum-šu in é-kiš-nu-gál ú-da-aš-ši*
18) *ša u*$_{4}$*-mi* 3 UDU.NÍTA *e-le-*⸢*en*⸣ UDU.NÍTA *gi-na-a la-bi-ri* (erasure) *a-na* ^{d}30 *ù* ^{d}*nin-gal* EN-*e-a lu ú-ki-in*
19) *bu-ša-a ma-ak-ku-ru qé-re-eb é-kiš-nu-gál ú-da-aš-ši*

ii 15–19) At that time, with regard to the god Sîn and the goddess Ningal, my lords, I made their *sattukku*-offerings more abundant than (they were) in the past. I made everything there is copious in Ekišnugal. Per day, I indeed established for the god Sîn and the goddess Ningal, my lords, three sheep above the original *ginû*-offering of a (single) sheep. I made possessions (and) property copious inside Ekišnugal.

20) *aš-šum bur-sag-ge-e ul-lu-li-im-ma ḫi-ṭi-ti la ra-še-e*
21) *ra-am-ku-ut é-kiš-nu-gál ù* É.MEŠ DINGIR.MEŠ
22) *e-nu i-šip-pí* ZABAR.DAB.BA LÚ.KUL.LUM LÚ.*en-gi-su*
23) LÚ.*a-ri-ru* LÚ.GAL-DÙ LÚ.ŠITIM LÚ.KISAL.LUḪ-*ḫa* (erasure) Ì.DU$_{8}$.GAL-*lum*
24) LÚ.*ti-ir* É LÚ.*la-ga-ru šá-ki-nu taq-ri-ib-ti*
25) LÚ.NAR.MEŠ *mu-ḫa-ad-du-ú lìb-bi* DINGIR.MEŠ
26) LÚ.*ki-ni-iš-tum šu-ut na-bu-ú šu-ma-an-šu-un*
27) *i-li-ik-šu-nu ap-ṭu-ur-ma* ŠU.BAR.RA-*šu-nu* ⸢*aš*⸣*-ku-un* (erasure) *ub-bi-*⸢*ib-šu*⸣*-nu-ti-ma*
28) *a-na* ^{d}EN.ZU *ù* ^{d}*nin-gal* EN.MEŠ-*e-a ú-zak-ki-šu-nu-ti*

ii 20–28) In order to keep the *bursaggû*-offerings pure and to avoid cultic mistake(s), I released the *ramku*-priests of Ekišnugal and the temples of the (other) gods (at Ur), (as well as) the *ēnu*-priest, the purification priest, the *zabarbaddu*-official, the brewer, the cook, the miller, the *rab-banî*-official, the builder, the courtyard sweeper, the head doorkeeper, the *tīru*-official of the house, the *lagaru*-priest who performs the *taqribtu*-ritual, the singers who please the heart(s) of the gods, the lower-ranking priesthood who are named (here) by their title(s), from their corvée labor and established their freedom from service obligations. I cleared them (of legal claims) and set them free for the god Sîn and the goddess Ningal, my lords.

29) ^{d}EN.ZU DINGIR *el-lu* EN *a-gi-i nu-úr te-né-še-e-ti*

ii 29–32) May the god Sîn, the bright god, the lord of

30) DINGIR *šu-ur-bu-ú šá qí-bi-it ki-na-at*
31) *a-na e-ep-še-ti-ia li-iḫ-du-ma li-ir-a-am šar-ru-ti*
32) *ba-la-ṭa*$_4$ *da-rí-a še-bé-e li-it-tu-tu a-na ši-ri-ik-tim liš-ru-kam*
33) *a-a ú-ša-ab-šá-a šá-ni-nu ma-ḫi-ri a-a ar-ši*
34) *e-ma* ITI *liš-tap-pa-a i-da-a-ti du-um-qí-ia*
35) *a-ge-e šar-ru-ti-ia a-na da-rí-a-tim lu-ki-in ra-šu-ú-a*
36) GIŠ.GU.ZA *be-lu-ti-ia šu-úr-ši-id a-na aḫ-ra-a-tu* UD.MEŠ
37) *e-ma* ITI *i-na i-te-ed-du-ši-ka*
38) *ṣa-ad-da-ka da-mi-iq-tim gi-na-a lu-ut-tap-la-as*
39) ^{d}*nin-gal* GAŠAN *šur-bu-tum ma-ḫa-ar-ki li-ta-ma-a* SIG$_5$*-tì*
40) *en-níg-al-di-*^{d}*nanna* DUMU.MUNUS *na-ra-am-ti lib-bi-ia*
41) *ma-ḫa-ar-ku-nu li-bur-ma li-kun qí-bi-is-su*
42) *e-ep-še-tu-šu li-ṭi-ba el*-ku-un*
43) *a-a ir-šá-a ḫi-ṭi-ti*

the crown, the light of the people, the supreme god who(se) command is firm, be happy with my deeds so that he loves my royal majesty. May he grant me a long life (and) the attainment of very old age.

ii 33) May he not bring a rival into existence for me (so that) I do not have opponents.

ii 34–36) Each month, may he make signs of my well-being manifest. May he firmly establish on my head the crown of my royal majesty forever. Make the throne of my lordly person secure in the days to come.

ii 37–38) Every month, when you renew yourself, may I always behold your auspicious sign(s).

ii 39) May the goddess Ningal, the supreme lady, say good things about me in your presence.

ii 40–43) May En-nigaldi-Nanna, the beloved daughter of my heart, remain in good health in your presence and may her command(s) be firm. May her deeds be pleasing to you (and) may she avoid cultic mistake(s).

35

A fragment of a two-column clay cylinder discovered at Ur preserves part of an Akkadian inscription written in archaizing Neo-Babylonian script. The attribution to Nabonidus is not entirely certain, but very plausible given the prominence of the moon-god Sîn in the extant text; note that C.J. Gadd (UET 1 p. 96) and P.-A. Beaulieu (NABU 1989 p. 45 no. 66) propose that the inscription dates to the reign of Cyrus II, but this seems unlikely, as already pointed out by H. Schaudig (Inschriften Nabonids p. 480). This text is sometimes referred to as the "Ur Cylinder" in scholarly literature.

CATALOGUE

Museum Number	Excavation/ Registration No.	Provenance	cpn
BM 120526	1928-10-9,9; U 8837	Ur, ziggurat, southeast side	c

BIBLIOGRAPHY

1928 Gadd, UET 1 p. 96 and pl. 58 no. 307 (copy)
1989 Beaulieu, NABU p. 45 no. 66 (study)
2001 Schaudig, Inschriften Nabonids pp. 480–481 no. 2.24[a] and 760 figs. 38–39 (edition)
2010 Heller, Spätzeit p. 245 (study)

34 ii 42 *el*-ku-un* "to you (pl.)": Here, the plural "you" (*-kun*) refers to the god Sîn and the goddess Ningal.

TEXT

Col. i
Lacuna
1′) ù ni-⸢ši-im⸣
2′) šu-um ṭa-biš im-bu-ú
3′) ^{d}EN.ZU ^{d}ŠEŠ.KI-a-rá
4′) AN-e ù KI-tim
5′) i-na GISKIM-šu SIG$_5$-tim
6′) kib-ra-a-tim er-bet-ti
7′) [a]-⸢na⸣ qá-ti-ia ú-mál-li-ma
8′) [DINGIR].⸢DINGIR⸣ a-na ki-iṣ-ṣi-šu-⸢nu ú⸣-ter-⸢ma⸣
9′) [...] ⸢ú-še-šib⸣

Lacuna
i 1′–9′) [When ...] gladly called (me) by name [for ruling over the land] and people, the god Sîn, the light of heaven and earth, through his auspicious omens, placed [i]n my hands the four quarters (of the world) and (thereby) I returned the [go]ds to their shrines a[nd] had (them) reside [...].

Col. ii
Lacuna
1′) [x x] x x x
2′) ⸢ba-la⸣-ṭa UD.MEŠ
3′) ru-qu-ú-tu
4′) ku-un-nu GIŠ.GU.ZA
5′) la-ba-a-ru BALA-e
6′) LUGAL-ú-tu la ša-na-an
7′) a-na ši-ri-ik-ti
8′) šu-úr-kam

Lacuna
ii 1′–8′) [...] ... granted me a long life (lit. "a life of distant days"), a firmly secured throne, a long-lasting reign, (and) a kingship without rival.

36

A diorite door socket unearthed at Ur bears an eight-line Akkadian inscription of Nabonidus written in archaizing Neo-Babylonian script. The text records that the king granted the *ramku*-priests of the Ekišnugal temple at Ur exemption from taxes and corvée labor. The object was likely commissioned during the second half of Nabonidus' second regnal year (554), when he consecrated his daughter En-nigaldi-Nanna as the *ēntu*-priestess of the moon-god Sîn at Ur and renovated and decorated her residence Egipar (*gipāru*-house); see Beaulieu, Nabonidus p. 42 and Schaudig, Inschriften Nabonids p. 48. In previous editions and studies, this text is referred to as "Nabonidus Door Socket 1" and "[Nabonidus] Inscription 3." The present edition is based on the photograph of BM 116417 published by C.J. Gadd in UET 1 (pl. W).

35 Lacuna before i 1′ Following H. Schaudig (Inschriften Nabonids p. 480), the translation assumes that the two now-missing lines before i 1′ contained *ì-nu-um ... a-na be-lu-ut ma-a-ti* "[When ... for ruling over the land]."
35 ii 1′–8′ Compare Neriglissar 1 (Esagil Inscription) ii 33–35, where that Babylonian king also asks for "a life of long days, the attainment of very old age, a firmly secured throne, and a long-lasting reign." Based on that inscription, possible restore ii 1′ as *ḫa-di-iš na-ap-li-is-ma* "look with pleasure."

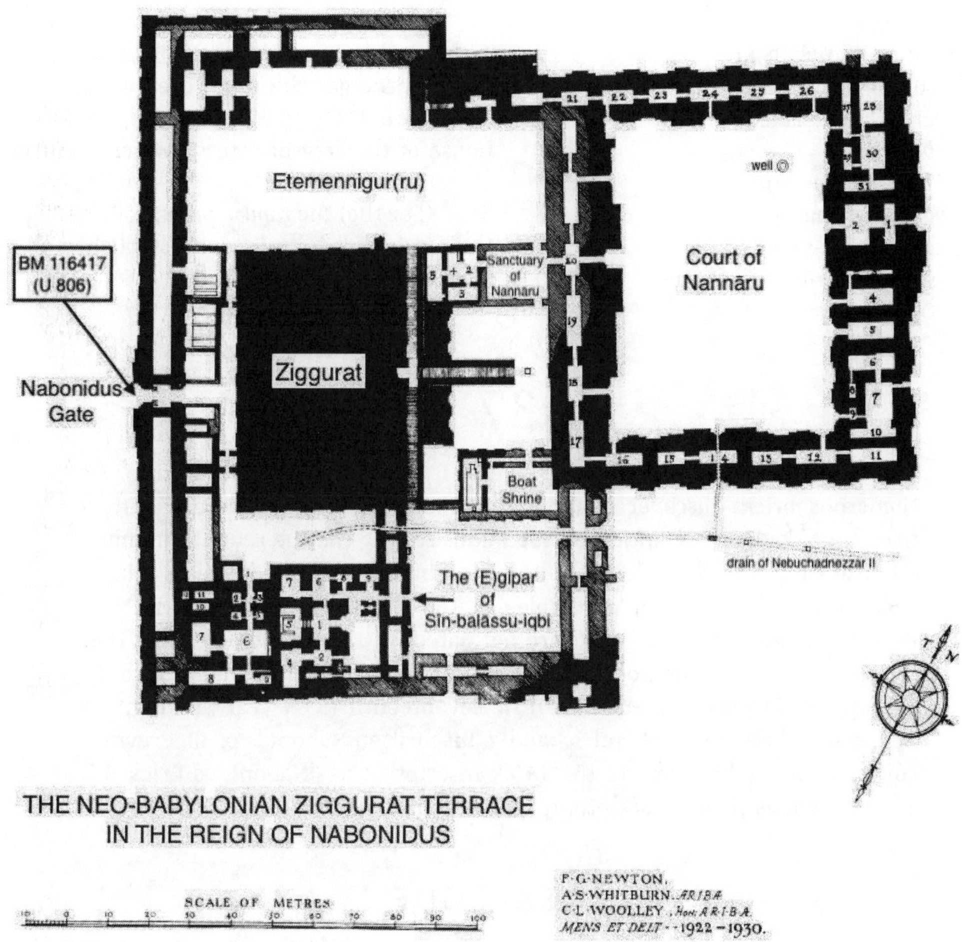

Figure 19. Plan of the ziggurat terrace at Ur during the reign of Nabonidus, with the find spot of BM 116417 (U 806; Nabonidus no. 36). Adapted from Wolley, UE 5 pl. 75.

CATALOGUE

Museum Number	Excavation/ Registration No.	Provenance	cpn
BM 116417	1923-11-10,2; U 806	Ur, ziggurat, 'Nabonidus Gate'	p

BIBLIOGRAPHY

1928 Gadd, UET 1 p. 57 and pls. W and 47 no. 187 (photo, copy, edition)
1939 Woolley, UE 5 p. 119 (study)
1962 Woolley, UE 9 pp. 11 and 18 (translation, study)
1973 Berger, NbK p. 344. Nbn. Türangelstein 1 (study)
1989 Beaulieu, Nabonidus pp. 23–24 Inscription 3 (edition)
2001 Schaudig, Inschriften Nabonids p. 344 no. 1.12[a] (edition)

TEXT

1) [^{d}]⸢AG⸣-I LUGAL KÁ.DIŠ.DIŠ.KI
2) *[pa-liḫ]* ^{d}30 ^{d}*nin-gal ana-ku*
3) *[é]-⸢gi$_{6}$⸣-pàr* É NIN.DINGIR.RA
4) *[ša] qé-reb úri*.KI
5) *[a]-⸢na⸣* ^{d}30 *be-lí-ia e-pu-uš*
6) *⸢ra⸣-am-ku-ut é-giš-nu$_{11}$-gal*
7) *ki-di-nu-ut-su-nu ak-ṣur-ma*
8) *šu-ba-ra-šu-un aš-ku-un*

1–2) [Nab]onidus, king of Babylon, [the one who reveres] the god Sîn (and) the goddess Ningal, am I. 3–5) [Fo]r the god Sîn, my lord, I built [Eg]ipar, the house of the *ēntu*-priestess, [which] is inside Ur.

6–8) (For the) the *ramku*-priests of Ekišnugal, I secured their privileged status and established their freedom from service obligations.

37

Numerous bricks discovered at various spots at Ur are inscribed with a five-line Akkadian inscription of Nabonidus stating that he rebuilt Enunmaḫ ("House of the Exalted Prince"), the *ḫilṣu*-building of the goddess Ningal inside the Ekišnugal temple complex at Ur. The script is archaizing Neo-Babylonian. Although the bricks are not dated, scholars generally think that this inscription was composed after Nabonidus' thirteenth regnal year (543), perhaps during his sixteenth (540) or seventeenth (539) year as king; see Beaulieu, Nabonidus p. 42 and Schaudig, Inschriften Nabonids p. 48. Previous editions and studies refer to this brick inscription as "Nabonidus Brick B I, 2," "Nabonidus [Brick Inscription] 14," and "[Nabonidus] Inscription 19."

CATALOGUE

Ex.	Museum Number/ Source	Excavation/ Registration No.	Provenance	Lines Preserved	cpn
1	BM 90149	51-1-1,287	Ur, mound south of the ziggurat	1–5	p
2	BM 90150	1979-12-20,72	As ex. 1	1–5	p
3	BM 90470 + BM 90713 + BM 90753	1979-12-20,268	As ex. 1	1–5	p
4	BM 114287	1919-10-11,4718	As ex. 1	2–5	p
5	BM 114288	1919-10-11,4719	As ex. 1	1–5	p
6	BM 137361	1919-10-11,5366	As ex. 1	1–5	p
7	BM 137362	1919-10-11,5367	As ex. 1	1–5	p
8	BM 137363	1919-10-11,5368	As ex. 1	—	n
9	BM 137364	1919-10-11,5369	As ex. 1	2–5	p
10	BM 137365	1919-10-11,5370	As ex. 1	1–5	p
11	BM 114339	1918-10-12,676	Ur	1–5	p
12	BM 137451	1919-11-11,1709	As ex. 11	—	n
13	UET 1 no. 189	U —	Ur, ziggurat and Enunmaḫ, in situ	1–5	n
14	Ash 1964-462	—	Probably Ur	—	n
15	MM 715.8	—	As ex. 14	—	n
16	YBC 16951	—	As ex. 14	1–4	p
17	YBC 16952	—	As ex. 14	3–5	p
18	YBC 16953	—	As ex. 14	3–5	p
19	CBS 16495	U 2862	As ex. 11	1–5	n
20	CDLI P498499	—	As ex. 11	1–5	p
21	X.3.335	—	As ex. 11	1–5	p

Figure 20. BM 114288 (Nabonidus no. 37 ex. 5), a brick discovered at Ur with an inscription stating that the king rebuilt Enunmaḫ, a building of the goddess Ningal inside the Ekišnugal temple complex. © Trustees of the British Museum.

COMMENTARY

The square-shaped bricks vary marginally in size. The largest and smallest bricks measure 34×33.5×7 cm and 32.5×32.5×6 cm respectively. The stamped area in which the inscriptions are written measure between 19 and 20.1 cm in length and 9 and 10 cm in height.

Following the edition of H. Schaudig (Inschriften Nabonids p. 340), the master text and lineation follow ex. 13, the brick(s) still embedded in the ruined mud-brick structures of the ziggurat and Enunmaḫ copied by C.J. Gadd in UET 1 (pl. 47 no. 189). No score of the inscription is given on Oracc since scores are not provided for texts on bricks (following the model of RIM and RINAP). In addition, no minor (orthographic) variants are given in the critical apparatus at the back of the book.

BIBLIOGRAPHY

1861 Rawlinson, 1 R pl. 68 no. 6 (exs. 1–3, copy)
1863 Oppert, EM 1 p. 262 (exs. 1–3, translation)
1875 Ménant, Babylone p. 253 (exs. 1–3, translation)
1890 Peiser in Schrader, KB 3/2 pp. 96–97 (exs. 1–3, edition)
1912 Langdon, NBK pp. 58 and 296–297 Nbd. no. 14 (exs. 1–3, edition)
1920 Thompson, Arch. 70 p. 125 fig. 13, p. 115 fig. 6 and p. 142 (exs. 11–12, copy; ex. 12, edition)
1928 Gadd, UET 1 p. 58 and pl. 47 no. 189 (ex. 13, copy, study)
1973 Berger, NbK p. 351 Nbn. Backsteine B I, 2 (exs. 1–13, study)

1981 Walker, CBI pp. 92–93 no. 112 Nabonidus 14 (exs. 1–15, transliteration, study)
1988 Beckman, ARRIM 6 pp. 1–2 (exs. 16–18, study)
1989 Beaulieu, Nabonidus pp. 37–38 and 214 Inscription 19 (exs. 1–15, edition; study)
1997 Márquez Rowe, AuOr 15 p. 89 (ex. 15, transliteration, study)
2001 Schaudig, Inschriften Nabonids pp. 339–340 no. 1.6[a] (ex. 13, edition; exs. 1–18, study)
2010 Heller, Spätzeit pp. 362 and 422 (study)

TEXT

1) [d]AG-*na-ʾi-id* LUGAL ŠÁR
2) LUGAL KÁ.DINGIR.RA.KI
3) *ša é-nun-maḫ* É *ḫi-il-ṣi*
4) *qé-reb é-giš-nu-gál*
5) *a-na* [d]*nin-gal* GAŠAN-*šu i-pú-šu*

1–5) Nabonidus, king of the world, king of Babylon, the one who built Enunmaḫ, the *ḫilṣu*-building (that is) inside Ekišnugal, for the goddess Ningal, his lady.

38

This Akkadian inscription is written on the faces of numerous bricks discovered at Ur; the script of this five-line text is archaizing Neo-Babylonian. The text states that Nabonidus renovated Elugalgalgasisa ("House of the King who Lets Counsel Flourish"), the ziggurat of the god Sîn at Ur. These bricks might have been stamped with this short text after Nabonidus' thirteenth regnal year (543), perhaps during his sixteenth (540) or seventeenth (539) year as king; for this opinion, see Beaulieu, Nabonidus p. 42 and Schaudig, Inschriften Nabonids p. 48. This inscription is referred to as "Nabonidus Brick B I, 1," "Nabonidus [Brick Inscription] 13," and "[Nabonidus] Inscription 18" in scholarly literature.

CATALOGUE

Ex.	Museum Number/ Source	Excavation/ Registration No.	Provenance	Lines Preserved	cpn
1	BM 90148	1979-12-20,71	Ur, ziggurat	1–5	p
2	BM 90161	1979-12-20,77	As ex. 1	1–5	p
3	BM 90162	1979-12-20,78	As ex. 1	1–5	p
4	BM 90712	1979-12-20,319	As ex. 1	1–5	p
5	BM 114283	1919-10-11,4714	As ex. 1	1–5	p
6	BM 114284	1919-10-11,4715	As ex. 1	1–5	p
7	BM 114285	1919-10-11,4716	As ex. 1	1–5	n
8	BM 114286	1919-10-11,4717	As ex. 1	1–5	p
9	BM 137346	1935-01-13,6; U 2863	As ex. 1	1–5	p
10	BM 137360	1919-10-11,5365	As ex. 1	1–5	p
11	BM 137404	1979-12-18,39	As ex. 1	1–5	p
12	BM 137450	1919-11-11,1708	Ur	1–2	p
13	UET 1 no. 188	U —	Ur, ziggurat, in situ	1–5	n
14	MM 715.21	—	Probably Ur	—	n
15	CBS 16561a	U —	As ex. 14	1–5	p
16	CBS 16561b	U —	As ex. 14	—	n
17	CBS 15328	U —	As ex. 14	1–5	p
18	CBS 15889	U —	As ex. 14	—	n
19	CBS 15378	U —	As ex. 14	—	n

20	UM 84-26-20	U —	As ex. 14	1–5	p
21	UM 84-26-44	U —	As ex. 14	1–5	p
22	IMJ 80.36/1	—	As ex. 14	1–5	p
23	YBC 17100	—	As ex. 14	1–5	p

COMMENTARY

This inscription appears on square bricks and rectangular half-bricks. Bricks of the former type measure between 32×32×6.5 cm and 31.5×29.5×5.5 cm, while the one known exemplar of the latter type (ex. 9 [BM 137346]) measures 32×15×6 cm. The rectangular stamped area in which the inscriptions are written vary marginally in size. The lengths measure between 11.7 and 12.5 cm and the heights measure between 8.8 and 9.3 cm.

As in the edition of H. Schaudig (Inschriften Nabonids p. 340), the master text and lineation follow ex. 1 (BM 90148). No score of the inscription is given on Oracc since scores are not provided for texts on bricks. Moreover, no minor (orthographic) variants are given in the critical apparatus at the back of the book.

Ex. 22 (IMJ 80.36/1) and ex. 23 (YBC 17100) were collated from photographs kindly provided L. Peri and K. Wagensonner respectively. IMJ 80.36/1 is currently on long-term loan in the Israel Museum (Jerusalem); the brick was purchased by Rev. Robert Craig for St. Andrew's Memorial Church, Church of Scotland (Jerusalem).

BIBLIOGRAPHY

1861 Rawlinson, 1 R pl. 68 no. 5 (exs. 1, 3–4, copy)
1863 Oppert, EM 1 p. 262 (exs. 1, 3–4, translation)
1875 Ménant, Babylone p. 253 (exs. 1, 3–4, translation)
1912 Langdon, NBK pp. 58 and 296–297 Nbd. no. 13 (exs. 1, 3–4, edition)
1920 Thompson, Arch. 70 p. 115 fig. 6 (ex. 12, copy)
1928 Gadd, UET 1 p. 57 and pl. 47 no. 188 (ex. 13, copy)
1973 Berger, NbK p. 350 Nbn. Backsteine B I, 1 (exs. 1–13, study)
1981 Walker, CBI p. 92 no. 111 Nabonidus 13 (exs. 1–13, transliteration, study)
1989 Beaulieu, Nabonidus p. 37 Inscription 18 (exs. 1–13, study)
1997 Márquez Rowe, AuOr 15 pp. 88–89 (ex. 14, transliteration, study)
2001 Schaudig, Inschriften Nabonids pp. 340–341 no. 1.7[a] (exs. 1, 3–4, edition; exs. 1–14, study)

TEXT

1) ^{d}AG-I LUGAL E.KI
2) *za-nin úri*.KI
3) *é-lugal-galga-si-sá*
4) *ziq-qur-rat é-giš-nu-gál*
5) *ud-diš-ma ana* KI-*šú* GUR

1–5) Nabonidus, king of Babylon, the one who provides for Ur, renovated and restored Elugalgalgasisa, the ziggurat of Ekišnugal.

39

This Akkadian inscription in archaizing Neo-Babylonian script is presently known from nine stamped bricks found at Ur. This five-line text records that Nabonidus rebuilt Egipar (*gipāru*-house), the residence of his daughter En-nigaldi-Nanna as the *ēntu*-priestess of the moon-god Sîn in the Ekišnugal temple complex at Ur. The bricks were probably stamped with this text during the second half of Nabonidus' second regnal year (554), when the king was rebuilding Egipar for his daughter. In previous editions and studies, this text is referred to as "Nabonidus Brick B I, 3," "Nabonidus [Brick Inscription] 15," and "[Nabonidus] Inscription 4."

CATALOGUE

Ex.	Museum Number/ Source	Excavation/ Registration No.	Provenance	Lines Preserved	cpn
1	BM 90151	1979-12-20,73	Ur, southeast mound	1–5	p
2	BM 90152	1979-12-20,74	As ex. 1	1–5	p
3	BM 90153	53-10-14,22	As ex. 1	1–5	p
4	BM 90154 + BM 90400	53-10-14,23	As ex. 1	1–5	p
5	UET 1 no. 186	U —	Ur, Egipar, in situ	1–5	n
6	MM 715.5	—	Ur, in the floor of a modern house in Nasiriyeh	1–5	n
7	CBS 16494	U 2863	Ur	1–5	p
8	CBS 16560a	U 2883a	As ex. 7	1–5	n
9	CBS 16560b	U 2883b	As ex. 7	1–5	n

COMMENTARY

The square-shaped bricks vary marginally in size. The largest and smallest bricks measure 37.5×37×7 cm and 37×36×6 cm respectively. The stamped area in which the inscriptions are written measure between 20.4 and 20.8 cm in length and 9.8 and 10.3 cm in height.

Following the edition of H. Schaudig (Inschriften Nabonids p. 342), the master text and lineation follow ex. 5, the in situ brick(s) copied by C.J. Gadd in UET 1 (pl. 47 no. 186). No score of the inscription is given on Oracc. In addition, no minor (orthographic) variants are given in the critical apparatus at the back of the book.

BIBLIOGRAPHY

1861 Rawlinson, 1 R pl. 68 no. 7 (exs. 1–2, 4, copy)
1863 Oppert, EM 1 p. 262 (translation, study)
1875 Ménant, Babylone p. 254 (translation)
1890 Peiser in Schrader, KB 3/2 pp. 96–97 (exs. 1–2, 4, edition)
1912 Langdon, NBK pp. 58 and 296–297 Nbd. no. 15 (exs. 1–2, 4, edition)
1928 Gadd, UET 1 pl. 47 no. 186 (ex. 5, copy)
1962 Wooley, UE 9 pp. 18, 36 and 41 (translation, study)
1973 Berger, NbK p. 352 Nbn. Backsteine B I, 3 (exs. 1–5, study)
1981 Walker, CBI p. 93 no. 113 Nabonidus 15 (exs. 1–5, transliteration, study)
1989 Beaulieu, Nabonidus pp. 24–25 Inscription 4 (exs. 1–5, study)
1997 Márquez Rowe, AuOr 15 p. 89 (ex. 6, transliteration, study)
2001 Schaudig, Inschriften Nabonids pp. 341–342 no. 1.8[a] (ex. 5, edition; exs. 1–6, study)

TEXT

1) ^{d}AG-*na-'i-id* LUGAL KÁ.DINGIR.RA.KI
2) *za-nin é-sag-íl ù é-zi-da*
3) *é-gi$_6$-pàr* É NIN.DINGIR.RA
4) *ša qé-re-eb úri*.KI
5) *a-na* ^{d}EN.ZU EN-*ia e-pú-uš*

1–2) Nabonidus, king of Babylon, the one who provides for Esagil and Ezida.
3–5) For the god Sîn, my lord, I built Egipar, the house of the *ēntu*-priestess that is inside Ur.

40

A rounded-top stele discovered in the Eanna ("House of Heaven") temple complex at Uruk was once inscribed with an inscription of a Babylonian king, possibly Nabonidus, written in archaizing Neo-Babylonian script. The entire inscription had been obliterated by a later ruler. The assignation to Nabonidus, rather than some other first-millennium ruler (for example, the eighth-century king Marduk-apla-iddina II) is based on the carved image of the king on the upper part of the stele, which is very similar to that of other, better preserved images of this king. Following, U. Moortgat-Correns (SMEA 39 [1997] pp. 111–116) and H. Schaudig (Inschriften Nabonids p. 535), this effaced stele is tentatively edited as an object bearing an inscription of Nabonidus; J. Börker-Klähn (Börker-Klähn, Bildstelen p. 228 no. 258) argues that it dates to the reign of Marduk-apla-iddina II (721–710 and 703). Although its inscription is not preserved, Schaudig (Inschriften Nabonids p. 48) suggests that the stele was engraved between Nabonidus' thirteenth (543) and sixteenth (540) regnal years on the basis of a letter written by the Babylonian king to Kurbanni-Marduk, the administrator of the Eanna temple, ordering that official to erect a stele on his behalf (YOS 3 no. 4). This stele is sometimes referred to as the "Uruk Stele" in scholarly literature. Because traces of only a few signs of this inscription are legible, no edition is provided in this volume.

CATALOGUE

Museum Number	Excavation Number	Provenance	cpn
IM —	W 18221	Uruk, Eanna, Qb XIV 5	c

BIBLIOGRAPHY

1956 Lenzen, UVB 12/13 p. 42 and pls. 21b, 22a and 23a (photo, study)

1982 Börker-Klähn, Bildstelen p. 228 no. 258 (study)

1993 Becker, AUWE 6 p. 60 and pls. 48–49 no. 794 (photo, study)

1997 Moortgat-Correns, SMEA 39 pp. 111–116 and figs. 3a–b (photo, study)

2001 Schaudig, Inschriften Nabonids p. 535 no. 3.6 (study)

41

A fragment from the first column of a two-column clay cylinder preserves part of an Akkadian inscription of Nabonidus written in contemporary Neo-Babylonian script. The text is not sufficiently preserved to be able to determine which building project of the king it commemorated. The extant text includes only Nabonidus' unusually long list of titles and epithets.

CATALOGUE

Museum Number	Registration Number	Provenance	cpn
BM 47814	81-11-3,521	Registered as coming from Ur	c

COMMENTARY

R. Da Riva (GMTR 4 p. 131) tentatively proposes that BM 47814 and BM 38696 belong to the same cylinder. Given that there is a ca. 2–3 cm gap between the two pieces, that BM 47814 is registered as coming from Ur and BM 38696 is said to have come from Borsippa, and that little of BM 38696 can be read because its surface is badly damaged, it is not yet possible to confirm Da Riva's proposed join between the two pieces. The online British Museum Collection website (March 2020) states that BM 38696 is inscribed with a hitherto unidentified text of Nebuchadnezzar II, however, the legible passages of that fragment seem to indicate that it could also be attributed to Nabonidus. Since the authors are unable to prove that BM 47814 and BM 38696 belong to one and the same cylinder, it is best to edit them separately. The former is edited here, while the latter is edited as text no. 1002.

The inscription, as far as it is preserved, is currently unparalleled by other Nabonidus texts and is unusual since it not only mentions the plague-god Erra and the goddess Ištar as the lady of battle, but also includes a petition to the gods to kill the king's enemies. The warlike elements included in this text might indicate an early date of composition for the text, although this cannot be proven with any degree of certainty given the poor state of preservation of the Nabonidus Chronicle.

BIBLIOGRAPHY

2008 Da Riva, GMTR 4 p. 131 no. 1b (study)

TEXT

Col. i

1) ^{d}AG-*na-ʾi-id* LUGAL TIN.TIR.KI *ru-bu-ú na-a-du*
2) *eṭ-lu šu-us-su-mu bi-nu-ut* ^{d}AG EN
3) *ša* IGI.GÁL-*li* DINGIR.MEŠ ^{d}AMAR.UTU *ú-šar-bu-ú zi-kir šu-mi*
4) [*ú-šá*]-⸢*ti*⸣-*ru ši-mat-*⸢*su be-lu*⸣-*ut* KUR *i-qí-pu-ma*
5) [...] *x x x x x x* (traces)

Lacuna

1′) [...] *x x* [...]
2′) [*x*-(*x*)]-*ri ka-la mi-*⸢*im-ma*⸣ [...]
3′) [*i*]-⸢*na*⸣ *bi-ri šu-ú sa x* KU *x* [...]
4′) ^{d}*èr-ra a-na šá-ga-áš za-*⸢*ʾi*⸣-[*i-ri*]
5′) ḪUL-*te lu e-ek-du-ti** GIŠ.TUKUL.MEŠ-*šu x x* [...]
6′) ^{d}INANNA *be-let* MÈ *mu-ka-an-ni-šá-at* ZA AG

i 1–5) Nabonidus, king of Babylon, attentive ruler, most befitting warrior who is the creation of the god Nabû, (my) lord, whose fame the wisest of the gods, the god Marduk, made great, whose lot [he made surpas]sing, (to whom) he entrusted the rule over his land and [...] ...

Lacuna

i 1′–12′) [...] everything there is [...] ... [...] ... [...] the god Erra, to kill [my] ene[my] ... his weapons [...] the goddess Ištar, the lady of battle who subdues ... [...] ..., the true shepherd, the one who provides for Esagil and Ezida, the ruler who provides (and) provides abundantly for all temples, the ... who brings gifts

i 4 [*ú-šá*]-⸢*ti*⸣-*ru ši-mat-*⸢*su*⸣ "whose lot [he made surpas]sing": No parallels of this expression are known in other Neo-Babylonian royal inscriptions, but *ušātirū nabnīti* "they made my form surpassing" possibly appears in two inscriptions of the Assyrian king Sîn-šarru-iškun (text no. 1 line 9 and text no. 6 line 10); see respectively http://oracc.org/rinap/Q003862/ and http://oracc.org/rinap/Q003867/ [2020].

i 2′ *ka-la mi-*⸢*im-ma*⸣ "everything there is": This expression is also attested in an inscription of Sîn-šarru-iškun (text no. 18 line 4); see http://oracc.org/rinap/Q003879/ [2020].

i 5′ *e-ek-du-ti** "wild": The cylinder has *e-ek-du-*MI. The term *ekdu* is usually attested in Neo-Babylonian royal inscriptions in connection with copper(-plated) statues of wild bulls (*rīmu*) set up in gateways of temples.

i 6′ After *mukannišat* ("the one who subdues"), one expects *za-i-ri* or *za-ʾi-i-ri* ("enemies").

⸢*ṣu*$^{?}$⸣ [...]
7′) *x x* DINGIR-*ti-iš* ID A RU MA Ú RA *x x*
8′) *re-é-*⸢*ú-um*⸣ *ki-i-ni za-nin é-sag-íl ù* ⸢*é*⸣-[*zi-da*]
9′) ÉNSI *za-ni-nu mu-ṭaḫ-ḫi-id gi-mi-ir* É.KUR
10′) *i-x ba-bi-il* IGI.SÁ-*e a-na* DINGIR.MEŠ GAL.MEŠ
11′) *áš-ru ka-an-šu pa-li-iḫ* DINGIR.MEŠ *u* ^{d}INANNA$^{?}$
12′) *ša* u_4*-mi-šá-am a-na zi-in-na-a-ti e x x na-a-du*$^{?}$
Col. ii
Completely missing

to the great gods, the humble (and) submissive one who reveres the gods and *goddess(es)*, who ... daily the provisioning of ...

Completely missing

42

This Akkadian inscription is known from a fragment from the left side of a two-column clay cylinder. Thirteen lines from the inscription's prologue are preserved and these parallel (with variation) Nabonidus' titulary in text no. 16 ([Larsa Cylinder] i 2–12), an inscription commemorating the restoration of Ebabbar ("Shining House"), the temple of the sun-god Šamaš at Larsa. Because nothing of the building report is preserved, it is not known if this inscription also recorded work at Larsa or if it commemorated construction in some other Babylonian city. The script is contemporary Neo-Babylonian. The edition is based on an unpublished transliteration of R. Da Riva.

CATALOGUE

Museum Number	Registration Number	Provenance	cpn
BM —	—	—	c

BIBLIOGRAPHY

2008 Da Riva, GMTR 4 p. 131 sub Nabonidus 1c (study)

TEXT

Col. i
Lacuna
1′) ⸢*mi*⸣*-gi-ir* ^{d}AMAR.UTU
2′) ⸢*ša*⸣*-ak-ka-na-ku za-ni-nu*
3′) ⸢*mu*⸣*-ud-di-iš é-sag-íl*
4′) ⸢*ù*⸣ *é-zi-da áš-ri pa-al-ḫa*
5′) *šá a-na ṭè-e-mi* DINGIR.DINGIR *pu-tu-qu*
6′) *i-da-an za-ni-na-a-ti*
7′) ⸢*mu-ud*⸣*-di-iš ma*-ḫa-zi*
8′) ⸢*iš*⸣*-ša-ak-ku ṣi-i-ri*

Lacuna
i 1′–13′) the favorite of the god Marduk, [the go]vernor who provides, the one who renovates Esagil and Ezida, the humble (and) reverent one who is constantly attentive to the will of the gods, (the one who has) generously providing hands, the one who renovates cult centers, the exalted ruler who provides abundantly for all temples, the indefatigable envoy who (succeeds) in reaching high mountains, the shep-

41 i 8′ *re-é-*⸢*ú-um*⸣ *ki-i-ni* "true shepherd": This epithet is rarely attested in extant Neo-Babylonian royal inscriptions (for example, Nabopolassar 4 i 5), but is frequently found in Neo-Assyrian royal inscriptions.

9′) *mu-ṭaḫ-ḫi-id gi-mir* É.KUR 10′) ⸢*na*⸣-*áš-pa-ri la a-ne-ḫa* 11′) ⸢*ka*⸣-*ši-id šá-di-i e-lu-ti* 12′) ⸢RE⸣.É.UM *mu-uš-ta-lu* 13′) [*mu-uš-te-ši-ir ni*]-⸢*ši ma-a*⸣-[*ti*]	herd who deliberates (and) [sets the people o]f (his) lan[d on the right path],
Lacuna	Lacuna
Col. ii Completely missing	Completely missing

Figure 21. BM 90837 (Nabonidus no. 43), the top part of a rounded-top stele that was purchased by C. Rich in 1811.

43

The upper, right edge of a broken, rounded-top stele purchased by C. Rich in 1811 preserves sixteen lines of an Akkadian inscription of Nabonidus.

The extant text, which is written in contemporary Neo-Babylonian script, records the prices for various commodities, including barley, dates, oil, wool, and tin. As only the upper part of this basalt (or trachyte) stele survives and because only a small portion of the inscription remains, it is uncertain if this monument comes from Babylon, as Rich claims, or from elsewhere in Babylonia. Affinities between this text and text no. 47 (Ḫarrān Stele), seem to suggest that the stele was commissioned by Nabonidus after his thirteenth (543) regnal year, perhaps in his fourteenth (542) or fifteenth (541) year as king; for this opinion, see Beaulieu, Nabonidus p. 42 and Schaudig, Inschriften Nabonids p. 48. In scholarly publications, this text is referred to as "Nabonidus Stele Fragment 1," "[Nabonidus] Inscription 14," and the "Tarif(f) Stele."

CATALOGUE

Museum Number	Registration Number	Provenance	cpn
BM 90837	25-5-3,99 (R 99)	Purchased by C. Rich in 1811, reportedly from Babylon	p

COMMENTARY

BM 90837 is one of the first Babylonian antiquities to have reached Europe; it is now housed in the British Museum (London). The face of the stele, as far as it is preserved, is engraved with a relief of Nabonidus standing before symbols of the moon (Sîn), sun (Šamaš), and Venus (Ištar). The left-facing king holds his staff in his left hand and addresses the gods with his right hand. Nothing of the inscription below the relief, assuming that surface was engraved with text, is preserved. That now-missing part of the inscription might have aided in determining where Nabonidus had that stele erected and when it was inscribed. The inscription was collated from legible photographs of the stele in print and online.

BIBLIOGRAPHY

1818 Rich, Second Memoir on Babylon pls. 2a–b (copy [Bellino])
1839 Rich, Narrative Babylon pls. 2a–b after p. 191 (copy [Bellino])
1852 Grotefend, Erläuterungen pp. 8–12 and fig. 1 (copy, edition)
1912 King, BBSt pp. 128–129 no. 37 and pls. 93–94 (photo, edition)
1918 Meissner, OLZ 21 pp. 119–123 (edition)
1936 Meissner, Warenpreise pp. 5, 8 and 10–11 (study)
1947 Landsberger, Studies Edhem p. 148 (study)
1956 Borger, Asarh. p. 121 §107 (study)
1958 Gadd, AnSt 8 pl. IIIa (photo)
1964 Röllig, ZA 56 pp. 247–249 (edition)
1973 Berger, NbK p. 382 Nbn. Stelen-Fragment 1 (study)
1975 Orthmann, Der alte Orient pp. 326–327 no. 251 and fig. 251 (photo, study)
1982 Börker-Klähn, Bildstelen pp. 230–231 no. 266 (study)
1986 Hawkins, Studies Mellink p. 94 (i′ 2–12, edition; study)
1989 Beaulieu, Nabonidus pp. 32–34 Inscription 14 (i′ 2–5, edition; study)
1990 Powell, AoF 17 pp. 93–94 (study)
1997 Moortgat-Correns, SMEA 39 pp. 111–133 and fig. 2 (photo, study)
2001 Schaudig, Inschriften Nabonids pp. 530–532 no. 3.4 (edition)
2007 Beaulieu, Representations of Political Power pp. 140, 148–149, 152 and 163 (study)
2008 André-Salvini and Beaulieu, Babylone p. 186 no. 108 (photo, study)
2008 Marzahn, Babylon: Wahrheit p. 117 fig. 48 and p. 124 no. 10 (photo, study)
2008 Finkel, Babylon: Myth and Reality p. 165 and fig. 152 (photo, study)
2008 Finkel and Seymour, Babylon: Mythos pp. 208–209 and fig. 1 (photo, study)
2009 Winter, On Art in the Ancient Near East 2 pp. 470 and 479 (photo, study)

TEXT

Lacuna

Col. i′

1) *ep-še-ti-ia* SIG$_5$.MEŠ *ḫa-diš ip-pa-lis-ma*

2) *a-ra-ku* [UD.MEŠ-*ia*] *i-qí-šá-an-ni ina a-mat* ^{d}30

3) LUGAL ⸢DINGIR⸣.MEŠ ^{d}IŠKUR ŠÈG *ú-*[*maš*]*-ši-ra-am-ma*

4) ^{d}*é-a ú-paṭ-ṭi-ra nag-bu-šú meš-ru-u*

5) *nu-uḫ-šú u* ḪÉ.GÁL-*la ina* KUR-⸢*ia*⸣ *iš-ku-un*

6) 1 GUR NIGIDA BANEŠ ŠE.BAR *a-na* 1 GÍN KÙ.BABBAR 1 GUR NIGIDAMIN BANEŠ ZÚ.LUM

7) [*a*]-*na* 1 GÍN KÙ.BABBAR NIGIDA BANIA ŠE.GIŠ.Ì *a-na* 1 GÍN KÙ.BABBAR

8) [*x*] BANEŠ *ú-le-e a-na* 1 GÍN KÙ.⸢BABBAR⸣ 5 MA.NA SÍG.ḪI.A

9) *a-na* 1 GÍN KÙ.BABBAR 1-*en* MA.NA ⸢AN?.NA?⸣ *a-na* 1 GÍN KÙ.BABBAR

10) ⸢GEŠTIN⸣ KAŠ.SAG KUR-*i šá ina qé-reb* KUR-*ia ia-a-nu*

11) ⸢BANEŠ?⸣ GEŠTIN *a-na* 1 GÍN KÙ.BABBAR KI.LAM *ina qé-reb* KUR-*ia*

12) [*ṭù*?]-⸢*uḫ*?-*du u meš-ru-ú ina* KUR-*ia*⸣ *iš-ku-un*

13) [UN.MEŠ] KUR-URI.KI *i-piš-tú* ^{d}30 *ip-pal-su-*⸢*ma*⸣

14) [*ip-la-ḫu* DINGIR]-*ut-su* GAL-*tú u* ^{d}⸢30⸣ LUGAL DINGIR.MEŠ

15) [...] *x šá ri* [*x x*] *ib-ši-ma*

16) [...] *x x x*

Lacuna

Lacuna

i′ 1–5) He (the god Sîn) looked with pleasure upon my good deeds and he granted me the lengthening of [my days]. By the word of the god Sîn, king of the gods, the god Adad re[lea]sed (his) rains (and) the god Ea opened up his springs. He established wealth, abundance, and prosperity in my land.

i′ 6–11a) One *gur*, one (bushel), and eighteen (*sila*) of barley (could be purchased) for one shekel of silver; one *gur*, two (bushels), and eighteen (*sila*) of dates (could be purchased) [f]or one shekel of silver; one (bushel) and thirty (*sila*) of sesame (oil) (could be purchased) for one shekel of silver; [... (bushel(s))] and eighteen (*sila*) of the finest oil (could be purchased) for one shekel of silver; five mina of wool (could be purchased) for one shekel of silver; one mina of *tin* (could be purchased) for one shekel of silver; [wi]ne, mountain beer, which does not exist in my land, eighteen (*sila*) (could be purchased) for one shekel of silver.

i′ 11b–12) (These are) the market price(s) in my land. He (the god Sîn) established plenty and riches in my land.

i′ 13–14a) [The people] of the land Akkad looked upon the deed(s) of the god Sîn a[nd became afraid of] his great [divi]nity.

i′ 14b–16) Moreover, the god Sîn, king of the gods, [...] ... [...] came to be and [...] ...

Lacuna

44

A fragmentarily preserved, single-column clay tablet is inscribed with a draft or archival copy of the beginning of an Akkadian inscription of Nabonidus; the script is contemporary Neo-Babylonian. The upper, left, and right edges, as well as parts of the first thirty-one and the last twenty lines written on the tablet are preserved. The inscription, as far as it is preserved, included Nabonidus' titulary and filiation, as well as the beginning of the building report, which may have recorded this king's work on Ezida ("True House"), the temple of the god Nabû at Borsippa, since that building's access way (*tallaku*) is mentioned. It is clear from the last line on the tablet (rev. 20′), which reads "[...] as utensils," that this tablet did not have the entire inscription written on it, but only the first part of it. The tablet inscribed with the rest of the text is still missing. The text is sometimes referred to as "[Nabonidus] Inscription G" in scholarly literature.

CATALOGUE

Museum Number	Registration Number	Provenance	cpn
BM 34706	Sp 2,194	Purchased	c

BIBLIOGRAPHY

1972 Walker, CT 51 pl. 24 no. 75 (copy)
1989 Beaulieu, Nabonidus p. 40 Inscription G (study)
2001 Schaudig, Inschriften Nabonids pp. 474–475 no. 2.20 (edition)
2005–06 George, AfO 51 p. 88 (obv. 23, 27–29, edition)

TEXT

Obv.

1) [... *ti*]-*ri-iṣ* ŠU.II ^{d}⸢*nisaba**⸣
2) [... *ni*]-⸢*bi-it*⸣ ^{d}*na-bi-*⸢*um*⸣
3) [...] DINGIR.MEŠ *u* ^{d}IŠ.TAR
4) [... *šá ra-šu*]-⸢*ú*⸣ *pu-luḫ-ti* DINGIR-<*ti*>-*šú* ⸢GAL-*tú*⸣
5) [... ^{d}]⸢*iš*⸣-*tar šá-aḫ-*⸢*ṭu*⸣
6) [...] x ⸢*si-iq*⸣-*ra-šú-*⸢*un*⸣
7) [...] ⸢^{d}ŠEŠ.KI⸣ x x ⸢*an*⸣-*ni-*⸢*ta*⸣
8) [...] ⸢*ip*?-*tíq*? / *ib*?-*ní*?⸣ *pa-*⸢*da-at-ti*⸣
9) [...] x *a-a it-bá-al*
10) [x x ŠU.II-*su*?] ⸢*ta*⸣-*ap-ri-ik pa-nu-*⸢*ú*⸣-*a*
11) [x x *šá mam-ma-an*] ⸢*la*?⸣ *i-lam-ma-du ina ḫu-*⸢*ṭù-ri*⸣
12) [...] ⸢*šu-ru-ba*⸣ DA LA ⸢URU BIŠ⸣ ŠI ⸢BIŠ⸣ *ma-na-ma*
13) [...]-⸢*ti*⸣ *ra-bi-iš ú-*⸢*mál-la*⸣
14) x MI NA IR ⸢BE SI DU⸣ *šá* ^{d}UTU *u* ⸢^{d}AMAR.UTU⸣
15) *ina na-*⸢*gab* te-né-še**⸣-*e-ti ma-*⸢*la* ib*⸣-*na-a* ⸢*qa*⸣-[*ta*]-⸢*a-šú*⸣
16) *a-*⸢*na*⸣ *be-lu-ut* KUR ⸢*iš*⸣-*šá-an-ni x x* ⸢LUGAL-*ú**⸣-[*ti*]-⸢*ia**⸣
17) ⸢*id*⸣-*di-na* GIŠ.NÍG.GIDRU* *i-*⸢*šar**⸣-*ti mu-*⸢*ra*-ap*-pi-šat*⸣ [KUR] *x x-né-e-ti*
18) *uš-pa-ra mu-kan-niš za-i-ri ú-šá-at-mi-ḫa* ⸢*qá*⸣-*tu-ú-a*
19) *re-e-ú-ut* KUR-*šú-*⸢*un*⸣ *ia-a-ti* ⸢*iš*⸣-*ru-kam*
20) ⸢DUMU ^{d}⸣AG-⸢*ba-lat-su-iq*⸣-*bi* ⸢NUN⸣ *pa-liḫ* DINGIR.MEŠ GAL.MEŠ *a-na-ku*
21) [*i-nu*]-⸢*um* ^{d}AMAR.UTU LUGAL?⸣-[*ú*]-⸢*ti*⸣ *ba-ú-la-a-ti*
22) [*e-pe-šú ana da*]-⸢*ri*?⸣-*a-ti* ⸢*ia*⸣-*a-ti iš-ru-kam*
23) [*a-na ud-du*]-⸢*šú*⸣ *tal-lik-*⸢*ta é*-zi*⸣-*da na-šá-an-ni* ⸢*lìb*⸣-*bi*

Obv. 1–6) [Nabonidus, ..., pr]otégé of the goddess Nisaba, [..., ch]osen by the god Nabû, [... of] the gods and goddesses, [..., who] fears his great divinity, [..., who] humbly [... the goddess I]štar, [...] their utterance(s)

Obv. 7–19) [...] the god Nannāru [...] this ..., [...] *he created* my figure, [...] he did not take away, [... p]laced [*his hand*] across my face, [... that] *no*[*body*] understands, with a staff [...] make enter ... nobody, [...] magnificently filled [...] ... of the gods Šamaš and Marduk, among all of humankind, as many as his h[an]ds had created, he raised me up to rule over the land, gave the ... of my royal maje[sty], let my hands grasp a just scepter that widens [the] ... [land] (and) a staff that subdues enemies, (and) gave me the shepherdship of their land (as a gift),

Obv. 20) son of Nabû-balāssu-iqbi, the prince who reveres the great gods, am I.

Obv. 21–26) [Whe]n the god Marduk gave me (the gift of) [exercising] *king*[*sh*]*ip* over (his) subjects [for *ete*]*rnity*, my heart wanted me [to renova]te the processional way of Ezida (and) my mind was focused [on constantly seeking out] the sanctuaries of the gods,

Obv. 1 [*ti*]-*ri-iṣ* ŠU.II ^{d}⸢*nisaba**⸣ "[pr]otégé of the goddess Nisaba": Literally "the one to whom the goddess Nisaba stretches out her hand." For details on this rarely used epithet, see the on-page note to text no. 2 (Emašdari Cylinder) i 17. ^{d}⸢*nisaba**⸣ "the goddess Nisaba": The tablet has visually similar ^{d}⸢TE-NAGA*⸣

Obv. 17 GIŠ.NÍG.GIDRU* *i-*⸢*šar**⸣-*ti* "a just scepter": The tablet has GIŠ.NÍG.Ú *i-*⸢QA⸣-*ti*.

24) [*a-na ši-te-e'-ú*] *eš-re-e-ti* DINGIR.⸢MEŠ*⸣ *ba-šá-a* ⸢*uz*⸣*-na-a-a*
25) [*pa-li-iḫ-ma*] ⸢*lìb*⸣*-bi a-na e-*⸢*pe*⸣*-eš ši-ip*-ri-šú-un*
26) [*a-na la ra-še-e*] ⸢*ḫi**⸣*-ṭi-ti gi-na-a ú-*⸢*sa-ap-pa*-a**⸣
27) [*é-sag*]-⸢*íl*⸣ *a-na* ⸢*šu*⸣*-ul-lu-mi ì*-lí** [GAL.MEŠ]
28) [*a-ši-bu-tú šá*] ⸢*si*⸣*-ḫi-*⸢*ir*⸣*-ti é-temen-an-*⸢*ki eš*⸣-[*šiš*]
29) [*e-pu-uš* ...]-*li* ⸢*gi-nu*⸣*-ú a-na na-*[*x x*]
30) [...] *x x* IT AM* *x* [*x*]
31) [...] *x x x* [*x x*]
Lacuna
Rev.
Lacuna
19 fragmentary lines
20′) [...] ⸢*a-na*⸣ *ú-*⸢*na*⸣*-a-ti*

(but) my heart [was afraid] (at the thought of) undertaking work on them and I constantly prayed [so that no] cultic mistake(s) [would occur].

Obv. 27–31) [I built Esag]il a[new] to ensure the well-being of the [great] gods [who reside] in the perimeter of Etemenanki. [...] to [...] *ginû*-offering(s) [...] ... [...] ... [...]

Lacuna

Lacuna
19 fragmentary lines
Rev. 20′) [...] as utensils.

45

A small piece of a (multi-column?) clay tablet is inscribed with a collection of Akkadian inscriptions of Nabonidus written in contemporary Neo-Babylonian script. Only the final three lines (the concluding formulae) of one text and the first three lines (the prologue) of a second text remain. Not enough of the contents of either text is preserved to be able to suggest which building projects of Nabonidus the inscriptions commemorate or to propose when the tablet was inscribed.

CATALOGUE

Museum Number	Registration Number	Provenance	cpn
BM 58756	82-7-14,3165	Possibly Sippar	c

COMMENTARY

BM 58756 is a little unusual since its obverse is rounded and its reverse is flat; one expects the opposite, for the obverse to be flat and the reverse to be rounded. Moreover, the reverse, as far as it is preserved, has been carefully smoothed and is not inscribed. A horizontal ruling separates the two inscriptions written on the obverse.

44 obv. 25 *ši-ip*-ri-šú-un* "work on them": The tablet has visually similar *ši-*LU*-ri-šú-un*.
44 obv. 27 *ì*-lí** "gods": The tablet has visually similar DÙ-DÙ. A.R. George (AfO 51 [2005–06] p. 88) has suggested that [u ^{d}15] ("and goddesses") should be restored at the end of the line, instead of [GAL.MEŠ] ("great").

BIBLIOGRAPHY

2001 Schaudig, Inschriften Nabonids pp. 477 no. 2.22 and 759 fig. 36 (copy, edition)

TEXT

Lacuna

1′) [...] *x* [...]

2′) [*x x*] ⸢^{d}⸣IDIM ^{d}UTU *u* ⸢^{d}⸣[...]

3′) ⸢*ur-ri*⸣-*ik* UD.MEŠ-*ia* ⸢MU⸣.[AN.NA.MEŠ-*ia* ...] *lu-lab-bi*-⸢*ir*⸣ [...]

4′) ^{md}AG-I LUGAL ⸢E.KI⸣ *em*$_4$-*qa mu-ut*-⸢*nen*⸣-[*nu-ú* ...]

5′) *x x x* [*x*] KU MU TE *x* [...]

6′) [...] ^{d}*x* [...]

Lacuna

Lacuna

1′–3′) [...] the gods Ea, Šamaš, and [...] prolong my days (and) [...] my y[ears ...] so that I may grow old [...].

4′–6′) Nabonidus, king of Babylon, the wise (and) pio[us one, ...] ... [...] the deity [...]

Lacuna

46

A fragment of a clay cylinder found at Ḫarrān preserves part of an inscription of Nabonidus commemorating his renovation of Eḫulḫul ("House which Gives Joy"), the temple of the moon-god Sîn in that city. The extant text, which is written in contemporary Neo-Babylonian script, contains part of a dialogue between Nabonidus and Marduk, the patron god of Babylon, discussing the rebuilding of Eḫulḫul, which had lain in ruins for fifty-four years, and the return of the statues of its deities (Sîn, Ningal, Nusku, and Sadarnunna); this text is presently one of the few extant inscriptions of Nabonidus that specifically mention the statues of these four deities. Because the inscription records work at Ḫarrān, it is fairly certain that the text was composed after Nabonidus' thirteenth regnal year (543), possibly in his sixteenth (540) year as king; see Schaudig, Inschriften Nabonids p. 48. In previous editions and studies, this text is referred to as "[Nabonidus] Fragment 3" and the "Ḫarrān Cylinder." For other inscriptions recording the renovation of Eḫulḫul, see text nos. 28–29 (Eḫulḫul Cylinder), 47 (Ḫarrān Stele), and 2001 (Adad-guppi Stele).

CATALOGUE

Museum Number	Excavation Number	Provenance	cpn
—	Hr 85/46	Ḫarrān	n

COMMENTARY

In earlier scholarly literature, Hr 85/46 is erroneously said to have been a fragment of a clay tablet; see Yardımcı, AnSt 36 (1986) p. 194. Moreover, the excavation number is Hr 85/46, not Hr 85/76, as reported in Donbaz, Varia Anatolica 1 p. 19. Because the original object was not available for study, since the present whereabouts of the cylinder fragment is not known, the edition presented here is based on V. Donbaz's published, hand-drawn facsimile of the inscription.

As for the date this still-incomplete text was composed, P.-A. Beaulieu (Nabonidus pp. 240–241) and H. Schaudig (Inschriften Nabonids p. 48) disagree. The former suggests that it was written during Belshazzar's regency (553–543), while the latter proposes that it was composed only after Nabonidus' thirteenth regnal year (543), probably during his sixteenth year as king (540). Beaulieu argues that the inscription written on Hr 85/46 was composed before Nabonidus' return to Babylon since "among the monumental inscriptions of Nabonidus, only those written during Belshazzar's regency fully acknowledge Marduk as supreme god with a befitting array of titles and epithets, while relegating Sîn to a subordinate position." While there is little doubt that the cylinder to which Hr 85/46 belongs was intended to be deposited in the structure of Eḫulḫul during its reconstruction, it is less certain when that took place. This may have been after 543, perhaps in 540, as Schaudig proposes, or earlier, in 549 or 548, as Beaulieu suggests. Beaulieu further explains his dating as follows: "rebuilding the temple was entirely Belshazzar's responsibility and was completed while the king was still in Teima, or it was initiated by Belshazzar but completed by Nabonidus after his return to Babylon. The second alternative has the advantage of harmonizing the contradictory data of the Eḫulḫul inscriptions in that it explains how Nabonidus could claim in inscription 13 [= text no. 47 (Ḫarrān Stele)] to have restored the Eḫulḫul after he left Teima, while at the same time the funerary stela of Adad-guppi [= text no. 2001] could insist that she witnessed the rebuilding before her death in the middle of Belshazzar's regency." Beaulieu further proposes that the inscription written on Hr 85/46 might have been a *Vorlage* (model) to all of the 'Eḫulḫul Inscriptions,' that is text nos. 17 (Larsa Stele), 28 (Eḫulḫul Cylinder), 43 (Tarif Stele), 47 (Ḫarrān Stele), and 2001 (Adad-guppi Stele). Given the poor state of preservation of this inscription and the uncertainties about exactly when Nabonidus had Eḫulḫul rebuilt, it is difficult to assign a firm date of composition to this text. Tentatively, Schaudig's suggested date is followed here.

BIBLIOGRAPHY

1986 Yardımcı, AnSt 36 p. 194 (study)
1987 Donbaz, Varia Anatolica 1 pp. 15–21 (copy, edition)
1989 Beaulieu, Nabonidus pp. 239–241 Frgm. 3 (study)
1993 Lee, RA 87 p. 132 (i′ 5′–7′, edition)
2001 Schaudig, Inschriften Nabonids pp. 472–474 no. 2.19 (edition)

TEXT

Lacuna
Col. i′
Lacuna
1′) [ALAM] ⸢^{d}⸣30 ^{d}⸢*nin*⸣-*gal* ⸢^{d}*nusku*⸣ [*u* ^{d}*sa-dàr-nun-na*]
2′) [*šá it-ti*] ⸢DINGIR⸣.MEŠ *šu-ut* URU.KASKAL *ina* ⸢*qer**⸣-[*bi-šú ú-ṣu-ú*]
3′) [*ud-du-uš-su-un šá*] ⸢*taq*⸣-*bu-ú ép-pu-uš-ma x* [...]
4′) [*x x a-na*] ⸢*qí-bi**⸣-*ti-ka ṣir-tú ul e*-⸢*eg*?⸣-[*gi ul a-še-et*]
5′) [*a-ḫi ul a-nam-di ki-ma*] ⸢*ṣi*⸣-*it pi-i-ka* ⸢ALAM⸣ ^{d}30 ^{d}⸢*nin*⸣-[*gal*]

Lacuna

Lacuna
i′ 1′–3′) [(As for) the statue(s) of] the deities Sîn, Ningal (Nikkal), Nusku, [and Sadarnunna, who had come out] of [it (Eḫulḫul/Ḫarrān) with the (other) g]ods of the city Ḫarrān, I will [renovate them as] you (Marduk) have commanded and [...].

i′ 4′–7′a) [...] I will not be *la*[*zy*, negligent, (or) careless with regard to] your exalted command. [According to] your decree, I will renovate the statue(s) of the deities Sîn, Ni[ngal (Nikkal), Nusku], Sadarnunna, and

i′ 4′ ⸢*qí-bi**⸣-*ti-ka* "your command": The copy has ⸢*qí*-MA⸣-*ti-ka*. H. Schaudig (Inschriften Nabonids p. 473 n. 652) tentatively suggests reading the signs as ⸢*a*!-*ma*⸣-*ti-ka* "*your* [*w*]*ord*."

6′) [^{d}*nusku*] ^{d}*sa-dàr-nun-na u* DINGIR.⌜MEŠ *šu*⌝*-ut* URU.⌜KASKAL⌝ [(*x*)]
7′) [...] *ud-da-áš-ma ú-šak-la-*⌜*lu ši-pir*⌝*-šú-un* é-ḫúl-*⌜*ḫúl*⌝
8′) [*ḫa-an-ṭiš*] ⌜*e**⌝*-pu-uš-ma ina qer*-bi-šú* ⌜*šu-úr*?-ma-a šu-bat-sú-un*⌝
9′) [*pal*]*-ḫi*?-iš a-ta-ma-a a-na* ^{d}EN.LÍL DINGIR.MEŠ* ^{d}⌜AMAR.UTU⌝
10′) [EN] EN.EN *reme*-nu-ú* ^{d}AMAR.UTU ⌜*um**⌝*-ma* URU *u* ⌜É* *šú-a-tú*⌝
11′) [*šá e*]-⌜*peš*⌝*-su taq-bu-ú iš-šak-nu ina pi-i-*⌜*ka**⌝
12′) [ERIM-*man*]-⌜*da*⌝ *sa-ḫir-šum-ma pu-ug-gu-lu* ⌜*e-mu-qa-a-šú*⌝
13′) [...] *x-ma šá-ni-ni ul i-ši ki-ki-i*
14′) [... ^{m}]⌜*iš*⌝*-tu-me-gi* LUGAL ERIM**-man-da íp-pu-šú* É
15′) [DINGIR.MEŠ *šu-ut* URU].⌜*ḫar-ra*⌝*-nu ú-šeš*-še-bu qé-*⌜*reb*⌝*-*[*šú*]
16′) [...] ⌜*it*?⌝*-ti*-ía e-*⌜*muq*?⌝ [...]
17′) [...] *x* [...]

Lacuna

Col. ii′

Lacuna

1′) [*a-na*] *si-mat* DINGIR-⌜*ti*⌝*-*[*šú* ...]
2′) ⌜*ki*⌝*-ma* ^{d}UTU-*ši šip-ri-šú a-*[...]
3′) ⌜*el-ṣi*⌝*-iš ud-diš-ma* [...]
4′) *ina qí-bit* ^{d}⌜AMAR.UTU⌝ [...]
5′) *re-eš* ⌜*mi*?⌝*-*[*im-ma-a-a dam-qa* ...]
6′) *ra-x* [...]
7′) *i-x* [...]

Lacuna

the (other) gods of the city Ḫar[rān, ...], and complete their work.

i′ 7′b–8′) (The god Marduk said to me:) "[Quickly] (re)build Eḫulḫul and have (them) take up residence in their dwelling place(s) inside it."

i′ 9′–13′a) I spoke [*rever*]*ently* to the Enlil of the gods, the god Marduk, (saying): "[O Lord] of lords, merciful Marduk, now, as for the city and that temple [who]se (re)building you have commanded, (whose renovation) has issued from (lit. "be placed in") your mouth — [a barbarian hor]de (the Medes) is all around it and its forces are powerful. [...] and it has no rivals."

i′ 13′b–16′) "How then [...]? Will [A]styages (Ištumegu), king of a barbarian horde (the Medes), (re)build th(at) temple (and) allow [the gods of the city Ḫa]rrān to dwell ins[ide it? ... w]*ith* me, *force*(*s*) *of* [...]."

Lacuna

Lacuna

ii′ 1′–3′) [... as] an appropriate symbol of [his] divinity [...] like the god Šamaš, *whose work* [...] I joyously renovated [...] and [...].

ii′ 4′–7′) By the command of the god Marduk [...] the best of ever[ything good ...] ... [...] ... [...]

Lacuna

47

This Akkadian inscription of Nabonidus is engraved on two rounded-top, basalt steles that were later reused to build the Great Mosque at Ḫarrān. The upper parts of both monuments are engraved with an image of the king standing before symbols of the moon (Sîn), sun (Šamaš), and the planet Venus (Ištar); the king faces left on both steles. This three-column text, which is written in contemporary Neo-Babylonian script, gives an account of the ten years that Nabonidus spent on the Arabian peninsula and states that after he returned to Babylon he rebuilt Eḫulḫul ("House which Gives Joy"), the temple of the moon-god Sîn at Ḫarrān, and returned that holy building's divine statues. With regard to his long stay in Tēmā, this text records that it was the god Sîn who made Nabonidus live there because the

---

46 i′ 8′ ⌜*šu-úr*?-ma-a*⌝ "have (them) take up residence": The copy looks more like ⌜*šu*-TU-*ma-a*⌝.
46 i′ 9′–12′ This passage also appears in text no. 28 (Eḫulḫul Cylinder) i 21–23.
46 i′ 10′ *reme*-nu-ú* "merciful": The copy has ŠU-*nu-ú*. ⌜*um**⌝*-ma* "now": For the use of *umma* in this passage not being used to introduce direct speech, but rather in the sense of Assyrian accentuating *mā* ("now"), see Schaudig, Inschriften Nabonids p. 276 §V.9.4 (with references to the relevant grammatical studies).
46 ii′ 2′ *šip-ri-šú* "*whose work*": Or possibly *me-re-šú* "*whose wisdom*." It is not certain how the signs are to be read here, as already pointed out by H. Schaudig (Inschriften Nabonids p. 473).

citizens of Babylon were so sinful towards the moon-god. Moreover, unlike text nos. 28 (Eḫulḫul Cylinder) and 46 (Ḫarrān Cylinder), this inscription states that it was Sîn, not Marduk (Babylon's tutelary deity), who spoke to Nabonidus in his dreams about restoring Eḫulḫul and returning its divine occupants from Babylon. Because the inscription explicitly states that the project was undertaken after the king's return to Babylon after his ten-year sojourn in Tēmā, the date of composition can be securely assigned to after the month Tašrītu (VII) of Nabonidus' thirteenth (543) regnal year. As little information is given on the reconstruction of Eḫulḫul, some scholars generally think that the steles were engraved during his fourteenth (542) or fifteenth (541) year as king; for this opinion, see Beaulieu, Nabonidus p. 42 and Schaudig, Inschriften Nabonids p. 48. This well-known text is referred to as "Nabonidus Stele Fragments III, 1," "[Nabonidus] Inscription 13," and the "Ḫarrān Stele."

CATALOGUE

Ex.	Museum Number	Excavation Number	Provenance	Lines Preserved	cpn
1	—	—	Ḫarrān, Great Mosque, east entrance, pavement	i 1–ii 42, iii 1–38	n
2	—	—	Ḫarrān, Great Mosque, west entrance, upper step of staircase	i 1–iii 5, 7–36	n

COMMENTARY

The line arrangement, when possible, follows ex. 1; the distribution of text varies between the two copies of the inscription. Ex. 2 cols. i and ii begin respectively with ex. 1 i 41 and ii 40. Neither exemplar of this inscription is complete and, therefore, the master text is a conflation of exs. 1 and 2; preference is given to ex. 1, the better preserved exemplar. A score is presented on Oracc and the minor (orthographic) variants are given in the critical apparatus at the back of the book.

BIBLIOGRAPHY

1957 Rice, ILN 231 p. 468 and figs. 5 and 10 (exs. 1–2, photo)

1958 Gadd, AnSt 8 pp. 35–36, 38–45, 56–69 and 79–92 and pls. II and IX–XVI (exs. 1–2, photo, edition)

1959 Moran, Orientalia NS 28 pp. 130–135 and 138–140 (iii 16–27, 34–35 transcription, study)

1959 Vogt, Biblica 40 pp. 92–102 (translation, study)

1960 Lambert, BWL p. 284 note to p. 52 (iii 0–2, study)

1960 Moran, Biblica 41 p. 296 (ii 15–18, study)

1964 Galling, Studien pp. 6–8, 10–12, 15–19 and 37 (study)

1964 Röllig, ZA 56 pp. 218–260 (edition)

1965 Landsberger, Brief p. 15 (i 14–17, study)

1965 Tadmor, Studies Landsberger p. 356 (iii 17–24 transcription, study)

1967 Borger, Orientalia NS 36 pp. 429–431 (i 21, study)

1969 Oppenheim, ANET³ pp. 562–563 (translation)

1972 Lambert, Arabian Studies 2 pp. 59–62 (study)

1973 Baltzer, WO 7 p. 91 (study)

1973 Berger, NbK p. 383 Nbn. Stelen-Fragmente III, 1 (study)

1979 Galling, Textbuch³ pp. 79–80 (i 7–27, ii 3–12, iii 11–24, translation)

1982 Börker-Klähn, Bildstelen p. 229 nos. 263–264 (study)

1988 Funk, Das Altertum 35 pp. 53 and 58–59 (study)

1989 Beaulieu, Nabonidus pp. 32, 59–63, 67, 146, 149–152, 172–173 and 213 Inscription 13 (i 1–4, 7–9, 11–19, 22–ii 26, iii 1–16, 34–38, edition; study)

1989 Dandamaev, Political History pp. 39–40 (study)

1994 D'Agostino, Nabonedo pp. 90–92 and 122 (i 7–11, 14–27, 45–ii 10, edition; study)

2001 Schaudig, Inschriften Nabonids pp. 486–499 no. 3.1 (edition)

2007 Beaulieu, Representations of Political Power pp. 137–163, esp. 140–152 (i 1–22, ii 14–20, edition; study)

2007 Ehring, Rückkehr JHWHs p. 99 (study)

2008 André-Salvini, Babylone p. 237 (photo)

2008 Finkel and Seymour, Babylon: Mythos p. 208 (i 16–24, translation)

2010 Heller, Spätzeit pp. 172, 181, 183, 185–186 and 193 (study)

— Schaudig in Eichmann and Hausleiter, Tayma 2 fig. 1.3 (ex. 2, drawing)

TEXT

Col. i

1) *i-piš-ti* ^{d}30 GAL-*ti šá* DINGIR.MEŠ *ù* ^{d}IŠ.TAR
2) *ma-am-ma-an* NU ZU-*šú šá ul-tu* u_4-*mu* *ru-qu-tu*
3) *a-na* KUR *la tu-ri-du u* UN.MEŠ KUR <*la*> *ip-pal-su-ma*
4) *i-na ṭup-pi la iš-ṭu-ru-ma la iš-tak-ka-nu*
5) *a-na* u_4-*mu ṣa-a-ti* ^{d}30 EN DINGIR.MEŠ *u* ^{d}INANNA *a-ši-bu-tú*
6) *šá* AN-*e šá ina pa-ni* ^{md}MUATI-NÍ.TUKU LUGAL TIN.TIR.KI
7) *ul-tu* AN-*e tal-li-ku a-na-ku* ^{md}MUATI-I
8) DUMU *e-du šá mam-ma-an la i-šu-ú šá* LUGAL-*u-tú*
9) *ina lìb-bi-ia la tab-šu-ú* DINGIR.MEŠ *u* ^{d}INANNA *a-na* UGU-
10) -⸢*ia*⸣ *ú-ṣal-lu-ú ù* ^{d}30 *a-na* LUGAL-*ú-ti*
11) ⸢*im*⸣-*ba-an-ni ina šá-at mu-ši* MÁŠ.GI_6 *ú-šab-ra-an*-⸢*ni*⸣
12) *um-ma é-ḫúl-ḫúl* É ^{d}30 *šá* URU.KASKAL *ḫa-an-ṭiš*
13) *e-pu-uš* KUR.KUR.MEŠ *ka-la-ši-na a-na* ŠU.II-*ka*
14) *lu-mál-la* UN.MEŠ DUMU.MEŠ TIN.TIR.KI *bár-sipa*.KI
15) NIBRU.KI *úri*.KI UNUG.KI *larsa*.KI LÚ.SANGA.MEŠ
16) UN.MEŠ *ma-ḫa-zi* KUR-URI.KI *a-na* DINGIR-*ú-ti-šu*
17) GAL-*ti iḫ-ṭu-ʾi-i-ma i-še-ti u ú-gal-li-lu*
18) *la i-du-u e-ze-es-su* GAL-*tú šá* LUGAL DINGIR.MEŠ ^{d}ŠEŠ.KI-*ri*
19) *par-ṣi-šú-nu im-šu-ʾi-i-ma i-dab-bu-bu sur-ra-a-tú*
20) *u la ki-na-a-tú ki-ma* UR.GI_7 *it-ta-nak-ka-lu*
21) *a-ḫa-míš di-ʾu u* SU.GU_7-*ú ina lìb-bi-šú-nu*
22) *ú-šab-šu-ú ú-ṣa-aḫ-ḫi-ir* UN.MEŠ KUR *u ana-ku*
23) *ul-tu* URU-*ia* TIN.TIR.KI *ú-še-ri-qa-an-ni-ma*
24) *ú-ru-uḫ* URU.*te-ma-a* URU.*da-da-nu* URU.*pa-dak-ku*
25) URU.*ḫi-ib-ra-a* URU.*ía-di-ḫu u a-di* URU.*ía-at-ri-bu*
26) 10 MU.AN.NA.MEŠ *at-tal*-⸢*la-ku*⸣ *qé-reb-šú-un a-na*
27) URU-*ia* TIN.TIR.KI *la e-ru-ub ina a-mat* ^{d}30
28) LUGAL DINGIR.MEŠ EN EN.EN *šá* DINGIR.MEŠ *u* ^{d}INANNA *a-ši-bu-ti*
29) *šá* AN-*e ú-šal-lim-u qí-bit* ^{d}30 ^{d}ŠEŠ.KI-*ri*

i 1–7a) The great deed of the god Sîn, which none of the gods and goddess(es) knew, which since distant days had not descended (from heaven) into the land, and (which) the people of the land had <not> seen, written down on a (clay) tablet, nor deposited for eternity, (that) you, the god Sîn, lord of the god(s) and goddess(es) who reside in heaven, have come (down) from heaven in the time of Nabonidus, king of Babylon.

i 7b–11a) I am Nabonidus, an only son who has no one, in whose heart (lit. "my heart") (the thought of) being king did not exist — the gods and goddess(es) (however) prayed for me and (therefore) the god Sîn called me to be king.

i 11b–14a) During the night, he showed m[e] a dream, saying: "Quickly, build Eḫulḫul, the temple of the god Sîn of the city Ḫarrān. I will place all of the lands into your hands."

i 14b–18) The people, the citizens of Babylon, Borsippa, Nippur, Ur, Uruk, (and) Larsa, the priests, (and) the people of the cult centers of the land of Akkad neglected his great divinity, *disregarded* (it), and sinned (against it). They did not know about the great anger of the king of the gods, the god Nannāru.

i 19–22a) They forgot their cultic rites and were speaking lies and untruths. They were eating one another like dogs, (and) created *di'u*-disease and famine among them. He (Sîn) reduced the people of the land.

i 22b–27a) Moreover, I — he (Sîn) took me far away from my city Babylon and, for ten years, I walked the road between the cities Tēmā, Dadānu, Padakku, Ḫibrā, Yadīḫu, and (then) as far Yatribu. I did not enter my city, Babylon.

i 27b–31a) By the word of the god Sîn, king of the gods, lord of lords, whose — the god Sin's, the god Nannāru's — command the gods and goddess(es) residing in heaven carry out in full, the deities Šamaš,

---

i 17 and 19 *iḫ-ṭu-ʾi-i-ma* "they neglected and" and *im-šu-ʾi-i-ma* "they forgot and": These two forms combine Akkadian final-weak verbal forms with Aramaic suffixes (*iḫṭûhēma* and *imšûhēma* respectively). For further details on these Aramaisms, see Schaudig, Inschriften Nabonidus p. 310 §VII.2.3.e.

i 23 *ú-še-ri-qa-an-ni-ma* "he (Sîn) took me far away and": Following the CAD (R p. 268), the verb is understood here as a Š-stem of the Akkadian verb *rêqu*, although the expected form of the word is *ušrīqannima*, not *ušerīqannima*. Alternatively, H. Schaudig (Inschriften Nabonids p. 312 §VII 2.5.a) has suggested that this verb may be an Aramaic loanword *erēqu* "to flee" and, if this proves correct, then *ú-še-ri-qa-an-ni-ma* should be translated as "he (Sîn) allowed me to flee and."

30) ^{d}UTU ^{d}INANNA ^{d}IŠKUR *u* ^{d}U.GUR EN.NUN-*tì šu-lum u* TIN
31) ⸢*ip*⸣-*qí-du it-ti-ia ina* MU *šá-a-šú ina* ITI.BÁRA
32) *u* ITI.DU$_6$ UN.MEŠ KUR-URI.KI *u* KUR.*ḫat-ti ḫi-ṣib* KUR-*i*
33) *u tam-tim i-leq-qu-nim-ma ina dan-na-tú um-ma-a-tú*
34) ITI.SIG$_4$ ITI.ŠU ITI.NE ITI.KIN ITI.DU$_6$ *ina* ITI.MEŠ *an-nu-tú*
35) *ina kal* MU.AN.NA.MEŠ *an-na-a-ti la ba-ṭa-a-lu*
36) *ina qí-bit* ^{d}30 ^{d}IŠKUR GÚ.GAL AN-*e u* KI-*tim* A.MEŠ
37) ŠÈG *i-šá-aq-qí-šu-nu-ti* NÍG.MEŠ$^{?}$-*šú-nu u bu-šá-šú-nu*

Ištar, Adad, and Nergal appointed me a guard for (my) well-being and (my) life.
i 31b–38a) In that year, in the months Nisannu (I) and Tašrītu (VII), the people of the lands of Akkad and Ḫatti took away for me the yield(s) of the mountains and sea(s), and, by the command of the god Sîn, the god Adad, the canal inspector of heaven and earth, gave them rainwater to drink during the scorching summer heat of the months Simānu (III), Duʾūzu (IV), Abu (V), Ulūlu (VI), (and) Tašrītu (VII), during these months, during all of those years, without ceasing. Their property and goods entered my presence intact.

38) *ina šu-lum ir-ru-bu-nu a-na maḫ-ri-ía ina a-mat*
39) ^{d}30 *u* ^{d}INANNA *be-let* MÈ *šá nu-kúr-ti u su-lum-mu-ú*
40) *ina ba-li-šu ina* KUR *la ib-ba-áš-šu-u ù kak-ku*
41) *la in-né-ep-pu-šu* ŠU.II-*su* ⸢*àna muḫ*⸣-*ḫi-šú-nu*
42) *ta-ap-ri-ik-ma* LUGAL KUR.*mi-ṣir* ⸢KUR⸣.*ma-da-a-a*
43) KUR.*a-ra-bi u nap-ḫar* LUGAL.MEŠ *na-ki-ru-tú a-na*
44) *su-lum-mu-ú u ṭu-ub-ba-a-ti* ⸢*i-šap*⸣-*pa-ru-nu*

i 38b–45a) By the command of the god Sîn and the goddess Ištar, the lady of battle without whom hostility and peace do not exist in the land and no war is fought, she (Ištar) laid her hand over them, and (then) the kings of the lands Egypt, Media, (and) Arabia, and all of the hostile kings sent (their envoys) into my presence for (establishing) goodwill and peace.

45) *a-na maḫ-ri-*⸢*ia* UN⸣.MEŠ ⸢KUR.*a-ra-bi šá* GIŠ.TUKUL⸣
46) *iš gal* [...] ⸢*šá* KUR-*ak-ka-di-i*.KI⸣
47) [...] x x *a-na*
48) ⸢*ḫa-ba-ti u la-qé-e*⸣ *šá bu-še-e iz-zi-*⸢*zu-ma*⸣

Col. ii

1) *i-na a-mat* ^{d}30 ^{d}U.GUR *kak-ki-šu-nu*
2) *ú-šab-bir-ma nap-ḫar-šú-nu ik-nu-šú a-na* GÌR.II-*a*$^{?}$

i 45b–ii 2) The people of Arabia, who ... [...] weapon(s) [...] of the land of Akkad [...] ... for robbing and taking away the possessions that they had available, but, by the word of the god Sîn, the god Nergal broke their weapons and they bowed down at *my* feet.

3) ^{d}UTU EN *ur-ti šá ina ba-li-šú pu-ú*
4) *la ip-pát-tu-ú u pu-u la uk-ta-at-ta-mu*
5) *mu-šal-lim qí-bit* ^{d}ŠEŠ.KI-*ri* AD ⸢*ba-ni-šú*⸣
6) UN.MEŠ KUR-URI.KI *u* KUR.*ḫat-ti šá ú-mál-lu-u*
7) ŠU.II-*ú-a pu-ú u lìb-bi ki-nim* ⸢*it-ti-ia*⸣
8) *iš-kun-šú-nu-ti-ma i-na-aṣ-ṣa-ru* EN.NUN-⸢*tì*⸣
9) *ú-šal-la-mu qí-bi-ti ina pi-rik* KUR-*i*.MEŠ
10) *né-su-ti ur-ḫu pa-rik-tú šá at-tal-la-ku*

ii 3–11) The god Šamaš, the lord of command(s) without whom no mouth is opened and no mouth is closed, the one who fully carries out the command(s) of the god Nannāru, the father who created him, made the people of the lands of Akkad and Ḫatti, whom he had placed in my hands, have common cause with and a loyal heart towards me so that they can fulfill (their) duties to m[e] (and) fully carry out (all of) my commands in the remote mountains region(s and on) the obstructed road(s) that I marched on for ten years.

11) 10 MU.AN.NA.MEŠ *ik-šu-dam-ma a-dan-nu*
12) *im-lu-u u*$_4$*-mu šá iq-bu-u* LUGAL DINGIR

ii 11b–26a) The appointed time arrived and the days that the king of the god(s), the god Nannāru, had

i 30 EN.NUN-*tì* "a guard for": M. Worthington (Textual Criticism p. 288 §5.4.8) suggests that the TIM sign is used as follows in first-millenium texts: "There is a peculiarity to the use of the sign TIM when it is ostensibly used as a phonetic complement to sumerograms: on manuscripts which otherwise give genitives the ending -*i*/*e*, TIM is used as a complement even for words which stand in the nominative and accusative. The use of TIM does not, then, indicate pronunciation /ti(m)/. Rather, it has simply become a standard spelling accompanying the sumerogram: a fossilised spelling. Rykle Borger called sign groups such as ZI-*tim* and KI-*tim* 'logographische Einheiten'. Why did such cases come into being? In our view, they are aids to reading. In the first millennium, the sign TIM is very rarely required to represent the spoken sounds /tim/ or /dim/. Therefore, readers knew as a rule of thumb that, whenever they saw it, there was a good chance it was being used as phonetic complement to a sumerogram. From here it is only a short step to using it as a marker of sumerography." Following the editorial practices of RINBE, RINAP, and RIM, the reading *tì* is used, when the pronunciation /ti/ or /tī/ is expected. For the use of logograms and the use of feminine ending *tì*, see also Schaudig, Inschriften Nabonids p. 103 §II.2.c and p. 169 §IV.2.4.2.e.

^{d}ŠEŠ.KI-*ri*
13) *ina* ITI.DU$_{6}$ UD.17.KAM *u*$_{4}$-*mu* ^{d}30 *im-ma-ag-gàr*
14) *pi-šìr-šú* ^{d}30 EN *šá* DINGIR.MEŠ *šá ina* UD.1.KAM
15) TUKUL ^{d}*a-nim zi-kir-šu* AN-*e ta-lap-pa-tú*
16) *u* KI-*tim ta-ḫe-ep-pu-ú ḫa-mi-im* GARZA
17) ^{d}*a-nù-ú-tú mu-gam-mi-ir* GARZA ⸢^{d}EN.LÍL⸣-*ú-tú*
18) *le-qu-ú pa-ra-aṣ* ^{d}*é-a-ú-ti*
19) *šá nap-ḫar gi-mi-ir pa-ra-aṣ* AN-*e ina* ŠU.II-*šú*
20) *tam-ḫu* ^{d}EN.LÍL DINGIR.MEŠ LUGAL LUGAL.LUGAL EN EN.EN
21) *šá a-na qí-bi-ti-šu la i-tur-ru*
22) ⸢*ù*⸣ *a-mat-su la ta-qab-bu-*⸢*ú*⸣ 2-*šú*
23) *šá pu-luḫ-ti* DINGIR-*ti-šú* GAL-*ti* AN-*e*
24) *u* KI-*tim ma-lu-ú ki-ma zi-mi-šú* AN-*e*
25) *u* KI-*tim saḫ-pu šá la ka-a-šu man-nu*

commanded had elapsed. In the month Tašrītu (VII), (on) the seventeenth day, whose interpretation is "the day the god Sîn is favorable," the god Sîn, the lord of the gods, whose name on the first day is "the *weapon* of the god Anu," *you* (*who*) *touch* the sky and break the earth, the one who has gathered (to himself all of) the divine offices of highest rank, the one who has collected (all of) the divine offices of supreme power, the one who has taken (for himself all of) the divine offices of the role of the god Ea, who grasps in his hands the totality of all of the divine offices of heaven, the Enlil of the gods, the king of kings, the lord of lords, who does not retract his command(s) (and) does not say his word(s) twice, the reverence of whose great divinity fills heaven and earth (and) covers heaven and earth like his appearance — what can be done without you?

26) *mi-na-a ip-pu-uš* KUR *šá lìb-bi-ka a-šab-šú*
27) *ub-lu pu-luḫ-tú* DINGIR-*ti-ka* GAL-*ti ina lìb-bi-šú*
28) *ta-šak-kan-ma a-na u*$_{4}$-*mu ru-qu-ti*
29) SUḪUŠ.MEŠ-*šú i-ku-un-nu* KUR *šá lìb-ba-ka*
30) *ḫa-pu-šú ub-lu pu-luḫ-ta-ka ul-tu*
31) *lìb-bi-šú ta-né-es-se-e-mu ta-na-an-di-iš*

ii 26b–32a) (As for) the land where your heart desired to reside, you placed reverence for your great divinity inside it so that its foundations are firmly established until distant days. (As for) the land that your heart desired to destroy, you withdrew your reverence from inside it (and) abandoned it until distant days.

32) *a-na u*$_{4}$-*mu* SÙ.MEŠ *šá nap-ḫar* DINGIR.MEŠ *u* ^{d}15
33) *a-ši-bu-*⸢*ti*⸣ *šá* AN-*e i-na-aṣ-ṣa-ru*
34) *ṣi-it pi-i-šú ú-šal-la-mu qí-bi-ti*
35) ^{d}ŠEŠ.KI-⸢*ri*⸣ AD *ba-ni-šú-un mu-ga-mi-ir*
36) GARZA AN-*e u* KI-*tim šá a-bal qí-bi-ti-šú*
37) *ṣir-tú šá u*$_{4}$-*mi-šam-ma ina šá-ma-mi*
38) *i-qab-bu-u* KUR *la ta-an-na-du-u*
39) *u nu-úr ina* KUR *la ib-ba-áš-šu-ú*

ii 32b–39) (You,) whose pronouncement(s) all of the gods and goddess(es) who reside in heaven honor (and) who fully carry out the command(s) of the god Nannāru, the father who created them, the one who has collected (all of) the divine offices of heaven and earth, without whose exalted command, which he speaks in heaven daily, no land is founded and no light in the land comes comes into existence —

40) ⸢DINGIR⸣.MEŠ GIM GI *i-šub-bu i-na-ar-ru-ṭu*
41) ^{d}*a-nun-na-ki šá la-pa-ni qí-bit* DINGIR-*ti-šú*
42) ⸢GAL-*ti*⸣ *šá la* ⸢*in*⸣-*nen-nu-*⸢*u*⸣ x x ⸢KUR-*i*⸣

ii 40–42) The gods were quivering like reed(s), the Anunnakū gods, who (...) in front of the command(s) of his great divinity, which cannot be changed, were trembling, ... mountain(s)

(8 lines illegible)

(8 illegible lines)

Col. iii
0) ⸢*it-ti* LÚ.ḪAL *u*⸣
1) LÚ.ENSI *a-lak-tú ul par-sat* ⸢*at*⸣-*til-ma*
2) *ina šat mu-ši* MÁŠ.GI$_{6}$ *pár-da-at a-di a-mat* $^{d?}$x x x
3) ⸢*im*⸣-*li* MU *ik-šu-du a-dan-nu šá* [*iq-bu-ú* ^{d}ŠEŠ.KI]-⸢*ri*⸣
4) *ul-tu* URU.*te-ma-a ú-*[...]

iii 0–4) (my) path did not stop with the diviner or the *dream-interpreter*. I laid down and, during the night, (my) dream was frightening, until the word of the god ... The year elapsed. (When) the appointed time that the god Nannāru had commanded arrived, [...] from the city Tēmā.

5) TIN.TIR.KI URU *be-lu-*[*ti-ia* x x-*ú-a*]
6) ⸢*i-mu-ru-ma*⸣ x x x

iii 5–11a) (As for the citizens of) Babylon, the city of [my] lordly maje[sty], they saw [my ...] and ... [...]

ii 15 TUKUL ^{d}*a-nim* "the *weapon* of the god Anu": It is uncertain exactly how one should understand the logogram TUKUL. One possibility is to emend the text to GIŠ.TUKUL.<DINGIR> (*miṭṭi anim*) "scimitar of of the god Anu." See Schaudig, Inschriften Nabonids pp. 491–492 n. 700 for further information on the many different scholarly interpretations of TUKUL ^{d}*a-nim*, which has been translated as "scimitar of the god Anu," "crescent moon of the god Anu," "princely seed," and "trustworthy one." P.-A. Beaulieu (Representations of Political Power p. 152), who also reads the sign in question as TUKUL and translates the pairing as "the weapon of the god Anu," understands *kakki anim* as the name of the moon-god on the first day of the month; he also notes that one expects *uskar anim*, which would be written logographically as U$_{4}$.SAKAR, not as KU (= TUKUL).

ii 36 *a-bal* "without": For the use of *abal* here, instead of *bala*, see Schaudig, Inschriften Nabonids p. 255 §V.6 sub *balu* d.

iii 0–1 These lines are a verbatim quote of Ludlul Bēl Nēmeqi I line 52.

7) [...] *àna šul-ma-*[*nu*] *u kád-ra-a*
8) ⸢*il-lu*?*-u*⸣ *a-na* ⸢*maḫ-ri-ía*⸣ LUGAL.MEŠ *qer-bu-tú*
9) *il-lu-nim-ma u-na-áš-šá-*⸢*qu* GÌR.II-*a*⸣
10) *u ru-qu-tú iš-mu-u ip-la-ḫu* DINGIR-*ut-su* GAL-
11) -*tú* DINGIR.MEŠ *u* ^{d}⸢IŠ.TAR⸣ *šá ip-par-du-ma i-re-qa*
12) *is-saḫ-ru-nim-ma i-qab-bu-*⸢*ú*⸣ *ba-ni-ti*
13) *ina* ⸢*pi-i*⸣ LÚ.ḪAL *iš-šá-kin* UZU *dum-qí-ía ina nu-uḫ-šú*
14) *ṭuḫ-du u* ḪÉ.GÁL-*la* UN.MEŠ-*ía ina* KUR-*i*.MEŠ *né-su-ti*
15) *ar-te-ed-dam-ma ina šá-lim-ti aṣ-bat ú-ru-uḫ*
16) *ma-ti-ia a-mat* DINGIR-*ti-šú* GAL-⸢*tú*⸣ *at-taṣ-ṣa-ar-ma*
17) *la e-gi la a-šit a-ḫi la ad-du* ⸢*ú*⸣*-šad-kam-ma*
18) UN.MEŠ KUR-URI.KI *u* KUR.*ḫat-ti ul-tu pa-aṭ* KUR.*mi-ṣir*
19) *tam-tim e-lit a-di tam-tim šap-lit šá* ^{d}30 LUGAL DINGIR
20) *ú-mál-lu-u* ŠU.II-*ú-a é-ḫúl-ḫúl* É ^{d}30 *eš-šiš*
21) *e-pu-uš ú-šak-lil ši-pir-šú* ŠU.II ^{d}30
22) ^{d}*nin-gal* ^{d}*nusku u* ^{d}*sa-dàr-nun-na ul-tu*
23) *šu-an-na* URU LUGAL-*ú-ti-ía a-ṣa-bat-ma ina ḫi-da-a-tú*
24) *u ri-šá-a-tú* ⸢*ú*⸣*-še-rib* ⸢*ú*⸣*-še-šib* BÁRA *da-ri-a-tú*
25) *ni-qu-u taš-*<*ri*>*-iḫ-tú ma-ḫar-šú-nu aq-qí-ma*
26) *ú-šar-ri-ḫi kád-ra-a é-ḫúl-ḫúl reš-*⸢*tú*⸣
27) *ú-mál-li-ma u-šá-li-iṣ lìb-bi* UN.MEŠ-*šú*
28) ⸢*ú*⸣*-šal-lim qí-bi-ti* ^{d}30 LUGAL DINGIR ⸢EN EN.EN⸣
29) *a-šib šá-ma-mu šá* DINGIR *šá* DINGIR.MEŠ *ina* AN-*e zi-kir-šú* ⸢*šu*⸣*-tuq*
30) ^{d}UTU *šá ni-bu-šú* ^{d}*nusku* ^{d}INANNA ^{d}IŠKUR *u* ^{d}U.GUR
31) *šá* ⸢*ú*⸣*-šal-lim-u' qí-bit* ^{d}ŠEŠ.KI-*ri*
32) *šu-tuq-šú-nu e-ma* GIŠ.TUKUL.MEŠ-*ía an-na-di-*⸢*iq*⸣*-ma*
33) *a-na e-peš* ⸢*ta-ḫa-zi*⸣ IGI-*ía áš-*⸢*kun-ma*⸣
34) *a-na šul-lu-mu qí-bit* ^{d}ŠEŠ.KI-*ri man-nu at-ta*
35) *šá* ^{d}30 *a-na* ⸢LUGAL-*u-ti*?⸣ *i-nam-bu-ka-ma*
36) DUMU-⸢*ú-ia-a*⸣*-ma i-qab-bu-ka aš-rat* ^{d}30
37) ⸢*a-šib šá-ma-me šá qí*⸣-[*bit-su la in*]-⸢*nen*⸣*-nu-ú*
38) ⸢*u a-mat*⸣*-su la ta-*[*qab-bu*]-⸢*u* 2⸣*-šú*
(5 lines illegible)

as a greeting-[gift] and a gift, they *came up* into my presence. The kings (living) nearby came up to me and kissed my feet. Moreover, the (kings) living far away heard (about it and) became frightened of his great divinity.

iii 11b–13a) The gods and goddesses who had cut themselves off and gone far away, turned favorably to me and said laudatory word(s) about me. My favorable omen(s) were placed in the mouth of the diviner.

iii 13b–17a) In the distant mountains, I constantly led my people in wealth, abundance, and prosperity, and I took the road (back) to my land in safety. I constantly observed the word(s) of his great divinity and I was not lazy, negligent, (or) careless.

iii 17b–20a) I mustered the people of the land of Akkad and Ḫatti, from the border of Egypt (and) the Upper Sea to the Lower Sea, which the god Sîn, king of the gods, had placed into my hands.

iii 20b–24) I built Eḫulḫul, the temple of the god Sîn, anew (and) completed its construction. I took the deities Sîn, Ningal, Nusku, and Sadarnunna by the hand, (leading them out) of Šuanna (Babylon), the city of my royal majesty, and I had (them) enter (and) reside on their eternal dais(es) during joyous celebrations.

iii 25–27) I offered sumptuous offerings before them (and) presented (them) with my gifts. I filled Eḫulḫul with joy and made the heart(s) of his people rejoice.

iii 28–32a) I fully carried out the command(s) of the god Sîn, king of the gods, lord of lords, the one who resides in heaven, whose name in heaven is "the god of gods," who surpasses the deities Šamaš — whose name is (also) Nusku — Ištar, Adad, and Nergal, who fully carry out the command(s) of the god Nannāru, who surpasses them.

iii 32b–34a) Whenever I put on my weapons and set my eyes on doing battle, (it was) to fully carry out the command(s) of the god Nannāru.

iii 34b–38) Whoever you are, whom the god Sîn names to be king and (then) calls you "my son," [...] the sanctuary of the god Sîn, the one who resides in heaven, wh[ose] com[mand(s) cannot be chan]ged and whose word(s) are not said twice,

(5 illegible lines)

---

iii 11 *ip-par-du-ma* "they had cut themselves off and": Following H. Schaudig (Inschriften Nabonids p. 313 §VII 2.5.f), this verb is understood here as an Aramaic loanword *parādu* "to separate oneself." At present, this is the only known attestation of that verb in Akkadian. It should not be confused with more frequently attested Akkadian of the same root, *parādu*, which means "to be fearful." Note that the CAD (P p. 144b) suggests emending this word to *ip-par-*<*ši*>*-du-ma*, understanding the verb as a form of *naparšudu* "to flee." Because both exemplars of this text write the word as *ip-par-du-ma*, Schaudig's suggestion that the word is an Aramaic loanword is preferred here, which would not be surprising since the inscription comes from Ḫarrān.

iii 28–32a The interpretation of the lines follows Schaudig, Inschriften Nabonids p. 499 (with nn. 726–727).

48

Part of one line of an inscription of Nabonidus written in contemporary Neo-Babylonian script is preserved on a small fragment of a piece of plaster found at Ḫarrān in 1959. The text is presently known only from H.W.F. Saggs' published edition, which he prepared from a squeeze made in the field. The inscription most likely dates to the last years of Nabonidus' reign, sometime after his return from the Arabian peninsula in the month Tašrītu (VII) of his thirteenth (543) regnal year. Because the original object was not available for study, the edition presented here is based on Saggs' edition.

CATALOGUE

Museum Number	Excavation Number	Provenance	cpn
—	—	Ḫarrān	n

BIBLIOGRAPHY

1969 Saggs, Iraq 31 p. 168 (edition)

2001 Schaudig, Inschriften Nabonids p. 547 no. 4.5 (edition)

TEXT

Lacuna
1′) DUMU ^{md}MUATI-⌜TIN$^{?}$⌝-[*su-iq-bi* ...]
Lacuna

Lacuna
1′) son of Nabû-ba[lāssu-iqbi, ...]
Lacuna

49

A stone fragment discovered at Ḫarrān in 1959 preserves parts of three lines of an Akkadian inscription of Nabonidus. The text, which is written in contemporary Neo-Babylonian script, is presently only known from the published copy and edition of H.W.F. Saggs, which he prepared from a squeeze made in the field. The inscription states that Nabonidus rebuilt Eḫulḫul ("House which Gives Joy"), the temple of the moon-god at Ḫarrān. Because the reconstruction of Sîn's temple took place after Nabonidus returned to Babylon after his ten-year sojourn in Tēmā, the inscription's date of composition can be securely assigned to after the month Tašrītu (VII) of his thirteenth (543) regnal year. As the present whereabouts of this stone fragment are not known, the edition presented in this volume is based on Saggs' copy and edition.

CATALOGUE

Museum Number	Excavation Number	Provenance	cpn
—	—	Ḫarrān	n

BIBLIOGRAPHY

1960 [Anonymus], AnSt 10 p. 8 no. 3 (translation [Saggs], study)

1969 Saggs, Iraq 31 pp. 166–169 and fig. 1 (copy, edition)

2001 Schaudig, Inschriften Nabonids p. 547 no. 4.4 (edition)

TEXT

Lacuna

1′) [...] *x x x*

2′) [...] *a-na-ku é-ḫúl-ḫúl* É* ^{d}30

3′) [*šá*? *qé-reb*? URU.*ḫar-ra-na*? *a-na*? ^{d}30? EN DINGIR.MEŠ *šá*] AN *u* KI-*tim* EN-*ía lu**-*ú e-pu-uš*

Lacuna

1′–2′a) [...] ... [...], am I.

2′b–3′) [*For the god Sîn*, lord of the gods of] heaven and earth, my lord, I indeed (re)built Eḫulḫul, the temple of the god Sîn [*that is inside the city Ḫarrān*].

50

A small inscribed piece of limestone was discovered during the third campaign of British excavations at Ḫarrān in 1959. Little of the text remains (only one word can be positively identified) and the attribution to Nabonidus is based on the fact that the inscription is written in contemporary Neo-Babylonian script and that other inscriptions of his were unearthed at the same time. If the identification proves correct, then the object was probably inscribed sometime after the month Tašrītu (VII) of Nabonidus' thirteenth (543) regnal year, when Eḫulḫul ("House which Gives Joy"), the temple of Sîn, was being rebuilt. Because the current whereabouts of the original object are not known, the present edition is based on H.W.F. Saggs' published copy and edition.

CATALOGUE

Museum Number	Excavation Number	Provenance	cpn
—	—	Ḫarrān	n

49 line 3′ The tentative restoration in line 3′ is based on text no. 51 line 3, a brick inscription from Ḫarrān.

BIBLIOGRAPHY

1969 Saggs, Iraq 31 p. 167 (edition)

2001 Schaudig, Inschriften Nabonids pp. 546–547 no. 4.3 (edition)

TEXT

Lacuna
1′) [...]-*ma a-si*?-[...]
2′) [...] *ti-iz-kar* [...]
3′) [...] *li* [...]
Lacuna

Lacuna
1′–3′) [...] ... [...] speak! [...]
Lacuna

51

About one hundred bricks found in the debris of the Islamic settlement of Ḫarrān are stamped with a four-line Akkadian inscription of Nabonidus stating that he rebuilt Eḫulḫul ("House which Gives Joy"), the temple of the moon-god Sîn. The script is contemporary Neo-Babylonian. Although the bricks do not bear a date, they were clearly made when Nabonidus was having Sîn's temple renovated, which, according to text no. 47 (Ḫarrān Stele), took place after he returned to Babylon in Tašrītu (VII) of his thirteenth regnal year (543). Therefore, this text was stamped on bricks sometime after that date. In scholarly literature, this inscription is sometimes referred to as "[Nabonidus] Fragment 2."

CATALOGUE

Museum Number	Excavation Number	Provenance	cpn
—	Hr 85/75	Ḫarrān, Squares 33 DD/36 GG, debris of Islamic settlement	(p)

COMMENTARY

Of the bricks discovered at Ḫarrān in 1985, 1989, and 1990, the excavation number for only one of them has ever been published: Hr 85/75. All of the partially-baked bricks, of which there appear to have been two different types (square and rectangular), are reported to have had the same four-line inscription on their faces. Four different stamps of equal size were used to impress the inscription; in most cases, the text was very faintly pressed into the face of the bricks. The square bricks measure 33.5×33.5×7 cm and the rectangular bricks measure 33.5×16.5×7 cm; the damaged brick Hr 85/75 measures 24×6×7 cm. The dimensions of the stamps themselves are not known.

The current whereabouts of the bricks used to build Eḫulḫul are unknown, but it is assumed that most were left in the field. The present edition is generally based on V. Donbaz's facsimile of the inscription (ARRIM 9 [1991] p. 12 and fig. 1), which is a composite made from over one hundred different bricks. The text could be partially collated from the published photograph of Hr 85/75 (Donbaz, Varia Anatolica 1 [1987] p. 21). From that photo it is clear that the name of Nabonidus' father in line 2 should be read as ^{md}MUATI-*ba-lat-su-iq-bi* ("Nabû-balāssu-iqbi"), and not ^{md}*nusku-ba-lat-su-iq-bi* ("Nusku-balāssu-iqbi") as copied and transliterated by Donbaz; for this reading of the name, see already Schaudig, Inschriften Nabonids p. 342.

No score of the inscription is given on Oracc and no minor (orthographic) variants are given in the critical apparatus at the back of the book. In the case of this text, this is because the inscription is known only from a composite copy and a photograph of a single exemplar.

BIBLIOGRAPHY

1987 Donbaz, Varia Anatolica 1 pp. 15, 19 and 21 (photo, copy, edition)
1989 Beaulieu, Nabonidus p. 239 Frgm. 2 (study)
1991 Donbaz, ARRIM 9 pp. 11–12 and fig. 1 (copy, edition)
2001 Schaudig, Inschriften Nabonids pp. 342–343 no. 1.9 (edition)
2007 Beaulieu, Representations of Political Power pp. 154–155 (study)

TEXT

1) ^{md}MUATI-*na-ʾi-id* LUGAL TIN.TIR.KI *za-nin é-sag-íl*
2) *u é-zi-da* DUMU ^{md}MUATI-*ba-lat-su-iq-bi* NUN *gít-ma-lum*
3) *é-ḫúl-ḫúl* É ^{d}30 *šá qé-reb* URU.*ḫar-ra-na a-na* ^{d}30
4) ^{d}*nin-gal* ^{d}*nusku u* ^{d}*sa-dàr-nun-na* EN.MEŠ-*a lu* DÙ-*uš*

1–2) Nabonidus, king of Babylon, the one who provides for Esagil and Ezida, son of Nabû-balāssu-iqbi, perfect prince.

3–4) For the deities Sîn, Ningal, Nusku and Sadarnunna, my lords, I built Eḫulḫul, the temple of the god Sîn that is inside the city Ḫarrān.

52

This bowl, which is said to have been made of *alallu*-stone (a light reddish brown stone that is 65 percent dolomite and 30 percent calcite), is inscribed with an Akkadian text of Nabonidus stating that he had this bowl and another bowl (a *šulpu*-vessel) dedicated to Sîn at Ḫarrān; the script is contemporary Neo-Babylonian. Both vessels were reported to have been used for hand-washing rituals performed at the ziggurat of Eḫulḫul ("House which Gives Joy"); this is the only cuneiform text mentioning a temple-tower at Ḫarrān. The present edition is based on the published photograph.

CATALOGUE

Museum Number	Registration Number	Provenance	cpn
SM 899.2.282	1660	Probably Ḫarrān	p

BIBLIOGRAPHY

1991 Dole and Moran, ZA 81 pp. 268–273 (photo, edition)

2001 Schaudig, Inschriften Nabonids pp. 545–546 no. 4.2 (edition)

Figure 22. SM 899.2.282 (Nabonidus no. 52), a fragment of a bowl dedicated to the god Sîn at Ḫarrān to be used during hand-washing rituals. Courtesy of the Semitic Museum, Harvard University.

TEXT

1) *a-na* ^{d}30 LUGAL *šá* DINGIR.MEŠ *a-šib* ⸢AN⸣-[*e* GAL.MEŠ EN *é-ḫúl-ḫúl šá qé-reb* KASKAL.KI EN-*ia*]

2) ^{d}MUATI-NÍ.TUKU LUGAL TIN.TIR.KI *za-nin é-*⸢*sag*⸣-[*íl u é-zi-da a-na-ku kal-lu u*]

3) *šul-pi šá* NA$_{4}$.*a-lál-lum a-na na-še-e me-*⸢*e*⸣ [ŠU.II *ina* ...]

4) *ziq-qur-rat é-ḫúl-ḫúl šá qé-reb* KASKAL.KI *e-pu-*⸢*uš*⸣-[*ma a-na si-mat* DINGIR-*ú-ti-šú*]

5) GAL-*ti šá u*$_{4}$-*mi-šam-ma ana gi-né-e ina šá-ma-mu a-*⸢*ma*⸣-[*at-su i-qab-bu-u*]

6) *u a-na qí-bit-šú* ⸢*la*⸣ [*i-tur-ru* ...]

1–2a) For the god Sîn, king of the gods, the one who resides [in the great] hea[vens, lord of Eḫulḫul, which is inside the city Ḫarrān, my lord]: Nabonidus, king of Babylon, the one who provides for E[sagil and Ezida, am I].

2b–6) I ma[de a *kallu*-bowl and] a *šulpu*-vessel of *alallu*-stone for carrying water for the [(washing of) hands in ...], the ziggurat of Eḫulḫul, which is inside (the city) Ḫarrān [and, as an emblem of his (Sîn's)] great [divinity], who daily and constantly [speaks his] wo[rd(s)] in the heavens and (who) does no[t go back] on his promise, [I ...].

53

This inscribed chalcedony bead, which is now in a private collection, was possibly found at Ḫarrān (or Ur). According to its Akkadian inscription, the bead was part of a dagger that Nabonidus dedicated to the statue of Sîn, after that god made this request in a dream. The script is presumed to have been contemporary Neo-Babylonian. Because the present whereabouts of the object are not known, the edition presented here is based on the published

52 line 6 The translation of *a-na qí-bit-šú* ⸢*la*⸣ [*i-tur-ru*] follows CAD T p. 258 3e.

transliteration of A.L. Oppenheim. This text is sometimes referred to in scholarly publications as the "Nabonidus Pearl" and "[Nabonidus] Inscription F."

CATALOGUE

Museum Number	Excavation/ Registration No.	Provenance	cpn
Private collection (anonymous)	—	Possibly Ḫarrān	n

COMMENTARY

H. Schaudig (Inschriften Nabonids pp. 48 and 545) suggests that the text was written in connection with the rebuilding of Eḫulḫul and the renovation of its divine statues and, therefore, postulates that this short inscription of Nabonidus was composed after that king's return to Babylon in his thirteenth regnal year (543). P.-A. Beaulieu (Nabonidus p. 40), on the other hand, notes that there "is no evidence to its date," since it original provenance is unknown. If the dagger in which this pearl was inlaid was indeed closely connected with this king's activities at Ḫarrān, then a late date of composition is expected. However, since Nabonidus was actively engaged with Sîn-related activities and construction at Ur starting in his second year as king (554), when he consecrated his daughter En-nigaldi-nanna as *ēntu*-priestess of the moon-god there, and since the dagger requested by Sîn to Nabonidus might have been associated with work at Ur, it is best not to assign a firm date of composition to this text. Tentatively, following Schaudig, the Pearl Inscription of Nabonidus is edited here together with that king's Ḫarrān inscriptions, rather than with those from Ur.

BIBLIOGRAPHY

1956 Oppenheim, Dream-book p. 192 (edition)
1973 Berger, NbK p. 343 Nbn. Perle (study)
1989 Beaulieu, Nabonidus p. 40 Inscription F (study)
1993 Berger, Rolle der Astronomie p. 281 (translation, study)
2001 Schaudig, Inschriften Nabonids p. 545 no. 4.1 (edition)

TEXT

1) GÍR *ḫi-šíḫ-ti* dEN.ZU EN DINGIR *šá ina* MÁŠ.GI_6 mdAG-I MAN TIN.TIR.KI *i-ri-šú*

1) (This is) the dagger, a request of the god Sîn, lord of the god(s), that he requested from Nabonidus, king of Babylon, in a dream.

54

In the spring of 2012, the Saudi Commission of Tourism and Antiquities discovered a badly weathered relief and Akkadian inscription of Nabonidus at al-Ḥā'iṭ (probably ancient Padakku), in an abandoned part of the modern city's palm oasis. The relief depicts a right-facing Nabonidus, who wears traditional Babylonian royal attire, holds a staff, and stands before four divine symbols, the moon (Sîn), the sun (Šamaš), the planet Venus (Ištar), and a U-shaped symbol (possibly the so-called 'omega'-shaped symbol representing a local Arabian deity). Little of the inscription, which is written in contemporary Neo-Babylonian script, remains; parts of the first twenty lines are preserved. Apart from the mention of Nabonidus, a few of his titles, the name of the city Padakku, and the name of the moon-god Sîn (who is called "king of the gods, lord of the gods"), little else about the inscription's contents is known. The text was composed either during Nabonidus' ten-year sojourn in Tēmā, between his third (553) and thirteenth (543) regnal years, during which time he conquered Padakku, or sometime after the month Tašrītu (VII) of his thirteenth (543) year as king, when he was rebuilding Eḫulḫul ("House which Gives Joy"), the temple of the moon-god Sîn at Ḫarrān. The edition presented in this volume is based on H. Schaudig's published copy.

CATALOGUE

Museum Number	Excavation Number	Provenance	cpn
—	—	al-Ḥāʾiṭ	n

BIBLIOGRAPHY

2014 Joannès, NABU pp. 83–84 no. 51 (study)
2014 Hausleiter and Schaudig, NABU pp. 114–115 no. 70 (study)
2016 Hausleiter and Schaudig, ZOrA 9 pp. 224–240 and figs. 9–16 (photo, copy, study)

TEXT

1) [(*x*)] DINGIR.⸢MEŠ⸣ [...]
2) [...].MEŠ [...]
3) [(*x*) *x*].MEŠ [(*x x*)] *x* [...]
4) [...]
5) [*ina*$^{?}$] ⸢*lìb*$^{?}$⸣-[*bi*$^{?}$] URU.⸢*pa*$^{?}$⸣-[*dak*$^{?}$-*ku*$^{?}$]
6) *x* ⸢URU$^{?}$⸣.[...]
7) *lìb-bi* URU ⸢EN⸣-[*ú-ti-*(*ia*)]
8) *ana* DÙ$^{?}$ [...]
9) [...]-⸢*ti*$^{?}$⸣ [...]
10) ^{d}⸢MUATI-I⸣ LUGAL E.KI [...]
11) LUGAL [GAL-*ú*$^{?}$] ⸢LUGAL KUR⸣-[*šu-me-ri*$^{?}$ *u*$^{?}$ KUR-URI.KI$^{?}$]
12) *x x* (*x*) [(*x*)] *x* (*x*) [...] *x* [...]
13) [*x* (*x*)] DINGIR GAL$^{?}$ [...]
14) [*x* (*x*)] *x-lu*$^{?}$-*tú*$^{?}$ *x* (*x*) A [...]
15) ⸢^{d}⸣30 ⸢LUGAL DINGIR⸣.MEŠ ⸢EN⸣ DINGIR.MEŠ [...]
16) [...] *x x* (*x*) [...]
17) [*x*] *x* ⸢*ša*$^{?}$⸣ *u* ^{d}[...]
18) [$^{d?}$]⸢30$^{?}$⸣ ^{d}*nusku* ^{d}[...]
19) [*x* (*x*)] NI $^{d?}$*x* ^{d}⸢15⸣ *u* ^{d}[...]
20) [...] *x* [...]

Lacuna

1–9) [(...)] gods [...] ... [... *in*]*side* the city *P*[*adakku*], the *cit*[*y* ...], in the city of [(my)] lordly ma[jesty], to *build* [...].

10–14) Nabonidus, king of Babylon, [..., *great*] king, king of the land of [*Sumer and Akkad*], ... [...] ... [...] ... [...]

15–20) The god Sîn, king of the gods, lord of the gods, [...] ... [...] ... [...] the deities [*Sî*]*n*, Nusku, [...] ..., Ištar, and [...]

Lacuna

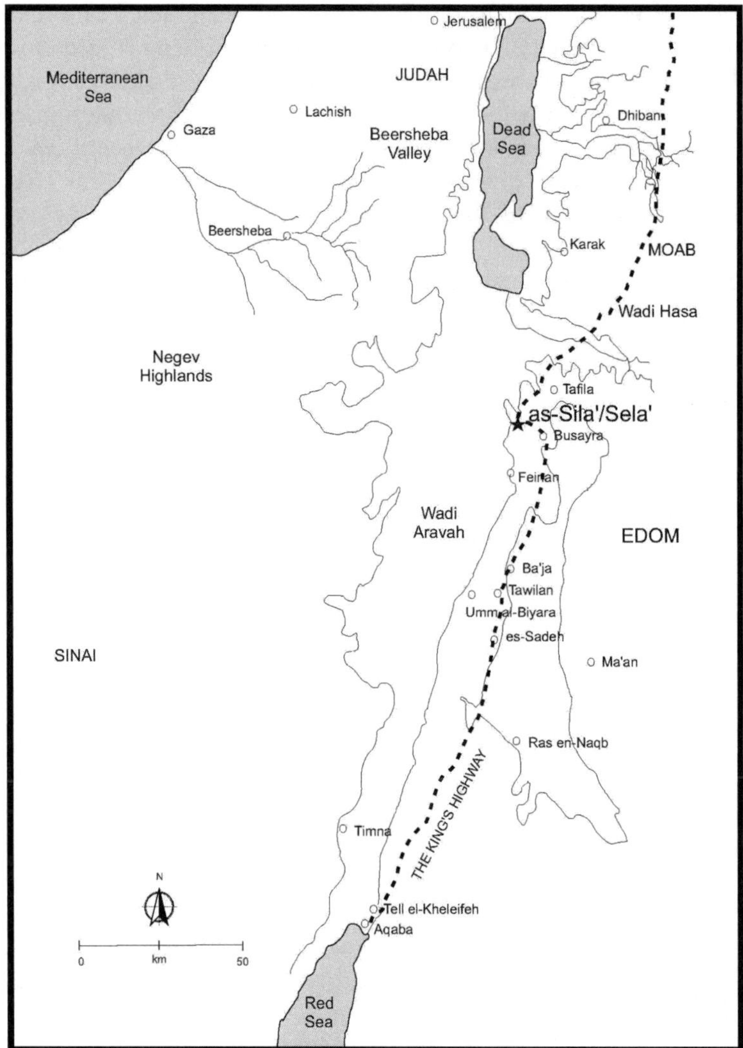

Figure 23. Map of Jordan showing the location of Sela'. Adapted from Porter, OJA 23 (2004) p. 375.

55

Nabonidus had one (or possibly two) Akkadian inscription(s) commemorating his deeds written on a high rock face at Sela' (Jordan). Because of the badly weathered condition of the monument, it is not possible to determine if the text in the left three columns (= cols. i–iii) and the text in the right two columns (= cols. iv–v) are parts of one and the same inscription or belong to two separate texts. The left-hand text, which is written in contemporary Neo-Babylonian script, is accompanied by an image of Nabonidus wearing traditional Babylonian royal attire, holding a staff, and standing before symbols of the moon (Sîn), sun (Šamaš), and the planet Venus (Ištar); the king faces right. The right-hand text, which was later added to the monument and also written in contemporary Neo-Babylonian script, was inscribed in two columns to the right of the original, three-column text. Scholars generally date the composition of the so-called "Sela' Inscription" between Nabonidus' third (553) and thirteenth (543) regnal years, during his ten-year sojourn in Tēmā. Since the left-hand text appears to mention the king's fifth year, the monument was probably originally carved during or after 551. The right-hand text was carved sometime later, although this is unclear as almost nothing survives today in cols. iv and v, apart from the the first four words, *anāku Nabium-na'id šar Bābili* ("I am Nabonidus, king of Babylon") in col. iv.

Figure 24. Annotated photo of the Sela' Inscription (Nabonidus no. 55) showing the four areas with traces of cuneiform text. © Sela Archaeological Project, Adrián Salgado, and Ramón Álvarez.

CATALOGUE

Museum Number	Excavation Number	Provenance	cpn
—	—	Sela', near Buṣayra, Jordan	c

COMMENTARY

In September 2018, R. Da Riva examined and photographed the badly-weathered inscription at Sela'. For a general description of the perilous expedition, which involved abseiling down to the monument with state-of-the-art climbing equipment and a team of skilled climbers trained in mountain rescue, see Da Riva, BAR 45 (2019) pp. 25–32 and Da Riva, ZA (forthcoming). The present edition is based on Da Riva's hand-drawn facsimiles, photographs, and transliteration of the Sela' Inscription, which she kindly provided prior to their publication in ZA. The authors would like to express their gratitude to her for allowing them access to this material prior to its publication.

BIBLIOGRAPHY

1997 Dalley and Goguel, ADAJ 41 pp. 169–176 and figs. 1–11 (photo, study)
1998 Roaf, RLA 9 p. 12 (study)
1999 Lindner, Nürnberger Blätter 15 p. 189 fig. 6 (photo)
1999 Vanderhooft, Neo-Babylonian Empire p. 57 (study)
1999 Zayadine, Syria 76 pp. 86–88 (study)
2001 Gentili, NABU 2001 pp. 84–85 no. 89 (study)
2001 Gentili and Saporetti, Geoarqueologia 2001/1 pp. 39–58 (photo, copy, edition)
2001 Raz, Raz, and Uchitel Cathedra 101 pp. 19–38 (edition [Hebrew])
2001 Schaudig, Inschriften Nabonids p. 544 no. 3.9 (iv 1, edition)
2006 Eichmann, Schaudig and Hausleiter, AAE 17 pp. 170–171 (study)
2007 Crowell, BASOR 348 pp. 75–88 (partial copy, edition)
2008 Beaulieu, Babylone p. 152 (drawing [after Börker-Klähn])
2010 Heller, Spätzeit p. 183 (study)
2019 Da Riva, BAR 45 pp. 25–32 (photo, study)
— Da Riva, ZA (photo, copy, edition)
— Schaudig in Eichmann and Hausleiter, Tayma 2 fig. 1.2 and 1.5–6 (drawing)

TEXT

Col. i
Lacuna
1′) *x x* [...]
2′) ⸢KASKAL$^{?}$⸣ *x x* [...]
3′) *x x* (*x*) *x* [...]
4′) *x x* (*x*) URU$^{?}$.*x* [...]
5′) *x* (*x*) *x* [...]
6′) [...]
7′) [...]
8′) *x* [...]
9′) ⸢*šu*$^{?}$⸣-*x* [(*x*)] *x* [...]
10′) [...]
11′) *x* ⸢KASKAL$^{?}$⸣ *x* [...]
12′) MU$^{?}$.5.KAM$^{?}$ [...]
13′) ⸢KI⸣ *a-ḫa-mi͗š* [...]
14′) *x x x* [...]
15′) LUGAL.MEŠ *x x* [(*x*)] *x* (*x*) BU [...]
16′) *x* [(*x*)] *x x x x* [...]
17′) *x* [...] *x* [(*x*)] *x* [...]
Lacuna

Lacuna
i 1′–11′) (No translation possible)

i 12′–17′) (*During my*) *fifth year* [...] with each other [....] ... [...] the kings of ... [...] ... [...]

Lacuna

Col. ii
Completely missing

Completely missing

Col. iii
1) [...]-IZ$^{?}$-*x*
2) [...] *x* (*x*) *x*
3) [...] *x* (*x*) *x*
4) [...] *x* [(*x*)]
5) [...] *x* [(*x*)]
6) [...] *x* [(*x*)] *x*
7) [...] ^{d}*na*$^{?}$-⸢*bi*$^{?}$-*um*$^{?}$⸣
8) [...] *x x x*
9) [...] *x x* (*x*) *x*

iii 1–21) (No translation possible)

10) [...] *x x x x* [*x*]
11) [...] *x* [...]
12) [...] *x* [...]
13) [...]
14) [...] RAB$^{?}$ *x* URU$^{?}$.*x* [...]
15) [...] *x x x* [...]
16) [... MU$^{?}$].5$^{?}$.KAM$^{?}$ [...]
17) [...] *x ra*$^{?}$ [...]
18) [...] AB (*x*) *x* [...]
19) [...].MEŠ *šá x x* (*x*) *x* [...]
20) [...] APIN$^{?}$ *x* [...]
21) [...] *x x x* [...]

Lacuna

Lacuna

Col. iv

1) ⸢*ana*⸣-*ku* ^{md}MUATI-⸢I⸣ LUGAL E.⸢KI⸣ *x* [...]
2) ⸢^{d}⸣UTU EN *x* [...]
3) ⸢^{d}EN$^{?}$⸣.[ZU ...]
4) *x x* [...]
5) [(*x*)] *x* [...]
6) [*x*] *ma*$^{?}$ *x* [...]
7) [(*x*)] *x* [...]
8) [(*x*)] *x* [...]

iv 1–3) I am Nabonidus, king of Babylon, [...] the god Šamaš, the [...] lord, [...], the god *S*[*în*, ...]

iv 4–8) (No translation possible)

Lacuna

Lacuna

Col. v

Completely missing

Completely missing

56

The upper part of a rounded-topped stele preserving part of an inscription of a late Babylonian king (almost certainly Nabonidus) was found during the 2004 German excavations at Tēmā. Both the relief — which depicts a right-facing king standing in front of symbols of the moon (Sîn), sun (Šamaš), and the planet Venus (Ištar) — and the Akkadian inscription — which is written in contemporary Neo-Babylonian script — are badly weathered. Little of the inscription itself remains and what is preserved records some of the king's deeds in Babylon. The attribution to Nabonidus is based on the iconography, the script, and the fact that Nabonidus lived on the Arabian peninsula for ten years (553–543). Although the inscription is not sufficiently preserved, the stele may have been inscribed either during his ten-year sojourn in Tēmā, between his third (553) and thirteenth (543) regnal years, or sometime after the month Tašrītu (VII) of his thirteenth (543) year as king, when he returned to Babylon and was engaged in rebuilding Eḫulḫul ("House which Gives Joy"), the temple of the moon-god Sîn at Ḫarrān.

CATALOGUE

Excavation Number	Provenance	cpn
TA 488	Tēmā, Qrayyah, Area E, within the debris outside the large public building (Building E-b1)	n

COMMENTARY

As far as the stele is preserved, it appears that only the face of the stele was inscribed. There are no traces of text on the sides or the back. Moreover, it is uncertain exactly what the complete inscription would have commemorated since much of the text is completely lost. H. Schaudig assumes that the now-missing portion of the inscription recorded Nabonidus' deeds in Babylonia, Syria, Arabia and Ḫarrān (especially the rebuilding of Eḫulḫul). If that proves correct, then the stele would have been inscribed sometime after Tašrītu (VII) 543. The edition presented here is based on Schaudig's published copy and edition of the inscription (AAE 17 pp. 169–173 and fig. 11).

BIBLIOGRAPHY

2006 Eichmann, Schaudig and Hausleiter, AAE 17 pp. 169–176 and figs. 8 and 11–13 (photo, copy, edition)

2008 al-Ghabban, Babylone pp. 231–232 (study)

2008 Finkel, Babylon: Myth and Reality p. 165 and fig. 154 (photo, drawing, study)

2008 Finkel and Seymour, Babylon: Mythos pp. 208–209 (study)

2008 Hausleiter, Babylone p. 187 no. 109 (photo, drawing, study)

2008 Marzahn, Babylon: Wahrheit p. 248 figs. 170a–c and pp. 273–274 no. 233 (photo, drawing, study)

2010 Hausleiter and Schaudig, Routes d'Arabie pp. 252–253 (photo, study)

2010 Schaudig, ATLAL 20 pp. 137–138 and pls. 4.15d–4.16c (photo, drawing, study)

2018 Schaudig in Hausleiter, ATLAL 25 p. 81 [Arabic section] and pp. 99–100 (study)

— Schaudig in Eichmann and Hausleiter, Tayma 2 no. 1 and figs. 1.1 and 1.5–6 (photo, copy, edition)

TEXT

1)	[*a-na-ku*$^{?}$ ^{md}MUATI-I$^{?}$ LUGAL$^{?}$ TIN.TIR.KI$^{?}$ ...]	1–7) [*I am Nabonidus, king of Babylon, ...*]
2)	[...]	
3)	[...]	
4)	[...]	
5)	[...]	
6)	[...]	
7)	[...]	
8)	[... *da*]-*ri-u*-⸢*tú*$^{?}$⸣ [...]	8–11) [... e]tern[al ...]
9)	[...]	
10)	[...]	
11)	[...] *x* [...] *x* (*x*) [...]	
12)	[...] ⸢^{d}⸣*x x* [...] ⸢*ra*⸣-*biš ú*-⸢*šak*⸣-[*lil*]	12–14) [...] the deity ... [...] I [mag]nificently com[pleted. ....] for the god Nabû ... [...] ... [...]... [...]
13)	[...] ⸢*a-na* ^{d}MUATI$^{?}$⸣ *x x* (*x*) *x* [...] *x x x* [*x x* (*x*)]	
14)	[...] *x x x* (*x*) *x* [*x* (*x*)] *x* (*x*) [...] *x x* [...]	
15)	[...] *šá* [...] ⸢NA$_4$⸣ *ni-siq-tú* NA$_4$ *šú*-[*qu-ru-tú*]	15–20) [...] *of* [...] precious [sto]ne(s), va[luable] stone(s), [...] ... [...] ... [... tal]ents (and) 6 minas of [...] ... [...] ... 6 *gur* of *al*[*abaster*(-stones), ...] 6,600 precio[us] *stones*, [...] ..., *pappardilû*-stone(s), ..., carnelian, lapis lazuli, ... [...] ... [...] revealed his [...] to [*me*].
16)	[...] ⸢NA$_4$$^{?}$⸣.*x* [...] *x* (*x*) *x* [...] *x x x* [...]	
17)	[...] ⸢GUN⸣ 6 MA.NA [...] *x x x x x x* NA$_4$.*x* [...] *x* [...]	
18)	[...] *x* ⸢6⸣ GUR NA$_4$.⸢GIŠ$^{?}$⸣.[NU$_{11}$$^{?}$.GAL$^{?}$ ...] ⸢6⸣ LIM 6 ME ⸢NA$_4$$^{?}$.MEŠ$^{?}$⸣ *ni-siq*-[*tú* ...]	

19) [...] (*x*) *x-qu*$^{?}$ NA$_4$.BABBAR.DILI [*x* (*x*) *x*] NA$_4$.⌜GUG NA$_4$.ZA.GÌN⌝ *x* (*x*) *x x* [...]

20) [...] *x x* [(*x*)] *x x x x* (*x*) *x-šu ud-du-nin-*⌜*ni a-na*⌝ [*ia-a-ti*$^{?}$]

21) [...] *x x x x x x x-su ra-biš ú-*⌜*ter*$^{?}$*-ma*$^{?}$ *a-na-ku*$^{?}$⌝

22) [...] ⌜*ú*⌝*-šá-lik* 1 NÍG.NA KÙ.GI SIKIL ⌜*ú-šag*$^{?}$*-me-er*$^{?}$⌝ *šu-bat* ^{d}AMAR.UTU ⌜^{d}*zar-pa-ni*⌝-[*tum*]

23) [...] *x x* ^{d}*x* (*x*) [(*x x*)] ⌜^{d}*taš*⌝*-me-tum* ^{d}*na-na-a* ⌜^{d}⌝[*x x* (*x*)]

24) [...] ⌜^{d}GAŠAN-*ía šá qé-reb é*$^{?}$*-bára*⌝-<*dúr*>*-gar-*⌜*ra*$^{?}$⌝ [*x* (*x*)]

25) [...] *x* (*x*) [...]

Lacuna

21–25) [...] ... I magnificently *returned* (it to) its ... *and* I [...] made (it) befitting. *I had* a censor of shiny gold *completed.* [...] the residence of the god Marduk (and) the goddess Zarpan[ītu ...] ... the goddesses Tašmētu, Nanāya, (and) [... of] Bēltīya (Zarpanītu), which is inside *Ebara<dur>gara*, [...] ... [...]

Lacuna

57

Two fragments of a sandstone pedestal discovered at Tēmā in 2006 and 2009 preserve part of a one-line Akkadian inscription of Nabonidus written in contemporary Neo-Babylonian script. As H. Schaudig has already suggested, these inscribed fragments might have been part of the pedestal on which the rounded-topped stele of Nabonidus discovered in 2004 or a hitherto undiscovered representation of him (perhaps an anthropomorphic statue) stood. This recently discovered inscribed object provides additional proof that Nabonidus resided in Tēmā.

CATALOGUE

Excavation Number	Provenance	cpn
TA 3656 + TA 9208	Tēmā, Qrayyah, Area E, Square E21, fill SU 2480 (south of the Building E-b1)	p

BIBLIOGRAPHY

2010 Hausleiter and Schaudig, Routes d'Arabie p. 253 no. 101 (photo, study)

2018 Schaudig in Hausleiter, ATLAL 25 p. 81 [Arabic section], pl. 2.20 figs. c–e and pp. 99–100 (photo, copy, edition)

— Schaudig in Eichmann and Hausleiter, Tayma 2 no. 2 and figs. 1.7–8 (photo, copy, edition)

TEXT

1) [(...)] DIŠ ⌜ALAM⌝ ^{md}MUATI-I ⌜LUGAL TIN.TIR⌝.KI LUGAL *dan-na* A ⌜^{m}⌝[^{d}MUATI-TIN-*su-iq-bi* ...]

1) [(...)] Statue of Nabonidus, kin[g of] Babylon, mighty king, son of [Nabû-balāssu-iqbi, ...].

58

A fragment of a stele discovered at Tēmā preserves parts of four lines of an inscription written in contemporary Neo-Babylonian script.

CATALOGUE

Excavation Number	Provenance	cpn
TA 3813	Tēmā, Qrayyah, Area E, Square E3, within the debris outside the large public building (Building E-b1), SU 243	p

COMMENTARY

Courtesy of H. Schaudig, text nos. 58–61 are included here prior to their publication. The authors would like to express their gratitude to him for allowing them to include these fragmentarily preserved inscriptions of Nabonidus prior to their publication. Full treatment of the texts — with photographs, hand-drawn facsimiles, and commentary — will appear in Schaudig's forthcoming contribution in Eichmann and Hausleiter, Tayma 2.

BIBLIOGRAPHY

— Schaudig in Eichmann and Hausleiter, Tayma 2 no. 3 and figs. 1.9–10 (photo, copy, edition)

TEXT

Lacuna
1′) [... *ù* ^{d}*iš-tar* GAŠAN] ⌜MÈ *ú-qa-ù*⌝-[*nin-ni* ...]
2′) [... DINGIR.MEŠ *a-ši*]-*bi é*-⌜*sag*⌝-*íl* ⌜*u é*⌝-[*zi-da* ...]
3′) [...] ⌜ŠÀ$^{?}$ *ik*⌝-*kud x* [...]
4′) [...] *x x* [...]
Lacuna

Lacuna
1′–4′) [... and the goddess Ištar, the lady of] battle, waited [for me ... the gods who resi]de in Esagil and E[zida ...] (*my*) *heart* was pounding, [...] ... [...]

Lacuna

59

A fragment from the left side of a stele found at Tēmā preserves the beginnings of six lines of an inscription of Nabonidus; the script is contemporary Neo-Babylonian. The stele fragments bearing this text and text no. 61 might come from one and the same monument. Since this cannot be proven with certainty, it is best to edit the two pieces separately.

CATALOGUE

Excavation Number	Provenance	cpn
TA 3833	Tēmā, Qrayyah, Area E, Square E3, within the debris outside the large public building (Building E-b1), SU 243	p

BIBLIOGRAPHY

– Schaudig in Eichmann and Hausleiter, Tayma 2 no. 4 and figs. 1.11–12 (photo, copy, edition)

TEXT

Lacuna
1′) *x x* [...]
2′) *qé-reb* [...]
3′) *ina qí-*⌜*bi*⌝-[*it* ...]
4′) *ina* ⌜*kal*?⌝ [...]
5′) *lu-be-*[*el* ...]
6′) *x* ⌜KUR / TE⌝ [...]
Lacuna

Lacuna
1′–6′) ... [...] inside [...], by the comm[and of ...] among *all of* [...] may I rule [over ...] ... [...]
Lacuna

60

A fragment of a stele bearing an inscription of Nabonidus written in contemporary Neo-Babylonian script was discovered at Tēmā. Despite that only the middle parts of seven lines are preserved, the attribution to Nabonidus is certain since the extant portion of the text states that the king who commissioned this monument restored Eḫulḫul ("House which Gives Joy"), the temple of the moon-god Sîn at Ḫarrān, and was the son of Nabû-balāssu-iqbi.

CATALOGUE

Excavation Number	Provenance	cpn
TA 11381	Tēmā, Qrayyah, Area E, Square E13, within the debris south of the large public building (Building E-b1), SU 2480	p

BIBLIOGRAPHY

— Schaudig in Eichmann and Hausleiter, Tayma 2 no. 5 and figs. 1.13–14 (photo, copy, edition)

TEXT

Lacuna
1′) [...] *x* [...]
2′) [...] *x* ⸢*mu*⸣-*šak*-⸢*lil*⸣ [*eš-re-e-ti*? ...]
3′) [... URU.*ḫar*]-⸢*ra*⸣-*na mu-ud-diš* ⸢*é-ḫúl*?⸣-[*ḫúl*? ...]
4′) [*ka-ši-id*? *šá-di-i*? *e*?]-*lu-ti mu*-⸢*ṭib lìb-bi*⸣ [...]
5′) [*za-nin é-sag-íl u é-zi*]-⸢*da*⸣ DUMU mdMUATI-⸢TIN⸣-[*su-iq-bi*]
6′) [... *a*]-⸢*na*⸣-*ku* d[...]
7′) [...] ŠI *x* [...]
Lacuna

Lacuna
1′–6′a) [...], the one who complet[es *sanctuaries*, ..., the one who ... the city Ḫar]rān, the one who renovates Eḫ[ulḫul, ..., *the one who (succeeds) in reaching h*]*igh* [*mountains*], the one who pleases the hea[rt(s) of ..., ..., the one who provides for Esagil and Ezid]a, the son of Nabû-balā[ssu-iqbi, ..., am] I.
6′b–7′) The god(dess) [...] ... [...]

Lacuna

61

A fragment from the left side of a sandstone stele of Nabonidus written in contemporary Neo-Babylonian script was discovered during the German excavations at Tēmā. Only the beginnings of six lines remain. This stele fragment and the one inscribed with text no. 59 might come from one and the same monument. Because the authors cannot prove that the two fragments originate from the same stele, it is best to edit the two pieces separately.

CATALOGUE

Excavation Number	Provenance	cpn
TA 17966	Tēmā, Qrayyah, Area E, Square E6, within the debris of SU 9650	p

BIBLIOGRAPHY

— Schaudig in Eichmann and Hausleiter, Tayma 2 no. 6 and figs. 1.15–16 (photo, copy, edition)

TEXT

Lacuna
1′) *mu*-[...]
2′) URU.[...]
3′) LUGAL [...]
4′) *ana ṣal*-⸢*ti*⸣ [...]
5′) *ina* ITI.[...]
6′) *x* [...]
Lacuna

Lacuna
1′–6′) the one who [...] the city [...] the king (of) [...] *for/into* batt[le ...] during the month [...]
Lacuna

1001

A fragment of a two-column clay cylinder bears an Akkadian inscription of a Neo-Babylonian king recording the restoration of a palace between the Šamaš Gate and the Euphrates River; the script is archaizing Neo-Babylonian. The text, which is sometimes referred to as the "Palace Cylinder" in scholarly literature, has been attributed to Nebuchadnezzar II (Unger and Weissbach), Amēl-Marduk (Weissbach), and Nabonidus (Berger, Beaulieu, Borger, George, and Schaudig). Following more recent scholarship, the text is tentatively included in this volume, as a 1000-number text of Nabonidus. Moreover, it is unclear where the royal residence whose rebuilding is being described here was located: Babylon (Berger, Beaulieu), Borsippa (Schaudig), Dilbat (Unger), Sippar (George), and Uruk (George) have all been suggested as possible locations.

CATALOGUE

Museum Number	Registration Number	Provenance	cpn
BM 38346	80-11-12,228	Possibly Babylon	c

COMMENTARY

The royal 'author' of the inscription and where the palace whose construction is described in this text was located have long been debated and there is no scholarly consensus on these two matters. Based on the script and shape of the cylinder, it is very plausible that BM 38346 was written in the name of Nabonidus; both are remarkably similar to the archaizing Neo-Babylonian copies of text no. 2 (Emašdari Cylinder; exs. 1–2). It is not impossible that the same scribe who inscribed VA Bab 2971 (text no. 2 ex. 1) and/or IM 95927 (text no. 2 ex. 2) also wrote out the inscription on BM 38346 (this text). Orthography and lexicography also point to this inscription probably being composed during Nabonidus' reign. At present, the following words/names are known only from positively identified inscriptions of Nabonidus and the text written on BM 38346: *rûmtu* ("darling") in i 7, *Gattu* ("Euphrates") in ii 1, and *urāšu* (a building) in ii 7. Many of the other extant words in this inscription are well attested in both the inscriptions of Nebuchadnezzar II and Nabonidus; *rebītu* ("street") and *teknû* ("care"), however, are only attested in the official inscriptions of Nebuchadnezzar II. Note that the word *gušūru* ("beam") is attested in one inscription of Nabopolassar and four inscriptions of Nabonidus, but usually written logographicly as GIŠ.ÙR; GIŠ.ÙR.MEŠ; it is not found in extant inscriptions of Nebuchadnezzar II or Neriglissar. Given the current evidence, it is very likely that the text written on BM 38346 dates to the time of Nabonidus, as P.-R. Berger, P.-A. Beaulieu, R. Borger, A.R. George, and H. Schaudig have already suggested. Based on the script and shape of the cylinder, both of which closely match those of two copies of the Emašdari Cylinder Inscription (text no. 2), it is possible that the palace whose restoration is commemorated in this text was located in Babylon, as already proposed by Berger and Beaulieu. This not only fits geographic information recorded in ii 1 — which would place the royal residence in western part of Babylon, in the Tuba district, near the Šamaš Gate and the Euphrates River — but also the fact that the word *rûmtu* ("darling") in i 7 is likewise attested in text no. 2 (Emašdari Cylinder; i 2), an inscription commemorating the rebuilding of the temple of the Ištar of Agade in Babylon. Therefore, it is not unreasonable to assume that this inscription was already composed to record work in Babylon. Because neither Nabonidus nor Babylon appear in the preserved text, the authors cannot prove with absolute certainty that this text was composed in the name of Nabonidus to record the renovation of a palace located in the Tuba district of Babylon. Therefore, it is best to edit this inscription as a 1000-number of Nabonidus, rather than as a 1000-number of Nebuchadnezzar II or Amēl-Marduk.

BIBLIOGRAPHY

1923 S. Smith, CT 37 pl. 21 (copy)
1924 S. Smith, RA 21 pp. 91–92 (ii 1–2, edition; study)
1933 Weissbach, ZA 41 pp. 267–268 (ii 1–8, study)
1967–75 Borger, HKL p. 492 (study)
1973 Berger, NbK p. 381 Nbn.? Zylinder-Fragment II, 1 (study)
1989 Beaulieu, Nabonidus pp. 41 and 99–100 Inscription Z (ii 1–8, edition; study)
1992 George, BTT p. 343 no. 56 and p. 365 no. 74 (study)
1995 Schaudig, AoF 22 p. 259 (ii 1, transliteration, study)
2001 Schaudig, Inschriften Nabonids pp. 483–484 no. 2.26[a] and 760 fig. 40 (edition; ii 8 collation)

TEXT

Col. i
1) [... LUGAL TIN].TIR.KI NUN *na-a-du*
2) [... *qar*]-⸢*ra*⸣-*du la ša-na-an*
3) [...] ⸢*e*⸣-*tel-lu qar-du*
4) [... *ša*]-⸢*ga*⸣-*pi-ru*
5) [...] TA A DAM
6) [...] ⸢*ša*⸣-*qu-ú* ^{d}AMAR.UTU
7) [...] *ru-um-tì* DINGIR GAL.GAL
8) [...] DINGIR.DINGIR ^{d}AG
Lacuna

i 1–8) [..., king of Bab]ylon, attentive prince, [...], unrivalled [wa]rrior, [...], valiant lord, [..., the maj]estic one, [...] ..., [..., the mo]st exalted of the god Marduk, [...], beloved of the great gods, [... of] the gods, the god Nabû,

Lacuna

Col. ii
1) *iš-tu* SILA.DAGAL KÁ.GAL-^{d}UTU *a-di ki-šá-*⸢*ad*⸣ *ga-at-ti*
2) *ša* LUGAL.MEŠ AD.MEŠ-*e-a qer-ba-šu i-pú-šu ga-nu-ni*
3) *tal-la-ak-ta-šu la šu-ud-du-la-at*
4) *la du-um-mu-qu ši-pí-ir-šu*
5) *in gu-šu-ur* GIŠ.EREN *ba-nu-ú ṣú-*⸢*lu*⸣*-ul-šu*
6) *ša* É.GAL *šu-a-tim šu-bat ḫi-*⸢*da*⸣*-a-tim*
7) *ú-ra-áš tak-né-e maš-ta-ku ri-ša-a-tim*
8) [*ú*]-⸢*te-ed-du-šu lìb*⸣*-bi ḫa-diš ub-lam-ma*
9) [...] *x x* [...]
Lacuna

ii 1–9) from the square of the Gate of the god Šamaš to the bank of the Gattu River (Euphrates), wherein the kings, my ancestors, had built private rooms — its processional way was not wide enough, its construction not well done, (and) its roof was built with beam(s) of cedar. My heart joyfully prompted me [to] renovate that palace, (that) seat of happiness, bedroom of pleasure, (and) chamber of joy, and [...] ... [...]

Lacuna

1002

A fragment from the second column of a two-column clay cylinder bears the second half of an Akkadian inscription of a Neo-Babylonian king, possibly Nebuchadnezzar II (as the British Museum Online Collection website suggests) or Nabonidus (as R. Da Riva [GMTR 4 p. 131] proposes); the script is contemporary Neo-Babylonian. The text, which is difficult to read because the surface of the piece is badly worn, is not sufficiently preserved to confidently identify the inscription's royal author or to determine which building project it commemorated. Since Da Riva suggests that BM 38696 bore an inscription of Nabonidus, it is tentatively included in the present volume as a 1000-number text of that king. An attribution to Nebuchadnezzar II cannot be entirely ruled out since he is also known to have sponsored construction at Borsippa, the purported find spot of this cylinder fragment.

CATALOGUE

Museum Number	Registration Number	Provenance	cpn
BM 38696	80-11-12,580	Registered as coming from Borsippa	c

COMMENTARY

R. Da Riva (GMTR 4 p. 131) tentatively proposes that BM 38696 came from the same two-column cylinder as BM 47814. Since the authors of the present volume cannot prove this, it is best to edit the two pieces separately; BM 47814 is edited in this volume as text no. 41. See the commentary of that inscription for further details.

BIBLIOGRAPHY

2008 Da Riva, GMTR 4 p. 131 no. 1b (study)

TEXT

Col. i
Completely missing
Col. ii
1) [...] x ⸢*ad-dì-in ki-ma x x-uš*⸣
2) [...] ⸢AḪ? ḪI⸣ x
3) [...].⸢MEŠ *šu-ú*⸣ *pa-*⸢*al*?⸣*-x x*
4) [...] (traces)
5) [...] (traces)
6) [...] x x x x (x)
7) [...] x x ⸢KI⸣
8) [...] ḪI *x-*⸢*a-ti*⸣
9) [...] x AB DÙ x
10) [...] ⸢*re*⸣*-e-ši-*⸢*ša*⸣
11) [...]-⸢*ti*⸣ *e-pu-uš-*⸢*ma*⸣
12) [...] x-BU *ri-ki-is-su*
13) [GIŠ.IG.GIŠ.IG? GIŠ].⸢EREN⸣ *taḫ-lu*-up-tì* ZABAR
14) [...] KÁ-*šu ú-rat-ti*
15) [... *ta-am*]-⸢*la*⸣*-a* <<MEŠ>> *ú-ma-al-li-ma*
16) [...] x *x-na ak-ṣu-úr*
17) [...]-*šu šá* KU MA ⸢ḪI⸣ *ia-ti*
18) [...] *e-lu-tim? qé-er-ba-šu*
19) [(...) *uš-ma*]*-al-la*
20) [...] *x-ti* KU$_6$.ḪI.A *u* ⸢MUŠEN?⸣.ḪI.A
21) [...] x *ma-ti-ia* ⸢*ú*?⸣*-da?-áš-ši*
22) [...] x *i-na?* x x IS ZI-*tim*
23) [...] x E ŠU x MU LA É x x (x)
24) [...] x *ir?-šu i-na* MU x x x x x

Completely missing

ii 1) [...] I gave [...] like ...
ii 2–9) (No translation possible)

ii 10–14) [...] its superstructure [...] I built and [...] ... its structure. I installed [in] its gate(s) [*doors* (made) of ced]ar with a facing of bronze [...].

ii 15–19) [...] I filled (it) in with [an inf]ill and I constructed [...] ... [...] ... (As for) me, [I had a] *high* [... fill]ed up inside it.

ii 20–21) I copiously supplied [...] ... fish and *birds*, [..., (and) the ...] of my land.
ii 22–24) (No translation possible)

ii 1 ⸢*ad-dì-in*⸣ "I gave": In the extant corpus of Neo-Babylonian royal inscriptions, the reading *dì* for the TI sign is presently otherwise attested only in two cylinder inscriptions of Nebuchadnezzar II: C26 i 10 and C34 i 10.
ii 13 *taḫ-lu*-up-tì* "a facing of": The cylinder has *taḫ*-KU-*up-tì*.
ii 20 KU$_6$.ḪI.A "fish": This spelling of the word is also known from Novotny and Jeffers, RINAP 5/1 p. 199 Ashurbanipal 9 (Prism F) iii 69.

25) [...] *x-bi-ma ú-da-⸢an⸣-ni-in né-re-⸢bi-šu*?⸣
26) [...] *x x na ši*? *im ru* DINGIR.MEŠ *ú*? d⸢IŠ⸣.[TAR]
27) [...] *x ep-še-ti-ia li-ṭí-ba* e-*<*li*>*-⸢ka⸣*
28) [... *re*]*-⸢e-ú⸣-si-⸢na⸣ ip-pu-šu li-ib-bi-⸢ia*?⸣
29) [...] *⸢li⸣-ri-ku* UD.MEŠ *ba-la-ṭe*$_4$*-ia*
30) [(...)] *⸢lu-uš-ba-a lit-tu-tu⸣*
31) [...] *x-ku ⸢li-na-ar⸣ a-a-⸢bi⸣*
32) [...] *x* ⸢Ú IL⸣ *x* ZA *x x x*

ii 25–26) [...] ... and (thereby) strengthened *its* entryways. [...] ... gods and goddesses.
ii 27–32) [O ...] may my deeds be pleasing to you [...] exercise their [she]pherdship, [...] *my* heart [.... M]ay the days of my life be long so that [(...) I] may be sated with old age. [...] kill my enemies [...] ...

1003

A small fragment from the right side of the front of a basalt stele preserves parts of ten lines of an inscription of a Neo-Babylonian king written in archaizing Neo-Babylonian script. Based on its phraseology (in particular, *la aqīpma* [*ar*]*taši niqitti* "I [d]id not believe (them) and [be]came distress[ed]" in lines 6′–7′) and contents (praying to the gods Adad and Šamaš for advice in lines 8′–10′), the text is usually attributed to Nabonidus, although this cannot be proven conclusively. Too little of the text remains to know what the inscription commemorated, nevertheless, H. Schaudig (Inschriften Nabonids p. 536) has tentatively proposed that it may have recorded work on Ebabbar ("Shining House"), the temple of the god Šamaš at Sippar. In addition, it has been suggested that this stele fragment may belong to the same stele upon which text no. 4, or possibly text no. 3 (Babylon Stele), is written. Given the fragmentary nature of the piece and the uncertainty of its attribution, this inscription is arbitrarily edited in this volume as a 1000-number of Nabonidus.

CATALOGUE

Museum Number	Excavation/ Registration No.	Provenance	cpn
VA 3217	—	—	c

BIBLIOGRAPHY

1907 Delitzsch, VAS 1 p. VIII and pl. 53 no. 56 (copy, transliteration, study)

2001 Schaudig, Inschriften Nabonids p. 536 no. 3.7[a] (edition)

TEXT

Lacuna
Col. i′
Lacuna
1′) [*x x*] (blank) [...]
2′) [*šá*] *⸢áš⸣-ra-*[*a-ti-šu-nu*]
3′) [*iš*]*-te-né-⸢e'⸣-ú ⸢a-na⸣-*[*ku*]

Lacuna

Lacuna
i′ 1′–3′) [..., (the one) who con]stantly seeks out [their] shri[nes], am I.

1002 ii 27 *li-ṭí-ba** "may (my deeds) be pleasing": The cylinder has *li-ṭí-*KU.

4′) [*a*]-⸢*ma*⸣-*a-ti-šu-nu*
5′) ⸢*eš*⸣-*te-né-em-me-e-ma*
6′) ⸢*la*⸣ *a-qí-ip-ma*
7′) [*ar*]-*ta-ši ni-qit*-⸢*ti*⸣
8′) [*a-na*] *mi-lik* ^{d}⸢UTU⸣
9′) [*ù*] ⸢^{d}⸣IŠKUR *ra-ba*-[*a*]
10′) [*aṣ-ba*]-⸢*at*⸣ *su-up*-⸢*pe*⸣-[*e*]
Lacuna

i′ 4′–7′) [I] was listening to their [wo]rds, but I [d]id not believe (them) and [be]came distress[ed].

i′ 8′–10′) [In order to] (receive) grea[t] advice from the gods Šamaš [and] Adad, [I start]ed pra[ying].

Lacuna

1004

This small piece of a clay cylinder was discovered by French excavators at Kish and preserves part of an Akkadian inscription of a Neo-Babylonian king written in contemporary Neo-Babylonian script. The text was originally dated to the reign of Nebuchadnezzar II, but this is unlikely, as P.-A. Beaulieu has already pointed out, since that ruler is mentioned as a previous king of Babylon, assuming that the Nebuchadnezzar mentioned in this inscription is the second, and not the first, king with that name. Therefore, the text must have been composed during the reign of Amēl-Marduk, Neriglissar, or Nabonidus. Since other cylinder fragments of Nabonidus were found by British excavators at Kish (text no. 14 [Kish Cylinder]) and since an inscription from Marad (text no. 19 [Eigikalama Cylinder]) records that he worked on that city's wall (Melem-kurkurra-dulla) and renovated its *akītu*-house, an attribution to Nabonidus seems plausible. If that attribution proves correct, then this inscription might have commemorated work on one of those two structures at Kish. Given the scant available evidence, one cannot entirely rule out an attribution to Amēl-Marduk or Nerglissar. Because the original was not avliable for study, the present edition is based on H. de Genouillac's published copy. This inscription is sometimes referred to as "Nabonidus Cylinder Fragment I, 1" and "[Nabonidus] Inscription X" in scholarly literature.

CATALOGUE

Museum Number	Excavation Number	Provenance	cpn
Ki 724	—	Kish, surface, in the area of the palace	n

BIBLIOGRAPHY

1924 de Genouillac, Kich p. 34 no. 136 and pl. 14 no. B 136 (copy)
1973 Berger, NbK p. 379 Nbn. Zylinder-Fragment I, 1 (study)
1989 Beaulieu, Nabonidus pp. 40–41 Inscription X (study)
2001 Schaudig, Inschriften Nabonids p. 484 no. 2.27 (edition)

TEXT

Lacuna
1′) [...] *x x x* [...]
2′) [...] 5 LIM GUR ŠE.[BAR ...]
3′) [... LUGAL] *maḫ-ri* LUGAL TIN.⸢TIR⸣.[KI ...]
4′) [... ^{md}AG-NÍG.GUB]-⸢ÙRU⸣ LUGAL TIN.TIR.KI [...]
5′) [...] *x-šú u pa-⸢li-iḫ⸣ x* [...]
6′) [...] *ṭù-⸢uḫ⸣-[ḫu-da-ku*$^{?}$ ...]
7′) [...] *x x* [...]
Lacuna

Lacuna
1′–7′) [...] ... [...] 5,000 gur of bar[ley ...], a former [king] (who was) the king of Babylon, [... Nebuchadnezz]ar (II), king of Babylon [...] ... and the one who reveres [..., ... I] lavish[ly provide ...] ... [...]
Lacuna

1005

A fragment of a brick found at Tell el-Laḥm (probably to be identified with ancient Kissik) preserves part of an inscription of a Babylonian king, perhaps Nabonidus since at least one inscription of his was found there. The text is not sufficiently preserved to confirm the attribution of the inscription with certainty. The edition is based on C.B.F. Walker's transliteration.

CATALOGUE

Museum Number	Registration Number	Provenance	cpn
BM 137452	1919-11-11,1751	Kissik	n

BIBLIOGRAPHY

1920 Thompson, Arch. 70 p. 115 fig. 6 and p. 141 (copy, study)

1981 Walker, CBI pp. 93–94 no. 114 Nabonidus X (transliteration, study)

TEXT

Lacuna
1′) ⸢*ša*⸣ [...]
2′) É *x* [...]
3′) ^{d}[...]
Lacuna

Lacuna
1′–3′) *w[ho ...] house/temple of* [...] the god(dess) [...]
Lacuna

1006

A small fragment from the left side of a two-column clay cylinder preserves a small portion of a Neo-Babylonian royal inscription written in contemporary Neo-Babylonian script. Too little of the text is extant to be absolutely certain that the inscription was composed during the reign of Nabonidus, as R. Da Riva (GMTR p. 131 sub Nabonidus 1.a) suggests. However, since several inscriptions of his begin with *inum* DN ("when DN"), an ascription to Nabonidus is likely; compare text nos. 19 (Eigikalama Cylinder), 23 (Ebabbar Cylinder), and 34 (En-nigaldi-Nanna Cylinder).

CATALOGUE

Museum Number	Registration Number	Provenance	cpn
BM 40076	81-2-1,40	Purchased, possibly from Sippar	c

BIBLIOGRAPHY

2008 Da Riva, GMTR 4 p. 131 sub Nabonidus 1.a (study)

TEXT

Col. i
1) *ì-nu-um* ^{d}AMAR.UTU ⸢*be*$^{?}$⸣-*lí x* [...]
2) ^{d}EN.⸢LÍL DINGIR.DINGIR⸣ *x x* [...]
3) ⸢*ri*$^{?}$⸣-*x x* [...]
4) ⸢*ma*$^{?}$⸣-[...]
5) *ma-ḫa-zi* [...]
6) *ik*-[...]
7) *é*$^{?}$-*x* [...]
8) [*x*] *x* [...]
Lacuna
1′) [*x x*] *x* RI$^{?}$ *šu*$^{?}$ *x* [...]
2′) *a-na* RA$^{?}$ *za-ʾi-i-*⸢*ri*⸣-[*ia*$^{?}$ ...]
3′) *bi-la-at ša-di-im x* [...]
Col. ii
Completely missing

i 1–8) When the god Marduk, *my lord*, [...], the Enlil of the g[od]s, ... [...] ... [...] cult centers [...] *E*[...]

Lacuna

i 1′–3′) [...] ... [...] to ... [*my*] enemie[s ...] tribute of the mountain(s) [...]

Completely missing

1007

A badly damaged and abraded two-column clay cylinder bears a difficult-to-read Akkadian inscription of a late Neo-Babylonian king, possibly Nebuchadnezzar II or Nabonidus since the text appears to deal with the rebuilding of Ebabbar ("Shining House"), the temple of the god Šamaš at Sippar, which these two kings are known to have restored; the script is contemporary Neo-Babylonian. Following R. Da Riva (GTMR 4 p. 131), the inscription on BM 40532+ is edited here with the texts of Nabonidus, rather than with those of Nebuchadnezzar II.

CATALOGUE

Museum Number	Registration Number	Provenance	cpn
BM 40532 + BM 40581 + BM 40582 + BM 40583 + BM 41109 + BM 41136	AH 81-4-28,73 + AH 81-4-28,125 + AH 81-4-28,126 + AH 81-4-28,127 + AH 81-4-28,656 + AH 81-4-26,683	Probably Sippar	p

BIBLIOGRAPHY

2008 Da Riva, GMTR 4 p. 131 sub 1a (study)

TEXT

Col. i
Lacuna
1′) [...] *x*
2′) [...] *x x*
3′) [...] (traces)
4′) [...] (traces)
5′) [...] (traces)
6′) [...] (traces)
7′) [...] (traces)
8′) [...] (traces)
9′) (traces)
10′) (traces) ⌜*da-rí-a*⌝
11′) (traces) (*x*) *x-ia*
12′) *ina*? *x x* (traces) *x x x bi-ri*
13′) (traces)
14′) *x x x* (traces)
15′) (traces) [...] (traces)
16′) [...] *x x x*
17′) [...] (*x*) *x x x*
18′) [...] (*x*) *x x x*
19′) [...] *x x*-⌜*ti*?⌝
20′) [...] *x x x x*

Lacuna
i 1′–20′) (No translation possible)

Col. ii
1) (traces)

ii 1–21) (No translation possible)

2) (traces)
3) (traces)
4) (traces)
5) (traces)
6) (traces) [*x* (*x*)]
7) (traces) [*x* (*x*)]
8) (traces) [...]
9) (traces) [...]
10) (traces) [...]
11) (traces) [...]
12) (traces) [...]
13) *x* [...]
14) *x* [...]
15) *x* [...]
16) *x* [...]
17) *x* [...]
18) *x* [...]
19) *x* [...]
20) *x* [...]
21) *a-⸢na⸣* [...]
22) ^{d}UTU *be-lí-⸢ia⸣* [...] (*x*) *x*
23) *a-na x x x* [...] *x-ma*
24) *ba-la-ṭa*$_4$ <<*x*>> *u*$_4$*-⸢um ru-qu⸣-ú-tim*
25) *lu x* (*x*) *x ⸢ši⸣-[ri]-⸢ik⸣-tu-um-ma*
26) *i-na na-⸢am-ru⸣ nu-ú-ri-ka*
27) *x x x x x x x la x x* (*x*)
28) *⸢a-na še-be-e li⸣-[it-tu-ti]*
29) (traces) *a-na-áš-šu-⸢ka⸣* [*x* (*x*) *x*]
30) *⸢i-na⸣ x* (*x*) *x nim*? *ši x* [...]
31) *i-x* (traces) [...]

ii 21–25) *to/for* [...] the god Šamaš, m[y] lord, [...] *to* ... [...] and ... a [l]ong life (lit. "a life of [l]ong da[ys]") as a g[i]ft.

ii 26–31) With your br[igh]t light, ... for the atta[inme]nt of ve[ry old age], ... I raise up *my hand(s)* to y[ou ...] ... [...] ... [...].

1008

A fragment of a three-column clay cylinder preserves part of an inscription of a first-millennium-BC (Assyrian or Babylonian) king commemorating work undertaken on Ebabbar ("Shining House"), the temple of the sun-god Šamaš at Sippar; the script is archaizing Neo-Babylonian, but with some contemporary Neo-Babylonian signs. The assignment to Nabonidus is not entirely certain, but the style and contents of the extant text seem to indicate that the inscription was likely composed during Nabonidus' reign, perhaps at the end of his second year (554) as king, rather than during the reigns of Šamaš-šuma-ukīn (667–648) or his brother Ashurbanipal (668–ca. 631). Unlike other texts recording work on the Ebabbar temple at Sippar, this inscription mentions the Old Babylonian king Samsu-iluna (1749–1712) as a previous builder of the temple. In scholarly literature, this text is sometimes referred to as the "Stone Wall Cylinder."

CATALOGUE

Museum Number	Registration Number	Provenance	cpn
BM 56618	82-7-14,997	Probably Sippar	c

BIBLIOGRAPHY

1889 Bezold, PSBA 11 p. 86 (study)

1924 Smith, RA 21 p. 75 (study)

1925 Baumgartner, ZA 36 pp. 131–132 (iii 4′–9′, study)

2001 Schaudig, Inschriften Nabonids pp. 481–482 no. 2.25^{a} and 761 fig. 43 (copy, edition)

2004 George, Studies Grayson pp. 141–144 (copy [S. Smith], edition)

TEXT

Lacuna

Col. i′

Lacuna

1′) [...] *x*

2′) [...] *x-ki*

3′) [...] *x-ru*

4′) [...] *x-šu*

5′) [...] *x*

Lacuna

Lacuna

Lacuna

i′ 1′–5′) (No translation possible)

Lacuna

Col. ii′

Lacuna

1′) [...] *x-bu*

2′) [...] *x-ki*

3′) [...] ⸢*a-na*⸣ *dan-na-ti*

4′) *e-pu-uš-ma iš-di-šu*

5′) *i-na qaq-qa-ri ú-dan-ni-in*

6′) ^{d}UTU EN GAL DI.KU$_5$ MAḪ

7′) ^{d}*a-a ḫi-ir-tum*

8′) *na-ra-am-ta-ka*

9′) ⸢*a*⸣*-bu-ut* ZIMBIR.KI

10′) ⸢*ù*⸣ *é-babbar-*⸢*ra*⸣

11′) ⸢*li*⸣*-iṣ-bat-*⸢*su*⸣*-ma*

12′) ⸢*ri*⸣*-ši ta-a-a-ri*

13′) ⸢*áš*⸣*-šu* ⸢*ki*⸣*-iṣ-ṣí-*⸢*ka*⸣ SIKIL

14′) *a-*⸢*ḫu-la*⸣*-ap*

15′) *liq-bi-*⸢*ku-um*⸣*-ma*

16′) ⸢*li*⸣*-ši-ru iṣ-*⸢*ṣu*⸣*-šu*

17′) [...] *x x x*

Lacuna

Lacuna

ii′ 1′–5′) [...] ... [...] ... I built [...] *to the bottom of the foundation pit* and (thereby) reinforced its foundations in the ground.

ii′ 6′–17′) O Šamaš, great lord (and) exalted judge, may the goddess Aya, your beloved wife, intercede for Sippar and Ebabbar so that you have mercy (on me). With regard to your pure shrine, she may say "*Aḫulap!*" to you so that its wood stays in good condition (lit. "straight") [...] ...

Lacuna

Col. iii′

Lacuna

1′) [...] *x x*

2′) ⸢*taš-mi-ka sa-lim*⸣*-ka*

3′) *lu-mu-ur*

4′) *i-nu-*<*šu*> *i-na ku-šar-ti* ⸢*šu-a-tum*⸣

Lacuna

iii′ 1′–3′) [... *May I experience*] your grace (and) see your reconciliation.

iii′ 4′–11′) At that time, in that repaired part, I found

ii′ 14′ *a-*⸢*ḫu-la*⸣*-ap* "'*Aḫulap!*'": This Akkadian word is an exclamation used to express or seek compassion. A precise translation is impossible, but depending on the context it can be paraphrased as "Mercy!," "Have pity!," or "Enough!"

5′) *mu-sa-re-*⸢*e*⸣
6′) *sa-am-su-i-lu-ni*
7′) LUGAL *maḫ-ri*
8′) *a-bi-ia la-bi-ri*
9′) *a-mu-ur-ma*
10′) *šu-um-šu la ú-nak-kír*
11′) *i-na man-za-zi-šu-ma* ⸢*ú-ki-in*⸣
12′) *ù mu-sa-*⸢*re-a ši-ṭir šu-mi*⸣*-*[*ia*]
13′) *áš-ṭur-ma i-na* ⸢*ku-šar-ti*⸣
14′) ⸢*šu-a-tum it-ti* MU⸣.[SAR]
15′) ⸢*sa-am-su-i-lu-ni*⸣
16′) [LUGAL] ⸢*maḫ*⸣*-ra a-na* ⸢*da-ár*⸣
17′) [*lu-ú ú*]-⸢*kin*⸣
18′) [*ru-bu*]-⸢*ù*⸣ *ar-ku-*⸢*ú*⸣
19′) [*ša* ^{d}UTU *i*]*-nam-bu-šu-*⸢*ma*⸣
20′) [...] ⸢*é*⸣*-babbar-*⸢*ra*⸣
21′) [...]*-ru*
22′) [...] *x* [...]
Lacuna

an inscribed object of Samsu-iluna, a king of the past, an ancient ancestor of mine, and I did not change (the inscription bearing) his name, (but) firmly placed (it) in its (original) position.

iii′ 12′–17′) Moreover, I inscribed an object bearing [my] name and [indeed fi]rmly placed (it) in the repaired part, together with the ins[cribed object of] Samsu-iluna, [a king of] the past, forever.

iii′ 18′–20′) [Any] later [ru]ler [whom the god Šamaš n]ames and who [renov]ates the [dilapidated section(s) of] Ebabbar and [...]

Lacuna

1009

A tiny fragment of clay cylinder, possibly from Sippar, preserves parts of seven lines of an inscription of a Neo-Babylonian king written in archaizing Neo-Babylonian script. C. Bezold attributed the piece to Nabonidus, but this assignation is yet to be confirmed. BM 90907 has never been published and, unfortunately, can no longer be found in the collections of the British Museum (London), perhaps because it is now joined to another Nabonidus cylinder; see C.B.F. Walker's information about the fragment in Schaudig, Inschriften Nabonids p. 485. Because Nabonidus has been suggested as the text's royal author, this inscription is tentatively included in the volume. This text is sometimes referred to in scholarly publications as "Nabonidus Cylinder Fragment I, 2" and "[Nabonidus] Inscription Y."

CATALOGUE

Museum Number	Registration Number	Provenance	cpn
BM 90907 (BM 12035)	82-7-14,—	Probably Sippar	n

BIBLIOGRAPHY

1889 Bezold, PSBA 11 p. 86 (study)
1973 Berger, NbK p. 380 Nbn.? Zylinder-Fragment I, 2 (study)
1989 Beaulieu, Nabonidus p. 41 Inscription Y (study)
2001 Schaudig, Inschriften Nabonids p. 485 no. 2.28[a] (study)

1010

A fragment of a multi-column clay cylinder, perhaps a three-column cylinder, known only from an illegible photograph published in Sumer 46 (1989–90), preserves part of an inscription of Nabonidus or some other Neo-Babylonian king. It is uncertain if the piece is inscribed with a unique text or a duplicate of text no. 28 (Eḫulḫul Cylinder).

CATALOGUE

Museum Number	Excavation Number	Provenance	cpn
IM —	1640	Sippar, Ebabbar	n

BIBLIOGRAPHY

1989–90 Al-Ǧādir and ʿAbd-Allāh, Sumer 46 pp. 87–88 and pl. 24, 1 [Arabic section] (photo, study)

2001 Schaudig, Inschriften Nabonids p. 485 no. 2.29 (study)

1011

The obverse of a fragmentarily preserved clay tablet is inscribed with a text of a Neo-Babylonian king, possibly Nabonidus; the script is contemporary Neo-Babylonian. Based on the language of the text, especially that of lines 4′–5′, an attribution to Nabonidus is likely, as several certainly assigned texts of his use the expressions *imlû ūmū ša iqbû* ("the days that he had commanded had elapsed") and *adannu ikšudamma* ("the appointed time had arrived and"). Note, however, that these phrases are not unique to Nabonidus and, therefore, one cannot entirely rule out the possibility that this text should be assigned to an earlier first-millennium king, for example, Marduk-apla-iddina II, Esarhaddon, or Ashurbanipal; for details, see Schaudig, Inschriften Nabonids p. 478. Following, H. Schaudig, this inscription is tentatively assigned to Nabonidus and, therefore, included here as a 1000-number of that king.

CATALOGUE

Museum Number	Registration Number	Provenance	cpn
BM 76544	AH 83-1-18,1915	Sippar	c

BIBLIOGRAPHY

2001 Schaudig, Inschriften Nabonids pp. 478–479 no. 2.23 and 760 fig. 37 (copy, edition)

TEXT

Obv.

Lacuna

1′) [GÌR.NÍTA$^{?}$] ⸢*šaḫ-ṭu*⸣ <*šá*> ^{d}EN ^{d}NIN.LÍL *na-ram* ^{d}AMAR.UTU⸣ [...]

2′) [*šá* ^{d}]⸢EN⸣ *u* ^{d}AG GEŠTU.II *ra-*⸢*pa-áš*⸣*-tum ú-šat-li-mu-šu-ma i-ḫu-*⸢*zu ta*-šim*⸣-[*tú*]

3′) ⸢*na*⸣*-a*ʾ*-i-du* LÚ.ÉNSI *ṣi-i-ri šak-ka-*⸢*nak*⸣*-ku en-qi* ⸢*ana*$^{?}$*-ku*$^{?}$⸣

4′) [*im*]-⸢*lu*⸣*-ú* u_4*-mu* EŠ.BAR *šá iq-bu-ú* LUGAL DINGIR.⸢MEŠ⸣ [^{d}AMAR.UTU$^{?}$]

5′) [*a*]-⸢*dan*⸣*-nu ki-i-ni ik-šu-*⸢*dam*⸣*-ma šá iš-ku-nu a-na* ⸢*ra-ma*⸣-[*ni-šú*]

6′) [*šá*]-⸢*ma*⸣*-mi u qaq-qa-ri* ⸢*šá*⸣ [x] x-*ku* DINGIR-*ú-ti-šú it-ta-*[...]

7′) [*iḫ*]-⸢*su*$^{?}$⸣*-su* TIN.TIR.KI *dur*$^{?}$-[*an*]-*ki mar-ka-su* ⸢*kib-ra*⸣-[*a-ti*]

8′) [*ub*]-⸢*lu*⸣ *lìb-ba-šú* ⸢KÁ.KÁ⸣ *é-*⸢*sag*⸣*-íl* É.GAL DINGIR.MEŠ x x [x]

9′) [x] x GÌR.NÍTA *pa-*⸢*li-iḫ*⸣ *šá* ⸢DUMU ^{d}EN⸣ ^{d}x DINGIR *na-mur-*⸢*ra*⸣

10′) [x] x x x ^{d}AG *ina lìb-bi-ia ú-šab-šu-ú* SAG.II-*šú-nu* x x x [x]

11′) [x] x x *ina* ITI.GU$_4$ *ina bi-ri* ⸢*ú-mad-da*⸣ [...]

12′) [x] x x x *ú-qa*-*⸢ʾ*a-ni*⸣ x [...]

Lacuna

Rev.

Completely missing

Lacuna

1′–3′) respectful [*governor*] of the god Bēl (Enlil) (and) the goddess Mullissu, beloved of the god Marduk, [... whom the gods B]ēl (Marduk) and Nabû granted a broad mind and who learn[ed] good judgem[ent, the at]tentive one, exalted ruler, wise governor, *am I.*

4′–6′) The determined days (lit. "days of decision") that the king of the gods, [the god *Marduk*], had commanded had elapsed. The true [appo]inted time that he had set for [him]se[lf] arrived and [the hea]vens and earth, which ... [...] his divinity.

7′–8′) [*He rem*]*embered* Babylon, *Dur*[*an*]*ki*, the bond of the (four) qua[rters (of the world)]. His heart prompted (him). ... the gates of Esagil, the palace of the gods.

9′–12′) [...], the governor who reveres the Son-of-Bēl (Nabû) and deity ..., the awe-inspiring god, ... that the god Nabû brought into existence in my heart, their superstructures ... [...] ... in the month Ayyāru (II), he informed me through divination [...] ... he waited for me [...]

Lacuna

Completely missing

Obv. 4′ [^{d}AMAR.UTU$^{?}$] "[the god *Marduk*]": Or possibly restore [^{d}ŠEŠ.KI-*ri*$^{?}$] "[the god *Nannāru*]." It is impossible to know with any degree of certainty which god is mentioned here, Babylon's patron deity Marduk or the moon-god Nannāru. Because the text concerns work at Babylon, one might be inclined to restore the name of Marduk here. However, since *ša iqbû* ("who had commanded") usually occurs with the god Nannāru in extant inscriptions of Nabonidus, it might be better to restore the name of that god in this passage. The former is tentatively restored here.

Obv. 12′ *ú-qa*-*⸢ʾ*a-ni*⸣ "he waited for me": The tablet has *ú*-BAR-⸢ʾ*a-ni*⸣.

2001

Two rounded-top steles bearing an identical Akkadian inscription of Nabonidus' mother Adad-guppi (Hadad-ḫappī) were discovered in and near Ḫarrān, one of the primary cult centers of the moon-god Sîn. The first (= ex. 2) was found in 1906 being used as a doorstep in a house in the village Eski Ḫarrān, which is 10 km from ancient Ḫarrān, while the second (= ex. 1) was found in 1956 in the north entrance of the Great Mosque at Ḫarrān, where it was used as a paving stone. The first two-thirds of the inscription give an autobiographical account of Adad-guppi's 104-year life, from the twentieth regnal year of the Assyrian king Ashurbanipal (649) to the ninth regnal year (547) of her son Nabonidus, which she claims was entirely devoted to serving the gods of her birth city, Ḫarrān; Adad-guppi reiterates that she never abandoned her love of the god Sîn, even though his temple, Eḫulḫul ("House which Gives Joy"), had been destroyed by a barbarian horde (the Medes) and was in ruins to the time of her death. The last third of the text records the pomp-filled, seven-day-long funeral that Nabonidus held for his beloved mother during his ninth year as king. This text, which is generally referred to as the "Adad-guppi Stele [Inscription]" in scholarly literature, also states that Nabonidus had Eḫulḫul rebuilt and its tutelary deities (Sîn, Ningal, Nusku, and Sadarnunna) returned to their new sanctuaries. This "pseudo-autobiographical" text was composed after the fifth day of Nisannu (I) in Nabonidus' ninth regnal year (April 6th 547), perhaps at the same time as text no. 47 (Ḫarrān Stele), which may have been engraved on steles during his fourteenth (542) or fifteenth (541) year as king, when he was reconstructing Eḫulḫul; for this opinion, see Beaulieu, Nabonidus p. 68 n. 1 and Schaudig, Inschriften Nabonids p. 501.

CATALOGUE

Ex.	Museum Number	Excavation Number	Provenance	Lines Preserved	cpn
1	—	—	Ḫarrān, Great Mosque, north entrance, pavement	i 1–ii 50, iii 1–56	n
2	—	—	Near Eski-Ḫarrān	i 15–40, ii 10–32, 47–iii 19	n

COMMENTARY

Although the name of Nabonidus' mother is traditionally read as Adad-guppi in scholarly literature, her name should be better understood as West-Semitic Hadad-ḫappī ("The god Adad has saved/preserved"), as already argued fifty years ago by W. von Soden (Orientalia NS 37 [1968] p. 271) since the centenarian mother of Nabonidus was born at Ḫarrān (during the reign of the Assyrian king Ashurbanipal). Nevertheless, Adad-guppi is still used here, following Assyriological convention.

The arrangement of text, as well as the number of lines in each column, varies between the two known exemplars. Neither exemplar of this inscription is complete and, therefore, the master text is a conflation of exs. 1 and 2. A complete score is presented on Oracc and a list of minor (orthographic) variants is provided at the back of the book. Major (textual) variants are noted in the on-page notes.

BIBLIOGRAPHY

1907 Pognon, Inscriptions sémitiques pp. 1–14 and pls. 12–13 no. 1 (ex. 2, copy, edition)
1908 Dhorme, RB 5 pp. 130–135 (ex. 2, edition)
1912 Langdon, NBK pp. 57–58 and 288–295 Nbd. no. 9 (ex. 2, edition)
1912 Thureau-Dangin, RA 9 p. 84 (ex. 2, study)
1923 Boutflower, Book of Daniel pp. 107 and 113 (study)
1945–46 Lewy, HUCA 19 pp. 405–426 (ex. 2 i 15–21, ii 11–21, 23–29, 49–51, iii 9, translation, study)
1947 Dhorme, RA 41 pp. 1–21 (ex. 2, translation, study)
1947 Landsberger, Studies Edhem pp. 115–151 and pls. I–III (ex. 2, photo, edition)
1955 Oppenheim, ANET² pp. 560–562 (ex. 2, translation)
1956 Borger, Asarh. pp. 52–53 n. 74 (iii 6–7, study)
1957 Rice, ILN 231 pp. 466–469 and figs. 6 and 9 (ex. 2, photo, study)
1958 Gadd, AnSt 8 pp. 35–38, 44–57, 69–78, 89–92 and pls. I, IV–VIII (ex. 1, photo, edition)
1959 Moran, Orientalia NS 28 pp. 130–138 (ex. 1, study)
1959 Vogt, Biblica 40 pp. 88–92 and 95–102 (translation, study)
1960 Borger, JNES 19 p. 52 (iii 19, study)
1964 Galling, Studien pp. 7, 10–11 and 16–17 (exs. 1–2, study)
1964 Röllig, ZA 56 pp. 234–243 (study)
1965 Borger, JCS 19 pp. 60–62 and 71–74 (study)
1965 Tadmor, Studies Landsberger pp. 356–358 (i 42–44, ii 15–21, transcription; study)
1968 von Soden, Orientalia NS 37 p. 271 (exs. 1–2, study)
1972 Lambert, Arabian Studies 2 pp. 54 and 61 (exs. 1–2, study)
1973 Baltzer, WO 7 p. 91 (study)
1982 Börker-Klähn, Bildstelen p. 229 nos. 261–262 (study)
1988 Funk, Das Altertum 35 pp. 53–59 (i 1–6, 29–35, translation, study)
1988 Hecker, TUAT 2/4 pp. 479–485 (exs. 1–2, translation)
1988 Zawadzki, Fall of Assyria pp. 25–26, 34–35, 39 and 54–56 (study)
1993 Lee, RA 87 p. 134 (i 6–11, edition, study)
1998 Mayer, Studies Römer pp. 245–261 (exs. 1–2, study)
1989 Beaulieu, Nabonidus pp. 20, 68–75, 78–79 and 208–209 (exs. 1–2 i 1–39, ii 11–22, 28–29, 32–iii 4, edition; study)
1991 Longman, Autobiography pp. 97–193 and 225–228 (exs. 1–2, translation, study)
1994 D'Agostino, Nabonedo pp. 109–117 and 121–126 (i 29–37, ii 21–28, 40–44, 51–iii 4–16, 18–25, edition; study)
1989 Gerber, ZA 88 pp. 72–77, 79 and 85 (study)
1999 Mofidi-Nasrabadi, Bestattungssitten pp. 31–33 (iii 5–43, edition; study)
2000 Bonatz, Grabdenkmal pp. 70–71, 139–140 and 160 (ii 21–32, 48–iii 19, translation, study)
2001 Schaudig, Inschriften Nabonids pp. 500–513 no. 3.2 (exs. 1–2, edition)
2007 Beaulieu, Representations of Political Power pp. 145–146 (i 1–13, edition; study)
2007 Ehring, Rückkehr JHWHs pp. 99–101 and 112–116 (ii 17–21, edition; study)
2008 André-Salvini, Babylone p. 237 (partial translation)
2010 Heller, Spätzeit pp. 150, 172, 175, 186–187, 193 and 228 (study)

TEXT

Col. i

1) *a-na-ku* ^{fd}IŠKUR-*gu-up-pi-i'* AMA
2) ^{md}*na-bi-um-na-'i-id* LUGAL TIN.TIR.KI
3) *pa-li-iḫ-tu* ^{d}30 ^{d}*nin-gal* ^{d}*nusku*
4) *ù* ^{d}*sa-dàr-nun-na* DINGIR.MEŠ-*e-a*
5) *šá ul-tu mé-eṣ-ḫe-ru-ti-ia áš-te-e'-u*
6) DINGIR-*ú-ut-su-un šá ina* MU.16.KAM ^{d}MUATI-A-ÙRU
7) LUGAL TIN.TIR.KI ^{d}30 LUGAL DINGIR.MEŠ *it-ti* URU-*šu*
8) *ù* É-*šú iz-nu-ú i-lu-ú šá-ma-miš* URU *ù*
9) UN.MEŠ *šá ina lìb-bi-šú il-li-ku* kar*-mu-ti*

i 1–9) I am Hadad-ḫappī (Adad-guppi), mother of Nabonidus — king of Babylon — the one who reveres the deities Sîn, Ningal, Nusku, and Sadarnunna, my gods, whose divinity I have constantly sought out since my childhood. Because in the sixteenth year of Nabopolassar, king of Babylon, the god Sîn, king of the gods, became angry with his city and his temple (and) went up to heaven, the city and the people (living) inside it fell into ruins.

10) *ina lìb-bi šá aš-ra-a-tú* ^{d}30 ^{d}*nin-gal* ^{d}*nusku*
11) *u* ^{d}*sa-dàr-nun-na áš-te-e'-u pal-ḫa-ku* DINGIR-*ut-su-un*
12) *šá* ^{d}30 LUGAL DINGIR TÚG.SÍG-*šú aṣ-bat-ma mu-ši u ur-ra*
13) *áš-te-né-e'-a* DINGIR-*ut-su* GAL-*ti u*$_4$-*mi-šam la na-par-ka-a*
14) *šá* ^{d}30 ^{d}UTU ^{d}15 *u* ^{d}IŠKUR *ma-la bal-ṭa-ku*
15) *ina* AN-*e u* KI-*tim pa-li-ḫa-at-su-nu ana-ku mim-mu-u-a*
16) *dam-qa šá id-di-nu-nu u*$_4$-*mu u mu-ši* ITI *u* MU *ad-din-šú-nu-tú*

i 10–15a) On account of the fact that I have constantly sought out the sanctuaries of the deities Sîn, Ningal, Nusku, and Sadarnunna, worshipping their great divinity, I grasped the hem of the god Sîn, king of the gods, and constantly sought out his great divinity, night and day. Daily, without ceasing, I was the one who reveres the deities Sîn, Šamaš, Ištar, and Adad, as long as I was alive, in heaven and (on) earth.

i 15b–21a) All of my good things that they (the gods of Ḫarrān) had given me, I gave them (back) day and night, month and year. I grasped the hem of the god Sîn, king of the gods, and my eyes were on him

17) TÚG.SÍG ^{d}30 LUGAL DINGIR.MEŠ aṣ-bat-ma mu-ši u ur-ra
18) IGI.II-ia it-ti-šú ba-šá-a ina su-pe-e u la-ban ap-pi
19) ku-um-mu-sak ina maḫ-ri-šú-un um-ma ta-a-a-ru-tu-ku
20) a-na URU-ka lib-šá-ma ni-ši ṣal-mat qaq-qa-du
21) lip-la-ḫu DINGIR-ú-ut-ka GAL-ti a-na nu-uḫ-ḫu
22) ŠÀ DINGIR-ia u ^{d}15-ia lu-bu-šú SÍG SAG šu-kut-ti
23) KÙ.BABBAR u KÙ.GI ṣu-ba-a-ti eš-šú ŠIM.ḪI.A u Ì.GIŠ DÙG.GA
24) la ú-ṭaḫ-ḫa a-na zu-um-ri-ía ṣu-bat nak-su
25) la-ab-šá-ku-ma mu-⸢ṣe-e⸣-a saq-qu-um-mu a-dal-lal
26) da-li-li-šú-un ⸢ta-nit⸣-tú URU-ía u ^{d}IŠ.TAR-ía
27) ina lìb-bi-ia iš-šá-kin-ma EN.NUN-tì-šú-nu aṣ-ṣur
28) mim-mu-ú-a dam-qa la e-zib-ma na-šá-ku ma-ḫar-šú-un
29) ul-tu MU.20.KAM AN.ŠÁR-DÙ-A LUGAL KUR-aš-šur šá al-da-ku
30) a-di MU.42.KAM ⸢AN.ŠÁR⸣-DÙ-A MU.3.KAM AN.ŠÁR-e-tel-lu-DINGIR
31) DUMU-šú MU.21.KAM ^{d}MUATI-A-PAP MU.43.KAM ^{d}MUATI-NÍG.GUB-PAP
32) MU.2.KAM ^{m}LÚ-^{d}AMAR.UTU MU.4.KAM ^{md}U.GUR-LUGAL-ÙRU
33) ina 95 MU.MEŠ ^{d}30 LUGAL DINGIR.MEŠ šá AN-e u KI-tim
34) šá áš-ra-a-ti DINGIR-ú-ti-šú GAL-ti áš-te-e'-u
35) ép-še-ti-ía SIG$_5$.MEŠ ḫa-diš ip-pal-sa-an-ni-ma
36) su-pe-e-a iš-mu-u im-gu-ru qí-bi-ta$_5$ ug-ga-ti
37) lìb-bi-šú i-nu-uḫ-ma a-na é-ḫúl-ḫúl É ^{d}30
38) šá qé-reb URU.KASKAL šu-bat ṭu-ub lìb-bi-šú is-li-mu ir-šu-u
39) ta-a-a-ri ^{d}30 LUGAL DINGIR.MEŠ ip-pal-sa-an-ni-ma
40) ^{md}MUATI-I DUMU e-du ṣi-it ŠÀ-ía a-na LUGAL-u-tú
41) im-bé-e-ma LUGAL-⸢ú-ti KUR-šu⸣-me-ri u KUR-URI.KI
42) ul-tu ⸢pa-ṭu KUR.mi⸣-ṣir tam-tim e-lit a-di tam-tim
43) šap-li-ti ⸢nap-ḫar KUR.KUR⸣ ú-mál-la-a
44) ⸢ŠU.II-uš-šú qa-ta-a-a aš-ši-ma a-na ^{d}30 LUGAL DINGIR⸣
45) ⸢pal-ḫiš ina te-me-qa⸣ [...]
46) [... ṣi]-it [lìb-bi-ía ...]

Col. ii

1) ⸢at-ta a-na LUGAL-u-ti tam-bi-šu-ma taz-ku-ru zi-kir-šú⸣
2) ⸢ina qí-bit DINGIR-ú-ti-ka GAL-ti DINGIR.MEŠ GAL.MEŠ⸣

night and day. In prayer and (with) expressions of humility (lit. "stroking the nose"), I knelt down before them, saying: "May your return to your city happen so that the people, the black-headed, revere your great divinity."

i 21b–25a) To appease the heart(s) of my god (Sîn) and my goddess (Ningal), I did not allow a garment of fine wool, jewelry of silver or gold, new clothing, aromatics (perfume), and aromatic oil to touch (lit. "come near") my body, (but) dressed myself in a torn garment; my muṣû-garment was (made of) sackcloth.

i 25b–28) I sung their praise(s). Praise for my city(-god) and my goddess was placed in my heart and (therefore) I (continued) to serve them. I did not leave behind any of my good things and I brought (all of it) into their presence.

i 29–39a) From the twentieth year of Ashurbanipal, king of Assyria, (during) which I was born, until the forty-second year of Ashurbanipal, the third year of Aššur-etel-ilāni, his son, the twenty-first year of Nabopolassar, the forty-third year of Nebuchadnezzar (II), the second year of Amēl-Marduk, (and) the fourth year of Neriglissar, after (these) ninety-five years, (when) the god Sîn, king of the gods of heaven and earth, the sanctuaries of whose great divinity I constantly sought out, looked with pleasure upon my good deeds and (then) heeded my prayers (and) accepted my request(s), (when) the wrath of his heart was appeased, and (when) he became reconciled towards Eḫulḫul, the temple of the god Sîn which is inside the city Ḫarrān, the residence of his happiness —

i 39b–44a) (at that time,) the god Sîn, king of the gods, looked upon me and called Nabonidus, (my) only son, my own offspring, to be king and placed the kingship of the lands of Sumer and Akkad (and of) all of the lands from the border(s) of Egypt (and) the Upper to the Lower Sea in his hands.

i 44b–ii 4) I raised up my hands to the god Sîn, king of the gods, and, reverently, [...] through prayer(s) [..., my own of]fsp[ring, ..., (saying)]: "You called him (Nabonidus) to be king and mentioned (him) by his name. By the command of your great divinity, may the great gods march at his side (and) cut down his enemies. Do not forget Eḫulḫul. Carry out its perfect cultic rites fully."

---

i 27, ii 44, and ii 47 EN.NUN-tì-šú-nu "I (continued) to serve them": See the on-page note to text no. 47 (Ḫarrān Stele) i 30.

3) ⸢*i-da-a-šú lil-li-ku li-šam-qí-tú ga-ri-šú*⸣
4) ⸢*e tam-šú é-ḫúl-ḫúl ù šuk-lu-lu-tú* GARZA-*šú*⸣ *šul-lim*
5) ⸢*qa-ta-a-šú ina* MÁŠ.GI$_6$-*ia ki-i iš-šak-nu*⸣ ^{d}30 LUGAL ⸢DINGIR⸣.[MEŠ]
6) ⸢*i-qab-ba-a um-ma*⸣ *it-ti-ka ta-a-a-ra-tú* DINGIR.MEŠ
7) ⸢*šu-bat* URU.KASKAL *ina* ŠU.II ^{md}MUATI-I⸣ DUMU-*ka a-šak-kan*
8) ⸢*é-ḫúl-ḫúl ip-pu-uš-ma ú-šak-lal ši-pir-šú* URU.KASKAL⸣
9) ⸢UGU *šá ma-ḫar*⸣ *ú-šak-lal-ma a-na áš-ri-šú ú-ta-ri*
10) ⸢ŠU.II ^{d}30 ^{d}*nin-gal* ^{d}*nusku u* ^{d}*sa-dàr-nun-na*⸣
11) ⸢*i-ṣab-bat-ma a-na é-ḫúl-ḫúl ú-še-reb a-mat* ^{d}30⸣
12) ⸢LUGAL DINGIR.MEŠ *iq-ba-a at-ta-ʾi-id-ma a-mur a-na-ku*⸣
13) ⸢^{md}MUATI-NÍ⸣.TUKU DUMU *e-du ṣi-it lìb-bi-ía par-ṣi*
14) ⸢*ma-šu-ti šá* ^{d}30 ^{d}*nin-gal* ^{d}*nusku ù*⸣
15) ⸢^{d}*sa-dàr-nun-na ú-šak-lil é-ḫúl-ḫúl*⸣
16) *eš-šiš i-pu-uš-ma ú-šak-lil ši-pir-šú* URU.KASKAL *e-li*
17) *šá ma-ḫar ú-šak-lil-ma a-na áš-ri-šú ú-ter qa-ti*
18) ^{d}30 ^{d}*nin-gal* ^{d}*nusku u* ^{d}*sa-dàr-nun-na ul-tu*
19) *šu-an-na* URU LUGAL-*ú-ti-šú iṣ-bat-ma ina qé-reb* URU.KASKAL
20) *ina é-ḫúl-ḫúl šu-bat ṭu-ub lìb-bi-šú-nu ina ḫi-da-a-tú*
21) *u ri-šá-a-tú ú-še-šib šá ul-tu pa-na-ma* ^{d}30 LUGAL DINGIR
22) *la i-pu-šú-ma a-na mam-ma la id-di-nu ina na-ra-mi-ia*
23) *šá* DINGIR-*ut-su pal-ḫa-ku* TÚG.SÍG-*šú aṣ-ba-ti* ^{d}30 LUGAL DINGIR
24) *re-ši-ia ul-li-ma* MU DÙG.GA *ina* KUR *iš-ku-na-an-ni*
25) *u$_4$-me ár-ku-ti* MU.AN.NA.MEŠ *ṭu-ub* ŠÀ *uṣ-ṣi-pa-am*-⸢*ma*⸣
26) *ul-tu pa-ni* ^{m}AN.ŠÁR-DÙ-A LUGAL KUR-*aš-šur*.KI *a-di* MU.9.⸢KAM⸣
27) ^{md}MUATI-NÍ.TUKU LUGAL TIN.TIR.KI DUMU *ṣi-it lìb-bi*-⸢*ia*⸣
28) 1 ME 4 MU.AN.NA.MEŠ SIG$_5$.MEŠ *ina pu-luḫ-ti šá* ^{d}30 LUGAL DINGIR.MEŠ
29) *ina lìb-bi-ia iš-ku-nu ú-bal-liṭ-an-ni ía-a-ti ni-ṭi-il* IGI
30) *na-mir-ma šu-tu-rak* ⸢*ḫa*⸣-*si-si qa-ti u* GÌR.II

ii 5–11a) When his hands were placed in my dream, the god Sîn, king of the gods, said to me, saying: "The return of the gods is your responsibility. I will place (responsibility for my) residence in Ḫarrān into the hands of Nabonidus, your son. He will (re)build Eḫulḫul and complete its construction. He will make the city Ḫarrān more perfect than before and he will return (it) to its place. He will take the deities Sîn, Ningal, Nusku, and Sadarnunna by the hand and will have (them) enter Eḫulḫul."

ii 11b–12) I was attentive to the word(s) that the god Sîn, king of the gods, had spoken to me and I personally saw (these things happen).

ii 13–21a) Nabonidus, (my) only son, my own offspring, carried out the forgotten cultic rites of the deities Sîn, Ningal, Nusku, and Sadarnunna to perfection. He built Eḫulḫul anew and completed its construction. He made the city Ḫarrān more perfect than before and returned (it) to its place. He took the deities Sîn, Ningal, Nusku, and Sadarnunna by the hand, (leading them out) of Šuanna (Babylon), the city of his royal majesty, and had (them) reside inside in the city Ḫarrān, in Eḫulḫul, the residence of their happiness, during joyous celebrations.

ii 21b–29a) That which from the (distant) past the god Sîn, king of the gods, had not done nor given to anyone: out of (his) love for me, I who revered his divinity and grasped his hem, the god Sîn, king of the gods, elevated me (lit. "raised up my head") and (then) he established a good reputation for me in the land (and) added long days (and) years of happiness to my (life). From the time of Ashurbanipal, king of Assyria, until the ninth year of Nabonidus, king of Babylon, (my) son, my own offspring, he (Sîn) kept me alive for 104 good years on account of the reverence that the god Sîn, king of the gods, had placed in my heart.

ii 29b–35a) (As for) me, my eyesight was (still) sharp (lit. "bright"), my hearing/mental faculties was/were (still) surpassing, my hands and feet were (still) intact,

---

ii 23 *pal-ḫa-ku* "I who revered": Ex. 2 has *ap-la-ḫu* "that I revered."

ii 30 *šu-tu-rak* ⸢*ḫa*⸣-*si-si* "my hearing/mental faculties was/were (still) surpassing": Because *hasīsu* has the meaning of both "ear" and "wisdom, comprehension," it is uncertain if Adad-guppi is referring to her hearing or her mental faculties. Therefore, both possibilities are offered in the translation. One could tentatively lean towards "hearing" as the primary meaning of *hasīsī* if *nu-us-su-qa a-ma-tu-u-a* ("my words were (still) well-chosen") is a statement about her mental faculties, that is, Adad-guppi's mind was still sharp enough to speak clearly. Moreover, because *šūturāk hasīsī* appears between *niṭil īnī namirma* ("my eyesight was (still) sharp") and *qātī u šēpī šalimma* ("my hands and feet were (still) intact"), *hasīsu* may refer to hearing since Adad-guppi is describing her physical abilities.

šá-li-im-ma
31) nu-us-su-qa a-ma-tu-u-a ma-ka-le-e u maš-qí-ti
32) šu-lu-ku UGU-ia UZU.MEŠ-u-a ṭa-bu-ma ul-lu-ṣi lìb-bi
33) DUMU DUMU DUMU DUMU.MEŠ-ia* a-di 4 li-pi-ia bal-ṭu-ut-su-nu
34) a-mur-ma áš-ba-a lit-tu-tu ^{d}30 LUGAL DINGIR.MEŠ a-na SIG$_5$-ti
35) tap-pa-al-sa-⸢an-ni⸣-ma u$_4$-mi-ía tu-ri-ki ^{d}MUATI-I LUGAL ERIDU.KI
36) DUMU-ú-a a-na ^{d}30 EN-ia ap-qid a-di bal-ṭu
37) la i-ḫa-aṭ-<ṭa>-ak-ka ^{d}ALAD dum-qí ^{d}LAMMA dum-qí šá it-ti-ía
38) tap-qí-du-ma ú-šak-ši-dan-nu a-na lit-tu-tu it-ti-šú
39) pi-qid-ma ina qa$^{?}$-ti ḫi-ṭi šá DINGIR-ú-ti-ka ra-bi-ti
40) e-ṭir-šu-ma DINGIR-ú-ut-ka GAL-ti li-ip-làḫ ina 21 MU.MEŠ
41) šá ^{md}MUATI-A-ÙRU LUGAL TIN.TIR.KI ina 43 MU.MEŠ šá ^{md}MUATI-NÍG.GUB-PAP
42) DUMU ^{md}MUATI-A-ÙRU ù 4 MU.MEŠ šá ^{md}U.GUR-LUGAL-PAP LUGAL TIN.TIR.KI
43) LUGAL-ú-ti i-te-ep-pu-šu-u' 68 MU.AN.NA.MEŠ
44) ina gab-bi lìb-bi-ia ap-làḫ-šú-nu-ti EN.NUN-tì-šú-nu aṣ-⸢ṣur⸣-[ma]
45) ⸢^{md}MUATI-I DUMU ṣi-it lìb-bi-ía ana IGI ^{md}MUATI-NÍG.GUB-ú-ṣur⸣
46) ⸢DUMU ^{md}MUATI-A-ÙRU u ^{md}U.GUR-LUGAL-PAP$^{?}$ LUGAL TIN.TIR.KI uš-ziz-ma⸣
47) ⸢ur-ri u mu-ši EN⸣.NUN-tì-šú-nu iṣ-ṣur-ma
48) šá e-li-šú-nu ṭa-a-bi i-te-né-ep-pu-šú ka-a-a-na
49) MU-a bab-ba-nu-ú ina pa-ni-šú-nu iš-ku-un ki-ma
50) DUMU.MUNUS ṣi-it lìb-bi-šú-⸢nu⸣ ul-lu-ú re-⸢ši-ia⸣
51) ár-ka-niš šim-ti ú-bil-šú-nu-⸢ti⸣
52) ma-na-ma ina DUMU.MEŠ-šú-nu u mam-ma ni-⸢ši⸣-[šú-nu]
53) u LÚ.GAL.MEŠ-šú-nu šá ⸢i⸣-nu-ma re-ši-[šú-nu]
54) ul-lu-ú ina bu-šu-ú ù NÍG.GA
55) ú-at-ter-šú-nu-tú la iš-tak-⸢kan⸣-šú-nu-[tú]
56) qut-rin-nu ia-a-tú ⸢ITI⸣-šam-ma la na-par-⸢ka⸣-[a]
57) ina lu-bu-ši-ia dam-qu-ú-tú GU$_4$.MEŠ
58) UDU.NÍTA.MEŠ ma-ru-tú NINDA.ḪI.A KAŠ.SAG ⸢GEŠTIN⸣
59) Ì.GIŠ LÀL u GURUN GIŠ.KIRI$_6$ ⸢ka⸣-la-ma ki-is-⸢pi⸣

Col. iii
1) a-kàs-sip$_4$-šú-nu-ti-ma sur-qin-nu
2) ṭaḫ-du-tú i-ri-ši ṭa-a-bi
3) a-na gi-na-a ú-kin-šú-nu-ti-ma
4) áš-tak-kan ina maḫ-ri-šu-un
5) ina MU.9.KAM ^{md}MUATI-I
6) LUGAL TIN.TIR.KI ši-im-⸢tú⸣

my words were (still) well-chosen, food and drink were (still) agreeable to me, my body was (still) healthy, and my spirit was (still) joyful. I saw my children's children's children's children alive up to the fourth generation and (therefore) I attained a very old age. You, Sîn, king of the gods, looked at me with favor and made my days long.

ii 35b–40a) I entrusted Nabonidus, king of Babylon, my son, to the god Sîn, my lord. For his entire life, he will not sin against you. Entrust to him the good *šēdu* (and) the good *lamassu* that you had entrusted to me and who had helped me reach a very old age and save him from sinning (lit. "the *hand* of sin") against your great divinity so that he reveres your great divinity.

ii 40b–48) During the twenty-one years of Nabopolassar, king of Babylon, the forty-three years of Nebuchadnezzar (II), son of Nabopolassar, and the four years of Neriglissar, king of Babylon, (when) th(ose three kings) exercised kingship, I whole heartedly revered them (the gods of Ḫarrān) for sixty-eight years, (continued to) serve them, [and] pressed Nabonidus, (my) son, my own offspring, into the service of Nebuchadnezzar (II), son of Nabopolassar, and Neriglissar, king of Babylon. He served them day and night and constantly did what was pleasing to them.

ii 49–56a) He (Sîn) established my excellent name before them. Like a daughter, their own offspring, they elevated me (lit. "raised up my head"). Afterwards, fate carried them off. Not one of their descendants and not one of [their] people or their eunuchs, whom they had made richer in possessions and property when they elevated th[em] (lit. "raised up [their] heads"), set out incense(-offerings) for th[em].

ii 56b–iii 4) (But as for) me, monthly, without ceasing, (and dressed) in my (most) beautiful garments, I presented them with oxen, fattened sheep, bread, beer, wine, oil, honey, and fruit(s) of the orchard, all of this, as a funerary offering and I made an abundance of strewn offerings (with) a sweet scent permanent for them (and) placed (them) before them (forever after).

iii 5–16a) During the ninth year of Nabonidus, king of Babylon, fate carried her off, and Nabonidus, king of

7) *ra-man-ni-šú ú-bil-šu-*⌈*ma*⌉
8) ^{md}MUATI-NÍ.TUKU LUGAL TIN.[TIR.KI]
9) ⌈DUMU *ṣi-it*⌉ *lìb-bi-šú na-ra-*⌈*am*⌉ AMA-*šú*
10) ⌈ADDA-*su*⌉ *ú-kam-mis-ma lu-bu-šú*
11) ⌈SIG$_5$-*ti*⌉ *ki-tu-*⌈*u*⌉ *na-am-ri a-lu*
12) KÙ.GI *x x nam-ru-tú*
13) ⌈NA$_4$ SIG$_5$-*u-ti* NA$_4$⌉ *ni-siq-tú*
14) NA$_4$ *šu-qu-ru-ti* [...]
15) Ì.GIŠ DÙG.GA ADDA-*su ú-[pa-ši-iš-ma]*
16) *iš-ku-nu ina ni-ṣir-ti* GU$_4$.MEŠ
17) UDU.NÍTA.MEŠ *ma-ru-tú ú-ṭa-*⌈*ab*⌉*-bi-[iḫ]*
18) *ma-ḫar-šú ú-pa-ḫir-ma* LÚ
19) TIN.TIR.KI *u bar-sip*.KI *ma-*⌈*al*⌉*-[ki]*
20) *a-šib na-gi-i né-su-tú* [NUN.MEŠ]
21) *u* GÌR.NÍTA.MEŠ *ul-tu [pa-aṭ]*
22) KUR.*mi-ṣir tam-tim e-*⌈*li*⌉*-[ti]*
23) *ana tam-tim šap-li-ti ú-[šat-ba-am-ma]*
24) *si-pi-it-ti u* [...]
25) *bi-ki-ti* ⌈*ṣar*⌉*-piš* ⌈*iš*⌉*-[ku-nu-ma]*
26) *id-du-u ri-gim-šú-un* 7 ⌈*ur*⌉*-[ri]*
27) *ù* 7 *mu-šá-a-ti* ⌈*ma*⌉*-[li-ti]*
28) *uḫ-tal-li-lu lu-bu-[ši-šú-nu* SAḪAR]
29) *sa-aḫ-pu ina 7-i u*$_4$*-mu [ina ka-šá-du]*
30) ⌈UN⌉.MEŠ KUR *ka-la-ma pe-*⌈*re*⌉*-[ti]*
31) *ú-gal-li-bu-ma* [...]
32) *[lu]-bu-ši-šú-nu* TA *x x*
33) IS SU US UN *x* BU ŠI *x [x x]*
34) *u šu-ka-ni-šú-nu iš-*⌈*ku*⌉*-[nu-ma]*
35) *i-ru-bu-ni a-*⌈*na*⌉ [...]
36) *ina ma-ka-le-e* [...]
37) ŠIM *ḫal-ṣa ú-kam-*⌈*mir*⌉ *[x x]*
38) Ì.GIŠ DÙG.GA *a-na* SAG-⌈*šú*⌉*-[nu]*
39) *ú-šap-pi-ik lìb-[ba-šú-nu]*
40) *ú-šá-li-iṣ-ma ú-[nam-mir]*
41) ⌈*zi*⌉*-mi-šú-un ú-ru-uḫ* [KUR]-
42) -⌈*šú-nu*?⌉ *ú-šá-aṣ-bit-šú-nu-*⌈*ti*⌉*-[ma]*
43) *a-na a-šar-šú-nu i-tu-[ru man-nu]*
44) *at-ta lu-ú* LUGAL *lu-u* ⌈NUN⌉ *[x x]*
45) *x x* TI *x* BE ^{d}30 ⌈LUGAL⌉ [DINGIR]
46) EN DINGIR.MEŠ *šá* AN-*e u* ⌈KI⌉*-[tim]*
47) DINGIR-*ut-su* GAL-*ti mu-ši u* ⌈*ur*⌉*-[ra]*
48) ^{d}UTU ^{d}IŠKUR *u* ^{d}15 EN? [AN-*e u*]
49) KI-*tim šá x ma x x [x x]*
50) *[a]-šib é-sag-*⌈*íl*⌉ *u é-[ḫúl-ḫúl]*
51) *[pi]-làḫ-ma ina* AN-*e u* [KI-*tim*]
52) ⌈*su*⌉*-up-pi-šú-nu-ti-ma* ⌈*ṣi*?⌉*-[it]*
53) ⌈*pi*⌉*-i šá* ^{d}30 DINGIR *x [x x]*
54) *[x x]* (traces) [...]
55) *[x x]-ma* NUMUN-*ka x [x x]*
56) *[x x] ri x x x [x x]*

Bab[ylon], (her) son, her own offspring, the beloved of his mother, prepared her corpse for burial, [... (her)] with a beautiful garment, bright linen, an *ālu*-ornament of gold, bright ..., good quality stone(s), a choice stone, precious stone(s), [...], an[ointed] her corpse with aromatic oil, [and] placed (it) in a secluded place.

iii 16b–29a) He (Nabonidus) slaughte[red] oxen and fattened sheep. In her presence, he gathered the people of Babylon and Borsippa, rul[ers] who reside in remote mountains, [nobles] and governors from [the border(s) of] Egypt (and) the Upp[er] Sea to the Lower Sea, and (then) he [made (them) rise up, and ...] lamentations and [...]. Th[ey] wept bitterly [and] uttered their laments. For seven da[ys] and seven nights, they let (their) *lou[d cries]* sound forth shrilly. [Their] garme[nts] were covered [with dust].

iii 29b–43a) When the seventh day [arrived, the pe]ople of the land shaved off all of (their) ha[ir] and [...] their [ga]rments ... They pla[ced *their*] ... and their jewelry [and] entered into [...]. With food, [...], filtered oil, he (Nabonidus) heaped [up ...]. He poured aromatic oil onto the[ir] head(s), made [their he]arts rejoice, and ma[de] their [f]aces [light up]. He made them take the road (back) to *their* (own) [land(s) and] they retur[ned] to their places.

iii 43b–56) [Whoever] you are, whether king or rul[er ...] ..., night and d[ay], revere the great divinity of the god Sîn, ki[ng of the gods], lord of the gods of heaven and e[arth], the deities Šamaš, Adad, and Ištar, *lord(s)* [of heaven and] earth, who ... [... (and) who re]side in Esagil and E[ḫulḫul, p]ray to them in heaven and [(on) earth] and [...] the *pro[noun]cement(s)* of the god Sîn ... [...] ... [...] your seed [...] ... [...]

iii 11 *a-lu* "an *ālu*-ornament": For the interpretation of *ālu* as an ornament, see CAD A/1 pp. 374–375 sub *alu* A 2b and *alu* B, as well as CDA p. 13 sub *ālu* II. H. Schaudig (Inschriften Nabonids p. 508 n. 742) proposed that the word is connected to *ālu* ("city") and tentatively suggests translating the word as "*mural crown*" (*Mauerkrone*), a royal headdress worn by Neo-Assyrian queens in artistic representations of them.
iii 13–14 The mention of various stones here may have had a two-fold purpose: they were chosen for their beauty, as well as their for their magical powers; see Schuster-Brandis, AOAT 46.
iii 27 ⌈*ma*⌉-[*li-ti*] "*lou*[*d cries*]": Or possibly ⌈*ma*⌉-[*li-li*] "*ree*[*d pipes*]." Both *malītu* and *malīlu* are each only known from a handful of attestations; see CAD M/1 pp. 164–165. H. Schaudig (Inschriften Nabonids p. 509) restores ⌈*ma*⌉-[*li-li*], rather than ⌈*ma*⌉-[*li-ti*].

Minor Variants and Comments

Neriglissar No. 1

i 2.2 *ru-ba-a* for *ru-ba-a-am*. **i 2.2** ⸢*na*⸣*-a-du* for *na-a-da*. **i 3.2** *áš-ri* for *áš-ru*. **i 5.2** *be-lí-šu* for EN-*šu*. **i 7.2** *ra-bi-ú-*[*tim*] for *ra-bu-ù-tim*. **i 11.2** ^{md}EN-*šu-mi-iš-ku-un* for ^{md}EN-*šu-um-iš-ku-un*.

Neriglissar No. 3

i 3.2 *da-am-qá-a-tim* for *da-am-qá-a-ti*. **i 4.2**, 7 *e-p*[*é-*(*e*)*-š*]*u* and *e-pe-šu* respectively for *e-pe-e-šu*. **i 7.2** *e-pe-*⸢*šu*⸣ for *e-pé-e-šu*. **i 9.2**, 6 *qaq-qa-du* and SAG.DU respectively for *qá-qá-dam*. **i 9.2**, 6 *e-pe-šu* for *e-pé-e-šu*. **i 10.2** ^{d}*na-bi-um* for ^{d}AG. **i 10.2**, 6 *i-ša-ar-tim* for *i-ša-ar-ti*. **i 11.6** *qá-tu-uš-šu* for *qa-tu-uš-šu*. **i 12.6** MA.DA for *ma-a-ti*. **i 14.7** [^{d}EN-*šu*]*-um-iš-*[*ku-un*] for ^{d}EN-MU-IN.GAR. **i 24.4** ⸢*ú-uš*⸣*-*[*zi-zu*] for *uš-zi-zu*. **i 28.4** ⸢*ka*⸣*-*[*as-pu*] for KÙ.BABBAR. **i 30.4** ⸢*ki-sè*⸣*-*[*e*] for *ki-se-e*. **i 34.1** *za-am-mu-*<*uk-ku*> for *za-am-mu-uk-ku*. **i 38.5** The reading of the sign after [*šit*]*-*⸢*lu-ṭu*⸣ does not appear to be the I sign. **i 42.6** *ga-ap-šu-tim* for *ga-ap-šu-ti*.

ii 2.1 There is an erased sign between *is-su-ú* and *i-re-e-qu*. **ii 2.6** *i-re-qu* for *i-re-e-qu*. **ii 3.5–6** *la-bi-ri* for *la-bí-ri*. **ii 10.6** *na-pa-ar-ku-tim* for *na-pa-ar-ku-ti*. **ii 14.1**, 6 have *ka-a-*<*a*>*-nam* and *ka-a-a-*[*nam*] respectively. **ii 29.3** [*ši-i*]*-pí-šu* for *ši-i-pí-ša*. **ii 31.3** [^{d}]⸢EN⸣ for ^{d}EN.LÍL. **ii 31.3** DINGIR for DINGIR.DINGIR. **ii 32.3** AD.AD-*šu* for *ab-bé-e-šu*. **ii 33.3** *na-ka-ri* for *na-ak-ri*. **ii 34.3** *lu-uš-ba* for *lu-uš-bu*. **ii 36.3** [*li-it-tu-ú*]*-tu* for *li-it-tu-ú-ti*.

Nabonidus No. 1

i 2.2 Omits *a-na*. **i 3.2** *mu-ut-né-en-'u-ú* for *mu-ut-né-en-nu-ú*. **i 3.2** *mu-*⸢*uš-te*⸣*-*<*né*>*-'u-ú* for *mu-uš-te-né-'u-ú*. **i 3.2** *aš-ra-a-tú* for *aš-ra-a-tì*. **i 6.2** Copy has ÍL for *sa-niq*. **i 8.1** ^{d}ŠEŠ.KI-NIR for ^{d}ŠEŠ.KI-*ri*. **i 9.2** DINGIR GAL.GAL for DINGIR.MEŠ GAL.MEŠ. **i 12.2** ^{md}*na-bi-um*-TIN-*su-iq-bi* for ^{md}*na-bi-um-ba-lat-su-iq-bi*. **i 13.2** Omits *a-na*. **i 14.2–3** *šu-tu-ra-ku* for *šu-tú-ra-ku*. **i 15.3** *du-uš-šá-a-ku* for *du-uš-šá-ku*. **i 16.2**, 3 respectively *ṭú-uḫ-ḫu*-da*-ku* and ⸢*ṭú*⸣*-uḫ*-AG-ŠU for *ṭú-uḫ-ḫu-da-ak*. **i 17** Ex. 1 adds extra ^{d}EN.LÍL after *im-gur-*^{d}EN.LÍL. **i 18.3** ⸢*i*⸣*-qu-up-pu* for *i-qu-pu*. **i 19.2** *it-ru-*<*ur*>*-ma* for *it-ru-ur-ma*. **i 19.3** *né-mé-et-ti* for *né-mé-et-ta*. **i 20.3** *né-mé-et-ti* for *né-mé-et-ta*. **i 21.3** [*qu-up-p*]*u-tu* for *qu-up-pu-tu*. **i 21.2** *ad-ke*-DI-*ma* for *ad-ke-e-ma*. **i 22.1** <*ku*>*-du-ur-ru* for *ku-du-ur-ru*. **i 23.2** *pu-lu-uk-*<*ku*> for *pu-lu-uk-ku*. **i 25.2** *pi-i* for *pa-ni*. **i 25.1** ZA-*a-bi* for *a-a-bi*.

ii 1.1 *ma-ḫa*-A for *ma-ḫa-za*. **ii 1.1** ⸢*ba-ú*⸣*-la*-ZA-⸢*tú**⸣ for *ba-ú-la-a-ti*. **ii 4.2** *úḫu-*<*mi-iš*> for *úḫu-mi-iš*. **ii 4.1–2** *ú-šar-ši-id*-ŠU and *ú-šar-ši-id*-MA respectively for *ú-šar-ši-id-su*. **ii 4.2** *tab-ra-a-ti* for *tab-ra-a-tú*. **ii 5.2** *ša* for *šá* (both instances). **ii 5.2** *qé-re-eb-šu* for *qé-reb-šu*. **ii 7.2** *ša* for *šá*. **ii 8.2** *ap-kal-lu* for *ap-kal-lu*$_{4}$. **ii 10.2** *e-*⸢*te*⸣*-ep-pu-uš-šu* for *e-te-ep-pu-šu*. **ii 12.2** *ba-la-ṭu-ia* for *ba-la-ṭi-ia*. **ii 13.2** *šá-*<*ni*>*-na* for *šá-ni-na*. **ii 14.2** *re-é-ú-*<<*tì*>>*-si-na* for *re-é-ú-si-na*. **ii 18.1** MA-ME-*na-at-*<*tu*>*-ú* for *iš-ta-na-at-tu-ú*. **ii 18.2** *na-gab-bi* for *nag-bi*. **ii 22.2** *i-ba-il* for *i-ba-'i-il*.

Nabonidus No. 2

i 1.4 *šu-úr-bu-tum* for *šu-úr-bu-tim*. **i 1.4** *ru-um-ti* for *ru-um-tì*. **i 2.2** DINGIR.DINGIR for *ì-lí*. **i 2.4** *qá-ri-it-ti* for *qá-ri-it-tim*. **i 3.4** *ta-am-ḫa-ri* for *ta-am-ḫa-ru*. **i 4.3** *tu-qu-un-ti* for *tu-qu-un-tim*. **i 5.2–3** *na-mi-ir-tì* for *na-mi-ir-ti*. **i 6.2–3** Respectively *ša-qu-ti* and *ša-qu-tú* for *ša-qu-tì*. **i 6.2** ^{d}*i-gi*$_{4}$*-gi*$_{4}$ for *i-gi*$_{4}$*-gi*$_{4}$. **i 7.3** *ru-ba-a-at* for *ru-ba-a-tì*. **i 8.3–4** *na-ša-at* and *na-šá-at* respectively for *na-ša-a-at*. **i 9.2** GAŠAN for *be-el-tim*. **i 9.4** Has an erasure after *ša*. **i 9.4** *má-lam-mu-šá* for *mé-lam-mu-šu*. **i 10.2–4** *ša-mu-ú* for *ša-mu-ù*. **i 11.4** *nam-ri-ru-šá* for *nam-ri-ir-ru-šu*. **i 11.3–4** *er-ṣe-tim* for KI-*tim*. **i 11.3–4** *ra-pa-aš-tim* for DAGAL-*tim*. **i 11** After *sa-aḫ-pu* exs. 3–4 add *ka-ši-da-at a-a-bi mu-ḫal-li-qá-at za-ma-nu*; ex. 4 has *mu-ḫal-li-qa-at* for *mu-ḫal-li-qá-at*. **i 12.3** *be-le-et* for *be-let*. **i 12.3–4** *ta-ḫa-zi* for *ta-ḫa-za*. **i 13.2–3** *ṣu-la-a-tim* for *ṣu-la-a-ti*. **i 14.3** Omits *a-ši-ba-at é-máš-da-ri*. **i 15.3** Omits *ša qé-re-eb* KÁ.DINGIR.RA.KI GAŠAN-*ia*. **i 15.2** *qé-er-bi* for *qé-re-eb*. **i 15.4** Has an erasure before GAŠAN-*ia*. **i 16.4** Has an erasure at the beginning of the line. **i 16.3–4** ^{d}*na-bi-um-na-'i-id* for ^{d}AG-*na-'i-id*. **i 16.3** KÁ.DINGIR.RA.KI for TIN.TIR.KI. **i 17.4** *qa-at* for *qá-ti*. **i 18.4** *à-áš-ri* for *à-aš-ru*. **i 18.2** *pa-liḫ* for *pa-li-iḫ*. **i 19.4** *za-ni-nu* for *za-ni-nu-um*. **i 20.3–4** *ṭè-e-mi* for *ṭè-mi*. **i 20.2–4** *ì-lí* for DINGIR.MEŠ. **i 20.3–4** *pu-tu-uq-qú* and *pu-tuq-qu* respectively for *pu-tuq-qú*. **i 21.3–4** *ša-aḫ-ṭú* for *ša-aḫ-ṭa*. **i 21.3–4** *mu-ur-te-ed-du-ú* for *mur-te-ed-du-ú*. **i 21.4** ^{d}*iš-tar* for *iš-tar*. **i 22.3–4** *mu-ṭaḫ-ḫi-id* for *mu-ṭa-aḫ-ḫi-id*. **i 22.3** *sat-tuk-ku* for *sa-at-tu-uk-ku*. **i 23.3–4** *mu-šar-ri-iḫ* for *mu-ki-in*. **i 24.4** *iš-te-né-e'-ù* for *iš-te-né-e'-ú*. **i 25.2** *ma-ḫa-za* for *ma-ḫa-zi*. **i 25.2–4** DINGIR.DINGIR, *ì-*⸢*lí*⸣, and *ì-lí* respectively for DINGIR.MEŠ. **i 26.3** *in* for *i-na*. **i 26.2–3** *ì-*⸢*lí*⸣ and *ì-lí* for DINGIR.DINGIR. **i 26.3–4** Add *šu-tu-ru zi-in-na-a-tim* after DINGIR.DINGIR; ex. 4 has *zi-in-na-a-ti* for *zi-in-na-a-tim*. **i 27.2** *šu-úr-*⸢*ru*⸣*-ḫu* for *šu-ur-ru-ḫu*. **i 28.4** *ú-še-re-bu* for *ú-še-er-re-bu*. **i 28.3** *qé-reb-šu* for *qé-re-eb-šu*. **i 29.2** *eš-*⸢*re*⸣*-et* for *eš-re-e-ti*. **i 29.4** *ì-lí* for DINGIR.DINGIR. **i 29.3** *ka-la-ši-na* for *ka-li-ši-na*. **i 30.2** *šu-ul-*⸢*ma*⸣*-num* for *šu-ul-ma-nu*. **i 31.2**, 4 ^{md}AG-TIN-*su-iq-bi* and ^{d}*na-bi-um-ba-la-at-su-iq-bi* respectively for ^{md}AG-*ba-lat-su-iq-bi*. **i 32.2–3** NUN for *ru-bu-ù*; ex. 4 has *ru-ba-a*. **i 32** *e-em-qa*: Ex. 2 has *em-*⸢*qa*⸣, ex. 3 had *em-qa*, and ex. 4 has *e-em-qu-ma*. **i 32.4** Omits *a-na-ku*. **i 33.2–3** Add *ša qé-er-bi* KÁ.DINGIR.RA.KI after *a-kà-dè*.KI; ex. 4 has *qé-re-eb* for *qé-er-bi* and ex. 3 has KÁ.DINGIR.MEŠ.KI for and KÁ.DINGIR.RA.KI. **ii 34.4** Omits *-na-* in *in-na-mu-ú*.

ii 1.3–4 *kar-mi-iš* for *ka-ar-mi-iš*. **ii 2–3.4** Omits *li-ib-na-as-su id-ra-num iq-mu-ú di-ta-al-li-iš*. **ii 4.4** LA-*ud-du-ú* for *šu-ud-du-ú*. **ii 5.4** *ba-áš-mu* for *ba-aš-mu*. **ii 7.4** *na-par-ku-ú* for *na-pa-ar-ku-ú*. **ii 7.2** *qú-ut-re-num* for *qú-ut-re-nu*. **ii 8.4** *e-pé-eš* for *e-pe-eš*. **ii 8.3–4** *šu-a-ti* for *ša-a-tim*. **ii 8.2**, 4 *li-ib-bi* for *lìb-bi*. **ii 9.2**, 4 *ka-ba-at-ta* and *ka-ba-at-ti* respectively for *ka-ba-at-tì*. **ii 9.2** *ḫa-áš-ḫa-tu-šu* for *ḫa-áš-ḫa-tuš*. **ii 11.2**, 4 *te-me-en-šu* for *te-em-mé-en-šu*. **ii 13.4** *li-ib-na-at-šu* for *li-ib-na-as-su*. **ii 14.3–4** *qé-re-eb* for *qé-reb*. **ii 14.4** Omits KÁ.DINGIR.RA.KI. **ii 15.3–4** Add *uš-šu-šu uš-te-ši-ir ú-ki-in te-em-me-en-šu* after *e-eš-ši-iš e-pú-uš*; ex. 4 has *te-em-me-en-šu* for *te-em-mé-en-šu*. **ii 16.2–3** *šu-a-ti* and ⸢*šu-a*⸣*-ti* respectively for *šu-a-tim*. **ii 17.2–4** *ta-am-ḫa-ri* for *ta-am-ḫa-ru*. **ii 18.3–4** Respectively *ša-a-ti* and *šu-a-ti* for *ša-a-tim*. **ii 19.2** Omits *šu-ba-at na-ra-mi-ki*. **ii 19.3** *šu-bat* for *šu-ba-at*. **ii 19.3–4** *na-ar-mi-*⸢*ki*⸣ and *na-ar-mi-ki* respectively for *na-ra-mi-ki*. **ii 20** *ḫa-di*-iš*: All four exemplars have *ḫa*-MI-*iš*. **ii 20.2** *nap-li-si-ma* for *na-ap-li-si-ma*. **ii 22.4** *ur-ri-ku* for *úr-ru-ku*. **ii 23.3–4** *šu-um-ú-du* for *šu-um-ú-da*$_{4}$. **ii 24.3–4** *ì-lí* for DINGIR.DINGIR. **ii 25.4** *tam-mi-i* for *at-mi-i*. **ii 26.3–4** *a-šar* for *a-ša-ar*. **ii 26.3–4** *qá-*⸢*ab*⸣*-li* and *qab-lu* respectively for *qá-ab-lum*.

ii 27.3–4 *ta-ḫa-zi* for *ta-ḫa-zi-im*. **ii 28**.3 *i*-BA-*a-a* for *i-da-a-a*. **ii 30**.3 *lu-ša-am-qí-ti* for *lu-ša-am-qí-it*.

Nabonidus No. 8

3.6 *ana-<ku>* for *ana-ku*.

Nabonidus No. 14

i 11′.2 ⌜*zi-ik-ri*⌝ for *zi-ik-r*[*a*].

Nabonidus No. 16

i 34.2 ⌜ŠÀ⌝-*šu* for *lìb-bi-šú*. **i 41**.4 *e-pe-ru* for *e-pe-ri*. **i 42**.1 Omits *ša*. **i 44**.1 *pa-na-<a>* for *pa-na-a*.

ii 2.1, 3 respectively EN-*ti-tim* and ⌜*re-eš-ti-tim*⌝ for *reš**-*ti-tim*. **ii 3**.1,3 have ⌜*ge-gu*⌝-[*na*]-⌜*a*⌝-*šu* for [*g*]*e-gu-<na>-a-šu* respectively for ⌜*ge*⌝-*gu-<na>-a-šu*. **ii 4**.3 [*ul-l*]*i-i* for *ul-li-ma*. **ii 8**.3 [*lìb-bi-š*]*u* for *lìb-bi-šú*. **ii 12**.5 [*b*]*a-aṣ-ṣu* for *ba-aṣ-ṣa*. **ii 14**.5 [*k*]*i-iṣ-ṣa* for *ki-iṣ-ṣi*. **ii 56**.3 [*uš-ta*]*m-ḫir** for *uš-ta-*[*am*]-⌜*ḫir*⌝.

iii 6.3 ⌜*e-pu-uš-ma*⌝ for *e-pú-uš-ma*. **iii 9**.3 *ú-ul-la-a* for *ul-la-a*. **iii 11**.3 *e-pú-uš* for *e-pu-uš*. **iii 13**.3 *ṣi-ir-tim* for *ṣir-tim*. **iii 14**.3 *zi-qú-ra-tim* for *zi-qu-ra-tim*. **iii 19**.3, 6 *ḫu-ur-sa-ni-iš* for *ḫur-sa-ni-iš*. **iii 21**.3, 6 respectively *ra-bu-ú* and [*ra*]-*bu-ú* for GAL-*ú*. **iii 21**.3, 6 *ia-ti* for *ia-tim*. **iii 22**.3, 6 *i-ir-a-mu* for *i-ir-a-am*. **iii 25**.3,6 have *e-pu-uš-m*[*a*] and *e-pu-uš-ma* respectively for *e-pú-uš-ma*. **iii 27**.3, 6 *šu-um* for *šu-mi*. **iii 31**.3, 6 respectively *<ana>* and [*a-n*]*a*. **iii 31**.3 *u*$_{4}$*-mu* for *u*$_{4}$*-mi*.

Nabonidus No. 19

i 1.2 DINGIR.DINGIR for DINGIR.MEŠ. **i 5**.2 *šar-ru-ti-šú* for *šar-ru-ti-šu*. **i 8**.2 *né*-ŠI-*qí* for *né-me-qí*. **i 9**.2 *bu-na-an-né-e-šú* for *bu-na-an-né-e-šu*. **i 10**.2 *pa-qí-du* for *pa-qid*. **i 10**.1 There is an erased *-qí-du* after *pa-qid*. **i 10**.1 *iš-ru-uk-ša* for *iš-ru-uk-šu*. **i 11**.1 ^{d}⌜ŠEŠ.KI⌝ for ^{d}ŠEŠ.KI-*ri*. **i 14**.1 *iš-ru-uk-ša* for *iš-ru-uk-šu*. **i 15**.2 *ú-ma-šu* for *ú-ma-ša*. **i 15**.2 *ú-ša-ag-mi-ir-šú* for *ú-ša-ag-mi-ir-šu*. **i 16**.2 *ú-za-ʾi-in-šú* for *ú-za-ʾi-in-šu*. **i 16**.2 *me-lam* for *me-lam-mi*. **i 16**.2 LUGAL-*ú-tim* for LUGAL-*ú-tu*. **i 17**.2 *ši-tul-tim* for *ši-tul-tum*. **i 17**.2 *ár-ka-tim* for *ár-kát*. **i 18**.2 *re-ṣu-ut-su* for *re-ṣu-su*. **i 19**.2 *ru-ba-a* for *ru-bu-um*. **i 21**.2 *šá* for *ša*. **i 21**.2 *ṭè-me* for *ṭè-e-mu*. **i 22**.1 *iš*-NA-*né-eʾ-ú* for *iš-te-né-eʾ-ú*. **i 22**.2 DINGIR.DINGIR for DINGIR.MEŠ. **i 22**.2 ^{d}INANNA for ^{d}IŠ.TAR. **i 24**.2 Omits EN GAL-*ú*. **i 24**.2 *be-lu-tu* for *be-lu-tì*. **i 24**.2 *ma-a-tim* for *ma-a-ti*. **i 25**.2 *zi-ik-ri* for *zi-ik-ru*. **i 26**.2 *u*$_{4}$*-mi-šam-ma* for *u*$_{4}$*-mi-ša-am-ma*. **i 27**.2 *aš-te-né-ʾa-a* for *aš-te-né-ʾe-e*. **i 27**.2 *šá* for *ša*. **i 27**.2 *e-li-šú-nu* for *e-li-šu-nu*. **i 27**.2 *ṭa-a-bi* for *ṭa-a-bu*. **i 28**.2 *šu-tu-rak* for *šu-tu-ra-ku*. **i 28**.2 *zi-in-na-a-tú* for *zi-in-na-a-tim*. **i 29**.1–2 Both exemplars have *im-mi-ma-a-a* for *mi**-*im**-*ma-a-a*. **i 29**.2 *ú-še-er-re-bu* for *ú-še-er-re-eb*. **i 29**.2 *ma-ḫar-šu-un* for *ma-ḫa-ar-šu-un*. **i 30** *na-par-ka-a*: Ex. 1 has *na-par-<ka>-a* and ex. 2 has *na-par-ka-aʾ*. **i 31**.2 *ta-na-da-a-tú* for *ta-na-da-a-ta*. **i 32**.2 *da-ád*-BAR for *da-ád-me*. **i 33**.1–2 *ki-iṣ-ṣi*: Both exemplars have *ki-iṣ*-AD. **i 34**.2 LUGAL for *šar-ri*. **i 34**.2 *te-me-en-ša* for *te-me-en-šú*. **i 35**.2 Has *ú-qá-an-ni* (over erased *-ma*)*-ma*. **i 36**.2 *te-me-en* for *te-me-en-na*. **i 36**.1 *uš*-BA-MA for *uš-šu-šu*.

ii 1.2 *ú-ul-la-a* for *ul-la-a*; *re-e-ši-šu* for *re-ši-šu*. **ii 2**.2 *me-lam-kur-kur-<ra>-dul-la* for *me-lem*$_{4}$*-kur-kur-ra-dul-la*. **ii 2**.2 *ú-zaq-qí-ir* for *ú-za-aq-qí-ir*. **ii 3**.1 *<ga>-aš-ru* for *ga-aš-ru*. **ii 3**.2 *ta-<ap>-šu-uḫ-ti-šú* for *ta-ap-šu-uḫ-ti-šu*. **ii 4**.2 *la-bí-ri-im-ma* for *la-bi-ri-im-ma*. **ii 4**.2 *e-pu-uš* for *e-pú-uš*. **ii 5**.2 URU.*ú-ba-as-su* for URU.*ú-ba-as-si*. **ii 5**.1 for BÁR.ŠID.KI for *bár-sipa*.KI. **ii 6**.2 *ú-ul-li-ma* for *ul-li-ma*. **ii 7**.2 ^{d}INANNA for ^{d}*iš-tar*. **ii 7**.2 *ú-še-ri-bu* for *ú-še-ri-ib*. **ii 9**.2 *sat-tuk-ki-šu* for *sa-at-tuk-ki-šu*. **ii 9**.2 *ú-šar-ri-iḫ* for *ú-šar-ri-ḫu*. **ii 9**.2 *ni-id-bé-e-šu* for *ni-id-bé-e-šú*. **ii 10** *aš-te-né-eʾ-e-ma*: Ex. 1 has *<aš>-te-né-eʾ-e-ma* and ex. 2 has *aš-te-né-<eʾ>-e-<ma>*. **ii 11**.2 *e-riš-tum* for *e-ri-iš-ti*. **ii 11**.2 *i-ri-iš-an-ni* for *i-ri-ša-an-ni*. **ii 13**.2 *lìb-bi-iá* for *lìb-bi-ia*. **ii 13**.2 MU-*šú* for *šum-šú*. **ii 14**.2 *ú-še-ri-bu* for *ú-še-ri-ib*. **ii 14**.2 *ana* for *a-na*. **ii 14**.2 *ma-ḫaz* for *ma-ḫa-zi*. **ii 15**.1 *na*-ŠU-*an-ni* for *na-ša-an-ni*. **ii 17**.2 *eṭ-lu* for *eṭ-lu-um*. **ii 18**.2 *ez-zu* for *ez-zi*. **ii 18**.2 *ša* for *šá*. **ii 19**.2 *nu-kúr-tum* for *nu-kúr-ti*. **ii 19**.1 *é-igi-kalam*-ŠU for *é-igi-kalam-ma*. **ii 20**.2 EN-*ia* (erasure) <<EN-*ia*>> for *be-lí-ia*. **ii 20**.2 *i-lu-ti*-MA for *i-lu-ti-šu*. **i 21**.2 *qar-ra-du-ti-šú* for *qar-ra-du-ti-šu*. **i 21**.1 Has an erased *-šu* after *qar-ra-du-ti-šu*. **ii 22**.2 *ta-ḫa-za* for *ta-ḫa-zi*. **ii 22**.2 *ru-qú-tú* for *ru-qu-tú*. **ii 23**.2 LUGAL for *šar-ri* **ii 23**.2 *i-pu-šu* for *i-pú-šu*. **ii 23**.1 Has a superfluous I before *te-me-en*. **ii 24**.2 *te-eq-ni-šu* for *ti-iq-ni-šu*. **ii 24**.2 *šu-a-tim* for *šu-a-ti*. **ii 25**.2 *ab-nim* for *ab-ni*. **ii 25**.1 *<eb>-bi* for *eb-bi*. **ii 25**.1 *ni-sì-iq*-IN for *ni-sì-iq-tu*$_{4}$. **ii 26**.2 *ma-ḫa-ri-šú* for *maḫ-ri-šu*. **ii 26**.2 *ú-še-rib* for *ú-še-ri-ib*. **ii 27**.2 *ú-ul-lu-ú* for *ul-lu-ú*. **ii 28**.2 *ki-di-šu* for *ki-di-šú*. **ii 30**.2 *qa-a-a-pu-tu* for *qa-a-a-pu-ti*. **ii 31**.2 *te-me-en-<ni>-šu* for *te-me-en-ni-šu*. **ii 31**.2 *ab-né-e-ma* for *ab-ni-ma*. **ii 32**.2 *ma-aṣ-ṣar-ta-šú* for *ma-aṣ-ṣar-ta-ša*. **ii 32**.2 *ú-dan-<ni>-in* for *ú-dan-ni-in*. **ii 33**.2 *e-pu-uš-ma* for *e-pú-uš-ma*. **ii 33**.2 *ú-ul-la* for *ul-la-a*. **ii 33**.2 *mug-da-šir*$_{9}$ for *mug-da-aš-ri*. **ii 33**.2 *šu-a-tim* for *šu-a-ti*. **ii 34**.2 *ḫa-diš* for *ḫa-di-iš*; *ina* for *i-na*. **ii 34**.1 KÙ.BABBAR for *ḫa-diš*; ŠÁ-*lu-si-ka* for *nap-lu-si-ka*. **ii 35**.2 *ma-ḫar* for *ma-ḫa-ar*. **ii 35**.2 Has an erased ŠU before AN-*e*. **ii 35**.2 AN-*e* for AN. **ii 35**.2 KI-*tim* for KI. **ii 36**.2 *u*$_{4}$*-mu* for UD.MEŠ **ii 36**.2 TIN-*iá* for TIN-*ia*. **ii 36**.2 *ina* for *i-na*. **ii 36**.1 Omits *-ka* after GIŠ.TUKUL.MEŠ. **ii 37**.2 *šu-um-qí-ta* for *šu-um-qí-tu*. **ii 37**.2 *ḫul-liq* for *ḫu-ul-li-iq*.

Nabonidus No. 24

i 1.2 *ana* for ⌜*a-na*⌝; omits *ṭè-me*. **i 3**.2 *e-qá-em* for *e-em-qá*; *mu-<ud>-di-iš* for *mu-ud-di-iš*. **i 3**.2–3 *ma-ḫa-zi* for *ma-ḫa-zu*. **i 4**.1 *mu-šak-<<li>>-lil* for *mu-šak-lil*. **i 5**.2–3 Respectively *ni-ši* and [*ni-š*]*i*? for *ni-šì*. **i 6**.2–3 *bi-nu-ti* for *bi-nu-tu*; *qá-ta* for *qá-at*; *ša* for *šá*. **i 7**.2 *<ú>-ṣu-ra-a-ti* for *ú-ṣu-ra-a-ti*. **i 7**.3 *giš-ḫur-ru* for *giš-ḫur-ri*. **i 8**.2 BAR-*ri* for *šip-ri*. **i 9**.1 ḪÉ.NÍTA for GÌR.NÍTA. **i 9**.3 DINGIR.MEŠ *ù* for DINGIR.DINGIR *u*. **i 9**.2 *ana-ku* for *a-na-ku*. **i 10**.1 ^{d}E for ^{d}UTU. **i 10**.2 ^{d}UTU.MEŠ for AN.TA.MEŠ. **i 10**.3 *ù* for second *u*. **i 11**.2–3 *ša* for *šá*. **i 11**.3 *pu-ru-us-se-e* for *pu-ri-se-e*. **i 12**.2–3 *lìb-bi* for *lìb-ba*. **i 12**.2 *te*-UŠ-*e-ti* for *te-re-e-ti*; LUGAL-*ti-ía* for LUGAL-*ú-ti-ia*. **i 13**.2–3 *za-ʾi-ri-ia* for *za-ʾi-i-ri-ia*. **i 14**.2 *šá* for *ša*. **i 14**.2 *ra-bu-ú* for GAL. **i 14**.2–3 *lìb-bi-ia* for *lìb-bi-ía*. **i 14**.2 *ki-i-ni* for *ki-nim*. **i 15**.2 *aš-te-ʾe-e-ma* for *áš-te-ʾe-e-ma*. **i 16**.2 *at-nu-ma* for *at-ma-nu*; DINGIR-*ti-šú* for DINGIR-*ú-ti-šú*. **i 17**.2 DI-*iṣ-ṣi* for *ki-iṣ-ṣi*. **i 17**.2–3 KÙ for *el-lu*; *mu-ša-bu* for *mu-šab*. **i 17**.2 MU.LU-*ti-šú* for *be-lu-ti-šú*. **i 18**.2–3 *ma-du-tu* for *ma-aʾ-du-tu*. **i 18** *ú-ṣu-ra-tu-šú*: Ex. 1 has *ú* (over erased *uṣ*)*-ṣu-ra-tu-šú* and ex. 2 has *uṣ*-⌜RA-*tu**-UZ⌝. **i 19**.2 *maḫ-ri* for *ma-aḫ-ri*. **i 20**.2–3 *ra-ma-ni-šú* and [*r*]*a-ma-ni-šú* respectively for *ra-man-ni-šú*; *ú-še-piš-šam-ma* for *ú-še-piš-ma*. **i 20**.2 *bé-lu-ti-šú* for *be-lu-ti-šú*. **i 22**.2 *ut-tab-bi-ku* for *ut-tab-bi-ka*; *mé-la-a-šú* for *mé-la-šú*. **i 24**.2 *ú-ṣu-rat-ti* (or *ú-ṣu-ra-a-ti*) for *ú-ṣu-ra-at*. **i 24**.3 Omits *-šu* in É-*šu*. **i 25**.3 *si-ma-tu*$_{4}$ for *si-mat*. **i 25**.2 <DINGIR-*ú*>-*ti-šú* for DINGIR-*ú-ti-šú*. **i 25**.2–3 *e-pe-šu* for *e-pe-ša*. **i 26**.2–3 Respectively *ut-nen-ni-šum*-ŠU and *ut-nen-ni-šum-ma* for *ut-nen-šum-ma*. **i 26**.2 *aq-qí-šum*-ŠU for *aq-qí-šum-ma*; BAR-*ru-us-su* for *ap-ru-us-su*. **i 26**.3 adds a word divider after *ap-ru-us-su*. **i 27**.2–3 *ṣi-i-ri* and ⌜*ṣi*⌝-*i-ri* respectively for *ṣi-ri*. **i 27**.2 UD.MEŠ for UD.ME; *ú-qa-<wa*$_{6}$*>-an-ni* for *ú-qa-wa*$_{6}$*-an-ni*. **i 28**.2–3 Respectively *ša-lim-ti* and [*š*]*a-lim-ti* for *šá-lim-ti*. **i 28**.2 *ki-nam* for *ki-nim*. **i 28**.2–3 *šá-la-mu* for *ša-la-mu*; *šip-ri-ia* for *šip-ri-ía*; *ù* for *u*. **i 29**.2–3 *ú-šá-<áš>-ki-na* and *ú-šá-áš-ki-na* respectively for *ú-šá-áš-ki-nu*; respectively *ter-ti-ia* and *ter-<<te>>-ti*-⌜*ia*⌝ for *te-er-ti-ia*. **i 30**.2 EŠ.BAR-SU-*nu* for EŠ.BAR-*šu-nu*. **i 30**.2–3 *ša* for *šá*. **i 30**.1 *in-<nen>-nu-ú* for *in-nen-nu-ú*. **i 30** *qa-ti*: Ex. 1 *qa* (over erased ŠU)*-ti* and ex. 2 has TA-*ta*. **i 31**.2 Omits É. **i 31**.2–3 *ša-na-at* and ⌜*ša-na-at*⌝ respectively for *šá-na-at*; respectively *ú-še-šib-šu* and *ú-še*-⌜*ši-ib-šu*⌝ for *ú-še-šib-šú*. **i 31**.2–3 *ù* for *u* in both instances. **i 31**.2–3 *ar-ku* and ⌜*ar*⌝-*ku* respectively for *ár-ku*. **i 31**.2 Omits MEŠ after DU$_{6}$. **i 32**.2 *ḫi-<iṭ>-ṭa-tú* for *ḫi-iṭ-ṭa-tú*. **i 32**.1 *ú-pa-aḫ-ḫi-ir*-ŠU for *ú-pa-aḫ-ḫi-ir-ma*. **i 32**.2–3 *ši-bu-tu* and ⌜*ši-bu-tu*⌝ respectively for *ši-bu-ut*. **i 32**.2–3 Respectively KÁ*.DINGIR.RA.KI and ⌜KÁ.DINGIR.RA.KI⌝ for TIN.TIR.KI. **i 32**.2 Adds LÚ before DUB.SAR; ex. 4 has [(LÚ).DUB.SAR].⌜MEŠ⌝. **i 32**.4 *mi-na-a*-⌜*ta*⌝ for *mi-na-a-ti*. **i 33**.3 *en-qu-tu* for *en-qu-ú-tu*. **i 33**.2 Omits É. **i 33**.2–4 Respectively *na-ṣi-ir*, ⸢*na*⸣*-ṣi-ir*, and [*na-ṣi-r*]*u* for *na-ṣir*. **i 33**.2, 4 NA-*riš-ti* and *pi-ri-iš-tu*$_4$ respectively for *pi-riš-ti*. **i 33**.2 PA.<<NI>>.AN for GARZA. **i 34**.2, 4 *mi-<it>-lu-uk-ti* and [*mi*]*t-lu-uk-tum* respectively for *mi-it-lu-uk-ti*. **i 34**.2–4 Respectively *áš-pu-*LU*-šu-nu-ti-ma*, *áš-pu-ur-šu-nu-ti-ma*, and *áš-pur-šú-nu-ti-ma* for *áš-pur-šu-nu-ti-ma*. **i 34**.2–3 *az-ku-ur-šu-nu-ti* and ⸢*az-ku-ur-šu-nu-tu*⸣ respectively for *az-kur-šu-nu-ti*. **i 34**.4 *te-me-en-na* for *te-me-en*. **i 34** *ši-te-ʾe-ma*: Ex. 1 has *ši-te-<ʾe>-ma* and ex. 3 has *ši-te-*⸢*ʾa-a-ma*⸣. **i 35**.2–3 *ka-a-a-nu* for *da-a-a-nu*; *ù* for *u*. i 35.2 EN.MEŠ*-ú-a* for EN.MEŠ*-a*; *ep-pu-*RI for ⸢*lu*⸣*-pu-uš*. **i 36**.2–3 *i-na* for *ina*. **i 36**.2–4 Respectively *te-me-qu*, ⸢*te-me-qu*⸣, and ⸢*te*⸣*-me-qu* for *te-me*$_5$*-qu*. **i 36**.2–3 *ša* DINGIR.MEŠ GAL.MEŠ and ⸢*ša* DINGIR.MEŠ GAL.MEŠ⸣ respectively for *šá* DINGIR GAL.GAL. **i 36**.2 RA.ME.A for UM.ME.A. **i 37**.2, 4 *pa-pa-ḫu* and ⸢*pa*⸣*-pa-ḫa-ni* respectively for *pa-pa-ḫi*. **i 37**.4 *ù* for *u*. **i 37**.3 [*i-t*]*u-*⸢*ru-nim-ma*⸣ for *i-tu-ru-nim*; ⸢*iq-bu*⸣*-ú-ni* for *iq-bu-nu*. **i 38**.4 [*a*]*p-pa-*⸢*li*⸣*-is-ma* for *ap-pa-lis-ma*. **i 38**.2–3 *ša* and ⸢*ša*⸣ for *šá*; respectively *na-ra-am-*^{d}30 and ⸢*na-ra-am-*^{d}30⸣ for *na-ram-*^{d}30. **i 39**.2–3 *im-mé-ri* for *im-me-ri*; *pa-ni-ú*-a* and *pa-ni-ú-a* respectively for *pa-nu-ú-a*. **i 39**.2 MU.LU*-ti-šú* for *be-lu-ti-šú*. **i 39**.2–3 *ù* for *u*. **i 40**.2 *ri-ša-a-ti* for *ri-šá-a-ti*. **i 40**.2–3 *ad-da-a* and ⸢*ad-da-a*⸣ respectively for *ad-da*.

ii 1.1 *ú-dan-nin-*ŠU for *ú-dan-nin-ma*. **ii 1**.2 *ú-ul-la-a* for *ul-la-a*. **ii 1**.2–3 *re-ša-a-šu* for *re-šá-a-šú*. **ii 1**.1 É-ŠU for É-*su*. **ii 1**.2–3 *ša* for *šá*. **ii 2** *be-lu-ti-šu*: Exs. 1, 2, and 3 have *be-lu-ti-<šú>*, MU-LU-*ti-šú*, and *be-lu-*⸢*ti*⸣*-šú* respectively. **ii 2**.3 *mat-si* for *si-mat*. **ii 2**.1 <DINGIR*-ú*>*-ti-šú* for DINGIR*-ú-ti-šú*. **ii 2**.2–3 EN*-ia* and [EN*-i*]*a* respectively for EN*-ía*. **ii 2**.2–3 Respectively <<*re*>>*-eš-<ši>-iš* and ⸢*e-eš-ši-iš*⸣ for *eš-ši-iš*. **ii 2**.2 *ú-še-piš-*ŠU for *ú-še-piš-ma*. **ii 3**.2–3 respectively *šu-mi-šu-*ŠU and ⸢*šu-mi-šu*⸣ for *šu-ú*; respectively *u*$_4$*-miš* and ⸢*u*$_4$*-miš*⸣ for *u*$_4$*-mi-<iš>* and *ú-nam-mir-šu* and ⸢*ú*⸣*-nam-mir-šu* for *ú-nam-mir*-šú*. **ii 3**.2–3 *pa-ag*-lu-<tú>* and *pa-ag-lu-tu* for *pa-ag*-lu-tú*. **ii 3** GIŠ.Ù.SUḪ$_5$: Ex. 1 has GIŠ.Ù.ŠU and ex. 2 has *a-šu-ḫu*. **ii 3**.2–3 *ši-*RI*-ú-tu* and *ši-ḫu-ú-tu* respectively for *ši-ḫu-t*[*i*]. **ii 4** GIŠ.MES.MÁ.KAN.NA: Ex. 1 has GIŠ.MES.<MÁ>.KAN.NA and ex. two has <GIŠ>.MES.<MÁ>.KAN.NA. **ii 4**.2 Omits GIŠ before *tal-lu*. **ii 5**.2 GIŠ.UG.DU$_7$ for GIŠ.GAN.DU$_7$. **ii 5**.3 Omits *giš-* in *giš-šà-ká-na-ku*. **ii 5**.2 *ù* for *u*; *ṣu-lul** for *ṣu-lul-tu*$_4$. **ii 5** *ú-šat-mi-iḫ-ma*: Ex. 1 has *ú-šat-<mi>-iḫ*-*ŠU, ex. 2 has *ú*-šat-mi-ih*-*ŠU (followed by the word divider :), and ex. 3 has ⸢*ú-ša-at*⸣*-mi-iḫ-ma*. **ii 5**.1 GIŠ.LI for GIŠ.TIR. **ii 5**.3 ⸢*ḫa-šu-ru*⸣ for ḪA.ŠUR; ⸢*i-ri-su*⸣ for *i-ri-is-su*. **ii 6**.2 *e-*GIŠ for *e-ma* and SIG.ḪU.ŠI.ŠU for *ú-rat-ti-ma*. **ii 7**.2–3 Respectively *ri-ki-is* and *r*[*i-k*]*i-is* for *ri-kis*. **ii 7**.2–3 *pa-pa-ḫu* and (erased *pa-pa-ḫu*) *pa-pa-ḫu* for *pa-pa-ḫi*. **ii 7**.2 MU.LU*-ti-šú* for *be-lu-ti-šú*. **ii 7**.1 Omits *a-na*. **ii 8**.2 *ša-lum-ma-tum* for *ša-lum-ma-at*. **ii 8**.2–3 *i-na* for *ina* and *ù* for *u*. **ii 9**.1 *tab-rat-<<a-ti>>* for *tab-rat*. **ii 9**.3 *ni-ši* for *ni-ši*. **ii 9**.2 AD-AD*-a* for *la-la-a*. **ii 9** *uš-ma-al-la-a*: Ex. 1 has *uš-ma-al-<la-a>* and ex. 2 has *uš-mál-la-a*. **ii 9**.2–3 *ù* for *u*. **ii 9**.2 Omits *-ia* in LUGAL*-ú-ti-ia*. **ii 10**.1 PA*-ta-ku* for *maš-ta-ku*. **ii 10**.2–3 Respectively *la-le-e-šu* and *la-le-e-*⸢*šu*⸣ for *la-le-šú*. **ii 10**.2 *pa-pa-ḫi* for *pa-pa-ḫi*.MEŠ. **ii 10**.3 *u* for *ù*. **ii 10**.2 *i-na* for *ina*. **ii 10**.3 *ši-*QIR for *ši-ip-ri*. **ii 11**.2 <*ud*>*-di-iš-*ŠU for *ud-di-iš-ma*; *zi-i-*ME.U for *zi-i-me*; DI.<KU$_5$>.GAL for DI.KU$_5$.GAL. **ii 12**.3 *ù* for *u*. **ii 12**.2–3 Respectively EN.MEŠ*-ú-a* and ⸢EN⸣.MEŠ*-ú-a* for EN*-ú-a*. **ii 12** *ta-na-da-a-tú*: Ex. 1 has DA*-na-da-a-tú* and exs. 2 and 3 have *ta-na-da-a-ti*. **ii 13**.2–3 *ù* and ⸢*ù*⸣ for *u*. **ii 13**.1 Omits GIŠ before IG.MEŠ. **ii 13**.2 *ì-gul-la-a* for *ì-gu-la-a*. **ii 13**.2–3 *a-na* for *ana*. **ii 13**.2–3 DINGIR*-ú-ti-šú-nu* and ⸢DINGIR*-ú*⸣*-ti-šú* for DINGIR*-ú-ti-šu-nu*. **ii 14**.2 *si-<mat>* for *si-mat*; *i-ri-*DA for *i-ri-šu*; RA*-a-*TI for *ṭa-a-bi*. **ii 14**.3 <<EN>> EN*-ia* for EN*-ia*. **ii 15**.2–3 Respectively KÁ*.MEŠ*-šú* and ⸢KÁ⸣*-šú*. **ii 15**.2 *ri-ša-<a-ti>* (or *ri-ša-a-ta*) for *ri-ša-a-ti*. **ii 15**.2–3 *a-na* for *ana*. **ii 16**.1 Adds superfluous *šu-bat* before *tap-šu-uḫ-ti-ka*. **ii 16**.2 *tap-*⸢*šu**?*-uḫ*⸣*-ḫu-ti-ka* for *tap-šu-uḫ-ti-ka*. **ii 16**.2–3 *i-na* for *ina*. **ii 16**.2–3 *né-re-ba-nu* and *né-re-ba-nu* respectively for *né-re-bi*.MEŠ. **ii 16**.2 Omits *pa-pa-ḫi*. **ii 16**.2–3 *ù* for *u*. **ii 17**.2 *pa-<nu>-uk-*LAGAB for *pa-nu-uk-ki*; *li-ri-šu-ka* for *li-ri-ši-ku*. **ii 17**.2–3 *i-na* for *ina*. **ii 17**.2–3 Respectively *pa-pa-ḫu* and ⸢*pa*⸣*-pa-ḫu* for *pa-pa-ḫi*. **ii 17**.2 MU.LU*-ti-<ki>* for *be-lu-ti-ka*. **ii 18**.3 *da-a-a-nu-ti-ki* for *da-a-a-nu-ti-ka*. **ii 18**.2–3 *i-na* for *ina*. **ii 18**.2 *a-ša-bi-ka* for *a-šá-bi-ku*. **ii 18**.2–3 *ù* for *u*. **ii 18**.3 *li-šap-ši-ḫi* for *li-šap-ši-ḫu*. **ii 19** É.GI$_4$.A: Ex. 1 has KAL.GI$_4$.A and ex. 2 has É.GI$_4$.<A>. **ii 20**.2 *pa-ni-ka* for *pa-nu-ka*. **ii 20** *liq-bi-k*[*u*]: Ex. 1 has IB-*bi-k*[*u*] and ex. 2 has *liq-bi-ka*. **ii 21**.5 *nam-*⸢*ru*⸣*-t*[*i*] for *nam-ru-tu*. **ii 21**.2–3 *ḫi-du-ti* and [*ḫi*]*-du-ti* respectively for *ḫi-du-tu*. ii 21.2 qa-ti-ia for *qá-ti-ía*; *šu-qú-ru* for *šu-qu-ru*. **ii 22**.2 Omits *-a* in *e-ep-še-tu-ú-a*. **ii 22**.3 *dam-qa-a-ti* for *dam-qa-a-ta*. **ii 22**.5 [*ši*]*-ṭi-ir* for *ši-ṭir*; MU*-ia* for *šu-mi-ia*; ALAM for *ṣa-lam*. **ii 23** *na-ap-li-sa-a-ma*: Ex. 1 has *na-ap-<li>-sa-a-ma* and ex. 2 has *na-ap-li-sa-ma*. **ii 23**.5 *liš-ša-kin* for *liš-šá-kin*. **ii 23**.2–3 Respectively *šap-*PÚ*-ka* and ⸢*šap*⸣*-tuk-ka* for *šap-*PÚ*-ka* and *šap-tuk-ku*. **ii 23**.2–3 *a-na* for *ana*. **ii 24**.5 *e-pu-šu* for *e-pu-uš-šu*. **ii 23**.2–3 *lu-ub-bi-ir* for *lu-bi-ir*; ex. 5 has *lu-*⸢*ub*⸣*-b*[*i-ir*]. **ii 25**.3 AB.GAN.DU$_7$ for GIŠ.GAN.DU$_7$. **ii 25** *giš-šà-ká-na-ku*: Ex. 1 has *giš-šà-ká*-na-ku* and ex. 3 has *giš-<šà>-ká-na-ku*. **ii 25**.1 É.BAR for É.⸢ME⸣. **ii 25**.3 AŠ for *u*. **ii 26**.2 *li-iṣ-ṣuru*-ma*? for *li-iṣ-ṣi-ru*; *liš-*MI-⸢*ši*⸣-MA for *liš-te-ši-ru*. **ii 26**.2–3 *tal-la-ak-ki* and *tal-la-ak-*⸢*ti*⸣ respectively for *tal-la-ak-ka*. **ii 29**.2–3 ^{d}*mi-ša-ri* for ^{d}*mi-šá-ri*. **ii 29**.2 DINGIR.<MEŠ> for DINGIR.MEŠ. **ii 29**.2–3 *a-ši-ib* for *a-šib*. **ii 30**.2–3 *i-na* for *ina*. **ii 30**.3 GAL*-ti* for *ṣi-ir-ti*. **ii 30**.2–3 *ša* for *šá*. **ii 30**.1, 3 Omit DINGIR in DINGIR*-ti-ka*. **ii 30**.3 *ṣi-ir-ti* for GAL*-ti*. **ii 31**.1 Omits *la*. **ii 31**.2–3 ⸢*ù**⸣ and *ù* for *u*. **ii 31**.1 Adds U before *ù*. **ii 32**.2 KI*-šá-áš-ki-na* for *li-šá-áš-ki-na*; *še-pi-ía* for *še-pi-ia*. **ii 32**.2–3 NI*-kal-la-*ŠA and *suk-kal-la-ka* respectively for *suk-kal-la-ku*. **ii 32**.2–3 *ṣi-i-ri* for MAḪ. **ii 32**.2 Adds *ina* before *maḫ-ri-ku*. **ii 32**.2–3 *maḫ-ri-ka* for *maḫ-ri-ku*. **ii 33**.2–3 *ša* for *šá* in both instances; *ra-ki-ib* for *ra-kib*. **ii 33** *a-šib*: Ex. 1 *a-šib* written over an erased *-ši-* and exs. 2 and 3 have *a-ši-ib*. **ii 33**.2–3 *ša-as-su* for *sa-as-si*. **ii 33**.3 Omits *la*. **ii 33** *im-maḫ-ḫa-ri*: Ex. 1 has *im-maḫ-<ḫa>-ri*, ex. 2 has *im-ma-ḫa-ri*, and ex. 3 has *im-maḫ-ḫa-ra*. **ii 34**.2 AD for *la*. **ii 34**.2 Omits *-ḫu* in *in-na-ḫu*. **ii 34**.1 Omits *-un* in *bir-ka-šu-un*. **ii 35**.2–3 *i-na* for *ina*. **ii 35**.1 *a-*KA*-lu* for *a-la-ku*. **ii 35**.2–3 *ù* for *u*. **ii 35** *i-ša-ad-di-ḫu*: Ex. 1 has *i-ša-ad-<di>-ḫu* and ex. 3 has *i-šad-di-ḫu*. **ii 35**.2 <*maḫ*>*-ri-ka* for *maḫ-ri-ka*. **ii 36**.2–2 Respectively *i-na* and ⸢*i*⸣*-na* for *ina*. **ii 36**.2–3 *ù* for *u*. **ii 36**.2 *a-*NA*-ku* for *a-ra-ku*. **ii 36**.1 Omits *-ka* in *lim-ta-al-lik-ka*. **ii 38**.3 *ši-pir-ri-ka* for *ši-ip-ri-ka*; *li-*⸢*il-li*⸣*-ki* for *lil-lik-ki*; *re-ṣu-*⸢*tu*⸣ for *re-ṣu-ú-tu*. **ii 39**.2 *be-lu-ú-tu* for *be-lu-tu*. **ii 39**.2 *ša mi-na-ta* for *šá-lum-ma-at*. **ii 39**.3 *ša-lum-ma-ti* for *šá-lum-ma-at*. **ii 40**.2 *šu-li-ku* for *šu-lik-ki*. **ii 41**.2 *za-i-ri-ia* for *za-ʾi-ri-ia*. **ii 41**.2–3 Respectively *na-ki-ri-a* and *na-ki-ri-<ia>* for *na-ki-ri-ia*. **ii 41** *lu-ku*-ul*: Ex. 1 has *lu-*ŠU*-ul*, ex. 2 has *lu*-uš-lu*-ul*, and ex. 3 has ⸢*lu*⸣*-uš-lu-ul*. **ii 41**.2–3 ŠU*-ti-tan* and *ma-*⸢*a-ti*⸣*-tan* respectively for *ma-ti-tan*. **ii 42**.3 *lu-*⸢*ú*⸣*-še-ri-bi* for *lu-še-ri-bi*. **ii 42**.2 *qé-*É ŠU*-ti-ia* for *qé-reb ma-ti-ia*. **ii 42**.2 *lu* for *lu-ú*. **ii 42**.2–3 *za-ni-nu* and ⸢*za*⸣*-ni-*[*n*]*u* respectively for *za-ni-in*. **ii 43**.2–3 *mu-ud-di-iš* for *mu-diš*; respectively *ma-ḫa-zi* and *ma-*⸢*ḫa-zi*⸣ for *ma-ḫa-zu*. **ii 43**.2–3 UD.ME and UD.ME* for UD.MEŠ. **ii 44**.3 *li-nu-*⸢*uš*⸣*-šu* for *li-nu-šu*. **ii 45**.2 TAR*-du-du* for *liš-du-du*. **ii 46**.3 KÁ.DINGIR.RA.KI for TIN.TIR.KI. **ii 46** *li-bil-lu-nu*: Ex. 1 has *li-bil-<lu>-nu*, ex. 2 has *lu-bil-lu-ni*, and ex. 3 has *lu-bil-*⸢*lu-ni*⸣. **ii 46**.2–3 *maḫ-*⸢*ri-ia*⸣ and *maḫ-*⸢*ri*⸣*-ia* respectively for *maḫ-ri-ía*. **ii 47**.3 KÁ.DINGIR.RA.KI for TIN.TIR.KI. **ii 47**.2–3 *li-ku-un* for *li-kun*; *i-<na>* and *i-na* respectively for *ina*. **ii 47**.3 *e-tál-*⸢*lu-ku*⸣ for *a-tál-lu-ku*; *lu-uš-bi* for *lu-uš-bu*. **ii 48**.3 *ù* for *u*; ⸢*ša*⸣ for *šá*; *lu-lab-<bi>-ir* for *lu-lab-bi-ir*. **ii 49**.2–3 *maḫ-<ri>* and *ma-aḫ-ri* respectively for *maḫ-ri*. ii 49.2–3 ^{d}EN ^{d}AG *u* ^{d}U.GUR for *be-lum* ^{d}*na-bi-um u* ^{d}NÈ.ERI$_{11}$.GAL. **ii 50**.2 DINGIR.MEŠ*-e-<a>* for DINGIR.MEŠ*-e-a*. **ii 50**.2–3 *ù* for *u*. **ii 50**.1 Omits *-ti* in *si-ḫi-ir-ti*. **ii 50**.2–3 Add É before *á-ki-it*. **ii 50**.3 *ša* for *šá*. **ii 50**.2–3 ^{d}AMAR.UTU for ^{d}ŠÚ. **ii 51**.3 *ma-aṣ-ḫa-tum* for *ma-aṣ-ḫa-ti*. **ii 51**.2 *é-da-di-*AD*-gál* for *é-da-di-ḫé-gál*. ii 61.3 ⸢*ut-ne-en-ni*⸣ for *ut-nen-ni*.

Nabonidus No. 27

i 9.4 ^{md}AG-I for ^{md}AG-NÍ.TUKU. **i 10** *za-ni-in*: Ex. 1 has *za-ni*[*n*] and ex. 4 has [*za*]*-ni-in*. **i 10**.1, 4 *p*[*a-le-e-a*] and *pa-le-e-a* respectively for BALA*-e-a*. **i 10**.4 *ki-i-nim* for *ki-nim*. **i 11**.1, 4 *i-ra-*[*am-mu*] and *i-ra-am-mu* respectively for *i-ram-mu*. **i 11**.4 *šu-a-tim* for *šu-a-ti*. **i 43**.1 *pa-le-e* for BALA*-e*. **i 48**.1 *šá-a-šú* for *šu-a-tim*. **i 48**.1, 4 *ka-at-mu* for *kát-mu*. **i 49**.1, 4 *ḫi-iṭ-ṭa-ti* and *ḫi-iṭ-<ṭa>-ti* respectively for *ḫi-iṭ-ṭa-tum*. **i 50**.1 ^{m}*bur-na-bur-ía-a-àš* for ^{m}*bur-na-bur-ía-àš*. **i 51**.1 *maḫ-ri-ia* for *maḫ-ri-šú*. **i 52**.1, 4 Add *šá* after *te-me-en-na*. **i 52**.1 ^{m}*bur-na-bur-ía-a-àš* for ^{m}*bur-na-bur-ía-àš*. **i 54**.4 *uš-šu* for *uš-šú*. **i 54**.1, 4 *šu-a-tim* for *šu-a-ti*. **i 57**.4 GAL-*ú* for *ra-bu-ú*. **i 58**.4 *šub-tú* for *šub-tum*. **i 59**.4 ^{md}AG-I for ^{md}AG-NÍ.TUKU. **i 61**.1, 4 *pa-le-e-[a]* and *pa-l[e-e-a]* respectively for BALA-*e-a*. **i 61**.4 *ki-i-ni* for *ki-nim*. **i 62**.4 *i-ra-a[m-mu]* for *i-ram-mu*. **i 63**.1 *iḫ-su-us-<<su>>-ma* for *iḫ-su-us-ma*. **i 64**.3–4 *[i-t]a-⸢am-ma⸣-r[u-ni]* and *i-ta-am-ma-ru-[ni]* respectively for *i-tam-ma-ru-ni*. **i 65**.4 *te-me-en* for *te-me-en-na*. **i 68**.3 *⸢e-li⸣-tum* for *e-li-tú*. **i 68**.3 LÚ.ERIM.ḪI.A⸣-*i[a]* for UN.MEŠ. **i 69**.3 *šu-a-tim* for *šu-a-tum*.

ii 2 <*ša*>: Ex. 1 has [*š*]*a* and ex. 2 omits the word. **ii 3**.1 *[z]iq-qur-rat* for *ziq-qur-ra-tum*. **ii 4**.1 *i-pu-šu* for *i-pu-šú*. **ii 9**.1 *ú-ki-in* for *ú-kin*. **ii 10**.1 *e-pu-uš-<ma>* for *e-pu-uš-ma*. **ii 14**.1 *šu-a-tim* for *šu-a-tum*. **ii 14**.2 Omits *-ma* after *e-pu-uš*. **ii 16**.1 *lu-ú* for *lu*. **ii 16**.1 GAL-*ú* for *ra-bu-ú*. **ii 17**.1 *⸢u$_{4}$-mi-šam-mu⸣* for *⸢u$_{4}$⸣-mi-šam-ma*. **ii 17**.1 *⸢na-<par>-ka-a'⸣* for *na-par-ka-a'*. **ii 18**.1 *ina* for *i-na*. **ii 21**.1 ⸢DINGIR⸣-*ú-ti-ka* for DINGIR-*ú-ti-ku-nu*. **ii 23**.1 [^{m}]^{d}AG-NÍ.TUKU for ^{md}AG-I. **ii 23**.1 [DINGIR-*ú-ti*]*-ka* for DINGIR-*ú-ti-ku-nu*. **ii 23**.1 GAL-*ti* for GAL-*tú*. **ii 24**.1 [*ba-la*]*-ṭu* for TIN. **ii 26**.1 *ir-šá-a* for *ir-šá-a'*. **ii 27**.1 NA$_{4}$.*a-su-mit-ti* for NA$_{4}$.*a-su-mit-tum*. **ii 29**.1 Omits *šá*. **ii 31**.1 ^{md}AG-NÍ.TUKU for ^{md}AG-I. **ii 38**.1 DINGIR.<MEŠ> *kiš-<šat>* for DINGIR.MEŠ *kiš-šat*. **ii 38**.1 *ú-šat-lim-šú-nu-ti-ma* for *ú-šat-li-mu-šú-nu-ti-ma*. **ii 46**.1 [^{md}A]G-⸢IBILA⸣-ÙRU for ^{md}AG-A-ÙRU. **ii 47**.1 *te-me-en-na* for *te-me-en*. **ii 47**.1 *šu-a-tim* for *šu-a-tú*. **ii 51**.1 *za-ni-in* for *za-nin*. **ii 52**.1 *pa-le-e-a* for BALA-*e-a*. **ii 52**.1 *ki-i-ni* for *ki-nim*. **ii 52**.1 *i-na** for *ina*. **ii 52**.1 *pu-luḫ-ti* for *pu-luḫ-tú*. **ii 55**.1 Omits *šu-a-ti*. **ii 56**.1 *ina* for *i-na*. **ii 57**.1 LÚ.ERIM.ḪI.A-*ia* for LÚ.UN.MEŠ-*ia*. **ii 58**.1 Omits *é-ul-maš*. **ii 60**.2 Omits *-ma* after *aḫ-ṭu-uṭ*; *šu-me*-RI for *šu-me-lu*. **ii 61**.1 *u* for *ù*. **ii 62**.1 *šu-a-ti* for *šu-a-tú*. **ii 63**.1 *nu-ba-'i-i-ma* and *ni-mu-ur* for *nu-ú-ba-'i-i-ma* and *ni-mur*. **ii 65**.1 *⸢aq-bi-šú-nu-tú⸣* for *aq-bi-šú-nu-ti*.

iii 28.1 [KUR-*aš-šu*]*r*.⸢KI⸣ for KUR-*aš-šur*. **iii 32**.1 *pa-le-⸢e⸣-a* for BALA-*e-a*. **iii 33**.1 GAL-*ti* for GAL-*tum*. **iii 34**.1 *ina* for *i-na*. **iii 35**.1 *šu-a-ti* for *šu-a-tum*. **iii 36**.1 Omits *i-na šat*. **iii 39**.1 LÚ.UN.MEŠ-*ia* for LÚ.ERIM.ḪI.A. **iii 39**.1 *šu-a-tim* for *šu-a-ti*. **iii 40**.1 ^{m}*ša-ga-rak-ti-<šur>-ia-aš* for ^{m}*ša-ga-rak-ti-šur-ia-áš*. **iii 41**.1 *⸢ḫi⸣-iṭ-ṭa-ti* for *ḫi-iṭ-ṭa-tum*. **iii 41**.1 *šu-a-tú* for *šu-a-ti*. **iii 43**.1 *šá-ṭi-ir* for *šá-ṭir*. **iii 44**.1 ^{m}*ša-ga-rak-ti-šur-ia-aš* for ^{m}*ša-ga-rak-ti-šur-ia-áš*. **iii 45**.1 *mi-gi-ir* for *mi-gir*. **iii 46**.1 KUR for *ma-a-ti*. **iii 47**.1 *ṣe-re-ti* for *ṣer-ret*. **iii 47**.1 *qa-tu-ú-a* for ŠU.II-*ú-a*. **iii 51**.1, 4 *la-ba-ru* and *⸢la-ba⸣-ru* respectively for *la-bar*. **iii 52**.1, 4 *aq-qu-ur* for *aq-qur*. **iii 53**.4 *uš-<ši>-šú-nu* for *uš-ši-šú-nu*. **iii 53**.1 *e-ep-ti* for *e-ep-tú*. **iii 53**.1 *as-⸢suḫ-ma⸣* for *as-suḫ*; ex. 4 has *as-su-u[ḫ]*. **iii 55**.1, 4 *uš-ma-al-lu* and *uš-ma-al-li* respectively for *uš-mál-lu*. **iii 55**.1, 4 *e-pe-er* for *e-pe-ri*. **iii 55**.1, 4 *ú-te-er* for *ú-ter*. **iii 56**.4 *i-ga-ri-šu-nu* for *i-ga-ri-šú-nu*. **iii 56**.1, 4 *áš-ri-šú-un* and *áš-ri-šu-un* respectively for *áš-ri-šú-nu*. **iii 57**.4 *ši-kit-ta-šu-nu* for *ši-kit-ta-šú-nu*. **iii 57**.1, 4 UGU for *e-li*. **iii 57**.2 Omits *šá* before *pa-ni*. **iii 58**.4 *šá-at-t[ú]* for *šá-at-ti*. **iii 59**.1, 4 UD.MEŠ-*ia* for UD.MEŠ-*ía*. **iii 60**.1 *li-id-du-šu* for *li-id-du-šú*. **iii 60**.1 Omits u$_{4}$-*mu*. **iii 60**.1, 4 *ri-šá-a-<<a>>-ti* and *ri-šá-a-ti* respectively for *ri-šá-a-tú*. **iii 61**.4 MU.MEŠ for MU.AN.NA.MEŠ. **iii 61**.1 *ši-rik-tú* for *ši-rik-ti*. **iii 62**.1, 4 *⸢di⸣-i-ni* and *di-i-ni* respectively for *di-in*. **iii 63**.1 ^{m}*ša-ga-rak-<ti>-šur-ia-aš* for ^{m}*ša-ga-rak-ti-⸢šur⸣-ia-áš*. **iii 64**.1 *sip-par*.KI for ZIMBIR.KI. **iii 67**.1 *li-ib-na-[a]t-su* for SIG$_{4}$-*at-su*. **iii 70**.1 *ra-bi-ti* for GAL-*tú*. **iii 70**.1 *i-na* for *ina*. **iii 72**.1 DINGIR-*ú-ti-ka* for DINGIR-*ti-ku-nu*. **iii 73**.1 *iš-da-šú-nu* for SUḪUŠ.MEŠ-*šú-nu*. **iii 73**.1 *ù* for *u*. **iii 73**.1 *i-na* for *ina*. **iii 74**.1 UN.MEŠ-⸢*šu*⸣ for UN.MEŠ-*šú*. **iii 74**.1 *iš-da-šu-nu* for SUḪUŠ.MEŠ-*šú-nu*. **iii 75**.1 *li-kunu*^{nu} for *li-ku-nu*. **iii 75**.1 ^{md}AG-NÍ.TUKU for ^{md}AG-I. **iii 75**.1 [DINGIR-*ú-t*]*i-ka* for DINGIR-*ú-ti-ku-nu*. **iii 75**.1 GAL-*ti* for GAL-*tú*. **iii 76**.1 *reš-tu-ú* for *reš-tu-u*. **iii 77**.1 [*ir-šá*]*-⸢a⸣* for *ir-šá-a'*. **iii 78**.1 ZIMBIR.KI-^{d}*a-nu-ni-tum* for *sip-par-^{d}a-nu-ni-tum*. **iii 79**.1 ^{d}15 for ^{d}IŠ.TAR. **iii 79**.2 Omits *a-ši-bu-tú*. **iii 80**.4 *ù* for *u*. **iii 80**.1, 4 [NA$_{4}$.*a-s*]*u-mi-né-e-tum* and ⸢NA$_{4}$⸣.*a-su-mi-né-e-tum* respectively for NA$_{4}$.*a-su-mi-né-e-tú*. **iii 81**.1 Omits the first *šá*. **iii 81**.4 *áš-ṭu-ru* for *áš-ṭu-ru-ma*. **iii 81**.1, 4 *ár-ku-ti* for *ár-ku-tum*.

Nabonidus No. 28

i 1 ^{d}*na-bi-um-na-'i-id*: Ex. 31 has ^{d}AG-NÍ.TUKU. **i 1** *ra-bu-ú*: Exs. 20–21 have GAL-*ú*. **i 1** *dan-nu*: Ex. 16 has *⸢da-an-num⸣*. **i 2** *kiš-šá-ti*: Ex. 2, 17, 20 have *kiš-šá-tum*; ex. 3, 21 has [*kiš-šá*]*-tum*; ex. 8 has [*ki*]*š-šá-tum*; ex. 11 has *⸢kiš-šá-tum⸣*; ex. 16 has [*k*]*iš-šá-tum*; ex. 21 has [*kiš-šá-t*]*um*; ex. 29 has [*kiš-šá-tu*]*m*. **i 2** TIN.TIR.KI: Exs. 2, 5, 8, 11, 17 have KÁ.DINGIR.RA.KI; ex. 16 has KÁ.DINGIR.RA.⸢KI⸣; ex. 20 has K[Á.DINGIR.RA].⸢KI⸣; ex. 21 has KÁ.<DINGIR>.RA.KI. **i 2** *kib-ra-a-ti*: Ex. 5 has *kib-ra-a-tum*; ex. 11 has *kib-ra-a-tú*; ex. 20 has *kib-rat*. **i 2** *er-bet-ti*: Ex. 16 has *er-bé-et-tum*. **i 3** *é-sag-íl*: Ex. 16 has *é-sag-<íl>*. **i 4** *um-mi-šu*: Exs. 2, 18 have *um-mi-šú*; exs. 16–17 have AMA-*šu*; ex. 20 has ⸢AMA-*šu*⸣. **i 5** LUGAL-*ú-tu*: Ex. 2 has LUGAL-*ú-⸢ti⸣*; exs. 5, 11, 16 have LUGAL-*ú-ti*; ex. 21 has ⸢LUGAL-*ú*⸣*-ti*. **i 6** NUN: Exs. 5, 17, 20, 25 have *ru-bu-ú*, *⸢ru-bu-ú⸣*, *⸢ru⸣-bu-ú*, and *⸢ru-bu-ú⸣* respectively. **i 6** *e-em-qu*: Exs. 2, 16 have *e-⸢em⸣-qá*; exs. 5, 11 have *e-em-qá*; ex. 12 has *e-em-⸢qá⸣*; ex. 18 has [*e-em*]*-⸢qá⸣*. **i 6** *pa-li-iḫ*: exs. 2, 5, 11–12, 18, 31 have *pa-li-ḫu*; ex. 19 has *pa-⸢li-ḫu⸣*; ex. 23 has *pa-li-⸢ḫu⸣*. **i 6** DINGIR: Exs. 17 and 20 have ⸢DINGIR.DINGIR⸣ and DINGIR.DINGIR respectively. **i 7** *ša*: exs. 11, 20 have *šá*. **i 7** *qé-reb*: Exs. 2, 21 have [*q*]*é-re-eb*; exs. 5, 16, 18, 25 have *qé-re-eb*; ex. 11 has *qé-er-ba*; ex. 17 has *q*[*é-r*]*e-eb*. **i 7** URU.*ḫar-ra-nu*: Exs. 2, 12 have URU.*ḫar-ra-an*; ex. 19 has ⸢URU⸣.*ḫar-ra-an*. **i 8** u$_{4}$-*mu*: Ex. 16 has u$_{4}$-*um*; ex. 20 has u$_{4}$-*me*; ex. 21 has ⸢u$_{4}$⸣-*mi*. **i 8** *ṣa-a-ti*: Ex. 2 has *ṣa-a-⸢tu⸣*. **i 8** EN: exs. 2, 12, 18, 21, 25, 46 have *be-lu*; ex. 19 has *be-⸢lu⸣*. **i 8** *ra-bu-ú*: Exs. 11, 17, 29 have *ra-bí-ù*; ex. 20 has GAL-[*ú*]; ex. 21 has *ra-⸢bí⸣-[ù]*; ex. 23 has GAL-*ú*. **i 9** *lìb-bi-šu*: Ex. 2 has *li-i[b]-bi-šu*; ex. 18 has ⸢ŠÀ⸣-*šú* ex. 20 has *lìb-⸢bi⸣-šú*; exs. 23, 46 have *lìb-bi-šú*; ex. 25 has *lìb-⸢bi-šú⸣*. **i 9** *qé-re-eb-šú*: exs. 2, 12, 17 have *qé-reb-šu*; ex. 3 has *qé-⸢re-eb⸣-šu*; exs. 11, 18–19, 23, 26 has *qé-re-eb-šu*; exs. 16, 21 have *qé-⸢re-eb-šu⸣*; ex. 20 has *⸢qé-reb-šú⸣*; ex. 25 has *qé-re-⸢eb⸣-š[u]*; ex. 31 has *⸢qé-reb-šu⸣*; ex. 34 has [*qé-re-e*]*b-⸢šu⸣*. **i 10** URU: Ex. 21 has URU.⸢KI⸣. **i 10** *šá-a-šu*: Ex. 5 has *ša-a-⸢šu⸣*; exs. 10–11, 16–18, 25 have *ša-a-šu*; ex. 21 has *ša-a-ša*; ex. 26 has *ša-a-⸢šu⸣*.

i 11 LÚ.ERIM-*man-da*: Ex. 5 has [*u*]*m-ma-an-ma-an-du*; ex. 7 has [*u*]*m-⸢ma-an⸣-ma-an-du*; ex. 10 has [...*-a*]*n-du*; ex. 11 has *um-man-ma-⸢an-du⸣*; ex. 16 has [(KUR).*u*]*m-ma-an-ma-an-⸢da⸣*; ex. 18 has *⸢um-ma⸣-an-man-du*; ex. 20 has [*u*]*m-man-ma-an-du*; ex. 21 has [*u*]*m-⸢man⸣-ma-an-⸢du⸣*; ex. 25 has [...]*-⸢an-du⸣*; ex. 26 has *um-ma-an-man-du*; ex. 46 has [*u*]*m-ma-an-ma-an-d*[*u*]. **i 11** *ú-šat-ba-am-ma*: Ex. 16 has *ú-šá-at-ba-am-ma*. **i 11** *šu-a-tim*: Ex. 11 has *šu-a-tum*; ex. 16 has *⸢ša-a-tim⸣*; ex. 20–21 have *šu-a-ti*. **i 11** *ub-bi-it-ma*: Ex. 2 has *⸢ub-bit-ma⸣*; ex. 17 has [*ub-bi*]*t-ma*; exs. 18, 26 have *ub-bit-ma*; ex. 20 has *ub-bit-⸢ma⸣*; ex. 21 has *⸢ub-bit⸣-ma*. **i 12** *ú-ša-lik-šu*: Ex. 2 has *⸢ú-šá-lik⸣-šú*; exs. 5, 7, 20 have *⸢ú⸣-ša-li-ik-šu*; ex. 10 has [*ú-ša-l*]*i-ik-šu*; ex. 16 has *ú-ša-li-⸢ik⸣-šu*; ex. 17 has *ú-šá-lik-šu*; ex. 21 has *⸢ú⸣-šá-lik-šu*; ex. 25 has [*ú-š*]*a-li-ik-šu*. **i 12** *kar-mu-tu*: Ex. 2 has *kar-mu-ti*; exs. 5, 10, 25 have *ka-ar-mu-tu*; ex. 7 has *ka-a*[*r-mu-tu*]; ex. 17 has *kar-mu-tú*; ex. 20 has *ka-ar-mu-⸢tu⸣*. **i 12** *ki-i-nim*: Ex. 11 has DI-*i-nim*; ex. 20 has *ki-⸢nim⸣*. **i 13** ^{d}EN.ZU: Ex. 1 omits ZU. **i 13** EN: Ex. 2 has *be-lu*; exs. 5, 10, 18, 25 have *be-lí*; ex. 7 has *be-l*[*u*]; ex. 21 has *be-⸢lu⸣*. **i 13** GAL-*ú*: Exs. 2, 5, 10, 16–18, 25 have *ra-bu-ú*; ex. 19 has [GA]L; ex. 20 has *ra-bu-⸢ú⸣*; ex. 21 has *ra-bí-ù*. **i 13** *na-ra-am*: Ex. 31 has *⸢na⸣-ram*. **i 13** LUGAL-*ú-ti-ia*: Ex. 5 has LUGAL-*ti-ia*; exs. 7, 10, 25 have *šar-ru-ti-ia*; ex. 16 has *⸢šar⸣-ru-ti-ia*. **i 14** *šá-a-šu*: Exs. 2, 5, 10–11, 16, 18, 25 have *ša-a-šu*; ex. 21 has *⸢ša⸣-a-⸢ša⸣*. **i 14** *is-li-mu*: Ex. 7 has *⸢is⸣-si-li-mu*; ex. 20 has [*is*]*-si-li-mu*; ex. 21 has [*is*]*-si-⸢li-mu⸣*; ex. 25 has [*i*]*s-si-li-⸢mu⸣*. **i 15** LUGAL-*ú-ti-ia*: Ex. 16 has LUGAL-*ti-ia*. **i 15** *da-rí-ti*: Exs. 2, 20–21 have *⸢da⸣-ri-tum*; exs. 5, 7, 10, 16, 25 have *da-ri-ti*. **i 15** *ú-šab-ru-'i-in-ni*: Exs. 7 and 25 has *ú-šá-ab-ru-'i-i*[*n-ni*] and *ú-šá-ab-ru-'i-in-ni* respectively. **i 15** *šu-ut-ti*: Ex. 16 has M[ÁŠ.G]I$_{6}$. **i 16** EN: Exs. 12, 21 have *be-lu*. **i 16** GAL: Ex. 10 has [GAL/*ra-bu*]*-⸢ú⸣*; exs. 11–12, 31 have GAL-*ú*; ex. 21 has *⸢ra-bu-ú⸣*; ex. 26 has ⸢GAL⸣-*ú*; ex. 52 has GAL-⸢*ú*⸣. **i 16** AN-*e*: Ex. 16 has *ša-mé-e*. **i 16** KI-*tim*: Ex. 11 has DI-*tim*; ex. 16 has *⸢er-ṣe⸣-tim*; ex. 20 has KI-<*tim*>. **i 17** *iz-zi-zu*: Ex. 2 has *iz-zi-iz*-SU. **i 17** Ex. 16 has an erasure between ^{d}AMAR.UTU and *i-ta-ma-a*.

i 18 ^{d}AG-NÍ.TUKU: Ex. 10 has [^{m}*na-bi-u*]*m-na-ʾi-id*; ex. 16 has [^{m}*n*]*a-*⸢*bi-um-*NÍ⸣.TUKU; exs. 20, 25 have [^{m}*na-bi-um-n*]*a-ʾi-id*. i 18 Ex. 25 has an erasure before LUGAL. **i 18** TIN.TIR.KI: Ex. 10 has KÁ.DINGIR.RA.⸢KI⸣; ex. 25 has KÁ.DINGIR.RA.KI. **i 18** *ru-ku-bi-ka* in ex. 7 is written over an erasure. **i 19** *e-pu-uš-ma*: Ex. 31 omits *-ma* in *e-pu-uš-ma*. **i 19** ^{d}EN.ZU: Ex. 31 has ^{d}30. **i 19** EN: Ex. 18 has *b*[*e-lu*]; ex. 25 has *be-*⸢*lu*⸣. **i 19** GAL-*ú*: Ex. 17 has GAL; ex. 25 has *ra-b*[*u-ú*].

i 20 *qé-er-bi-šu*: Ex. 16 has ⸢*qé-er-bi-ša*⸣. **i 20** *šu-ur-ma-a*: Ex. 21 omits *-ma-* in *šu-ur-ma-a*. **i 20** *šu-ba-at-su*: Ex. 17, 18, 26, and 52 have ⸢*šu*⸣*-*[*ba*]*t-su*, *šu-bat-su*, *šu-bat-s*[*u*], and *šu-*[*bat-su*] respectively. **i 21** DINGIR.MEŠ: Ex. 7 has ⸢DINGIR.DINGIR⸣; exs. 16, 21 have DINGIR.DINGIR; ex. 17 has DINGIR; ex. 20 has [DINGIR].⸢DINGIR⸣. **i 22** *šu-a-tim*: Exs. 17, 21 have *šu-a-ti*; ex. 20 has *šu-a-tum*. **i 22** *ša*: Exs. 16, 52 have *šá*. **i 22** *taq-bu-ú*: Exs. 11, 17, 25, 48 have *ta-aq-bu-ú*; ex. 21 has ⸢*ta*⸣*-aq-bu-ú*; ex. 44 has [*t*]*a-aq-bu-ú*. **i 22** *e-pe-šu*: Ex. 16 has *e-pé-eš-su*; ex. 17 has *e-pe-eš*$_{15}$*-su*; ex. 18 has ⸢*e*⸣*-pe-eš*$_{15}$*-su*; ex. 20 has ⸢*e*⸣*-pé-eš*$_{15}$*-s*[*u*?]; ex. 21 has *e-pé-*⸢*eš*$_{15}$⸣*-su*; ex. 26 has [*e-p*]*é-eš*$_{15}$*-s*[*u*]; ex. 44 has *e-pé-*⸢*eš-su*⸣. **i 23** LÚ.ERIM-*man-da*: Exs. 11, 21 have [*u*]*m-man-ma-an-du*; exs. 14, 17 have *um-man-ma-an-du*; ex. 16 has [*un-m*]*a-an-ma-an-da*; exs. 18, 20 have *um-ma-an-man-du*; ex. 26 has *um-ma-*⸢*an*⸣*-*[...]; ex. 39 has LÚ.ERIM-*man-d*[*u*]; ex. 43 has *um-ma-*[...]; ex. 48 has LÚ.ERIM-*man-du*; ex. 52 has *um-man-ma-an-*[*da/du*] **i 23** *sa-ḫi-ir-šum-ma*: Ex. 20 has *sa-ḫi-ir-šu-um-ma*; ex. 21 has ⸢*sa-ḫi*⸣*-ir-šu-um-ma*; ex. 25 has ⸢*sa-ḫi-ir-šu-um-ma*⸣. **i 23** *e-mu-qá-a-šu*: Ex. 16 has *e-mu-qa-a-šu*; ex. 25 has ⸢*e-mu-qá*⸣*-šu*; ex. 44 has *e-mu-qa-a-šu*. **i 24** ^{d}AMAR.UTU-*ma*: Ex. 26 has ⸢^{d}⸣AMAR.UTU-LA. **i 24** *i-ta-ma-a*: Ex. 21 omits *-ta-* in *i-ta-ma-a*. **i 24** LÚ.ERIM-*man-da*: Exs. 11, 17, 21, 26 have *um-man-ma-an-du*; ex. 16 has *um-ma-an-ma-an-da*; ex. 18 has ⸢*um*⸣*-ma-an-*⸢*man*⸣*-du*; ex. 20 has *um-*⸢*ma-an*⸣*-ma-an-du*; ex. 25 has [...*-a*]*n-da*; ex. 42 has *u*[*m-*...]; exs. 44, 48 have LÚ.ERIM-*man-du*. **i 24** *šá*: Exs. 18, 20–21, 25–26 have *ša*; ex. 29 has [*š*]*a*. **i 24** *taq-bu-ú*: Ex. 20 has *ta-aq-*⸢*bu*⸣*-ú*; ex. 21 has *ta-aq-bu-ú*; ex. 25 has ⸢*ta-aq*⸣*-bu-ú*. **i 25** KUR-*šu*: Ex. 16 has KUR-*šú*; exs. 17, 42 have *ma-ti-šu*; ex. 21 has ⸢*ma*⸣*-ti-šu*; exs. 25, 46 have [*ma-t*]*i-šu*. **i 25** *a-lik*: Ex. 16 has *a-li-ku*. **i 25** *i-di-šu*: Exs. 11, 16, 20, 44 have *i-di-šú*; ex. 30 has *i-*⸢*di-šú*⸣. **i 26** *ša-lu-ul-ti*: Ex. 14 has *šá-lul-*⸢*ti*⸣; ex. 16 has *ša-lul-ti*; ex. 20 has *ša-*⸢*lul*⸣*-tum*; ex. 25 has [*ša-l*]*u-ul-tum*; ex. 26 has *ša-lu-ul-tu*; ex. 42 has ⸢*ša*⸣*-lu-*⸢*ul*⸣*-tum*; ex. 46 has [*ša-lu-u*]*l-*⸢*tum*⸣. **i 26** *ka-šá-du*: Ex. 4 has *ka-ša-*⸢*du*⸣; exs. 16, 25 have *ka-šá-di*; ex. 18 has *k*[*a*]*-*⸢*šá*⸣*-da*; ex. 20 has ⸢*ka-ša-du*⸣; ex. 26 has *ka-šá-da*; ex. 29 has *ka-ša-di*; ex. 44 has *ka-šá-du*. **i 27** *ú-šat-bu-niš-šum-ma*: Ex. 16 has *ú-šat-bu-ni-iš-šu-um-ma*; ex. 18 has *ú-šat-bu-niš-šu-*⸢*um*⸣*-m*[*a*]; ex. 20 has *ú-ša-at-bu-*⸢*ni*⸣*-iš-šu-um-ma*; ex. 25 has [*ú-šat-b*]*u-niš-šum-ma* (over erasure); ex. 29 has [*ú-ša*]*t-bu-ni-šu-um-ma*; ex. 42 has ⸢*ú*⸣*-šá-at-bu-ni-šu-um-ma*; ex. 46 has *ú-šá-at-*[*bu-ni-šu-um-ma*]. **i 27** *ṣa-aḫ-ri*: Ex. 17 has *ṣa-aḫ-ru*. **i 28** *um-ma-ni-šu*: Ex. 16 has *ni-ši-šu*; ex. 17 has *um-*<*ma*>*-ni-šu*; ex. 30 has [*u*]*m-ma-ni-šú*. **i 28** *i-ṣu-tu*: Ex. 25 has *i-ṣu-*SU. **i 28** LÚ.ERIM-*man-da*: Ex. 2 has *um-*⸢*ma*⸣*-a*[*n-*...]; exs. 11, 17 have ⸢*um-man-ma-an-du*⸣; ex. 16 has *um-ma-an-ma-an-da*; ex. 18 has *u*[*m-*...]*-*⸢*du*⸣; ex. 20 has *um-*⸢*ma-an-ma-an*⸣*-du*; ex. 21 has [*u*]*m-ma-an-ma-an-du*; exs. 25, 44 have [...*-d*]*u*?; ex. 26 has *um-ma-an-man-du*; ex. 29 has [...*-a*]*n-du*; ex. 42 has ⸢*um*⸣*-man-ma-an-du*; ex. 48 has LÚ.ERIM-*man-du*. **i 28** *rap-šá-a-ti*: Ex. 11 has ⸢*rap*⸣*-šá-a-ta*; ex. 17 has *rap-*<*šá*>*-a-tú*; ex. 18 has ⸢*rap*⸣*-šá-ti*; exs. 21, 25, 29, 42 have *rap-ša-a-ta*. **i 29** ^{m}*iš-tu-me-gu*: Ex. 16 has [^{m}*i*]*š-tu-me-gi*; ex. 17 has ^{m}*iš-tu-me-gi*; ex. 42 has ⸢^{m}⸣*iš-tu-me-e-gu*. **i 29** LÚ.ERIM-*man-da*: Ex. 2 has ⸢*um*⸣*-m*[*a-*...]; ex. 4 has [...*-a*]*n-du*; exs. 11, 21 have *um-man-ma-an-du*; ex. 16 has KUR.*um-ma-an-ma-an-da*; exs. 17–18, 26 have *um-ma-an-man-du*; exs. 20, 29, 42 have KUR.*um-man-ma-an-du*; ex. 22 has ⸢*um-man*⸣*-ma-*⸢*an*⸣*-du*; ex. 24 has [...]*-du*; ex. 25 has KUR.*um-man-ma-an-*⸢*du*⸣; ex. 48 has LÚ.ERIM-*man-du*. **i 29** *iṣ-bat-ma*: Exs. 4, 11, 16, 29, 42, 48 have *iṣ-ba-at-ma*; ex. 17 has *iṣ-ba-at-*⸢*ma*⸣; ex. 20 has *iṣ-*⸢*ba-at-ma*⸣; ex. 21 has *iṣ-*⸢*ba*⸣*-at-*⸢*ma*⸣; ex. 22 has *iṣ-ba-at-m*[*a*]. **i 29** KUR-*šu*: Ex. 4 has ⸢*ma-ti-šu*⸣; ex. 16 has ⸢*ma-ti*⸣*-šu*; exs. 17, 20, 22, 29, 42 have *ma-ti-šu*; ex. 21 has *ma-*⸢*ti*⸣*-šu*; ex. 25 has [*m*]*a-ti-š*[*u*]; ex. 46 has ⸢*ma*⸣*-*[*ti-šu*].

i 30 *a-mat*: Exs. 2, 46 have *a-ma-at*; ex. 4 has [*a-m*]*a-at*; ex. 16 has [*a*]*-ma-at*; ex. 20 has *a-*⸢*ma*⸣*-at*; ex. 21 has [*a-ma-a*]*t*; ex. 26 has ⸢*a-ma*⸣*-at*; ex. 29 has ⸢*a*⸣*-ma-at*. **i 30** ^{d}EN: Exs. 4, 16, 20, 22, 29, 46 have EN. **i 30** GAL-*ú*: Ex. 2 has GAL-*i*; exs. 20–21, 26, 42, 46 have GAL. **i 30** ^{d}EN.ZU: Ex. 22 has ^{d}30. **i 30** AN-*e*: Ex. 16 has *ša-mé-e*; ex. 29 has *ša-mé-*⸢*e*⸣. **i 30** KI-*tim*: Ex. 16 has *er-ṣe-*⸢*tim*⸣; ex. 20 has KI-<*tim*>; ex. 29 has *er-ṣe-tim*. **i 31** *šá*: Exs. 2, 46, 48 have *ša*; exs. 4, 18, 26, 42 have [*š*]*a*; ex. 41 has ⸢*ša*⸣. **i 31** *qí-bi-it-su-nu*: Exs. 2, 4, 18, 22, 26, 46 have *qí-bit-su-nu*; ex. 16 has [*q*]*í-bit-su-nu*; ex. 20 has ⸢*qí*⸣*-*<*bit*>*-su-nu*. **i 31** *qí-bi-ti-šú-nu*: Exs. 2, 26 have *qí-*É*-šu-nu*; ex. 16 has *qí-bi-ti-šu-nu*; ex. 18 has ⸢*qí-*É⸣*-šu-nu*; ex. 20 has ⸢*qí*⸣*-bi-ti-šu-nu*; ex. 53 has [*qí-bi-ti-š*]*u*?*-nu*. **i 31** *ṣir-ti*: Exs. 2, 16, 20, 29 have *ṣi-ir-ti*; ex. 4 has ⸢*ṣi*⸣*-ir-*⸢*ti*⸣; ex. 17 has *ṣi-ir-tum*; ex. 18 has *ṣi-ir-*⸢*tim*⸣ ex. 21 has ⸢*ṣi*⸣*-i*[*r-ti*]; ex. 26 has *ṣi-ir-t*[*i*]. i 31 Ex. 22 has three superfluous signs after *ṣir-ti*. **i 32** *na-qut-ti*: Exs. 2, 4, 16–18, 21, 48 have *na-qú-ut-ti*; ex. 4 written over an erasure; ex. 21 has *na-qú-*⸢*ut-ti*⸣; ex. 26 has ⸢*na*⸣*-qú-ut-ti*; ex. 42 has *na-qut-tum*. **i 32** *dul-lu-ḫu*: Ex. 20 has *d*[*u*]*-*⸢*ul-lu-ḫu*⸣. **i 32** *pa-nu-ú-a*: Ex. 20 has ⸢*pa-nu-ú-*<*a*>⸣. **i 33** *a-ḫi*: Ex. 4 has ⸢*a*⸣*-ḫa*; exs. 16–17, 25, 29 have *a-ḫa*; **i 33** *la* (second instnce): Ex. 1 had AD. **i 33** *ad-da*: Exs. 2, 20 have *ad-du*; ex. 4 has [*ad-d*]*i*?; exs. 16, 53 have *ad-*⸢*di*⸣; exs. 17, 25, 29, 42 have *ad-di*; ex. 18 has ⸢*ad*⸣*-di*. **i 33** *ú-šat-ba-am-ma*: Ex. 4 has [*ú-š*]*a-at-ba-am-ma*; ex. 16 has ⸢*ú*⸣*-šá-at-ba-am-ma*; ex. 20 has ⸢*ú-ša*⸣*-at-ba-am-*⸢*ma*⸣. **i 34** *rap-šá-a-ti*: Ex. 4 has ⸢*rap-šá-a*⸣*-ta*; ex. 16 has *ra-ap-ša-a-*⸢*ti*⸣; ex. 18 has *rap-šá-a-tu*; ex. 25 has *rap-*⸢*šá*⸣*-a-*⸢*ta*⸣; ex. 29 has ⸢*rap-šá*⸣*-a-ta*. **i 34** KUR.*ḫa-az-za-ti*: Ex. 2 has KUR.*ḫa-az-za-tu*; ex. 17 has *ḫa-az-za-*⸢*tum*⸣; ex. 20 has URU.*ḫa-az-za-*⸢*tum*⸣. **i 34** Ex. 22 has an erasure after KUR.*mi-ṣir*. **i 35** *e-li-ti*: Ex. 16 has *e-li-tim*; exs. 20, 42 have *e-li-tum*. **i 35** *a-bar-ti*: Ex. 4 has *a-ba-*⸢*ar*⸣*-ti*; ex. 16 has [*a-b*]*a-ar-ti*; exs. 20, 25 has *a-ba-ar-ti*; ex. 21 has *a-*⸢*ba-ar*⸣*-ti*; ex. 22 has ⸢*a*⸣*-bar-tú*; ex. 42 has [*a-ba*]*-*⸢*ar*⸣*-tum*; ex. 46 has *a-ba-ar-t*[*i*]; ex. 53 has *a-bar-*⸢*tu*?⸣. **i 35** ÍD.BURANUN.KI: ex. 11 has ⸢ÍD.BURANUN⸣.DI. **i 35** *šap-li-ti*: Exs. 16, 42 have *šap-li-tim*; exs. 17, 20 have *šap-*⸢*li*⸣*-tum*. **i 36** Exs. 20, 29 add *ù* before GÌR.NÍTA.MEŠ; exs. 4 and 25 have an erased *ù* after NUN.MEŠ. **i 36** *rap-šá-a-ti*: Exs. 11, 22, 25 have *rap-šá-a-ta*; ex. 16 has DAGAL.MEŠ. **i 37** *ša*: Exs. 20, 22 have *šá*. **i 37** ^{d}EN.ZU: Exs. 11, 22 have ^{d}30. **i 37** *ia-ti*: Ex. 2 has *ia-a-tu*; exs. 17, 20 have *ia-a-ti*; ex. 18 has *ia-*⸢*a-tu*⸣; ex. 19 has *ia-a-t*[*i*]; ex. 21 has *ia-a-*⸢*ti*⸣; ex. 22 has *ia-*⸢*a*⸣*-ti*; ex. 25 has [*i*]*a-a-ti*; ex. 42 has *ia-*(over erased *a*)*-ti*. **i 37** *i-qí-pu-nu*: Ex. 2 has *i-qí-pu-nim*; ex. 16 has ⸢*i-qí-pu-ni*⸣; ex. 18 has ⸢*i-qí-pu-nim*⸣. **i 38** *e-pe-šu*: Exs. 16, 42 have ⸢*e*⸣*-pé-šu*. **i 38** ^{d}EN.ZU: Ex. 22 has ⸢^{d}30⸣. **i 38** EN-*ia*: Ex. 2 has *be-li-ia*; ex. 16 has [*be*]*-lí-ia*; ex. 18 has *be-li-*⸢*ia*⸣; ex. 21 has *be-li-*[*ia*]. **i 38** *a-lik*: Exs. 16, 35 have *a-li-ku*; ex. 17 has *a-li-ka*; ex. 20 has [*a*]*-*⸢*li*⸣*-i*[*k*]; ex. 21 has *a-*⸢*li*⸣*-ku*; ex. 26 has [*a-l*]*i-k*[*u*]; ex. 41 has *a-l*[*i-ik/ku*]. **i 39** *ša* (first instance): Exs. 12, 16, 22 have *šá*. **i 39** *qé-reb*: Exs. 2, 17 have *qé-er-bi*; exs. 16, 18, 25–26, 42 have *qé-re-eb*; ex. 21 has *qé-*⸢*re*⸣*-eb*. **i 39** URU.*ḫar-ra-nu*: Ex. 2 has URU.*ḫar-ra-an*. **i 39** *šá* (second instance): Exs. 12, 17 have ⸢*ša*⸣; ex. 18 has [*š*]*a*; exs. 19, 21, 41 have *š*[*a*]. **i 39** ^{m}AN.ŠÁR-*ba-an*-IBILA: Ex. 17 has <^{m}>AN.ŠÁR-*ba-an*-IBILA; ex. 18 has ^{m}AN.ŠÁR-DÙ-IBILA; ex. 22 has [^{m}A]N.ŠÁR-DÙ-IBILA. **i 39** KUR-*aš-šur*.KI: ex. 11 has KUR-*aš-šur*.DI.

i 40 NUN: Exs. 16, 18 have [*r*]*u-bu-ú*; ex. 21 has *ru-*⸢*bu*⸣*-ú*; ex. 41 has ⸢*ru*⸣*-*[*bu-ú*]. **i 40** *a-lik*: Ex. 16 has *a-li-ku*; **i 40** *maḫ-ri-ia*: Ex. 17 has *maḫ-*<*ri*>*-*⸢*ia*⸣. **i 40** *i-pú-šu*: Ex. 2 has *i-pu-*[*šu*]; ex. 17–19, 21, 26 have *i-pu-šu*. **i 41** *šá-al-mu*: Exs. 16, 35 have *ša-al-mu*; ex. 21 has *šá-al-mi*; **i 41** *u*$_{4}$*-mu*: Ex. 1 has *u*$_{4}$*-*<*mi*>; ex. 16 has *u*$_{4}$*-um*; ex. 17 has UD; ex. 19 has *u*$_{4}$*-*⸢*mi*⸣; exs. 21, 26 have *u*$_{4}$*-mi*. **i 41** *še-mi-i*: Ex. 1 has <*še*>*-mi-i*; ex. 17 has [Š]E.GA. **i 41** *šá*: ex. 11 has *ša*; exs. 12, 17, 19 have ⸢*ša*⸣; ex. 41 has *š*[*a*]. **i 41** *ú-ad-du-ni*: Ex. 16 has *ú-ad-du-ú*; ex. 18 has [*ú*]*-*⸢*ad*⸣*-du-ú*; ex. 20 has ⸢*ú*⸣*-wa*$_{6}$*-ad-du-ú*; ex. 26 has *ú-ad-du-ú-ni*. **i 42** *né-me-qu*: Exs. 16–17, 20, 31 have *né-me-qí*; ex. 19 has [*n*]*é-me-qí*; ex. 47 has [*né*]*-*⸢*me*⸣*-qí*. **i 43** *ši-ip-ri*: Ex. 16 has *ši-pí-ir*. **i 43** *ù*: Ex. 25 has *ši-pir* instead of *ù*.

ii 1 *ni-siq-ti*: Exs. 16, 47 have *ni-sì-iq-ti*; ex. 25 has [*ni-s*]*ì-iq-ti*; ex. 31 has *ni-sì-iq-t*[*i*]. **ii 1** Ex. 8 has an erasue before *šu-qu-ru-tu*. **ii 1** *šu-qu-ru-tu*: Ex. 16 has *šu-*⸢*qu*⸣*-r*[*u-t*]*i*. **ii 1** *ḫi-biš-ti*: Exs. 17, 26 have *ḫi-bi-iš-ti*; ex. 18 has *ḫi-biš-tú*; ex. 20 has [*ḫi-b*]*i-*⸢*iš-ti*⸣; ex. 29

has ḫi-bi-i[š-ti]; ex. 31 has ḫi-bi-⸢iš⸣-t[i]; ex. 47 has [ḫi-bi]-iš-ti. **ii 2** ḫi-da-a-ti: Ex. 20 has ḫi-⸢da-a⸣-tu. **ii 2** ri-šá-a-ti: Exs. 3, 8, 47 have ri-ša-a-ti; ex. 10 has [ri-š]a-a-ti; ex. 19 has ri-šá-a-tú; ex. 25 has [r]i-ša-a-ti; ex. 26 has ri-ša-a-⸢ti⸣; ex. 29 has ⸢ri-ša⸣-a-ta. **ii 3** te-me-en-na: Exs. 16, 21 have te-me-en-<na>; ex. 20 has te-me-⸢en-<na>⸣. **ii 3** ša: Ex. 3 has ⸢šá⸣; exs. 8, 19 have šá. **ii 3** ^{m}AN.ŠÁR-ba-an-IBILA: Ex. 5 omits ^{m}. **ii 3** KUR-aš-šur.KI: Ex. 20 has ⸢KUR-aš-šur⸣. **ii 4** te-me-en-na: Ex. 16 has [t]e-me-1+EN-na; ex. 17 has te-me-en-<na>; ex. 20 has [t]e-me-en-<na>; ex. 21 has [te]-me-en-<na>. **ii 4** Ex. 16 adds šá before ^{m}šul-man-SAG.KAL. **ii 4** ^{m}šul-man-SAG.KAL: Ex. 3 has [^{m}šu]l-ma-an-SAG.KAL; ex. 5 has ^{m}šul-ma-[...]; ex. 8 has [^{m}šul]-⸢ma⸣-an-a-šá-⸢red⸣; ex. 11 has ^{m}šul-ma-an-a-šá-red; ex. 16 has ^{m}⸢sál⸣-ma-an-SAG.KAL; ex. 17 has ^{m}šul-ma-an-SAG.KAL; ex. 20 has ^{m}šul-ma-a[n-SAG].KAL; ex. 21 has ^{m}šul-ma-an-SAG.KAL; ex. 29 has ^{m}šul-ma-an-a-šá-⸢red⸣. **ii 4** ^{m}AN.ŠÁR-na-ṣir-IBILA: Ex. 21 has ^{m}AN.ŠÁR-na-<ṣir>-IBILA. **ii 5** ad-di-ma: Ex. 3 has [a]d-de-e-ma. **ii 5** ú-kin: Exs. 3, 10, 16–21, 23, 29 have ú-ki-in; ex. 11 has ú-⸢ki-in⸣; exs. 12, 32 have ⸢ú-ki-in⸣; ex. 25 has ú-ki-⸢in⸣. **ii 5** lib-na-at-su: Exs. 12, 16 have li-ib-na-at-su. **ii 5** KAŠ: Exs. 11–12, 19, 23, 29, 31 have KAŠ.SAG. **ii 5** LÀL: Ex. 20 has SISKUR. **ii 6** šal-la-ar-šú: Exs. 3, 11–12, 17–18, 21, 23, 29 have šal-la-ar-šu; ex. 10 has [ša]l-la-ar-šu; ex. 16 has ⸢šal⸣-la-ar-⸢šu⸣; ex. 20 has ⸢šal⸣-la-⸢ar-šu⸣; ex. 25 has [ša]l-⸢la-ar⸣-šu. **ii 6** ab-lu-ul: Ex. 31 has ab-lul. **ii 7** šá: Exs. 17–18, 20–21, 29 have ša. **ii 7** ab-bé-e-a: Exs. 2, 18 have AD.MEŠ-e-a; ex. 16 has AD.MEŠ-⸢e⸣-a. **ii 7** ép-še-ti-šu: Ex. 2 has e-⸢ep⸣-š[e-ti-šu]; ex. 5 has ep-še-t[i-šu]; exs. 16–17, 29 have ep-še-ti-šu; ex. 18 has ⸢e⸣-ep-še-ti-⸢šu⸣; ex. 19 has ⸢ép-še-ti-šú⸣; ex. 21 has e-ep-še-ti-⸢šu⸣; ex. 25 has ep-še-ti-⸢šu⸣; ex. 31 has e-ep-še-ti-šú. **ii 7** ú-dan-nin-ma: Exs. 10, 25 have ú-da-an-ni-in-ma; ex. 16 has ú-d[a-ni]-⸢ni-in⸣-ma; ex. 29 has ú-da-an-ni-⸢in⸣-ma. **ii 8** ú-nak-ki-lu: Ex. 2 has ú-nak-ki-⸢il⸣; exs. 16, 29 have ú-na-ak-ki-lu; ex. 17 has ú-na-ak-ki-il; ex. 18 has ⸢ú-nak⸣-ki-⸢il⸣; ex. 20 has ú-na-ak-ki-⸢lu⸣; ex. 21 has ú-na-ak-ki-⸢il⸣; ex. 23 has [ú-n]a-ak-ki-lu. **ii 8** ši-pí-ir-šú: Exs. 2, 17 have ši-pí-ir-⸢šu⸣; ex. 6 has [š]i-pí-ir-šu; ex. 10 has [ši-p]í-ir-šu; exs. 11, 23, 25 have ši-pí-ir-šu; ex. 16 has ši-⸢pí⸣-ir-šu; ex. 18 has ⸢ši⸣-pi-ir-⸢šu⸣; ex. 20 has ši-pí-⸢ir-šu⸣; ex. 21 has ši-⸢pí⸣-ir-š[u]; ex. 29 has ši-pí-ir-[š]u. **ii 8** šu-a-tim: Exs. 17, 21 have šu-a-⸢ti⸣; ex. 31 has šu-a-ti. **ii 8** te-me-en-ni-šu: Ex. 3 has te-me-en-<ni>-šú; ex. 17 has te-⸢me⸣-e[n-n]i-šú. **ii 9** gaba-dib-bi-šú: Ex. 6 has [gaba]-dib-bi-šu; ex. 10 has [gab]a-dib-bi-šu; exs. 11, 23, 25 have gaba-dib-bi-šu; ex. 17 has gaba-d[ib-b]í-šu; ex. 18 has gaba-dib-bi-⸢šu⸣; ex. 21 has gaba-dib-bi-š[u]; ex. 29 has gaba-dib-bi-[š]u. **ii 9** e-eš-ši-iš: Ex. 1 has e[š-ši-iš]; exs. 12, 16, 23 have eš-ši-iš; ex. 17 has e-eš-šiš; exs. 19–20 have ⸢eš⸣-ši-iš. **ii 9** ú-šak-lil: Ex. 2 has ú-šá-a[k-li-i]l; ex. 18 has ú-ša-⸢ak-li⸣-il; ex. 19 has ú-šak-l[i-il]; ex. 20 has [x (x) x]-⸢li-il⸣; ex. 21 has ú-šá-ak-li-il; ex. 23 has ú-š[a]k-li-il; ex. 25 has ú-ša-ak-li-il; ex. 29 has ⸢ú-ša-ak-li-il⸣. **ii 9** ši-pir-šu: Exs. 2, 32 have ⸢ši⸣-pí-ir-šu; ex. 6 has [ši-p]í-ir-šu; ex. 10 has [š]i-pí-ir-šu; exs. 17, 29 have ši-⸢pi-ir-šu⸣; ex. 18 has ši-pí-ir-⸢šu⸣; ex. 20 has ši-pí-i[r-šu]; ex. 21 has ši-pí-⸢ir⸣-š[u]; exs. 23, 25 have ši-pí-ir-šu; ex. 48 has ši-pí-ir-š[u].

ii 10 GIŠ.ÙR: Exs. 2, 21 have GIŠ.ÙR.MEŠ; ex. 20 has ⸢GIŠ⸣.ÙR.MEŠ. **ii 10** ṣi-ru-tu: Ex. 2 has ⸢ṣi⸣-ru-ti; ex. 3 has ṣi-ru-tú; exs. 18, 21 have ṣi-ru-ti; ex. 31 has ṣi-ru-t[i]. **ii 10** ta-ar-bi-it: Ex. 17 has tar-bit. **ii 10** KUR.ḫa-ma-nu: Ex. 17 has KUR.ḫa-ma-ni; ex. 18 has URU.ḫa-⸢ma⸣-nu; exs. 23, 48 have URU.ḫa-ma-nu. **ii 11** ú-ša-at-ri-iṣ: Ex. 16 has ⸢ú-šá-at⸣-ri-iṣ. **ii 11** Ex. 29 has an erasure between GIŠ.IG.MEŠ and GIŠ.EREN. **ii 12** ša: Exs. 2, 17 have ⸢šá⸣; ex. 20 has šá. **ii 12** i-ri-is-si-na: Ex. 2 has ⸢i-ri-si-na⸣; ex. 18 has i-ri-is-sì-⸢na⸣. **ii 12** KÁ.MEŠ-šú: Ex. 3 has KÁ.MEŠ-ša; ex. 6 has KÁ.MEŠ-šu; ex. 10 has KÁ.KÁ-⸢šu⸣; exs. 11, 17, 25 have KÁ.KÁ-šu; ex. 16 has ⸢KÁ.MEŠ-šu⸣; ex. 18 has ⸢KÁ⸣.MEŠ-šu; ex. 20 has KÁ.MEŠ-⸢šu⸣; ex. 32 has KÁ.⸢MEŠ⸣-šu. **ii 13** ù: Exs. 2, 17, 25, 34 omit ù. **ii 13** É.GAR$_8$.MEŠ-šu: Exs. 2, 12, 17, 19–20, 23 have É.GAR$_8$.MEŠ-šú; ex. 10 has [i]-⸢ga-ra⸣-a-ti-šu; ex. 16 has i-ga-⸢ra⸣-a-ti-šu; ex. 25 has i-ga-ra-a-t[i]- ⸢šu⸣; ex. 29 has [i-g]a-ra-a-ti-šu; ex. 46 has ⸢i⸣-[ga-ra-a-ti-šu]. **ii 13** ú-šal-biš-ma: Exs. 10, 25, 29 have ú-šá-al-bi-iš-ma; ex. 16 has ú-šá-al-bi-iš-⸢ma⸣; ex. 17 has ⸢ú⸣-šá-al-bi-iš-⸢ma⸣. **ii 13** ú-šá-an-bi-iṭ: Ex. 18 has ú-ša-an-bi-ṭu. **ii 13** šá-áš-šá-ni-iš: Ex. 6 has ⸢^{d}UTU-ši-niš⸣; exs. 10, 25, 29 have ša-aš-ša-ni-iš; ex. 11 has ^{d}UTU-ši-niš; ex. 16 has ša-aš-ša-ni-i[š]; ex. 20 has ^{d}⸢UTU⸣-š[i-niš] ex. 23 has šá-⸢áš-šá⸣-niš; ex. 31 has ša-áš-š[a-ni-iš]; ex. 32 has šá-áš-šá-⸢niš⸣; ex. 48 has šá-áš-šá-niš. **ii 14** ri-i-mu: Exs. 17 and 31 have ⸢AM.MEŠ⸣ and AM.MEŠ respectively. **ii 14** za-ḫa-le-e: Ex. 34 has za-ḫa-le-<e>. **ii 14** eb-bi: Ex. 10 has eb-⸢ba⸣; exs. 25, 29 have eb-ba. **ii 14** mu-nak-kip: Ex. 2 has mu-na-ak-⸢ki-ip⸣; ex. 3 has [mu-na-ak-k]i-ip; ex. 16 has mu-nak-ki-ip; ex. 18 has mu-na-ak-ki-ip; ex. 32 has [mu-na]k-ki-ip. **ii 17** ZAG: Ex. 16 has i-mit-ti; exs. 20, 25 have im-ni. **ii 17** GÙB: Ex. 3 has ⸢2⸣.30; exs. 10, 46 have [2].⸢30⸣ ; ex. 16 has šu-me-⸢lu⸣; exs. 20, 25 have šu-me-lu; ex. 29 has 2.30. **ii 18** qá-tì: Exs. 5, 10 have qa-at; ex. 6 has ⸢qá⸣-at; ex. 31 has ŠU.II. **ii 18** ^{d}30: Ex. 2 has ⸢^{d}EN⸣.ZU; ex. 5 has ^{d}⸢EN⸣.[ZU]; ex. 10 has ⸢^{d}EN.ZU⸣; exs. 16, 18, 25 have ^{d}EN.ZU; ex. 20 has ^{d}EN.Z[U]; ex. 29 has [^{d}EN].⸢ZU⸣. **ii 18** Ex. 25 adds ù after ^{d}EN.ZU.**ii 19** šu-an-na.KI: Exs. 16, 17 have ba-bi-lam.KI and TIN.TIR.KI respectively. **ii 19** LUGAL-ú-ti-ia: Exs. 11, 25 have LUGAL-ti-ia; ex. 17 has šar-ru-ti-ia; ex. 29 has LUGAL-⸢ti-ia⸣.

ii 20 aṣ-ba-at-ma: Ex. 2 has ⸢aṣ-bat-ma⸣; exs. 10–11, 18 have aṣ-bat-ma; ex. 17 has aṣ-bat-⸢ma⸣. **ii 20** Ex. 25 has an erasure before ù. **ii 20** ri-šá-a-ti: Ex. 2 has ⸢ri⸣-šá-a-t[u]; exs. 3, 14, 17 have ri-ša-a-⸢ti⸣; ex. 10 has [r]i-ša-a-ti; ex. 16 has ri-⸢ša-a-ti⸣; ex. 25 has ri-⸢ša-a⸣-[ti]; ex. 29 has ri-ša-⸢a-ti⸣; ex. 46 has [ri-šá-a]-tu. **ii 21** šu-ba-at: Ex. 31 has šu-bat. **ii 21** lìb-bi: Exs. 2, 17, 18, 19 have respectively ⸢li-ib⸣-b[i], lib-bi, lib-⸢bi⸣, ŠÀ. **ii 21**.11 Has an erasure between lìb-bi and qé-er-ba-šu. **ii 21** qé-er-ba-šu: Ex. 2 has [q]é-er-ba-šú; ex. 3 has [qe]r-ba-šu; ex. 17 has qer-ba-šu; ex. 20 has ⸢qer-ba-šu⸣; ex. 31 has qer-ba-š[u]. **ii 21** ú-še-ši-ib: Ex. 3 has ú-še-šib. **ii 22** UDU.SÍSKUR: Exs. 16, 29, 31 have ⸢UDU.SISKUR⸣, ⸢UDU⸣.SISKUR, and ⸢ni-qu⸣-ú respectively. **ii 22** taš-ri-iḫ-ti: Exs. 2, 14, 29 have ta-áš-ri-iḫ-ti; ex. 10 has ta-áš-ri-iḫ-⸢ti⸣. **ii 22** eb-bi: Ex. 10 has ⸢e⸣-[eb-bi]; exs. 14, 17, 31 have eb-ba; ex. 16 has ⸢eb⸣-ba; ex. 29 has e-eb-bi; ex. 46 has ⸢e⸣-eb-bi. **ii 22** ma-ḫar-šú-nu: Exs. 2, 14, 16–17, 29, 45–46, 48 have ma-ḫar-šu-nu; ex. 10 has [ma-ḫ]ar-šu-nu; ex. 18 has ⸢ma⸣-ḫar-šu-nu; ex. 25 has [m]a-⸢ḫar⸣-šu*-nu. **ii 23** ú-šam-ḫi-ir: Ex. 2 has ú-⸢šam⸣-ḫi-ra; ex. 9 has ⸢ú-šá-am-ḫi-ir⸣; ex. 10 has ú-⸢ša⸣-am-ḫi-ir; exs. 16, 29 have ⸢ú⸣-ša-am-ḫi-ir; ex. 16 has ú-šá-⸢am-ḫi⸣-ra; ex. 17 has ú-⸢ša⸣-am-ḫi-ir; ex. 18 has ú-šam-ḫi-ra; ex. 19 has ú-šam-ḫir; exs. 45, 48 have ú-šá-am-ḫi-ir. **ii 23** kád-ra-a-a: Ex. 2 has ka-⸢ad⸣-ra-a-a; exs. 3, 11, 14 have ka-ad-ra-a-a; ex. 9 has ⸢ka-ad-ra-a-a⸣; exs. 10, 16 have ⸢ka⸣-ad-ra-a-a; ex. 17 has ka-ad-ra-⸢a-a⸣; ex. 18 has ka-ad-⸢ra-a⸣-a; ex. 29 has ka-ad-⸢ra⸣-[a-a]. **ii 23** re-eš-tum: Ex. 3 has [r]e-eš-ti; exs. 11, 14, 17, 29 have re-eš-ti; ex. 16 has re-eš-⸢ta⸣; exs. 45, 48 have re-eš$_{15}$-ti. **ii 23** ú-mál-li-ma: Ex. 2 has ú-ma-al-⸢la⸣; exs. 3, 14, 16 have ú-ma-al-li-ma; ex. 10 has ⸢ú-ma⸣-al-li-ma; ex. 17 has ú-ma-al-⸢li-ma⸣; ex. 29 has ú-⸢ma⸣-a[l-li-ma]. **ii 24** URU.ḫar-ra-an: ex. 3 has [URU.ḫar-ra-n]u; exs. 10–11, 18 have URU.ḫar-ra-nu; exs. 14, 17 have ⸢URU⸣.ḫar-ra-nu; ex. 16 has [U]RU.KI ḫar-ra-nu; ex. 31 has URU.ḫar-ra-nu.KI. **ii 24** gi-im-ri-šu: Exs. 3, 10–11, 16 have gi-mi-ri-šu. **ii 25** Ex. 16 has an erasure after ITI. **ii 25** ú-nam-mi-ir: Ex. 10 has ú-⸢na⸣-am-mi-NI; ex. 31 has ú-na-am-m[i-ir]. **ii 25** ša-ru-ru-šu exs. 11 and 17 have šá-ru-ru-šu and š[á]-ru-ru-šu respectively. **ii 26** ^{d}EN.ZU: Ex. 31 has ⸢^{d}⸣30. **ii 26** DINGIR.MEŠ: Exs. 11, 17, 31 have DINGIR.DINGIR. **ii 26** šá (first instance): Exs. 2, 16, 18, 31 have ša; ex. 10 omits this šá. **ii 26** AN-e: Ex. 31 has šá-me-⸢e⸣. **ii 26** šá (second instance): Exs. 2, 10–11, 20–21, 31, 45 have ša; ex. 14 has [š]a; exs. 17–18 have ⸢ša⸣. **ii 26** ul-la-nu-uš-šu: Ex. 17 has ul-la-<<ku>>-nu-uš-šu (or ul-la-nu$_{10}^{nu}$-uš-šu). **ii 27** URU: Ex. 20 has URU.KI. **ii 27** KUR: Exs. 2 and 16 have respectively ma-a-ti and ma-a-⸢ti⸣. **ii 27** in-nam-du-ú: Exs. 10, 25, and 29 have in-na-an-du-⸢ú⸣, in-na-an-du-ú, and in-⸢na⸣-a[n-du-ú] respectively. **ii 27** Ex. 2 has an erasure after la. **ii 27** i-tur-ru: Exs. 2–3, 16 have i-tu-ru; exs. 10–11, 14, 17 have i-tu-ur-ru; ex. 20 has i-t[u-ur-r]u; ex. 31 has i-⸢tu-ur⸣-ru. **ii 28** šu-bat: Ex. 2 has ⸢šu-ba⸣-at; exs. 3, 10–11, 18, 20, 25, 29 have šu-ba-at. **ii 28** la-le-e-ka: ex. 11 has la-le-ka. **ii 28** e-re-bi-ka: Ex. 20 has e-re-bi-ku*. **ii 29** SIG$_5$-tì: Exs. 2, 25 have ⸢da⸣-mi-iq-ti; ex. 4 has ⸢da⸣-m[i-iq-ti]; ex. 10 has ⸢da-mi-iq-ti⸣; ex. 14 has [d]a-⸢mi-iq-ti⸣; ex. 17 has da-mi-iq-⸢ti⸣; ex. 18 has [da-mi-i]q-⸢ti⸣; ex. 29 has da-mi-iq-ti; ex. 31 has SIG$_5$-ti. **ii 29** URU: Exs. 25, 29 have URU.KI. **ii 29** šá-a-šu: Ex. 2 has *ša-a-*⌜*šu*⌝; ex. 10 has ⌜*ša-a-šu*⌝; exs. 14, 17, 25, 29, 31, 46 have *ša-a-šu*. **ii 29** *liš-šá-ki-in*: Ex. 4 has *li-*⌜*iš-šá*⌝*-ki-in*; exs. 3, 10–11, 25, 29 have *li-iš-šá-ki-in*; ex. 14 has ⌜*li-iš-šá-ki*⌝*-i*[*n*]; ex. 16 has ⌜*li*⌝*-iš-*⌜*šá-ki-in*⌝; ex. 17 has *li-iš-ša-ki-in*; ex. 18 has [*l*]*i-iš-šá-ki-in*; ex. 20 has *li-*⌜*iš*⌝*-šá-kin*; ex. 21 has *l*[*i-iš-šá-ki-in*]; ex. 31 has ⌜*li*⌝-[*iš-šá-ki-in*]. **ii 29** *šap-tu-uk-ka*: Ex. 10 has ⌜*šap-tuk-ka*⌝; exs. 11, 18, 20 have *šap-tuk-ka*; ex. 17 has ⌜*ša*⌝*-ap-tu-uk-*⌜*ka*⌝; ex. 25 has *šap-*⌜*tuk*⌝*-ka*; ex. 29 has *ša-ap-tu-uk-ka*; ex. 50 has [*ša*]*p-tuk-ku*.

ii 30 *a-ši-bu-tu*: Ex. 2 has [*a-š*]*i-bu-*⌜*ú*⌝*-tu*; exs. 14, 25, 29 have *a-ši-*<*bu*>*-tu*; exs. 16, 45 have *a-ši-bu-ú-tu*; ex. 18 has *a-ši-bu-*⌜*ú-tu*⌝; ex. 23 has [*a-ši*]*-bu-ú-tu*; ex. 48 has ⌜*a*⌝*-š*[*i-bu*]*-*⌜*ú*⌝*-tu*. **ii 30** *ša*: Ex. 2–3, 10–11, 14, 16–17, 20, 25, 29, 45, 48 omit *ša*; exs. 18 and 23 have ⌜*šá*⌝ and *šá* respectively. **ii 30** KI-*tim*: Ex. 23 has *e*[*r*]*-*⌜*ṣe*⌝*-tim*. **ii 31** *li-ik-ta-ra-bu*: Ex. 2 and 11 have respectively [*li-i*]*k-ta-ra-bi* and *li-ik-ta-ra-bi*; ex. 16 has *lik-tar-ra-bu*. **ii 31** ^{d}EN.ZU: Exs. 11, 17 have ^{d}30. **ii 31** *a-bi*: Ex. 17 has *a-ba*. **ii 31** *ba-ni-šu-un*: Ex. 20 has *ba-ni-šú-un*. **ii 32** *ia-ti*: Ex. 2 has [*ia*]*-*⌜*a*$^{?!}$⌝*-ti*; exs. 3, 14, 18 have [*i*]*a-a-ti*; ex. 4 has *ia-a-*⌜*ti*⌝; exs. 11, 16, 20, 25 have *ia-a-ti*; ex. 17 has ⌜*ia*⌝*-a-ti*; ex. 29 has ⌜*ia-a-ti*⌝. **ii 32** ^{d}AG-NÍ.TUKU: Ex. 3 has {d}*na-bi-um-na-'i-id*; ex. 16 has ^{md}⌜AG-NÍ⌝.TUKU; ex. 20 has ^{d}*na-bi-um-*⌜NÍ.TUKU⌝; ex. 25 has ^{d}*na-bi-*⌜*um*⌝*-*[*na*]*-*⌜*'i*⌝*-id*. **ii 32** TIN.TIR.KI: Ex. 3 has KÁ.DINGIR.RA.⌜KI⌝; ex. 10 has KÁ.DINGIR.⌜RA⌝.KI; exs. 25, 29 have KÁ.DINGIR.RA.KI. **ii 32** *mu-šak-lil*: Ex. 2 has *mu-šak-*⌜*li-il*⌝; ex. 3 has [*m*]*u-šak-li-il*; ex. 14 has *mu-šá-a*[*k-li-il*]; ex. 16 has *mu-šá-ak-li-*⌜*il*⌝; ex. 17 has ⌜*mu*⌝*-ša-ak-li-il*; ex. 20 has *mu-šá-ak-*⌜*li*⌝*-il*; ex. 25 has *mu-šá-ak-li-il*; ex. 29 has *mu-šá-ak-*⌜*li-il*⌝. **ii 32** *šu-a-tim*: Ex. 2 has ⌜*šu*⌝*-a-ti*; ex. 17 has *šu-*⌜*a-ti*⌝; ex. 20 has ⌜*šu-a-ti*⌝. **ii 33** ^{d}EN.ZU: ex. 11 has ^{d}30. **ii 33** *šá*: Exs. 2, 25 have [*š*]*a*; exs. 3–4, 16–18 have *ša*; exs. 14, 20 have ⌜*ša*⌝. **ii 33** KI-*tim*: Ex. 29 has ⌜*er-ṣe-tim*⌝. **ii 33** *i-ni-šú*: Exs. 2–3, 11, 14, 17, 25, 45 have *i-ni-šu*; exs. 4, 18 have ⌜*i-ni-šu*⌝; ex. 16 has *i-ni-*⌜*šu*⌝; ex. 23 has [*i*]*-*⌜*ni-šu*⌝. **ii 33** SIG$_5$.MEŠ: Ex. 2 has *dam-*⌜*qá*⌝*-*[*a*]*-*⌜*tu*⌝; ex. 18 has ⌜*dam-qa-a-ti*⌝. **ii 34** *lip-pal-sa-an-ni-ma*: Ex. 16 has ⌜*lip*⌝*-*<*pal*>*-sa-an-ni-ma*. **ii 34** *ár-ḫi-šam-ma*: Ex. 4 has *ar-ḫi-*⌜*šam-ma*⌝; exs. 14, 25, 29 has *ar-ḫi-šam-ma*; ex. 17 has ⌜*ar-ḫi*⌝*-ša-am*; ex. 20 has ⌜*ar*⌝*-ḫi-*⌜*šam*⌝. **ii 34** *ni-ip-ḫi*: Ex. 2 has *ni-ip-ḫu*. **ii 34** *ri-ba*: Exs. 2, 4, 18 have *ri-bi*; ex. 17 has [*r*]*i-bi*; exs. 25, 46 have *ri-*⌜*bi*⌝; ex. 33 has [*ri*]*-*⌜*bi*$^{?!}$⌝. **ii 35** *li-dam-mi-iq*: Ex. 4 has ⌜*li-da-am-mi-qu*⌝; ex. 14 has *li-da-am-mi-q*[*u*]; ex. 16 has *li-da-am-*⌜*mi-iq*⌝; ex. 20 has *l*[*i-da-am*]*-mi-qu*; ex. 25 has *li-da-am-mi-*⌜*qu*⌝; ex. 29 has *li-da-am-mi-qu*. **ii 35** UD.MEŠ-*ia*: Exs. 2 and 18 have ⌜*u*$_4$⌝*-mi-ia* and *u*$_4$*-*⌜*mi-ia*⌝ respectively. **ii 35** *li-šá-ri-ik*: Ex. 4 has ⌜*li-ša-ri-ik*⌝; ex. 16 has ⌜*li*⌝*-šá-rik*; ex. 18 has ⌜*li-šá*⌝*-ri-ik*; exs. 25, 29 have *li-ša-ri-ik*. **ii 36** MU.AN.NA.MEŠ-*ia*: ex. 11 omits MEŠ. **ii 36** *li-šá-an-di-il*: Exs. 16 and 18 have respectively *li-ša-an-di-il* and *li-šá-*⌜*an-di*⌝*-lu*. **ii 36** *lu-ki-in*: Exs. 11, 19–20, 29 have *li-ki-in*; ex. 25 has ⌜*li-ki-in*⌝; ex. 42 has *li-k*[*i-in*]. **ii 37** LÚ.*na-ak-ru-ti-ia*: Ex. 4 has ⌜*na-ak-ru-ti-ia*⌝; ex. 11 has ⌜*nak*⌝*-ru-ti-ia*; ex. 14 has *na-ak-ru-t*[*i-ia*]; ex. 16 has LÚ.*nak-ru-*⌜*ti*⌝*-ia*; ex. 20 has *nak-ru-ti-*⌜*ia*⌝; ex. 25 has *na-ak-ru-ti-ia*; ex. 29 has *na-ak-*⌜*ru*⌝*-ti-ia*; ex. 49 has *na-a*[*k-ru-ti-ia*]. **ii 37** *lik-šu-ud*: Ex. 2 has *l*[*i-ik-šu-u*]*d*; ex. 4 has ⌜*li-ik-šu-ud*⌝; ex. 25 has *li-ik-šu-ud*; ex. 27 has *li-ik-šu-du*; ex. 29 has *li-*⌜*ik*⌝*-*[*šu-ud*]; ex. 37 has [*l*]*i-ik-šu-ud*. **ii 37** LÚ.*za-ma-ni-ia*: Ex. 4 has ⌜*za-ma*⌝*-ni-*[*ia*]; exs. 20, 29 have *za-ma-ni-ia*; ex. 37 has *za-ma-n*[*i-ia*]; ex. 42 has *za-ma-ni-i*[*a*]; ex. 49 has [*za-m*]*a-ni-ia*. **ii 37** *li-šá-am-qit*: Ex. 4 has [*l*]*i-*⌜*šá-am-qí-it*⌝; exs. 11, 29 have *li-šá-am-qí-it*; ex. 14 has [*li-šá-a*]*m-qí-it*; ex. 17 has *li-ša-am-qit*; ex. 18 has ⌜*li-šá-am-qí-it*⌝; ex. 19 has ⌜*li*⌝*-šá-am-q*[*í-i*]*t*; ex. 20 has ⌜*li*⌝*-šam-qí-it*; ex. 23 has *li-šá-am-qí-i*[*t*]; ex. 25 has [*li-š*]*á-am-*⌜*qí*⌝*-it*; ex. 49 has *li-šam-qit*. **ii 38** *ga-ri-ia*: Ex. 2 has LÚ.*g*[*a-ri-ia*]; ex. 11 has LÚ.*ga-ri-ia*. **ii 38** AMA: Exs. 2 and 16 have ⌜*um-mi*⌝ and *um-*⌜*mi*⌝ respectively. **ii 38** DINGIR GAL.GAL: Exs. 2 and 23 have respectively ⌜DINGIR.MEŠ⌝ [GAL.MEŠ] and DINGIR.MEŠ GAL.MEŠ. **ii 39** *ma-ḫar*: Ex. 4 has *ma-*⌜*aḫ*⌝*-ri*; ex. 14 has *ma-ḫ*[*a-ar*]; ex. 16 has ⌜*maḫ-ri*⌝; ex. 23 has *maḫ-ri*; exs. 25, 27, 29 have *ma-ḫa-ar*; ex. 37 has [*ma*]*-*⌜*aḫ*⌝*-ru*. **ii 39** ^{d}EN.ZU: Exs. 11 and 50 have ^{d}30 and [^{d}3]0*. **ii 39** *na-ra-mi-šú*: Exs. 11, 29 have *na-ra-mi-šu*; ex. 18 has *na-ra-mi-*⌜*šu*⌝; ex. 19 has ⌜*na-ar*⌝*-mi-šu*; ex. 23 has ⌜*na*⌝*-ar-mi-šu*. **ii 39** *li-iq-ba-a*: Ex. 16 has *liq-*⌜*ba*⌝*-a*; exs. 18–19 have *liq-ba-a*; ex. 27 has [*l*]*i-iq-ba-*<*a*>. **ii 39** *ba-ni-ti*: Ex. 4 has ⌜*ba-ni*⌝*-tum*; exs. 11, 20, 27, 29, 49 have *ba-ni-tum*; ex. 16 has *ba-ni-tú*; ex. 18 has *ba-ni-*⌜*tú*⌝; ex. 25 has *ba-*⌜*ni*⌝*-*[*t*]*um*; exs. 33, 50 have [*ba-ni-tu*]*m*.

ii 40 Ex. 29 has an additional *ù*. **ii 40** ^{d}*iš-tar*: Ex. 17 has [^{d}1]5. **ii 40** ŠÀ-*šú*: Exs. 4, 19, 23, 27 have ⌜*lìb-bi-šu*⌝; exs. 11, 25 have *lìb-bi-šu*; exs. 16, 29 have *lib-bi-šú*; ex. 17 has [*lìb-bi-š*]*u*; ex. 18 has ⌜*lib*⌝*-bi-šu*; ex. 29 has *lib-bi-šú*; ex. 37 has *lìb-b*[*i-šu*]. **ii 40** *na-am-ra*: Exs. 4, 27 have ⌜*na-am-ru*⌝; exs. 11, 16 have *nam-ri*; ex. 20 has *nam-ru*; ex. 25 has ⌜*na*⌝*-a*[*m*]*-*⌜*ru*⌝. **ii 41** ^{d}EN.ZU: Exs. 29, 49 have ^{d}30; ex. 37 has ⌜^{d}⌝30. **ii 41** *a-bi*: Ex. 17 has [*a*]*-*⌜*ba*⌝. **ii 41** *ba-ni-šu-nu*: Exs. 11, 20, 49 have *ba-ni-šú-un*; ex. 17 has *ba-*BI*-*⌜*šu-un*⌝; exs. 18, 23, 29, 36 have *ba-ni-šu-un*; ex. 19 has ⌜*ba*⌝*-ni-šu-un*; ex. 25 has [*ba*]*-*⌜*ni*⌝*-šu-un*; ex. 27 has [*b*]*a-*⌜*ni*⌝*-šu-un*. **ii 41** *li-iq-bu-ú*: Exs. 16 and 49 have respectively ⌜*liq-bu-ú*⌝ and *liq-bu-ú*. **ii 41** SIG$_5$-*tì*: Ex. 18 has *da-mi-iq-ti*; ex. 25 has *d*[*a*]*-*⌜*mi-iq*⌝*-ti*; ex. 29 has *da-mi-iq-*⌜*ti*⌝. **ii 42** SUKKAL: Ex. 2 has *suk-ka*[*l-lum*]; exs. 16, 18–19, 23 have *suk-kal-lum*; ex. 48 has *suk-kal-l*[*um*]. **ii 42** *su-pe-e-a*: Ex. 20 has *su-pu-e-a*. **ii 42** *li-iš-me-e-ma*: Exs. 17 and 49 have *liš-me-*⌜*e-ma*⌝ and *liš-me-e-ma*. **ii 43** *li-iṣ-ba-at*: Exs. 17–18 have ⌜*li-iṣ-bat*⌝; ex. 48 has *li-iṣ-ba-t*[*u*]; ex. 49 has *li-iṣ-bat*. **ii 43** *a-bu-tu*: Ex. 16 has *a-bu-ú-tu*; ex. 17 has ⌜*a-bu-tú*⌝; ex. 20 has *a-*⌜*bu*⌝*-ú-*⌜*ti*⌝; ex. 25 has *a-bu-ta*; ex. 38 has *a-bu-*⌜*ta*⌝. **ii 43** *mu-sa-ru-ú*: Exs. 16, 18, 20, 22 have MU.SAR-*ru-ú*; ex. 17 has ⌜MU⌝.[SAR-*ru-ú*]; ex. 49 has [MU].SAR-*ru-ú*. **ii 43** *ši-ṭi-ir*: Exs. 11, 20, 22, 49 have *ši-ṭir*; ex. 17 has [*š*]*i-ṭir*. **ii 43** *šu-um*: Ex. 49 has *šu-mi*. **ii 44** *šá*: Exs. 4, 11, 27, 29, 36, 38, 53 have *ša*; exs. 16, 18, 23, 25 have ⌜*ša*⌝; ex. 19 has [*š*]*a*. **ii 44** ^{m}AN.ŠÁR-*ba-an*-IBILA: Ex. 17 has <^{m}>AN.ŠÁR-DÙ-IBILA; exs. 27, 49 have ^{m}AN.ŠÁR-DÙ-IBILA; ex. 38 has ^{m}AN.ŠÁR-DÙ-⌜IBILA⌝; ex. 53 has ^{m}AN.ŠÁR-DÙ-[IBILA]. **ii 44** KUR-*aš-šur*.KI: Ex. 20 has KUR-*aš-š*[*u*]*r*. **ii 44** *a-mu-ur-ma*: Exs. 13, 20, 29, 42 have *a-mur-ma*; ex. 17 has *a-mur-m*[*a*]; ex. 49 has *a-mur-*⌜*ma*⌝. **ii 45** *ú-nak-ki-ir*: Ex. 16 has ⌜*ú*⌝*-na-ak-ki-ir*; ex. 20 has *ú-nak-kìr*; ex. 38 has *ú-na-a*[*k*]*-ki-ir*. **ii 45** UDU.SÍSKUR: Ex. 18 has ⌜UDU.SISKUR⌝; ex. 20 has UDU.SISKUR; ex. 25 has *ni-qu-*⌜*ú*⌝; ex. 29 has *ni-*⌜*qu-ú*⌝; ex. 36 has [*ni-q*]*u-ú*; ex. 38 has ⌜*ni-qu-ú*⌝. **ii 45** *aq-qí*: Exs. 18 and 49 have ⌜*aq-qu*⌝ and *aq-qu* respectively. **ii 46** *mu-sa-re-e-a*: Ex. 11 has MU.⌜SAR⌝*-re-e-a*; ex. 16 has MU.⌜SAR⌝*-e-a*; ex. 17 has M[U.S]AR*-e-a*; ex. 18 has MU.SAR*-e-*⌜*a*⌝; ex. 20 has ⌜MU.SAR-*ru*⌝*-e-a*; ex. 49 has MU.SAR*-re-e-a*. **ii 46** *áš-kun-ma*: Exs. 11, 49 have *áš-ku-un-ma*; exs. 18, 25 have *áš-ku-un-*⌜*ma*⌝; ex. 19 has *áš-k*[*u-un-ma*]; ex. 27 has [*áš-k*]*u-un-ma*; ex. 29 has *áš-ku-*⌜*un-ma*⌝. **ii 46** *ú-te-er*: Exs. 20, 22 have *ú-ter*; ex. 27 has *ú-*DI*-er*. **ii 46** *áš-ru-uš-šu*: Ex. 38 has *aš-ru-uš-šu*. **ii 47** Ex. 16 has an erasure after ^{d}UTU. **ii 47** *ša*: Exs. 11, 13, 19–20, 22, 49 have *šá*; ex. 36 omits *ša*. **ii 47** *ù*: Ex. 22 has *u*. **ii 48** *šá*: Exs. 11, 13, 17–18, 20, 25, 29, 38, 53 have *ša*; ex. 16 has ⌜*ša*⌝. **ii 48** *qé-reb*: Exs. 11, 16, 18, 38 have *qé-re-eb*; exs. 20, 29 have *qé-re-*⌜*eb*⌝; ex. 25 has ⌜*qé*⌝*-r*[*e*$^{?}$*-eb*]; ex. 53 has ⌜*qé*$^{?}$*-re*$^{?}$*-eb*$^{?!}$⌝. **ii 49** *šá*: Exs. 4, 11, 13, 16–17, 25, 29, 42 have *ša*; exs. 20, 28, 38 have ⌜*ša*⌝. **ii 49** ^{md}AG-NÍG.GUB-ÙRU: ex. 11 has ^{d}AG-⌜NÍG.GUB⌝-ÙRU; ex. 16 has ^{md}⌜AG-*ku-dúr*⌝*-ri*-ÙRU; ex. 17 has ^{d}AG-NÍG.GUB-Ù[RU]; ex. 25 has ^{md}AG-[*ku-dú*]*r-*⌜*ri-ú*⌝*-ṣu-úr*; ex. 38 has ^{d}⌜AG⌝*-ku-dúr-ri-ú-ṣu-úr*; ex. 42 has ^{md}AG-*ku-dúr-r*[*i-ú-ṣu-úr*]. **ii 49** *maḫ-ri*: Exs. 17, 25 have *ma-aḫ-ri*; ex. 27 has *ma-*⌜*aḫ*⌝*-ri*; ex. 29 has *ma-*⌜*aḫ*⌝*-r*[*i*]; ex. 49 has *maḫ-ra*. **ii 49** *i-pu-šu-ma*: Exs. 17, 25 have *i-pú-šu-ma*; ex. 27 has *i-p*[*ú-šu-ma*]; ex. 29 has [*i*]*-*⌜*pú-šu-ma*⌝; ex. 38 has *i-pú-šu-*<*ma*>.

ii 50 *te-me-en-šu*: Ex. 16 has *te-me-*⌜*en-šú*⌝; ex. 20 has *te-me-en-šú*; ex. 25 has *te-me-en-n*[*a-š*]*u*. **ii 50** *ú-ba-'u-ú*: Exs. 11, 16, 18, 25, 49 have *ú-ba-'u-ú-ma*; ex. 17 has ⌜*ú*⌝*-ba-'u-ú-ma*; ex. 20 has *ú-ba-'u-*⌜*ú*⌝*-*[*ma*]; ex. 22 has ⌜*ú*⌝*-ba-'u-ú-*⌜*ma*⌝; ex. 27 has [*ú-ba-'u*]*-ú-ma*; ex. 38 has *ú-ba-'u-*⌜*ú*⌝*-ma*. **ii 51** *šu-a-tim*: Ex. 16 has ⌜*šu*⌝*-a-tu*; exs. 17, 22 have *šu-a-ti*. **ii 51** *i-pu-uš-ma*: Ex. 17 has *i-*⌜*pú*⌝*-uš-ma*; ex. 18 has ⌜*i-pu*⌝*-šu-*⌜*ma*⌝; ex. 20 has *i-pu-šu-ma*; ex. 22 has *i-pú-uš-ma*. **ii 52** *ša*: Ex. 4 has *šá*; ex. 13 has [*š*]*á*. **ii 52** *šu-a-tim*: Exs. 2, 6 have *šu-a-tu*; exs. 4, 25, 29 has *ša-a-tim*; ex. 17 has *šu-a-*⌜*ti*⌝; ex. 18 has ⌜*šu-a*⌝*-tu*; exs. 20, 22 have *šu-a-ti*; ex. 49 has *šá-a-šu*. **ii 52** Ex. 25 has an erasure after *i-qu-pu*. **ii 52** *i-ga-ru-šu*: in ex. 11 *i-ga-ri-šu* is written over an erasure. **ii 53** *na-qut-ti*: Exs. 2, 16, 25 have *na-qú-ut-ti*; ex. 11 has *na-*⌜*qú*⌝*-ut-ti*; ex. 18 has ⌜*na-qú*⌝*-ut-ti*; ex. 20 has *na-qú-ut-t*[*i*]; ex. 28 has [*n*]*a-qú-ut-ti*; ex. 29 has *na-qú-*⌜*ut*⌝*-*[*ti*]. **ii 53** *ar-še-e-ma*: Ex. 16 has *ar-še-e-*ŠU. **ii 54** *qé-er-bi-šu*: In ex. 11

the -šu of qé-er-bi-šu is written over an erased ú-; ex. 13 has qé-er-bi-šú; ex. 16 has qé-re-bi-šú; ex. 20 has qé-bi-ir-šu; exs. 25, 27 have qé-re-bi-šu; ex. 29 has ⸢qé-re-bi-šu⸣; ex. 38 has qe-re-⸢bi⸣-šu. **ii 55** šá-nim-ma: Ex. 2 has ⸢ša⸣-nim-⸢ma⸣; ex. 17 has ⸢ša-ni?-im?-ma⸣; ex. 18 has ša-nim-⸢ma⸣; exs. 25, 29 have ša-ni-im-ma; ex. 27 has ⸢ša-ni-im-ma⸣; ex. 38 has šá-ni-⸢im⸣-ma. **ii 55** šu-a-tim: Ex. 4 has šú-a-tim; ex. 13 has šu-a-⸢tú⸣; ex. 16 has šu-a-tu; ex. 17 has šu-a-ta; exs. 18, 20 have šu-a-ti; exs. 25, 29 have šu-a-⸢ti⸣. **ii 56** te-me-en-šu: Ex. 17 has te-me-en-šú; ex. 20 has te-ŠI-en-šú; ex. 23 has [te]-⸢me⸣-en-šú. **ii 56** la-bi-ri: Ex. 2 has [l]a-bi-ru; ex. 38 has [l]a-⸢bi⸣-ri. **ii 56** ú-ba-ʾi-ma: Exs. 2, 25 have ú-ba-ʾi-i-⸢ma⸣; ex. 3 has [ú-ba-ʾ]i-i-ma; exs. 11, 16, 20, 29 have ú-ba-ʾi-i-ma; ex. 17 has ú-ba-ʾi-[i-m]a; ex. 19 has ⸢ú-ba-ʾi-i-ma⸣. **ii 56** qá-qá-ri: Ex. 16 has ⸢qá-qá-ru⸣. **ii 57** ú-šap-pi-il-ma: Ex. 2 has ú-šá-a[p-p]i-⸢il-ma⸣; exs. 11, 20, 25 have ú-šap-pil-ma; ex. 13 has ⸢ú-šap-pil⸣-ma; ex. 16 has ⸢ú-šap⸣-pil-ma; ex. 17 has ú-ša-ap-pi-⸢il⸣-[m]a; ex. 19 has ú-šap-<pi>-il-⸢ma⸣; ex. 29 has ú-⸢šap⸣-pil-ma; ex. 38 has [ú-š]ap-pil-ma. **ii 57** te-me-en-na: Ex. 2 has [te]-me-en-<na>; exs. 16, 20 have te-me-en-<na>; ex. 18 has ⸢te-me-en-<na>⸣. **ii 57** Ex. 18 adds ⸢šá⸣ before na-ram-^{d}EN.ZU. **ii 57** ^{m}na-ram-^{d}30: Ex. 2 has ^{m}na-ra-am-^{d}EN.ZU; ex. 11 has ^{m}na-ram-^{d}EN.ZU; ex. 13 has [^{m}na-ra]-⸢am-^{d}30⸣; exs. 16, 20, 29 have ^{m}na-ra-am-^{d}EN.ZU; ex. 17 has ^{m}na-ra-am-^{d}30; ex. 18 has na-ram-^{d}EN.ZU; ex. 25 has ^{m}na-ra-am-⸢^{d}⸣[EN.ZU]. **ii 58** ša: Exs. 11, 20 have šá; exs. 12, 29 have ⸢šá⸣. **ii 58** MU.AN.NA.MEŠ: Ex. 20 has MU.MEŠ. **ii 58** a-lik: Ex. 17 has [a]-⸢li-ik⸣. **ii 58** la: ex. 11 omits la before i-mu-ru. **ii 59** EN: Exs. 16, 18 have be-lu; ex. 17 has be-lum. **ii 59** GAL-ú: Ex. 2 has [r]a-bí-⸢ù⸣; exs. 6, 16, 19–20 have GAL; ex. 17 has ⸢ra⸣-[b]í-ù; ex. 18 has ra-bu-ú. **ii 59** É: Exs. 2, 17 have É-su. **ii 59** šu-bat: Ex. 11 has [šu-ba-a]t; ex. 17 has šu-⸢ba⸣-at; ex. 25 has šu-ba-⸢at⸣; ex. 29 has [šu-b]a-at. **ii 59** ŠÀ-šú: Ex. 2 has lib-b[i]-⸢šu⸣; exs. 11–12, 18, 23 have lìb-bi-šu; ex. 17 has lìb-⸢bi⸣-šu; ex. 19 has [lìb-b]i-šu; ex. 25 has ⸢lìb-bi-šú⸣; ex. 29 has lìb-bi-šú; ex. 38 has ⸢ŠÀ⸣-šu.

ii 60 ú-kal-lim-an-ni: Ex. 3 has [ú-ka]l-li-ma-an-ni. **ii 60** ia-a-ši: Exs. 2, 17, 29 have ia-a-šu; ex. 25 has ia-a-ti. **ii 60** ITI.DU$_6$: Ex. 12 has ITI.KU. **ii 60** šal-mu: Exs. 2, 18, 20 have šá-al-mu; exs. 6, 32 have [ša/šá-a]l-mu; exs. 11–12, 19, 23, 25, 50 have ša-al-mu; exs. 16–17 have ⸢šá-al⸣-mu; ex. 29 has ša-⸢al⸣-mu. **ii 60** UD: Exs. 2, 50 have u$_4$-mi; exs. 3, 16, 18 have u$_4$-mu; ex. 25 has ⸢u$_4$⸣-mu. **ii 60** ŠE.GA: Exs. 3 and 16 have še-mi-i and ma-ag-ru respectively. **ii 61** ša: Exs. 16, 25, 29 have šá; ex. 50 has ⸢šá⸣. **ii 61** ú-ad-du-ni: Exs. 2, 16, 18, 20 have ú-ad-du-ú; **ii 62**.11 Has an erased ù between KÙ.BABBAR and KÙ.GI. **ii 62** ni-siq-ti: Exs. 10 and 16 have [ni-si-i]q-ti and ni-s[i-iq-ti] respectively. **ii 62** šu-qu-ru-tu: Exs. 10 and 19 have šu-qú-ru-tu and ⸢šu-qú⸣-ru-tu. **ii 62** ḫi-biš-ti: Ex. 10 has ḫi-bì-iš-⸢tu⸣; ex. 17 has ḫi-bi-iš-ti; ex. 29 has ḫi-⸢bi⸣-iš-tu; ex. 35 has ⸢ḫi⸣-bi-i[š-ti/tu]; ex. 50 has ḫi-bì-iš-ti. **ii 63** ḫi-da-a-ti: Ex. 20 has ḫi-da-a-tu. **ii 63** ri-šá-a-ti: Exs. 3, 50 have ri-ša-a-⸢ti⸣; ex. 10 has ri-ša-a-ta; exs. 11–12, 29 have ri-ša-a-ti; ex. 17 has ri-⸢ša-a⸣-ta. **ii 63**.50 Has U after ri-ša-a-⸢ti⸣. **ii 64** e-li: Ex. 11 omits e-li; ex. 16 has ⸢UGU⸣. **ii 64** te-me-en-na: Ex. 2 has ⸢te⸣-me-en-<na>; ex. 12 has te-me-en-DI; exs. 18, 20 have te-me-en-<na>. **iii 64**.17 Adds ša after te-me-en-na. **ii 64** ^{m}na-ra-am-^{d}EN.ZU: Ex. 3 has [^{m}na-ra-am/ram]-⸢^{d}⸣30; ex. 6 has ^{m}na-⸢ra⸣-[am]-^{d}30; ex. 12 has <^{m}>na-⸢ram⸣-^{d}30; ex. 17 has ^{m}na-ra-am-^{d}30; ex. 19 has ^{m}⸢na⸣-ram-^{d}30. **ii 64** DUMU: Ex. 29 has IBILA*. **ii 65** a-ṣe-e: Ex. 17 has a-ṣe-<e>. **ii 65** e-re-bi: Exs. 10, 50 have e-re-bu. **ii 65** ú-kin: Ex. 2 has ⸢ú⸣-ki-in; exs. 10, 23 have ú-⸢ki-in⸣; exs. 3, 6, 11, 17–19, 25, 29, 50 have ú-ki-in; ex. 12 has ⸢ú⸣-[k]i-in; ex. 16 has ú-ki-i[n]. **ii 65** lib-na-at-su: Ex. 2 has li-ib-na-at-su; ex. 10 has [li-i]b-na-at-su; ex. 25 has li-ib-n[a-at-su]; exs. 29, 50 have ⸢li⸣-ib-na-at-su.

iii 1 GIŠ.EREN: Exs. 16 and 18 have respectively GIŠ.EREN.MEŠ and GIŠ.⸢EREN⸣.MEŠ. **iii 1** dan-nu-tu: Ex. 2 has dan-nu$_4$-tim; ex. 10 has ⸢da-nu$_4$⸣-tim; ex. 17 has dan-nu-tum; exs. 18, 23, 25, 29 have da-nu$_4$-tim; ex. 50 has dan-nu-ti. **iii 1** ṣu-lu-li-šú: Ex. 2 has ṣu-lu-li-šu; ex. 12 has [ṣ]u-lu-li-šu; ex. 17 has ṣu-lu-li-ša; ex. 18 has ⸢ṣu⸣-lu-li-šu; ex. 23 has ṣú-⸢lu⸣-li-šu. **iii 1** ú-šat-ri-iṣ: Ex. 23 has ú-šá-at-ri-iṣ. **iii 2** GIŠ.IG.MEŠ: Ex. 23 has GIŠ.IG.GIŠ.IG. **iii 2** ṣi-ra-a-ti: Ex. 3 has ṣi-⸢ra⸣-a-tú; ex. 12 has [ṣi-r]a-a-tú; ex. 16 has ṣi-r[a]-⸢a-tim⸣. **iii 2** as-kup-pu: Ex. 23 has as-ku-up-pu. **iii 3** KÁ.MEŠ-šu: Ex. 11 has KÁ.KÁ-šu; ex. 12 has KÁ.MEŠ-šú; ex. 16 has KÁ.M[EŠ]-⸢šú⸣; ex. 17 has ⸢KÁ⸣.KÁ-šu; ex. 19 has ⸢KÁ.MEŠ-šú⸣. **iii 4** a-di: Ex. 18 has a-di-i. **iii 4** ziq-qur-ra-ti-šú: Exs. 2–3, 6, 10–12, 16, 32 have ziq-qur-ra-ti-šu; ex. 17 has ⸢ziq⸣-qur-⸢ra⸣-ti-šu; ex. 18 has ziq-qur-ra-ti-⸢šu⸣; ex. 20 has [ziq-qur-ra]-⸢ti-šu⸣; ex. 23 has zi-qú-ra-ti-šu; ex. 29 has ziq-qur-⸢ra⸣-ti-⸢šu⸣. **iii 5** eš-ši-iš: Ex. 2 has e-eš-š[i-iš]; exs. 3, 10, 16, 23, 25, 29, 32, 50 have e-eš-ši-iš; ex. 17 has e-e[š-ši-iš]; ex. 18 has ⸢e⸣-[e]š-ši-iš. **iii 5** e-pu-uš-ma: Ex. 10 has e-pú-⸢uš⸣-ma; exs. 16, 23 have e-pú-uš-ma; exs. 25 and 32 have ab-ni-ma and ab-ni-⸢ma⸣. **iii 5** ú-šak-lil: Ex. 2 has ú-šak-li-il; ex. 16 has ú-ša-ak-⸢li⸣-lu; ex. 18 has ú-⸢šak-li⸣-il; ex. 23 has ú-ša-ak-li-il. **iii 5** ši-pí-ir-šu: Exs. 2, 11 have ši-pi-ir-šu; ex. 3 has ši-pir-šu; ex. 18 has ši-pi-ir-⸢šu⸣; ex. 32 has ši-pi-ir-šú. **iii 6** qá-at: Exs. 2, 17 have qá-t[ì]; ex. 3 has qá-⸢tì⸣; exs. 10, 25, 32 have qá-tì; exs. 18, 20, 29 have ⸢qá-tì⸣; ex. 50 has qá-ti. **iii 6** aṣ-bat-ma: Ex. 12 has [a]ṣ-⸢ba⸣-at-ma; exs. 16, 23 have aṣ-ba-at-ma; ex. 17 has [aṣ-ba]-⸢at⸣-ma; ex. 32 has aṣ-ba-a[t-ma]. **iii 6**.16 Has an erasure after ⸢ḫi⸣-da-a-ti. **iii 6** ri-šá-a-ti: Exs. 3, 16, 29 have ri-ša-a-ti; ex. 10 has ri-⸢ša-a⸣-[ti]; ex. 17 has [ri-ša/šá-a]-⸢ta⸣; ex. 20 has ri-šá-a-tú; ex. 50 has ri-ša-⸢a-ti⸣. **iii 7** lìb-bi: Ex. 2 has lib-bi; ex. 20 has ⸢ŠÀ⸣. **iii 7** qé-er-ba-šu: Ex. 16 has qer-ba-ša. **iii 8** ši-ṭi-ir: Ex. 2 has ⸢ši⸣-[ṭi]r; exs. 3, 10, 20, 23 have ši-ṭir; ex. 6 has ši-⸢ṭir⸣; ex. 17 has ši-ṭ[ir?]; ex. 25 has ši-KI-ir. **iii 8** šu-um: Exs. 25, 50 have šu-mi; ex. 29 has ⸢šu⸣-mi; ex. 46 has [šu-m]i. **iii 8** šá: Exs. 2–3, 6, 10, 18, 23, 46, 50 have ša. **iii 8** ^{m}na-ra-am-^{d}30: Exs. 2, 25, 50 have ^{m}na-ra-am-^{d}EN.ZU; ex. 6 has ^{m}na-ram-⸢^{d}EN.ZU⸣; ex. 10 has ^{m}na-ram-^{d}30; ex. 16 has ⸢^{m}⸣na-ra-am-^{d}EN.ZU; ex. 18 has ⸢^{m}na-ra-am⸣-^{d}EN.ZU; ex. 20 has ^{m}na-ra-⸢am-^{d}EN⸣.ZU; ex. 29 has ^{m}⸢na⸣-r[a-a]m-^{d}EN.ZU. **iii 8** a-mu-ur-ma: Ex. 2 has a-mur-⸢ma⸣; exs. 3, 20, 29 have a-mur-ma; ex. 6 has ⸢a-mur⸣-ma; ex. 10 has a-mur-m[a]; exs. 18, 50 have a-⸢mur-ma⸣. **iii 9** ú-nak-ki-ir: Ex. 2 has ⸢ú⸣-na-ak-ki-ir; ex. 16 has ú-na-ak-ki-⸢ir⸣; ex. 20 has ú-nak-kìr; ex. 23 has ú-na-ak-[ki-ir]. **iii 9** ap-šu-uš: Exs. 10, 16 have ap-<šu>-uš. **iii 9** UDU.SÍSKUR: Exs. 2, 18, 20 have UDU.SISKUR; exs. 16, 23 have ni-qu-ú.

iii 10 mu-sa-re-e-a: Exs. 2, 18 have MU.SAR-e-a; ex. 3 has MU.SAR-re-e-a. **iii 10**.16, 20 Have erasures after mu-sa-re-e-a. **iii 10** áš-ku-un-ma: Exs. 2–3 have áš-kun-ma; ex. 6 has ⸢áš-kun-ma⸣. **iii 10** ú-te-er: Exs. 18 and 50 have respectively ú-te$_9$-er and ú-KI-er. **iii 10** áš-ru-uš-šu: Ex. 16 has aš-ru-uš-šu. **iii 11** GAL-ú: Ex. 6 has ⸢GAL⸣; exs. 10, 16, 18–20, 23, 29, 50 have GAL. **iii 11** šá: Ex. 3 has ⸢ša⸣; exs. 10, 18, 23, 25, 29, 50 have ša. **iii 11** KI-tim: Ex. 2 has er-ṣe-ti. **iii 11** nu-úr: Ex. 2 has ⸢nu⸣-ú-ru; exs. 17, 50 have nu-ú-ru; ex. 23 has [nu-ú-r]u. **iii 11** DINGIR.MEŠ: Exs. 3, 16, 20, 23 have DINGIR.DINGIR **iii 11** ab-bé-e-šu: Exs. 29 and 50 have [AD].⸢MEŠ-šu⸣ and AD.MEŠ-šu respectively. **iii 12** lìb-bi: Exs. 2, 10, 16 have lib-bi; ex. 3, 20 have ŠÀ; ex. 17 has lib-⸢bi⸣. **iii 12** ša: Exs. 16, 19 have ⸢šá⸣ and šá. **iii 12** ^{d}EN.ZU: Exs. 6, 19, 48 have ^{d}30. **iii 13** na-ra-mi-ka: Exs. 19 and 48 have respectively ⸢na-ar-mi⸣-ka and na-ar-mi-k[a]. **iii 15** ia-ti: Exs. 2, 17, 32 have ia-a-ti; ex. 3 has ⸢ia-a-ti⸣; ex. 16 has ⸢ia-a-tú⸣; ex. 18 has ia-a-tú; ex. 20 has [ia]-⸢a-ti⸣; ex. 25 has ia-⸢a-ti⸣; ex. 29 has ia-a-⸢ti⸣. **iii 15**.51 Appears to have an erasure before ^{d}AG-NÍ.TUKU. **iii 15** ^{d}AG-NÍ.TUKU: Exs. 23 has ^{d}na-bi-um-na-ʾ[i-id]. **iii 15** TIN.TIR.KI: Ex. 23 has [K]Á.⸢DINGIR⸣.RA.⸢KI⸣. **iii 15** NUN: Exs. 2, 18, 23, 50 have ru-bu-ú. **iii 15** za-ni-in-ka: Exs. 3, 16, 18 have za-nin-ka; ex. 20 has ⸢za⸣-nin-k[a]; ex. 50 has za-nin-⸢ka⸣. **iii 16** lìb-bi-ka: Exs. 2, 10, 16, 18 have lib-bi-ka; ex. 17 has [l]ib-bi-⸢ka⸣; ex. 20 ŠÀ-ka; ex. 23 has [l]i-ib-bi-⸢ka⸣; ex. 32 has lib-⸢bi-ka⸣. **iii 16** e-pí-iš: Exs. 23, 32 have e-pi-iš and e-piš respectively. **iii 17** ép-še-tu-ú-a: Exs. 2, 10–11, 16, 18 have e-ep-še-tu-ú-a; ex. 3 has e-ep-⸢še⸣-tu-ú-a; ex. 17 has ⸢e-ep-še⸣-tu-ú-a. **iii 17** SIG$_5$.MEŠ: Exs. 2, 23, 51 have respectively dam-qá-a-ti, dam-qa-⸢a-ti⸣, and dam-qa-a-ti. **iii 17** na-ap-li-is-ma: Ex. 16 has nap-li-is-ma. **iii 18** u$_4$-mi-šam-ma: Ex. 2 has u$_4$-mi-šá-am-ma; ex. 10 has u$_4$-mì-šam-ma; exs. 16, 50 have u$_4$-mi-šam; ex. 18 has u$_4$-⸢mì?-šam⸣-ma; ex. 20 has [u$_4$-mi]-⸢šam⸣. **iii 18** ni-ip-ḫi: Exs. 2, 32 have ni-ip-ḫu; ex. 51 has [ni]-⸢ip-ḫu⸣. **iii 18** ri-ba: exs. 2–3, 11, 18 have ri-bi; ex. 20 has ⸢ri⸣-bi. **iii 18** šá-ma-mi: Exs. 29, 50 have ša-ma-mi. **iii 18** qá-qá-ri: Ex. 3 has ⸢qaq⸣-qa-ri; exs. 11, 50 have qaq-qa-ri; ex. 20 has qaq-qa[r]; ex. 23 has qaq-qa-[ri]; ex. 32 has qaq-qar. **iii 19** un-nin-

ni-ia: Ex. 3 has *un-*⌜*ni*⌝*-ni-*⌜*ia*⌝.

iii 20 *mu-gu-ur*: Ex. 17 has *m*[*u-ug-r*]*a*. **iii 20** *ta-aṣ-li-ti*: Ex. 20 has *ta-aṣ-*⌜*li*⌝*-tum*. **iii 20** *ki-i-nim*: Ex. 32 has *ki-i-ni*. **iii 21** *šá*: Exs. 10, 18, 25 have *ša*; ex. 14 has *š*[*a*]; exs. 16, 29 have ⌜*ša*⌝. **iii 21** *tu-šat-mi-ḫu*: Ex. 3 has *tu-š*[*at*]*-mi-*RI; exs. 10, 25, 29 have *tu-šat-mi-ḫa*; exs. 11, 16 have *tu-šat-mi-ḫi*; ex. 17 has ⌜*tu-šat*⌝*-mi-ḫi*; ex. 50 has [*t*]*u-šat-mi-ḫa*. **iii 21** *qa-tu-ú-a*: Ex. 2 has *qá-tu-*⌜*ú*⌝*-*[*a*]; ex. 3 has *qá-tu-ú-a*; ex. 16 has *qá-tu-*⌜*ú*⌝*-a*; ex. 20 has ⌜ŠU.II*-ú*⌝*-a*. **iii 21** *lu-bé-el*: Exs. 3, 17, and 20 have respectively [*l*]*u-bi-il*, *lu-bi-il*, and [*lu-bi-i*]*l*. **iii 21** *du-ú-ri*: Exs. 2, 17, 19–20, 50 have *du-ur*; exs. 3, 23 have [*d*]*u-ur*; ex. 16 has *du-*⌜*ur*⌝; ex 18 has *du-ri*; ex. 29 has ⌜*du-ur*⌝. **iii 21**.16 Has an erasure before *da-a-ri*. **iii 22** ^{d}*a-nu-ni-tum*: Ex. 19 has ^{d}*a-nu-*<*ni*>*-tum*. **iii 22** GAŠAN: Exs. 2, 18 have *be-le-et*; exs. 3, 10, 29, 50 have *be-let*; ex. 6 has *be-*⌜*le*⌝*-e*[*t*]; exs. 16–17 have *be-le-*⌜*et*⌝; ex. 23 has [*b*]*e-le-et*; ex. 25 has *be-*[*let*?]. **iii 22** MÈ: Exs. 2, 18 have *ta-ḫa-*⌜*zi*⌝; ex. 3 has *ta-ḫa-z*[*i*]; ex. 10 has ⌜*ta*⌝*-*[*ḫa-zi*]; exs. 16–17 have *ta-ḫa-zi*; ex. 23 has *ta-ḫa-*[*zi*]; exs. 29, 50 have *ta-ḫa-za*. **iii 22** *na-šá-ta*: Ex. 3 has [*n*]*a-šá-at*; ex. 16 has ⌜*na*⌝*-šá-at*; ex. 17 has *na-*ZA*-a-ta*; exs. 18, 20 have *na-šá-at*; exs. 23, 29 have *na-šá-a-ta*; ex. 46 has *na-ša-a-t*[*a*]; ex. 50 has *na-šá-*⌜*a-ta*⌝. **iii 22** *iš-pa-ti*: Ex. 3 has *iš-pa-tum*; ex. 19 has *iš-pa-ta*; ex. 29 has [*i*]*š-pa-*⌜*ta*⌝; ex. 32 has *iš-pa-*⌜*ta*⌝; ex. 50 has ⌜*iš*⌝*-pa-ta*. **iii 23** *mu-šal-li-ma-at*: Ex. 2 has *mu-šal-li-ma-*(over erasure)*-at*; ex. 6 has [*m*]*u-šal-li-mat*; ex. 23 has *mu-šá-al-li-ma-*⌜*at*⌝; ex. 48 has [*mu-š*]*al-li-mat*. **iii 23** *qí-bi-it*: Exs. 2, 6, 18, 29, 50 have *qí-bit*; ex. 3 has *qí-*⌜*bit*⌝; ex. 16 has ⌜*qí*⌝*-bit*; ex. 23 has [*qí-b*]*i-ti*; ex. 40 ⌜*qí-bit*⌝. **iii 24** LÚ.*na-ak-ru*: Exs. 2–3, 6, 11, 18–19 have *na-ak-ru*; ex. 10 has *n*[*ak-ri*]; ex. 16 has *na-ak-*⌜*ru*⌝; ex. 17 has *na-ak-ri*; ex. 23 has *na-*[*a*]*k-ri*; ex. 25 has *nak-r*[*i*]; ex. 29 has *nak-ri*; ex. 40 has ⌜*nak-ri*⌝; ex. 50 has IŠ*-ri*. **iii 24** *mu-ḫal-li-qa-at*: Exs. 23, 40 have respectively [*mu-ḫa*]*-al-l*[*i-qa-at*] and *mu-ḫal-*⌜*li-qá-at*⌝. **iii 24** *ra-ag-gu*: Ex. 3 has <*ra*>*-ag-gu*; exs. 11, 17, 20 have *rag-gu*; ex. 18 has *rag-*⌜*gu*⌝; ex. 29 has ⌜*ra*⌝*-ag-ga*; ex. 32 has *rag-*⌜*gu*⌝; ex. 50 has *ra-ag-ga*. **iii 25**.11 Has an erasure between *a-li-ka-at* and *maḫ-ri*. **iii 25** *maḫ-ri*: Ex. 2 has *ma-aḫ-ru*; ex. 10 has *m*[*a-aḫ-ri*]; ex. 23 has *ma-aḫ-r*[*i*]; ex. 25 has ⌜*ma*⌝*-*[*aḫ-ri*]; exs. 29, 50 have *ma-aḫ-ri*; ex. 40 has *ma-*⌜*aḫ*⌝*-ri*. **iii 25** *ša*: Exs. 6, 19 have *šá*. **iii 25** DINGIR.DINGIR: Exs. 11, 18–19 have DINGIR.MEŠ. **iii 26** *ša*: Exs. 6, 19 have *šá*. **iii 26** *i-na*: Ex. 11 omits *i-na*. **iii 26** ^{d}UTU.È: Ex. 2 has ^{d}UTU.È.A. **iii 26** *ú-dam-ma-qu*: Ex. 2 has [*ú-d*]*a-am-ma-qu*; ex. 3 has ⌜*ú*⌝*-da-am-ma-*⌜*qu*⌝; ex. 16 ⌜*ú-da-am-ma-qu*⌝; exs. 17–19 have *ú-da-am-ma-qu*; ex. 20 has [*ú-d*]*am-ma-*⌜*qa*⌝; ex. 32 has *ú-da-am-ma-*⌜*qu*⌝. **iii 26** *it-ta-tu-ú-a*: Ex. 25 has *it-*<*ta*>*-*⌜*tu-ú*⌝*-*[*a*]. **iii 27** *šá* (first instance): Exs. 2, 11, 16–18 have *ša*; exs. 3, 32 have ⌜*ša*⌝; ex. 6 has [*š*]*a*. **iii 27** ZIMBIR.KI-^{d}*a-nu-ni-tum*: Ex. 32 has ZIMBIR.⌜KI⌝-^{d}*a-nun-*⌜*ni*⌝*-tum*. **iii 27** *šá* (second instance): Ex. 2 has [*š*]*a*; exs. 10–11, 17–18, 23, 32, 50 have *ša*; exs. 16, 20, 25 have ⌜*ša*⌝. **iii 27** MU.AN.NA.MEŠ: Exs. 2, 16, 20 have MU.MEŠ. **iii 28** ^{m}*šà-ga-rak-ti-šur*-ia-áš*: Ex. 1 has ^{m}*šà-ga-rak-ti-*BUR*-ia-*ÍA; exs. 2–3, 16–18 have ^{m}*šag-*BI-<*rak*>*-ti-*BUR*-ia-áš*; ex. 6 has ^{m}*šà-ga-*⌜*rak-ti*⌝*-*BUR*-*⌜*ia*⌝*-àš*; exs. 11, 50 have ^{m}*šà-ga-rak-ti-*BUR*-ia-áš*; ex. 12 has [^{m}*šà-g*]*a-rak-ti-*BUR*-ia-áš* ; ex. 19 has ^{m}*šà-*^{ga}*gar-rak-ti-*BUR*-ia-áš*; ex. 20 has ^{m}*šag-*BI-<*rak*>*-ti-*BUR*-ia-*⌜*áš*⌝; ex. 25 has ^{m}*šà-ga-rak-ti-*BUR*-*⌜*ia-àš*⌝; ex. 29 has [^{m}*šà-g*]*a-rak-ti-*BUR*-ia-àš*; ex. 32 has ⌜^{m}*šà*⌝*-ga-rak-ti-*⌜BUR*-ia-àš*⌝; ex. 38 has ^{m}*šà-ga-rak-*⌜*ti*⌝*-*BUR*-*⌜*ia*⌝*-àš*; ex. 40 has ^{m}*šà-ga-rak-ti-*BUR*-ia*⌝*-á*[*š*]. **iii 29** ^{m}NÍG.GUB-^{d}EN.LÍL: Exs. 17, 19 have ^{m}*ku-dúr-ri-*^{d}EN.LÍL. **iii 29** *i-pu-šu*: Ex. 19 has *i-pú-*⌜MA⌝; ex. 32 has ⌜*i-pú-šu*⌝; ex. 38 has *i-pú-šu*.

iii 30 *te-me-en-šu*: Exs. 2, 16 have [*t*]*e-me-en-šú* and *te-me-en-šú* respectively. **iii 30** *la-bi-ri*: Exs. 19 and 32 have respectively *la-bí-ri* and ⌜*la*⌝*-bí-ri*. **iii 30** *aḫ-tu-uṭ-ma*: Exs. 17, 20 have *aḫ-ṭu-*<*uṭ*>*-ma*. **iii 31** *te-me-en-na*: Exs. 2, 16, 18 have *te-me-en-*<*na*>. **iii 31** Exs. 2, 16, 50 add *šá* after *te-me-en-*<*na*>; ex. 33 has *ša*. **iii 31** ^{m}*šà-ga-rak-ti-šur*-ia-áš*: Ex. 1 has ^{m}*šà-ga-rak-ti-*BUR*-*⌜*ia*⌝*-áš*; exs. 2–3, 16–18 have ^{m}*šag-*BI-<*rak*>*-ti-*BUR*-ia-áš*; ex. 6 has ^{m}*šà-*⌜*ga-rak-ti-*BUR⌝*-ia-áš*; exs. 11, 19, 40 have ^{m}*šà-ga-rak-ti-*BUR*-ia-áš*; ex. 12 has [^{m}*š*]*à-ga-rak-ti-*BUR*-ia-áš*; ex. 20 has ^{m}⌜*šag-*BI⌝-<*rak*>*-ti-*⌜BUR*-ia-áš*⌝; ex. 25 has ^{m}*šà-*⌜*ga*⌝*-rak-ti-*BUR*-ia-àš*; ex. 29 has [^{m}*šà-ga-rak-t*]*i-*BUR*-ia-àš*; ex. 32 has ^{m}*šà-ga-rak-ti-*⌜BUR⌝*-*[*ia-àš*]; ex. 33 has ^{m}*šà-g*[*a-rak-ti-*BUR*-ia-àš*]; ex. 38 has [^{m}*šà-g*]*a-*⌜*rak*⌝*-ti-*BUR*-ia-a-*⌜*àš*⌝; ex. 50 has ^{m}*šà-ga-rak-*⌜*ti*⌝*-*BUR*-ia-áš*. **iii 31** Ex. 3 has an additional DIŠ before ^{m}NÍG.GUB-{d}EN.LÍL. **iii 31** ^{m}NÍG.GUB-^{d}EN.LÍL: Exs. 2, 18–19 have ^{m}*ku-dúr-ri-*^{d}EN.LÍL, ^{m}*ku-dúr-ri-*^{d}EN.⌜LÍL⌝, and ^{m}*ku-dúr-ri-*^{d}⌜EN.LÍL⌝ respectively. **iii 32** *ú-ki-in*: Exs. 6, 20 have *ú-*⌜*kin*⌝ and *ú-kin*. **iii 32** *lib-na-at-su*: Ex. 50 has *lib-na-*SI*-su*. **iii 33** *šá-a-šu*: Ex. 2 has *šu-a-tum*; ex. 11 has *šu-a-tim*; ex. 16 has *ša-a-ša*; ex. 17 has *šu-a-t*[*i*]; ex. 18 ⌜*šu*⌝*-a-tu*; ex. 19 has ⌜*ša*⌝*-a-šu*; ex. 32 has *šu-*⌜*a*⌝*-tim*. **iii 33** *eš-šiš*: Exs. 2, 16, 18, 20, 25, 32, 50 have *e-eš-ši-iš*; ex. 3 has [(*e*)*-eš-ši*]*-*⌜*iš*⌝; exs. 11, 19, 33 have *eš-ši-iš*; ex. 17 has [(*e*)]*-eš-ši-iš*; ex. 38 has ex. 3 has [(*e*)*-eš-ši*]*-iš*. **iii 33** *e-pu-uš-ma*: Ex. 1 omits the *-ma*; exs. 3, 16, 19–20, 40, 50 have *e-pú-uš-ma*; ex. 25 has *e-pú-uš-*⌜*ma*⌝; ex. 32 has ⌜*e*⌝*-pú-uš-ma*; ex. 38 has *e-pú-*⌜*uš-ma*⌝. **iii 33** *ú-šak-lil*: Ex. 16 has *ú-šak-l*[*i-il*]; ex. 17 has *ú-ša-*[*ak-l*]*i-il*; ex. 19 has *ú-šak-*⌜*li-il*⌝; ex. 32 has *ú-ša-ak-li-il*. **iii 33** *ši-pí-ir-šú*: Ex. 2 has *ši-pi-ir-šu*; exs. 3, 16–17, 20 have *ši-pí-ir-šu*; exs. 6, 11 have *ši-pir-šú*; ex. 18 has *ši-pí-ir-š*[*u*]; ex. 19 has ⌜*ši-pir*⌝*-š*[*u*]; ex. 25 has ⌜*ši-pí-ir*⌝*-*[*šu*?]; ex. 32 has *ši-*⌜*pí*⌝*-ir-šu*; ex. 50 has *ši-pí-*⌜*ir*⌝*-š*[*u*]. **iii 34** ^{d}*a-nu-ni-tum*: Ex. 16 has ^{d}*a-nun-ni-tum*. **iii 34** GAŠAN: Exs. 2, 6, 18–19 have *be-let*; exs. 16–17, 32, 38 have *be-le-et*. **iii 34** MÈ: Exs. 2, 17–18, 32 have *ta-ḫa-zi*; exs. 3, 16 have *ta-ḫa-za*; ex. 38 has *ta-ḫa-*⌜*zi*⌝. **iii 34** *mu-šal-li-mat*: Ex. 1 omits the *-šal-*; ex. 16 has *mu-šal-li-ma-*[*at*]; ex. 17 has *mu-šal-li-ma-*⌜*at*⌝; exs. 18–19 have *mu-šal-li-ma-at*; ex. 32 has *mu-ša-al-li-ma-at*; ex. 38 has [*mu-šal-l*]*i-*⌜*ma*⌝*-at*. **iii 34** *qí-bit*: Exs. 17, 32 have *qí-bi-it*; ex. 20 has *qí-*⌜*bi-it*⌝; ex. 25 has ⌜*qí*⌝*-bi-it*. **iii 34** *a-bi-šu*: Exs. 6, 11–12, 20 have *a-bi-šú*; ex. 16 has *a-bi-*⌜*šú*⌝. **iii 35** LÚ.*na-ak-ru*: Exs. 2, 11, 16, 19–20, 25, 32, 38, 50 have *na-ak-ru*; ex. 6 has *na-*⌜*ak-ru*⌝; ex. 17 has LÚ.KÚR; ex. 18 has *na-*⌜*ak*⌝*-ru*; ex. 33 has *na-ak-*⌜*ru*⌝. **iii 35** *mu-ḫal-li-qa-at*: Ex. 17 has *mu-ḫa-a*[*l*]*-*⌜*li*⌝*-qa-at*. **iii 35** *rag-gu*: Exs. 3, 19, 32, 38 have *ra-ag-ga*; exs. 6, 12 have *ra-ag-gu*; ex. 16 has [*r*]*a-ag-g*[*a*]; ex. 18 has *ra-ag-*⌜*gu*⌝. **iii 36** *maḫ-ri*: Ex. 17 has *ma-aḫ-ru*; exs. 32, 38 have *ma-aḫ-ri*. **iii 36** *šá*: Exs. 17, 32, 40 have ⌜*ša*⌝; exs. 19–20, 25, 38, 50 have *ša*. **iii 36** DINGIR.MEŠ: Exs. 19–20, 38, 50 have DINGIR.DINGIR; ex. 32 has ⌜DINGIR⌝.DINGIR. **iii 36** *ú-šar-ma-a*: Exs. 17, 38 have *ú-ša-ar-ma-a*; ex. 32 has ⌜*ú-ša-ar*⌝*-ma-a*. **iii 36** *šu-ba-at-su*: Exs. 2–3, 11–12, 18, 20, 50 have *šu-bat-su*; exs. 16, 40 have *šu-bat-s*[*u*]; ex. 25 has ⌜*šu-bat-su*⌝. **iii 37** *nin-da-bé-e*: Ex. 17 has *ni-in-*⌜*da*⌝*-*[*bé-e*]. **iii 37** *šá*: Exs. 2–3, 17, 19, 25, 40, 50 have *ša*; exs. 16, 20 have [*š*]*a*; ex. 18 has ⌜*ša*⌝. **iii 37** *maḫ-ri*: Ex. 2 has *ma-*⌜*ḫar*⌝; ex. 17 has *ma-ḫa-ar*; ex. 18 has *ma-aḫ-*⌜*ri*⌝; ex. 19 has *ma-*⌜*aḫ*⌝*-ri*; ex. 32 has ⌜*ma*⌝*-aḫ-ri*. **iii 37** *ú-šá-te-er-ma*: Ex. 16 has *ú-ša-te-er-m*[*a*]; ex. 17 has *ú-*⌜*ša*⌝*-*[*te-er-ma*]; ex. 18 has *ú-ša-t*[*e-e*]*r-ma*; exs. 19, 32 have *ú-ša-te-er-ma*; exs. 20, 25 have *ú-ša-te$_{9}$-er-ma*; ex. 33 has [*ú-š*]*a-te-*⌜*er*⌝*-ma*; ex. 50 has ⌜*ú*⌝*-ša-te$_{9}$-*⌜*er*⌝*-ma*. **iii 38** *ú-kin*: Exs. 2, 25, 32, 50 have *ú-*⌜*ki*⌝*-in*; ex. 3 has [*ú-ki-i*]*n*; exs. 11–12, 17, 19–20, 38 have *ú-ki-in*; ex. 16 has ⌜*ú*⌝*-ki-*⌜*in*⌝; exs. 18, 33 have *ú-ki-*⌜*in*⌝; ex. 40 has ⌜*ú-ki-in*⌝. **iii 38** *ma-ḫar-šú*: Ex. 2 has *ma-ḫar-*⌜*šu*⌝; exs. 3, 38 have *ma-ḫa-ar-šu*; exs. 11–12, 50 have *ma-ḫar-šu*; ex. 16 has [*ma*]*-*⌜*ḫa-ar*⌝*-*[*šu*]; ex. 17 has *ma-ḫa-*[*a*]*r-*[*šu*]; exs. 18, 40 have ⌜*ma-ḫar-šu*⌝; ex. 19 has *ma-ḫa-ar-*⌜*šu*⌝; ex. 20 has [*ma*]*-ḫar-*⌜*šu*⌝; ex. 25 has *m*[*a-ḫar*]*-šu*; ex. 32 has ⌜*ma*⌝*-ḫa-ar-*⌜*šu*⌝. **iii 38** ^{d}*a-nu-ni-tum*: Ex. 16 has ^{d}*a-nun-*[*ni-tu*]*m*?. **iii 38** GAŠAN: Ex. 17 has ⌜*be-el-tum*⌝; ex. 32 has ⌜*be*⌝*-el-ti*; ex. 38 has *be-el-ti*; ex. 40 has *be-let*; ex. 50 has *be-*⌜*el-ti*⌝. **iii 38** GAL*-ti*: Ex. 6 has ⌜*ra-bi-ti*⌝; ex. 11 has *ra-bi-ti*; ex. 17 has ⌜*ra-bi*⌝*-*[*ti*]; ex. 32 has *ra-bi-tum*; ex. 38 has ⌜*ra*⌝*-bi-ti*. **iii 39** *šu-a-tim*: Ex. 2 has ⌜*šu-a-tu*⌝; ex. 6 has [*š*]*u-*⌜*a*⌝*-tú*; ex. 16 has *šu-*⌜*a-tú*⌝; ex. 18 has ⌜*šu-a*⌝*-tu*; ex. 19 has *ša-a-š*[*u*]; ex. 20 has <*šu*>*-a-t*[*im*]; ex. 25 has [*š*]*u-*⌜*a-šu*⌝; ex. 40 has *šá-a-tú*; ex. 50 has *šá-a-šu*.

iii 40 *ép-še-tu-ú-a*: Exs. 2, 20, 38, 50 have *e-ep-še-tu-ú-a*; ex. 3 has ⌜*e-ep*⌝*-*[*še-tu-ú-a*]; ex. 16 has *e-*⌜*ep-še-tu*⌝*-ú-a*; ex. 17 has ⌜*e*⌝*-e*[*p-še*]*-*⌜*tu*⌝*-ú-a*; ex. 18 has *e-ep-še-*⌜*tu*⌝*-ú-a*; ex. 25 has *e-ep-*⌜*še-tu*⌝*-ú-a*; ex. 32 has [*e-e*]*p-še-*⌜*tu-ú-a*⌝; ex. 40 has ⌜*e-ep-še-tu-ú-a*⌝. **iii 40** SIG$_{5}$.MEŠ: Ex. 16 has *dam-qa-a-ti*; ex. 17 has *da-am-qá-a-*[*ti*]; ex. 25 has ⌜*da-am-qá*⌝*-a-ti*; ex. 32 has ⌜*dam*⌝*-qa-a-ti*; ex. 40 has [*da-am*]*-*⌜*qá-a-ti*⌝; ex. 50 has [*d*]*a-am-qá-a-ti*. **iii 40** *na-ap-li-si-ma*: Ex. 20 has *nap-l*[*i-s*]*i-*[*ma*]. **iii 41** *ár-ḫi-šam-ma*: Exs. 2, 16, 18, 20, 25 have ⌜*ar*⌝*-ḫi-šam-ma*; ex. 3 has *ar-ḫi-š*[*am-ma*]; ex. 17 has ⌜*ar-ḫi-šam*⌝*-ma*; ex. 29 has *a*[*r-ḫi-šam-ma*]; ex. 32 has ⌜*ar-ḫi*⌝*-šam-*⌜*ma*⌝; ex. 38 has *ar-ḫi-šá-am-ma*; ex. 50 has [*a*]*r-ḫi-*⌜*šam*⌝*-ma*. **iii 41**

^{d}UTU.È: Ex. 20 has ^{d}UTU.DU. **iii 42** *šu-uq-ri-ba*: Ex. 3 has [*šu-uq-r*]*i-bi*; ex. 16 has *šu-uq-ri-*[*b*]*i*; ex. 17 has *šu-*[*u*]*q-ri-bi*; ex. 23 has *šu-*⸢*uq*⸣*-ri-bi*; exs. 25, 32, 38, 50 have *šu-uq-ri-bi*. **iii 42** SIG$_{5}$-*tì*: Exs. 3, 32, 38 have *da-mi-iq-ti*; ex. 16 has *da-mi-i*[*q-tì*]; ex. 17 has *d*[*a*]*-mi-*⸢*iq*⸣*-tì*; ex. 18 has *da-mi-iq-tì*. **iii 43** *man-nu*: Ex. 23 has *ma-an-nu*. **iii 43** *šá*: Exs. 2, 16–18, 25, 32 have *ša*; exs. 3, 50 have ⸢*ša*⸣; ex. 29 has [*š*]*a*. **iii 43** ^{d}30: Exs. 2, 16, 18, 20, 29, 32, 50 have ^{d}EN.ZU; ex. 17 has ^{d}E[N.Z]U; ex. 25 has ^{d}EN.[ZU]; ex. 38 has ⸢^{d}EN.ZU⸣ **iii 43** LUGAL-*ú-tu*: Ex. 3 has [LUGAL]-*ú-ti*; ex. 16 has LUGAL-*ú-*[*t*]*i*$^{?}$; ex. 17 has *šar-ru-ú-t*[*u*]; exs. 18, 23, 25, 38 have LUGAL-*ú-ti*; ex. 32 has LUGAL-*ú-*⸢*ti*⸣; ex. 50 has [LUGAL]-⸢*ú*⸣*-ti*. **iii 44** *pa-le-e-šú*: Exs. 2–3, 16–17, 20, 38 have *pa-le-e-šu*; ex. 18 has *pa-*⸢*le*⸣*-e-šu*; ex. 25 has *pa-le-*KAL-*šu*; ex. 32 has *pa-le-e-*⸢*šu*⸣; ex. 50 has [*pa*]-⸢*le-e*⸣*-šu*. **iii 44** *šu-a-tim*: Exs. 17, 18 have *šu-a-*⸢*ti*⸣ and *šu-a-tu* respectively. **iii 44** *eš-šiš*: Exs. 11, 19, 32 have *eš-ši-iš*; ex. 20 has *e-eš-*⸢*ši*⸣*-i*[*š*]; ex. 38 has *e-eš-ši-iš*; ex. 50 has *e-*⸢*eš*⸣*-ši-iš*. **iii 44** *ip-pu-šu*: Ex. 38 has *i-ip-pu-šu*. **iii 45** *mu-sa-ru-ú*: Exs. 17, 20 have MU.SAR-*ru-ú*; ex. 25 has ⸢MU.SAR-*ru*⸣*-ú*. **iii 45** *ši-ṭir*: Ex. 2 has ⸢*ši-ṭi-ir*⸣; exs. 3, 11, 16–18, 20, 38, 50 have *ši-ṭi-ir*; ex. 32 has *ši-*⸢*ṭi*⸣*-ir*. **iii 45** *li-mur-ma*: Ex. 2 has ⸢*li-mu-ur*⸣*-ma*; ex. 3 has [*li-mu-u*]*r-ma*; ex. 12 has [*l*]*i-*⸢*mu*⸣*-ur-ma*; ex. 16 has *li-mu-*⸢*ur*⸣-[*ma*]; ex. 17 has *li-mu-ur-*⸢*ma*⸣; exs. 18–19, 25, 29, 38 have *li-mu-ur-ma*; ex. 32 has ⸢*li-mu-ur-ma*⸣. **iii 45** Ex. 50 has an erasure before *la*. **iii 45** *ú-nak-ka-ar*: Ex. 23 has ⸢*ú*⸣*-na-ak-k*[*a-ar*]; ex. 32 has *ú-na-ak-ka-ar*; ex. 38 has *ú-na-ak-ka-*⸢*ar*⸣. **iii 46** *lip-šu-uš*: Ex. 2 has *li-ip-*⸢*šu*⸣-[*u*]*š*; ex. 3 has *li-ip-šu-u*[*š*]; exs. 16, 18, 32, 38 have *li-ip-šu-uš*. **iii 46** UDU.SÍSKUR: Exs. 16, 18 have UDU.SISKUR; exs. 32, 38 have *ni-qu-ú*. **iii 46** *li-iq-qí*: Ex. 2 has BAL-*qí*; exs. 10–11, 29, 50 have *li-iq-qu*. **iii 47** *mu-sa-ru-ú*: Exs. 2, 17 have *mu-sa-re-*⸢*e*⸣; ex. 3 has *mu-*⸢*sa-re*⸣-[*e*]; exs. 6, 38 have *mu-sa-re-e*; ex. 16 has [*mu-sa-r*]*e-*⸢*e*⸣; ex. 20 has [MU.S]AR-*re-e*; ex. 23 has *mu-sa-*⸢*re*⸣*-e*; ex. 25 has [*mu-sa*]-⸢*re*⸣*-e-*⸢*a*⸣; ex. 29 has *mu-sa-*⸢*re-e*⸣*-a*; ex. 32 has ⸢*mu-sa*⸣*-re-*⸢*e*⸣; ex. 50 has [*m*]*u-*⸢*sa*⸣*-re-e*. **iii 47** *ši-ṭir*: Ex. 2 has [*ši*]-⸢*ṭi*⸣*-ir*; exs. 11, 18–19, 25, 32, 38, 50 have *ši-ṭi-ir*; ex. 17 has *š*[*i*]-⸢*ṭi-ir*⸣; ex. 20 has *ši-ṭi-*⸢*ir*⸣; ex. 23 has *ši-*⸢*ṭi-ir*⸣; ex. 29 has *ši-*⸢KI-*ir*⸣. **iii 47** *šu-mi-šú*: Exs. 3, 10–11, 13, 17, 19, 25, 29, 32, 50 have *šu-mi-šu*; ex. 12 has ⸢*šu*⸣*-mi-šu*; ex. 18 has *šu-*⸢*mi-šu*⸣; ex. 20 has ⸢*šu*⸣-[*mi-š*]*u*; ex. 23 has [*šu-mi-š*]*u*; ex. 38 has *šu-mi-*⸢*šu*⸣. **iii 47** *liš-kun-ma*: Ex. 2 has *li-iš-kun-m*[*a*]; ex. 3 has *li-iš-*⸢*ku*⸣*-u*[*n-ma*]; ex. 6 has [*li-iš*]-⸢*ku*⸣*-un-ma*; exs. 11–12 have *liš-ku-un-ma*; exs. 16, 18, 29, 38 have *li-iš-ku-un-ma*; ex. 17 has ⸢*li-iš*⸣*-ku-un-*⸢*ma*⸣; ex. 19 has *li-i*[*š-ku-un/kun-ma*]; ex. 20 has *li-*[*iš-k*]*u-un-ma*; ex. 23 has *li-iš-ku-un-m*[*a*]; ex. 32 has *li-iš-*⸢*kun-ma*⸣; ex. 50 has [*li-iš-k*]*u-un-ma*. **iii 47** *lu-ter*: Ex. 2, 6, 11, 16–17, 20, 32, 38, 50 have *lu-te-er*; exs. 19, 25 have ⸢*lu*⸣*-te-er*; ex. 23 has [*lu*]-*te-er*; ex. 29 has ⸢*lu-te*⸣*-er*. **iii 47** *áš-ru-uš-šu*: Ex. 10 has *áš-ru-uš*-MA; ex. 16 has *aš-ru-uš-šu*; ex. 32 has *aš-*⸢*ru*⸣*-uš-*⸢*šu*⸣; ex. 38 has *aš-ru-uš-*⸢*šu*⸣. **iii 48** ^{d}*a-nu-ni-tum*: Ex. 20 has ^{d}*a-*<*nu*>*-ni-tum*. **iii 48** *su-pu-ú-šu*: Ex. 2 has *su-pu-šu*; ex. 3 has [*s*]*u-pu-ú-šú*; ex. 6 has ⸢*su*⸣*-pe-e-šu*; ex. 16 has *su-pu-ú-šú*; ex. 19 has *su-pe-e-šu*; ex. 50 has *su-pu-ú-*<*šu*>. **iii 48** *li-iš-mu-ú*: Ex. 2 has *liš-*⸢*mu*⸣*-ú*; exs. 3, 6, 10-11, 16–17, 19–20, 25, 20, 50 have *liš-mu-ú*. **iii 49** *li-im-gu-ra*: exs. 11, 23, 32 have *li-im-gu-ru*; ex. 16 has *li-im-gu-r*[*u*$^{?}$]; ex. 25 has ⸢*li-im*⸣*-gu-ru*; exs. 29, 38 have ⸢*li*⸣*-im-gu-ru*; ex. 50 has [*li*]-*im-gu-ru*. **iii 49** *qí-bit-su*: Ex. 38 has *qí-bi-it-su*. **iii 49** *i-da-a-šú*: Exs. 2, 17, 19, 23, 29, 32 have *i-da-a-šu*; ex. 20 has *i-*⸢*da*⸣*-a-šu*; ex. 38 has [*i-d*]*a-a-šu*; ex. 50 has [*i-d*]*a-*⸢*a*⸣*-šu*. **iii 49** *lil-li-ku*: ex. 11 has *lil-li-ka*; ex. 17 has *lil-*⸢*li*⸣*-ka*; exs. 20, 23, 32, 38, 50 have *li-il-li-ku*; ex. 29 has *li-il-li-*⸢*ku*⸣. **iii 50** *li-šá-am-qí-ta*: Ex. 2 has *li-ša-am-*⸢*qí*⸣*-it*; ex. 3 has ⸢*li-šam-qí*⸣*-t*[*a*]; ex. 10 has [*l*]*i-šam-qí-tu*; exs. 11, 25, 50 have *li-šam-qí-tu*; ex. 12 has *li-šá-am-qí-ta*; exs. 16, 20 have *li-šam-qí-ta*; ex. 18 has *l*[*i*]*-šam-qit*; ex. 23 has *li-ša-am-qí-tu*; ex. 29 has *li-šam-*⸢*qí*⸣*-tu*; ex. 32 has *li-*⸢*šam*⸣*-qí-tu*; ex. 38 has [*li-ša-a*]*m-qí-tu*. **iii 50** *ga-ri-šú*: Exs. 2, 6, 10–11, 16, 20, 23, 29, 32, 38, 50 have *ga-ri-šu*; ex. 17 has *ga-*⸢*ri*⸣*-šu*; ex. 18 has TA-*ri-šú*; ex. 25 has *ga-ri-š*[*u*]. **iii 50** *u*$_{4}$*-mi-šam-ma*: Exs. 2, 23 have *u*$_{4}$*-mi-šá-am-ma*; ex. 16 has *u*$_{4}$*-mi-šam*; ex. 17 has *u*$_{4}$*-mì-šam-ma*; ex. 18 has *u*$_{4}$*-mu-šam-ma*; ex. 20 has ⸢*u*$_{4}$*-mi*⸣*-šam*; ex. 32 has DI-*mi-šam-ma*; ex. 50 has [*u*$_{4}$*-mi-š*]*am*. **iii 50** ^{d}EN.ZU: Exs. 3, 6, 29 have ^{d}30; ex. 17 has ^{d}⸢30⸣; ex. 50 has ⸢a-na ^{d}EN.BI⸣ **iii 51** *ba-ni-šu-un*: Ex. 2 has *ba-ni-ši-na* (with *-ši-na* over an erased *-šu-un*); exs. 3, 20 have *ba-ni-ši-na*; ex. 18 has *ba-ni-šú-nu*. **iii 51** *da-mi-iq-ta-šú*: Exs. 2, 17, 23, 32 have *da-mi-iq-ta-šu*; ex. 10 has [*da-mi-iq-ta*]-*šu*; ex. 20 has SIG$_{5}$-*tì-šu*; ex. 29 has *da-*⸢*mi*⸣*-iq-ta-šu*; ex. 50 has [*da-mi-i*]*q-ta-šu*. **iii 51** *li-iq-bu-ú*: Ex. 2 has *liq-ba-a*; exs. 3, 6, 11–12, 17 have *liq-bu-ú*; ex. 19 has *liq-*⸢*bu*⸣-[*ú*]; ex. 20 has *liq-ba-a'-šú*; ex. 29 has *liq-bu-*⸢*ú*⸣; ex. 50 has *liq-*⸢*bu-ú*⸣.

Nabonidus No. 32

i 1.11 [^{m}]⸢^{d}AG⸣-I for ^{md}AG-NÍ.TUKU. **i 2**.6 *za-nin* for *za-ni-in*. **i 10**.6, 11 ^{m}*šul-gi* for ^{md}*šul-gi*. **i 11**.4 I-*sa-re-e* for *mu-sa-re-e*. **i 12**.6, 11 ^{m}*šul-gi* for ^{md}*šul-gi*. **i 13**.11 *ziq-qur-ra-ti* for *ziq-qur-rat*. **i 15**.6, 11 ^{m}*šul-gi* for ^{md}*šul-gi*. **i 16**.1 *šu-a-tú* for *šu-a-ti*. **i 17**.1, 6 *il-lik-ma* for *il-li-ik-ma*. **i 18**.11 *te-*⸢*me-en*⸣ for *te-me-en-na*. **i 19**.6 ^{m}*šul-gi* for ^{md}*šul-gi*. **i 22**.11 *i-*<*na*> for *i-na*. **i 22**.9–10, 12–13 *u* for *ù*. **i 23**.4–6, 9–13 *ba-ta-aq-šu* for *ba-ta-aq-šú*. **i 24**.6, 11 *ù* for *u*. i 25.3 *é-giš-nu-gál* for *é-giš-nu*$_{11}$*-gál*.

ii 3.6 *be-lí* for EN. **ii 6**.6 *a-šib* for *a-ši-ib*. **ii 6**.11 *é-giš-nu*$_{11}$*-gál* for AN-*e* GAL.MEŠ. **ii 12**.6 ⸢*šap*⸣*-tu-uk-ka* for *šap-tuk-ka*. **ii 14**.4–5, 8–10, 12–13 GAL-*tú* for GAL-*ti*. **ii 15**.11 *šu-uš-ki-in-ma* for *šu-uš-ki-in-ma*. **ii 17**.6 *iš-da-šu-nu* for *iš-da-šú-nu*. **ii 18**.4–5, 8–10, 12–13 *ia-a-ti* for *ia-ti*. **ii 19**.14 [^{m}]⸢^{d}⸣AG-NÍ.TUKU for ^{md}AG-I LUGAL. **ii 19**.6 *ra-bi-ti* for GAL-*ti*. **ii 22**.6, 12 have respectively *ru*-BI-*ti* and *ru-qu-tu* for *ru-qu-ti*. **ii 24**.6 *pu-luḫ-tú* for *pu-luḫ-ti*. **ii 25**.4, 11–13 GAL-*tú* for GAL-*ti*. **ii 26**.11 *ḫi-ṭi-tú* for *ḫi-ṭi-ti*.

Nabonidus No. 47

i 1.2 ^{d}15 for ^{d}IŠ.TAR. **i 3**.2 *ma-a-tu* for KUR. **i 4**.2 *ina* for *i-na*. **i 5**.2 ^{d}15 for ^{d}INANNA. **i 8**.2 *i-šu-u* for *i-šu-ú*. **i 11**.1 *ú-šab-ra-an-*<*ni*> for *ú-šab-ra-an-n*[*i*]. **i 12**.2 KASKAL.II.KI for URU.KASKAL. **i 12**.2 *ḫa-*⸢*an-ṭi-iš*⸣ for *ḫa-an-ṭiš*. **i 16**.2 *ma-ḫa-zu* for *ma-ḫa-zi*. **i 12**.2 DINGIR-ti-*šu* for DINGIR-*ú-ti-šu*. **i 17**.2 GAL-*tú* for GAL-*ti*. **i 12**.2 *ú-gal-li-lu-u'* for *ú-gal-li-lu*. **i 18**.2 *e-ze-es-sú* for *e-ze-es-su*. **i 18**.1 Omits GAL-*tú*. **i 20**.2 *i-ta-na-kal* for *i-ta-na-ka-lu*. **i 21**.2 *su-gu-u* for SU.GU$_{7}$-*ú*. **i 22**.2 *ú-ṣa-ḫi-ri* for *ú-ṣa-aḫ-ḫi-ir*. **i 23**.2 URU-*ía* for URU-*ia*. **i 24**.2 URU.*te-ma-a'* for URU.*te-ma-a*. **i 24**.1 URU.*da-da-*<*nu*> for URU.*da-da-nu*. **i 24**.2 URU.*pa-dak-ka* for URU.*pa-dak-ku*; that ex. also places this city name after URU.*ḫi-ib-ra-a* rather than after URU.*da-da-nu*. **i 25**.2 URU.*ḫi-bi-ra-a* for URU.*ḫi-ib-ra-a*. **i 25**.2 URU.*pa-dak-ka* for URU.*pa-dak-ku*. **i 26**.2 *at-tal-lak* for ⸢*at-tal-la-ku*⸣. **i 27**.2 URU-*ía* for URU-*ia*. **i 28**.2 ^{d}IŠ.TAR for ^{d}INANNA. **i 28**.2 *a-ši-bu-tú* for *a-ši-bu-ti*. **i 29**.2 *ú-šal-li-mu-u'* for *ú-šal-lim-u*. **i 30**.2 ^{d}15 for ^{d}INANNA. **i 31**.2 *it-ti-ía* for *it-ti-ia*. **i 31**.2 MU.AN.NA for MU. **i 31**.2 Omits *šá* in *šá-a-šú* and *ina* before ITI.BÁRA. i 32. UN.<MEŠ> for UN.MEŠ. **i 32**.2 KUR.MEŠ for KUR-*i*. **i 33**.2 *dan-na-ti* for *dan-na-tú*. **i 35**.2 *an-na-a-tú* for *an-na-a-ti*. **i 35**.2 Adds *a-na* before *la ba-ṭa-lu*. **i 35**.2 *ba-ṭa-lu* for *ba-ṭa-a-lu*. **i 37**.2 *i-šaq-qí-šú-nu-tú* for *i-šá-aq-qí-šu-nu-ti*. **i 37**.2 NÍG-*šú-nu* for NÍG.MEŠ$^{?}$-*šú-nu*. **i 38**.2 IGI-*ia* for *maḫ-ri-ía*. **i 39**.2 ^{d}*iš-tar* for ^{d}INANNA. **i 39**.2 *ta-ḫa-zu* for MÈ. **i 39**.2 [*nu*]-*kúr-tú* for *nu-kúr-ti*. **i 39**.2 *su-lum-mu-u* for *su-lum-mu-ú*. **i 40**.2 *ba-li-šú* for *ba-li-šu*. **i 40**.2 GÁL-*ú* for *ib-ba-áš-šu-u*. **i 40**.2 *u* for *ù*. **i 41**.2 *in-né-ep-pu-šú* for *in-né-ep-pu-šu*. **i 41**.2 *a-na* for ⸢*àna*⸣. **i 42**.2 URU.*ma-da-a-a* for ⸢KUR⸣.[*ma*]-⸢*da*⸣*-a-a*. **i 46**.2 ⸢KUR-URI.KI⸣ for ⸢KUR-*ak-ka-di-i*.KI⸣.

ii 2.2 ⸢*ina*$^{?}$⸣ for *i-na*. **ii 7**.2 *ki-i-nim* for *ki-nim*. **ii 9**.2 *qí*-É for *qí-bi-ti*. **ii 10**.2 *pa-rik-ti* for *pa-rik-tú*. **ii 11**.2 Omits *-ma* after *ik-šu-dam*. **ii 14**.2 DINGIR.<MEŠ> for DINGIR.MEŠ. **ii 15**.2 *zi-kìr-šú* for *zi-kìr-šu*. **ii 16**.2 *ta-ḫe-ep-pu-u* for *ta-ḫe-ep-pu-ú*. **ii 17**.2 ^{d}*a-nù-tú* for ^{d}*a-nù-ú-tú*. **ii 17**.2 *mu-gam-mi-ru* for *mu-gam-mi-ir*. **ii 17**.2 *pa-ra-aṣ* for GARZA. **ii 18**.2 *le-qu-u* for *le-qu-ú*. **ii 18**.2 GARZA for *pa-ra-aṣ*. **ii 18**.2 ^{d}IDIM-*ú-tu* for ^{d}*é-a-ú-ti*. **ii 19**.2 GARZA for *pa-ra-aṣ*. **ii 19**.2 *qa-ti-šú* for ŠU.II-*šú*. **ii 22**.2 *u* for *ù*. **ii 22**.2 *ta-qab-bu-u* for *ta-qab-bu-ú*. **ii 25**.2 *ka-a-šú* for ⸢*ka-a*⸣*-šu*. **ii 28**.2 *ru-qu-tú* for *ru-qu-ti*. **ii 29**.2 *i-ku-un-na* for *i-ku-un-nu*. **ii 30**.2 *ub-la* for *ub-lu*. **ii 30**.2 *pu-luḫ-ta-ku* for *pu-luḫ-ta-ka*. **ii 33**.2 *a-ši-bu-tú* for ⸢*a-ši-bu-ti*⸣. **ii 34**.2 *qí-bit* for *qí-bi-ti*. **ii 35**.2 ^{d}ŠEŠ.KI-*ru* for ⸢^{d}ŠEŠ.KI-*ri*⸣. **ii 35**.2 *mu-*

gam-mir for *mu-ga-mi-ir*. **ii 37**.2 *šá-ma-mu* for *šá-ma-mi*. **ii 38**.2 *tan-na-an-du-u* for *ta-an-na-du-u*. **ii 39**.2 *ma-a-tú* for KUR. **ii 39**.2 *ib-ba-šu-u* for *ib-ba-áš-šu-ú*. **ii 42**.2 ⸢*šá-di-i*⸣ for ⸢KUR-*i*⸣.

iii 1.2 ⸢*a-lak?-ti*⸣ for *a-lak-tú*. **iii 8**.2 ⸢IGI-*ía*⸣ for ⸢*maḫ-ri-ía*⸣. **iii 9**.2 *še-pi-ía* for ⸢GÌR.II-*a*⸣ **iii 11**.2 ^{d}INANNA for [^{d}]⸢IŠ.TAR⸣. **iii 12**.2 *i-qab-bu-u* for *i-qab-bu*-⸢*ú*⸣. **iii 14**.2 Adds *u* before *ṭuḫ-du*. **iii 14**.2 *né-su-tú* for *né-su-ti*. **iii 15**.2 *aš-te-ed-dam-ma* for *ar-te-ed-dam-ma*. **iii 15**.2 Omits *ú-* in *ú-ru-uḫ*. **iii 16**.2 KUR-*ia* for *ma-ti-ia*. **iii 16**.2 GAL-*ti* for GAL-⸢*tú*⸣. **iii 16**.2 *at-taṣ-ṣa-ar-mu* for ⸢*at*⸣*-taṣ-ṣa-ar-ma*. **iii 17**.2 *u-šad-kam-ma* for ⸢*ú*⸣*-šad-kam-ma*. **iii 20**.2 *u-mál-lu-u* for *ú-mál-lu-u*. **iii 21**.2 *u-šak-lil* for *ú-šak-lil*. **iii 23**.2 LUGAL-*u-ti-ía* for ⸢LUGAL⸣-*ú-ti-ía*. **iii 24**.2 *u-še-rib u-še-šib* for ⸢*ú-še-rib ú-še-šib*⸣. **iii 26** *ú-šar-ri-ḫi*: Ex. 1 has *ú-šar-r*[*i-ḫi*] and ex. 2 has *u-šar-ri-ḫi*. **iii 27** *ú-mál-li-ma*: Ex. 1 has *ú-mál-l*[*i-ma*] and ex. 2 has *u-mál-li-ma*. **iii 28** ⸢*ú*⸣*-šal-lim*: Ex. 1 has ⸢*ú-šal*⸣-[*lim*] and ex. 2 has *u-šal-lim*. **iii 28**.2 EN EN for ⸢EN EN.EN⸣. **iii 29**.2 DI-*tuq* for ⸢*šu*⸣*-tuq*. **iii 30**.1 Omits *u* before ^{d}U.GUR. **iii 31** ⸢*ú*⸣*-šal-lim-u'*: Ex. 1 has ⸢*ú*⸣-[*šal-lim-u'*] and ex. 2 has *u-šal-lim-u'*. iii 32 *an-na-di*-⸢*iq*⸣*-ma*: Ex. 1 has [*an*]-⸢*na-di-iq-ma*⸣ and ex. 2 has *an-na-di-*<*iq*>*-ma*. **iii 33**.2 MÈ* for ⸢*ta-ḫa-zi*⸣. **iii 33**.1 [IGI-*i*]*a* for IGI-*ía*. **iii 33**.2 *áš-ku-un-ma* for *áš*-⸢*kun-ma*⸣. **iii 35**.2 ⸢LUGAL⸣-*u-tú* for ⸢LUGAL-*u-ti*$^{?}$⸣. **iii 33** *i-nam-bu-ka-ma*: Ex. 1 has [*i-nam-bu*]*-ka-ma* and ex. 2 has *i-nam-bu-ka-mu*. **iii 36**.2 DUMU-*u-ía-a*$^{?}$*-ma*$^{?}$ for DUMU-⸢*ú-ia-a*⸣*-ma*.

Nabonidus No. 2001

i 15.2 *a-na-ku* for *ana-ku*. **i 16**.2 *da-an-qa* for *dam-qa*. **i 16**.1 *u*$_4$*-*<*mu u*> for *u*$_4$*-mu u*. **i 16**.2 MU.AN.NA for MU. **i 17**.2 DAB-*ma* for *aṣ-bat-ma* **i 18**.2 IGI-*ía* for IGI.II-*ia*. **i 18**.2 KI-*šú* for *it-ti-šú*. **i 19**.2 *ta-a-a-ru-tu-ka* for *ta-a-a-ru-tu-ku*. **i 20**.2 ⸢*lib*⸣*-šá-a-ma* for *lib-šá-ma*. **i 20**.2 SAG.DU for *qaq-qa-du*. **i 21**.2 DINGIR-*ut*-⸢*ka*⸣ for DINGIR-*ú-ut-ka*. **i 21**.2 *nu*-⸢*uḫ*⸣*-ḫi* for *nu-uḫ-ḫu*. **i 22**.2 DINGIR-*ía* for DINGIR-*ia*. **i 22**.2 *lu-bu-uš* for *lu-bu-šú*. **i 22**.2 [*šu-kut*]*-tú* for *šu-kut-ti*. **i 23**.2 *ṣu-ba-a-tú* for *ṣu-ba-a-ti*. **i 23**.2 Omits *u* before Ì.GIŠ. **i 24**.2 *zu-um-ri-ia* for *zu-um-ri-ía*. **i 25**.2 *la-ab*-⸢*šá*⸣*-ku-ú-ma* for *la-ab-šá-ku-ma*. **i 26**.2 ⸢*ta-nit*⸣*-ti* for ⸢*ta-nit*⸣*-tú*. **i 26**.2 URU-*ia* for URU-*ía*. **i 27**.2 ⸢*lìb*⸣*-bi-ía* for *lìb-bi-ia*. **i 27**.2 *iš-šak-*<*kin*>*-ma* for *iš-šá-kin-ma*. **i 27**.2 [*aṣ-ṣ*]*ur-ma* for *aṣ-ṣur*. **i 28**.2 *mim-mu-u-a* for *mim-mu-ú-a*. **i 29**.2 ⸢TA⸣ for *ul-tu*. **i 30**.2 [AN.ŠÁR]*-e-tel-lu-*DINGIR.MEŠ for AN.ŠÁR-*e-tel-lu*-DINGIR. **i 31**.2 [^{d}MUATI-A]-ÙRU for ^{d}MUATI-A-PAP. **i 31**.2 ^{d}MUATI-NÍG.GUB-ÙRU for ^{d}MUATI-NÍG.GUB-PAP. **i 32**.2 ^{md}U.GUR-LUGAL-PAP for ^{md}U.GUR-LUGAL-ÙRU. **i 34**.2 [*áš-ra-a*]*-tú* for *áš-ra-a-ti*. **i 36**.2 *qí-bi-ti* for *qí-bi-ta*$_5$. **i 39**.2 [*ta-a-a-r*]*ì* for *ta-a-a-ri*.

ii 13.2 ^{md}MUATI-I for ⸢^{md}MUATI-NÍ⸣.TUKU. **ii 13**.2 Adds LUGAL TIN.TIR.KI after ^{md}MUATI-I. **ii 13**.2 Omits *e-du*. **ii 14**.2 *ma-šu-tú* for ⸢*ma-šu-ti*⸣. **ii 14**.2 Omits ⸢*ù*⸣ after ^{d}*nusku*. **ii 16**.2 DÙ-*uš-ma* for *i-pu-uš-ma*. **ii 16**.2 URU.*ḫar-ra-nu* for URU.KASKAL. **ii 21**.2 DINGIR.MEŠ for DINGIR. **ii 22**.2 *i-pu-šu-ma* for *i-pu-šú-ma*. **ii 22**.2 *na*-⸢*ra*⸣*-mi-ía* for *na-ra-mi-ia*. **ii 23**.2 DINGIR-*ú-ut*-ŠU for DINGIR-*ut-su*. **ii 23**.2 *ap-la*-⸢*ḫu*⸣ for *pal-ḫa-ku*. **ii 23**.2 *aṣ-ba*-⸢*tu*$_4$⸣ for *aṣ-ba-ti*. **ii 23**.2 [DINGIR.M]EŠ for DINGIR. **ii 25**.2 *ár*-⸢*ku*⸣*-tú* for *ár-ku-ti*. **ii 26**.2 MU.MEŠ for MU.AN.NA.MEŠ. **ii 26**.2 *lìb-bi* for ŠÀ. **ii 26**.2 *a-di-i* for *a-di*. **ii 27**.2 *lìb-bi-ía* for *lìb-bi-i*[*a*]. **ii 28**.2 MU.MEŠ for MU.AN.NA.MEŠ. **ii 29**.2 *iš-ku-nu-ma* for *iš-ku-nu*. **ii 29**.2 *ia-a-ti* for *ía-a-ti*. **ii 29**.2 *ni-ṭi-lu* for *ni-ṭi-il*. **ii 29**.2 IGI.II for IGI. **ii 30**.2 *še-e-pi* for GÌR.II. **ii 30**.2 *šá-li-im-mu* for *šá-li-im-ma*. **ii 31**.2 *a-mat-ú-a* for *a-ma-tu-u-a*. **ii 32**.2 UGU-*ía* for UGU-*ia*. **ii 32**.2 [*ṭa*]-⸢*bu*⸣ for *ṭa-bu-ma*. **ii 33** DUMU.MEŠ-*ia**: Ex. 1 has DUMU.MEŠ-DUMU. **ii 48**.2 DÙG.GA for *ṭa-a-bi*. **ii 48** *i-te-né-ep-pu-šú*: Ex. 1 has *i-te-*<*né*>*-ep-pu-šú* and ex. 2 has ⸢*i*⸣*-te-né*-⸢*ep*⸣*-pu*-⸢*uš*⸣. **ii 49**.2 IGI-*šú-nu* for *pa-ni-šú-nu*.

iii 2.1 [*ṭaḫ*]*-du-ti* for *ṭaḫ-du-tú*. **iii 6**.2 E.KI for TIN.TIR.KI. **iii 7**.2 *ra-áma*-⸢*ni*⸣*-šú* for *ra-man-ni-šú*. **iii 8**.2 E.KI for TIN.[TIR.KI]. **iii 10**.2 *šal-mat-*[*su*] for ⸢ADDA-*su*⸣. **iii 11**.2 SIG$_5$-*ú-tú* for ⸢SIG$_5$-*ti*⸣. **iii 11**.2 *ki-tu-ú* for ⸢*ki-tu-u*⸣. **iii 13**.2 NA$_4$.MEŠ for ⸢NA$_4$⸣. **iii 13**.2 SIG$_5$-*ú-tú* for ⸢SIG$_5$-*u-ti*⸣. **iii 15**.1 Omits GA in DÙG.GA. **iii 15**.2 *šal-mat-su* for ADDA-*su*. **iii 17**.2 UDU.NÍTA.<MEŠ> for UDU.NÍTA.MEŠ. **iii 19**.2 *šu-*[*an-na*.KI] for TIN.TIR.KI. **iii 19**.2 *ù* for *u*. **iii 19**.2 *bár-sip*$_4$.KI for *bar-sip*.KI.

Index of Museum Numbers

Ankara, Archaeological Museum

Atlanta, Michael C. Carlos Museum, Emory University

Babylon, Nebuchadnezzar Museum

Baghdad, Iraq Museum

Barcelona, Montserrat Museum

Berlin, Vorderasiatisches Museum

Berlin, Private Collection

Cambridge, Massachusetts, Harvard Semitic Museum

Cambridge, UK, Fitzwilliam Museum (loan from Trinity College)

Istanbul, Archaeological Museum

Jerusalem, St. Andrew's Memorial Church, Church of Scotland

Leiden, Böhl Collection

London, British Museum

New Haven, Yale Babylonian Collection

New York, Metropolitan Museum of Art

Oslo, Schøyen Collection

Oxford, Ashmolean Museum

Paris, Louvre

Philadelphia, University of Pennsylvania Museum of Archaeology and Anthropology

No.	RINBE 2	No.	RINBE 2	No.	RINBE 2
CBS 15328	Nabonidus 38.17	CBS 16108	Nabonidus 1.1	CBS 16561a	Nabonidus 38.15
CBS 15378	Nabonidus 38.19	CBS 16494	Nabonidus 39.7	CBS 16561b	Nabonidus 38.16
CBS 15617	Nabonidus 33	CBS 16495	Nabonidus 37.19		
CBS 15618	Nabonidus 32.14	CBS 16560a	Nabonidus 39.8	UM 84-26-20	Nabonidus 38.20
CBS 15889	Nabonidus 38.18	CBS 16560b	Nabonidus 39.9	UM 84-26-44	Nabonidus 38.21

Saint Louis Public Library, St. Louis

No.	RINBE 2	No.	RINBE 2
Grolier 9	Neriglissar 7	SPL W 2/8	Neriglissar 7

Turin, Institute of Archaeology, University of Turin

No.	RINBE 2
—	Nabonidus 8.7

Uncertain, Private collection

No.	RINBE 2
—	Nabonidus 53

Urfa, Urfa Museum

No.	RINBE 2	No.	RINBE 2		
—	Nabonidus 47.1	—	Nabonidus 47.2	—	Nabonidus 2001.1

Index of Excavation Numbers

Seleucia

Sippar

Tēmā

Ur

Uruk

Index of Names

Personal Names

Geographic, Ethnic, and Tribal Names

Divine, Planet, and Star Names

Gate, Palace, Temple, and Wall Names

Concordances of Selected Publications

Beaulieu, Nabonidus pp. 20–40 and 239–241 (Appendix 2)

P.	No.	RINBE 2
20–22	Inscription 1	Nabonidus 3
22–24	Inscription 2	Nabonidus 34
23–24	Inscription 3	Nabonidus 36
24–25	Inscription 4	Nabonidus 39
25	Inscription 5	Nabonidus 24
25–26	Inscription 6	Nabonidus 25
26–27	Inscription 7	Nabonidus 19
27	Inscription 8	Nabonidus 26
27–29	Inscription 9	Nabonidus 16
28–30	Inscription 10	Nabonidus 15
30–31	Inscription 11	Nabonidus 23
31–32	Inscription 12	Nabonidus 18
32	Inscription 13	Nabonidus 47
32–34	Inscription 14	Nabonidus 43
34	Inscription 15	Nabonidus 28
34–35	Inscription 16	Nabonidus 27
35–37	Inscription 17	Nabonidus 32
37	Inscription 18	Nabonidus 38
37–38	Inscription 19	Nabonidus 37
38–39	Inscription A	Nabonidus 1
39	Inscription B	Nabonidus 2
39	Inscription C	Nabonidus 7
39–40	Inscription D	Nabonidus 8
40	Inscription E	Nabonidus 9
40	Inscription F	Nabonidus 53
40	Inscription G	Nabonidus 44
40	Inscription H	Nabonidus 6
40–41	Inscription X	Nabonidus 1004
41	Inscription Y	Nabonidus 1009
41	Inscription Z	Nabonidus 1001
239	Fragment 1	Nabonidus 17
239	Fragment 4	Nabonidus 10
239–240	Fragment 2	Nabonidus 51
239–241	Fragment 3	Nabonidus 46

Berger, NbK

P.	No.	RINBE 2
325	A-M. Gefäß I, 1	Amēl-Marduk 3
326	A-M. Gefäß I, 2	Amēl-Marduk 4
327	A-M. Gefäß I, 3	Amēl-Marduk 5
328	A-M. Gefäß I, 4	Amēl-Marduk 6
329	A.-M. Pflasterstein I	Amēl-Marduk 2
330	A.-M Backstein A I, 1	Amēl-Marduk 1
333	Ner. Gefäß I	Neriglissar 9
334	Ner. Backsteine A I, 1	Neriglissar 4
335	Ner. Backsteine A I, 2	Neriglissar 5
336	Ner. Zyl. II, 1	Neriglissar 1
337	Ner. Zyl. II, 2	Neriglissar 2
338–339	Ner. Zyl. II, 3	Neriglissar 3
340	Ner. Zyl.-Frgm. II, 1	—
341	Ner. Zyl.-Frag II, 2	Neriglissar 6
343	Nbn. Perle	Nabonidus 53
344	Nbn. Türangelstein 1	Nabonidus 36
345	Nbn. Pflasterstein U	Nabonidus 6
346	Nbn. Backsteine A I, 1	Nabonidus 7
347	Nbn. Backsteine Ap I, 1	Nabonidus 8
348–349	Nbn. Backsteine Ap I, 2	Nabonidus 18
350	Nbn. Backsteine B I, 1	Nabonidus 38
351	Nbn. Backsteine B I, 2	Nabonidus 37
352	Nbn. Backsteine B I, 3	Nabonidus 39
353	Nbn. Backsteine U	Nabonidus 9
354	Nbn. Zyl. II, 1	Nabonidus 1
355–359	Nbn. Zyl. II, 2	Nabonidus 32
360	Nbn. Zyl. II, 3	Nabonidus 2
361	Nbn. Zyl. II, 4	Nabonidus 26
362	Nbn. Zyl. II, 5	Nabonidus 19
363	Nbn. Zyl. II, 6	Nabonidus 15
364	Nbn. Zyl. II, 7	Nabonidus 34
365–366	Nbn. Zyl. II, 8	Nabonidus 25
367–368	Nbn. Zyl. II, 9	Nabonidus 24
369–370	Nbn. Zyl. III, 1	Nabonidus 16
371–375	Nbn. Zyl. III, 2	Nabonidus 28
376	Nbn. Zyl. III, 3	Nabonidus 23
377–378	Nbn. Zyl. III, 4	Nabonidus 27
379	Nbn. Zyl.-Frgm. I, 1	Nabonidus 1004
380	Nbn. Zyl.-Frgm. I, 2	Nabonidus 1009
381	Nbn. Zyl.-Frgm. II, 1	Nabonidus 1001
382	Nbn. Stelen-Fragment 1	Nabonidus 43
383	Nbn. Stelen-Fragmente III, 1	Nabonidus 47
384–386	Nbn. Stelen-Fragment XI	Nabonidus 3
387	Nbd. Tfl-Frgm. VI, 1	Nabonidus 27.4
388	Nbd. Tfl-Frgm. VI, 2	—

Da Riva, SANER 3 pp. 106–144

P.	No.	RINBE 2	P.	No.	RINBE 2
106	3.1 (B1)	Amēl-Marduk 1	114–120	4.2.1 (C21)	Neriglissar 1
107	3.2.1 (V1)	Amēl-Marduk 3	120–124	4.2.2 (C22)	Neriglissar 2
107–108	3.2.2 (V2)	Amēl-Marduk 4	124–135	4.2.3 (C23)	Neriglissar 3
108–109	3.2.3 (V3)	Amēl-Marduk 5	135–138	4.2.4 (C011)	Neriglissar 7
109–110	3.2.4 (V4)	Amēl-Marduk 6	138–140	4.2.5 (C021)	—
110–111	3.3 (PS1)	Amēl-Marduk 2	140–143	4.2.6 (C022)	Neriglissar 6
112–113	4.1.1 (B1)	Neriglissar 4	143–144	4.3 (V1)	Neriglissar 8
113–114	4.1.2 (B2)	Neriglissar 5			

Langdon, NBK

P.	No.	RINBE 2	P.	No.	RINBE 2
45	Ner. No. 1	Neriglissar 3	208–215	Ner. No. 1	Neriglissar 3
45–46	Ner. No. 2	Neriglissar 1	214–219	Ner. No. 2	Neriglissar 1
46	Ner. No. 3	Neriglissar 4	218–219	Ner. No. 3	Neriglissar 4
46–47	Nbd. no. 1	Nabonidus 28	218–229	Nbd. no. 1	Nabonidus 28
47	Nbd. no. 2	Nabonidus 26	230–235	Nbd. no. 2	Nabonidus 26
47	Nbd. no. 3	Nabonidus 16	234–243	Nbd. no. 3	Nabonidus 16
48	Nbd. no. 4	Nabonidus 27	242–251	Nbd. no. 4	Nabonidus 27
49	Nbd. no. 5	Nabonidus 32	250–253	Nbd. no. 5	Nabonidus 32
49–50	Nbd. no. 6	Nabonidus 24	252–261	Nbd. no. 6	Nabonidus 24
50–53	Nbd. no. 7	Nabonidus 25	263–271	Nbd. no. 7	Nabonidus 25
53–57	Nbd. no. 8	Nabonidus 3	270–289	Nbd. no. 8	Nabonidus 3
57–58	Nbn. no. 9	Nabonidus 2001.2	288–295	Nbn. no. 9	Nabonidus 2001.2
58	Nbd. no. 10	Nabonidus 8	294–295	Nbd. no. 10	Nabonidus 8
58	Nbd. no. 11	Nabonidus 7	294–295	Nbd. no. 11	Nabonidus 7
58	Nbd. no. 12	Nabonidus 18	294–295	Nbd. no. 12	Nabonidus 18
58	Nbd. no. 13	Nabonidus 38	296–297	Nbd. no. 13	Nabonidus 38
58	Nbd. no. 14	Nabonidus 37	296–297	Nbd. no. 14	Nabonidus 37
58	Nbd. no. 15	Nabonidus 39	296–297	Nbd. no. 15	Nabonidus 39

Schaudig, Inschriften Nabonids

P.	No.	RINBE 2	P.	No.	RINBE 2
335	1.1[a]	Nabonidus 31	384–394	2.9	Nabonidus 24
335	1.2[a]	Nabonidus 7	395–397	2.10[a]	Nabonidus 13
336	1.3[a]	Nabonidus 20	397–409	2.11	Nabonidus 16
336–337	1.4[a]	Nabonidus 8	409–440	2.12	Nabonidus 28–29
337–338	1.5[a]	Nabonidus 18	440–445	2.13	Nabonidus 23
339–340	1.6[a]	Nabonidus 37	445–466	2.14	Nabonidus 27
340–341	1.7[a]	Nabonidus 38	467	2.15[a]	—
341–342	1.8[a]	Nabonidus 39	468–469	2.16	—
342–343	1.9	Nabonidus 51	469–470	2.17	Nabonidus 10
343	1.10	Nabonidus 9	471–472	2.18	Nabonidus 14
343	1.11	Nabonidus 6	472–474	2.19	Nabonidus 46
344	1.12[a]	Nabonidus 36	474–475	2.20	Nabonidus 44
345–350	2.1	Nabonidus 1	476	2.21	Nabonidus 5
350–353	2.2	Nabonidus 32	477	2.22	Nabonidus 45
353–358	2.3[a]	Nabonidus 2	478–479	2.23	Nabonidus 1011
358–362	2.4	Nabonidus 26	480–481	2.24[a]	Nabonidus 35
362–370	2.5	Nabonidus 19	481–482	2.25[a]	Nabonidus 1008
370–372	2.6	Nabonidus 15	483–484	2.26[a]	Nabonidus 1001
373–377	2.7	Nabonidus 34	484	2.27	Nabonidus 1004
378–384	2.8[a]	Nabonidus 25	485	2.28[a]	Nabonidus 1009

P.	No.	RINBE 2	P.	No.	RINBE 2
485	2.29	Nabonidus 1010	537–543	3.8[a]	Nabonidus 4
486–499	3.1	Nabonidus 47	544	3.9	Nabonidus 55
500–513	3.2	Nabonidus 2001	545	4.1	Nabonidus 53
514–529	3.3[a]	Nabonidus 3	545–546	4.2	Nabonidus 52
530–532	3.4	Nabonidus 43	546–547	4.3	Nabonidus 50
532–534	3.5	Nabonidus 17	547	4.4	Nabonidus 49
535	3.6	Nabonidus 40	547	4.5	Nabonidus 48
536	3.7[a]	Nabonidus 1003			

Walker, CBI

P.	No.	RINBE 2	P.	No.	RINBE 2
91–92	110 (Nabonidus 12)	Nabonidus 18	93	113 (Nabonidus 15)	Nabonidus 39
92	111 (Nabonidus 13)	Nabonidus 38	93	114 (Nabonidus X)	Nabonidus 1005
92–93	112 (Nabonidus 14)	Nabonidus 37